AMERICA'S
Wonderful
LITTLE
HOTELS
& INNS
Fourteenth Edition

The West Coast

States and Canadian Provinces
Covered in This Edition

Alaska   WESTERN CANADA
California   Alberta
Hawaii   British Columbia
Oregon
Washington

Also in This Series

America's Wonderful Little Hotels & Inns, U.S.A. and Canada
America's Wonderful Little Hotels & Inns, New England
America's Wonderful Little Hotels & Inns, The Middle Atlantic
America's Wonderful Little Hotels & Inns, The Midwest
America's Wonderful Little Hotels & Inns, The Rocky Mountains and The Southwest
America's Wonderful Little Hotels & Inns, The South
Europe's Wonderful Little Hotels & Inns, Great Britain & Ireland
Europe's Wonderful Little Hotels & Inns, The Continent

AMERICA'S
Wonderful
LITTLE
HOTELS
& INNS
Fourteenth Edition

The West Coast

Edited by Sandra W. Soule

Associate Editors:
Nancy P. Barker, June C. Horn,
Alexandra Brady, Meg Cassidy, Abby Humphrey,
Betsy Sandberg

Contributing Editors:
Suzanne Carmichael, Susan Waller Schwemm, Linda
Goldberg, Gail Davis, Pam Phillips, Matthew Joyce, Mary
Ann Boyle

Editorial Assistant:
Jeffrey Soule

St. Martin's Press
New York

This book is dedicated to the people who take the time and trouble to write about the hotels and inns they've visited, and to my children—Hilary and Jeffrey—my husband, and my parents.

The cover photograph shows the Agate Cove Inn, Mendocino, California.

ISBN 0-312-11238-6

First Edition: December 1994

10 9 8 7 6 5 4 3 2 1

Maps by David Lindroth, © 1994, 1992, 1991, 1990, 1989, 1988, 1987 by St. Martin's Press.

Contents

Acknowledgments

We would like again to thank all the people who wrote in such helpful detail about the inns and hotels they visited. To them belong both the dedication and the acknowledgments, for without their support, this guide would not exist. If I have inadvertently misspelled or omitted anyone's name, please accept my sincerest apologies.

I would also like to thank Hilary Rubinstein, who originated the concept for this series. Also thanks to my helpful and supportive editors Anne Savarese and Helen Packard; to my wonderful colleagues Nancy Barker, June Horn, Alex Brady, Meg Cassidy, Betsy Sandberg, Mary Ann Boyle, Suzanne Carmichael, Susan Schwemm, Nancy Debevoise, Gail Davis, Linda Goldberg, Tina Kirkpatrick, and Diane Wolf; and to faithful respondents Peg Bedini, John Blewer, Robert Boas, Donna Bocks, Pat Borysiewicz, John Chiles, Ann Christofferson, Rose Ciccone, Marjorie Cohen, Happy and Ernie Copley, Dianne Crawford, Brian Donaldson, Sally Ducot, Ellie & Robert Freidus, Allan Hay, BJ Hensley, Stephen Holman, William Hussey, Linda Intaschi, Keith Jurgens, Al and Lauren Kenney, Daena Klugel, Zita Knific, Bradley Lockner, Bill MacGowan, Carolyn Mathiasen, Celia McCullough, Mark Mendenhall, Michael and Dina Miller, Carolyn Myles, Betty Norman, Bill Novack, Marilyn Parker, Pam Phillips, Adam Platt, Jill Reeves, Stephanie Roberts, Mary Louise Rogers, Duane Roller, Marion Ruben, Joe and Sheila Schmidt, Fritz Shantz and Tara O'Neal, Mary Jane Skala, Jeanne Smith, Ruth Tilsley, Lee Todd, Wendi Van Exan, Hopie Welliver, Rose Wolf, Karl Wiegers and Chris Zambito, and the many others who went far beyond the call of duty in their assistance and support.

Introduction

Reading the Entries

Each entry generally has three parts: a description of the inn or hotel, quotes from guests who have stayed there, and relevant details about rooms, rates, location, and facilities. Occasionally you may find that no general description is given or that the factual data are incomplete. There are two reasons for this: Either the descriptions supplied by guests made this unnecessary, or the facility failed to supply us with adequate information. Please remember that the length of an entry is in no way a reflection of that inn or hotel's quality. Rather, it is an indication of the type of feedback we've received both from guests and from the innkeepers themselves. Some hotel owners are totally unaware of this guide; others take an active role in encouraging their guests to write.

Wherever a location is of particular tourist interest, we've tried to include some information about its attractions. If we have only one listing for a town, this description usually falls within the body of the entry. If there is more than one inn or hotel listed for a town, the description of the town and information about its location precede the individual entries.

In some areas the magnet is not a particular town but rather a compact, distinct region. Travelers choose one place to stay and use it as a base from which to explore the area. But because this guide is organized by town, not by region, the entries are scattered throughout the chapter. When this applies, you will see the name of the region noted under the "Location" heading; check back to the introduction for a description of the region involved. When an inn is located in a small village close to a better-known town, cross-references are provided to make the process easier.

The names at the end of the quotations are those who have recommended the hotel or inn. Some entries are entirely or largely quoted from one report; if several names follow the quotation, we have distinguished the writers of the quoted material by putting their names first. Some writers have requested that we not use their names; you will see initials noted instead. *We never print the names of those who have sent us adverse reports, although their contributions are invaluable indeed.*

Although we have tried to make the listings as accurate and complete as possible, mistakes and inaccuracies invariably creep in. The most significant area of inaccuracy applies to the rates charged by each establishment. In preparing this guide, we asked all the hotels and inns to give us their 1995–1996 rates, ranging from the least expensive room in the off-season to the most expensive peak-season price. Some did so, while others just noted the 1994 rate.

Some of the shorter entries are marked "**Information please:**" or "**Also recommended:**" The former usually refer to establishments which have just come to our attention, as well as those that were listed in past editions. The latter are sometimes too big or small for a full entry, or those that have been recommended just as we were going to press.

Please remember that the process of writing and publishing a book takes nearly a year. *You should always double-check the rates when you make your reservations; please don't blame the hotel or this guide if the prices are wrong.* On the other hand, given the current level of inflation, you should not encounter anything more than a 5% increase, unless there has been a substantial improvement in the amenities offered or a change of ownership. Please let us know immediately if you find anything more than that!

If you find any errors of omission or commission in any part of the entries, we urgently request your help in correcting them. We recognize that it takes extra time and effort for readers to write us letters or fill in report forms, but this feedback is essential in keeping this publication totally responsive to consumer needs.

The Fifteen Commandments of Vacation Travel

We all know people who come back from a vacation feeling on top of the world, and others who seem vaguely disappointed. Here's how to put yourself in the first category, not the second.

1. Know yourself. A successful vacation is one that works for the person you are, not the person you think you should be. Confirmed couch potatoes who resent having to walk from the far end of the parking lot will not find true fulfillment on a trek through the Himalayas. If privacy is a top priority, a group tour or communal lodge will turn fantasy into frustration. Acknowledge your own comfort levels. How important is it for you to be independent and flexible? Structured and secure? How essential are the creature comforts when it comes to sleeping, eating, and bathing? Would you rather have one week of luxury travel or two weeks of budget food and accommodation? And remember that while your personality doesn't change, your needs do. The type of vacation you plan for a romantic getaway is totally different from a family reunion.

2. Know your travel companions. Adjust your plans to accommodate your travel partners. Whether you are traveling with friends, spouse, children, and/or parents, you'll need to take their age, attention span, agility, and interests into account. If you're traveling with the kids, balance a morning at an art museum with an afternoon at the zoo; if you're spending time with elderly parents, make sure that they can stroll a country lane while you go rock-climbing; if your group includes skiers and non-skiers, pick a resort that has appealing shops and other activities.

3. Plan ahead: anticipation is half the fun. Enjoy the process. The more you know about an area you're going to visit, the more fun you'll have. Skim a guidebook; get a calendar of events; write to the local chamber of commerce and tourist offices; read a novel set in the region; talk to friends (or friends of friends) who have been there recently.

4. Don't bite off more than you can chew. Keep your itinerary in line with the amount of time and money available. Focus on seeing a smaller area well, rather than trying to cover too much ground and seeing nothing but interstate highways. Don't overprogram; allow yourself the luxury of doing nothing.

5. Avoid one-night stands. Plan to stay a minimum of two nights everywhere you go. A vacation made up of one-nighters is a prescription for exhaustion. You will sleep poorly, spend most of your time in transit, and will get only the smallest glimpse of the place you're visiting. If it's worth seeing, it's worth spending a full day in one place.

6. Travel off season. Unless your vacation dates are dictated by the school calendar, off-season travel offers many advantages: fewer crowds, greater flexibility, and a more relaxed atmosphere. Learn to pick the best dates for off-season travel; typically these are the weeks just before and after the rates change. Off-season travel offers big savings, too; for example, most ski areas are delightful places to visit in summer, and offer savings of 50% or more on accommodations.

7. Book well ahead for peak season travel. If you must travel during peak periods to popular destinations, make reservations well in advance for the key sites to avoid aggravation, extra phone calls, and additional driving time.

8. Take the road less traveled by. Get off the beaten path to leave the crowds behind. Instead of booking a room in the heart of the action, find a quiet inn tucked in the hills or in a neighboring village. If you visit the Grand Canyon in August, at the height of the tourist season, stay at the North Rim, which attracts 90% fewer visitors than the South Rim.

9. Ditch the car. Sure you need a car to get where you're going. But once you're there, get out and walk. You'll see more, learn more, experience more at every level, while avoiding crowds even at the most popular destinations. We promise. Car travel is an isolating experience, even when you're in bumper-to-bumper traffic.

10. Hang loose. The unexpected is inevitable in travel, as in the rest of life. When your plans go astray (and they will), relax and let serendipity surprise you. And keep your sense of humor in good working order. If possible, travel without reservations or a set itinerary.

11. Carpe diem—seize the day. Don't be afraid to follow your impulses. If a special souvenir catches your eye, buy it; don't wait to see if you'll find it again later. If a hiking trail looks too inviting to pass up, don't; that museum will wait for a rainy day.

12. Don't suffer in silence. When things go wrong—an incompetent guide, car troubles, a noisy hotel room—speak up. Politely but firmly express your concern then and there; get your room changed, ask for a refund or discount, whatever. Most people in the travel business would rather have you go away happy than to leave grumbling.

13. Remember—being there is more than seeing there. People travel to see the sights—museums and mountains, shops and scenery—but it is making new friends that can make a trip memorable. Leave a door open to the people-to-people experiences that enrich travel immeasurably.

14. Don't leave home to find home. The quickest way to take the wind out of the sails of your trip is to compare things to the way they are at home. Enjoy different styles and cultures for what they are and avoid comparisons and snap judgments.

15. Give yourself permission to disregard all of the above. Nothing is immutable. If you find a pattern that works for you, enjoy it!

Inngoers' Bill of Rights

We've read through a lot more brochures for inns and hotels than the average bear, and can attest to the fact that not one makes mention of its possible drawbacks, however slight. Furthermore, unlike this guidebook, *which accepts no fee of any kind for an entry*, most inn guidebooks charge a listing or membership fee of some kind, making them basically paid advertisements. Despite brochure promises and glowing listings in other books, we all know that perfection isn't possible in this world, but we feel that (despite the irate reactions of some innkeepers) complete and honest reporting will give readers *reasonable* expectations, ones that are often surpassed in the best of hostelries.

On the other hand, travelers have the right to expect certain minimum standards. These rights are especially important in hotels and inns at the top end of the rate scale; we don't expect as much from more modestly priced places, although it certainly is often received.

So, please use this Bill of Rights as a kind of checklist in deciding how you think a place stacks up on your own personal rating scale. And, whether an establishment fails, reaches, or exceeds these levels, be sure to let us know. We would also hope that innkeepers will use this list to help evaluate both the strong points and shortcomings of their own establishments, and are grateful to those who have already done so.

The right to suitable cleanliness: An establishment that looks, feels, and smells immaculate, with no musty, smoky, or animal odors.

The right to suitable room furnishings: A firm mattress, soft pillows, fresh linens, and ample blankets; bright lamps and night tables on each side of the bed; comfortable chairs with good reading lights; and adequate storage space.

The right to comfortable, attractive rooms: Guest rooms and common rooms that are as livable as they are attractive. Appealing places where you'd like to read, chat, relax.

The right to a decent bathroom: Cleanliness is essential, along with reliable plumbing, ample hot water, good lighting, an accessible electric outlet, space for toiletries, and thirsty towels.

The right to privacy and discretion: Privacy must be respected by the innkeeper and ensured by adequate sound-proofing. The right to discretion precludes questions about marital status or sexual preference. No display of proselytizing religious materials.

The right to good, healthful food: Fresh nutritious food, ample in quantity, high in quality, attractively presented, and graciously served in smoke-free surroundings.

The right to comfortable temperatures and noise levels: Rooms should be cool in summer and warm in winter, with windows that open, and quiet, efficient air-conditioning and heating. Double windows, drapes, and landscaping are essential if traffic noise is an issue.

The right to fair value: Prices should be in reasonable relation to the facilities offered and to the cost of equivalent local accommodation.

The right to genuine hospitality: Innkeepers who are glad you've come and who make it their business to make your stay pleasant and memorable; who are readily available without being intrusive.

The right to a caring environment: Welcoming arrivals with refreshments, making dinner reservations, providing information on activities, asking about pet allergies and dietary restrictions, and so on.

The right to personal safety: A location in a reasonably safe neighborhood, with adequate care given to building and parking security.

The right to professionalism: Brochure requests, room reservations, check-ins and outs handled efficiently and responsibly.

The right to adequate common areas: At least one common room where guests can gather to read, chat, or relax, free of the obligation to buy anything.

The right of people traveling alone to have all the above rights: Singles usually pay just a few dollars less than couples, yet the welcome, services, and rooms they receive can be inferior.

The right to a reasonable cancellation policy: Penalties for a cancellation made fewer than 7-14 days before arrival are relatively standard. Most inns will refund deposits (minus a processing fee) after the deadline only if the room is rebooked.

The right to efficient maintenance: Burnt-out bulbs and worn-out smoke detector batteries are the responsibility of the innkeeper—not the guest. When things go wrong, guests have the right to an apology, a discount, or a refund.

Of course, there is no "perfect" inn or hotel, because people's tastes and needs vary so greatly. But one key phrase does pop up over and over again: "I felt right at home." This is not written in the literal sense—a commercial lodging, no matter how cozy or charming, is never the same as one's home. What is really meant is that guests felt as welcome, as relaxed, as comfortable, as they would in their own home.

What makes for a wonderful stay?

We've tried our best to make sure that all the hotels and inns listed in this guide are as wonderful as our title promises. Inevitably, there will be some disappointments. Sometimes these will be caused by a change in ownership or management that has resulted in lowered standards. Other times unusual circumstances will lead to problems. Quite often, though, problems will occur because there's not a good "fit" between the inn or hotel and the guest. Decide what you're looking for, then find the inn that suits your needs, whether you're looking for a casual environment or a dressy one, a romantic setting or a family-oriented one, a vacation spot or a business person's environment, an isolated country retreat or a convenient in-town location.

We've tried to give you as much information as possible on each hotel

5

or inn listed, and have taken care to indicate the atmosphere each inn-keeper is trying to create. After you've read the listing, write, if there is time, for a copy of the establishment's brochure, which will give you more information. Finally, feel free to call any inn or hotel where you're planning to stay, and ask as many questions as necessary.

Inn etiquette

A first-rate inn is a joy indeed, but as guests we need to do our part to respect its special qualities. For starters, you'll need to maintain a higher level of consideration for your fellow guests. Century-old Victorians are noted for their nostalgic charms, not their sound-proofing; if you come in late or get up early, remember that voices and footsteps echo off all those gleaming hardwood floors and doors. If you're going to pick a fight with your roommate, pull the covers up over your head or go out for a walk. If you're sharing a bath, don't dawdle, tidy up after yourself, and dry your hair back in your room. If you've admired the Oriental carpets, antique decor, handmade quilts, and the thick fluffy towels, don't leave wet glasses on the furniture, put suitcases on the bed, or use the towels for removing make-up or wiping the snow off your car. After all, innkeepers have rights too!

Hotels, inns . . . resorts and motels

As the title indicates, this is a guide to exceptional inns and hotels. Generally, the inns have 5 to 25 rooms, although a few have only 2 rooms and some have over 100. The hotels are more often found in the cities and range in size from about 50 to 200 rooms.

The line between an inn or hotel and a resort is often a fine one. There are times when we all want the extra facilities a resort provides, so we've added a number of reader-recommended facilities. We've also listed a handful of motels. Although they don't strictly fall within the context of this book, we've included them because readers felt they were the best option in a specific situation. Some entries are members of the Best Western chain. Please don't be put off by this; Best Western is a franchise operation, with no architectural unity from one property to the next. Those listed in this guide have substantial architectural or historical appeal, and concerned, professional management.

Although we do not provide full coverage of hotel chains, we do want to point out that the Four Seasons and Ritz-Carlton hotels are almost impossible to beat at the luxury end of the spectrum. Readers consistently rave about their unbeatable combination of unparalleled service and plush accommodation; weekend rates make them an exceptional value.

What is a B&B anyway?

There are basically two kinds of B&Bs—the B&B homestay and the B&B inn. The homestay is typically the home of an empty nester, who has a few empty bedrooms to fill, gaining some extra income and pleasant company. B&B inns are run on a more professional basis, independently marketed and subject to state and local licensing. Guests typically have dedicated common areas for their use, and do not share the hosts' living quarters, as in a homestay. We list very few homestays in this guide. Full-service or country inns and lodges are similar to the B&B inn, except that they serve breakfast and dinner on a regular basis, and may be somewhat larger in size; dinner is often offered to the public as well as to house guests. The best of all of these are made special by resident owners bringing the warmth of their personalities to the total experience. A B&B is *not* a motel that serves breakfast.

Rooms

All hotel and inn rooms are not created equal. Although the rooms at a typical chain motel or hotel may be identical, the owners of most of the establishments described in this book pride themselves on the individuality of each guest room. Some, although not all, of these differences are reflected in the rates charged.

More importantly, it means that travelers need to express their needs clearly to the innkeepers when making reservations and again when checking in. Some rooms may be quite spacious but may have extremely small private baths or limited closet space. Some antique double beds have rather high footboards—beautiful to look at but torture for six-footers. Many inns are trading their double beds in for queens and kings; if you prefer an oversize bed, say so. If you want twin beds, be sure to specify this when making reservations and again when you check in; many smaller inns have only one or two twin-bedded rooms.

Some rooms may have gorgeous old bathrooms, with tubs the size of small swimming pools, but if you are a hard-core shower person, that room won't be right for you. Many others have showers but no baths, which may be disappointing if you love a long, luxurious soak in the tub. If you are traveling on business and simply must have a working-size desk with good lighting, speak up. Some rooms look terrific inside but don't look out at anything much; others may have the view but not quite as special a decor. Sometimes the largest rooms are at the front of the house, facing a busy highway. Decide what's important to you. Although the owners and staff of the hotels and inns listed here are incredibly hard-working and dedicated people, they can't read your mind. Let your needs be known, and, within the limits of availability, they will try to accommodate you.

Our most frequent complaints center around beds that are too soft and inadequate reading lights. If these are priorities for you (as they are for us), don't be shy about requesting bedboards or additional lamps to remedy the situation. Similarly, if there are other amenities your room is lacking— extra pillows, blankets, or even an easy chair—speak up. Most innkeepers would rather put in an extra five minutes of work than have an unhappy guest.

If your reservation is contingent upon obtaining a particular room, make this very clear to the innkeeper. Some inns will not accept such reservations, feeling that they are too difficult to guarantee. Those that do accept them have an obligation to meet their guarantee; if circumstances prevent them from following through on the promised room, make it clear that you expect some sort of remuneration—either the return of your deposit or a reduction in the price of another room.

If you really don't like your room, ask for another as soon as possible, preferably before you've unpacked your bags. The sooner you voice your dissatisfaction, the sooner something can be done to improve the situation. If you don't like the food, ask for something else—in other words, you're the guest, make sure you get treated like one. If things go terribly wrong, don't be shy about asking for your money back, and be *sure* to write us about any problems.

What is a single? A double? A suite? A cottage or cabin?

Unlike the proverbial rose, a single is not a single is not a single. Sometimes it is a room with one twin bed, which really can accommodate only one person. Quite often it is described as a room with a standard-size double bed, in contrast to a double, which has two twin beds. Other hotels call both of the preceding doubles, although doubles often have queen- or even king-size beds instead. Many times the only distinction is made by the number of guests occupying the room; a single will pay slightly less, but there's no difference in the room.

There's almost as much variation when it comes to suites. We define a suite as a bedroom with a separate living room area and often a small kitchen, as well. Unfortunately, the word has been stretched to cover other setups, too. Some so-called suites are only one large room, accommodating a table and separate seating area in addition to the bed, while others are two adjacent bedrooms which share a bath. If you require a suite that has two separate rooms with a door between them, specify this when you make reservations.

Quite a few of our entries have cabins or cottages in addition to rooms in the main building. In general, a cabin is understood to be a somewhat more rustic residence than a cottage, although there's no hard-and-fast rule. Be sure to inquire for details when making reservations.

Making reservations

Unless you are inquiring many months in advance of your visit, it's best to telephone when making reservations. This offers a number of advantages: You will know immediately if space is available on your requested dates; you can find out if that space is suitable to your specific needs. You will have a chance to discuss the pros and cons of the available rooms and will be able to find out about any changes made in recent months—new facilities, recently redecorated rooms, nonsmoking policies, even a change of ownership. It's also a good time to ask the innkeeper about other concerns—Is the neighborhood safe at night? Is there any renovation or construction in progress that might be disturbing? Will a wedding reception or bicycle touring group affect use of the common areas during your visit? If you're reserving a room at a plantation home that is available for public tours, get specifics about the check-in/out times; in many, rooms are not available before 5 P.M. and must be vacated by 9 A.M. sharp. The savvy traveler will always get the best value for his accommodation dollar.

If you expect to be checking in late at night, *be sure to say so;* many inns give doorkeys to their guests, then lock up by 10 P.M.

We're often asked about the need for making advance reservations. If you'll be traveling in peak periods, in prime tourist areas, and want to be sure of getting a first-rate room at the best-known inns, reserve at least three to six months ahead. This is especially true if you're traveling with friends or family and will need more than one room. On the other hand, if you like a bit of adventure, and don't want to be stuck with cancellation fees when you change your mind, by all means stick our books in the glove compartment and hit the road. If you're traveling in the off-season, or even midweek in season, you'll have a grand time. But look for a room by late afternoon; never wait until after dinner and expect to find something decent. Some inns offer a discount after 4:00 P.M. for last-minute bookings; it never hurts to ask.

Payment

The vast majority of inns now accept credit cards. A few accept credit cards for the initial deposit but prefer cash, traveler's checks, or personal checks for the balance; others offer the reverse policy. When no credit cards are accepted at all, you can settle your bill with a personal check, traveler's check, or even (!) cash.

When using your credit card to guarantee a reservation, be aware that most inns will charge your card for the amount of the deposit, unlike motels and hotels which don't put through the charge until you've checked in. A few will put a "hold" on your card for the full amount of your entire stay, plus the cost of meals and incidentals that you may (or may not) spend. If you're using your card to reserve a fairly extended trip, you may find that you're well over your credit limit without actually having spent a nickel. We'd suggest inquiring; if the latter is the procedure, either send a check for the deposit or go elsewhere. If you have used American Express, Diners Club, Mastercard, or Visa to guarantee your reservation, these companies guarantee if a room is not available, the hotel is supposed to find you a free room in a comparable hotel, plus transportation and a free phone call.

Rates

All rates quoted are per room, unless otherwise noted as being per person. Rates quoted per person are usually based on double occupancy, unless otherwise stated.

"Room only" rates do not include any meals. In most cases two or three meals a day are served by the hotel restaurant, but are charged separately. Average meal prices are noted when available. In a very few cases no meals are served on the premises at all; rooms in these facilities are usually equipped with kitchenettes.

B&B rates include bed and breakfast. Breakfast, though, can vary from a simple continental breakfast to an expanded continental breakfast to a full breakfast. Afternoon tea and evening refreshments are sometimes included as well.

MAP (Modified American Plan) rates are often listed per person and include breakfast and dinner. Only a few of the inns listed serve lunch, although many will prepare a picnic on request for an additional charge. Full board rates include three squares a day, and are usually found only at old-fashioned resorts and isolated ranches.

State and local sales taxes are not included in the rates unless otherwise indicated; the percentage varies from state to state, city to city, and can reach 20% in a few urban centers, although 10–15% is more typical.

When inquiring about rates, always ask if any off-season or special package rates are available. Sometimes discounted rates are available *only* on request; seniors and AAA members often qualify for substantial discounts. During the week, when making reservations at city hotels or country inns, it's important to ask if any corporate rates are available. Depending on the establishment, you may or may not be asked for some proof of corporate affiliation (a business card is usually all that's needed), but it's well worth inquiring, since the effort can result in a saving of 15 to 20%, plus an upgrade to a substantially better room.

A number of companies specialize in booking hotel rooms in major cities at substantial discounts. Although you can ask for specific hotels by name, the largest savings are realized by letting the agency make the selection; they may be able to get you a discount of up to 65 percent. **Hotel Reservations Network** (8140 Walnut Hill Lane, Dallas, Texas 75231; 800–96–HOTEL) offers discount rates in over 20 U.S. cities plus London and Paris; **Quikbook** (381 Park Avenue South, New York, New York 10016; 800–789–9887) is a similar service with competitive rates. **Express Reservations** (3800 Arapahoe, Boulder, Colorado 80303; 800–356–1123) specializes in properties in New York City and Los Angeles. For San Francisco, try **San Francisco Reservations** (22 Second Street, Fourth Floor, San Francisco, California 94105; 800–677–1550).

Another money-saving trick can be to look for inns in towns a bit off the beaten path. If you stay in a town that neighbors a famous resort or historic community, you will often find that rates are anywhere from $20 to $50 less per night for equivalent accommodation. If you're travelling without reservations, and arrive at a half-empty inn in late afternoon, don't hesitate to ask for a price reduction or free room upgrade. And of course, watch for our ¢ symbol, which indicates places which are a particularly good value.

If an establishment has a specific tipping policy, whether it is "no tipping" or the addition of a set service charge, it is noted under "Rates." When both breakfast and dinner are included in the rates, a 15% service charge against the total bill—not just the room—is standard; some inns are charging 18–20%. A number of B&Bs are also adding on a service charge, a practice which also sits poorly with us. If you feel—as many of our readers do—that these fees are a sneaky way of making rates seem lower than they really are, let the innkeeper (and us) know how you feel. When no notation is made, it's generally expected that guests will leave $1–3 a night for the housekeeping staff and 15% for meal service. A number of inns have taken to leaving little cards or envelopes to remind guests to leave a tip for the housekeepers; most readers find this practice objectionable. If you welcome a no-tipping policy and object to solicitation, speak up.

While the vast majority of inns are fairly priced, there are a few whose rates have become exorbitant. Others fail to stay competitive, charging top weekend rates when a nearby luxury hotel is offering a beautiful suite at a lower price. No matter how lovely the breakfast, how thoughtful the innkeepers, there's a limit to the amount one will pay for a room without an in-room telephone, TV, or a full-size private bathroom. We recently learned about a B&B that has the nerve to charge $125 for a room with shared bath, and asks you to bring your own pool towels during the summer!

Deposits and cancellations

Nearly all innkeepers print their deposit and cancellation policies clearly on their brochures. Deposits generally range from payment of the first night's stay to 50% of the cost of the entire stay. Some inns repeat the cancellation policy when confirming reservations. In general, guests canceling well in advance of the planned arrival (two to four weeks is typical) receive a full refund minus a cancellation fee. After that date, no refunds are offered unless the room is resold to someone else. A few will not refund *even if the room is resold,* so take careful note. If you're making a credit card booking over the phone, be sure to find out what the cancellation policy is.

We would like to applaud the inns which require only two to seven days' notice of cancellation, and would love to see other areas follow suit. We also feel strongly that even if you cancel on short notice, you should be given the opportunity to rebook within a reasonable time period rather than losing your entire deposit.

Sometimes the shoe may be on the other foot. Even if you were told earlier that the inn at which you really wanted to stay was full, it may be worthwhile to make a call to see if cancellations have opened up any last-minute vacancies.

Minimum stays

Two- and three-night minimum weekend and holiday stays are the rule at many inns during peak periods. We have noted these when possible, although we suspect that the policy may be more common than is always indicated in print. On the other hand, you may just be hitting a slow period, so it never hurts to call at the last minute to see if a one-night reservation would be accepted. Again, cancellations are always a possibility; you can try calling on a Friday or Saturday morning to see if something is available for that night.

Pets

Very few of the inns and hotels listed accept pets. When they do we've noted it under "Extras." On the other hand, most of the inns listed in this book have at least one dog or cat, sometimes more. These pets are usually found in the common areas, sometimes in guest rooms as well. If you are highly allergic to animals, *we strongly urge that you inquire for details before making reservations.*

Children

Some inns are family-style places and welcome children of all ages; we've marked them with our ♦ symbol. Others do not feel that they have facilities for the very young and only allow children over a certain age. Still others cultivate an "adults only" atmosphere and don't even welcome children at dinner. When inns and hotels do not encourage all children, we've noted the age requirement under the heading "Restrictions." If special facilities are available to children, these are noted under "Facilities" and "Extras." If an inn does not exclude children yet does not offer any special amenities or rate reductions for them, we would suggest it only for the best-behaved youngsters.

Whatever the policy, you may want to remind your children to follow the same rules of courtesy toward others that we expect of adults. Be aware that the pitter-patter of little feet on an uncarpeted hardwood floor can sound like a herd of stampeding buffalo to those on the floor below. Children used to the indestructible plastics of contemporary homes will need to be reminded (more than once) to be gentle with antique furnishings.

State laws governing discrimination by age are affecting policies at some inns. To our knowledge, both California and Michigan now have such laws on the books, although this was rarely reflected in the brochures sent to us by inns in those states. Some inns get around age discrimination by limiting room occupancy to two adults. This discourages families by forcing them to pay for two rooms instead of one. Our own children are very clear on their preferences: although they've been to many inns that don't encourage guests under the age of 12, they find them "really boring"; on the other hand, they've loved every family-oriented place we've ever visited.

Porterage and packing

Only the largest of our listings will have personnel whose sole job is to assist guests with baggage. In the casual atmosphere associated with many inns, it is simply assumed that guests will carry their own bags. If you do need assistance with your luggage, don't hesitate to ask.

If you're planning an extended trip to a number of small inns, we'd suggest packing as lightly as possible, using two small bags rather than one large suitcase. You'll know why if you've ever tried hauling a 50-pound oversize suitcase up a steep and narrow 18th-century staircase. On he other hand, don't forget about the local climate when assembling your wardrobe. In mountainous and desert regions, day- and nighttime temperatures can vary by as much as 40 degrees. Also, bear in mind that Easterners tend to dress more formally than Westerners, so pack accordingly.

Meals

If you have particular dietary restrictions—low-salt, vegetarian, or religious—or allergies—to caffeine, nuts, whatever—be sure to mention these when making reservations and *again* at check-in. If you're allergic to a common breakfast food or beverage, an evening reminder will ensure that you'll be able to enjoy the breakfast that's been prepared for you. Most innkeepers will do their best to accommodate your special needs, although, as one innkeeper noted tartly, "we're not operating a hospital."

In preparing each listing, we asked the owners to give us the cost of prix fixe and à la carte meals when available. An "alc dinner" price at the end of the "Rates" section is the figure we were given when we requested the average cost of a three-course dinner with a half bottle of house wine, including tax and tip. Prices listed for prix fixe meals do not include wine and service. Lunch prices, where noted, do not include the cost of any alcoholic beverage. Hotels and inns which serve meals to the public are noted with the ✕ symbol.

Dinner and lunch reservations are always a courtesy and are often essential. Most B&B owners will offer to make reservations for you; this can be especially helpful in getting you a table at a popular restaurant in peak season and/or on weekends. Some of the establishments we list operate restaurants fully open to the public. Others serve dinner primarily to their overnight guests, but they also will serve meals to outsiders; reservations are essential at such inns, usually eight or more hours in advance.

A few restaurants require jackets and ties for men at dinner, even in rather isolated areas. Of course, this is more often the case in traditional New England and the Old South than in the West. Unless you're going only to a very casual country lodge, we recommend that men bring these items along and that women have corresponding attire.

Breakfast: Breakfast is served at nearly every inn or hotel listed in this guide. Those that do not, should. No inn is truly "wonderful" if you have to get in your car and drive somewhere for a morning meal. Nor do we consider the availability of coffee and tea alone an appropriate substitute. The vast majority of lodgings listed include breakfast in their rates. Whenever possible we describe a typical breakfast, rather than using the terms "continental" or "full" breakfast.

Continental breakfast ranges from coffee and store-bought pastry to a lavish offering of fresh fruit and juices, yogurt and granola, cereals, even cheese and cold meats, homemade muffins and breads, and a choice of decaffeinated or regular coffee, herbal and regular tea. There's almost as much variety in the full breakfasts, which range from the traditional eggs,

13

bacon, and toast, plus juice and coffee, to three-course gourmet extrava-
ganzas.

We've received occasional complaints about breakfasts being too rich
in eggs and cream, and too sweet, with no plain rolls or bread. A dietary
splurge is fun for a weekend escape, but on a longer trip we'd advise
requesting a "healthy breakfast" from your innkeeper. You can be sure
that they don't eat their own breakfasts every day! Equally important to
many guests are the timing and seating arrangements at breakfast. As one
reader put it: "We stayed at a B&B where breakfast is served at one large
table, promptly at 8:30 A.M. This is a mixed blessing. The breakfast was
lovely and fresh, and the setting encouraged a convivial meal with the
other guests. But there are those who consider any conversation prior to
a second cup of coffee to be barbaric. More importantly, this doesn't allow
for different time schedules." *(William Hussey)*

Lunch: Very few of the inns and hotels listed here serve lunch. Those
that do generally operate a full-service restaurant or are located in isolated
mountain settings with no restaurants nearby. Quite a number of B&B
inns are happy to make up picnic lunches for an additional fee.

Dinner: Meals served at the inns listed here vary widely from simple
home-style family cooking to gourmet cuisine. We are looking for food
that is a good, honest example of the type of cooking involved. Ingredients should be fresh and homemade as far as is possible; service and
presentation should be pleasant and straightforward. We have no interest
in the school of "haute pretentious" where the hyperbolic descriptions
found on the menu far exceed the chef's ability.

Drinks

With a very few exceptions (noted under "Restrictions" in each listing)
alcoholic beverages may be enjoyed in moderation at all of the inns and
hotels listed. Most establishments with a full-service restaurant serving
the public as well as overnight guests are licensed to serve beer, wine, and
liquor to their customers, although "brown-bagging" or BYOB (bring
your own bottle) is occasionally permitted, especially in dry counties. Bed
& breakfasts, and inns serving meals primarily to overnight guests, do not
typically have liquor licenses, although most will provide guests with
setups, i.e., glasses, ice, and mixers, at what is often called a BYO (bring
your own) bar.

Overseas visitors will be amazed at the hodgepodge of regulations
around the country. Liquor laws are determined in general by each state
but individual counties, or even towns, can prohibit or restrict the sale o
alcoholic beverages, even beer.

Smoking

The majority of B&Bs and inns prohibit indoor smoking entirely, allowing
it only on porches and verandas; a few don't allow smoking anywhere on
the grounds. Larger inns and hotels usually do permit smoking, prohibit

ing it only in some guest rooms, and dining areas. Where prohibitions apply we have noted this under "Restrictions." We suggest that confirmed smokers be courteous or make reservations elsewhere. If there is no comment about smoking under "Restrictions," non-smokers should ask if smokers are in residence.

Physical limitations and wheelchair accessibility

We've used the well-known symbol ♿, to denote hotels and inns that are wheelchair accessible. Where available, additional information is noted under the "Extras" heading. Unfortunately, what is meant by this symbol varies dramatically. In the case of larger hotels and newer inns, it usually means full access; in historic buildings, access may be limited to the restaurant and public rest rooms only, or to a specific guest room but not the common areas. *Call the inn/hotel directly for full details and to discuss your needs.*

If you do not need a wheelchair but have difficulty with stairs, we urge you to mention this when making reservations; many inns and small hotels have one or two rooms on the ground floor, but very few have elevators. Similarly, if you are visually handicapped, do share this information so that you may be given a room with good lighting and no unexpected steps.

Air-conditioning

Heat is a relative condition, and the perceived need for air-conditioning varies tremendously from one individual to the next. If an inn or hotel has air-conditioning, you'll see this listed under "Rooms." If it's important to you, be sure to ask when making reservations. If air-conditioning is not available, check to see if fans are provided. Remember that top-floor rooms in most inns (usually a converted attic) can be uncomfortably warm even in relatively cool climates.

Transportation

A car is more or less essential for visiting most of the inns and hotels listed here, as well as the surrounding sights of interest. Exceptions are those located in the major cities. In some historic towns, a car is the easiest way to get there, but once you've arrived, you'll want to find a place to park the car and forget about it.

If you are traveling by public transportation, check the "Extras" section at the end of each write-up. If the innkeepers are willing to pick you up from the nearest airport, bus, or train station, you'll see it noted here. This service is usually free or available at modest cost. If it's not listed, the innkeeper will direct you to a commercial facility that can help.

Parking

Although not a concern in most cases, parking is a problem in many cities, beach resorts, and historic towns. If you'll be traveling by car, ask the innkeeper for advice when making reservations. If parking is not on-site, stop at the hotel first to drop off your bags, then go park the car. In big cities, if "free parking" is included in the rates, this usually covers only one arrival and departure. Additional "ins and outs" incur substantial extra charges. Be sure to ask.

If on-site parking is available in areas where parking can be a problem, we've noted it under "Facilities." Since it's so rarely a problem in country inns, we haven't included that information in those listings. Regrettably, security has become an issue in most cities. Never leave anything visible inside the car; it's an invitation for break-in and theft.

Christmas travel

Many people love to travel to a country inn or hotel at Christmas. Quite a number of places do stay open through the holidays, but the extent to which the occasion is celebrated varies widely indeed. We know of many inns that decorate beautifully, serve a fabulous meal, and organize all kinds of traditional Christmas activities. But we also know of others, especially in ski areas, that do nothing more than throw a few token ornaments on a tree. Be sure to inquire.

Ranch vacations

Spending time on a ranch can give you a real feel for the West—far more than you could ever experience when driving from one tourist attraction to the next. Many families find a ranch they like and return year after year, usually for the same week, and eventually become close friends with other guests who do the same. When booking a ranch vacation, it's wise to ask about the percentage of return guests, and to get the names and telephone numbers of some in your area. If the return percentage is low, or the telephone numbers of recent guests are "unavailable," try another ranch. When reading a glossy brochure, make sure that the pictures shown were taken on the ranch, and clearly show its cabins (both interior and exterior), horses, and other facilities, rather than generic Western pictures available anywhere.

While wonderful, ranch vacations are expensive, especially when you're budgeting for a family. When toting up the costs, remember to add on 10–15% for gratuities to the wranglers and staff—this is standard at almost every ranch but is not always mentioned in the rate information. When comparing prices, keep in mind that a ranch with a four-diamond AAA rating, gourmet cuisine, and resort facilities will not be in the same ballpark as a working ranch with comfortable but more basic food, accommodation, and activities. Finally, make sure that you pay for the things you want. A ranch with a full-fledged children's program is likely to cost more than one with a more casual approach. The cost of a ranch which includes unlimited riding will inevitably be higher than one that charges for riding by the hour. If you live and breathe horses, unlimited riding is clearly a better value. If one or two rides is all you have in mind, then the à la carte approach makes better sense. Read the fine print to be sure of exactly what is included. By the way, if you or another member of your family is not too keen on horses, look for a ranch that offers other activities—tennis, water sports, and hiking—or for a ranch that is near a major city or tourist center.

Is innkeeping for me?

Many of our readers fantasize about running their own inn; for some the fantasy may soon become a reality. Before taking the big plunge, it's vital to find out as much as you can about this demanding business. Begin by reading *How to Start and Run Your Own Bed & Breakfast Inn* by long-time innkeepers Ripley Hotch and Carl Glassman, covering everything from financing to marketing to day-to-day innkeeping responsibilities. ($14.95; Stackpole Books, P.O. Box 1831, Harrisburg PA 17105; 800–732–3669). The two best sources for in-depth information are the Professional Association of Innkeepers, International (PAII—pronounced "pie") and Oates and Bredfeldt Consultants. PAII co-directors Pat Hardy and Jo Ann Bell publish *Innkeeping Newsletter,* various books for would-be innkeepers, and coordinate workshops for aspiring innkeepers. For details contact them at PAII, P.O. Box 90710, Santa Barbara, CA 93190; 805–569–1853. An equally good source, especially in the East, are consultants Bill Oates and Heide Bredfeldt. Contact them at P.O. Box 1162, Brattleboro, VT 05301; 802–254–5931 to find out when and where they'll be offering their next seminar entitled "How to Purchase and Operate a Country Inn." Bill and Heide are highly respected pros in this field and have worked with innkeepers facing a wide range of needs and problems; his newsletter, *Innquest,* is written for prospective innkeepers looking to buy property.

For more information

The best sources of travel information in this country and in Canada are absolutely free; in many cases, you don't even have to supply the cost of a stamp or telephone call. They are the state and provincial tourist offices.

For each state you'll be visiting, request a copy of the official state map, which will show you every little highway and byway and will make exploring much more fun; it will also have information on state parks and major attractions in concise form. Ask also for a calendar of events and for information on topics of particular interest, such as fishing or antiquing, vineyards or crafts; many states have published B&B directories, and some are quite informative. If you're going to an area of particular tourist interest, you might also want to ask the state office to give you the name of the regional tourist board for more detailed information. You'll find the addresses and telephone numbers for all the states and provinces covered in the Appendix at the back of this book.

You may also want to contact the local chamber of commerce for information on local sights and events of interest or even an area map. You can get the necessary addresses and telephone numbers from the inn or hotel where you'll be staying or from the state tourist office.

If you are one of those people who never travel with fewer than three guidebooks (which includes us), you will find the AAA and Mobil regional guides to be helpful references. The Mobil guides can be found in any bookstore, while the AAA guides are distributed free on request to members. Both series cover hotels, restaurants, and sightseeing information, although we find the AAA guides to offer wider coverage and more details. If you're not already an AAA member, *we'd strongly urge you join before your next trip;* in addition to their road service, they offer quality guidebooks and maps, and an excellent discount program at many hotels (including a number listed here).

Guidebooks are published only once every year or two; if you'd like to have a more frequent update, we'd suggest one of the following:

Country Inns/Bed & Breakfasts (P.O. Box 182, South Orange, NJ 07079; 201–762–7090), $18, 6 issues annually. You know what they say about a picture being worth 1000 words. A must for inngoers.

Yellow Brick Road (2445 Northcreek Lane, Fullerton, CA 92631; 714–680–3326 or 800–79 B and B), $46 for 12 issues annually, $4 single copy. Focuses on inns and special events in the western states and Hawaii.

Where is my favorite inn?

In reading through this book, you may find that your favorite inn is not listed, or that a well-known inn has been omitted from this edition. Why? Two reasons, basically: In several cases, establishments have been dropped because our readers had unsatisfactory experiences. Feel free to contact us for details. Other establishments have been omitted because we've had no reader feedback at all. This may mean that readers visiting these hotels and inns had satisfactory experiences but were not sufficiently impressed to write about them, or that readers were pleased but just assumed that someone else would take the trouble. If the latter applies, please, please, do write and let us know of your experiences. We try to visit as many inns as possible ourselves, but it is impossible to visit every place, every year. So please, keep those cards, letters, and telephone calls coming! As an added incentive, we will be sending free copies of the next edition of this book to our most helpful respondents.

Little Inns of Horror

We try awfully hard to list only the most worthy establishments, but sometimes the best-laid plans of mice and travel writers do go astray. Please understand that whenever we receive a complaint about an entry in our guide we feel terrible, and do our best to investigate the situation. Readers occasionally send us complaints about establishments listed in *other* guidebooks; these are quite helpful as warning signals.

The most common complaints we receive—and the least forgivable— are on the issue of dirt. Scummy sinks and bathtubs, cobwebbed windows, littered porches, mildewed carpeting, water-stained ceilings, and grimy linens are all stars of this horror show.

Next in line are problems dealing with the lack of maintenance: peeling paint and wallpaper; sagging, soft, lumpy mattresses; radiators that don't get hot and those that make strange noises; windows that won't open, windows that won't close, windows with no screens, decayed or inoperable window shades; moldy shower curtains, rusty shower stalls, worn-out towels, fluctuating water temperatures, dripping faucets, and showers that only dribble, top the list.

Food complaints come next on this disaster lineup: poorly prepared canned or frozen food when fresh is readily available; meals served on paper, plastic, or worst of all, styrofoam; and insensitivity to dietary needs. Some complaints are received about unhelpful, abrasive, or abusive innkeepers, with a few more about uncaring, inept, or invisible staff. Complaints are most common in full-service inns when the restaurant business preoccupies the owners' attention, leaving overnight guests to suffer. Last but not least are noise headaches: trucks and trains that sound like they're heading for your pillow, and being awakened by the sound of someone snoring—in the next room. More tricky are questions of taste—high Victorian might look elegant to you, funereal to me; my collectibles could be your Salvation Army thriftshop donation. In short, there are more than a few inns and hotels that give new meaning to the phrase "having reservations"; fortunately they're many times outnumbered by the many wonderful places listed in this guide.

Pet peeves

Although we may genuinely like an inn, minor failings can keep it from being truly wonderful. Heading our list of pet peeves is inadequate bedside reading lights and tables. We know that there is not always room for a second table, but a light can always be attached to the wall. For reasons of both safety and comfort, a lamp should be at every bedside. Another reader is irked by inadequate bathroom lighting: "I think it must be an innkeepers' conspiracy to keep me from ever getting my makeup on properly." *(SU)* Equally annoying is the addition of fancy amenities when the basics are inadequate. As one reader put it: "Brandy by the bed and chocolates on the pillow are no excuse to overlook all other aspects of an enjoyable stay. When everything else is perfect, the small touches make a hotel magical, but in the absence of solid comfort the extras are mostly jarring." *(Robert Freidus)* Other readers object to overly friendly innkeepers: "The innkeeper chatted with us all during breakfast, and was disappointed that we didn't plan to go in to say goodbye after we loaded up the car. Innkeepers should remember that the guests are customers, not long-lost relatives." *(Karl Weigers & Chris Zambito)* Another common gripe concerns clutter: "Although pretty and interesting, the many collectibles left us no space for our personal belongings." And: "Instructions were posted everywhere—how to operate door locks, showers, heat, air-conditioning, and more." Anything you'd like to add?

Glossary of Architectural and Decorating Terms

We are not architectural experts, and when we started writing *America's Wonderful Little Hotels & Inns*, we didn't know a dentil from a dependency, a tester from a transom. We've learned a bit more since then, and hope that our primer of terms, prepared by associate editor Nancy Barker, will also be helpful to you.

Adam: building style (1780–1840) featuring a classic box design with a dominant front door and fanlight, accented by an elaborate surround or an entry porch; cornice with decorative moldings incorporating dentil, swag, garland, or stylized geometric design. Three-part Palladian-style windows are common.

antebellum: existing prior to the U.S. Civil War (1861–1865).

Arts and Crafts movement: considered the first phase of the Modern movement that led to the Prairie style (1900–20) of Frank Lloyd Wright in Chicago, and the Craftsman style (1905–30) of the Greene brothers in Southern California. In the Arts and Crafts style, historical precedent for decoration and design was rejected and ornamentation was "modernized" to remove traces of its historic origins. It features low-pitched roofs, wide eave overhangs, and both symmetrical and asymmetrical front façades.

beaded board: simple ornamented board, with a smooth, flat surface alternating with a half-round, rod-like carving (bead) running the length of the board. Common wainscoting or panelling in Victorian-era homes.

carpenter Gothic: *see* country, folk Victorian.

chinoiserie: imitation of Chinese decorative motifs; i.e., simulated Oriental lacquer covering pine or maple furniture. See also Chinese Chippendale below.

Chippendale: named for English furniture designer, Thomas Chippendale, of the Queen Anne period (1750–1790); the style varies from the Queen Anne style in ornamentation, with more angular shapes and heavier carving of shells, leaves, scrolls. Chinese Chippendale furniture employs chiefly straight lines, bamboo turnings, and as decoration, fluting, and fretwork in a variety of lattice patterns.

Colonial Revival: building style (1880–1955) featuring a classic box design with a dominant front door elaborated with pilasters and either a pediment (Georgian-style) or a fanlight (Adam-style); double-hung windows symmetrically balanced.

corbel: an architectural member that projects from a wall to support a weight and is stepped outward and upward from the vertical surface.

Corinthian: column popular in Greek Revival style for support of porch roofs; the capitals are shaped like inverted bells and decorated with acanthus leaves.

cornice: projecting horizontal carving or molding that crowns a wall or roof.

country, folk Victorian: simple house form (1870–1910) with accents of Victorian (usually Queen Anne or Italianate) design in porch spindlework and cornice details. Also known as carpenter Gothic.

Craftsman: building style (1905–1930) with low-pitched, gabled roof and wide, unenclosed eave overhang; decorative beams or braces added under gables; usually one-story; porches supported by tapered square columns.

dentil: exterior or interior molding characterized by a series of small rectangular blocks projecting like teeth.

dependencies: buildings that are subordinate to the main dwelling; i.e., a detached garage or barn. *See* also garçonnière.

Doric: column popular in Greek Revival style for support of porch roofs; the simplest of the three styles, with a fluted column, no base, and a square capital.

Eastlake: architectural detail on Victorian houses, commonly referred to as "gingerbread." Typically has lacy spandrels and knob-like beads, in exterior and interior design, patterned after the style of Charles Eastlake, an English furniture designer. Eastlake also promoted Gothic and Jacobean Revival styles with their strong rectangular lines; quality workmanship instead of machine manufacture; and the use of varnished oak, glazed tiles, and unharmonized color.

Eclectic movement: architectural tradition (1880–1940) which emphasized relatively pure copies of Early American, Mediterranean, or Native American homes.

eyebrow dormer: a semi-circular, narrow window over which the adjoining roofing flows in a continuous wave line; found on Shingle or Richardsonian Romanesque buildings.

faux: literally, French for "false." Refers commonly to woodwork painted to look like marble or another stone.

Federal: *See* Adam.

four-poster bed: variation on a tester bed but one in which the tall corner posts, of equal height, do not support a canopy. Carving of rice sheaves was a popular design in the Southern states, and signified prosperity.

Franklin stove: metal heating stove which is set out into the room to conserve heat and better distribute it. Named after its inventor Benjamin Franklin; some designs resemble a fireplace when their front doors are open.

gambrel roof: a two-slope, barn-style roof, with a lower steeper slope and a flatter upper one.

garçonnière: found on antebellum estates; a dependency housing unmarried male guests and family members.

Georgian: building style (1700–1830) featuring a classic box design with a dominant front door elaborated with pilasters and a pediment, usually with a row of small panes of glass beneath the crown or in a transom; cornices with decorative moldings, usually dentil.

Gothic Revival: building style (1840–1880) with a steeply pitched roof, steep gables with decorated vergeboards, and one-story porch supported by flattened Gothic arches. Windows commonly have pointed-arch shape.

Greek Revival: building style (1825–1860) having a gabled or hipped roof of low pitch; cornice line of main and porch roofs emphasized by a wide band of trim; porches supported by prominent columns (usually Doric).

half-tester bed: a bed with a low footboard and a canopy projecting from the posts at the head of the bed. Pronounced "half tee'-stir."

Ionic: column popular in Greek Revival style for support of porch roofs; the caps of the column resemble the rolled ends of a scroll.

Italianate: building style (1840–1885) with two or three stories and a low-pitched roof with widely overhanging eaves supported by decorative brackets; tall, narrow windows arched or curved above with elaborate crowns. Many have a square cupola or tower.

keeping room: in a Colonial-era home, the equivalent of a modern family room; it was usually warm from proximity to kitchen, so infant and the ill were "kept" here.

kiva: stuccoed, corner beehive-shaped fireplace common in adobe homes in Southwestern U.S.

latillas: ceiling of unpeeled, rough sticks, supported by vigas (rough beams); seen in flat-roofed adobe homes

Lincrusta (or Lincrusta-Walton): an embossed, linoleum-like wallcovering made with linseed oil, developed in 1877 in England by Frederick Walton.

lintel: horizontal beam, supported at both ends, that spans an opening

mansard roof: having two slopes on all sides with the lower slope steeper than the upper one.

Mission: building style (1890–1920) with Spanish mission-style parapet; commonly with red tile roof, overhanging, open eaves, and smooth stucco finish. In furniture, the Mission style is best represented by the work of designer Gustav Stickley. Using machine manufacture, he utilized simple, rectangular lines and favored quarter-sawn white oak for the rich texture of the graining.

Palladian window: typically a central window with an arched or semicircular head.

Pewabic (tile): glazed tiles made in the Detroit, Michigan, area, in the first half of the 1890s, whose unique manufacturing process has been lost

pocket doors: doors that open by sliding into a recess (pocket) in the wall.

portal: (or *portale*) in Spanish-style homes, the long, narrow porch that opens onto an internal courtyard; it functions as a sheltered passageway between rooms.

post and beam: building style based on the Medieval post-and-girder method, where upper loads are supported by heavy corner posts and cross timbers. In contemporary construction, the posts and beams are often left exposed on the interior.

Prairie: building style (1900–1920) with low-pitched roof and widely overhanging eaves; two stories with one-story wings or porches; façade detailing that emphasizes horizontal lines; massive, square porch supports

Pueblo Revival: building style (1910 to present) with flat roof, parapet above; corners and edges blunted or rounded; projecting vigas, stepped back roof lines, and irregular stucco wall surfaces. Influenced by the flat-roofed Spanish Colonial buildings and Native American pueblos; popular in Arizona and New Mexico; common in Santa Fe and Albuquerque

Queen Anne: building style (1880–1910) with a steeply pitched roof of irregular shapes; an asymmetrical façade with one-story porch; patterned shingles, bay windows, single tower. In furniture design the Queen Anne style was prevalent from 1725 to 1750, characterized by a graceful unadorned curve of the leg (known as cabriole) and repeated curve of the top crest and vase-form back (splat) of a chair.

quoin: wood, stone, or brick materials that form the exterior corner of

22

a building and are distinguishable from the background surface because of texture, color, size, or material.

rice-carved bed: *See* four-poster bed.

Richardsonian Romanesque: building style (1880–1900) with massive masonry walls of rough, squared stonework and round-topped arches over windows, porch supports, or entrances; round tower with conical roof common.

Santa Fe: *see* Pueblo Revival.

Second Empire: building style (1855–1885) with mansard roof adorned with dormer windows on lower slope; molded cornices above and below lower roof, and decorative brackets beneath eaves.

Shaker: style of furniture which represents the Shaker belief in simplicity. The finely crafted pieces are functional, without ornamentation. Chairs have ladder backs, rush seats, and simple turned legs; tables and cabinets are angular, with smooth surfaces.

Sheraton: named for English furniture designer, Thomas Sheraton, of the Federal period (early 1800s); style marked by straight lines, delicate proportions, wood inlays, and spare use of carving; characteristically tapered legs.

Shingle: building style (1880–1900) with walls and roofing of continuous wood shingles; no decorative detailing at doors, windows, corners, or roof overhang. Irregular, steeply pitched roof line and extensive porches common.

shotgun: simple 19th century house form suited to narrow urban lots, featuring a single-story, front gable building one room wide. Rooms and doorways are in a direct line, front to back; theorectically, a bullet fired through the front door would travel through the house unobstructed.

spandrel: decorative trim that fits the top corners of doorways, porches, or gables; usually triangular in shape.

Spanish Colonial: building style (1600–1900) of thick masonry walls, with low pitched or flat roof, interior wooden shutters covering small window openings, and multiple doorways. Pitched roof style often has half-cylindrical tiles; flat style has massive horizontal beams embedded in walls to support heavy roof of earth or mortar. Internal courtyards or cantilevered second-story porches are common.

Stick: building style (1860–1890) with a steeply pitched, gabled roof, usually with decorative trusses at apex; shingle or board walls interrupted by patterns of boards (stickwork) raised from the surface for emphasis.

Territorial: a variation of the Spanish Colonial building style found in New Mexico, western Texas, and Arizona. The flat roof and single story are topped by a protective layer of fired brick to form a decorative crown.

tester bed: a bed with a full canopy (the tester), supported at all four corners by tall posts. Pronounced "tee'-stir."

transom: usually refers to a window placed above a doorway.

trompe l'oeil: literally, French for "to trick the eye." Commonly refers to wall paintings that create an optical illusion.

Tudor: building style (1890–1940) with steeply pitched roof, usually cross-gabled; decorative half-timbering; tall, narrow, multi-paned windows; massive chimney crowned with decorative chimney pots.

vergeboard: decorative trim extending from the roof overhang of Tudor, Gothic Revival, or Queen Anne-style houses.

vernacular: style of architecture employing the commonest forms, materials, and decorations of a period or place.

viga(s): exposed (interior) and projecting (exterior) rough-hewn wooden roof beams common in adobe homes in Southwestern U.S.

wainscoting: most commonly, narrow wood paneling found on the lower half of a room's walls.

widow's walk: a railed observation platform built above the roof of a coastal house to permit unobstructed views of the sea. Name derives from the fate of many wives who paced the platform waiting for the return of their husbands from months (or years) at sea. Also called a "captain's walk."

Windsor: style of simple chair, with spindle back, turned legs, and usually a saddle seat. Considered a "country" design, it was popular in 18th and early 19th century towns and rural areas.

For more information:

A Field Guide to American Houses (Virginia and Lee McAlester, New York: Alfred A. Knopf, 1984; $19.95, paperback) was an invaluable source in preparing this glossary, and is highly recommended. Its 525 pages are lavishly illustrated with photographs and diagrams.

Clues to American Architecture (Marilyn W. Klein and David P. Fogle, Washington, D.C.: Starrhill Press, 1985; $6.95, paperback) is a handy, affordable 64-page pocket guide to over 30 architectural styles, from the Colonial period to contemporary construction. Each is clearly described in easy-to-understand language, and illustrated with numerous detailed sketches. Also in the same style and format is *Clues to American Furniture* (Jean Taylor Federico, Washington, D.C.: Starrhill Press, 1988; $6.95) covering design styles from Pilgrim to Chippendale, Eastlake to Art Deco. If your bookstore doesn't stock these titles, contact Starrhill directly at P.O. Box 32342, Washington, D.C. 20007; 202–387–9805.

Regional itineraries

Contributing editor Suzanne Carmichael has prepared these delightful itineraries to lead you from the best-known towns and cities through beautiful countryside, over less-traveled scenic highways to delightful towns and villages, to places where sights both natural and historic outnumber the modern "attractions" that so often litter the contemporary landscape.

To get a rough idea of where each itinerary will lead you, take a look at the appropriate map at the back of this book. But to really see where you'll be heading, pull out a detailed full-size map or road atlas, and use a highlighter to chart your path. (If you're hopeless when it comes to reading maps, ask the AAA to help you plan the trip with one of their Triptiks.) Some of our routes are circular, others are meant to be followed from one end to another; some are fairly short, others cover hundreds of miles. They can be traveled in either direction, or for just a section of the suggested route. You can sample an itinerary for a weekend, a week, or even two, depending on your travel style and the time available. For information on what to see and do along the way, refer to our state and local introductions and to a good regional guidebook. For a list of places to stay en route, see the list of towns at the end of each itinerary, then refer to the entries in the state chapters for full details.

Northwest Mountain and River Route Most visitors to the Northwest head for the fabled Oregon coast, friendly but sophisticated Seattle, the Olympic Peninsula, or Washington's San Juan Islands. Our route introduces you to less-traveled areas in the Cascade Mountains, along the Columbia River—even through rarely visited ancient lava beds.

Start your route in Portland, heading south on I-5 through the Willamette Valley past Albany to Eugene. Stop in Eugene to picnic in one of the parks along the Willamette River; in spring, visit Hendricks Park Rhododendron Garden to see over 6000 plants in dazzling bloom. Head east on Route 126, which winds along the scenic McKenzie River. A few miles past the town of McKenzie Bridge, turn east on Route 242, which emerges from deep forest to pass miles of black lava set against a Cascade Mountain backdrop.

At Sisters, turn south on Route 20 to Bend, a small resort town near Mount Bachelor ski resort. Take a brief detour south 15 miles on Route 97 to see both the Lava River Cave and the Lava Cast Forest, two unique formations left by ancient volcanoes.

Continue north on Route 97 to Madras where you have your choice of two routes to the Columbia River. Either follow Route 97 through the almost-ghost town of Shaniko and up to Biggs, then west along the river on I-94 to Hood River, *or* follow Route 26 across the Warm Springs Indian Reservation to Timberline Lodge at the foot of Mt. Hood, and then take Route 35 to Hood River. If you choose Route 97, detour on Route 218 to see the unusual John Day Fossil Beds National Monument.

Oregon's apple and winter pear orchards surround Hood River, a pleasant river town. Cross over the Columbia here to Washington state where you can take a side trip north on Route 141 to Trout Lake, a jumping off point for Mt. Adams wilderness explorations. To continue on our route, follow Route 14 east along the Columbia River, stopping at Maryhill, a bizarre mansion built by Samuel Hill in 1907 and now housing an eclectic art collection (don't miss Hill's version of Stonehenge, one mile east).

Turn north on Route 97 through Goldendale, following it through Toppenish, stopping to visit the Yakima Indian Nation Museum, and proceeding to Yakima, gateway to Washington's wine country. Hop on I-82, exiting almost immediately on scenic Route 281. If you have the time, loop north from Ellensburg on Route 97 past Bavarian-esque Leavenworth, to Chelan, at the base of skinny, 55-mile long Lake Chelan. Board an excursion boat to Stehekin at the tip of the lake, then return down Route 97, and go west on Route 970 to Cle Elum. If time is short, head west from Ellensburg on Route 10 through the Cascade foothills to Cle Elum.

INTRODUCTION

I-90 west is your route to Seattle, passing towering Cascade Mountain peaks, and local ski areas near Snoqualmie Pass. Exit at North Bend to visit Snoqualmie (where the TV series *Twin Peaks* was filmed), or stop in Issaquah to see clusters of gift-shop malls. Our route ends in Seattle, but if you need to return to Portland, follow I-5 south, stopping to see what remains of Mount St. Helens and visiting the new National Volcanic Monument, just east of Castle Rock.

Bed down for the night at accommodations in any of these towns (in order of their appearance above): Portland, Eugene, Sisters, Bend, Warm Springs, Timberline Lodge, Government Camp, Hood River (all in Oregon); Leavenworth, Chelan, Stehekin, Cle Elum, Snoqualmie, Seattle.

Northwest Ferry Tale   You can't experience the essence of the Northwest without getting out *on* the water. Small forested islands, busy Puget Sound ship traffic, and vistas of distant snowcapped peaks are all best sampled from a water vantage. Our route takes you on a series of ferries through some of the region's prettiest waterscapes and most imposing vistas. Before embarking, make sure you have sunglasses, binoculars (to spot whales and eagles), a sweater, and ferry schedules.

Begin in Seattle heading north on I-5 past Everett to Burlington. In spring, consider a side trip on Route 20 to Anacortes past fields of commercially grown daffodils and tulips. From Anacortes you can take a separate ferry trip to and through the San Juan Islands (see description in Washington state chapter). From Burlington take Route 11 north along the forested Puget Sound shoreline, which offers excellent views of the San Juan Islands. Route 11 ends in Bellingham, where you can stop by Fairhaven, a restored business district, or take a tiny ferry to Lummi Island, a quiet, pastoral isle once inhabited by local Native Americans.

Continue north on I-5 to Blaine, crossing point to British Columbia. Be aware that there's often a backup at customs, especially on holiday weekends. Across the border, go north on Route 99 to the city of Vancouver, which is worth several days of exploration itself. Tear yourself away, head south on Route 99, then take Route 17 to the Tsawwassen ferry terminal. From here huge ferries depart for Vancouver Island. Our suggestion: Make a reservation on one that stops midway (in the Strait of Georgia) at one of the quiet, forested Gulf Islands. Stay over night on Mayne Island or hop to the other Gulf Islands on small, interisland ferries.

After visiting the Gulf Islands, ferry to Sidney, just north of Victoria. Give yourself at least a full day to explore very-British Victoria, then book passage on the ferry that crosses the Strait of Juan de Fuca to Port Angeles, Washington. Before heading east, drive up to Hurricane Ridge (directly south of Port Angeles) for impressive views of the Olympic Mountains' highest peaks.

Take Route 101 east to Sequim where we recommend you follow a side road north to Dungeness Spit, a wisp of sand that sticks out 7 miles into the Strait, the longest natural sandspit in the U.S. Return to Route 101 past scenic bays and quiet coves, then turn north on Route 20 to Port Townsend. Restored Victorian homes line the high bluff above tiny downtown Port Townsend, a lively artists' community.

Board your next ferry at Port Townsend for Keystone on Whidbey

Island, Puget Sound's largest island. Turn northward first past Coupeville to Deception Pass State Park near the northern end of the island. After gaping at the Deception Pass chasm, head back south on Routes 20 and 525 through small island towns like Greenbank, Freeland, and Langley. Take one last ferry from Clinton to Mukilteo on the mainland, then follow I-5 south, back to Seattle.

Sample American and Canadian hospitality at accommodations in these towns/islands (in order of their appearance above): Seattle, Everett, Anacortes, Bellingham, Lummi Island, Blaine (Washington state); Vancouver, Gulf Islands (Mayne, Galiano, Salt Spring), Victoria (Mill Bay and Sooke also near Victoria, Canada); Port Angeles, Sequim, Port Townsend, Coupeville, Greenbank, Freeland, Langley (Washington state).

You'll need to call the numbers listed below for ferry schedules and reservations:

Lummi Island: Private ferry, no reservations available. Hourly sailings. For schedule call 206–671–3990.

Vancouver to Vancouver Island or Vancouver to Vancouver Island via Gulf Islands: Operated by BC Ferries. Reservations *not* available for Tsawwassen-Schwartz Bay (Vancouver Island); reservations *are required* for Tsawwassen-Gulf Islands (604–669–1211); reservations *not* available for inter-Gulf Island ferries. **Victoria to Port Angeles:** Operated by Black Ball Ferry. Reservations *not* available but call for schedule. Get to dock *hours* ahead of time during peak seasons (206–457–4491). **Port Townsend to Keystone; Clinton to Mukilteo; and Anacortes-San Juan Islands.** All operated by Washington State Ferries. No reservations available except from Anacortes to Sidney, BC. Clinton to Mukilteo route is very busy during commuter hours. Arrive at all three way ahead of scheduled sailing. (800–843–3779 in Washington state; 206–464–6400, out of state).

Sip-to-Shore Loop   The only way to grasp California's multiple personalities is to plan individual trips to each of its distinct regions, or combine no more than two in a single sojurn. Anchored in San Francisco, our suggested loop takes you through the region's famous wine country, then whisks you down California's rugged north coast. Because there is so much for the palate and eyes to sample on this route, it could be tasted briefly in a long weekend or savored over two weeks.

Begin by crossing the San Francisco Bay Bridge north to Sausalito, an artists' enclave where studios vie for space with stylish boutiques and small outdoor cafés. From here follow Route 101 past Ignacio, then Route 37 east to Sears Point. Turn north toward California wine country on Route 121. Stop in Sonoma to visit local vineyards as well as excellent Sonoma State Historic Park. North on Route 121, just past Glen Ellen (Jack London's home), turn east on an unnumbered road to Oakville (ask locally for directions if necessary). One of the prettiest backroads in the area, this route winds through hills of vineyards, with occasional, sweeping glimpses of the entire Napa valley.

At Oakville turn south on Route 29 if you want to visit wineries in Yountville and Napa, or follow our suggested route north on Route 29, tippling your way through Rutherford to St. Helena and Calistoga. Take a dip in Calistoga's mineral springs, slather yourself with its "restorative" mud, visit local geysers, or soar the skies in a glider. Set your compass northwest now, following Route 128 through Geyserville, into southern redwood country at Boonville.

Route 128 ends at the Pacific Ocean. Turn north on Route 1, passing through Albion and Little River to Mendocino. Although popular with tourists, Mendocino's charm penetrates even crowded summer sidewalks. An optional side trip is to follow Route 1 north from Mendocino past Fort Bragg and Westport, then Route 101 deep into redwood forests. Turn west at Alton to Ferndale, known for its "butterfat palaces" built by prosperous local dairymen. Return to Route 101 by following lightly traveled Route 211 through Capetown, Petrolia, and Bull Creek.

South from Mendocino, Route 1 hugs the northern coast, providing photogenic seascapes and sweeping panoramas; green hills, cut only by the highway, plunge directly into the sea. After passing through Elk, stop in Gualala to walk its nearby beaches, at Sea Ranch to view a planned community (west-coast style), and at Ft. Ross to visit a one-time Russian toehold in America.

Return to San Francisco on Route 1, passing through Bodega Bay and Inverness, taking detours to Pt. Reyes Light Station (south of Inverness), Muir Woods National Monument, and Muir Beach. For a final adventure in your sip-to-shore loop, head to Point San Pedro to embark on an overnight adventure on a San Francisco Bay island.

Spend your evenings in comfort at accommodations in the following towns (in order of their appearance above): San Francisco, Sausalito, Sonoma, Glen Ellen, Santa Rosa (northwest of Glen Ellen on Route 101), Yountville, Napa, St. Helena, Angwin, Calistoga, Geyserville, Healdsburg (south of Geyserville on Route 101), Boonville, Albion, Little River, Mendocino, Fort Bragg, Leggett, Westport, Ferndale, Elk, Gualala, Sea Ranch, Cazadero (east of Route 1, south of Sea Ranch), Bodega Bay, Inverness, Olema, Muir Beach.

Criteria for entries

Unlike many guidebooks, *we do not collect a membership or listing fee of any kind from the inns and hotels we include.* What matters to us is the feedback we get from you, our readers. This means we are free to write up the negative as well as the positive attributes of each inn listed, and if any given establishment does not measure up, there is no difficulty in dropping it.

Free copy of *INNroads* newsletter

Want to stay up-to-date on our latest finds? Send a business-size, self-addressed, stamped envelope with 52 cents postage and we'll send you the latest issue, *free!* While you're at it, why not enclose a report on any inns you've recently visited? Use the forms at the back of the book or your own stationery.

Key to Abbreviations and Symbols

For complete information and explanations, please see the Introduction.

¢ Especially good value for overnight accommodation.

⋔ Families welcome. Most (but not all) have cribs, baby-sitting, games, play equipment, and reduced rates for children.

✗ Meals served to public; reservations recommended or required.

⚘ Tennis court and swimming pool and/or lake on grounds. Golf usually on grounds or nearby.

♿ Limited or full wheelchair access; call for details.

Rates: Range from least expensive room in low season to most expensive room in peak season.

Room only: No meals included; European Plan (EP).

B&B: Bed and breakfast; includes breakfast, sometimes afternoon/ evening refreshment.

MAP: Modified American Plan; includes breakfast and dinner.

Full board: Three meals daily.

Alc lunch: À la carte lunch; average price of entrée plus nonalcoholic drink, tax, tip.

Alc dinner: Average price of three-course dinner, including half bottle of house wine, tax, tip.

Prix fixe dinner: Three- to five-course set dinner, excluding wine, tax, tip unless otherwise noted.

Extras: Noted if available. Always confirm in advance. Pets are not permitted unless specified; if you are allergic, ask for details; *most innkeepers have pets.*

We Want to Hear from You!

As you know, this book is effective only with your help. We really need to know about your experiences and discoveries. If you stayed at an inn or hotel listed here, we want to know how it was. Did it live up to our description? Exceed it? Was it what you expected? Did you like it? Were you disappointed? Delighted? Have you discovered new establishments that we should add to the next edition?

Tear out one of the report forms at the back of this book (or use your own stationery if you prefer) and write today. *Even if you write only "Fully endorse existing entry" you will have been most helpful.*

Thank You!

Alaska

Glacier Bay Country Inn, Gustavus

Alaska is one of our most extraordinary states and a fantastic place to visit. Its size and scope are difficult to imagine: It encompasses an area one-fifth the size of the continental United States and has 3,000 rivers, 3 million lakes, 19 mountains higher than 14,000 feet, and more than 5,000 glaciers—one of which is larger than the state of Rhode Island.

Peak travel season to Alaska is during the summer months, when the weather is warmest and the days are the longest. Travelers are learning that the weather can be nearly as nice in the late spring and early fall, when the need for advance reservations is less pressing.

Alaska is the only state that Americans tend to visit by cruise ship and tour bus—as though it were some exotic foreign country. While it's true that old "Sourdoughs" refer to the U.S. as the "Lower 48" and anyplace outside of Alaska as "Outside," the fact remains that the state is easily accessible by air, road, and ferry. The people speak English, willingly accept U.S. dollars, and are extremely friendly and hospitable!

For more information, contact the Alaska Tourism Marketing Council (P.O. Box 110801, Juneau, AK 99811–0801; 907–465–2010), for a copy of the helpful "Alaska Official Vacation Planner." Both the state of Alaska and the province of British Columbia maintain extensive schedules on their modern, well-equipped liners; contact them at Alaska Marine Highway, P.O. Box 25535, Juneau 99811 (907–465–3941 or 800–642–0066); and BC Ferries, 1112 Fort Street, Victoria, BC, V8V 4V2, Canada (604–386–3431 or 206–624–6663). It's also worthwhile getting information on the AlaskaPass (P.O. Box 351, Vaslion, WA 98070; 907–766–3145 or 800–248–7598) offering unlimited travel within a specified time period on 10 Alaska surface transport companies, including Alaska and BC ferries and rail companies, as well as numerous bus routes. Whatever your route, early reservations are *essential* for peak season travel; cabins on the ferries are often fully booked before February for summer sailings, as are rooms in the most desirable inns and B&Bs in popular destinations.

Reader tips: For planning your Alaska trip, our highest recommendations go to Pat Niven of **Alaska Northwest Travel Service** (130 Second Avenue South, Edmonds, Washington 98020; 206–775–4504 or 800–533–7381). "Our trip included travel by plane (jet and prop), ferry (we loved it), train, bus, and van, and included stops in Anchorage, Denali, Kotzebue, Juneau, Glacier Bay, and Vancouver, among others, with accommodations exclusively small hotels, inns, and B&Bs." *(SWS, also Susan Prizio)*

"Although the views were unsurpassed and the price was right, don't expect anything remotely resembling a cruise on the Alaska ferries. The facilities were spartan, sometimes old and frayed around the edges. Cleanliness could have been better, and often the staff was less than available. Omnipresent video games and average cafeteria food were typical. BC Ferries are far better kept up, appointed and the staff was friendlier." *(AP)*

Note: Special thanks to *Pat Niven* (see above) for her invaluable suggestions in preparing this chapter.

ANCHORAGE

With nearly 250,000 inhabitants, Anchorage is Alaska's largest and most cosmopolitan city. Its modern skyscrapers contrast vividly with the surrounding miles of wilderness—it's not unheard of for a moose to take a wrong turn and come wandering into town. Anchorage is the gateway to South Central Alaska, and is a key stopover for anyone heading north to Denali and Fairbanks, the Arctic Circle, or south to the Kenai Peninsula.

Reader tips: "Anchorage has plenty of traffic, and diesel buses and trucks can endanger your sleep far more than the proverbial midnight sun. If you're a light sleeper, *insist* on an upper-floor room, away from the street, for any of the downtown hotels." *(DK)* "A 'don't miss' excursion from Anchorage is the easy day trip to the Portage Glacier. The visitor's center offers an exceptional (free) movie, and we followed a wonderful hiking trail to the base of the Byron Glacier, where our grandchildren had a snowball fight. Though expensive, the *Ptarmigan* boat trip to the face of the Portage Glacier is well worth it." *(Rose Wolf)*

Also recommended: An appealing and affordable homestay B&B is **Kathy's B&B** (2430 Sunny Circle, 99502; 907–248–6171). "Our quarters included the entire downstairs, with a bedroom, living room with small stocked refrigerator, and bathroom/laundry. Lovely home; extremely clean and fresh smelling. There was even a porch swing outside the sliding glass doors. Breakfast is prepared to order from a wide choice of entrées. Seating is upstairs at the kitchen table which makes one feel part of the family. Kathy and Hal are pleasant, easy-going innkeepers, and the B&B is just eight minutes from the airport in a residential neighborhood." *(Susan Prizio)* B&B double rates are $65.

On a return trip to Anchorage, this same reader was equally delighted with **Slim Waltson's B&B** (611 M Street, #4, 99501; 907–277–8215). Accommodations include a two-bedroom suite, an efficiency apartment, and a second-floor double with a king-size bed; Double rates are $80–130, including a breakfast of cereal, fresh fruit, yogurt, muffins, and eggs (on request). "Clean, spacious accommodations. Good lighting, and beautiful views of Cook's Inlet from the kitchen/living room. Slim was willing to please; he asked what we liked to eat and provided that for breakfast. The downtown location made for easy access to many activities." *(Susan Prizio)* *Pat Niven* (see chapter introduction) suggests the following B&Bs, located in the residential areas near the airport: The **Fancy Moose** (3331 West 32nd Avenue, 99517; 907–243–7596) is a beautiful home, built as a B&B, with three guest rooms, each with private bath; B&B double rates are $95. **The Glacier Bear B&B** (4814 Malibu Road, 99517; 907–243–8818) has five guest rooms with private and semi-private baths; the $80–90 double rate includes a continental breakfast and airport pickups.

Information please: A downtown possibility is the **Arctic Fox Inn** (326 East Second Court, 99501; 907–272–4818) offering ten double rooms and apartments, at B&B double rates of $50–90, including a continental breakfast, served in the dining room. Guests can relax in the living room with cable TV, or in the recreation room, with pool table.

Anchorage Hotel ♿	*Tel:* 907–272–4553
330 E Street, 99501	800–544–0988
	Fax: 907–277–4483

Built in 1916, the Anchorage was remodeled in 1993 with contemporary furnishings, decorated in muted shades of dusty green, pink, and taupe. Televisions are discreetly tucked away in oak cabinets, and the rates include a light continental breakfast and the morning paper, delivered to your door.

"Elegant but friendly, with a convenient location for exploring the downtown area. Although the hotel has no restaurant, just around the corner is the Downtown Deli, with delicious homemade food." *(PN, also Karen Buchsbaum)* More comments needed.

Open All year.
Rooms 11 suites, 16 doubles—all with private bath and/or shower, telephone, radio, TV, desk, fan. Suites with refrigerator, honor bar, microwave, coffee maker.
Facilities Bar/lounge, elevator. Room service 6 A.M.–10 P.M. Off-street parking.
Location City center, 4th Ave. & E St. Next to Convention Center.
Restrictions Smoking restricted. No elevator.
Credit cards All major.
Rates B&B, $119–179 suite, $99–169 double, $89–159 single. Extra person, $10. AAA, AARP discount.

Voyager Hotel	*Tel:* 907–277–9501
501 K Street, 99501	In U.S.: 800–247–9070
	In AK: 800–478–9501

This sturdy brick and concrete four-story building has a small but pleasant lobby with ample couches for comfortable seating. Coffee, tea, and cocoa are available here in the morning. Most of the spacious guest rooms have two double beds, one set up much like a couch. There's a sturdy table to use for eating or as a desk. Each has a kitchenette, with plates and cutlery free on request. The decor is pleasant if unremarkable, with good lighting, firm beds, flowered spreads and matching drapes, and sturdy, well-made furnishings. The bathrooms are small but functional; there's a little sign on the mirror noting that toothbrushes, toothpaste, and razors are free at the desk if you forgot yours. The showers offer strong water pressure, steady hot water (no fluctuations) in ample supply. Owner Stan Williams is often at the front desk, available to answer questions and chat. He bought the hotel in 1977, when it was a rundown boarding house, and each year has worked to upgrade some facet of the hotel." (SWS)

"We've returned often to the Voyager because of its staff, excellent value, and facilities. The hotel's location is another plus. It's set on the edge of what passes for downtown Anchorage, across the street from the well-known Captain Cook Hotel." (Stephen Holman) "Our non-smoking room was impeccably clean, with lots of fluffy towels and plenty of hot water. The pleasant staff was more than willing to help out." (Susan Prizio, also Jean Irmischer) "Well-priced in an expensive area." (Wayne Stephenson) Comments appreciated.

Worth noting: Sixty percent of the hotel's rooms—those on the second and third floors—are reserved for non-smokers. While every effort is made to honor requests for these rooms, there's no guarantee, especially in the peak summer months.

Open All year. Closed Christmas.
Rooms 38 doubles—all with full private bath, telephone, radio, TV, desk, kitchenette, hair dryer. Fan on request.
Facilities Restaurant, bar/lounge with TV, lobby, parking lot. Valet service. Parks, walking trails nearby.
Location City center. Junction K and 5th Sts., near Cook Inlet.
Restrictions Traffic noise in lower-floor rooms. 60% non-smoking rooms.
Credit cards Amex, DC, Discover, MC, Visa.
Rates Room only (includes morning coffee), $79–135 double, $74–115 single. Extra person, $10. 10% senior discount. Off-season weekend specials.
Extras Crib.

DENALI NATIONAL PARK

Denali National Park covers 5.7 million acres of land and is home to 35 kinds of mammals, from grizzly bears to caribou and moose, plus a variety of bird and plant life. Mosquitoes are probably the most populous species in the park; fortunately they diminish by the latter part of the season. Private cars are discouraged in the park; shuttle buses bring guests to campgrounds and transport visitors to places of interest throughout. Area activities include hiking, canoeing, natural history and photography trips, rafting, bicycling, fishing, and panning for gold. The park is 240 miles north of Anchorage, 120 miles southwest of Fairbanks.

Reader tips: "Although there are spectacular views of Mt. McKinley to be had on the trip up from Anchorage, you can't see the mountain from

Denali Station or any of the nearby hotels; some brochures are quite misleading in this regard." *(RSS)*

Information please: Kantishna Roadhouse (P.O. Box 130, Denali National Park, 99755 or in winter, P.O. Box 80067, Fairbanks 99708; 800–942–7420 or in summer 907–683–2710) offers daily guided hikes and horse-drawn wagon trips for sightseeing and gold panning; every evening is a program with naturalists or photographers. There are 27 cabins with private bath, a lodge with family-style dining room and saloon, and a sauna along the creek. Rates, including bus transportation for the 90-mile trip from Denali Depot, all meals and activities, are $520 per day for two people. Additional feedback needed.

The **Denali Crow's Nest Cabins** (Mile 238.5 Parks Highway, P.O. Box 70, 99755; 907–683–2723) sit on Sugar Loaf Mountain, overlooking Horseshoe Lake and the Nenana River, close to the entrance to Denali National Park. The Crow's Nest spreads over five levels (plenty of steps), with two hot tubs offering great views from the top terrace. The adjacent Overlook Bar & Grill, open from 11 A.M. to midnight, garnishes the view with steaks, burgers, chicken, and seafood, plus picnic lunches on request.

For a truly remote getaway, consider the **Denali Wilderness Lodge** (P.O. Box 50 Denali Park, 99755 or P.O. Box 71784, Fairbanks, 99707; 907–683–1287 or 800–541–9779), 30 miles by air from Denali Station. Built as a hunting camp in the early 1900s, accommodations are offered in restored log cabins, now supplied with electricity and indoor plumbing. The rates of $295 per person cover all food, accommodations, and activities, including the round-trip flight and guided horseback rides into the surrounding 2,000 acres of wilderness.

A small wilderness lodge about 40 miles west of Denali, the **Denali West Lodge** (Lake Minchumina, 99757; 907–674–3112 or 907–276–5853) is run by full-time Alaskan residents Jack and Sherri Hayden. Moose, black bear, caribou and wolves all live nearby in the tundra, woodlands, and rivers. Weekend packages, per person based on double occupancy, including guided activities, meals, lodging, saunas, showers and laundry service, are $975.

Denali Riverview Inn 👫   *Tel:* Summer: 907–683–2663
Summer: Mile 238.5 Park Highway, 99755   *Fax* 907–683–2423
Winter: 6159 Evergreen Way,   Winter: 206–384–1078
Ferndale WA 98248

Recently built by Ford and Karen Reeves, the Denali Riverview Inn is comprised of two-story timber buildings set among the evergreens; the balconies offer lovely views of the Nenana River and the National Park (though not of Mt. McKinley). Rooms are motel-like, with soft blue fabrics complementing the natural birch and pine furnishings.

"Nice, new hotel owned by a lovely family. There's no restaurant, but you can get pizza delivered or a hotel with restaurants is a short walk away." *(Karen Buchsbaum)* "Clean, attractive, fine place to stay if you have a car." *(Pat Niven)*

Open Late May–mid-Sept.
Rooms 12 doubles—with private bath, TV, balcony.

Facilities Lobby.
Location George Parks Hwy, close to park entrance.
Credit cards CB, DC, MC, Visa.
Rates Room only, $85–115. Extra person, $5. No charge for children under 5.
Extras Crib.

North Face Lodge/Camp Denali 👫

P.O. Box 67, Denali National Park, 99755

Tel: 907–683–2290
603–675–2248
Fax: 907–683–1568
Fax: 603–675–9125

Imagine waking from a good night's sleep, throwing back the covers of your handmade down-filled quilt, and stepping outside to watch the sun transform Mt. McKinley's 20,000 feet of majestic whiteness to a rosy pink. Then add a caribou grazing in the foreground to complete this idyllic picture, and you'll be on your way to understanding what it's like to stay at either the North Face Lodge or Camp Denali.

Longtime owners Wallace and Jerryne Cole have done an exceptional job of creating two havens from which to enjoy the wilderness. Their first effort, Camp Denali, consists of a central dining room, living room, and restroom/shower buildings along with the cabins, scattered along a high ridge. While rustic, calico curtains, firm beds, and Denali-made quilts make them very inviting. In 1987, the Coles renovated nearby North Face Lodge, offering wilderness luxury. An L-shaped building, the lodge consists of a spacious living/dining area, with the smallish guest rooms making up the long end of the L. A covered veranda provides an ideal place to relax and enjoy the view. Electricity to power everything from the reading lights to the pumps that supply hot water for your bath is produced by the inn's own generators. Despite the fact that the nearest major supply source is 200 miles away, the kitchen staff manages to provided three tasty meals daily. A hearty breakfast is served promptly at 7:30 A.M.; at 8:30 A.M., the lunch fixings are set out, so that guests can pack up a portable meal; at 6:30 P.M., the single-entrée dinner is served.

But the Denali experience is more than good food and comfortable lodging. From the knowledgeable naturalist/drivers who escort you from Denali Station on a 5½-hour photographic safari back to the lodge, to the guided nature hikes, to the evening film or lecture, the Coles are eager for their guests to appreciate the surrounding wilderness and its inhabitants. To facilitate area explorations, they maintain a storeroom filled with L.L. Bean duck boots, sturdy daypacks, rain pants, ponchos, and more.

"Our room had a down comforter, four pillows on the firm queen-sized bed, and bedside lamps and tables on each side of bed. Soft shades of dusty pink and blue contrasted with the rustic pine paneling. The chairs on the porch outside our room were perfect for reading or chatting in the long evenings—sunset in mid-August came around 10:30.

"We breakfasted on French toast one day and eggs the next. We made our own lunches from a buffet of cheese, ham, and tuna spreads, home-made bread, sprouts, apples, oranges, cookies, plus plastic bottles to fill with water or lemonade. Dinner included halibut in sour cream sauce, rice, carrots and snow peas, and Waldorf salad, with strawberry rhubarb pie for dessert. The delightful staff mixed easily with guests at meals and during other activities, creating a warm, friendly, and knowledgeable atmosphere. The living room is handsomely furnished with plenty of comfortable couches, chairs, tables for games, and a stone fireplace." *(SWS)* "Our naturalist/driver was superb and truly made the long trip to the lodge an unforgettable experience." *(Janet & Howard Emery)*

"Everything was spit-shine clean, and the hot water supplies were ample. One evening slide presentation covered the wolves of Denali, the other the four seasons of Alaska. Our guided nature hike up Cranberry Ridge was fascinating. We flew around Mt. McKinley with Lowell Thomas, Jr., an incredible experience." *(Susan Prizio)*

Open Early June–early Sept.
Rooms North Face Lodge: 1 suite, 14 twins—all with full private bath. Camp Denali: 18 cabins—each with wood-burning stove, running water, gas hot plate, propane lights, outhouse. Shared shower facility.
Facilities Both lodge & cabins: Dining rooms, library/living rooms, natural history resource room, darkroom. Naturalist program in evenings. Pond, hiking trails. Daypacks, fishing poles, raingear, boots provided.
Location In center of park, 90 m W of Denali Station.
Restrictions No smoking. Alcoholic beverages permitted in cabin/room only. No fresh milk served. Children over 7 preferred.
Credit cards None accepted.
Rates Full board: Lodge, $275 per person, double, $375 single; Camp Denali, $240 per person double, $340 single. Family, children's rates. 2–3 night minimum stay.
Extras Narrated safari and picnic from Denali Station included in rates. Crib. French spoken.

FAIRBANKS

When you consider the fact that Fairbanks is America's northernmost city, just 150 miles south of the Arctic Circle, it's not surprising that the local baseball team can play a midnight game on June 21 without the benefit of artificial light. Fairbanks was settled in 1901, and was first populated by gold miners. A second wave of growth came in 1968, with the discovery of gold in Prudhoe Bay and the building of the Alaska Pipeline. Sights of interest include the University of Alaska Museum, depicting the state's natural history; a 36,000-year-old preserved bison, killed by a lion, is the star attraction. Families will enjoy a visit to the pioneer theme park, Alaskaland, offering historic buildings, a sternwheeler, trains, and a salmon bake.

Information please: The **Chokecherry Inn** (946 North Coppet, 99709; 907–474–9381), is recommended as being a "large, lovely home, with a variety of rooms, some with private bath, and a spacious suite on the lower level." B&B double rates are approximately $100 including a full breakfast.

A conveniently located downtown B&B is **Ah, Rose Marie** (302 Cowles Street, 99701; 907–456–2040), a friendly homestay named for owner John Davis' mother. Most of the seven guest rooms have semi-private baths, and all have a TV and a clock. Guests can relax in the ample common areas, or outside in the gazebo. B&B double rates range from $50–70, including breakfasts of muffins, pastries, cereal, eggs and juice, served anytime after 6:30 A.M.

Alaska's Seven Gables B&B ¢ ♿   *Tel:* 907–479–0751
4312 Birch Lane, P.O. Box 80488, 99708   *Fax:* 907–479–2229

Despite its name, the Seven Gables doesn't really have seven gables, but 14, seven along the front of this 7,000-square-foot Tudor-style house and another seven along the back. Custom-built by Paul and Leicha Welton in 1982, this B&B has many other unusual touches, including a flower-filled two-story atrium greenhouse, a foyer with a seven-foot rock water-fall and stained glass ceiling insets, and a living room with a cathedral ceiling 23 feet high. The Weltons' home is simply furnished with contemporary decor. The well-equipped bedrooms are compact, and most have queen or twin-size beds with cheerful floral bedspreads and curtains.

"An enormous home, built for B&B, with excellent soundproofing between rooms. A full breakfast is served at 7:15; although a continental breakfast is available for late risers, early birds are well rewarded. The first morning we had a delicious meal of cheese-baked eggs with freshly baked apple muffins; the second we feasted on crepes stuffed with a cream cheese and pecan mixture, topped with peach sauce. The Weltons are friendly, hospitable innkeepers, eager to introduce visitors to Fairbanks." *(Pat Niven)* "We explored Fairbanks via the inn's canoes and bicycles." *(AS)* "The owners are considerate, the custom-designed rooms immaculate, and the breakfasts exceptional." *(Dr. C.L. Ping, also HG)*

Open All year.
Rooms 4 suites with full private bath, refrigerator, deck; 5 doubles with private Jacuzzi bath; 3 doubles share 3 European-style baths. All with telephone, clock/radio, TV, desk, fan. 2 suites in annex.
Facilities Living room with piano, balcony, books; dining room, garden solarium, multipurpose room with fireplace. 2 Jacuzzis, laundry privileges. Guitar, piano entertainment evenings. $1\frac{1}{2}$ acres with canoes, bicycles, children's play equipment. Off-street parking.
Location From Parks Hwy., turn onto Geist Rd. Go right at Loftus Rd., left at Birch Lane to inn on left. Walking distance to U. of Alaska/Fairbanks.
Restrictions Smoking in 2 suites only.
Credit cards Amex, DC, Discover, MC, Visa.
Rates B&B, $65–110 suite, $45–95 double, $40–85 single. Extra person, $10. No tipping. Weekly, seasonal discounts.
Extras Wheelchair access. Airport/station pickup, $5. Outdoor pets welcome. Crib. Spanish, German spoken.

GUSTAVUS

Gustavus is a small and isolated community on southeast Alaska's famed Inside Passage, about 50 miles west of Juneau. Located on a large sandy plain created by receding glaciers, the area contrasts with the typical rocky wooded shoreline of southeast Alaska. There are no roads or ferry service—the only way to get here is by plane; the only paved surface in town is the landing strip.

The key attraction here is Glacier Bay National Park, a series of fjords and active tidewater glaciers extending over 65 miles. Activities include hiking in the rain forests of hemlock, spruce, and pine; cruising up the bay to watch for whales, bald eagles, black bear, deer, and 200 varieties of birds; or climbing into a kayak for a close-up look at the seals and porpoises that will accompany you. Fishermen will opt for deep-sea and river fishing for salmon, halibut, cutthroat, and Dolly Varden trout, while winter visitors can add cross-country skiing to the recreation list. Another highlight is a bush plane flightseeing tour of the park, revealing the bay's deep crevasses, enormous ice fields, jagged peaks, and breathtaking beauty. Berry-picking and picnicking on the beach are a delight for children of all ages.

Although outdoor activities are limitless, one thing Gustavus does not have is a liquor store; if you enjoy a glass of wine with dinner, bring your own. Remember that the weather can be cool and damp even in summer, so bring along warm and waterproof clothing, including hat and gloves.

Reader tip: "Don't come to Glacier Bay for the weather; it's often cold and rainy, with low clouds obscuring the views. Bring warm clothes and foul weather gear."

Information please: Listed in past editions, we need current reports on the **Gustavus Inn** (P.O. Box 60, 99826; 907–697–2254 or, in winter, 913–649–5220). In 1968 Jack and Sally Lesh bought this old Alaska homestead, built in 1928 for a family of 11, and started the inn. Ten years later, their son David and his wife JoAnn took over its management. Guest rooms are simply decorated with pretty stenciling and quilts. Dave does the cooking—featuring fresh seafood and fruits and vegetables from their own garden. Full board rates are about $125, per person, double occupancy.

Glacier Bay Country Inn †𝕩

P.O. Box 5, 99826
Off season: P.O. Box 2557, St. George UT 84771

Tel: 907–697–2288
Off-season: 801–673–8480
Fax: 907–697–2289
Fax: 801–673–8481 (Oct.–Apr.)

"Al Unrein met us at the airport in his van. We bumped along the dusty roads deep into the woods to their beautiful rustic inn, which the Unreins built of logs cut and milled on the land they cleared. Arriving just in time for lunch, we sipped homemade soup and savored salmon and fennel salad sandwiches; the chef agreeably made up French bread pizzas just for the kids. As we ate, we looked out through the wide windows past split rail fences to the sunny meadow beyond, and watched a young black bear ambling through. After lunch, we were driven over to Glacier Bay National Park to take a ranger-led walk through the rain forest, then returned to the inn to explore and relax. At night, we dined on Dungeness crab and rice, with delicious chocolate cake and raspberries for dessert. Salads were a highlight, with nasturtiums and a variety of greens, just picked from their extensive garden of flowers, fruits, and vegetables. The next day we cruised in Glacier Bay, and were rewarded with sightings of calving glaciers, hundreds of seals, and two humpback whales. The Unreins are wonderful hosts. Al is a casual guy, open and down-to-earth; Annie is as sweet and helpful as could be. Their two kids are just as cute, though they were never around to disturb any kid-phobic guests. Our children loved this place, from the garden, to the bear, to the play fort and swings in the front yard." *(SWS, and others)*

"The inn is an eclectic assortment of old and new—white walls, wooden beams, and firm mattresses with flannel sheets, country-print comforters, antique furniture, hand-stenciling, and unusually shaped large windows overlooking pastures and snow-covered mountains." *(Kim & Ann Hutchinson)* "Our charming room had an antique dresser, needlepoint samplers, and fresh wildflowers." *(Corine Geldhof)* "The delicious meals included steamed wild ferns. The staff was happy to serve the wine we had brought." *(Janet Emery)* "Annie meets with guests to discuss the next day's activities—kayaking, fishing, whale watching, park tours, and more. The staff will even wake you to see the Northern Lights!" *(Mary Johnson)* "The inn's location is remote yet convenient, with bald eagles regularly in view." *(Jack & Patricia Horn)* "The inn has lots of nooks and crannies so that people can find a private corner, yet everyone gets together in friendly groups at mealtime." *(Shirley Holmgreen)*

"Jan met us at the airport and drove us directly to the dock for an afternoon whale-watching trip. We were given tasty bag lunches with whitefish sandwiches, chips, potato salad, cookies, fruit, and soda. The excursion was breath-taking; we saw humpbacks feeding and saw one breaching. Sea lions played around the boat, and we also saw porpoises, puffins, cormorants, and an eagles' nest. We returned to the inn in time for tea and just-baked cookies; a delicious salmon and rice dish was served for dinner. Just before dessert, we saw a wolf on the airstrip behind the inn. Our immaculate room overlooked the front gardens, and had a comfortable bed and a rocking chair. Plenty of hot water and nice towels in the bathroom." *(Susan Prizio)* "The chef was attentive and accommodating; the owners are 'hands on' folks who work to make your stay everything Alaska should be." *(Linda Alfonso)*

Open May–Sept.
Rooms 1 suite, 7 doubles, 1 single—7 with private shower, 1 with private tub, 1 with shared sink/toilet downstairs; shares staff shower. All with desk; some with fan. Add'l. B&B & condo lodging at Whalesong Lodge.
Facilities Dining room, living room with games, library. 160 acres with gardens, bicycles, hiking trails, creeks, ponds. Fishing, whale-watching, kayaking, glacier trips available.
Location 4 miles from park headquarters. Take main road toward park, turn left at inn sign and follow to end.
Restrictions No smoking.
Credit cards None accepted.
Rates Room only, $155 double, $80 shared single, $110 single; B&B, $167 double, $86 shared single, $116 single; MAP, $207 double, $136 single; Full board, $223 double, $144 single. Extra adult, $35–69; extra child under 12, $20–54. Lunch, $10; dinner, $24. Whalesong Lodge: B&B, $140 double; 3-bedroom condo, $225–300.
Extras Airport/dock/Nat'l Park pickups. Crib, babysitting by arrangement.

HAINES

Haines abounds with breathtaking views, wildlife, recreational possibilities, and photographic opportunities. The Chilkat River runs nearby, and every autumn over 3000 bald eagles congregate along its banks to spend the winter. In mid-August of each year the town hosts the Southeast Alaska State Fair. Haines is also home of historic Fort William H. Seward, where you can visit a recreated native village, and watch traditional wood carvers at work.

Information please: Listed in past editions, we need current reports on **The Summer Inn B&B** (P.O. Box 1198, 247 Second Avenue, 99827; 907–766–2970). Named for owners Bob and Mary Ellen Summer (not the climate), the inn was built at the turn of the century by Tim Vogel, a member of Skagway's infamous Soapy Smith gang. Situated in downtown Haines, the inn overlooks the Lynn Canal and provides a central location for enjoying the sites of the Chilkat Valley. B&B double rates for the five guest rooms are $65, including hearty breakfasts of sausage and pancakes, juice, fruit, and muffins.

HOMER

Homer makes a delightful base for touring the beautiful Kenai Peninsula. Set on Kachemak Bay, it's about an hour south of Anchorage by plane or about a five-hour drive (225 miles on a paved road), following Cook Inlet much of the way to Homer. From Homer, intrepid adventurers can visit one of the wilderness lodges noted below, or can take the Alaska Marine Highway to Kodiak, home of the Alaskan brown bear.

Reader tip: "Homer is the halibut capital of the world; at the docks, we saw three 120-pound halibut, and were told that this was not unusual." *(Ann La Posta)* And: "Unless you're staying at a fly-in lodge, you'll need a car when you're in Homer."

Kachemak Kiana B&B   *Tel: 907–235–8824*
Mile 5, East Road, 99603
Mailing address: P.O. Box 855, 99603

Long-time Alaska resident Amy Springer notes that if you drive as far west as you can on Alaska's highway system you'll end up in Homer; keep on going and you'll be at Kachemak Kiana B&B. Her B&B occupies the entire second floor of her handsome contemporary home, and offers beautiful views of the bay and mountains beyond. Amy notes that "wild game—moose, coyotes, and pheasant—often come into the yard. Winter visitors can drive onto the Homer Spit and see hundreds of bald eagles who congregate there to be fed by Jean Keane (the Eagle Lady)." The breakfast of cereal, juices, fresh fruit, bagels, cream cheese, muffins, toast, jams and jellies, coffee, milk is available all morning, so guests can rise early or sleep in.

"Amy Springer is a gracious hostess, welcoming us by name as we walked in the door. We weren't surprised to learn that Kiana means 'welcome.' Our room, the Master Suite, had an incredible view of Kachemak Bay. It had a walk-in cedar closet, king-size bed with built-in reading lights, a small sitting area and a large bathroom with lots of towels and plenty of hot water. Breakfast each day was a feast of breads, muffins, fruits, cereals, juices, and coffee or tea. All the guests sit together at a long

41

dining room table to share conversation and food. We followed Amy's recommendations for dining and activities and were delighted. The inn is spanking clean and the common areas are comfortable. The kitchen is open for guests' use and is stocked with teas, coffee, hot chocolate, juices, and fruits." *(Susan Prizio)*

Open All year.
Rooms 1 cabin, 3 doubles—all with private bath and/or shower, clock. Cabin with TV, refrigerator, balcony.
Facilities Living room with fireplace, den with fireplace, VCR/TV, books; deck. $3\frac{1}{2}$ acres with hot tub. 8 m from boat harbor. Cross country skiing, hiking, fishing nearby.
Location 5 m E of town.
Restrictions No smoking. Children over 12.
Credit cards None accepted.
Rates B&B, $55–95 cabin, $60–90 double, $50–70 single. Extra person, $20.

Tutka Bay Lodge
Tel: 907–235–3905
P.O. Box 960, 99603

Jon and Nelda Osgood moved to Tutka Bay on a year-round basis in 1983, and have worked every year to improve the quality of their lodge and cabins. Jon's 14,000 flight hours stand him in good stead when he flies guests on a helicopter tour of the glaciers in the nearby Harding Ice Field. Nelda, who grew up in Kodiak, reports that "we emphasize learning about and appreciating the natural history of our area—marine mammals, birds, intertidal plants and animals, glaciers, forests, tides and weather. Guests observe and participate in harvesting clams, shrimp, crab, fish and berries in season."

"Lovely quiet retreat, surrounded by water, with cabins hidden in a forest of fern and spruce. Very clean. We dug for clams at low tide, pulled up crab and shrimp traps." *(Mr. & Mrs. Carl Verheyen)* "Fresh seafood from the Osgood's dock was deliciously prepared for our meals. The Osgoods are totally committed to running a first-quality lodge, as evidenced in their energy, cleanliness, maintenance, and continuing improvement projects." *(J.D. Worrell)* "The owners have worked hard to make a wonderful place even more special. An excellent value." *(PN)*

Open All year.
Rooms 2 1–2 bedroom cabins, 2 doubles—all with private bath and/or shower, radio, deck, electric heat. Some with woodstove, refrigerator.
Facilities Dining room, deck, sauna. 7 acres with picnic area, hiking trails, floating deepwater dock, guided boating, fishing, sea kayaking, mountain biking.
Location 200 m S of Anchorage. 9 m S of Homer by boat or air.
Restrictions No smoking. No children under 12.
Credit cards None accepted.
Rates Full board, $500–550 per person, 2 days/2 nights. Rates include accommodations, family style meals, some activities. 10–40% discounts Sept.–June 15.
Extras Airport/station pickup.

JUNEAU

Set at the northern end of Southeast Alaska, Juneau is Alaska's capital city. It is the only state capital unreachable by road, and has the additional distinction of having a glacier (the Mendenhall) just 12 miles from town. The city dates to 1880, when gold was discovered by Joe Juneau and Dick Harris. Mining provided the underpinnings of the local economy for years; these days, government jobs provide most paychecks.

Reader tips: "Be sure to drive up to the site of the AJ Mine, either for the salmon bake or to picnic. You can pan for gold or hike one of the many trails. The setting is beautiful—steep forested hillsides and dozens of waterfalls." *(Lewis Bennett)*

Also recommended: The **Prospector Hotel** (375 Whittier Street, 99801; 907–586–3737 or 800–331–2711) is a clean, comfortable 60-room hotel, with a convenient location, next to the Alaska State Museum, a short walk from downtown. Its recently refurbished guest rooms each have a full private bath, cable TV, and two queen-size beds; rates range from $60–125. *(Jean Irmischer)*

Information please: For a quiet but convenient location, within walking distance of downtown, try **Mullins House B&B** (526 Seward Street, 99801; reservations through Alaska B&B Association, 907–586–2959). "Pleasant older home overlooks city, next to a totem pole and a Russian Orthodox church. Friendly, helpful hosts; comfortable, clean rooms; super breakfast; clean, convivial atmosphere." *(W.R. Weber)* Double rates for this four guest room, two-bath B&B range from $60–70.

Dawson's B&B ¢ ♔   *Tel: 907–586–9708*
1941 Glacier Highway, 99801

Dave and Velma Dawson "try our best to make our guests' stay pleasant" in their B&B, set on a wooded hillside. Always pleased to provide information, they are knowledgeable about sights and activities of interest.

"Don't come to Dawson's for the decor—and you won't find candy on your pillow or little carafes of sherry on the night stand, but you will find comfortable beds, great showers with strong water pressure, and the nicest 'amenity' of all—use of a washer and dryer. Velma's breakfasts are cooked to order, almost anytime from 7 to 9 A.M., and include your choice of hot cakes, eggs any style, French toast, and our favorite—her cheese/onion/pepper omelets. She even went out and bought a box of Cocoa Krispies to please one young guest. The living room and the two front bedrooms have lovely views of Gastineau Channel and the Douglas Mountains. The guest rooms are well equipped with such extra touches as an ice pack in the refrigerator for picnics and night lights in the bathrooms." *(SWS)*

"On the first day, Mr. Dawson drove us across the bay up to Blueberry Hill so we could see Juneau at its best. He pointed out the major attractions, then drove us around the town for a closer look—all without asking. The inn itself is very unpretentious; when we returned after an overnight excursion we felt like we were coming home. Flowers abound on the inside and out." *(Rose Halper)* "Dave is a retired tour guide, Velma is a cook with many years' experience—what more could you ask for?" *(Charles Moebim)* "I hope my husband and I talk the way Dave and Velma Dawson talk after 39 years of marriage. Lots of laughter, interruptions, stories, and genuine affection. They also know everything about Juneau and Alaska, and were patient with our millions of questions." *(Penny Poirier)*

Open All year.
Rooms 5 doubles—3 with private bath, 2 with a maximum of 4 people sharing 1 bath. All with telephone, radio, TV; 2 with refrigerator.
Facilities Breakfast room, sitting room, deck. Laundry facilities. 8 m to skiing.
Location SE AK. 2 m to town; 7 m to airport.
Restrictions No smoking in dining room.
Credit cards MC, Visa.
Rates B&B, $65–75 double, $55–65 single. Extra person, $10. No charge for children under 6. 2-night minimum.
Extras Airport/ferry pickups. Bus stops (on request) in front of house.

KATMAI NATIONAL PARK

Also recommended: "Since the well-known Brooks Lodge was full, we stayed at the **Katmai-Quinnat Landing Hotel** (in summer—P.O. Box 418, King Salmon 99613; 907–246–3000 or 800–770–FISH or in winter—5520 Lake Otis Parkway, Suite 101, Anchorage 99507; 907–561–2310), and were delighted we did. This modern 48-room hotel provides all comforts and amenities, at rates ranging from $165–190. Food in the restaurant was fine, and we enjoyed exploring this little town. Katmai is just 15 minutes away by float plane." *(PN)*

Brooks Lodge	*Tel:* 907–243–5448
Mailing address: 4700–WI Aircraft Drive	800–544–0551
Anchorage 99502	*Fax:* 907–243–0649

Built in 1950, Brooks Lodge has a spectacular view of aquamarine Naknek Lake and is adjacent to the Brooks River, famous for its trout and salmon fishing. Inside guests gather around the large circular stone fireplace to swap fish and bear stories. Katmailand is the authorized concessionaire for Katmai Park, operating three lodges in the park, of which Brooks is the largest, as well as four-wheel bus tour programs to the "Valley of 10,000 Smokes," which last erupted in 1912. The lodge is reached by float plane from King Salmon airport, 35 miles away, with connecting flights to Anchorage; rates include air transportation between Anchorage and Brooks.

"Though it's rustic, the operators attempt to compensate with generous quantities of food, clean rooms, and a welcoming atmosphere. Enthusiasts of three kinds jam the place—fishermen, photographers, and wildlife lovers—sometimes in combination, sometimes a bit wary of one another. It's expensive, but is worth it for a once-in-a-lifetime experience. Fishing is strictly catch and release, with barbless hooks. The brown bear watching is fabulous. Sometimes they wander through the lodge grounds, but their behavior at Brooks Falls is memorable." *(Steve Holman)* Reports needed.

Open June 1–Sept. 10.
Rooms 16 cabins/rooms (for 2 to 4 people)—each with private shower, toilet.
Facilities Restaurant, bar, sitting room with stone fireplace. Flightseeing, fishing, hiking. Interpretive ranger programs. Sportfishing, boat guides.

Location SW AK. 265 m SW of Anchorage. Inside Katmai National Park.
Credit cards Amex, MC, Visa accepted only at lodge, not for reservations.
Rates 1-night room/airfare package, $520–530 per person, for a double; $446 per child under 12. 4-night June, Sept. specials. Valley of Smokes tour, $50–57. Flightseeing tour, $85. Alc breakfast, $8–10; alc lunch, $10–12; alc dinner, $16–22. Fishing, wildlife packages.
Extras Airport pickups. Crib.

KENNICOTT

Information please: In the adjacent town of McCarthy is the **McCarthy Lodge** (mailing address: P.O. Box 870393, Wasilla 99687; 907–333–5402) built in 1916. Double rates range from $105; with breakfast and dinner, it's $175. Rooms are basic but comfortable, and the large and lively bar is the center of night life in town.

If you're traveling the Richardson Highway between Valdez and Fairbanks, consider a stop for food or accommodation at the historic **Copper Center Lodge** (Drawer J, Copper Center 99573; 907–822–3245), dating back to the Klondike Gold Rush of 1898. The full-service dining room is open from 7 A.M. to 9 P.M.; double rates for the 19 guest rooms are $70. Sourdough pancakes with century-old starter are a breakfast specialty, while steak or halibut, fries and salad, make up the dinner menu.

Kennicott Glacier Lodge 🏃 ✕   *Tel:* 907–258–2350
P.O. Box 103940, Anchorage 99510   *Fax:* 907–248–7975

Wrangell-St. Elias National Park is vastness on a scale that's hard for non-Alaskans to grasp. Its acreage exceeds that of Connecticut, Massachusetts, and Rhode Island combined; the park contains nine of the 16 tallest peaks in the U.S., with glaciers each five times the size of Manhattan. In 1900, the Kennicott Mining Company began shipping huge quantities of copper ore by rail to ships waiting at Cordova. The high-grade ore was played out by the 1930s, and when the mining company moved out its 800 workers, Kennicott became a ghost town overnight.

Rich and Jody Kirkwood, who built the lodge in 1986, note that Kennicott is a National Historic Landmark, located in the center of the Wrangell-St. Elias National Park. We offer guided glacier treks, historic tours of the ghost town, horseback riding, nature hikes, flightseeing, photography, and more." They go on to explain that the park is reached by car with surprising ease in summer via the Glenn Highway from Anchorage or the Richardson Highway from Valdez. The road from Anchorage is paved up to the park entrance; the next 60 miles are a state-maintained gravel road. At the end of the road, near McCarthy, park your car, call the lodge on the "bush phone" and cross the Kennicott River in hand-powered, two-person cable trams. The lodge staff will pick you up in their shuttle van after you've crossed over.

"Along with commanding views of the Kennicott Glacier and the Wrangell Mountains, the lodge offers a comfortable oasis for recouping from the rigors of hiking mountain trails, glacier treks, and old mining camp rambles. Kennicott is early Alaska history, and the lodge illustrate life there from 1911 to 1938. The current lodge structure is a faithful reproduction of the housing for staff families of the Kennecott Copper Corporation (the original structure was destroyed by fire in 1983). Its walls are decorated with artifacts of mining life. A comfortable gathering area within the lodge opens onto a long porch with magnificent views. The porch also has benches, tables and chairs for outdoor dining.

"Our lower level room was comfortable with a firm bed, a cold water sink, and an adequate clothing storage area. It opened out to the inner hall and outdoor porch. Across the hall from our room was an immaculate bathroom with toilet and hot and cold water sink; there are two hot showers at the end of the hall. A plus was Rich's considerable library of Kennicott and Wrangell/St. Elias books, pamphlets, and maps." *(Mr. & Mrs. John A. Lamb)* "Our cozy room was small but immaculate. Delicious meals were served family style—as much as you could eat. Those looking for luxury will be disappointed, but anyone looking for a new experience will be delighted. Rich and Jody were considerate, caring, and willing to make your stay special." *(Inger Ricci, also PN)* Reports appreciated.

Open May 15–Sept. 20
Rooms 25 doubles share 6 shower rooms. 7 with deck.
Facilities Dining room, meeting room, living room with fireplace, books; porches. Hiking, rafting, games, picnic area, flightseeing.
Location S central AK. 320 m E of Anchorage (approx. 8 hrs.), 170 NE of Valdez.
Restrictions No smoking.
Credit cards Amex, MC, Visa.
Rates Room only, $139 double, $119 single. Extra person, $30. Full board, $220 double, $150 single. Extra person, $75. Children age 4–12 in parents' room, ½ price. Alc lunch, $10. Prix fixe dinner, $20.

KETCHIKAN

Main Street B&B ¢   *Tel:* 907–225–8484
437 Main Street, P.O. Box 7473, 99901

Ketchikan is famous for its totem poles, and at the Main Street B&B, you'll see the Kyan totem just outside the front door. Built as a private home in 1906, long-Alaska residents Greg and Harriet Zerbetz, opened this B&B in 1986. The interior is equally Alaskan, with carved totems and other local collections; guest rooms are highlighted by Harriet's handmade quilts. Breakfast is served at 8 A.M., and the tempting menus vary daily, perhaps sliced melon, apple puff pancakes, mustard-glazed ham, lemon-blueberry muffins with homemade jam; followed the next day by vegetable frittata, reindeer sausage, fresh fruit, and oatmeal biscuits. Continental breakfast is set out for guests catching early morning flights or ferries.

"A delightful B&B with comfortable rooms, pleasant owners, and a convenient location. For dinner, we like Annabelle's Restaurant, in the old Gilmore Hotel." *(PN)* Comments welcome.

Open May 15–Sept. 30
Rooms 2 doubles in main house share 1 bath—each with clock, TV, desk. 2 with fireplace. Apartment in adjacent home with kitchen, living room, private bath.
Facilities Living/dining room, library with books, piano; family room with wood-stove, TV/VCR; deck. Pocket gardens, deck, courtyard. Limited off-street parking. Beach, fishing, hiking nearby.
Location SE AK, Inside Passage. Historic hillside district. 2 blocks to bus. 5 min. walk to docks, galleries, park. 20 min. walk to hiking trail, shopping mall. 2 m to ferries. Call for directions by car, bus, taxi.
Restrictions Covered porch for smokers.
Credit cards None accepted.
Rates B&B, $60–80 apartment, $55–70 double, $50–65 single. Extra person, $15. No tipping.
Extras Crib, "very rusty" German spoken.

KODIAK

A Wintel's B&B ¢   *Tel:* 907–486–6935
1612 Mission Rd, P.O. Box 2812, 99615

Located within walking distance of Kodiak's famous fishing fleet, this contemporary home has been owned by Willie and Betty Heinrichs since 1989. Betty reports, "Our B&B attracts outdoor people. Favorite activities are fishing, hunting, hiking, photography, visiting archaeological digs, and watching bears, migrating birds, killer whales, and gray whales." Breakfast includes fresh fruit, juice, sourdough pancakes, eggs, sausage, ham, or bacon; a fresh fruit basket is found in each guest room. For those in search of an authentic souvenir, the inn features gift items by Kodiak artisans: trading bead jewelry, hand-woven sea grass baskets, and Alaska fur articles.

"The charming hosts, Willie and Betty, have the ability to tell stories and draw everyone out. There is always a hot fresh drink of your choice with several choices of fresh baked goodies." *(Susan Stanford & Walt Cunningham)* "A home-cooked breakfast with delightful side order of local history! Relaxing atmosphere." *(Jeff Knights)* "The large, windowed living room offered a view of the ocean and several bald eagles could be seen soaring over nearby trees." *(Ron Scherzinger)* "Great breakfasts. Warm, inviting setting; clean rooms; helpful area information." *(Roger Lucas)*

Open All year.
Rooms 1 suite with private bath, 3 doubles, 1 single share 1 bath. All with telephone, radio, desk, fan.
Facilities Breakfast room, living room with fireplace, TV; family room with games, sun porch, gift shop, indoor hot tub, sauna. Surf fishing, beach combing nearby.
Location S AK, NE Kodiak Island. ¾ m from town center, dock.
Restrictions No smoking. Children over 5.
Credit cards None accepted.
Rates B&B, $90 suite, $55–70 double, $50 single. Extra person, $25. Box lunch on request, $9.
Extras Airport pickup. German, Spanish spoken.

KOTZEBUE

Nullagvik Hotel ✕ &
P.O. Box 336, 99752

Tel: 907–442–3331
Fax: 907–442–3340

The second largest Eskimo village in Alaska, Kotzebue has a population that is over 80 percent Inupiaq Eskimo. Easily reached by commercial flights from Anchorage and Nome, it's worth a brief visit for a taste of life north of the Arctic Circle; be sure to visit the NANA Museum of the Arctic. Because the entire village rests on the permafrost, all permanent structures are built on raised columns to prevent the buildings' heat from melting the ground, which would cause them to sink. The Nullagvik was built in 1977 by the Inupiaq-owned Nana Development Corporation, and is a modern, functional hotel; Gaylen Hanna is the manager.

"Unexpectedly well maintained hotel. Our simply furnished room had a view of Kotzebue Sound, and was supplied with ample towels, lots of lighting. The entire hotel was very clean, an especially hard task with all the dust from the village's dirt roads. The restaurant was clean, with seafood and reindeer specials, and the staff accommodating. We hit a heat wave in Kotzebue—80°F. The locals were swimming in Kotzebue Sound because it was so hot!" *(Susan Prizio)*

Open All year. Closed Christmas. Restaurant closed Sun./Mon. Oct.–April.
Rooms 75 doubles—all with full private bath, telephone, radio, clock, TV, desk.
Facilities Restaurant, laundry, deck.
Location NW Alaska. 550 miles NW of Anchorage, 30 m N of Arctic Circle.
Restrictions Some non-smoking rooms available.
Credit cards DC, MC, Visa.
Rates Room only, $150 double, $125 single. Tips welcome.
Extras Wheelchair access; some rooms equipped for disabled.

PETERSBURG

Jewell's by the Sea ¢
806 Nordic Drive, P.O. Box 1662, 98833

Tel: 907–772–3620
Fax: 907–772–9339

"A picturesque fishing and logging town, Petersburg makes a pleasant stop when traveling the Inside Passage on the ferry. Major points of interest include the Laconte Glacier and Devils Thumb Mountain, while charter sport fishing is a key activity. A stroll through town will give you a glimpse of Petersburg's Norwegian heritage, seen in the traditional rosemaling adorning the older buildings. Jewell Dean Herbranson welcomes guests to her art gallery and B&B, with its ringside view of the Wrangell Narrows. Jewell notes that 'float planes vie with eagles for air space in front of our house.' Fishing boats and snowcapped mountains complete the view you'll have while relaxing in her living room or eating a home-cooked breakfast of Belgian waffles topped with blueberries or strawberries. A pleasant, friendly hostess, Jewell and her son built this house in 1982; they opened it as a B&B in 1985." *(SWS)* "Jewell Dean, as she tells everyone to call her, goes out of her way to make sure you're happy and comfortable." *(Erik Lie-Nielsen)* "Comfortable and quiet. Good breakfast; beautiful views overlooking the Wrangell Narrows beneath Petersburg Mountain." *(Thomas Jahnke)*

Open All year. Closed 2 P.M. Fri.–11 P.M. Sat.
Rooms 3 doubles share 2 baths. All with telephone.
Facilities Living room with TV, dining room, deck, art gallery. Laundry facilities. Fishing nearby.
Location SE AK, Inside Passage. 1/4 m from ferry dock, 3/4 m from downtown.
Restrictions No smoking or alcoholic beverages. No children.
Credit cards Amex, Discover, Visa.
Rates B&B, $50–60 double, $45–50 single. Extra person, $5. Weekly rates.
Extras Ferry pickup.

SEWARD

Also recommended: Right at the harbor is the **Harborview B&B** (900 Third Street at 'C' Street, 99664; 907–224–3217), with four comfortable guest rooms and an apartment good for a family. B&B double rates are approximately $75. *(PN)*

SITKA

Along the western edge of the archipelago which dots the Inside Passage is the town of Sitka, known for its Russian heritage.

Information please: The **Biorka B&B** (611 Biorka Street, 99835; 907–747–3111) is owned by Stephanie Vieira, and offers two guest rooms, each with private bath, telephone, and TV. The $65 rates includes a continental breakfast.

Sitka House B&B ¢   *Tel: 907–747–4937*
325 Seward Street, 99835

"Dorothy Breedlove is a gracious hostess, informative and accommodating. Her home is immaculate both inside and out, furnished with some antiques and Alaskana. Sitka is a wonderful town right on the ocean. The harbor area is filled with sailboats of all sizes, and there are plenty of walking trails and little shops. Dorothy picked us up at the airport and arranged for her daughter to drive us to the ferry the day we left. Our spacious room had an African theme with masks and animal pelts, a comfortable bed, sitting area, and lots of light; the bathroom had great towels and plenty of hot water. Breakfast was served on the sunporch; both quantity and quality were excellent—salmon quiche one day, sourdough pancakes the next, with homemade bread or sweet rolls." *(Susan Prizio)*

Open May–mid-Sept.
Rooms 2 doubles with private bath.

Facilities Dining room, sunporch, deck with hot tub; guest freezer.
Location Walking distance to historic sites, waterfront.
Credit cards None accepted.
Rates B&B, $65 double, $55 single.
Extras Airport/ferry pickups.

SKAGWAY

Information please: A beautifully restored B&B inn, the **Skagway Inn** (7th and Broadway, P.O. Box 500, 99840; 907–983–2289 or 800–478–2290 in AK) offers 12 handsome guest rooms, all with shared baths, plus a home-cooked breakfast included in the $60–75 double rates.

For a clean, comfortable motel accommodation, two good choices are available. The **Gold Rush Lodge** (6th and Alaska Streets, P.O. Box 514, 99840; 907–983–2831) is owned by the accommodating Harry and Vicki Bricker. Coffee, juice, and rolls are set out in the lobby every morning for guests. Twelve units are available at rates of $45–75 double, depending on season. An equally good choice (especially if you have a car) is the recently built **Wind Valley Lodge** (22 & State Streets, P.O. Box 354-B, 99840; 907–983–2236), with an attractive rustic setting, including a gazebo, and spacious motel-style guest rooms with one or two queen-sized beds. *(PN)*

SOLDOTNA

Information please: For a truly remote escape, consider **Haeg's Wilderness Lodge** (Chinitna Bay via P.O. Box 338, 99669; 907–262–9249) on remote Chinitna Bay in Lake Clark National Park, about 60 miles west of Homer. Bears and other wild animals, birds and fish far outnumber the handful of people in this park, which has no roads. The Haeg family has built a cluster of log cabins, and offer comfortable accommodation, meals with the freshest of seafood, homemade breads and jams, and such activities as bird-, bear-, or whale-watching, hiking and berry-picking amid the 10,000-foot Chigmit mountains, plus fishing for halibut, shark, salmon and Arctic char.

TOK

Information please: At the junction of the Routes 1 (the Al-Can) and 2 (Glenn Highway) is Tok, the trade town for nearby Athabascan villages, and the "dog capital of Alaska," a center for dog breeding, training, and mushing. The annual Tok Race of Champions, in March, is one of the oldest and largest sled dog races in the state. The **Cleft in the Rock Inn** (Sundog Trail, P.O. Box 122, Tok 99780; 907–883–4219 or in AK 800–478–5646) offers "clean accommodations and warm, friendly, Christian hospitality" in a guest room, apartment, or cabin set in a spruce forest. Rates of $50–85 include a home-cooked hot breakfast.

VALDEZ

Also recommended: *Pat Niven* (see chapter introduction) recommends two B&Bs in Valdez. **Gussie's Lowe Street Inn** (354 Lowe St. 99686; 907–835–4448) offers guest rooms with shared and private baths, and B&B rates of $80; the **Cliff House B&B** (P.O. Box 1995, 99686; 907–835–5244) has two beautifully furnished guest rooms (each with queen-size bed and private bath), and spectacular views of Prince William Sound, at B&B double rates of $125, including breakfast.

Information please: One block from the small boat harbor, museum, restaurants, and shops, and ten-minutes walk from the ferry is the **Downtown B&B Inn** (P.O. Box 184, 99686; 907–835–2791 or 800–478–2791), offering clean, comfortable motel-style rooms, some with private baths, and bay or mountain views. The $65–90 double rate includes a breakfast of fresh fruit and juice, yogurt, cereal, rolls, and muffins, coffee and tea.

WASILLA

Also recommended: In Palmer, about 40 miles east of Wasilla, is the **Glacier House B&B** (P.O. Box 660, Palmer 99645; 907–745–4087 or 800–745–4087), offering two lovely guest rooms, one with a private bath, at B&B double rates of $100.

Yukon Don's ¢ ♦	*Tel:* 907–376–7472
Yukon Circle, 1830 East Parks Highway	In Alaska: 800–478–7472
Suite 386, 99654	*Fax:* 907–376–6515

Yukon Don is a real Alaskan character and his personality is evident in this B&B inn, a 10,000-square-foot converted farm building. Each log-walled guest room has a sitting area and Alaskan decorations like bear skins, mounted salmon, moose racks, old tools, and even a dog sled. Rates include a self-service continental breakfast.

"Set in the valley at the edge of a bluff, Yukon Don's enjoys a spectacular view of the Chugach Mountains and the Matanuska Valley. Although there is no restaurant on the property, there are plenty of places to eat nearby." *(Linda Lockwood)* "Our accommodations were clean, nicely decorated, and the lodge was full of authentic Alaskan artifacts and collectibles." *(Timothy Jorstad)* "Appreciated the flexibility of the self-service breakfast. We enjoyed meeting Don and his friendly family." *(Wayne Krieger)* "Pleasant, quiet location; our hosts had a vast knowledge of Alaska." *(Jon & Penny Lyn Andreasen)*

Open All year.
Rooms 1 apartment with kitchen, laundry. 1 suite, 3 doubles. Apt., suite with full private bath. 3 rooms share 2 baths. All with radio, table, telephone. Fan available.
Facilities Common room with woodstove, pool table, snack bar, library, TV/VCR; deck, sauna, exercise room. 2 acres with horseshoes, croquet, swing set.
Location Matanuska Valley. 40 min N of Anchorage. 5 m from Wasilla.

Restrictions Interior walls are not soundproof. No smoking.
Credit cards None accepted.
Rates B&B, $80–105 suite, apt.; $55 double. Extra person, $10; children under
free.
Extras Train pickups.

We Want to Hear from You!

As you know, this book is effective only with your help. We really need to know about your experiences and discoveries. If you stayed at an inn or hotel listed here, we want to know how it was. Did it live up to our description? Exceed it? Was it what you expected? Did you like it? Were you disappointed? Delighted? Have you discovered new establishments that we should add to the next edition?

Tear out one of the report forms at the back of this book (or use your own stationery if you prefer) and write today. *Even if you write only "Fully endorse existing entry" you will have been most helpful.*

Thank You!

California

Gingerbread Mansion, Ferndale

California is the nation's third largest state and the most populous. Its terrain is incredibly diverse, offering virtually every possible land- and seascape, much of great interest to tourists. Though the clock puts them three hours behind the East Coast, Californians tend to think of themselves as being ahead of the rest of the country. Many of the country's dominant trends got their start here and spread eastward across the country—not the least of them being the popularity of the small hotels and inns described in this guide. Small wonder then that this is our longest chapter.

There is one category for which we'd really like to request more recommendations: inns that actually *welcome* children! We're all in favor of romantic adult getaways, but there are regions of California—the Wine Country, for example—where there is hardly a place that will tolerate children, let alone welcome them. Perhaps as a reaction to this, a law was recently passed in California making it illegal for hotels and inns to discriminate on the basis of age. As a result, when we note under Restrictions "No children under 12," this has no legal bearing whatsoever. It is rather an indication given to us by the inns involved that they feel their property is more appropriate for older children. We have mixed feelings on this whole subject; sometimes a kid-free atmosphere is valid, other times we feel it's a cheap substitute for proper soundproofing on the innkeepers' part. An alternative is **Kids Welcome** (3924 East 14th Street, Long Beach CA 90804–2933; 310–498–0552 or 800–383–3513), a reservation service specializing in "family-friendly" B&B homestays. Give them a call and they'll book you into a comfortable place; although they

53

cover the whole state, their list is especially strong in southern Californi

In general, there's not too much seasonal variation in the rates o
California's inns and hotels, although they do tend to be 10% to 20
higher on weekends in most areas. Exceptions are the North Coast regio
where midweek rates are lower off-season (November to March), and th
desert areas, where brutal summer heat cuts rates in half.

Another source of information is available through the California Asso
ciation of B&B Inns: an information and reservation service available 2
hours a day. Dial 800–284–INNS for a detailed recorded message descril
ing the inns, their prices, and interesting events, anywhere in the stat
Once you've found a place that interests you, your call can be transferre
directly to the inn for a reservation.

The California Office of Tourism divides the state into 12 distin
regions; we've noted them below, along with a few annotations an
subdivisions of our own. At the end of each region, we list the towns wi
recommended inns and hotels, to help you in using this chapter. Whe
reading the entries, you'll see the 12 regional divisions noted in th
"Location" heading for each entry. Check back to these thumbna
sketches if you are liable to get Monterey mixed up with Mendocino

Finally, please note that most of the greater Los Angeles area (exclu
ing Orange County) is listed under Los Angeles, so you don't need
look through the entire chapter to find out what's available in this mo
sprawling of cities.

Shasta-Cascade   This relatively undiscovered region in north-centr
and northeast California offers a dramatic introduction to California
wilderness and geologic past. Best known is the Whiskeytown-Shast
Trinity National Recreation Area, near 14,000-foot Mt. Shasta, where yc
can backpack or rent a houseboat on Lake Shasta. At Lassen Volcan
National Park, see the strange formations and caves left by wide-rangir
volcanic activity. Even more unusual is Lava Beds National Monumer
near the Oregon border, where the Modoc Indians made their last stan
using volcanic rubble for protection. This area fronts on Tule Lake, whe
over one million waterfowl visit each fall and huge populations of ba
eagles spend the winter. At the southern edge of this region, take Rou
70 through Quincy and the spectacular Feather River Canyon.

North Coast   This region has three distinct subregions. The **Win
Country** is located northeast of San Francisco, along Routes 29 and 1
In addition to over 200 wineries with free tours and tastings, there a
rolling green hills, mud baths in Calistoga, gliding, and ballooning. Nc
to be missed is Petaluma Adobe, a restored 1840s headquarters of th
Vallejo agricultural empire.

Not surprisingly, food is taken as seriously here as wine, and the are
is noted for its many outstanding restaurants. *If you'll be visiting on
weekend, be sure to ask your host to make your dinner reservations when yc
book your room.* Keep in mind that the Napa Valley, in particular, surpass
Disneyland in popularity with tourists; unless heavy traffic is your thin
avoid fall weekends when everyone goes wine-tasting!

The **Coast** area on Highway 1 north of San Francisco includes world-class scenery, shorelines, and accommodations. Near Jenner the road cuts through steep green slopes that sweep down to the sea. Close by is Fort Ross, an 1812 Russian trading post, complete with onion-domed Orthodox church. To the north are tiny towns and perfect beachcombing shores near Sea Ranch and Gualala, Elk, Little River, and trendy Mendocino. The area then becomes more remote and wild as it passes through Westport. One recommended side trip for the experienced driver is the back road to Ferndale (from South Fork past Cape Mendocino), which winds up high bluffs with superb ocean views.

The Redwood Empire on Highway 101 stretches from Piercy to Crescent City. It's worth putting up with the cutesy tourist offerings to see the real scenery. Especially recommended are Avenue of the Giants near Pepperwood; Big Tree at Prairie City, north of Orick; and the Jedediah Smith area east of Crescent City.

North Coast towns with inns/hotels listed: Wine Country: Angwin, Boonville, Calistoga, Cazadero, Geyserville, Glen Ellen, Glenhaven, Guerneville, Healdsburg, Napa, St. Helena, Santa Rosa, Sonoma, Ukiah, Yountville.**Coast:**Elk, Ferndale, Fort Bragg, Gualala, Inverness, Leggett, Little River, Mendocino, Muir Beach, Olema, Westport. **Redwood Empire:** Eureka, Garberville, Trinidad, Vichy Springs.

San Francisco Bay Area   Here and elsewhere along the coast, fog often shrouds the area in spring and early summer. To some this means unwanted cool weather only miles away from a sunny, warm interior. To others this underlines the special romance and mystery of the area. Although few cities can surpass San Francisco for culture, shopping, and sightseeing (see description in listings), there is more to the Bay Area. Across the Golden Gate Bridge are Sausalito and Tiburon, both artists' colonies with unusual homes clinging to the cliffsides. Nearby Muir Woods provides an easy introduction to the giant redwoods. The East Bay includes Berkeley with its hillside residential area, lively university district, and excellent botanical garden. To the south, stroll the pretty seaside boardwalk at Santa Cruz, and visit Año Nuevo State Reserve to see lolling elephant seals and rocks covered with fossilized seashells.

San Francisco Bay Area towns with inns/hotels listed: Alameda, Aptos, Berkeley, Davenport, Half Moon Bay, Montara, Moss Beach, Palo Alto, San Francisco, Point San Pablo, San Gregorio, San Jose, Santa Cruz, Saratoga, Sausalito.

Central Valley   Extremely hot during the summer, this region offers comparatively little of interest to tourists. Extending south from Chico through the central portion of California to Bakersfield, this area has over 11 million acres of rich farmland, and produces an astonishing variety of fruits, nuts, and vegetables. Worth seeing: the Chinese temple in Oroville; Old Sacramento (take the walking tour); and Route 160 from Sacramento to Isleton, which winds along dikes, past almond and fruit groves, and through Locke, a bizarre, two-block, two-level town built in 1915 by

Chinese workers. In the south, Bakersfield is near California's oil fields and is known as the state's country music center.

Central Valley towns with inns/hotels listed: Coalinga, Kernville, Oroville, Red Bluff, Redding, Sacramento.

Gold Country   Gold mining brought thousands of people to this region in the 1850s, but these days the only thing that is mined there are the tourists. Overcrowded with visitors in the summer, this area nevertheless has retained a genuine Old West flavor and should not be missed. Be sure to get off Route 49 to some of the smaller towns like Murphys and Volcano; see nearby Grinding Rocks State Park where the Mi-Wok Indians lived for centuries, and the restored town of Columbia, now a state historical park. Don't avoid the unnumbered back roads that wind up hills and through picturesque farms. To the north, visit Downieville, which is tucked into the northern Sierras, then take passable dirt roads to Malakoff Diggings to see how hydraulic placer mining washed away a mountainside.

Gold Country towns with inns/hotels listed: Amador City, Coloma, Columbia, Grass Valley, Ione, Jackson, Murphys, Nevada City, Oroville, Quincy, Sonora, Sutter Creek, Tuolumne, Volcano.

High Sierras   For 400 miles, the Sierra Nevada mountain range defines eastern California, from north of Lake Tahoe to the northern terminus of the desert region. Yosemite, Kings Canyon, and Sequoia national parks provide unlimited outdoor opportunities for everyone from car window sightseers to rugged backpackers. See 14,495-foot Mt. Whitney, giant sequoias and torrential waterfalls, or ski at one of 20 areas. Lake Tahoe provides resort offerings, with famous casinos, gambling, and glitzy shows nearby at Stateline Nevada. The crowning jewel here is Emerald Bay. For a bizarre foray into history, visit Donner Memorial Park, two miles west of Truckee, where an 1846 pioneer group, stranded by heavy winter snows, resorted to cannibalism.

High Sierras towns with inns/hotels listed: Bishop, Bridgeport, Fish Camp, Groveland, Hope Valley, Quincy, Tahoe City, Yosemite.

Central Coast   This photogenic region stretches from the Monterey Peninsula south to Santa Barbara. Inland, Pinnacles National Monument's volcanic spires, bluffs, and crags are worth a visit. On the coast, from Monterey (see description in listings), tour the peninsula via Seventeen-Mile Drive (a toll is charged) past Pebble Beach, wind-sculptured cypresses, cavorting otters, and on to Carmel. Highway 1 cuts through misty, ragged cliffs that rush into the sea. This is Big Sur—wild, beautiful, with almost no off-road access and too many crowds in the summer. To view the excesses of the rich, visit Hearst's San Simeon Castle (reservations required). To the south, Morro Bay marks the start of the renowned California beaches. Stop to see Solvang, a 1911 Danish settlement, and Santa Barbara, the heart of Spanish Mission country.

Central Coast towns with inns/hotels listed: Big Sur, Ballard, Baywood Park, Cambria, Carmel, Montecito, Monterey, Ojai, Pacific Grove, San Luis Obispo, Santa Barbara, Solvang.

Greater Los Angeles   This city-region includes not only LA itself but the myriad surrounding cities, beaches, and islands. For relaxation, sail or fly to Santa Catalina Island, one of the top resort locations in the country. See listings for more information about the area.

   Greater Los Angeles area towns with inns/hotels listed: Avalon, Los Angeles (also includes Beverly Hills, Hollywood, North Hollywood, Santa Monica).

Orange County   Welcome to the California of commercials and legend. Here you can experience the mythic and somewhat crazed California beach life at Newport, Laguna, and Balboa. It's all here: sun, sand, surfers, theme parks (Disneyland, Knott's Berry Farm, Magic Mountain), nouveau everything, Super Hype. Your children will love it, but you may need a week on a desert island to recover.

   Orange County towns with inns/hotels listed: Dana Point, Laguna Beach, Newport Beach.

Inland Empire   From the San Gabriel Mountains in this region you can look down over Los Angeles. Route 2, east of Pasadena, twists through the mountains and past ski areas. East of San Bernardino, Route 18 is called the Rim of the World Drive. Although an overstatement, it is a pretty mountain road that leads to overdeveloped Lake Arrowhead and Big Bear Lake resort area. Southwest is Riverside, California's "citrus capital" and home of the famous Mission Inn, touted by Will Rogers.

   Inland Empire towns with inns/hotels listed: Big Bear Lake, Lake Arrowhead, Orland, Redwood, Riverside, Skyforest.

San Diego County   Although San Diego (see description in listings) is the star of this region, there are several nearby areas in the county worth noting. La Jolla's natural caverns, formed by waves pounding against the sandstone cliffs, and the Mingei International Museum of prehistoric and contemporary crafts make for a special stop. I-8, which becomes Route 79, is a pretty drive to the old mining town of Julian. Farther on is the retirement community of Borrego Springs, with its superb Anza-Borrego Desert State Park. Stop at the headquarters for an excellent introduction to the varied plant and animal life of California's desert country.

   San Diego County towns with inns/hotels listed: Coronado, Julian, La Jolla, Rancho Santa Fe, San Diego, Temecula, Valley Center.

The Deserts   From posh Palm Springs to Nevada, from Mexico to Death Valley, this region is unlike anything else on earth. Since the desert area covers almost one-sixth of the state, it is important to plan your itinerary carefully. Unless you are a dedicated desert aficionado, it can get repetitive. South of Palm Springs, don't miss the enormous date groves near Thermal and Mecca, or the restaurants offering date milkshakes and date pecan pies. Just to the south, senior citizen communities dot the shoreline of Salton Sea, created in 1905 by human error during the construction of the Colorado River aqueduct. To the east are the Chocolate Mountains and the sprawling Sand Hills. North is Joshua Tree National Monument, best in spring when the cacti blossom. Finally there is Death Valley, a bewitching place of startling contrasts in altitude, colors, vegetation, formations, and texture. A few reminders: Try not to visit this region in the summer, always heed the warning to stay on the highway, and carry extra water in your car.

Desert Country towns with inns/hotels listed: Death Valley, Desert Hot Springs, Idyllwild, Nipton, Palm Springs.

ALAMEDA

Garratt Mansion   *Tel:* 510–521–4779
900 Union Street, 94501   *Fax:* 510–521–6796

Although many people think of B&Bs only for weekend getaways, they're equally popular with business travelers who value the warm hospitality inns offer. The Garratt Mansion, built in 1893 and named for a turn-of-the-century industrialist, is just such a refuge. In 1977, after 50 years as a boarding house, Royce and Betty Gladden bought this Colonial Revival home, restoring it as a B&B in 1983. Betty notes that "we have lived in this area all our lives and have explored public transportation, theaters, restaurants, museums, parks and tourist attractions. Our day trip suggestions help guests maximize their time and enjoyment." Rooms are furnished primarily with period antiques, and the architectural detailing includes a carved oak stairway lined with beveled and stained glass windows. Breakfast is served at guests' convenience at the large dining room table, and might include freshly squeezed orange juice, sliced kiwi and mango, scalloped potatoes, banana bread, scrambled eggs with fresh chives and ham, or perhaps Dutch baby pancakes with sautéed apples.

"Hospitable hostess; room sunny and beautifully decorated. Thick towels, fresh flowers, homemade cookies and drinks always available, delicious breakfast, warm, friendly environment, helpful suggestions for local restaurants." *(SB)* "Great neighborhood for jogging, walking, exploring." *(P.J. Hoffer)*

Open All year.
Rooms 1 suite, 6 doubles—5 with private bath and/or shower, 2 with maximum of 4 people sharing bath. All with radio, clock. 5 with telephone, desk; 3 with fan, 1 with fireplace.
Facilities Dining room, living room with books, stereo, games; Den with TV/VCR, guest pantry. Patio, porch, lawn swing. On-street parking. 2 blocks to park, tennis; 4 blocks to beach for wind-surfing, paved walking trail.
Location San Francisco Bay area. 15 m E of San Francisco; 12 m S of Berkeley. 8 blocks from center. Corner of Union & Clinton; call for directions.
Restrictions No smoking. Children over 6.

Credit cards Amex, DC, MC, Visa.
Rates B&B, $130 suite, $95 double, $85 single. Extra person, $15. 2-night minimum holidays, graduation.
Extras Spanish spoken.

AMADOR CITY

Imperial Hotel ¢ ✗
14202 Highway 49, 95601, P.O. Box 195

Tel: 209–267–9172
Fax: 209–267–9249

With about 150 inhabitants, Amador City is California's smallest city; it seems only fitting that its grandly named hotel, the Imperial, offers all of six guest rooms! First built as a store, the Imperial opened as a hotel in 1879, and remained in operation until 1927. Bruce Sherrill and Dale Martin bought and restored the Imperial in 1988, and have decorated the guest rooms with Victorian antiques and reproduction furnishings; Oriental rugs contrast with the dark wood floors and exposed brick walls; the common areas are enlivened by contemporary artwork.

Breakfast entrées change daily, with smoked salmon Benedict, huevos rancheros, and spinach rice with tomatoes and feta cheese among the creative offerings, accompanied by fresh fruit, homemade fruit breads, and hot and cold beverages. The dinner menu might include lamb stew with chard and polenta; prawns with apricot curry sauce; and Dijon encrusted pork medallions.

"Our room had lots of sun, wicker furniture, a firm bed, and a good shower." *(Kathleen Lowe Owen)* "The trompe l'oeil painting is beautifully executed and lends a sense of whimsy to the hotel." *(Nan Spina)* "Beautiful long walks can be taken along a rural road near the hotel. Easy parking, in the shade." *(Gretchen Hackett)* "Early morning coffee and fresh fruit set in the hall; later we had a delicious orange liqueur French toast at a patio table near the waterfall." *(Linda Davis)* "The bathroom was airy and spotless with designer soaps, fluffy towels, and bath beads. Fine dinner with solicitous, yet unobtrusive, friendly, efficient service." *(NC)*

Open All year.
Rooms 6 doubles—all with private bath and/or shower, radio, air-conditioning, ceiling fan. 2 with balcony.
Facilities Restaurant, bar, breakfast room, library, balconies, patio. Limited off-street parking. River nearby for gold panning.
Location Gold Country. 40 m SE of Sacramento. Center of town.
Restrictions Traffic noise in front rooms midweek; noise from bar possible in guest rooms. Smoking (including cigars) permitted in bar, section of dining room, balconies. Room #5 is very small, with minimal storage space.
Credit cards Amex, DC, Discover, MC, Visa.
Rates B&B, $65–95 double, $60–90 single. Mid-week family rate. 2-night weekend/holiday minimum. Alc dinner, $28; Sunday Brunch, $9.
Extras Airport/station pickup.

ANGWIN

Forest Manor
415 Cold Springs Road, 94508

Tel: 707–965–3538
Tel: 800–788–0364
Fax: 707–965–3516

Innkeepers Harold and Corlene Lambeth traveled throughout the world and lived for many years in Thailand before returning to California. They built Forest Manor, a large English Tudor-style home, in 1980, and furnished it with pieces they collected during their travels, including English antiques, Persian rugs, and Asian art. True to its name, Forest Manor is surrounded by woods and vineyards, making it an exceptionally peaceful retreat.

"The spacious Somerset Suite has a king-size bed with a carved head-board and a free-standing fireplace faced by two swivel armchairs with reading lights and a sheepskin rug. The dresser was actually a mirrored dining room buffet, and an armoire contained the makings for hot drinks for use with the coffee maker in the bathroom. The bath was done in inch-square brown tiles, and had a double shower with two shower heads, a massive counter with two sinks, and a double whirlpool bath backed by mirrors. Towels were lush and plentiful. We breakfasted in our room by the sunny five-sided bay window overlooking the pool and hot tub." *(SHW)* "Unlike most Napa Valley inns, Forest Manor is set on a meander-ing country road. he sumptuous breakfast typically consisted of juice, coffee, fresh fruit salad, fresh baked muffins, an egg dish or waffles, and carried us through to dinner. Our room was supplied with terrycloth robes, and a welcoming fruit basket; cookies or snacks were always available on a plate in the foyer." *(Michael Milne)*

Open All year.
Rooms 5 suites—all with private bath, air-conditioning, radio, clock, coffee maker, refrigerator. Telephone, TV on request. 1 with Jacuzzi, deck, desk; 2 with fireplace.
Facilities Dining room, living room with fireplace, organ, library; game room. 20 acres with swimming pool, hot tub, walking trail. Vineyard, forest adjacent. Tennis nearby. 20 min. to Lake Berryessa for fishing, boating.
Location North Coast, Napa Wine Country. 70 m N of San Francisco; 7 m NE of St. Helena; 27 m N of Napa. 5 m from Silverado Trail. N on Rte. 29 through St. Helena, exit at Deer Park Rd. Turn right at red blinking light; continue 5 1/2 m to Angwin. Turn right on Cold Springs Rd & go 3/4 m to inn on left.
Restrictions No smoking. Children over 12.
Credit cards Amex, MC, Visa.
Rates B&B, $99–239 suite. Extra person, $25. 2-3 night weekend/holiday mini-mum.
Extras Spanish spoken.

APTOS

Aptos is located in the San Francisco Bay Area, 15 minutes east of Santa Cruz and 40 minutes north of Monterey. It's approximately 85 miles south of San Francisco. Set along the north side of Monterey Bay, it makes a convenient base for area explorations.

Apple Lane Inn ¢   *Tel: 408–475–6868*
6265 Soquel Drive, 95003

The Apple Lane Inn is a restored Victorian farmhouse, built in the 1870s; it's decorated with period antiques and hand-stenciled walls. The inn was purchased by Diana and Douglas Groom in 1990, and recent improvements include the Wine Cellar suite, with private garden entrance, two large stained glass windows, and wine memorabilia accenting the decor, plus a large, airy attic suite in the treetops. Diana's breakfasts vary with the seasons, but might include fresh raspberries with yogurt, souffléd eggs with ham and four kinds of cheese, accompanied by lemon and nut breads, hot muffins and tarts.

"Well maintained and extremely clean. The Grooms were warm and generous hosts. Our room had an antique four-poster bed with a magnificent white eyelet coverlet and matching canopy and an elaborately carved marble-topped dresser. Hot water was ample for a long soak in the deep, clawfoot tub and the hand-held shower made washing my hair easy." *(Peg Iversen)* "The resident sheep, horse, roosters and lop-eared rabbit add to the inn's homey farm atmosphere. You really feel like you're in the country, even though you're right off the main road and in town. My lovely room, Blossom, done in mauve shades, had a huge bathroom complete with skylight, wicker chaise lounge, and clawfoot tub supplied with apple-scented bath salts. Along with a cool breeze, Apples the cat came through the open window and made herself at home at the foot of my bed. Charming innkeepers." *(Gail Davis)*

Open All year.
Rooms 3 suites, 2 doubles—all with private bath and/or shower. Some with desk, fan; 1 with wet bar.
Facilities Main parlor, with library, fireplace, player piano; sitting room with guest refrigerator, supplies for coffee or tea. 3 acres with gazebo, patio, gardens, croquet, horseshoes, farm animals. Tennis, hiking, beach for fishing, swimming nearby. Walking distance to ocean.
Location From Hwy. 1, take Park Ave. N to Soquel Dr. Go right on Soquel to inn.
Restrictions No smoking. Children over 12 preferred.
Credit cards MC, Visa.
Rates B&B, $100–175 suite, $70–100 double. Extra person, $15. 15% midweek business discount.
Extras Local airport/station pickup; charge varies. Crib, babysitting by arrangement. Knowledge of American sign language. Spanish, German spoken.

AVALON, SANTA CATALINA ISLAND

We can't think of Catalina without remembering these words from the old song, "26 miles across the sea, Santa Catalina is a-waiting for me. . . ." Well, it's still waiting, and it remains a relatively unspoiled escape, easily accessible by ferry from San Pedro or Newport Beach. Most of the island is now owned by the Santa Catalina Conservancy, which keeps the terrain unchanged and uninhabited. William Wrigley, the chewing-gum magnate, purchased much of the island in 1919 and did quite an effective job of converting it into a California Riviera; be sure to visit the Wrigley Memorial and Botanical Garden, and the Casino, now a museum. Visitors today enjoy hiking and all water sports, especially fishing, scuba diving, and snorkeling, plus golf, tennis, horseback riding, and bicycling. Very few cars are permitted on the island, so most people get around on foot, bicycle, or golf cart.

Reader tips: "Avalon gets crowded on summer weekends; visit mid-week for reduced hotel rates and to avoid the mob scene. November through April is off-season; ask about package rates for substantial savings." *(MA)* Also: "We thought the price was high for our small, simple room, but then, everything has to be shipped from the mainland." *(AMA)*

Information please: Some of the 47 guest rooms of the **Hotel Metropole** (205 Crescent Avenue, P.O. Box 1900, 90704; 310–510–1884 or in CA, 800–541–8528) have balconies, ocean views, whirlpool tubs, king-size beds, and gas fireplaces; others overlook the Metropole Market right on the harbor; rates range from $85–275, and include a breakfast of fresh-squeezed orange juice, coffee, and croissants or pastries. Relax at the nearby beach, or in the rooftop hot tub.

Hotel Vista Del Mar

Tel: 310–510–1452

417 Crescent Avenue, P.O. Box 1979, 90704

Owners Jerry Dunn and Kelly Rowsey created this Mediterranean-style structure, originally built as the Hotel Campo Bravo, by gutting the interior and starting from scratch, reopening in 1988 as the Hotel Vista Del Mar. Rooms, which open onto a central plant-filled atrium (original to the 1930s structure), are decorated in soft pastels with wicker furnishings.

"Excellent ambience, decor, cleanliness, and amenities. Delicious breakfast of coffee, tea, fresh-squeezed orange juice, and croissants with jam and butter, served on the patio." *(Dr. & Mrs. Shneidman)* "Conveniently located; everything within walking distance; the sound of the ocean lulls you to sleep." *(Philonise Williams)* "Excellent on all counts. The owner, front desk staff, and reservation people were friendly, helpful, accommodating, and genuine. Even the cleaning staff were professional and unobtrusive." *(Kathleen Evans)*

Open All year.
Rooms 2 suites with balcony, double Jacuzzi; 13 doubles—all with full private bath, telephone, radio, TV, desk, air-conditioning, hair dryer. Most with wet bar, refrigerator, fireplace.
Facilities Library, garden atrium, lobby. 10 steps from sandy ocean beach (towels and beach chairs provided).
Location Center of town; at foot of pier. 2 blocks from ferry.
Restrictions Smoking in lobby, courtyard only.
Credit cards Amex, Discover, MC, Visa.

Rates B&B, $195–275 suite, $65–165 double. Extra adult, $15. 10% senior discount. Off-season midweek packages. 2-night weekend minimum.
Extras Airport, ferry pickup, $3–5. Crib. Spanish spoken.

Inn on Mt. Ada ✕
Tel: 310–510–2030

398 Wrigley Road, P.O. Box 2560, 90704

If you've always wanted to stay in the home of a multimillionaire, this may be your best chance. Chewing-gum magnate William Wrigley, Jr., built this Georgian colonial mansion in 1921; in 1985 it was restored by island residents at a cost of over $1 million. Town and ocean views from the inn are spectacular, and the decor is lavish, with flowered chintzes coordinating comforters and draperies, overstuffed couches and easy chairs. Rates include a full breakfast, a deli sandwich selection at lunchtime, evening wine, hors d'oeuvres, dinner, and a shuttle to and from town.

"We were greeted at the door as if we were the most important people ever to come to the inn, and our first view was of a lovely bouquet of flowers and a magnificent circular staircase. The inn is kept immaculately clean, yet the staff was almost invisible until we needed something. A canopied golf cart is provided for touring the island." *(Vivianne Fitzgerald)* "We ate in the cozy dining room and returned to our room (#3) on the corner and were delighted with the twinkling lights of Avalon and the sound of distant music and laughter." *(Jane & Melvin Mattoon)* "Dinners are an event, and I was impressed by the chef's talent. We visited with other guests, and enjoyed quiet time with each other." *(Linda Andrew)*

Open All year. Closed Dec. 24, 25.
Rooms 2 suites, 4 doubles—all with private bath and/or shower, radio, desk, fan. Telephone, TV on request.
Facilities Living room, dining room, den with TV, sun porch, decks, and terraces. 5½ acres with golf carts provided for local transportation.
Location On hill overlooking town.
Restrictions No smoking. No children under 14.
Credit cards MC, Visa.
Rates Full board, $370–590 suite, $230–490 double. Extra person, $100. 2-night weekend, holiday minimum.
Extras Free ferry/heliport pickup. Spanish spoken.

Zane Grey Pueblo Hotel
Tel: 310–510–0966

P.O. Box 216, 90704
310–510–1520

They say you can't make money in publishing (we can attest to that), but prolific Western author Zane Grey was one of the exceptions that proves the rule. By the time of his death in 1939, he had written 89 books, many of them best sellers; others fueled the TV series, the *Zane Grey Theater*. In 1926, he built this Hopi pueblo-style adobe home, and you can enjoy the same views of the ocean, cactus-covered hillside, harbor, and town below as the Grey family did.

"Copies of all Zane Grey's books are in the living room. The location keeps noise far away and allows for appreciation of the tranquil site, overlooking the harbor and canyon. Breakfast is a self-service toast and coffee affair. Each of the rooms is different, with a Western motif. We stayed in Mr. Grey's brother's room, which overlooks the canyon and has a sitting area and bedroom. We saw many of the other rooms and each was charming and clean. The inn is near the Wrigley clock, which chimes every 15 minutes until 10 P.M." *(Audrey Williams)*

Note: Although it's a steep walk up the hill to the hotel, guests are picked up at the boat dock, and free taxi service into town is scheduled for 8, 9 and 10 A.M. and 3, 5, and 6 P.M.

Open All year.
Rooms 17 doubles—all with private bath and/or shower.
Facilities Living room with piano, fireplace, TV. Guest microwave, refrigerator. Gardens, unheated swimming pool.
Location Atop hillside above Avalon Casino.
Credit cards Amex, MC, Visa.
Rates B&B, $55–125 double. Extra person, $35.
Extras Free ferry pickup.

BALLARD

Ballard Inn ♿
2436 Baseline Avenue, 93463

Tel: 805–688–7770
800–638–2466
Fax: 805–688–9560

To experience the pleasures of 27 award-winning wineries, plus fine food and quality lodging, head to the uncrowded Santa Ynez valley, an easy drive from Santa Barbara. Unlike the better-known Napa Valley vineyards, the Santa Ynez wineries are friendly, personal, and informal; tastings are free or modestly priced and typically include a souvenir wine glass. An excellent base for oenophilic explorations is the Ballard Inn, built by Larry Stone and Steve Hyslop; Kelly Robinson is the manager. Guest rooms are individually decorated, with queen- or king-size beds, highlighted with handmade quilts and antiques, reflecting the history of the Santa Ynez valley and its residents. Rates include a full breakfast, cooked to order from 8–10 A.M., and at 5 P.M., afternoon wine, tea, and hors d'oeuvres.

"Homey, informal atmosphere; lovely common areas; staff extremely friendly. Across the street is the Ballard Store restaurant, serving excellent French country food. Afternoon buffet and wine-tasting with high quality wines." *(Hugh Wilson Elliott)*

Open All year.
Rooms 15 doubles—all with private bath and/or shower, air-conditioning. 7 with wood-burning fireplace, 1 with balcony.
Facilities Living room with fireplace, dining room with fireplace, sitting room with TV, sun porch. Verandas with rockers. Bicycle rentals. Hiking, bicycling, horseback riding, fishing, boating nearby.
Location Santa Ynez valley. 35 m N of Santa Barbara. 3½ m N of Solvang via Alamo Pintado Rd., 2 m S of Los Olivos.
Restrictions No smoking.
Credit cards Amex, MC, Visa.
Rates B&B, $160–195 double. 10% service.
Extras Wheelchair access; 1 room specially equipped.

BAYWOOD PARK

Baywood B&B Inn 🛏 ✕ ♿.

1370 Second Street, 93402

Tel: 805–528–8888

"Almost halfway between San Francisco and Los Angeles, the Morro Bay area makes a great meeting point for families or friends from either area. Built originally for offices, the building was bought by Pat and Alex Benson in 1990. They turned it into a beautiful B&B, situated directly across from the bay and a little dock where birds gather. Each room has a outside entrance; those on the second floor are reached from a balcony which wraps around the building. Only a small tree-lined road separates the B&B and the bay; nearby are little shops and excellent seafood restaurants. We bought cups of steaming capuccino from a small coffee stand, and took them out to the dock to watch the sunset. This wonderful view and the tranquil environment made for a most romantic setting.

"The pastel-colored California Beach room has a high metal poster bed, sofa and table, large tiled bathroom, and a closet stocked with complimentary beverages and popcorn. Shell decorations and artificial palm trees reinforced the beach theme. At the 5 P.M. wine and cheese hour we tasted wine from a local winery and were able to tour the other rooms; the Williamsburg room, with flowered chintz and canopy bed, is among the most popular. Beds are turned down at 7:30, with a chocolate left on the pillow. Breakfast is served in the room at any time between 7 and 9 A.M.; you can also choose from the menu in the restaurant. Our breakfast came on a big tray with hot coffee in a thermos, juice, pastries, and mini-quiches. The staff was friendly and helpful. Close by is Montana de Oro park with hiking trails along the ocean." *(Wendy Kameda)*

Open All year. Restaurant closed Mon., Tues.

Rooms 8 suites, 7 doubles—all with full private bath, telephone, radio, clock, TV, desk, ceiling fan, wood-burning fireplace, refrigerator, microwave, hairdryer, balcony/patio.

Facilities Restaurant, living room, mezzanine with books, stereo; deck. Occasional poetry readings. Approx. 1 ½ bay front acres with patio, garden, off-street parking, canoeing, sailing. Beach, fishing, golf, hiking nearby.

Location Central coast. 12 m W of San Luis Obispo. Morro Bay.

Restrictions No smoking. Some morning noise along balcony when breakfast is delivered to rooms.

Credit cards MC, Visa.

Rates B&B, $140 suite, $80–120 double. Extra person, $15. No charge for children under 8. 2-night minimum preferred holiday weekends.

Extras Wheelchair access.

BERKELEY

Best known for its branch of the University of California, Berkeley is the place to go to find out what the rest of the country will be doing three years hence. Gardeners will especially enjoy a visit here, from the university's Botanical Garden to the city's Rose Garden. **Reader tip:** "Probably a minority opinion, but we prefer Berkeley to San Francisco any day; it's a warmer, more hospitable, friendlier place; much less puffed up about itself than SFO." *(EDF)*

Also recommended: Although it's too big for a full entry at 240 rooms, *Eric Friesen* recommends the **Claremont Resort** (Ashby & Domingo Avenues, Berkeley Hills, Oakland 94623–0363; 510–843–3000 or 800–551–7266): "An original place (reminiscent in appearance of the Del Coronado in San Diego) with a bar and superb restaurant with excellent views of the Bay looking back to San Francisco, great service and reasonable summer rates. This great dowager of a place is independently run by true hoteliers." This well-equipped resort is built around a handsome 1915 chateau, and has 22 landscaped acres, with two heated swimming pools, 10 tennis courts, and a recently built spa building. The creative restaurant menus offer guilt-free enjoyment; many dishes are available in "spa portions" with reduced calories, portions, and cost. Double rates range from $184–224, and children under 17 stay free; ask for information on special package rates.

Although a bit basic for some, budget travelers are consistently pleased with the **French Hotel** (1538 Shattuck Avenue, 94709; 510–548–9930) with comfortable rooms, reasonable rates, and a "fantastic location." *(Shirley Dittloff)*

Information please: Across the street from the University of California, Berkeley is the **Bancroft Club Hotel** (2680 Bancroft Way, 94704; 510–549–1000 or 800–666–6666), with 22 guest rooms, many with balconies or decks. Built in 1928 in the Arts and Crafts style and renovated in 1993, B&B double rates range from $90–110.

Another area possibility approximately 12 miles east in Walnut Creek is the **The Mansion at Lakewood**, a gracious 1861 Victorian manor house, set behind white cast iron gates in a quiet residential neighborhood (1056 Hacienda Drive, Walnut Creek 94598; 510–945–3600 or 800–477–7898) of Walnut Creek. The Mansion's guest rooms are elegantly furnished with period antiques, four-poster and canopy beds, plus down comforters and fluffy robes. A typical breakfast menu might include Dutch baby pancakes with warm berry sauce, lemon poppyseed muffins, fresh squeezed orange juice, coffee and English breakfast tea. Also provided is afternoon tea on the terrace.

For an additional area entry, see listing for **Alameda**.

Gramma's Rose Garden Inn 🏃 ♿   *Tel:* 510–549–214
2740 Telegraph Avenue, 94705   *Fax:* 510–549–108

"After the Loma Prieta earthquake of 1989, Gramma's expanded from two turn-of-the-century mansions to five buildings ringing a garden courtyard of lawns, flowers, and fruit trees. The two mansions reveal their Victorian charm with leaded and stained glass windows, elaborate wainscoting, inlaid hardwood floors, and tiled fireplaces. Their guest rooms, although smaller, are furnished with antiques. Rooms in the three newer buildings are light and spacious, with scrubbed pine furnishings, French doors, and large windows draped with lace. My favorite room was #7 in the Fa

House, with a large stained-glass window, marble fireplace, and a curved bay window with an attached bench, perfect for reading the morning paper. The king-size bed came equipped with reading lights on both sides, and the desk was good for working. Breakfast is available in the glass-ceilinged dining room or outside on the redwood deck." *(Matt Joyce)*

"We prefer the rooms in the main house—#5 is our favorite. Wine and cheese is available every evening: we love to sit in front of the fire to relax and enjoy. There's always fresh coffee and cookie jars filled with home-made goodies. The breakfast buffet includes fresh juice and fruit, cereal, toppings of chopped walnuts, raisins, brown sugar, and yogurt; fluffy homemade croissants, plus muffins and scones. Sometimes an omelet, quiche, or buttermilk hot cakes are offered. Concerned, helpful staff." *(Billie & Cliff Lundin, also Norman Hughes)*

Open All year.

Rooms 6 suites, 34 doubles—all with private bath and/or shower, telephone, radio, TV. Some with desk, fan, fireplace, deck, 1 with kitchenette. 11 rooms in main house, 29 rooms in 4 other buildings.

Facilities 2 living rooms with fireplace, breakfast room, decks. 1.4 acres with garden, patios. Swimming pool, tennis courts, jogging trails nearby. Off-street parking.

Location Bay Area, 15 m E of San Francisco. 5 blocks from center; 9 blocks to campus. Exit I-80 at Ashby Ave. (Rte. 580). Go E to Telegraph Ave., then N (left) to inn on left.

Restrictions Traffic noise in some rooms. No smoking.

Credit cards Amex, CB, DC, MC, Visa.

Rates B&B, $150–175 suite, $85–125 double, single. Extra person, $10. Corporate rates. 10% AARP, senior discount. Sunday brunch, $19.

Extras Wheelchair access. Crib, babysitting. Some Spanish spoken.

BIG BEAR LAKE

Also recommended: On a quiet street one block from the lake and shopping village, **Janet Kay's B&B** (695 Paine Road, P.O. Box 3874, 92315; 909–866–6800 or 800–243–7031) offers 17 fully equipped guest rooms, many with double whirlpool tubs, gas fireplaces, and decks. Each guest room has a different theme, from the king-size reproduction sleigh bed in the Victorian room to the mosquito netting draping the bed in the Jungle Room. The two suites on the top floor have lake views. B&B double rates range from $59–169; suites from $119–219.

Information please: The **Eagle's Nest** (41675 Big Bear Boulevard, P.O. Box 1003, Big Bear Lake, 92315; 909–866–6465), is a rustic log home and cottages, set in the pine-covered mountains. The cozy living room is furnished invitingly with antiques, and has a huge stone fireplace. Rates of $75–165 include a continental breakfast, hot or cold beverages throughout the day and afternoon hors d'oeuvres.

Two appealing B&Bs can also be found in nearby Fawnskin. The **Windy Point Inn** (39263 North Shore Drive, P.O. Box 385, Fawnskin 92333; 909–866–2746) sits right on Windy Point, overlooking the lake, framed by mature pine trees and bordered by sandy beaches. This contemporary lodge offers six guest rooms with lake and mountain views, private baths, refrigerators, fireplaces, and queen- or king-sized beds. The master suite is ideal for honeymoons and anniversaries with its skylight, panoramic lake views, stereo, and Jacuzzi tub. The $135–275 rates include a full breakfast and afternoon hors d'oeuvres. "Val & Kent Kessler are incredibly gracious hosts. We can't wait to return." *(Janet Emery)*

Set in a pine forest, **The Inn at Fawnskin** (880 Canyon, P.O. Box 378, Fawnskin 92333; 909–866–3200) is a contemporary log lodge with a baby grand piano by the fireplace in the living room, and a game room with full-size pool table and oversize TV. Four guest rooms are available, and the $75–165 rates include a full breakfast (home-baked cinnamon rolls a specialty) and afternoon refreshments.

BIG SUR

Novelist Henry Miller, Big Sur resident for 20 years, noted that "There being nothing to improve on in the surroundings, the tendency is to set about improving oneself." Unfortunately, news of Big Sur's breathtaking beauty is now well known, and summer traffic jams often clog the hairpin turns of Highway 1. Our advice is to travel off-season, or to leave the crowds behind by hiking the beautiful trails of Pfeiffer–Big Sur State Park, Julia Pfeiffer Burns State Park, and the Ventana Wilderness. May and October are probably the best times for minimal crowds and maximal weather.

Reader tip: "Just up the road from Deetjen's is the Nepenthe restaurant, in a house built by Orson Welles for Rita Hayworth. For brunch, I had a delicious chile relleno quiche, freshly squeezed orange juice, and good coffee. The terrace has a fabulous 20-mile coastal view." *(Bob Freidus)*

Also recommended: Although it is not quite right for a full entry, readers are delighted with the **Big Sur Lodge** (Hwy. 1, P.O. Box 190, 93920; 408–667–3100 or 800-4-BIG SUR). "A reasonably priced motel with nice large rooms. It's in the center of Pfeiffer Big Sur State Park, across from the ocean. Their restaurant serves good food at reasonable prices." *(Jocelyn Luff)* Also: "It was wonderful being in the redwoods with the Big Sur River flowing by. Our spacious room had a fireplace, sofa, table, and small deck. The lodge entrance is separate from the main park entrance." *(Mr. & Mrs. John Keele)* Depending on the season, rates for its 61 units and condo-style cottages range from $70–175. A swimming pool, grocery store, and hiking trails make it a fine family choice.

Those willing to forgo double Jacuzzi tubs in their search for a taste of the "old California" can try **Deetjen's Big Sur Inn** (Highway 1, 93920; 408–667–2377), a 20-room rustic retreat built in the early 1930s by Helmuth and Helen Deetjen, Norwegian immigrants. While not fancy, rooms rent for $44–125, and the restaurant has a good reputation. "Fun but very basic. Lots of wood supplied for the stove to keep you warm. No soundproofing between rooms," said one reader, while another recommended the tiny Petite Cuisine room as a terrific value for a single traveler.

Information please: At the opposite end of the luxury scale is the ultra-chic, ultra-chère **Post Ranch Inn**, (408–667–2200 or 800–527–2200) just across Highway One from the Ventana. This "environmentally sensitive" luxury retreat will pamper you with magnificent cliffside ocean views, polished wood and natural stone decor, in-room slate-lined Jacuzzi tubs, designer robes, and fold-away massage tables, but you'll have to be "green" financially as well as ecologically: rates range from $255–495 for the 30 rooms either set on stilts or burrowed into the hillside, to minimize environmental impact. The restaurant offers both meat and vegetarian prix fixe menus at $45, with ocean views from every table.

Ventana Inn ✕ ૭   *Tel:* 408–667–2331
Highway One, 93920   800–628–6500

A long-time reader favorite, the Ventana was built in 1975, and has been expanded several times under the longtime management of Robert Bussinger. The architecture is California-modern, with tall ceilings, large exposed beams, and natural woods, and the rooms are spread over 12 buildings on very ample grounds. Rooms have a modern, country look; 34 have ocean vistas, while the remainder overlook the mountains or forest. The restaurant, one-eighth of a mile from the inn, has spectacular views of the Pacific and specializes in California cuisine, with an emphasis on fresh seafood, vegetables, and fruits; advance reservations are essential. Rates include breakfast, with fresh fruits and home-baked breads and pastries, brought to your room or available buffet-style in the lobby, and an afternoon wine and cheese buffet. Careful attention to detail in all areas—service, comfort, cuisine, and atmosphere—produces consistently positive reports from all sources:

"The ambience is one of sophistication, privacy, romance, and discretion." *(Howard Wechsler)* "My room, a lower unit in Bay House, had spectacular views from the hot tub of the sun setting over the Pacific 1,000 feet below. Inside and out, the air smelled wonderfully fresh and woodsy. The chef prepared an outstanding vegetarian dinner at my request. The staff is dedicated to providing the optimum in comfort and service." *(Gail Davis)*

Open All year.
Rooms 5 suites, 55 doubles—all with full private bath, telephone, TV/VCR, radio, desk, air-conditioning, refrigerators. Many with fireplace, deck, wet bar, hot tubs. Rooms located in 12 buildings.
Facilities Breakfast room/lobby with fireplace, restaurant with 3 fireplaces, library, porch. 243 acres with 2 heated swimming pools, sauna, Japanese hot baths, hiking trails. 3 m to ocean beaches for swimming, fishing.
Location Central Coast. 150 m S of San Francisco, 310 m N of Los Angeles. On scenic Hwy. 1, 28 m S of Carmel. 2½ m S of Pfeiffer–Big Sur State Park entrance.
Restrictions No smoking in common areas. Children definitely not encouraged.
Credit cards All major.
Rates B&B, $310–785 suite, $165–475 double. Extra person, $50. 2–3-night minimum weekends/holidays. Alc lunch $18, alc dinner $39.
Extras Wheelchair access; some rooms equipped for disabled. Spanish, French spoken.

BISHOP

Chalfant House ¢   *Tel:* 619–872–1790
213 Academy Street, 93514

The Chalfant House was built in 1898 by P.A. Chalfant, editor and publisher of the first newspaper in the Owens Valley, and was restored as a B&B in 1986 by Fred and Sally Manecke.

"We were greeted with a homemade fruit drink and introduced to the other guests. Next to the house is a well-lighted parking lot; the location set back from the main street makes for a quiet and restful night. My favorite breakfast is French toast with peach jam, fresh peaches, topped with whipped cream." *(James Rez)* "Guest rooms have antique beds with beautiful quilts, ceiling fans, lovely accent pieces, and color-coordinated curtains and linens. Spotless bathrooms with fresh towels daily. The wood-burning stove in the antique-filled sitting room created a friendly ambiance. Helpful restaurant and sightseeing recommendations." *(Jane Walpin)* "Sally offers cookies and hot or cool drinks every afternoon, and ice cream sundaes in the evening." *(TF)* "Fred is a craftsman—everything is in top-notch working order." *(Mr. & Mrs. Joseph Pehl)* "Nice firm mattresses. Modern heating and plumbing systems. Within walking distance of downtown Bishop." *(Kay Balian)* "Enjoyed the pictures on display depicting the history of the area. The inn is in a commercial area, but noise was not a factor." *(Shirley & George Wright)*

Open All year.
Rooms 3 suites, 4 doubles—all with private bath and/or shower, telephone, air-conditioning, fan.
Facilities Dining room, living room with TV, games, library. Fish cleaning sink, freezer. Antique shop. Lake nearby for water sports.
Location High Sierras, E central CA. 200 m W of Reno, NV, 300 m NE of Los Angeles. Inyo County; Owens Valley, between White Mts. and Sierra Nevadas. From Los Angeles take Rte 395 N to Bishop. 2 blocks past first signal, turn left on Academy St. Go W 1 block to inn on right.
Restrictions No smoking. Prefer children over age 8.
Credit cards Amex, MC, Visa.
Rates B&B, $70–90 suite, $65 double, $55 single. Extra person, $15. 3-night minimum Memorial Day weekend.
Extras Free local airport/station pickup.

BOONVILLE

The Anderson Valley lies just 11 miles southeast of Mendocino, and offers quiet pleasures to travelers. Now reached by winding Highway 128, this valley was once so isolated that it developed its own dialect, called Boontling. Known primarily for its high-quality vineyards (sparkling wines a specialty), apple orchards, and sheep ranches, visitors will enjoy the low-key atmosphere of the wine-tasting rooms, roadside apple stands, and vistas of grazing sheep in this rural setting. Two good dining choices are found at the Boonville Hotel and the Floodgate Store and Grille.

Information please: The spacious **Anderson Creek Inn** (12050 Anderson Valley Way, Boonville 95415; 707–895–3091 or 800–LLAMA–02) offers four spacious guest rooms in a rambling contemporary room, each with full private bath and king-size bed. After a breakfast of organic juices, house-blend coffee, home-baked bread, and perhaps eggs Benedict or fruit-topped baked pancakes, guests follow owners Ed and Lee Lewis outside to feed the inn's herd of llamas. The $120–175 double rates also include use of the inn's bicycles, swimming pool, and hot tub, plus afternoon hors d'oeuvres. Also in Boonville is the "downtown" **Boonville Hotel** (Highway 128 at Lambert Lane, P.O. Box 326, Boonville 95415; 707–895–2210) with simply furnished but comfortable rooms, a popular bar, and an excellent restaurant, open for dinner Wednesday through Sunday. Rates for the seven guest rooms and suites range from $70–150, including a breakfast of fresh-baked scones with local jam, local apple juice, and coffee. Another intriguing choice in nearby Philo is the **Philo Pottery Inn** (8550 Highway 128, P.O. Box 166, Philo 95466; 707–895–3069), a redwood farmhouse built in 1888, and used as a stagecoach stop on the road to the north coast. Four guest rooms and one cottage are available at double B&B rates of $80–95, including a breakfast of home-baked treats, local juices, and hearty entrées, plus after-dinner sherry and home-baked cookies. Guest rooms are comfortably furnished with patchwork quilts, comfortable antiques, and down comforters. After a day of exploration, guests can relax on the back porch overlooking the gardens. For the privacy of your own contemporary cottage, the **Sheep Dung Estates** (Route 128, P.O. Box 49 Yorkville, 95494; 707–894–5322) is a delightful choice. A hilltop setting offers lovely views from the many windows, and the contemporary decor is spare and restful. A mini-kitchen is stocked with breakfast fixings, and dogs are welcome. All this for $75 (no extra charge for the great name).

BRIDGEPORT

The Cain House
P.O. Box 454, 93517

Tel: 619–932–7040
Fax: 619–932–7419

Built in 1925, The Cain House was converted into an inn in 1989, by owner Marachal Gohlich. The guest rooms are individually furnished in wicker, oak, or white-washed pine, with some antiques.

"Marachal greeted us warmly, and recommended the Bridgeport Inn for an excellent dinner. At 5 P.M. she served wine and cheese in the living room, as classical music played softly in the background. Our room was adequate in size, highlighted by an antique doll and a beautiful comforter. During the night, we heard cows mooing in a distant pasture, plus a coyote serenade. Breakfast is served between 8–10 A.M.; guests were asked upon arrival about their dislikes and dietary requirements. We enjoyed the quaintness of this little town (population 500), as well as its proximity to Bodie (a wonderful old ghost town), Mammoth Lakes, and Mono Lake." *(Patricia King)* "The well-equipped rooms are supplied with terrycloth bathrobes and huge, fluffy towels. Marachal's wonderful breakfast started with freshly squeezed orange juice, accompanied by burritos filled with bacon, scrambled eggs, cheddar and jack cheese, chiles, and salsa; we never felt rushed or pressured." *(Jean Hembree)*"Fully endorse existing entry. Immaculate B&B; great hostess." *(JTD)*

Open April 15–Nov. 15.
Rooms 7 doubles—all with full private bath, TV, fan, coffee/tea maker.
Facilities Living room with games, TV/VCR; breakfast room, deck. Lawn games, off-street parking. 100 yds. to tennis court. 10 m to cross-country skiing. Hiking, fishing nearby.
Location Eastern Sierras. 113 m S of Reno NV, via Hwy 395. 120 m NE of Yosemite Village. In center.
Restrictions No smoking.
Credit cards Amex, CB, DC, Discover, MC, Visa.
Rates B&B, $79–130 double. "No tipping necessary."
Extras Airport/station pickup, $10. Limited German, Spanish spoken.

CALISTOGA

Set in the North Coast's Wine Country, Calistoga is located at the northern end of the Napa Valley, about 75 miles north-northeast of San Francisco. Nestled in the foothills of Mt. St. Helena, it was founded in 1859 by Sam Brannan, a New Englander who moved west and started California's first newspaper. Brannan was familiar with New York State's Saratoga Springs, and his goal was to make the mineral springs of Calistoga equally well known. People still come for the spas—to sit and soak in tubs filled with volcanic-ash mud and naturally heated mineral water and in mineral-water whirlpools.

Other area attractions include the dozens of area wineries, many first-class restaurants and shops, a petrified forest, a lake for water sports, and a geyser, along with hot-air ballooning and gliding, bicycling, and outdoor summer concerts. The Sharpsteen Museum depicts Calistoga's early days. Summer and fall weekends are very busy; visit during the spring if possible. To reach Calistoga, take Route 29 (St. Helena Highway) north from Napa.

Also recommended: For a different experience, *Mark Mendenhall* suggests **Indian Springs** (1712 Lincoln Avenue, 94515; 707–942–4913), California's oldest continuously operating spa facility, with its own 120 by 600 foot steaming spring-fed mineral pool, using 100% volcanic ash in its mud baths. "Indian Springs, with its white adobe cottages all in a row, looks more like a Florida beach resort of the '40s than a hot springs resort of the '90s. The studio and 1-bedroom cottages have wide-board bleached wood floors, pale pink walls, and many built-in cabinets, with big brass beds and floral patterned comforters. Each room has large closets, terrycloth robes, and thick towels. We visited in February; the pool was revitalizing in the grey gloom and moderate chill of northern California." The rates for the cottages, ranging from a studio to a 2-bedroom unit, are $95–150 double occupancy; the midweek off-season rate includes free mud bath treatments.

Information please: For a change of pace from omnipresent Victorian frills, try the **Calistoga Country Lodge** (2883 Foothill Boulevard, 94515; 707–942–5555) offering six guest rooms handsomely decorated in Southwest/Santa Fe style, a sunny common room where a continental breakfast and evening refreshments are served, and an inviting swimming pool set among century-old oaks. Rae Ellen is the innkeeper, and rates range from $95–125. An easy walk from Calistoga's restaurants, shops, and spas, is the **Scott Courtyard** (1443 Second Street, 94515; 707–942–0948), offering six suites, furnished with tropical-style Art Deco antiques and collectibles; each has a sitting room, queen-size bed, private bath and entrance. The inn occupies four buildings, centered around a latticed courtyard garden and swimming pool. The $110–135 double rates (less in winter) include a full buffet-style breakfast. The **Silver Rose Inn** (351 Rosedale Road, 94515; 707–942–9581 or 800–995–9381) is an airy, contemporary structure sets on an oak-studded knoll, landscaped with roses, a rock garden, and a waterfall. Each of the guest rooms have a special theme, and most have queen- or king-size beds, fireplaces, balconies, and whirlpool tubs. The $115–200 double rates include a continental buffet breakfast and 5:30 P.M. wine and cheese.

The Elms	*Tel: 707–942–9476*
1300 Cedar Street, 94515	*Fax: 707–942–9479*

The Elms was built by Judge A.C. Palmer and his bride soon after returning from France in 1871; to signal its completion, European elm seedlings were planted, which today stand as the largest elms in the Napa Valley. A Second Empire-style home (also known as French Victorian), complete with mansard roof, the Elms has long been a B&B. In 1993, Elaine Bryant bought the house and furnished it with antiques. She notes that "assistant innkeeper Boomer, a gentle, laid-back black German shepherd, is available for petting and walking." Rates include breakfast, early morning coffee or tea in your room, afternoon wine and cheese in the parlor, and evening port and chocolates.

"The Nouveau Dream room has a comfortable, king canopy bed, a marble fireplace, and a small, wisteria-draped balcony, where we enjoyed viewing the waterfall birdbath during a balmy summer evening. Lovely scented bath towels." *(Irene Kolbisen)* "We were greeted with both wine and Calistoga sparkling water, and a fruit and cheese platter. Delicious breakfast of granola yogurt parfaits; croissants; an egg, cheese, and turkey sausage casserole; and chocolate chip raisin bread pudding." *(Nanci Sullivan)*

Open All year.
Rooms 1 cottage, 6 doubles—all with private bath and/or shower. 3 rooms in carriage house. 5 with fireplace, TV, 1 with balcony, 1 with kitchenette.
Facilities Parlor with fireplace, dining room. Garden.
Location ½ block from main st.; next to park on the river.
Restrictions No smoking in guest rooms. No children.
Credit cards None accepted.
Rates B&B, $140–160 cottage, $95–115 double.

Foothill House
3037 Foothill Boulevard, 94515

Tel: 707–942–6933
800–942–6933

Foothill House was bought by Doris and Gus Beckert in 1992; this little B&B is acclaimed for its comfortable, well-equipped rooms, excellent food, and attentive service. Rates include a breakfast of homemade breads and muffins, freshly squeezed orange juice, fresh fruit compote with raspberry sauce, French toast served with chicken turkey sausage and sundried tomatoes or perhaps a Hungarian casserole and later, evening refreshments.

"The guest rooms are on the ground level, with outside entrances, but all rooms open through sliding glass doors to a covered porch. The spacious, well-insulated guest rooms have every amenity one could dream up: the fire ready-laid, bottled water in the room's refrigerator, coffee-maker, cloth-wrapped soaps, stationery, individual reading spotlights on each side of the bed in addition to nightstand lamps and lots of magazines." *(SHW)*

"The Evergreen Suite is decorated with quilts, antiques, and had a special reading nook with built-in bookcase, loveseat, and wingback chair." *(Theresa Baker & Steve Chambers, and others)* "Doris trained at the California Culinary Academy, so breakfasts are spectacular, with never a repeat." *(Mary Lyndon Haviland)* "The Quail's Roost is elegantly furnished with a king-size bed and two-sided fireplace facing both the sitting area and the bathroom, which also had a shower for two facing a lighted outdoor waterfall." *(Sheri & Richard DeBro)*

"Responsive to my requests for low-fat, vegetarian meals." *(Ann Bach)* "Elegant hot hors d'oeuvres and wine are served in the congenial sun room each night at 6 P.M. Doris is knowledgeable about dining all over Napa and Sonoma; Gus is familiar with the area wineries." *(Mary Lynch)* "Doris turns down the bed, dims the lights, sets soft music playing, and leaves an evening treat of cookies and sherry." *(Terry & Lisa Beth Howland)* "The grounds and garden are small, but appealing with a waterfall, gazebo, and swing." *(Kathi Ann Brown, also Amy Siegal)*

And a word to the wise: "Watch carefully for the inn's sign if you're arriving after dark."

Open All year. Closed Dec. 23–26.
Rooms 2 suites, 1 cottage—all with full private bath, telephone, radio, desk, fireplace, air-conditioning, ceiling fan, refrigerator, mini-stereos with cassette players & tapes. TV on request.
Facilities Dining/breakfast room with fireplace, sitting area, patio. 1½ acre with gardens, waterfall, picnic area. Swimming, tennis, golf nearby.
Location 1½ m from center, on left past Petrified Forest Rd.
Restrictions No smoking. No children.
Credit cards Amex, MC, Visa.
Rates B&B, $115–220 suite, double, $110–215 single. Extra person, $35. 2-day weekend minimum. 10% senior discount midweek.

Quail Mountain Inn
4455 North St. Helena Highway, 94515

Tel: 707–942–0316

"A modern structure built for the specific purpose of providing bed and breakfast accommodations, Quail Mountain enjoys an idyllic setting on a orested mountaintop between St. Helena and Calistoga." *(J. H. Schoggen)* The dining room and living room of this contemporary home are divided y a free-standing fireplace. The large windows and wood paneling con- ey the feeling of an elegant country lodge. The bedrooms are entered om a glass hallway running along the front of the house. The guest ooms are medium-size with cathedral ceilings, private decks, king-size rass beds, goosedown duvets, and bathrobes." *(SHW)*

"The rooms are spotless with excellent bedside reading lights; the athrooms modern and sparkling." *(Susan & Stuart Gellman)* "Our room ad a large dressing area with excellent luggage storage space." *(David iroen)* "We were served wine and snacks in the solarium each evening." *Harold & Verdell Pierce)* "Alma and Don are a wonderful source of infor- nation when planning daily excursions. Fresh flowers in our room every ay. The grounds are enchanting with wonderful views of hummingbirds eeding and the sun setting through the pines." *(Suzanne & Richard Misher)*

"You can count on fresh-squeezed orange juice, just-picked fruit, piping ot coffee, and breakfast served on beautiful china place settings." *(Dale Nelson)* "Thoughtful touches included inquiries about food allergies, and vase of roses at each table setting." *(JBG)* "The location 300 feet up from he valley floor made us feel like we were in a quiet forest, yet you are nly minutes from town." *(Lynn & Mike Zeigler)*

Open All year.
Rooms 1 suite, 2 doubles—all with private bath and/or shower, telephone, ir-conditioning, refrigerator. 2 with private entrance.
Facilities Dining room with fireplace, solarium with games. 26 acres, heated ouble-lane lap pool, hot tub, picnic tables, hammock, garden, vineyard, streams. iolf, tennis nearby.
Location 6 m N of St. Helena. From Calistoga, go S on Rte. 29 1½ m to riveway on right. Go ⅓ m up mountain to inn.
Restrictions No smoking. No children.
Credit cards MC, Visa.
Rates B&B, $125 suite, $100–110 double, $90–115 single. Extra person, $25. No pping. 2-night weekend minimum.

Scarlett's Country Inn 🏨 ♿   *Tel: 707–942–6669*
918 Silverado Trail North, 94515

A turn-of-the-century farmhouse, Scarlett's Country Inn is built on the site •f a Wappo Indian settlement; obsidian arrowheads are still to be found n the grounds. A breakfast of freshly squeezed orange juice, fresh fruit nd a main dish of French toast, oatmeal or pancakes is served at your hoice of times between 8–10 A.M. "Reached by a winding path off the nain road. Our first view was of an inviting porch tucked amid the trees. he main house is set behind the guest cottage; a beautiful deck surrounds he swimming pool." *(Dr. & Mrs. Joseph Drugay)* "Scarlett is terrific with eferrals for everything from restaurants to babysitters." *(Bill & Cheryl ihonborn)* "Secluded and charming. The Silverado Trail is a much quieter oad, traffic-wise, for winetasting than Highway 29." *(JG)* "Scarlett ouldn't have been nicer; excellent breakfast of Dutch babies with berry auce, fresh fruit and juice; peaceful poolside area with patio and surround- ng gardens. Our kids loved the swimming pool, the apple tree from which they could pick delicious apples, and the roaming rooster and hens." *(EL)*

Open All year.
Rooms 2 suites in guest cottage, 1 double in main house—all with private shower and/or bath, telephone, radio, TV, desk, air-conditioning, fan, refrigerator, microwave, private entrance. 2 with deck, 1 with fireplace.
Facilities Dining room, decks; play equipment, games. 1 acre with flower gardens, swimming pool.
Location From St. Helena, go N on Hwy. 29 to Bale Lane. Turn right on Bale, then left on Silverado Trail. Go 1/2 m. Turn right on dirt road with sign '3918' on fence under tree. House is yellow 2-story farmhouse.
Restrictions No smoking.
Credit cards None accepted.
Rates B&B, $115–150 suite, $95 double, $85 single. Extra adult $20; extra child no charge.
Extras Wheelchair access. Crib, babysitting. Spanish spoken.

CAMBRIA

Cambria is a good base from which to visit Hearst Castle in San Simeon, six miles to the north and Morro Bay and San Luis Obispo to the south; it's located on the Central Coast, midway between Los Angeles and San Francisco. Winter visitors should take time to visit the town's seaside parks for a glimpse of sea otters and migrating gray whales. Take time to drive inland 25 miles to the Paso Robles wine country to visit the dozen of area wineries; you'll find enthusiastic vintners, uncrowded tasting rooms, and reasonable prices.

Reader tip: "The view from Moonstone Drive is exquisite. Trails follow the bluffs, and paths lead to the rock outcroppings and tidepools where you can watch the seals sun or frolic in the water. Surfers are a little farther away, and there's plenty of beachcombing to be done." *(Erika Holm, also Patricia Nye)*

Also recommended: Moonstone Drive, just across the road from the ocean, is home to a number of motel-cum-inns which some readers adore while others are left cold. While the architecture is basic motel, most have an appealing common area where breakfast and tea is served, and guest rooms done in French country decor—"Laura Ashleyfied to the max" as one correspondent put it. Typically, these properties are not owner operated, but do have friendly, accommodating innkeepers and home made breakfasts. The majority of guest rooms have canopy beds, ocean views, gas fireplaces, whirlpool tubs, refrigerators, telephones, and color cable television with VCRs—perfect for travelers who value modern conveniences over historic ambience. Here are some recommended choices for this type of lodging:

Blue Dolphin Inn (6470 Moonstone Beach Drive, 93428; 805–927–3300). 18 rooms; B&B, $75–185 double.

Blue Whale Inn (6736 Moonstone Beach Drive, 93428; 805–927–4647). 6 rooms; B&B, $125–175.

White Water Inn (6790 Moonstone Beach Drive, 93428; 805–927–1066). 17 rooms; B&B, $85–160.

In San Simeon, eight miles north of Cambria and two miles from Hearst

Castle, is the **Cavalier Inn** (9415 Hearst Drive, San Simeon 93452; 805–927–4688 or 800–826–8168, a Best Western motel recommended by *Peggy Vaughn*): "Dogs welcome; outstanding service and efficiency; spacious guest room with nice bathrooms; right above the beach for lovely views." Facilities include a fitness center, two swimming pools, guest laundry, and a restaurant; guest rooms are equipped with refrigerator, honor bar, TV, and queen- or king-size beds, and some also have a wood-burning fireplace, wet bar, and private patio.

Olallieberry Inn ♿	*Tel:* 805–927–3222
2476 Main Street, 93428	*Fax:* 805–927–0202

"A darling Greek revival-style house built in 1873, the Olallieberry Inn is filled with Victorian antiques and country charm. Our room was clean, comfortable, with good lighting in the bathroom." *(Gail Davis)* "The marvelous back porch and yard with flower gardens and flowing stream is perfect for relaxing." *(Nancy Wood)*

"Just a short walk to restaurants and shops. The sitting room has an antique sofa and chairs, and is a quiet place for reading. The bedrooms are beautifully furnished with antique beds, dressers, armoires, and chairs. The Harmony Room was fresh and immaculate with an English carved wooden double bed, rocking chair, armoire, and dresser. The bed had a peach-colored patchwork quilt, plenty of soft pillows, and rose-patterned cotton sheets. Fresh flowers in a vase and chocolates were set on the dresser. The bathroom had a claw foot tub with shower and a pedestal sink. Although each room has a private bath, some are a few steps down the hall, and guests are given thick terry robes to use.

"Breakfast is served family-style from 8–9 A.M., around the long wooden table in the kitchen, and includes homemade olallieberry jam, gourmet coffee, pastries, fresh fruit, and a hot entrée—perhaps stuffed French toast or an egg casserole. Wine and appetizers are served in the late afternoon, along with juice, hot tea, mineral water, and little snacks. The friendly owners, Peter and Carol Ann Irsfeld, are always around to help with reservations or other information." *(Wendy Kameda)*

Open All year.
Rooms 6 doubles—all with private bath and/or shower. 3 with fireplace.
Facilities Dining room with fireplace, parlor, porch, deck. ½ acre with lawn games, gardens, stream.
Location East Village. In Cambria, turn E on Main St. Go 1 m to inn on left (watch for redwood tree in front of inn).
Restrictions No smoking. "Not really suitable for children, over age 10 preferred."
Credit cards MC, Visa.
Rates B&B, $85–120 double. 10% senior discount.
Extras Wheelchair access; 1 room equipped for disabled.

CARMEL

Carmel dates back to the early 1900s when it was an artists' colony and popular summer resort for well-to-do San Franciscans. Opinion is di-

vided on Carmel—most people think it's a charming seaside town fille
with darling shops and beautiful art galleries; others find it a bit muc
Whatever your opinion, there's no lack of suitable accommodation
Carmel probably has more attractive inns in its zip codes than any othe
town in the country except Cape May, New Jersey! A number of ther
were built in the 1950s as motels and have since been renovated as inn
making for an interesting hybrid—the mood, decor, and amenities of a
inn, added to the convenience and privacy found in a motel.

Location is important when booking an inn in Carmel. Parking in tow
is *impossible* on busy weekends, so be sure to book a place that's "withi
walking distance" of the places you want to see.

Other than shops and art galleries, Carmel's attractions include th
historic Carmel Mission, golf and tennis, music festivals, and excursion
to Big Sur, Monterey, and the Seventeen-Mile Drive. Both Carmel Beac
and Point Lobos State Reserve are nice for walking, but the water
generally too cold for swimming, and the undertow is treacherous.

Carmel, also known as Carmel-by-the-Sea, is located just south of th
Monterey Peninsula, 120 miles south of San Francisco. Most of Carmel
laid out in a grid pattern, with numbered avenues running east/wes
starting at First in the north end of town and ascending as you go sout
The exception is Ocean, the town's main east/west thoroughfare. Stree
are named and run north/south; Junipero is the main drag. The center c
town is Carmel Plaza, where Junipero and Ocean avenues meet.

Word to the wise: Most Carmel inns define a two-night weeken
minimum as being either Thursday and Friday nights *or* Saturday an
Sunday nights; some charge a premium for a Friday/Saturday combina
tion. Call to double-check and plan accordingly.

Reader tips: "Carmel has a marvelous climate—cool, clean air encou
ages the lush growth of beautiful trees and abundant flowers. Rolling sur
and clean white beaches where evenings find couples, families, and lon
strollers. Excited dogs chase waves or fetch driftwood." *(Dianne Evan.
*"Carmel is still relatively unspoilt—no longer an artist colony but fille
with well regulated, affluent, bourgeois charm." *(Hugh & Marjorie Smit

Also recommended: Although too big at 144 rooms, *Jane & Ric
Mattoon* recommend the spa suites at the **Highlands Inn** (Highway
P.O. Box 1700; 408–624–3801 or 800–538–9525): "Our suite had
double whirlpool tub, a fireplace, kitchen area, and patio with Pacific view
The restaurant perches on the cliff, 200 feet about the ocean's edge for
breathtaking vista." Double rates start at $225; suites at $325. A luxuriou
resort, the **Quail Lodge** (8205 Valley Greens Drive, 93923; 408–624
1581 or 800–538–9516) offers a full range of activities and amenities i
a beautifully landscaped environment. The 100 guest rooms are decorate
with a light airy look, featuring original artwork, fresh flowers, paste
colors, and all conceivable amenities. The elegant Covey Restaurant offer
an ambitious menu with creative dishes like shrimp and sole mousse i
puff pastry; veal with morel mushrooms, brandy, and cream; duck wit
black currant sauce; and a variety of tempting desserts. The resort's 60
acres offer a full range of resort activities—swimming, tennis, golf, bicy
cling, hiking, and more.

Information please: Renovated in 1992 by film director, actor, an former Carmel mayor Clint Eastwood is the **Mission Ranch** (26270 Dolores Street, Carmel 93923; 408–624–6436 or 800–538–8221). The expression, "Meet you at the ranch," is said to have originated here. Rescued from a condo developer's wrecking ball, the ranch has 31 guest rooms, located in the original 1860s farmhouse, bunkhouse and in several newer buildings; furnishings combine antiques and custom-designed ranch-style pieces. Guests have use of the tennis courts and exercise room. The popular restaurant has an informal piano bar nightly and two barns accommodate private events for up to 50 people.

Dating back to the 1900s, the **Pine Inn** (Ocean Avenue and Lincoln, P.O. Box 250, 93921; 408–624–3851 or 800–228–3851), offers low-key, turn-of-the-century charm. Rooms are furnished with period antiques (many original to the building) and reproductions. The inn's restaurant serves traditional American cuisine and California specialties under a dome that opens to the sky. Decorated in Laura Ashley and Ralph Lauren style, **Los Laureles** (Carmel Valley Road, Carmel Valley 93924; 408–659–2233) offers a variety of accommodations including rooms in the renovated former horse stables. Located in nearby Carmel Valley, the inn has beautiful mountain views, walking trails, restaurant, comfortable parlor and a gift shop. Double rates are $80–135, and children under 18 stay free; golf packages available.

The Cobblestone Inn

Junipero and Eighth Avenues,
P.O. Box 3185, 93921

Tel: 408–625–5222
Fax: 408–625–0478

The Cobblestone, built as a motel in 1950, is an example of traditional "Carmel architecture"—two stories with a balcony surrounding a courtyard with garden and patio. The inn was renovated in 1984, and includes an English garden with over 50 varieties of flowers.

"Perfect location, two blocks from the shopping area and about eight blocks from the beach. The tasty buffet breakfast is beautifully presented, with a hot dish, muffins or biscuits, cereal, fruit, and juice. Tea, coffee, ice water, soft drinks, and fruit are always available; a jar is kept full with freshly baked cookies. In the late afternoon wine, cheese, crackers, veggies and dip are served. After dinner sherry and cookies are set out. Teddy bears are everywhere; you can even adopt them to bring home." *(Jennie & Jim Brick)* "We enjoy having breakfast in our room though it is also served in the beautifully appointed sitting room and on the garden patio." *(John & Teri Sabio)* "Our suite had all the amenities—stocked refrigerator, remote-controlled TV hidden in an armoire, fluffy towels, night-time mints, and morning newspaper." *(Trudy Reid)* "Our suite had a cobblestoned fireplace in both the bedroom and sitting room; the second bathroom is convenient for a traveling family. Parking is on the street but was not a major problem once we'd unloaded our bags. Everything you'd want to see in Carmel is within reasonable walking distance." *(Carol & Gordie Dinmore)* "Many rooms feature subtle hand-painted motifs, perhaps a wreath painted on a bathroom wall or a group of wildflowers 'growing' from the wainscoting. Evenings, when the innkeepers turn down the beds, they leave a fresh rose, a chocolate, and a card with the next day's forecast." *(Dianne Evans)*

Open All year.
Rooms 3 suites, 21 doubles—all with private shower and/or bath, telephone, radio, TV, desk, gas fireplace, refrigerator.
Facilities Living room/lounge/breakfast area; patio. Limited parking facilities.
Location In heart of town. From Hwy. 1 turn W on Ocean Ave. Continue down Ocean to Junipero & turn left; go 2 blocks to inn at corner of 8th Ave.
Restrictions Street noise could disturb light sleepers in 3 rooms. No smoking in common rooms.
Credit cards Amex, MC, Visa.
Rates B&B, $175 suite, $95–160 double. Extra person, $15. Picnic baskets on request.
Extras Crib, babysitting. French spoken. Four Sisters Inns.

Cypress Inn
Lincoln & 7th, P.O. Box Y, 93921

Tel: 408–624–3871
800–443–7443
Fax: 408–624–8216

Noted for its Moorish-Mediterranean facade when it was constructed as a hotel in 1929, the Cypress Inn is decorated with contemporary and reproduction French pieces, soothing color schemes and coordinating floral curtains and bedspreads. "Wonderful, with a friendly atmosphere and convenient location in the center of Carmel. Our room was large, with double bed, separate living room, and large bath. For breakfast you go across the road to the inn's library or have it brought to your room." *(Stephanie Blanc)* "Appealing architectural style, wonderful roof, flower-laden courtyard, and impressive portico. The public rooms are spacious, the decor elegant, the furnishings rich. Our enormous, well appointed suite had a large dining alcove overlooking the street; a decanter of sherry and a basket of fruit were on the table. The continental breakfast could be taken outside to the courtyard to enjoy. We thought the best rooms were those on the second floor, overlooking the courtyard, with a balcony from which one could see the ocean." *(Hugh & Marjorie Smith)*

Open All year.
Rooms 6 suites, 27 doubles—all with private bath and/or shower, telephone, TV.
Facilities Bar/lounge, living room with fireplace, garden courtyard. Limited off-street parking.
Location Town center, 1 block S of Ocean Ave.
Credit cards Amex, MC, Visa.
Rates $174–185 suite, $98–129 double. Extra person, $15.
Extras Pets with permission, $15.

La Playa Hotel ♔ ✕ ♿
Camino Real and 8th Street, P.O. Box 900, 93921

Tel: 408–624–6476
800–582–8900
Fax: 408–624–7966

Fully restored and expanded in 1983, La Playa was built in 1904 as a private Spanish-style mansion. The warm and inviting lobby is decorated in pastel shades, with a variety of neo-classical Greek, Mediterranean, and contemporary elements. Guest rooms are also done in soft colors, with good lighting and Spanish mission-style furniture hand-carved with the hotel's mermaid motif. The hotel restaurant offers a choice of creatively prepared dishes, such as crab ravioli or seared pork loin with a spiced Jack Daniels sauce.

"Charming, Mediterranean-style small hotel a few blocks from the sea (upper rooms have distant ocean views). Much quieter than some of Carmel's other inns and hotels on the main streets, plus easy parking, a real plus in Carmel. Our spacious room at the rear of the property faced the swimming pool and magnificent terraced gardens ablaze with color. It had an open fireplace, separate dining room, and large bathroom. Excellent dining room which features wonderful regional wines." *(Lorraine Gillespie)* "Superb colorful, well-kept garden, well-equipped rooms. Excellent restaurant with well-presented desserts." *(P. Bottomley)*

Open All year.
Rooms 2 suites, 73 doubles, 5 cottages—all with full private bath, telephone, radio, clock, TV, desk, refrigerator. Some cottages with kitchen, wet bar, patio, fireplace.
Facilities Restaurants, bar/lounge, heated dining terrace, lobby with fireplace, conference rooms. Concierge service. 2 acres with gardens, gazebo, heated swimming pool. Limited off-street parking.
Location 4 blocks from center; 2 blocks from ocean.
Credit cards All major cards.
Rates Room only, $195–300 suite, $110–210 double. Extra person, $15. 10% AAA discount. 2-3 night weekend/holiday minimum. Alc breakfast, $8–10; alc lunch, $8–15; alc dinner, $30–35; early bird dinner, $10.
Extras Wheelchair access; some rooms specially equipped. Crib, babysitting by arrangement. French, German, Spanish spoken.

Lobos Lodge ¢
Ocean Avenue & Monte Verde,
P.O. Box L–1, 93921

Tel: 408–624–3874
Fax: 408–624–0135

"Lobos Lodge is structured like a Mediterranean village, with multilevel, oddly arranged cubes painted white and framed with foliage, mostly multi-colored impatiens, begonias, geraniums and the like. Convenient location; it's the last commercial structure at the bottom of the main street that leads west to the beach. The street corner entrance opens onto several shops and a beauty parlor. The walls and draperies in the guest rooms are done in cheerful bright greens and yellows. Most have small porches, some with ocean views and a lounge area with a coffee table and spacious closets. No two rooms are the same shape. Some have partial views to the west and the ocean/sunset, while others look inward onto little patios and walkways. The rooms are very comfortable, encouraging one to spend time there. A continental breakfast of tea or coffee, juice and locally baked pastry is brought to your room between 8:00–9:15, along with the *San Francisco Bay Examiner*. The courteous staff meets all requests immediately; the housekeepers are exceptionally thorough. This reasonably priced inn is popular with returning guests, so make advance reservations in peak periods." *(Steve Holman)*

Open All year.
Rooms 30 suites, doubles—all with private bath and/or shower, telephone, TV, gas fireplace, refrigerator.
Facilities Garden, off-street parking.

Location 3 blocks to center; across street from Pine Inn.
Credit cards Amex, MC, Visa.
Rates B&B, $140–170 suite, $93–125 double. Extra person, $25.

San Antonio House
Tel: 408–624–4334

San Antonio by Ocean Avenue, P.O. Box 3683, 93921

Readers recommend the San Antonio for its wonderful balance of small-scale charm and guest privacy. Built in early 1920s, the house is set among aged Monterey Pines, stone walkways, flower gardens and ivy covered walls; inside, rooms are furnished with period antiques and flowered chintz fabrics. Rates include a breakfast tray of fresh pastries, eggs, fruit, juice, and coffee, plus the morning paper, brought to your room each morning.

"One of Carmel's loveliest inns." *(Gail Clark)* "Quiet and relaxing." *(MP)* "Treetops, overlooking the garden, is my favorite, but all the guest rooms are nice. Delicious breakfast." *(PM)* "Books up months in advance; plan ahead." *(LW)*

Open All year.
Rooms 2 suites, 2 doubles—all with private bath and/or shower, telephone, TV, refrigerator, wood-burning fireplace, private entrance, breakfast patio. 1 room in carriage house.
Facilities Library, gardens, patios.
Location At corner of Ocean & San Antonio, between Carmelo & Scenic Rd. 1 block from beach, 3 blocks from village. Close to Pebble Beach golf course entrance.
Restrictions Children over 12.
Credit cards MC, Visa.
Rates B&B, $130–155 suite, $110–145 double. Extra person, $20. 2-night minimum weekends, special events.

Sea View Inn ¢
Tel: 408–624–8778

Camino Real, between 11th and 12th Streets, P.O. Box 4138, 93921

Marshall and Diane Hydorn have been welcoming guests to the Seaview since 1975. Guest rooms in this Victorian home are decorated with four-poster canopy beds and other antiques, Oriental rugs, fresh flowers, and whimsical toys. Rates include a weekday breakfast of juice, fresh fruit, yogurt, cereal, muffins, toast, and bagels, with a hot dish, such as quiche served on Sundays. Afternoons you'll find tea and coffee set out, and in the evening, sherry is enjoyed by the parlor fire.

"Located in a pleasant old neighborhood a few blocks from the beach and the main part of town." *(Deborah Waller)* "Quiet street with lovely plantings and flowers. Marshall is an artist and his paintings adorn the walls; he and Diane made us feel that we left as friends. The neighbor's cat, Crash, has been known to visit your room too—another friend." *(Patty Gibian)* "Our room was well-appointed and immaculate; careful attention to detail." *(Glenn Simplicio, also Cathy Ford)* Reports requested.

Open All year.
Rooms 8 doubles—6 with private bath and/or shower, 2 with a maximum of 4 people sharing bath. Some with desk.
Facilities Dining room, living room both with fireplace; library, porch. Garden, patio, picnic area. Deep sea fishing, whale watching, golf nearby.

ocation 120 m S of San Francisco. 5 blocks to center, 3 blocks to beach. From
Hwy 1, Take Ocean Ave. W to Camino Real. Turn left, go S 5½ blocks to inn
on left between 11th and 12th.
Restrictions No smoking. Prefer children over 12.
Credit cards MC, Visa.
Rates B&B, $85–120 double, $80–110 single. 2-night holiday/weekend mini-
mum.
Extras Limited French spoken.

Vagabond's House   *Tel:* 408–624–7738
Fourth and Dolores Streets, P.O. Box 2747, 93921   800–262–1262

A brick half-timbered English Tudor country inn, the Vagabond's guest
rooms are furnished with antiques, with decorating themes ranging from
nautical American to English hunt. Under the same management is the
Lincoln Green Inn, with a similar English theme to the architecture and
decor of its steeply peaked cottages.

"Our brightly decorated room had freshly cut flowers, sherry, a fruit
basket, books, coffee and teas. The bath was supplied with lavender soap
and thick towels. At our request, our breakfast tray of coffee, hard-boiled
eggs, fresh rolls, and the morning newspaper was served to us in the
flower-filled courtyard." *(Mr. & Mrs. Paul Petrenk)* "On one visit we had
a small but cozy room done in white wicker with yellow and blue
accessories; on a return trip we had a large and airy corner room done in
knotty pine." *(John & Sandra Nelipovich)* "The cooperative staff made
dinner reservations and provided information." *(Pat & Peter Maschi)* "The
flagstone courtyard is dominated by large oak trees, offering a shady place
to read and relax." *(Laura Scott)* "Quiet location, yet close to shops and
restaurants." *(Kathy & Roger Knieth)* Reports welcome.

Open All year.
Rooms 11 doubles—all with private bath and/or shower, telephone, radio, TV,
desk, refrigerator, fireplace. Some with kitchen.
Facilities Parlor with fireplace. Courtyard with waterfall. 8 blocks to beach.
Off-street parking.
Location 2 blocks from center. From Hwy. 1, turn W onto Ocean Ave., then turn
right on Dolores.
Restrictions Some street noise in two rooms. No children under 12.
Credit cards Amex, MC, Visa.
Rates B&B, $79–150 double. Extra person, $20. 2-night weekend minimum.
Midweek rates off-season.
Extras Pets by arrangement, $10 extra. Spanish, Korean spoken.

CAZADERO

Timberhill Ranch ✕ 🏹   *Tel:* 707–847–3258
35755 Hauser Bridge Road, 95421   *Fax:* 707–847–3258

When Tarran McDaid and Michael Riordan, with Frank Watson and
Barbara Farrell, built the Timberhill in 1985, they had a clear vision of
what they wanted their resort to be: intimate, elegantly adult, energizing
and relaxing, providing comfortable surroundings and fine cuisine. The

CALIFORNIA

six-course dinners are served with quality china, linens, and crystal, an
might include seafood sausage, apple and squash bisque, watermelon an
sweet onion salad, and ginger pear sorbet.

The main house is "California-style" with lots of glass, natural woo
and stone, while the spacious cedar cottages combine cathedral ceiling
and sliding glass doors with country quilts and comfortable seating. Hig
on the Ridge at Timber Cove, 1100 feet above the water, the ranch is s
among redwoods and meadows, above the coastal fog and wind.

"Exploring the ranch with its menagerie of horses, llamas, ducks, goat
dogs, and cats was a real treat. Our attractive cabin had a stone firepla
and a deck overlooking the trees. The meals are delicious, beginning wit
breakfast, delivered to your cabin at your choice of time, through lunc
to the romantic candlelit dinner. One day we took a picnic hampe
complete with linen tablecloths and napkins, bouquet of flowers, wine, an
lunch, to a scenic spot overlooking the ocean." (Joe & Margaret Flore
"Cozy, 'upscale-rustic' cottages, accommodating service and outstandin
views from a beautiful mountaintop location." (LI)

Minor niggles: "At $350 per night, we resented being charged $2 f
a glass of iced tea." And: "I assume the lack of bathtubs is the result o
water shortages."

Open All year.
Rooms 15 cottages—all with private shower, radio, desk, fireplace, refrigerato
deck.
Facilities Dining room with fireplace, lobby with library, meeting room, firepla
decks. 80 acres with heated swimming pool, hot tub, 2 tennis courts, pond, stable
Golf, hiking, riding, bicycling nearby. Salt Point State Park & Kruse Rhododendro
Reserve adjacent.
Location North Coast. 2½ hrs. N of San Francisco, 1½ hrs. NW of Santa Ros
From San Francisco, take the Golden Gate Bridge N via Hwy. 101 to 5 m pa
Santa Rosa. Turn onto River Rd. through Russian River area to Jenner. Follo
Hwy. 1 N, & go right on Meyers Grade Rd. 5 m N of Jenner (1st right aft
Seaview Plantation Rd.). Ranch is 13.7 m from Hwy 1. Meyers Grade Rd. chang
name to Seaview, then Hauser Bridge Rd.
Restrictions No smoking except in designated areas. Request no children.
Credit cards MC, Visa.
Rates MAP, $296–350 double, $275 single. 2–3-night holiday/weekend mir
mum. 15% service. Picnic lunches by request. Alc lunch, $10–25; prix fixe dinn
$40.
Extras Wheelchair access. French, Spanish spoken.

COALINGA

The Inn at Harris Ranch ₡ ♀ ✕ ♿   Tel: 209–935–071
24505 W. Dorris,   In CA: 800–942–233
Highway 198 and Interstate 5   Fax: 209–935–506
Mailing address: Route 1, Box 777, 93210

Veteran drivers of California's interminable Interstate 5 will particular
welcome the discovery of Harris Ranch. Set in the heart of the San Joaqu
Valley, halfway between San Francisco and Los Angeles, the inn offe
Mexican-American cuisine and overnight accommodations in an ear

California setting. The architecture of the inn resembles a Spanish hacienda with adobe walls, red tile roofs and floors, and the main buildings
center around a garden courtyard and swimming pool. Guest rooms have
high ceilings, double basin baths, pine furnishings, and floral print decor.

"We loved our room, the pool, the grounds, the restaurant, and the
shop where they sell baked goods and beef from their cattle ranching
operations." *(Lee Todd)* "Given its excellent restaurant, comfortable if
unimaginative rooms, and delightful swimming pool, Harris Ranch is a
destination as much as a stop on the interstate. A few miles north, the
Harris Ranch operates an enormous feedlot (for 100,000 head of cattle)
which is worth seeing." *(W. Parker)* "Everything about this oasis—and on
I-5 it is a true oasis—was as described in your book. Excellent breakfast
and dinner." *(Eric Friesen)*

Open All year.

Rooms 28 suites, 95 doubles—all with private bath and/or shower, telephone,
TV, desk, air-conditioning, refrigerator, mini-bar. Some with radio, patio, balcony.
with fireplace, whirlpool. Rooms in 5 buildings.

Facilities 2 restaurants, lobby with fireplace, bar/lounge with weekend entertainment, gift shop, meat market. 1 acre with heated swimming pool, hot tub, courtyard, garden, airstrip. Golf nearby.

Location Central Valley. 60 m SW of Fresno, 13 m E of Coalinga. SE corner of
I-5 and Hwy. 198 (Dorris Ave.).

Restrictions Smoking restricted to some guest rooms.

Credit cards All major.

Rates Room only, $90–225 suite, $81–90 double, $78–87 single. Extra person,
$8. No charge for children under 12. 10% senior, AAA discount. Alc lunch, $8–17;
alc dinner, $8–26.

Extras Wheelchair access. Spanish spoken.

COLOMA

With only 175 inhabitants today, it's hard to believe that Coloma's
population reached nearly 20,000 shortly after James Marshall discovered
gold in the American River near Sutter's Mill. The Marshall Gold Discovery State Historic Park now offers a replica of the mill and Marshall's
cabin, as well as a museum and visitor center devoted to local history.

Information please: Just up the hill from the Visitor Center is the
Coloma Country Inn (345 High Street, Box 502, 95613; 916–622–6919),
a farmhouse built in 1856. Its sunny guest rooms and ample common areas
are handsomely furnished with American antiques, highlighted by hand-
pieced quilts and folk art in bright and cheerful colors. Rates include a
breakfast of fresh fruit, homemade baked goods, juice and coffee, and
afternoon tea.

Vineyard House ¢ ✗
Cold Springs Road & Highway 49,
P.O. Box 176, 95613

Tel: 916–622–2217
800–762–2632

Among Coloma's thousands of gold diggers, Robert Chalmers was one of
the few who realized that the real profits were to be made from the miners,
not from the mines. In 1876, he built the Vineyard House, both as his

residence and to provide accommodations for visiting dignitaries (inclu
ing President Ulysses S. Grant in 1881). After his death, his widow Loui
tried to keep the mansion by taking in boarders and even renting out th
wine cellar (now the saloon) for use as an auxiliary jail.

Restored in 1991 by Cindy and Paul Savage, the Vineyard Hou
remains a social center for El Dorado County, although today's atm
sphere is somewhat calmer. Guests are welcomed with afternoon sher
or tea from 4–6 P.M.; coffee and juice are available to early risers, wi
breakfasts of perhaps fruit smoothies, gingered pears, granola, oven-fre
bread, apple crepes, hash browns, and sausage. Best known for its resta
rant, Vineyard House has five period-furnished dining rooms; dinn
favorites include chicken and dumplings, prime rib, and such daily specia
as pork sausage with polenta or braised rabbit with garlic mashe
potatoes. Named for Gold Rush characters, the guest rooms have peric
decor, and most have queen- or king-size beds.

"We were welcomed with iced coffee and huge cookies by the hospit
ble owners. We stayed in Mrs. Chalmers' Room, with a comfortab
king-size canopy bed and a sitting area with chairs and a love seat. M
sister had the Lola Montez room, which was equally appealing, comple
with a clawfoot tub in the private bath. The food and service in th
restaurant downstairs were wonderful; the enormous breakfast w
equally good." *(Sharon Bielski)*

Open All year.
Rooms 7 doubles—1 with private bath, 6 with shared bath. All with air-con
tioning. Clock on request. 3 with balcony. 1 with fireplace.
Facilities Restaurant with fireplace, weekend music (until 11 P.M.); saloon, parl
with piano, fireplace, games; veranda. 5 acres with hot tub, gazebo, lawn game
carriage rides. On American River. Whitewater rafting, gold panning, balloonin
bicycling, hiking, swimming nearby.
Location Gold Country. Adjacent to Gold Discovery State Park. From Sa
ramento go E on Hwy. 50. Take Ponderosa/Shingle Springs exist (just pa
Cameron Park). Over the freeway, right on N. Shingle Rd. Left at 'Y' onto Lot
Rd. Right on Gold Hill Rd. Left at stop sign onto Cold Springs Rd.
Restrictions Smoking in saloon. Children over 6.
Credit cards MC, Visa.
Rates B&B, $80–100 double. Package rates. Alc dinner, $15–20. Senior, AA
discount. 2-night weekend minimum.

COLUMBIA

City Hotel ¢ ✕   *Tel:* 209–532–14:
Main Street, Columbia Historic Park   *Fax:* 209–532–70.
P.O. Box 1870, 95310

A gold-rush town, founded in 1850, Columbia is now a historic pa
owned by the state of California and restored to its 1860s condition wi
authentic, museum-quality period antiques. Managed by Tom Bend
some staff members are hotel management students from Columbia C
lege. The hotel is well known for its restaurant, open for dinners ar
Sunday brunch; a recent meal included angel hair pasta with duck, su

dried tomatoes, and goat cheese; greens with orange-ginger vinaigrette; salmon Wellington with mushrooms and leeks; and apple tart with caramel sauce.

"We had one of the balcony rooms overlooking the peaceful main street, which is closed to car traffic. The arrangement of a half-bath in our room and the shower at the far end of the parlor worked out fine—the hotel provides a basket with robe, slippers, towels, and Neutrogena soap and shampoo to carry back and forth." *(Linda Bair)* "Although the two best guest rooms are the ones at the front of the hotel, all are adequate. Ours had an elaborately carved headboard over six feet high; in the morning, we opened the French doors and stepped out onto our balcony, watching the early morning sun illuminate the silent streets. The simple breakfast buffet, set up in the spacious upstairs parlor, included orange juice, sliced cheddar, sourdough bread, cinnamon rolls, and freshly baked muffins and breads.

"Service at dinner was friendly yet professional. The prix fixe dinner was delicious and an excellent value, enhanced by a local wine, chosen from the first-rate wine list. In contrast to the formal atmosphere of the restaurant, the saloon is a completely casual local hangout." *(SWS, also Jerry Turney)*

Minor niggles: Better reading lights in the bedrooms and parlor. Typical of old hotels, the walls are thin. Don't pick a fight with your roommate—anyone sitting in the parlor will hear every word.

Open All year. Closed Dec. 24 & 25, Jan. 1 through Jan. 7. Restaurant closed Mon. from Sept. through May.

Rooms 10 doubles—all with private half-bath; 2 showers in hall. All with desk, air-conditioning. 2 with balcony.

Facilities Restaurant, saloon, parlor with games, balcony. Tennis nearby. Lake, river nearby for boating, swimming.

Location Central Valley; Gold Country, Sierra foothills. 120 m E of San Francisco. 4 m N of Sonora, off Hwy. 49.

Restrictions Room above saloon might have some noise. Smoking in saloon only.

Credit cards Amex, MC, Visa.

Rates B&B, $70–90 double, $65–85 single. Extra person, $15. Prix fixe dinner, $29. Theater, Victorian Christmas packages.

Extras Station/local airport pickup by prior arrangement. Crib.

CORONADO

Also recommended: The **Hotel Del Coronado** (1500 Orange Avenue, 92118; 619–522–8000 or 800–HOTEL DEL), located on the beach, is a large turn-of-the-century seaside resort with over 500 rooms in the original towered Victorian building and the modern complex. "Stunning wood paneled lobby with beautiful period furniture and chandelier; wonderful view of the Pacific from our room in the Victorian building; attentive staff.' *(Debbie Bergstrom)* Note: Not all rooms at the Del are equal in size, comfort, sound-proofing, or view; ask for details.

Coronado Village Inn ¢   *Tel:* 619–435–9318
1017 Park Place, 92118

Built in 1928, the Coronado Village Inn has been owned since then by the Bogh family; Tony and Leanne DiFulvio are the managers at this Coronado Historical Landmark. Breakfast includes homemade muffins, fresh fruit, juice, coffee, and tea, plus assorted snacks, set out in the guest kitchen.

"This three-story brick building has a lot of character, with tiny balconies at the end of each hallway and an old elevator with a grated sliding door. The bathrooms have been refurbished with new tile and fixtures." *(Maureen Hickler)* "Convenient location on a quiet street that feeds into a small park and residential area, yet close to shops and the beach. My cozy little room was clean, light, and airy with wicker furniture; the bathroom had efficient plumbing and was stocked with shampoo and bubble bath. Tony and Leanne were always there to see to our comfort. Delicious blueberry muffins for breakfast." *(Nola Hoffman)* "Ask for room #207, with a canopy bed and a whirlpool tub." *(DN)*

Open All year.
Rooms 15 doubles—all with full private bath, TV, ceiling fan. 11 with telephone, 2 with whirlpool.
Facilities Breakfast room/guest kitchen, sitting room. Limited off-street parking. Park, tennis, swimming, golf nearby. 1 block to ocean beach; beach towels, chairs, umbrellas provided.
Location 4 m SW of downtown San Diego, in center of village. 3 blocks from Del Coronado. From I-5, exit at Coronado Bridge 75. Go to Orange Ave. & turn left. Go to Park Place (2nd little street past 10th St.) & turn right.
Restrictions Smoking allowed.
Credit cards Amex, MC, Visa.
Rates B&B, $50–80 double. 7th night free. 2-night weekend minimum preferred.
Extras Airport/station pickup. Crib.

DANA POINT

Blue Lantern Inn   *Tel:* 714–661–1304
34343 Street of the Blue Lantern, 92629

Reflecting the Cape Cod atmosphere of Dana Point, the Blue Lantern features traditional New England furnishings, original art, print wallpapers, and handmade quilts, complemented by the colors of the coast—seafoam green, lavender, periwinkle, sand.

"Perched on a cliff overlooking the harbor. A delicious afternoon treat of wine, cheese, vegetables, and homemade banana bread started our evening." *(Janet Emery)* "Our Pacific Edge room was spotless and spacious, with TV and refrigerator hidden in an armoire, a flick-of-a-switch fireplace, closets that light up when you open the door, and an oceanview balcony with a nice wood table and chairs. The bathroom was large, with lots of glass and mirrors and little extras like bubble bath and Q-tips. Breakfast was a tasty Mexican egg pie with cheese, chilis, and salsa, plus melon, raisin scones, yogurt, and granola. Although we could have eaten in our room, we enjoyed sitting in the dining room, with glass double doors to let in sea breezes and views of both the harbor and ocean." *(Jennifer Ball)*

"Well-organized and professionally run, with an efficient front desk, and the atmosphere of a small hotel." *(Willis Frick)* "Our bicycles were securely stored, and we were shown around the inn. Restaurant recommendations were forthcoming and reservations made. Though at the lower end of their price range, our room was comfortable, beautifully appointed, and well equipped." *(JTD)* "Marvelous staff, generous afternoon tea, and thoughtful evening turndown service with chocolates left on our pillows." *(Shiin Wright, also IKM)*

Open All year.

Rooms 1 suite, 28 doubles—all with full private bath, telephone, radio, TV, desk, air-conditioning, gas fireplace, refrigerator, Jacuzzi tub. 12 with balcony.

Facilities Dining room, living room with fireplace, library with fireplace, deck. Exercise, conference rooms. Boat charters, windsurfing, sailing nearby.

Location Orange County, 20 m S of Newport Beach. From Hwy. 1 go W on St. of the Blue Lantern.

Restrictions Light sleepers should request rooms away from parking lot. No smoking.

Credit cards Amex, MC, Visa.

Rates B&B, $350 suite, $135–250 double. Extra person, $15. 30% senior discount midweek. Corporate rates.

Extras Wheelchair access. Crib, babysitting. Spanish spoken.

DAVENPORT

New Davenport B&B ¢ ✕ &.   *Tel:* 408–425–1818
31 Davenport Avenue (Highway 1), Box J, 95017   408–426–4122

After operating a pottery school for 15 years, Marcia and Bruce McDougal built the New Davenport Cash Store in 1977 as an outlet for their pottery and craft interests. They ended up with a mini-complex housing a B&B, a restaurant and bakery, and the Cash Store, a craft shop where African and Asian art is a specialty.

The McDougals describe the Davenport area as being a "rural-coastal environment in a rugged, outdoor area. There are endless beaches and mountain paths for hiking. It's eight miles to the Año Nuevo State Elephant Seal Reserve, and you can see the whales migrating from January through May." The rates include a welcome bottle of champagne, $5 credit toward breakfast in the restaurant weekdays, and on weekends a breakfast of hard-boiled eggs, fresh granola, yogurt, fresh-baked pastry, fruit, juice, and coffee.

"The the best rooms are above the restaurant and shop, most with ocean views. The Whale Watcher Room has lovely antique furniture, high stained-wood ceilings, skylights, and a modern bath. Breakfast choices included omelets, blueberry pancakes, and waffles. Although the inn is directly on Highway 1, I heard no traffic noise. Lovely, accommodating innkeeper." *(Gail Davis)* "Captain Davenport's Retreat is a corner room with two walls of floor-to-ceiling glass and a large sitting area with a

CALIFORNIA

high-backed rattan chair and sofa. Comfortable chairs and coffee tables are
arranged along the brick-walled porch making it a pleasant place to relax;
a double-paned wall of glass cuts the ocean wind and most of the traffic
noise, without obstructing the fantastic views of the cliffs and sea." *(Matt
Joyce)* "I had an ample salad, fresh-baked bread, and delicious swordfish."
(Barbara Occhiogrosso)

Minor niggle: "Our room had wall pegs but no closet in which to hang
clothes."

Open All year. Restaurant closed Christmas, Thanksgiving.
Rooms 1 suite, 11 doubles—all with private shower and/or bath, telephone, desk.
Some with fan, balcony. 4 rooms in annex.
Facilities Restaurant, coffee bar, gallery, wraparound porch, common room with
games, reading materials; patio. Ocean beach across street. Hiking, beachcombing,
fishing, windsurfing, hang-gliding, bicycling nearby.
Location San Francisco Bay Area. 60 m S of San Francisco. 9 m N of Santa Cruz,
halfway between San Francisco and Carmel. "Big brick building on Hwy. 1 in
Davenport (only 2 blocks long)."
Restrictions No smoking. Traffic noise in some rooms. Some rooms equipped for
families.
Credit cards Amex, MC, Visa.
Rates B&B, $60–115 double. Extra person, $10. Prix fixe lunch, $6–8; prix fixe
dinner, $15. Alc lunch, $6–7; alc dinner, $17–20.
Extras Wheelchair access. Crib. Spanish spoken.

DEATH VALLEY

Furnace Creek Inn & Ranch Resort 🛅 ✕ 🎿   *Tel:* 619–786–2345
P.O. Box 1, 92328   *Fax:*619–786–2307

Death Valley—the name still conjures up the hardships endured by America's pioneers. Travelers return today to explore this national monument
and to learn about its geological and ecological wonders as well as its
mining history, including 20-mule-team borax wagons and famous
Scotty's Castle. Although Death Valley is America's hottest place in the
summer, the desert climate is inviting from October to early May.

The Furnace Creek Inn and Ranch Resort is owned by operated by
AMFAC/Fred Harvey Resorts. Use the same address and phone number
for information on the Ranch, a more casual, motel-like structure with 225
guest rooms. Although children are welcome at the inn, the ranch is
perhaps a better choice.

Built in 1927, the inn is a Spanish-style adobe villa overlooking Death
Valley with a spectacular view of the valley and surrounding mountains.
Remodeled many times over the years, the resort remains a luxurious one,
set in an unlikely location. Guest rooms are simply furnished, each with
twin or king-size beds.

"Hillside setting overlooking the valley, with fabulous sunset views of
the desert. The building itself is a labyrinth of passageways and walkways
built into the hillside. Lovely gardens step down the hillside; after dinner
we enjoyed strolling past the little waterfalls and lush plantings to the big
old swimming pool and shuffleboard court." *(JWM)* "The restaurant and

grounds are outstanding. We were there for nearly a week, and the food was varied and consistently high in quality." *(Duane Roller)* "The breakfast special (served before 8 A.M.) is a good deal and makes sense when there's so much to see. For dinner, we preferred the Italian restaurant downstairs for delicious pasta." *(Kathleen Lowe Owen)*

Open Mid-Oct.–mid-May.
Rooms 1 suite, 67 doubles—all with full private bath, telephone, TV, desk, air-conditioning.
Facilities Inn dining room, Italian restaurant, lounge with live music, library, sun deck. Barber shop, service station. 85° naturally spring-fed swimming pool, waterfall, hot tub, lighted tennis courts, golf, hiking, trail rides.
Location Desert Country, SE CA. 140 m NW of Las Vegas, NV; 300 m NE of Los Angeles. From Los Angeles, take I-15 to Baker. From Baker, follow 127/190 to Furnace Creek. 1 m from National Park Visitor Center and Museum.
Restrictions No jeans at dinner; men must wear a jacket.
Credit cards All major.
Rates MAP, $325 suite, $243–325 double, $210–285 single. Extra adult, $50; extra child ages 5–12, $25; children under 5, free. 15% suggested service. Alc lunch, $10, alc dinner, $20–40.
Extras Crib, $15.

DESERT HOT SPRINGS

Travellers Repose ¢   *Tel: 619–329–9584*
66920 First Street, P.O. Box 655, 92240

Built in 1986, Travellers Repose is a neo-Victorian home complete with gingerbread trim and fish-scale shingles. The interior decor includes ceiling fans, lace window treatments, iron and brass beds, and pull-chain toilets, complemented by country-floral wallpapers and hardwood floors. Innkeepers Marian and Sam Relkoff serve a breakfast of fresh fruit and juice, homemade granola, and a variety of home-baked muffins, plus afternoon tea.

"Accented by bay windows and stained glass, much of the furniture was hand-crafted by Sam himself." *(Toni Smith)* "Our room offered a spectacular view of Mt. Jacinto and the desert." *(Christina & David Martinez)* "Just a hop, skip and a jump from the freeway system, Palm Desert, and Palm Springs." *(Kimberley Klein)* "A serene setting away from the congestion and glitz of Palm Springs." *(Richard & Catherine McCarthy)* "Marian's flair for decorating and color is evident. These accommodating people enjoy their work." *(Suzanne Rios)* "Outstanding breakfast with home-baked breads and granola." *(Hester Robbizo)* "Our room, Buttons & Bows, had lovely lace curtains, comfortable queen-size brass and iron bed. The house has a heart theme throughout; ask Marian to show you the heart-shaped shadow which forms each night on their walkway. A visit to Sam's workshop is a treat." *(Gail Davis)*

Open Sept. through June.
Rooms 3 doubles—1 with private bath, 2 sharing bath. All with air-conditioning, ceiling fan.

Facilities Dining area, living room with games, books. Patio, heated swimming pool, hot tub, gardens.

Location Desert Country. 12 m N of Palm Springs, 3 blocks from town center. From I-10 take exit for Palm Dr., go N 5 m to Pierson Blvd, turn right. Go E 3 blocks, turn left on First St. to inn on right.

Restrictions No smoking. No children under 12.

Credit cards None accepted.

Rates B&B, $55–75 double, $46–68 single. No tipping. Weekly rates.

Extras Airport pickup, $5.

ELK

Elk is located in Mendocino County on the northern California coast just 15 miles south of Mendocino. (See Mendocino for more information on area attractions.) This tiny hamlet developed as a logging town, and most of its inns were originally built of redwood by a local lumber company. It's 145 miles north of San Francisco, a 4½-hour drive by Highway 1, or just over three hours by way of Highway 101 to Cloverdale. From there take Route 128 to the coast, then 5 miles south on Highway 1 to Elk.

Information please: Set high on a bluff, the **Greenwood Pier Inn** (5928 Highway One, Box 36, 95432; 707–877–9997 or 707–877–3423) offers unsurpassed views of spectacular rock formations and the ocean. Some rooms have cathedral ceilings, multi-level architecture, free-standing rock fireplaces, and bay windows. There's a variety of seating areas for enjoying the gorgeous setting, all decorated with warm colors and soft, inviting fabrics that contrast with the natural wood walls and exposed beams; decks overlook the rock formations. B&B rates for the 11 guest rooms range from $90–195.

Harbor House ✗
5600 South Highway 1, P.O. Box 369, 95432

Tel: 707–877–3203

Certainly no one would want to miss seeing a redwood forest on a trip to California, and a visit to the Craftsman-style Harbor House will give you a chance to see what a house built entirely of virgin redwood is like. As is the case with several other homes in the area, the Harbor House was originally built as an executive residence and guest house by a local lumber company. Now owned by Dean and Helen Turner, the inn has a footpath winding down the bluff to the beach below.

The innkeepers raise many of the inn's vegetables, and the rest of its food is purchased from local sources. Breakfast, served from 8:30 to 9:30 A.M., might include pears cooked in wine, eggs du bois, banana sesame bread, and freshly ground coffee or tea, while the dinner menu might entice you with carrot soup, garden salad with feta, marinated ling cod, broccoli timbales, herb bread, and apricot cake roll with whipped cream.

"Set on a bluff with a breathtaking location overlooking the Pacific. The Turners make you feel like their personal house guests." *(Mary Steiss)* "Gracious, cordial owners; pleasant accommodations; gracious dining overlooking the water." *(Susan Schwemm, also Dana McLaughlin)* "Wonderful food, fabulous views, comfortable rooms. The guests are warm and friendly, the staff unobtrusive and professional." *(Mary Eleanor Haenggi, also Joy Sugg)*

Open All year.
Rooms 10 doubles, including 4 cottages—all with private bath and/or shower. 9 with fireplace, 5 with sun deck.
Facilities Dining room, living room with games, piano, guitar, record collection. 5 acres with gardens, path to private beach. Fishing, tennis, golf, hiking, canoeing, white-water kayaking nearby.
Location North Coast. At N edge of town.
Restrictions No smoking. Not recommended for children under 14. Minimal traffic noise; quiet after 10 P.M.
Credit cards None accepted.
Rates MAP, $135–250 double, $99–214 single. Extra person, $45. 2-night weekend minimum if Sat. included. Prix fixe dinner by reservation only, $26.

Sandpiper House Inn   *Tel: 707–877–3587*
5520 South Highway 1, P.O. Box 149, 95432

Claire and Richard Melrose describe their inn as having a "serene location at the edge of rugged bluffs above Greenwood Cove, with magnificent views of off-shore rock formations, wave-hewn tunnels, and the Pacific. A cottage garden surrounds the house and continues to the edge of the cliffs, where a series of walkways and steps lead to a deck and down to a private beach in the cove below." The inn was built in 1916 by the Goodyear Redwood Lumber Company, and has been owned by the Melroses since 1987. Breakfast favorites include lemon pancakes with raspberry sauce, or an egg and cheese puff with sausage. Highlighted by ornate redwood paneling, the rooms are furnished with antiques, and beds are topped with down comforters.

"Exceptional breakfasts, myriads of multicolored flowers, the warm glow of the fire on chilly evenings, a bouquet of roses at your bedside table, and falling asleep to the gentle sound of the sea." *(Carol Glen)* "Warm, inviting common areas, with wood-paneled walls and beamed ceilings. Guest rooms are spotless, thoughtfully equipped with fresh flowers, wine, and excellent lighting; the bathrooms have luxurious towels, Q-tips, lotion, shampoo, and more. At breakfast, guests are seated around a single large table, or at tables for two. We had orange-peach juice; then puréed strawberries with bananas, topped with a cinnamon sugar wafer; followed by baked Finnish pancakes, topped with apples sautéed in rum and accompanied by chicken-apple sausage. Claire uses low-calorie, low-cholesterol ingredients, though you would never know it. Afternoon tea is available with a variety of teas and homemade ginger cookies and lemon bars; homemade spiced pecans and sherry were also available. Exceptional hospitality." *(Linda Goldberg)*

Open All year.
Rooms 5 doubles—all with private bath and/or shower, with desk, refrigerator. 3 with fireplace, 2 with patio/balcony, 1 with double soaking tub.
Facilities Dining room, living room with fireplace, books; porch, deck. 1/2 acre with private beach.
Location In village center.
Restrictions No smoking. Not suitable for children under 12.

Credit cards MC, Visa.
Rates B&B, $110–195 double, $100–185 single. Extra person, $20. 2-3 night weekend/holiday minimum.

EUREKA

Visitors come to Eureka, still a major lumbering center and fishing port, to wander through its restored Old Town—once home to the area's many lumber barons—hike in the area's parks and forests, and fish in Humboldt Bay. Eureka is located on the North Coast (Redwood Country), 250 miles (5 hours) north of San Francisco. To reach Eureka from the north or south, take Highway 101; from the east, follow Route 299 to 101. The town is laid out in a grid, with the numbered streets running north/south, parallel to the water, and the lettered streets running east/west.

Information please: Just a few blocks from Old Town, the **Iris Inn** (1134 H Street, 95501; 707–445–0307) is a Queen Anne Victorian home built in 1900. Rooms are furnished with antiques and contemporary art, and the $65–90 double rates include breakfast, afternoon tea, and an evening nightcap. "Friendly owners; Brie and crackers in the afternoon; delicious breakfast of waffles and poached pears." *(DL)*

An Elegant Victorian Mansion   *Tel:* 707–444–3144
1406 C Street, 95501   707–442–5594

This Queen Anne–influenced, Eastlake Victorian inn was built in 1888 for Eureka mayor and county commissioner William S. Clark; the inn is listed on the National Register of Historic Places, and has been owned by Doug and Lily Vieyra since 1989.

"My immaculate bedroom had an antique bed with a firm queen-size mattress, two bedside reading lights, overstuffed chairs, and a desk. Our afternoon croquet game was followed by tea and delicious scones. After dinner, I was offered sherry and enjoyed an evening of listening to tapes of old radio shows in the sitting room. Breakfast included freshly squeezed orange juice, fresh-ground coffee, Austrian apple strudel, eggs Benedict, fruit, and homemade chocolate croissants." *(Cindy Jansen)* "After dinner, we found scrumptious chocolates placed beside our down-turned bed." *(Janell & Carlton Conner)* "Doug is an enthusiastic font of information about the area and the Victorian era." *(Lee Todd)*

"The immaculate Lilly Langtry room has an old-fashioned bath with a clawfoot tub, assorted soaps and lotions, and oodles of pink towels." *(Jack Thurbon)* "Thoughtful touches, like the stamped stationery in our room, a tuxedo-clad Doug carrying in our bags, Lily serving ice-cream sodas on the veranda, and Doug's tour of Eureka in his 1928 Ford highlighted our stay." *(Roger & Mary Wabeke)* "Doug and Lily provided us with a selection of menus from local restaurants and helped us make an excellent choice." *(Bernard & Catherine Bishop)* "Secure garaged parking protected our bicycles and the complimentary laundry service was a godsend." *(Bill & Gail Smithman)* "The inn is in a modest residential district, a 10-12 block walk to restaurants." *(Heath Allen)* "Bookshelves full of topical books and well-kept Victorian gardens surrounding the inn." *(Lola & Philip Sherlock)*

Open All year.
Rooms 1 suite, 3 doubles—1 with private bath, 3 sharing 3 baths. All with desk, air-conditioning.
Facilities Dining room, breakfast room with fireplace, living room with fireplace, books, TV/VCR, stereo; parlors, masseuse service, laundry service. Evening movies, chamber music weekly. Gazebo, Victorian flower garden, croquet, sauna, bicycles. Off-street garage parking. Tennis, health club nearby.
Location From Hwy. 101, go S on C St. to inn at 14th St.
Restrictions No smoking. No children under 15.
Credit cards MC, Visa.
Rates B&B, $95–135 suite, $79–105 double, $69–90 single. Midweek, off-season rate. Extra person in suite, $30.
Extras Station pickup; airport pickup, $25. Dutch, French, German spoken.

Hotel Carter ✕ ও.

301 L Street, 95501

Tel: 707–444–8062
Fax: 707–444–8062

Mark and Christi Carter opened the Hotel Carter in 1986, offering period atmosphere with all modern comforts. The decor is an unusual mix of period pieces, primitive antiques, and modern art; peach and white tones predominate. A sample dinner might include a tomato fennel soup or baby greens; grilled salmon with mustard rosemary sauce or marinated rack of lamb; and wild berry cobbler with lemon curd sauce.

Under the same ownership is **Carter House,** a Victorian reproduction B&B, located at 1033 Third Street, Eureka 95501; 707–445–1390 and the Belle House, a neighboring Victorian home with guest kitchen, living room, and three bedrooms, each with private bath.

"Mark is enthusiastic and hospitable. He conducted us and other guests on a tour of the hotel, inn, garden and greenhouse. We had a delightful time with the other guests gathered around the wine and hors d'oeuvres; at 9 P.M., everyone returns for tea and cookies." *(Eileen O'Reilly)* "The food was healthy, hearty, homemade, and beautifully presented. The hotel's atmosphere was welcoming and comfortable, with classical music playing softly in the background, art and flowers set strategically around the rooms, and the fireplace burning." *(BA)*

From the Nothing's Perfect Department: "We spent a night at Carter House, and although our suite was lovely and the breakfast good, the staff seemed cool and impersonal." Also: "Better soundproofing between guest rooms."

Open All year. Restaurant closed Tues. & Wed.
Rooms 4 suites, 18 doubles—all with full private bath, telephone, radio, TV, desk. Suites with double Jacuzzis, double-headed showers, CD stereo, fireplace, mini-bar.
Facilities Dining room with weekend entertainment, lobby with fireplace. Charter fishing nearby.
Location 3 blocks to Old Town.
Restrictions No smoking in guest rooms. Street noise in some street-level rooms.
Credit cards Amex, CB, DC, Discover, MC, Visa.
Rates B&B, $135–300 suite, $79–115 double, $69–110 single. Extra person, $20. Family, senior discounts. Alc dinner, $35.
Extras Wheelchair access; elevator; 1 room equipped for disabled. Crib. Spanish spoken.

CALIFORNIA

A Weaver's Inn ¢
Tel: 707–443–811?
1440 B Street, 95501

Although comfortable accommodations, good food, and warm hospitality are all B&B essentials, the chance to enjoy the individual talents of the innkeepers themselves is equally important. Bob and Dorothy Swendman bought this B&B in 1990; Dorothy is a fiber artist, weaver, spinner, quilter and paper maker, who has crafted most of the textiles of the inn, including lamp shades, tapestries, and some of its painting. In addition to his role as head of the inn's "building and maintenance department," Bob loves to entertain guests on the parlor piano from his collection of old sheet music.

Built as a Queen Anne in 1883 and remodeled in 1907 with Colonial Revival elements, original 19th century elements include the faux graining in the entrance hall, wallpaper in one bedroom, and the oversize windows of hand-rolled glass brought around the Horn. Breakfast varies daily, but might include white grape juice; fruit compote with mint marinade; chili cheese bake with fresh salsa, sour cream and tortillas, and corn muffins.

"The Swendmans gave us a tour of their spacious garden, and showed us Dorothy's prizewinning fiber artwork. Bob's piano playing created a relaxed atmosphere during a delicious breakfast. The Pamela Suite includes a bedroom with queen-size bed, down comforters and pillows, plus a sitting room with sofa bed and fireplace. Lovely antiques, linens, and fresh flowers throughout; careful attention to detail." *(Barbara & David Engen)*

Open All year.
Rooms 1 suite, 3 doubles—2 with private bath and/or shower, 2 with maximum of 4 people sharing bath. All with radio, clock. 1 with desk, 2 with fireplace, 1 with double soaking tub.
Facilities Dining room, living room with fireplace, family room with piano, weaving studio. Limited off-street parking, garden, croquet. Tennis, golf, fishing nearby.
Location 1 m from downtown. Between 14th & 15th Sts.
Restrictions No smoking.
Credit cards Amex, Discover, MC, Visa.
Rates $85 suite, $60–70 double, $45–80 single. Extra person, $15. 10% service
Extras Airport/station pickup, $15. Pets by arrangement, $15.

FERNDALE

Thought by many to be California's best-preserved Victorian village, the entire village of Ferndale is registered as a State Historic Landmark. The town has more than its share of pretty Victorian homes, originally called "butterfat palaces," since their owners made their money in the dairy industry. At the midpoint of Redwood Country, set off the tourist trail, Ferndale is a perfect town for an overnight stay. Although activities are planned year-round, a special effort is made for Christmas, highlighted (literally) by a 125-foot spruce, decorated with over 900 lights. Be sure to stop in at any shop for a free walking-tour brochure. Ferndale is located in the North Coast region (Redwood Country), 260 miles north of San Francisco, 15 miles south of Eureka, and five miles from Highway 101.

Reader tips: "During the late spring, Ferndale's rhododendrons are in

96

bloom; each home seems to have huge bushes of gorgeous flowers out in front." *(Erika Holm)* "Bibo's restaurant was superb." *(Margaret Sievers)*

The Gingerbread Mansion *Tel:* 707–786–4000
400 Berding Street, P.O. Box 40, 95536

Within seconds of your first glimpse of the Gingerbread Mansion, you'll know why owner-innkeeper Ken Torbert chose that name and why this is the most photographed Victorian in northern California!

"This ornate gingerbread mansion is painted soft yellow and peach, and is surrounded by beautiful English gardens. It's located off the main street in a quiet, well-lit residential neighborhood close to the well-preserved historic downtown area. Tea and coffee were brought to the landing for early risers." *(Patrick & Gloria Smith)* "Ken is well-informed about local history and current attractions, but we were content just sitting around the house doing jigsaw puzzles and wandering in the gardens." *(Caroline & John Blattner)* "The Fountain Suite was spacious and beautifully decorated with antiques. The gigantic bathroom had a pair of side-by-side clawfoot tubs, a modern shower stall, large wall mirrors, night light, and a gas fireplace next to the chaise lounge. The staff was pleasant and friendly; we met Ken Torbert at breakfast. Breakfast was served family-style at two large tables in the dining room. The first day we had juice, a fruit bowl, pumpkin ginger bread, poppy seed cake, and individually baked French toast with hot maple syrup. The second day featured juice, fruit, cheddar cheese muffins, coffee cake, eggs Florentine, and homemade granola." *(Karl Wiegers & Chris Zambito)*

"We stayed in the Rose Suite with a fantastic mirrored bathroom, complete with an enormous claw-foot tub and shower." *(Jan & Barry Olsen)* "Afternoon tea included such homemade goodies as bourbon balls and petit fours. Ken and Sandie were gracious hosts, attentive to the smallest detail." *(Marilyn Maxwell)* "On a stroll through town you may pass a candy shop where you can watch the workers hand-dip chocolates; at night, you'll find these same delicious chocolates by your pillow." *(Erika Holm)* "All that you described and more." *(Margaret Sievers)*

Open All year.
Rooms 4 suites, 5 doubles—all with private bath and/or shower. 3 with gas fireplace. Some with desk, twin claw-foot tubs.
Facilities 4 parlors with 2 fireplaces and library, dining room, porches. Formal English gardens, fountain, bicycles. Ocean, river, wilderness park nearby.
Location Take Ferndale exit off Hwy. 101, 5 m to Main St. Turn left at Bank of America; 1 block to inn.
Restrictions No smoking. Children over 10 preferred.
Credit cards Amex, MC, Visa.
Rates B&B, $110–205 suite, $90–160 double, $65–135 single. Extra person, $35. 2-night holiday/weekend minimum.

FISH CAMP

Thirty-five miles south of Yosemite Valley, Fish Camp sits just outside the southern entrance to Yosemite National Park on Route 41, one of three park access roads open year-round. A few miles north is the one of th finest giant sequoia groves in the Sierras, the Mariposa Grove, with th Grizzly Giant (with a diameter of 30 feet) and the tunneled Californi Tree, so large that a car could drive through.

Also recommended: Without exception, readers are delighted wit the dinners at **The Narrow Gauge Inn** (48571 Highway 41, Fish Cam 93623; 209–683–7720), a motel combining western-style architectur with Victorian decor, most of the latter obtained from the now-defunc Pony Express Museum. One reader was pleased with "a rustic cabin calle 'Sleepy Hollow.' Although furnished in 'early miscellaneous,' it was clear extremely quiet, with a lovely setting in the woods. We ate in th restaurant every night, enjoying the well prepared food, the friendl service, and the views of the moonlight on the mountains through th large windows." *(Carol Dinmore)* "Our room was furnished in 'basic mote but the view of the Sierra National Forest from our balcony made up fo it. The nicely landscaped grounds and swimming pool provided an invi ing setting. Not to be missed is a ride on the Narrow Gauge Railroa through the forest into the canyon." *(Glenn Roehrig)*

Another possibility is **Karen's B&B** (1144 Railroad Avenue, 9362 209–683–4550 or 800–346–1443), a simple contemporary home on High way 41, just a mile south of the park entrance. The three guest rooms hav private baths, and the $85 rate for this homestay B&B includes a fu breakfast and afternoon refreshments. "You can visit with the owners an guests, watch TV, play games, or feed the raccoons which visit nightl Children are welcome, and breakfasts include waffles, pancakes, or baco and eggs. The knowledgeable owners grew up in the area." *(Sharon Crair* "There is an upstairs guest sitting area outside of the family quarters." *(ACR*

Thirteen miles to the south in Oakhurst is the **Château du Sureau** (4868 Victoria Lane, P.O. Box 577, Oakhurst 93644; 209–683–6860), constructe to resemble a manor house from the south of France, complete with stucc facade and tile roof. The nine luxuriously appointed rooms are complet with stereo/CD system, imported linens, woodburning fireplace, and ma ble bathrooms. The estate's restaurant, Erna's Elderberry House, is wel regarded for its innovative and elegant cuisine. Double rates of $250–35 include a European-style breakfast with cold meats, cheeses, fruit, freshl baked breads, and coffee. "Our six course prix-fixe meal at Erna's wa spectacular, in a dining room reminiscent of a European chateau." *(ACR)*

Information please: Thirteen miles south of Fish Camp, and 2½ mile from Highway 49 is **The Homestead** (41110 Road 600, Ahwahne 93601; 209–683–0495), four recently constructed cottages, made c adobe, stone, and cedar, each peaceful and private, with beautiful view The decor is accented with tiled floors, peeled log beds, antiques; each un has a living/dining area, fireplace, kitchen, bedroom, bathroom, televisio and air-conditioning. Double rates are $125.

Apple Tree Inn   *Tel:* 209–683–511
1110 Highway 41, P.O. Box 41, 93623

Surrounded by the Sierra National Forest, the Apple Tree Inn offe abundant tranquility and privacy in its cottages, built in 1945. "We ha a spacious but cozy cabin, with a modern bathroom. The wonderful basket of homemade muffins, juice, fresh fruit, and coffee was brought to us in the morning by friendly, helpful owner Gerry Smith. For dinner, Gerry reserved a table for us at the Narrow Gauge Inn, where the food was surprisingly good." *(Stephanie Roberts)* "Even better than I expected from your description. The cottages are set on a forested hillside and are separated from one another for quiet and privacy. Ours was roomy and comfortably furnished with a nice sitting area, with corner windows looking out to the forest. Even in late May our well-stocked fireplace was welcome in the evening. My favorite feature was the busy hummingbird feeder near the front porch of each cottage." *(JTD)*

Open All year.
Rooms 6 cottages—all with private shower, radio, deck, parking space, TV. 4 with desk or fireplace. 2 with refrigerator.
Facilities 7 acres surrounded by Sierra National Forest.
Location High Sierras. 2 m S of south entrance to Yosemite National Park.
Restrictions No smoking in 3 cottages. 1 family cottage.
Credit cards Amex, MC, Visa.
Rates B&B, $100–130 family cottage, $80–95 double, $70–85 single. 2-night holiday minimum.

FORT BRAGG

Located in the Mendocino section of the North Coast, Fort Bragg is 8 miles north of Mendocino and approximately 160 miles northwest of San Francisco. The town's best-known tourist attraction is the scenic "Skunk Train" through the redwood forest to Willits; its name came from the smell of its original gas-powered engines. Also of interest in Fort Bragg is the Mendocino Coast Botanical Gardens, where flowers frame ocean views nearly year-round; and in March, the Whale Festival, celebrating the migration of the California grey whale.

Reader tips: "Fort Bragg is 8 miles and many dollars away from Mendocino. If you're on a tight budget, stay here and visit there." Also: "The town isn't particularly scenic, so don't plan to spend much time here. Take a quick look at the Noyo harbor and wharf area, and snap a few pictures of the sea lions barking on the docks." *(LG)*

Also recommended: If you're looking for an affordable alternative to high-priced coastal accommodations, or need a break when driving Highway 101, consider the **Baechtel Creek Inn** (101 Gregory Lane, Willits, 95490; 707–459–9063 or 800–459–9911), just off 101, 35 miles east of Fort Bragg via Route 20. "Jane and Robert Rodriguez run this attractive motel like a Swiss watch. Excellent housekeeping, hospitality; tasty continental breakfast." *(Frank Byrnes)* The 46 guest rooms have private bath, TV, and telephone; B&B double rates are $65. Although the inn is just behind McDonald's and Taco Bell, it has an attractive swimming pool and a pleasant creekside location.

Also recommended: The **Pudding Creek Inn** (700 North Main Street, 95437; 707–964–9529 or 800–227–9529), originally built by

"Bottle Brown," an immigrant from Russia who grew wealthy from the success of his bottling plant. Guest rooms are decorated with Victorian antiques, floral comforters and wallpapers. Breakfast includes juice, fresh fruit, home-baked coffee cake or muffins, and an egg dish such as asparagus and Canadian bacon strata; afternoon beverages are served in the parlor, accompanied by fresh fruit and cheese. B&B rates for the 10 guest rooms ranges from $65–125. "Beautifully decorated; immaculately clean; excellent service." *(Gilbert Deyler)* "Within walking distance of beach and town. Delicious breakfast." *(Nadine Jasmin)*

The **Avalon House** (561 Stewart Street, 95437; 707–964–5555 or 800–964–5556) is a restored 1905 Craftsman home, carefully soundproofed, with modern bathrooms and antique decor. "Sits on a quiet residential street, its garden filled with flowering trees and bushes." *(Ester & Harold White)* "Great bed, with a firm mattress and down comforter, cozily set in front of the fireplace." *(Rory Krememer)* "The Yellow Room has a canopy bed and chairs made from tree branches, a fireplace and a double whirlpool bath right in the room." *(Linda Goldberg)* B&B double rates for the six guest rooms range from $70–135.

Overlooking the harbor is the **Noyo River Lodge** (500 Casa del Noyo Drive, 95437; 800–628–1126). B&B rates are $90–140, with the most expensive accommodations offering water views, fireplaces, soaking tubs and private decks. Weather permitting, breakfast is served on the sheltered decks overlooking the river, while the 'evening social hour features entertainment by sea lions, seals, and sea gulls." Offering views of the ocean (with migrating whales from December to March) and flower-filled meadows, the **Jughandle Beach Country B&B Inn** (32980 Gibney Lane, 95437; 707–964–1415) is a restored Victorian farmhouse. Jughandle State Park is right across the street for hiking. This B&B has four guest rooms (two have ocean views), all with queen-size beds, private baths, coffee makers, and FM radios; rates of $75–85 include a full breakfast.

The Grey Whale Inn ¢ ♿	*Tel:* 707–964–0640
615 North Main Street, 95437	800–382–7244
	Fax: 707–964–4408

A classic-style structure of old-growth redwood, the Grey Whale Inn has been a Mendocino Coast landmark since 1915. Innkeepers John and Colette Bailey converted the building into an inn in 1978 and have been fixing it up ever since. The breakfast buffet changes daily and includes such entrées as Greek frittata, zucchini pie, or potato egg casserole, plus fresh fruit, cinnamon prunes, juices, hot and cold cereals, non-fat milk, home-baked coffee cake, toasting bread, homemade jams, house-blend coffee, teas, and hot chocolate.

"The hallways and entrance are decorated with fine prints, paintings, and old photographs of logging days and of the great whales. Helpful, candid, guest critique book of local restaurants." *(Donald Hook)* "Most guest rooms are spacious and pleasantly decorated with antiques and reproduction furnishings, redwood paneling, and coordinating wallpapers, window treatments, and comforters. Breakfast is served buffet-style from 7:30 to 10 A.M., and although only four tables await guests, you can easily take breakfast to your room. After breakfast, we walked along the cliffs and down the walking path. Colette is knowledgeable about area activities and the inn's history. The Sunrise Suite features a king-size bed with hand-embroidered pillows and a matching quilt, comfortable chairs for reading, a table and chairs, an armoire, and a space heater for chilly fog-bound evenings, and ample bedside reading lights. The bathroom has a huge whirlpool tub and separate shower. Large windows look out onto a private deck with patio furniture and views of town and the ocean. Although slightly smaller, the Sunset is also popular because of its excellent ocean views and dramatic sunset vistas. It has a private deck, king-size bed, and lots of large windows." *(Matthew Joyce)* "Colette handled our request for information with amazing warmth and speed. The Railway Suite was beautiful and spacious with a king-size bed, sofa, table and chairs, and fireplace." *(Julie & Doug Philips)* "A clever and tasteful adaptation of an old commercial building." *(Jean Rees)*

Open All year.
Rooms 6 suites, 8 doubles—all with private bath and/or shower, telephone, clock radio. 6 with TV; 3 with fireplace; 1 with whirlpool tub. 3 with balcony or patio.
Facilities Parlor, breakfast room, lounge with fireplace, guest refrigerator, recreation room with pool table, conference room, TV/VCR room. Garden, lawns. 4 blocks to ocean.
Location North Coast. On Hwy. 1.
Restrictions Street noise in some rooms might disturb light sleepers. No smoking. "Facilities for children very limited."
Credit cards Amex, MC, Visa.
Rates B&B, $132–160 suite, $83–160 double, $60–130 single. Extra person, $20. 2–3 night weekend, holiday minimum. Winter midweek rate.
Extras Wheelchair access; 1 room equipped for disabled. Airport/station pickup. Spanish spoken.

GARBERVILLE

Benbow Inn ✖   *Tel: 707–923–2124*
445 Lake Benbow Drive, 95542

Owned since 1977 by Chuck and Patsy Watts, the Benbow is a National Historic Landmark. Rates include in-room coffee and sherry, afternoon tea and scones, and evening hors d'oeuvres.

"The feel of a grand English manor, with an expansive terrace, sweeping lawns, and gardens. The guest rooms have books, comfortable chairs, good lighting for reading, and a basket of amenities in the bathroom." *(Norma & Bill Hodge)* "A wonderful lobby full of antiques, a game table for puzzles or chess, a large castle-like fireplace, and French doors opening to the patio. The front porch, furnished with wicker, is a comfortable place to sip a cocktail or enjoy the view." *(Sally Brown)* "My parents stayed in a spacious, handsomely decorated suite, overlooking the river and lawns. Our room in the new wing was moderate in size and splendidly appointed. A private balcony overlooked the peaceful grounds. The food and service in the lovely dining room (or on the patio) are excellent and the maitre d' was extremely helpful and accommodating. Reservationists are especially accommodating, and the desk staff is friendly and courteous. Rooms in the front don't enjoy as lovely a view as those to the back. While the entire inn is quite close to a highway, we had no noise problem, even with the windows open." *(Sally Ducot)* "Inviting common area—fire going in the fireplace, many comfortable spots to sit. Good food." *(Mary Karrick)* "A great place to go for Christmas, complete with Yule Log and caroling." *(E.H. Buckingham)*

Open Mid-April–late Nov.; Dec. 20–Jan. 2.

Rooms 1 cottage, 3 suites, 52 doubles—all with private bath and/or shower, air-conditioning. Some with terrace, fireplace, TV/VCR, or refrigerator. Cottage with wet bar, Jacuzzi, fireplace.

Facilities Restaurant, bar/lounge with videotape library, lobby, terrace, gardens. Lake for fishing, swimming, boating. 9-hole golf course, hiking, tennis, horseback riding, bicycling nearby.

Location North Coast, Redwood Empire. 200 m N of San Francisco. 10 m S of Valley of the Giants. Opposite Benbow Lake State Recreation Area on Eel River, just off Hwy. 101.

Restrictions No smoking.

Credit cards MC, Visa.

Rates Room only, $250 cottage, $140–180 suite, $98–130 double. Extra person, $15. Midweek packages, off-season. Alc breakfast, $4–9; alc lunch, $7–12, alc dinner, $25–40. Picnic lunches with 12-hr. notice.

Extras Babysitting by arrangement. German, French spoken.

GEYSERVILLE

People go to the Sonoma Valley to explore the area wineries, visit the Russian River resorts, and enjoy the area's inns and restaurants. In general, the pace here is quieter and slower than in the neighboring Napa Valley.

Geyserville is located in the North Coast region, in the center of Sonoma County Wine Country, Alexander, and Dry Creek Valleys. It's 75 miles north of San Francisco and eight miles north of Healdsburg.

Campbell Ranch Inn 🏕
1475 Canyon Road, 95441   *Tel: 707–857–3476*

Campbell Ranch Inn is a large, comfortable home, set on a canyon hillside surrounded by gardens, terrace, and deck. The rooms are immaculate, all with comfortable king-size beds, quality linens, fresh fruit and flowers.

"Breakfast includes a choice of fruits and cereals, omelets, fried eggs, or an egg puff with chilies or mushrooms, plus homemade jam, muffins and breads, served at guests' convenience from 8–10 A.M. In the evening Mary Jane serves fresh, delicious desserts—apple, peach, apricot, blackberry, blueberry pies, chocolate or apple walnut cake." *(Phyllis & Walt Reichle)* "Unforgettable views of rolling hills covered with vineyards or a thickly wooded ravine. The second-story bedrooms have balconies, and the tree-shaded terrace is equally inviting." *(Stephen & Judy Gray)* "Extremely comfortable beds, bathrobes, extra large pool towels, fresh flowers, and of course, the desserts." *(JMB)*

"The good-sized rooms are quiet and well-insulated, with good temperature control. Jerry and Mary Jane have great recommendations for touring, restaurants, and local wineries. Breakfasts are outstanding, with such extras such as homemade salsa and raspberry jam. The breakfast table is set for ten; guests may eat together or take their food to individual tables on the deck or around the pool. My favorite rooms were #4 for privacy and #2 for the larger bathroom and the views. All rooms have comfortable king-size beds, luggage racks, tissues, two wastebaskets, and pink glycerine soaps." (SHW)

Open All year.
Rooms 1 2-bedroom cottage, 4 doubles—all with private bath and/or shower, air-conditioning. Cottage with cassette player, fireplace, deck; 4 with desk, balcony.
Facilities Living room with fireplace, family room with fireplace, games, TV; dining room, terrace. 35 acres with flower gardens, heated swimming pool, hot tub, tennis court, aviary. Ping-Pong, horseshoes, bicycles. 3 m to Lake Sonoma for boating, swimming, fishing; 3 m to Russian River for fishing, canoeing.
Location 2 m from town. Take Canyon Rd. exit off Hwy. 101, go 1.6 m W to inn.
Restrictions No smoking. Young children not encouraged.
Credit cards MC, Visa.
Rates B&B, $100–165 double, $90–155 single. Extra person, $25. 2–3-night weekend/holiday minimum.
Extras Local airport/station pickup.

The Hope-Merrill & Hope-Bosworth House   Tel: 707–857–3356
21253/21238 Geyserville Avenue,   800–825–4BED
P.O. Box 42, 95441   Fax: 707–857–HOPE

Facing each other across Geyserville Avenue are the Hope-Bosworth House, a Queen Anne Victorian—a pattern book house built entirely of redwood in 1904—and the Hope-Merrill House, a 19th century Eastlake Stick-style house. Owned since 1981 by Bob and Rosalie Hope, with Kim Taylor as the long-time manager, both inns have been fully restored and decorated in period; the Hope-Merrill features striking Victorian revival wallpapers designed by Bruce Bradbury and original Lincrusta paneling, while the Hope-Bosworth has antique light fixtures and the original oak-grained woodwork. Breakfast is served at 9 A.M., and includes juice, fresh fruit, a hot entrée, homemade bread and jams.

"Well-run inn; personable owners. Enjoyed talking with the other guests at breakfast." (Shirley Dittloff) "Guest rooms are Victorian masterpieces. Immaculate housekeeping. Rosalie's delicious breakfasts are accompanied by lively conversation." (Noel Gentry)

Open All year.
Rooms 1 suite, 11 doubles—all with full private bath. 10 with fan, 3 with fireplace, whirlpool tub. Rooms in 2 buildings.
Facilities Dining room, living room, library, porch. 12 acres with heated swimming pool. Golf, river, lake nearby.
Location From Hwy. 101, take Geyserville exit. Go N on Geyserville Ave. 1 m to inns.
Restrictions No smoking.
Credit cards Amex, MC, Visa.

Rates B&B, $95–140 suite, double. Extra person, $20. 2-night minimum March–Nov. Picnic, $30 for two.
Extras Limited wheelchair access. Spanish spoken. Airport pickup.

GLEN ELLEN

A quiet base for a tour of the Sonoma Valley, Glen Ellen's main claim to fame—other than its vineyards and wineries—is the Jack London State Historic Park, comprising the author's home and ranch, with a museum of his papers, personal belongings, and mementos. Its 800 acres also offer ample opportunities for walking, hiking, and riding. Glen Ellen is located in the Wine Country area of the North Coast, 55 miles north of San Francisco and 15 minutes north of Sonoma. From San Francisco, take Highway 101 north. Before Novato, take Highway 37 to Highway 121 toward Sonoma. Then take Highway 116 for a short distance and go right (north) on Arnold Drive to Glen Ellen.

Gaige House
13540 Arnold Drive, 95442

Tel: 707–935–0237
800–935–0237
Fax: 707–935–6411

The Gaige House, an Italianate Queen Anne Victorian home built in 1890, was restored as an inn in 1980, and has been owned by Ardath Rouas since 1993. The decor combines Victorian antiques with Oriental rugs and an eclectic collection of art acquired by Ardath during her travels. A breakfast of fresh squeezed orange juice, seasonal fruit, and entrées of pancakes, waffles or eggs accompanied by chicken sausage or turkey bacon is served at separate tables in the dining room and on the terrace on summer mornings. Local wine and imported cheeses are served by the fire on cool evenings, or on the terrace when it's warm.

"Attentive staff. Ardath has mastered the art of being friendly without being intrusive. Well-kept house and grounds. The delicious breakfasts are never repeated during your stay." *(Jerome & Carol Haydon)* "Great location for touring area wineries; good restaurants nearby. We enjoyed the early morning coffee and relaxing by the pool." *(George Clendenin)*

Open All year.
Rooms 1 suite, 8 doubles—all with private bath and/or shower, telephone, radio, clock, air-conditioning. Some with desk, fan, balcony/deck; 2 with fireplace, 1 with whirlpool tub. 3 rooms in carriage house.
Facilities Parlor with fireplace, books, TV/VCR, stereo; dining room, guest refrigerator, deck. 1 1/4 acres with lawns, creek, heated swimming pool. Off-street parking.
Location 6 m from Sonoma Plaza. From Plaza, take W. Napa to Hwy 12. Go N on Hwy to signs for "Glen Ellen" and "Lodging," 2 m past turnoff to Jack London Sate Park, & turn left on Arnold Dr. Go 0.6 m to inn on right.
Restrictions Occasional traffic noise in front room. No smoking. Children over 12.
Credit cards Amex, Discover, MC, Visa.
Rates B&B, $195–225 suite, $100–175 double, $90–158 single. Extra person, $25. 2-night weekend minimum Nov.–March.

Glenelly Inn ¢   *Tel: 707–996–6720*
5131 Warm Springs Road, 95442

This southern-style house, encircled by verandas on both the first and
second floors, was built as an inn in 1916; in those days guests arrived via
the Southern Pacific Railroad. Completely renovated in 1985, it was
purchased in 1990 by mother and daughter, Kristi and Ingrid Hallamore,
who added Scandinavian down comforters, terrycloth robes, comfortable
seating on the verandas, an outdoor Jacuzzi, and extensive gardens with
benches for quiet times under the fruit trees. A recent breakfast included
baked fruit with cream, leek tart with ham, brioches, granola and yogurt.

"Our delightfully peaceful room had a garden view and was charmingly
furnished with a wicker settee, small rocker, queen-size brass bed, an old
oak washstand as a dresser and an antique armoire as a closet." *(Lynne
Derry)* "Affectionate inn cats." *(Yvonne Sullivan)* "Inviting, well-tended
grounds." *(Margaret Sievers)* "Guests gather in the appealing common
room to enjoy wine, cheese and crackers, or sherry and tea; the buffet
breakfast is also served here." *(Eileen O'Reilly)* "Kristi is friendly yet not
intrusive, full of great restaurant recommendations. Our super breakfast
included melon, fig walnut bread, smoked chicken and apple sausage,
followed by peach raspberry cobbler with vanilla yogurt. Seating for
breakfast is at one large table, but guests are not forced to eat at the same
time. Each guest room has a private outside entrance, lamps on both sides
of the bed, luggage racks, thick white towels, and bathrobes." *(Susan W.
Schwemm)*

Open All year.
Rooms 3 suites, 5 doubles—all with full private bath, fan, balcony, private
entrance. 2 with fireplace. 2 rooms in annex.
Facilities Dining room, common room with fireplace, books, games, verandas. 1
acre with Jacuzzi, fruit trees, rose gardens. Golf, tennis, hot air ballooning, wineries
nearby.
Location 2 blocks from center. Go N on Arnold Rd., then turn left at Warm
Springs Rd. to inn ⅓ m on right.
Restrictions No smoking. Children welcome by prior arrangement. Daytime
traffic noise in some rooms.
Credit cards MC, Visa.
Rates B&B, $130 suite, $95–105 double. 2-night holiday/weekend minimum.
10% discount for 4-night stay. Off-season discount.
Extras Norwegian spoken.

GLENHAVEN

Also recommended: The **Kristalberg B&B** (715 Pearl Court, 95443;
707–274–8009) was built as a B&B in 1987, and offers panoramic views
of Clear Lake, known for its excellent fishing. The living room and three
guest rooms are decorated with Victorian and European furnishings, and
the B&B double rates range from $60–150. "Clean, attractive rooms. A full
German breakfast was served in the dining room, which has a wonderful
view of the lake. Later we enjoyed refreshments in the parlor. The house

CALIFORNIA

is located high on a hill with unobstructed views." *(LaRee Keller)* "Gracious innkeeper who respected our need for quiet and privacy." *(David Walrath)*

GRASS VALLEY

Murphy's Inn   *Tel: 916–273–6873*
318 Neal Street, Grass Valley 95945

At Murphy's Inn, the first thing you'll notice is the ivy. Thick "columns" of ivy accent the veranda, punctuated by hanging ivy topiary baskets. Sketches of the building from 1882 show the same plantings in an earlier stage of growth. Built in 1866 as the home of Edward Coleman, gold-baron owner of the North Star and Idaho mines, the inn has been owned by Tom and Sue Myers since 1991. Rooms are furnished with pine, oak, and mahogany antiques. Breakfast is served at individual tables, and might include eggs Benedict, country French toast with homemade blackberry syrup, sausage and hash browns, or Belgian waffles.

"Sue Myers is a gracious owner, as is innkeeper Linda Jones. The comfortable parlor is done in mauve tones, with period furnishings. The breakfast room has attractively set tables with white lace cloths and fresh flowers. Chilled wine and soft drinks are available, as are homemade snacks, cookies and sherry. Most guest rooms have queen- or king-size beds, antique furnishings, and floral wallpapers, with good bedside lighting. The cozy Maid's Quarters is a good value, with a skylight, white wicker chairs, fancy carved wooden headboard, and floral accents, while the Hanson Suite in the Donation Day House has more space, including an appealing bathroom with an antique vanity and a tiled double shower." *(Linda Goldberg)* Comments welcome.

Open All year.
Rooms 4 suites, 4 doubles—all with private shower and/or bath, air-conditioning. 4 with fireplace, 2 with TV, 1 with refrigerator, deck. 2 suites in cottage across street.
Facilities Breakfast room, parlor with fireplace, deck. golf, fishing, swimming nearby. Off-street parking.
Location 60 m E of Sacramento. 3 blocks from center. From Hwy. 20/49, take Colfax 174 exit. Left on S Auburn, left on Neal.
Restrictions No smoking. Children by arrangement.
Credit cards Amex, MC, Visa.
Rates B&B, $115–140 suite, $75–100 double. Extra person, $18. 2-night weekend/holiday minimum.
Extras Airport pickup.

GROVELAND

Groveland Hotel ¢ ✗ &   *Tel: 209–962–4000*
18767 Main Street, P.O. Box 289, 95321   800–273–3314
                                          Fax: 209–962–6674

Groveland, once known as Savage's Diggings, experienced two building booms, one with the Gold Rush and a second when the Hetch Hetchy

106

alley to the east was dammed to create a reservoir for the city of San rancisco. Now a popular stop en route to Yosemite, the town has a istoric main street that reflects these important periods in its existence. he Groveland Hotel was built of adobe (with walls 18 inches thick) in 849, and its 1914 wood-frame annex was constructed with Queen Anne tyling. Owner Peggy Mosley restored the inn in 1992. The guest rooms ave coordinating floral fabrics and wallpapers, antique beds (most queen-ize or twins), down comforters and robes. Lyle's Room is a favorite of uests, not just because of its decor, but because of its resident ghost, the ponymous Lyle, a gold prospector who died (of natural causes) in this oom in 1927.

Rates include continental breakfast, with brunch offered on Sundays. he restaurant features seasonal California cuisine, with such seafood and asta favorites as mushroom and black pepper linguine in cheddar sauce, r mahi mahi with pineapples in black bean sauce.

"Our spotless room was decorated with period furniture, with an ndividual thermostat. Groveland is also home to California's oldest sa-oon, the Iron Door." *(E.R. Taft)* "Good location, with Yosemite close by nd several restaurants within walking distance." *(Steve Talton)* "Friendly wners and staff, excellent restaurant." *(Burma Workman)*

Open All year.
Rooms 3 suites, 14 doubles—all with private bath and/or shower, telephone, adio, air-conditioning, ceiling fan, balcony. TV on request. Suites with fireplace, acuzzi. 13 rooms in annex.
Facilities Restaurant/saloon with weekend entertainment, parlor with fireplace, aundry, porch, deck. Conference facilities, fitness center. ½ acre, hot tub, gazebo, ourtyard. Mt. Lake, Tuolumne River for water sports & rafting; golf nearby.
Location High Sierras, 145 m E of San Francisco Bay area, 23 m W of Yosemite ark, on Rte. 120.
Restrictions Traffic noise in front rooms. No smoking. Prefer children over 10.
Credit cards Most major credit cards.
Rates B&B, $145–165 suite, $75–95 double. Extra person, $15. MAP, full board ates. Golf package. Alc lunch, $8; alc dinner, $25.
Extras Limited wheelchair access. Free Pine Mt. Lake Airport pickup. Pets by rrangement. Crib.

GUALALA

ronounced "wa-*la*-la," the unusual name of this town may be derived rom an Indian word meaning "water coming down place;" others think he name originated with the early German and Spanish settlers, who may ave thought this area resembled heaven, or Valhalla.

Gualala is located in the Mendocino area of California's North Coast, hree hours north of San Francisco and two hours west of the Napa Valley. To reach Gualala, take Highway 101 to Petaluma and proceed west hrough Two Rock and Valley Ford to Bodega Bay. Follow Highway 1 orth to Gualala.

The "banana belt" climate here is mild and mostly free of coastal fog. Golf, tennis, hiking, whale watching, fishing, swimming, and diving are all opular activities. For more information on area attractions, please see the :hapter introduction.

CALIFORNIA

Reader tip: "Great area for R&R, but not if you want to be constantly on the go. Many art galleries in the area, most open Thursday through Monday. Visit the Food Company for a picnic lunch." *(AR)*

Also recommended: Those for whom an ocean view is more important than a private bath will enjoy **The Old Milano Hotel** (38300 Highway 1, 95445; 707–884–3256), a Victorian landmark overlooking the Pacific and decorated in period. Six guest rooms share two modern bathrooms with two-person showers (B&B, $80–110); top choice accommodation is the romantic and authentic Caboose (B&B, $135), set in the woods. Breakfast, served in the restaurant or brought to your room, might include home-baked breads, fresh fruit, blueberry pancakes and bacon. "Dinner was excellent. Guest rooms are small but pleasant, intensely Victorian. Spectacular views of the ocean and Castle Rock." *(Duane Roller)* "A secluded hot tub from which to watch the stars and ocean. Charming perennial gardens. Our room had a private bath, great views, and funky '60s-style Victorian furnishings." *(MEH)*

Several miles to the south, **The Sea Ranch Lodge** (60 Sea Walk Drive, P. O. Box 44, Sea Ranch 95497; 707–785–2371 or 800–732–7262), originally a 17,000-acre Mexican land grant, still encompasses 10 miles of coastline. The ranch is a second-home colony, developed in the early 1970s with the intent of disturbing the environment as little as possible. Lodge guests are able to use all the facilities of the ranch. The lodge restaurant serves American food, with an emphasis on fresh ingredients, homemade breads and desserts, and a good selection of California wines; reader opinions on the food have been mixed. "Simple but adequate accommodations; most with an ocean view; breathtaking scenery. Perfect place for a quiet retreat." *(Diana Chang)*

Information please: A recently built inn, the **Breakers Inn** (Highway One, P.O. Box 389, 95445; 707–884–3200) offers oceanfront guest rooms with 180° water views, private balconies, king-size poster or sleigh beds, fireplaces, double whirlpool tubs, color TV, telephones, coffee-makers and a wet bar. Meals are available from the adjacent Captain's Quarters Restaurant. Doubles rates range from $65–265, depending on view, room, and season.

North Coast Country Inn
34591 South Highway 1, 95445

Tel: 707–884–4537
800–959–4537

The North Coast Country Inn is composed of several weathered buildings set on a redwood-forested hillside, and has been owned by Loren and Nancy Flanagan since 1984.

"Guest rooms are large, clean, and comfortable, with country antiques, braided rugs, handmade quilts, and unusual pictures and books. Private decks allow for quiet afternoons of reading and relaxing. Attractive landscaping with lots of flowers. Because of the inn's proximity to Highway One there is some traffic noise during the day, but it's quiet at night." *(Alice Boyer & Jim Martin)* "The Gallery room has a four-poster queen-size bed with handmade quilt. French doors open from a private deck into a fresh, bright sitting room/bedroom with a fireplace and a generous supply of wood. A short walk through the trees along a softly lit path leads to

private open-air hot tub; the sound of barking sea lions drifts through
e redwoods." *(Ginny Anderson)* "My favorite rooms are the Aquitaine
oom with its French antiques and Oriental rugs, and the Quilt Room,
th its country flavor. Nearly all the guest rooms have high, exposed
am ceilings. Breakfast included a croissant, baked egg with cheese, and
apefruit slices." *(Linda Goldberg)* "Careful attention to detail, from the
ell-stocked kitchen, to the large closet with two luggage racks and ample
ngers, to the extra heaters in bedroom." *(Emmett & Carol Cooke)* "Nancy
d Loren are attentive while respecting guests' privacy." *(Mark Steisel)*

pen All year.
ooms 4 doubles—all with private shower, fireplace, deck, kitchenette. 1 with
ylight.
cilities Antique shop. 1 acre with garden, gazebo, hot tub, picnic table.
cation 4 m N of Gualala on Hwy 1. at Fish Rock Rd. ¼ m N of Anchor Bay.
strictions No smoking. No children under 13.
edit cards Amex, MC, Visa.
ttes B&B, $135 double. 2–3-night weekend, holiday minimum.
tras Local airport pickup.

Orres ¢ ✕
601 South Highway 1,
O. Box 523, 95445

Tel: 707–884–3303
707–884–3335 (restaurant)
Fax: 707–884–3903

arked by the influence of Russian settlers, the inn's onion-dome architec-
re is unusual. The main building houses the inn's well-known restaurant
d some guest rooms; the remainder are in cottages scattered throughout
e property and hidden in the redwood forests. Although all offer access
the sun deck, sauna, and hot tub, the simplest cottage has a woodstove
d an outdoor hot-water shower; the most luxurious has a fireplace, full
th, and wet bar.

The restaurant is extremely popular; make a reservation when you
ok your accommodations. The menu changes seasonally and offers a
de choice of entrées, from quail marinated in tequila and garlic, served
th green onion pancakes; to beef filet with mustard and green pepper-
rns; to a vegetable tart of corn, mushrooms, and peppers accented with
smoked tomato sauce. Irresistible desserts include bread pudding with
n-dried cherries, currants, and almonds and huckleberry tart with creme
glaise.

"Fantastic three-story onion-domed dining room. Rooms are on the
all side but comfortably appointed, with hand-crafted wood walls and
cally handmade comforters." *(SC)* "Our cabin overlooked the fern can-
n and a majestic redwood forest. A breakfast of fresh fruit and orange
ce, granola, scrambled eggs, and a delicious apple crisp was delivered
our door." *(Pam & Bob Hamilton, also Mark Mendenhall)* "Request a
bin a bit farther away from the restaurant—the quiet setting is well
rth the short walk. Go hiking after noon, when the fog burns off, and
rk up an appetite for the superb cuisine." *(Ron & Betsy Kahan)* "Sequoia
ttage has wood-trimmed walls and ceiling, a sunken sitting area with
eplace, a raised sleeping alcove with a skylight, and a luxuriously tiled

bathroom with a deep small tub and many windows." *(LG, also Leis* *Robinson)* Reports welcome.

Open All year.
Rooms 8 doubles sharing 3 baths; 11 cottages with private bath and/or showe
8 cottages with fireplace or woodstove, deck; 10 with wet bar or refrigerator.
Facilities Lobby, restaurant, wine bar, solarium. 42 acres with sauna, sun dec
massage room, hot tub (available for some cottages only), path to beach. Go
tennis nearby.
Location 2 m N of Gualala, on Hwy. 1.
Restrictions Kitchen noise could disturb light sleepers in hotel. No smoking
dining room. 2 cottages suitable for families. No children under 6 in dining roo
at dinner.
Credit cards None accepted in dining room; MC, Visa for lodging.
Rates B&B, $75–180 cottages, $50–65 doubles. Extra person, $15. 2-night wee
end minimum. Prix fixe dinner, $28.
Extras Local airport pickup.

Whale Watch Inn
35100 Highway 1, 95445

Tel: 707–884–366
800–WHALE–4

One of the area's most elegant—and expensive—inns, Whale Watch
located on the water side of the highway, and is composed of fiv
contemporary wooden buildings containing the luxurious guest room
most with spectacular ocean views. A full breakfast is delivered to you
room or served in the common room. Wine and cheese are served a
Saturday night socials with live classical and flamenco guitar perfo
mances. "A marvelous, romantic place on a bluff overlooking the Pacifi
The Silver Mist Room is a beautiful split-level room with a private dec
and a whirlpool tub positioned to see both the fireplace and the ocean
Lovely flower gardens and a scenic wooden staircase that winds down th
cliff to the ocean." *(Tom Wilbanks)* "Elegant lobby where you are we
comed with a glass of wine or locally made apple juice. Though my roo
was one of the less expensive ones, it lacked for nothing. It was adjacer
to the large living room with a panoramic ocean view. Our breakfa
consisted of fresh fruit, coffee, bagels, and a delicious omelet." *(AR)* "O
two-couple party stayed in Cliff Side and Morning Light; though th
smallest, they were closest to the ocean and we enjoyed (almost privately
the adjacent living room with a fireplace. We were amazed with th
ingenuity with which the designers incorporated the views into ever
room." *(Lee Todd)*

Open All year.
Rooms 6 suites, 12 doubles—all with private bath and/or shower, deck. Mo
with fireplace, some with double whirlpool tub, refrigerator. Rooms in 5 separat
buildings.
Facilities Lobby, living room with fireplace, telescope. Off-street parking, ga
dens, lawns, private beach, whale watching, .
Location Anchor Bay, 5 mi. N of Gualula on Hwy 1.
Restrictions No smoking.
Credit cards Amex, MC, Visa.

Rates B&B, $200–255 suite, $170–230 double. 2-3 night weekend/holiday mini-mum.

GUERNEVILLE

Guerneville is located in Sonoma County, 1½ hours north of San Fran-cisco. From Highway 101 go north to Guerneville/River Road exit, then go west to town.

Applewood—An Estate Inn ✕ &.   *Tel: 707–869–9093*
13555 Highway 116, Pocket Canyon 95446

Built in Guerneville's glory days in the 1920s, Applewood was bought by Darryl Notter and Jim Caron in 1985 and transformed into an elegant, yet comfortable inn. Before a roaring fire in the river-rock fireplace, guests sink into the down-filled cushions of the living room chairs and couches, or gather in the verdant solarium. Served from 9–10 A.M., a typical breakfast might include Grand Marnier French toast with strawberries, bacon or sausages, orange juice and dark French roast coffee. Dinners are just as special—tomato bisque, pear and Roquefort tarts with caramelized on-ions; lamb with mint pesto, carrot and potato gratin, and asparagus with lemon tarragon sauce; and white chocolate buttercream cake.

"Careful attention to detail: roses in our room, fine chocolates at night, newspaper at our breakfast table." *(Pam & Steve Levine)* "After an early dip in the swimming pool, Jim brought us Mimosas, coffee, and the morning paper. Terrific breakfasts of eggs Florentine, local berries, and fresh-baked bread. Wonderful dinners, especially the baked salmon with tomato and basil beurre blanc, and a strawberry cream cake with brandy sabayon." *(Melissa Hultgruen)* "Wonderful setting among the redwoods, perched on a hill; well maintained grounds. The inn is immaculate, and service is friendly, efficient and professional. The atmosphere is quiet and private." *(H. Leon Anderson)* Comments welcome.

Open All year. Restaurant open Mon., Wed., Sat.
Rooms 16 doubles—all with private bath and/or shower, telephone, TV. Some with desk, private entrance, patio, or balcony. 6 rooms in new building with fireplace, Jacuzzi.
Facilities Dining room, living room with fireplace, library, solarium with fireplace, stereo, breakfast room. 6 acres with redwood groves, vineyard, heated swimming pool, hot tub. Tennis, golf, horseback riding nearby. Fishing, canoeing in Russian River nearby.
Location North Coast, Sonoma wine country. In town, turn left on Rte. 116 & continue to inn.
Restrictions No smoking. No children.
Credit cards Amex, Discover, MC, Visa.
Rates B&B, $125–225 double. 2–3-night weekend/holiday minimum. Prix fixe dinner, $30.
Extras Wheelchair access; rooms equipped for the disabled. Local airport pickup.

Ridenhour Ranch House ¢ &.   *Tel: 707–887–1033*
12850 River Road, 95446

The Ridenhour Ranch House Inn, purchased in 1989 by Fritz and Diane Rechberger, has been welcoming guests since 1980. Austrian-born Fritz is an award-winning chef; the evening menu includes an entrée of lamb, chicken, venison, fish, beef, or veal accompanied by appetizers, soup or salad, sorbet, dessert, and coffee.

"The inn is located in a 1906 farmhouse and its eclectic antiques maintain the feeling of country charm throughout. It is located on the Russian River, adjacent to the Korbel Winery. Our small room was well appointed and comfortable. Our hosts' attention to detail extended from the complimentary beverages to bedtime mints." *(Larry Schoeneman)* "The comfortable living room is both a great gathering place for guests and a cozy reading room as well. Outside a hot tub and lawn chairs are relaxing after a day of wine tasting." *(Ken & Joan Masegian)* "Fresh-baked cookies always available. Diane and Fritz are helpful and knowledgeable about area activities." *(Chester & Velda Jasper)* "Fritz's meals are elegantly presented and delicious." *(Joseph Rosen)* "The Spruce Room is warm and bright with a queen-size bed, antique furnishings and a private view of woods and garden through the large window." *(Ralph Ridley)*

Open All year.
Rooms 1 suite, 5 doubles, 2 cottages—all with private bath and/or shower. Some with TV, fireplace, deck, fan.
Facilities Dining room, living room with fireplace, piano; game room, guest kitchen. 2 acres, hot tub, rose garden, orchard, picnic area. 200 yards to Russian River, 25 min. to ocean.
Location Sonoma wine country, 3 m E of Guerneville. 12 m W of River Road exit, adjacent to Korbel Winery.
Restrictions Street noise in some rooms. No smoking. Prefer children over 10.
Credit cards MC, Visa.
Rates $130 cottage, $120 suite, $95–130 double. Extra person, $15. 15% service. 2-night weekend minimum. Prix fixe dinner, by arrangement, $35.
Extras Wheelchair access; 1 room equipped for disabled. Airport pickup. German spoken.

HALF MOON BAY

Less than an hour south of San Francisco, this 50-mile section of coast—from Half Moon Bay to Santa Cruz—is rarely visited by travelers rushing down to Monterey and Carmel. Towns here still retain much of their character as sleepy fishing villages, but people are beginning to discover the area's nine state beaches (horseback riding is allowed at some), elephant seals (at Año Nuevo), and whale-watching tours. Bicyclists will enjoy following the horse trail for miles along the bluffs to Moss Beach.

Half Moon Bay—called the Cape Cod of California by some—is located in the San Francisco Bay Area, 28 miles south of San Francisco. Take Highway 1 south, or Highway 280 to Highway 92 west to Half Moon Bay.

For additional area entries, see listings for **Seal Cove Inn** in **Moss Beach,** six miles north, the **Goose & Turrets** in **Montara,** eight miles north, and the **Rancho San Gregorio**, ten miles south.

Cypress Inn ♿.   *Tel:* 415–726–6002
407 Mirada Road, 94019   In CA: 800–83–BEACH
                                              Fax: 415–712–0380

Set right on Miramar Beach, each individually decorated room at the Cypress Inn (built in 1989) has a deck with ocean view. The California Spanish-style decor features Mexican tiled floors, counters and showers; wicker and scrubbed wood furnishings with wonderful colors; and whimsical Mexican carved animals and primitive paintings. Breakfast entrées include omelets with Brie and roasted red peppers, Belgian waffles, or peaches and cream French toast, accompanied by fresh fruit and homemade breads, plus afternoon tea, wine, and hors d'oeuvres.

"Situated right on the Pacific, with unparalleled ocean views. We stayed in La Luna, on the first floor, with a tiled floor (with cozy radiant heating). Shuttered walls of windows face the ocean, with a clever latch that allows one to leave the shuttered glass door open just a crack to let in the sound and smell of the ocean, while retaining security and temperature. The inn is more modern and less frilly that many we've visited, a distinction I appreciate." *(Randy Delucchi)* "The sound of sea and surf put you at ease the moment you arrive. The fireplace is perfect for foggy days. Each room is painted a soft warm color to go with its Spanish name. The living room has an open-beam ceiling and giant skylight. Clean, uncluttered, and quiet." *(Matt Joyce)* "Our favorite activity was taking long walks on the beach across the street." *(Marion Richardson)*

Open All year.
Rooms 1 suite, 7 doubles—all with private full bath, telephone, radio, desk, gas fireplace, deck. Some with whirlpool tub, TV; 1 with refrigerator.
Facilities Dining room, living room with fireplace, laundry, masseuse. Water sports, whale watching, horseback riding, golf, wine tasting nearby.
Location From Hwy. 1, turn right on Medio St. Go W to Mirado Rd. to inn on left on Miramar Beach.
Restrictions No smoking. Children under 12 by arrangement.
Credit cards Amex, MC, Visa.
Rates B&B, $275 suite, $150–185 double. Extra person, $20. Senior, AAA discount. 2-3 night weekend/holiday minimum. Picnics. Midweek, off-season rates.
Extras Wheelchair access; some bathrooms specially equipped.

Old Thyme Inn   *Tel:* 415–726–1616
779 Main Street, 94019

The Old Thyme Inn is a Queen Anne home built in 1899 of redwood and hauled to this location by oxen; in 1986, it was completely renovated as a B&B, and was purchased by George and Marcia Dempsey in 1992. A typical breakfast might include fresh-squeezed orange juice, fresh fruit, yogurt, and such baked treats as lemon-thyme pound cake, frittata, or croissants baked with cheese and turkey.

"The well-maintained rooms (each with a resident teddy bear) vary considerably in size, and a few have the bathtub in the bedroom. The smaller rooms are cozy in feeling and are an excellent value, while the larger rooms, each with a fireplace, hardwood floors, and antique armoire and dressing table are elegant and comfortable. All rooms have freshly cut flowers, sherry, and lace curtains." *(MJ)* "Comfortable beds with goose-down pillows." *(Jean & Sol Cohen)* "We were greeted warmly and assisted with dinner reservations. Sherry, wine, and snacks were served in the early evening. Delicious bagels, scones, crumpets, muffins at breakfast." *(James & Elizabeth Smith)* "The honeymoon suite is lovely, with a canopy bed and sitting area all done in soft rose and cream." *(Irene Kolbisen)* "George gave me a tour of his herb garden and gave me a few cuttings to take home. The beach, interesting shops, and good restaurants nearby." *(Ruth Moran)* "Tasty homemade buttermilk-raisin scones and strawberries." *(Robert Nguyen)*

Open All year.
Rooms 1 suite, 6 doubles—all with full private bath. 3 with whirlpool bath, fireplace, 1 with refrigerator, TV/VCR, tape deck.
Facilities Living/breakfast room; herb garden. Video library.
Location Inn is 6 blocks S of Hwy. 92, 4 blocks E of Hwy. 1. 1 m from ocean.
Restrictions No smoking.
Credit cards Amex, Discover, MC, Visa.
Rates B&B, $165–220 suite, $75–150 double. 2-night holiday weekend minimum.
Extras Well-behaved pets by arrangement. French spoken.

Zaballa House
324 Main Street, 94019

Tel: 415–726–9123

Renovated in 1990, the Zaballa House was built in 1859 and overlooks a flower-filled public garden. It's owned by David Cresson and is managed by innkeepers Simon Lowings and Kerry Pendergast. Rates include a full breakfast and evening refreshments.

"The oldest structure in town, decorated with period antiques, old photographs and paintings. The inn is clean, well-maintained, and nicely decorated with floral wallpapers and some antiques." *(Matt Joyce)* "Delicious breakfast, with an egg and salsa dish, muffins and breads, fresh fruit, coffee and tea. Our room had satin hangers in the closet and interesting reading material." *(Lisa Gallagher)* "We liked the convenient fireplace—a flick of a switch and it was lit—and the oversized whirlpool tub." *(Debbie Sorich)* "Nice touches in my room included stuffed animals, candy, and a good book to read. I was not bothered by traffic noise when I stayed in the front room upstairs. Parking was excellent in a well lit area and the house is within walking distance of the beach or downtown." *(Barbara Jones)*

Open All year.
Rooms 9 doubles—all with full private bath. 4 with gas fireplace, 3 with double whirlpool tub, some with clock, TV.
Facilities Dining room, living room with fireplace, books. 1 acre with off-street parking, flower garden. Golf, tennis, boating, fishing nearby.
Location 3 blocks E of Hwy 1 & 1 block S of Hwy. 92.
Restrictions No smoking. Prefer children over 6.
Credit cards Amex, Discover, MC, Visa.

ates B&B, $65–165 double, $60–150 single. Extra person, $10. 2-3 night week-
nd/holiday minimum.
xtras Pets by prior arrangement.

HEALDSBURG

Taking a break from the serious business of wine tasting, visitors to
Healdsburg enjoy swimming, fishing, boating, and canoeing in the Rus-
ian River and Lake Sonoma, plus hot air ballooning, hiking, bicycling,
ennis, and golf. Five wine tasting rooms are right in town, with 50 more
within an easy drive.

Located in the Sonoma Valley, along the Russian River Wine Road in
California's North Coast region, Healdsburg is 70 miles north of San
Francisco, and 13 miles north of Santa Rosa, on Highway 101.

Reader tip: "We enjoyed dinner at Jacob Horner's and Tre Scalini."
(DCB) "Ravenous is an extraordinary local restaurant—eight tables, no
reservations, great food, low prices." (Phyllis Baldenhofer)

Camellia Inn ¢ ♿	Tel: 707–433–8182
211 North Street, 95448	800–727–8182
	Fax: 707–433–8180

Ray and Del Lewand opened this B&B in 1981 after a careful restoration
of their 1869 Italianate Victorian home. Antiques and Oriental rugs and
complemented by soft shades of salmon and peach to create a warm and
soothing atmosphere. The Lewands also own an inn in Puerto Vallarta,
Mexico; in the winter, you may find them there, while their daughter Lucy
hosts guests in California.

"The Royalty Room had a huge, comfortable maple tester bed from a
castle in Scotland. The ample breakfast was a group affair around a huge
table, a good time to plan your day." (Caroline & Jim Lloyd) "Our room
was wonderfully decorated with a brass bed, antique lamps and fixtures,
fresh flowers, and a bathroom which was once a sunporch. Breakfasts
include homemade jams and preserves, excellent breads, fresh fruit, yogurt, granola, cereals, juice, and a main dish, such as quiche or huevos
rancheros. Complimentary beverages, cheese, and crackers are served in
the early evening at the pool; the Lewands really know how to bring
people together for informal conversation." (Maria Castrulla) "Quiet
neighborhood, with colorful grounds. Our hosts were friendly, helpful,
and knowledgeable about the wine industry." (Ruth & Joe Cochrane) "The
inn is within walking distance of six or seven wine tasting rooms—no
need to be concerned about designating drivers." (DCB) "The pool is a
real plus on a 95° August day." (Brooke Abercrombie) Comments welcome.

Open All year.
Rooms 9 doubles—all with private bath and/or shower. Some with gas fireplace,
whirlpool tub for 2, ceiling fan, private entrance.
Facilities Double parlor with 2 fireplaces, books, games; dining room. ½ acre
with 50 varieties of camellias, swimming pool. Off-street parking.
Location 2 blocks from main plaza. Exit Hwy. 101N at central Healdsburg exit.

Go N 3 lights, turn right on North St. Go 2½ blocks to inn on left; parking rear.
Restrictions No smoking. Infants and children over 10 preferred.
Credit cards Amex, MC, Visa.
Rates B&B, $70–135 double. 2-night weekend/holiday minimum.
Extras Public rooms have wheelchair access; 1 guest room equipped for disable

George Alexander House	*Tel:* 707–433–13
423 Matheson Street, 95448	800–310–13
	Fax: 707–433–13

Readers are always delighted to discover a smaller B&B like the Geor Alexander House, owned by Phyllis and Christian Baldenhofer, that offe high-quality accommodations with the personal touch found only at owner-operated inn. This exuberantly ornamented 1904 Victorian hon which was built for the son of the area's first settler, has been furnishe with antiques and custom-made furniture, accented by stained glass an quatre foil windows. Phyllis and Christian bought the inn in 1991, an describe themselves as "San Francisco expatriates, with past experience the coffee roasting business." Guests report that the inn's best featur include the interesting collections of art and Oriental rugs, the comfo able beds, the tasty breakfasts and quality coffee (including espresso), t relaxing atmosphere, and the convenient location. "Our room, the Ba Porch, had a private entrance, a large sitting area, a wood-burning stov a wonderful bathroom with a double Jacuzzi, and a ceramic tile floor wi radiant heating. Delicious breakfast, convenient refrigerator stocked wi snacks, convenient location just a short walk from the town square *(Randy Delucchi)* "Just the right classical music in the background, plen of books on the shelves and comfortable places to sit. The surroundi gardens are well tended with many interesting plants." *(Steve & Juel Cra* "Mature shade trees provide a country feel to this quiet residential neig borhood. Phyllis and Chris are wonderful hosts, good cooks and know t best wineries and restaurants to visit." *(John Tugwell)*

Open All year.
Rooms 4 doubles—all with private bath and/or shower, air-conditioning. 2 wi fireplace/wood-burning stove, 1 with Jacuzzi, deck.
Facilities 2 parlors (1 with fireplace), dining room, music library, guest refrigera tor, porch. Laundry privileges. Off-street parking, patio, gardens. Off-street pa ing. Near Russian River for water sports.
Location 3 blocks from town center. From Healdsburg Ave. drive 3 blocks ea on Matheson to inn on left.
Restrictions No smoking.
Credit cards MC, Visa.
Rates B&B, $80–150 double, $70–140 single. Extra person, $25. No tippir Babies free. 2-night weekend/holiday minimum in two rooms.
Extras Local airport/station pickup. Crib; babysitting by arrangement.

Grape Leaf Inn	*Tel:* 707–433–81
539 Johnson Street, 95448	

A Queen Anne Victorian home built in 1900, the Grape Leaf Inn has bee owned since 1981 by Karen and Terry Sweet. Named after differe arieties of grapes, guest rooms are furnished with period antiques; those on the first floor have high ceilings and old-fashioned charm; those on the second are tucked under the eaves with skylight roof windows. Each evening, the Sweets hold a wine-tasting from 5–7 P.M., with a minimum of six wines, plus cheese and crackers. Breakfasts include vegetable and cheese frittatas, blueberry-pecan pancakes, or cinnamon raisin-walnut French toast, plus home-baked breads and muffins, with fresh fruit.

"The Sweets treat their guests like good friends. Wonderful selection of afternoon wines; beautifully maintained; scrumptious homemade breakfast. We especially appreciated the Gamay Rose room because of its comfy king-size bed." (CG)

Open All year.
Rooms 1 suite, 6 doubles—all with private bath and/or shower, air-conditioning. with double whirlpool tub.
Facilities Dining room, living room with fireplace, parlor, porch. Shaded lot with seating, off-street parking.
Location 4 blocks from town square. From Hwy. 101 N, take 'Central Healdsburg' exit. Go ³⁄₄ m to Grant St., turn right. Go 2 blocks to inn on right.
Restrictions No smoking. Children over 10.
Credit cards Discover, MC, Visa.
Rates B&B, $145 suite, $90–130 double, $60–95 single. Extra person, $35. 10% weekly discount in winter. 2-night minimum some weekends.

Healdsburg Inn on the Plaza & Tel: 707–433–6991
110/116 Matheson Street, P.O. Box 1196, 95448

Set in a turn-of-the-century structure, originally housing doctors, dentists, and a Wells Fargo office, the Healdsburg Inn has been owned by Genny Jenkins since 1981. Rates include a full breakfast served at 9 A.M. (continental breakfast available at 7:30 on weekdays), round-the-clock coffee and a never-empty cookie jar, afternoon snacks, popcorn, wine, and evening dessert buffet.

"Overlooking the plaza, a small park with trees, grass, and somnolent locals. The entrance to the inn is a storefront, with art and craft exhibits for sale around the reception area. All but one of its guest rooms are on the second floor, reached by an impressive staircase. Breakfast was excellent—orange juice and champagne, croissants, muffins, toast, fruit and a wonderful quiche. Staff were pleasant and helpful." (Hugh & Marjorie Smith) "Decorated in pastel Victorian style, the guest rooms have comfortable queen-size beds and ample seating. The bathrooms have large clawfoot tubs, showers, fluffy towels, lovely soaps and lotions, and whimsical rubber ducks. The main hall has comfortable seating for reading and jigsaw puzzle working. Genny and her friendly staff provide helpful information and amusing conversation." (Alan & Irma Judkins)

Open All year.
Rooms 9 doubles—all with private bath and/or shower, telephone, TV, air-conditioning. Some with fireplace.
Facilities Lounge with games, books, TV/VCR; solarium breakfast room with roof garden; lobby with art gallery, gift shop. Off-street parking ¹⁄₂ block away. m to Russian River.
Location Center of old town.

Restrictions Smoking on roof garden only. Children by arrangement. "T ground-floor guest room has little natural light."
Credit cards MC, Visa.
Rates B&B, $135–160 double. Extra person, $35. Off-season rates in early De Jan. 2-night holiday weekend minimum. Senior, AAA, off-season, midweek, corp rate rates. Discount for extended stays.
Extras 1 room wheelchair accessible.

Madrona Manor ✕ ᴦ   *Tel:* 707–433–42.
1001 Westside Road, P.O. Box 818, 95448   800–258–40(
                                          Fax: 707–433–07(

Originally built in the 1880s as a summer home by a wealthy S. Francisco businessman, Madrona Manor sits on a high knoll overloo ing the town of Healdsburg and nearby vineyards. In 1983 it w bought by John and Carol Muir, who have turned it into an elega country hotel. Most of the space on the first floor of the main buildi is devoted to dining rooms, although the front parlor has a five-pie Victorian suite with carved griffin arms. Guest rooms in the ma house are very large, and those on the first and second floors ha furnishings original to the house; those in the Carriage House are lu uriously furnished with more modern decor. Todd Muir is the exec tive chef, and a recent winter dinner included Dungeness crab mous with lobster sauce, acorn squash soup, rack of lamb with honey glaze root vegetables, and apple cheese roulade. The Manor is a busy pla in season, and reservations are essential for both the rooms and resta rant, especially on weekends.

"Through the French doors on either side of the 10-foot-high carve headboard in our bedroom was a terrace from which we could see acro the valley to the mountains." *(Virginia Severs)* "The buffet breakfast i cluded a variety of meats and cheeses, soft-boiled eggs, yogurts, grano melon, breads, rolls and several homemade preserves. We stayed or night in the best room in the mansion with a 12-foot headboard and pa green walls, and the second in a suite (#400) in the Carriage House, ar thoroughly enjoyed both." *(Rick & Cyndy Gould)* "We stayed at a nearl B&B, but were delighted with our elegant dinner." *(MW)* Commen welcome.

Open All year.
Rooms 3 suites, 15 doubles—all with full private bath, telephone, radio, des air-conditioning, fan. 18 rooms with gas fireplace, 5 with balcony. 9 rooms in ma house, 9 in Carriage House, 3 in 2 cottages.
Facilities 3 dining rooms, music room, lobby, terrace. 8 acres with garde orchard, walking trails, swimming pool. Golf, tennis, swimming, canoeing, hors back riding nearby.
Location ³⁄₄ m from town. From Central Healdsburg exit of Hwy. 101, go le on Mill St., which becomes Westside Rd.
Restrictions Occasional traffic noise midweek. No smoking.
Credit cards Amex, DC, MC, Visa.
Rates B&B, $200–225 suite, $135–185 double. Extra person, $30. 5-course pr fixe dinner, $50; alc dinner, 35–45. Sunday brunch, $15. Service additional.
Extras Wheelchair access. Local airport pickup, $25. Pets permitted by pri arrangement. Crib, babysitting. Spanish spoken.

HOPE VALLEY

Sorensen's Resort 👤 🍴
14255 Highway 88, 96120

Tel: 800–423–9949

Dating back to 1906, Sorensen's Resort was opened as an inn in 1982 by John and Patty Brissenden. The restaurant serves three meals daily, with such dinner entrées as veal Marsala, snapper with lemon and capers, and artichoke pasta.

"The Chapel cabin was originally built for Santa's Village, near Santa Cruz. When the village was torn down, Sorensen's had the opportunity to acquire several buildings, which were then rebuilt—log by log—at Sorensen's. The Chapel is delightful, with a high vaulted log ceiling with a double glazed clerestory window giving lots of space and light. The cozy loft bedroom is reached by a spiral staircase. Added pluses are the warm hospitality of John and Patty Brissenden, the hearty food at the café, plus beautiful surroundings and great skiing at Kirkwood." *(Craig Fusaro)* "The brook trickling by the front door of our cabin, Rock Creek, provided a calming lullaby each night." *(Barbara Gault)* "Friendly, smiling staff and management. Excellent meals, quality wines, and homemade desserts served in the cozy atmosphere of the dining room, with a fireplace and soft, live music in the background." *(Kay Danielson)*

Open All year. Closed Christmas Day.
Rooms 26 cabins, 3 doubles—27 with private bath and/or shower, 2 with maximum of 4 people sharing bath. Most with kitchen, porch. 18 with fireplace/woodstove. 1 with double Jacuzzi tub.
Facilities Restaurant, library, porch. 165 acres with fishing pond & stream, swimming holes, swings, gazebo, hiking; cross-country ski center with rentals, tours, instruction. 14 m to downhill skiing at Kirkwood. Tennis, golf nearby.
Location Sierra Nevada, 20 m S of Lake Tahoe. 26 m W of Genoa, NV.
Restrictions Traffic noise in some rooms. No smoking; $250 fine.
Credit cards Amex, MC, Visa.
Rates Room only, $55–300 cabin. B&B, $60–125 double. Extra person, $15–20. Tipping encouraged. No charge for children under 7. 2-4 night weekend/holiday minimum for advance reservations. Sleeping bags in dorm accommodations. Alc breakfast, $6; lunch, $6; alc dinner, $20. Mid-week Kirkwood ski packages.
Extras 1 cabin wheelchair accessible; bathroom specially equipped. Pets in 3 cabins with approval. Cribs, babysitting by arrangement. Spanish, French spoken.

IDYLLWILD

Set at an elevation of 5,500 feet, Idyllwild is a quiet resort village in the San Jacinto Mountains. Surrounded by thousands of acres of national forest, it's an ideal spot for fishing, hiking, and horseback riding. It's also the base of the Idyllwild School of Music and the Arts, which sponsors musical theater productions through the summer.

Located at the edge of Desert Country, Idyllwild is approximately one hour west of Palm Springs and two hours east of Los Angeles. From I-10, go south on Route 243 to Idyllwild. From Hemet or Palm Desert, take Route 74 to Mountain Center and go north on Route 243 to Idyllwild.

CALIFORNIA

Information please: Located in a secluded mountain setting, the Cedar Street Inn (25880 Cedar Street; P.O. Box 627, 92549; 909–659–4789) has been owned by Gary and Patty Tompkins since 1989, and is decorated with antiques and collectibles. Each guest room has a different country Victorian decor and all have queen-sized beds and setups for morning coffee and tea.

Reader tip: "This mountain retreat just east of San Bernardino makes a great stop between Los Angeles and Las Vegas, or is an alternative to Palm Springs. It's quiet, full of pines, and excellent for hiking. The town also has three or four good restaurants." *(Lon Bailey)*

Strawberry Creek Inn ♿   *Tel:* 909–659–3202
26370 Highway 243, P.O. Box 1818, 92549   800–262–8969

Set beside the stream that is its namesake, the Strawberry Creek Inn offers a quiet country retreat. Owned and run by Jim Goff and Diana Dugan, this rambling shingled home is decorated with antiques and handmade quilts.

"It was pleasant to sit in the parlor and read from the enormous library, ranging from current magazines to the classics. Great location, just a short walk along Strawberry Creek to town." *(Chris & Teresa Mackey)* "The relaxing outdoor areas include the patio and the secluded lawn swing under the pines." *(Daniel Martinez)* "The inn sits back from the road in a serene setting. A delicious breakfast was served in the sun room. The innkeepers visited each table to make sure everyone was well taken care of. They helped explain the best locations for hiking and exploring the area." *(Roberto & Linda Pagan)* "Jim and Diana are justly proud of their lovely antiques, handmade quilts, and spotless accommodations." *(Ken & Kim Williams)* "The tall pines give a wonderful scent to the air. The inn's living room is filled with sunlight on cool mornings, and is one I'd like to have in my own home." *(William MacGowan)*

Open All year.
Rooms 1 cottage, 9 doubles—all with private bath and/or shower, fan. Some with refrigerator, fireplace. Cottage with double whirlpool tub, fireplace, TV/VCR, kitchen. 6 rooms in annex.
Facilities Dining room, living room, library, music alcove with piano, guitar, stereo; decks. ½ acre with flower garden, creek for fishing. Cross-country skiing nearby.
Location From Hwy. 243 N go past South Circle Drive. Look for inn on right.
Restrictions No smoking. Street noise may disturb light sleepers.
Credit cards MC, Visa
Rates B&B, $135 cottage, $85–105 double. 2–4-night weekend/holiday minimum.
Extras Wheelchair access.

INVERNESS

Although Point Reyes almost became as developed as the rest of Marin County, it was saved by the environmental movement in the 1970s and was declared a National Seashore. Only an hour northwest of San Francisco, the area offers magnificent beaches, hiking trails in the forests, and

Inverness Ridge with abundant wildlife including deer, fox, rabbits, and birds.

Inverness is located in the southernmost part of the North Coast area, in west Marin County. Visitors frequently make Inverness their base for explorations of the Point Reyes National Seashore.

Reader tips: "Point Reyes is far more interesting and attractive than the stuffy, congested Wine Country, a two-hour drive." *(Adam Platt)* "Marin County is convenient but pricy; $110 is about the *least* you'll pay for a small double room with private bath and full breakfast." *(MD)* "About six miles from Inverness, in Point Reyes, is the Station House Café, a wonderful culinary experience." *(Bob Freidus)*

Also recommended: Just north of Point Reyes National Seashore and overlooking the bay, is the **Inn at the Tides** (800 Coast Highway 1, P.O. Box 640, Bodega Bay 94923; 707–875–2751 or 800–541–7788), composed of weathered shingled lodges, each housing several units, most with a view. The 86 guest rooms are decorated with contemporary decor and soft pastel colors, and each has a sitting area with queen-size sofa hide-a-bed. The inn's Bayview Restaurant serves Sonoma-style country cuisine, with fruits and vegetables from local farms, wines from Sonoma's best vineyards, and fish from Bodega boats. "Our immaculate room had a spectacular view. Beautifully maintained grounds. Breakfast overlooking the bay was delightful." *(Pat Malone)* Facilities include a heated indoor/outdoor swimming pool, sauna, and hot tub; B&B double rates are $120–190, and children under 12 stay free; golf, off-season packages available.

Information please: The **Holly Tree Inn** (3 Silver Hills Road, Inverness; mailing address: Box 642, Point Reyes Station, 94956; 415–663–1554), set amongst the trees, offers hospitality, firm beds, and a relaxing, quiet environment. The accommodations include a one-bedroom cottage with a fireside living room, and solarium set on pilings out in Tomales Bay. "Cozy, casual, comfortable. Friendly owners cooked a terrific breakfast. Lots of tasty snacks set out for guests." *(Diana Chang)* B&B rates for the six rooms range from $100–175.

Established in 1906, the **Hotel Inverness** (P.O. Box 780, Inverness 94937; 415–669–7393) is a shingle-style hotel on park-like grounds, within the historic section of Inverness. Guest rooms have queen-sized beds and private baths; the B&B double rates of $100–140 include a continental breakfast. A turn-of-the-century hunting lodge, **Manka's Inverness Lodge** (P.O. Box 1110, 94937; 415–669–1034) is family owned, offering "honest beds and phenomenal foods," according to owner Margaret Gradé. The acclaimed restaurant offers such entrées as duck with shiitake mushrooms and plum chutney, tuna with sauteed spinach and tomato aoli, and elk with sweet potato pancakes. B&B rates range from $65–160; two cabins with fireplace are available, while two guest rooms have decks with distant views of Tamale Bay.

For additional area entries, see **Olema.**

Ten Inverness Way
10 Inverness Way, 94937

Tel: 415–669–1648

Innkeeper Mary Davies writes that "guests come to enjoy the three nearby parks—seashore, bay, and redwoods—and gather around the

stone fireplace in the evenings to talk, read, or play the piano and guitar
The inn was built in 1904 and is decorated with comfortable antique
guest rooms are simply furnished with pastel-painted walls and quil
topped beds; some are quite small.

"We loved the woodsy seclusion. Guest rooms are furnished wi
beautiful quilts, hand-carved furniture, first-class linens and good toiletrie
Our room had a high window running the length of the room with a vie
of the back gardens. Breakfast was a hot croque monsieur sandwich wi
white sauce, fresh fruit, juice and coffee." *(Diane Schwemm)*

"I was welcomed with tea and delicious home-baked cookies. Th
living room was exceptionally homey and warm, with a beautiful stor
fireplace, Oriental rugs, a piano, plump sofas, and brass reading lamps. Th
guest rooms have excellent lighting and a variety of magazines. Super
breakfast of banana buttermilk buckwheat pancakes and chicken app
sausages." *(Linda Goldberg)* "Mary Davies took a personal interest in o
enjoyment, and make recommendations tailored to our interests." *(Gle
Roehrig)* "They mapped out excellent paths for us to hike, along ocea
shores teeming with wildlife." *(Heide Bredfeldt)*

Open All year.
Rooms 1 suite, 4 doubles—all with private bath and/or shower, clock/radi
fan/heater. Suite with sunroom, kitchen, private garden.
Facilities Sun-room with wood stove, living room with fireplace, piano, librar
1/4 acre with garden, hot tub.
Location From Olema, go N on Hwy. 1. Turn left for the National Seasho
Visitor's Center. Go 3 m to stop sign, turn left & continue into Inverness. Turn le
at Inverness Inn onto Inverness Way; inn is immediately on right.
Restrictions No smoking. Extremely small closets in most rooms.
Credit cards MC, Visa.
Rates B&B, $110–160 double, $100–150 single. Extra person, $15, 2-night wee
end minimum. 20% midweek discount to nurses, Nov.–May except holiday pe
ods.
Extras A little French spoken.

IONE

The Heirloom ¢ &.   *Tel: 209–274–44(*
214 Shakeley Lane, P.O. Box 322, 95640

One of the earliest settlers of the Gold Country built the Heirloom in t
1850s; Melisande Hubbs and Patricia Cross are its long-time owners. Th
inn's good-size rooms are furnished with antiques and quilts, includi
many family heirlooms. A typical breakfast might include fresh
squeezed orange juice, pears with raspberry sauce, apricot coffee cak
popovers, and spinach soufflé.

"Secluded charm, beautiful rose gardens. The friendly owners will dire
you to excellent local wineries, impressive underground caves, melodran
theater, antique stores galore, and beautiful outdoor recreational areas
(Jennifer & Jerry Wilhelm) "Breakfast is served in the dining room by th
fire, in the yard by the gazebo, on the upstairs veranda, or in bed—as y

wish." *(Mr. & Mrs. Robert Andrews)* "The cottage has adobe walls and a sod roof. Comfortable chairs, good lighting, and plenty of reading material made for a pleasant evening. The bath had a large tiled shower, a stained glass window and plenty of thick towels." *(Mary Moses)*

"A cool glass of lemonade awaits you on a warm summer afternoon or a glass of wine by the living room fire on a cold fall day. Tasty hors d'oeuvres tempt guests before dinner. Sandy and Pat stay current on local restaurants and have never steered us wrong; advance dinner reservations are made with pleasure. Breakfast are delicious, and carefully planned to avoid repeats for returning guests. Incredible Christmas decorations." *(Bob & Kim Stetson)*

Open All year. Closed Thanksgiving, Dec. 24, 25.
Rooms 6 doubles—4 with private bath and/or shower, 2 with maximum of 4 sharing bath. All with desk, fan; some with fireplace, balcony; 5 with air-conditioning. 2 rooms in cottage, each with woodstove.
Facilities Living room with fireplace, piano; dining room with fireplace. Verandas. 1½ acres with swings, hammocks, croquet, bicycles. Walking distance to golf course; tennis nearby. Lakes, rivers nearby for boating, fishing, swimming.
Location Gold Country. 45 min. SE of Sacramento. Ione is at the intersection of Rtes. 104 & 124.
Restrictions No smoking. No children under 10.
Credit cards Amex, MC, Visa.
Rates B&B, $74–92 suite; $60–92 double; $55–87 single. Extra person, $15. 2-night holiday, weekend minimum.
Extras Limited wheelchair access. Airport pickup. Portuguese spoken.

JACKSON

Jackson is located in Amador County, in the Gold Country; it's about one hour southeast of Sacramento via Route 16. Jackson Gate Road is a largely residential road, running roughly parallel with Highway 49 from Jackson partway to Sutter Creek.

Also recommended: Vic and Jeanne Beltz are warm hosts at **The Wedgewood Inn** (11941 Narcissus Road, Jackson, 95642; 209–296–4300 or 800–933–4393). "Delicious breakfast, careful attention to detail, hospitable innkeepers, peaceful setting with gazebo and rose arbor." *(Paula Beaumont)* The house, built in 1987 to replicate a Victorian farmhouse, is lavishly furnished in period with family heirlooms, antiques, and collectibles. Each guest room has a private bath (some with clawfoot tub); the $85–125 rates include a breakfast of fruit, juice, hot entrée, breads, and coffee.

JAMESTOWN

Founded as a mining camp during the 1848 gold rush, Jamestown looks much like a Western movie set—or should that be the other way around? That the town keeps this atmosphere owes much to the fact that it's bypassed by Highway 49—the main north/south route. Appealing shops invite you to browse, and crossing the street is not a life-endangering experience. Unlike the original miners, today's residents extract their gold quite painlessly from travelers who come to enjoy Jamestown's history and picturesque setting. **Information please:** We need current reports on the **National Hotel** (Main Street, P.O. Box 502, 95327; 209–984–3446), built in 1859, one of the oldest continuously operating hotels in California. Guest rooms are simply but attractively furnished with antique brass beds (with queen-size mattresses). Breakfast includes homemade breads, hard-boiled eggs, fresh fruit and juice, and the morning paper. The hotel restaurant is popular with locals and tourists alike, and dinners have an Italian accent, with fresh pasta and veal specialties. The saloon has a handsome redwood bar original to the hotel, while the grape-arbored patio is pleasant in warm weather. B&B double rates for the 11 guest rooms range from $65–80.

JULIAN

Julian Gold Rush Hotel ¢   *Tel:* 619–765–0201
2032 Main Street, P.O. Box 1856, 92036   In CA: 800–734–5854

Julian is an old mining town; gold was discovered here in 1868. In the 1880s Albert and Margaret Robinson, two freed slaves from Georgia, arrived and started a restaurant. Their reputation for good food grew, and in 1897 they decided to build a hotel. The Julian is now Southern California's oldest continuously operating hotel and is listed on the National Register of Historic Places. In 1976 it was purchased by Steve and Gig Ballinger, who furnished the rooms with authentic antiques and period wallpapers. Breakfast includes eggs, breads, fresh fruit and juices, and granola.

"Old-fashioned, charming rooms; good food; accommodating, courteous, and down-to-earth staff. They are knowledgeable about the town and glad to make reservations and inquire about schedules." *(Jock Crook)* "Rooms are small but comfortable, bathroom facilities adequate, and everything is immaculate." *(David & Ruth Davis)* "As is typical of the hotels of that period, rooms are on the small side, and the walls rather thin." *(MB)* "We stayed in the 'Honeymoon Cottage,' cozy and quaint with fireplace and clawfoot tub. Hospitable staff." *(Robert & Barbara Pavick)* "Clean and safe, delicious breakfast." *(Alice Chandler)*

Open All year.
Rooms 2 cottages (1 with fireplace), 12 doubles, 1 single—5 with private bath and/or shower, 13 with maximum of 6´sharing bath.
Facilities Lobby, parlor, dining room, deck, patios. Fishing, boating, cross-country skiing nearby.
Location San Diego County. 60 m NE of San Diego, at intersection of Hwys. 78 & 79.
Credit cards Amex, MC, Visa
Rates B&B, $95–145 cottage, $64–94 double, $38 single. 2-night weekend minimum. 15% senior discount midweek.

KERNVILLE

Kern River Inn ¢   *Tel: 619–376–6750*
119 Kern River Drive, P.O. Box 1725, 93238

The area around Kernville and the Kern River is rugged territory, bordered by Sequoia National Forest and the foothills of the Sierra Nevada Mountains. Mike Meehan and Marti Andrews, a husband and wife team, built the Kern River Inn in 1991, patterning it after a Victorian ranch house. Marti reports that "the area provides year-round activities from fishing in the river right in front of the inn, to panning for gold, to spending some gold in local antique shops. The high country and the giant redwoods are just a short drive." Guest rooms are accented with paintings and curios from local artists; some have handsome river rock fireplaces. Tea, crackers and cheese are served in the afternoon, and breakfast includes homemade granola and yogurt, stuffed French toast or waffles with fruit toppings, fruits and juices, freshly brewed coffee and a variety of teas.

"Delicious giant cinnamon rolls and fresh fruit bowl. Coffee and tea were always available in the country kitchen." *(Mr.& Mrs. C.F. Avery)* "Our friendly hosts were helpful with suggestions for dining and area activities." *(TA)* "They leave a selection of drinks in the fridge for those who might want something before bed. Our room was spotless, attractive, and cheerful with the morning sun pouring through the windows. Terrific half-way stop between Death Valley and the San Francisco area." *(Kathleen Lowe Owen)*

Open All year.
Rooms 6 doubles—all with full private bath, radio, air-conditioning. 3 with fireplace, 2 with whirlpool tub.
Facilities Dining room, living room with fireplace, stereo, TV/VCR, books, games. Flower garden, off-street parking. On Kern River for whitewater rafting, kayaking. Hiking, bicycling, golf, fishing nearby; 14 m to downhill, cross-country skiing.
Location Central Valley/S Sierra Nevada. 50 m NE of Bakersfield, in S section of Sequoia National Forest. From Bakersfield, take Rte. 178 E. to Rte. 155 N to Burland Rd. to Kernville. Turn right past golf course, onto Kern River Drive to inn on left. Walking distance to restaurants, shops, museum.
Restrictions No smoking.
Credit cards MC, Visa.
Rates B&B, $69–89 double, $59–79 single. Extra person, $15. 2-night weekend minimum April 1–Oct. 31.
Extras Wheelchair access; 1 room equipped for disabled. Local airport pickup.

LAGUNA BEACH

Laguna became popular as a resort at the turn of the century and was established as an art colony in the 1930s. It provides both beautiful

125

beaches and year-round sun, but life here isn't entirely without pressure—there are parking meters by the tennis courts to indicate remaining court time. Laguna offers theater and ballet as well as a number of arts and crafts festivals and plenty of shops. Of course, water sports, from surfing to scuba diving, are very popular.

Laguna Beach is located on the Orange County coast 11 miles south of Newport Beach, about 38 miles south of Los Angeles and about 60 miles north of San Diego on Coast Highway 1. From Los Angeles take Route 5 south to Irvine and then west on Route 133 to the coast. From San Diego, take Route 5 north to Capistrano Beach and continue north about 8 miles on Coast Highway 1.

Reader tip: "We like the Beach House for brunch, and Romeo's for lunch or dinner." *(MP)*

Information please: For lovely ocean views, try the **Casa Laguna Inn** (2510 South Pacific Coast Highway, 92651; 714–494–2996 or 800–233–0449), built in the 1930s in a combination of California mission and Spanish revival style, with rooms decorated with both antique and contemporary furnishings. The grounds are charmingly landscaped with plants, fountains, even a swimming pool and an aviary. Light sleepers should be sure to ask for a quiet room, since traffic on the PCH is heavy.

The Carriage House
1322 Catalina Street, 92651

Tel: 714–494–8945

One of Laguna's designated landmarks, the Carriage House has been owned by the Taylor family since 1981. The inn forms a "U" around a flower-filled courtyard with fountain; rooms are charming, spacious, and decorated with many antiques, as are the living and dining rooms. Each suite has an adequate kitchen and separate living area, making this inn a fine choice for families or longer stays. The inn is conveniently located within walking distance of town, in a quiet residential section.

"The house has an old New Orleans look about it with courtyard gardens, fountain and wrought iron. Our room was done in white wicker with palm fronds wallpaper. Breakfast was served family style with the other guests." *(Debbie Bergstrom)* "We were warmly welcomed with fruit and wine; the innkeepers were helpful with directions and area information. Good housekeeping and fresh flowers in our room. Ample parking and easy beach access." *(Elizabeth Twigg)*

Open All year.
Rooms 6 1- and 2-bedroom suites—all with sitting room, bedroom, full private bath, radio, TV; most with kitchen, desk.
Facilities Dining, breakfast room, courtyard with fountain. 3 blocks from beach. Tennis, golf, parks nearby.
Location Residential area, 1 m S of downtown. From PCH, turn E on Cress St.; go 2 blocks to inn.
Credit cards None accepted.
Rates B&B, $95–150. Extra person, $20. 2-day weekend minimum. 10% senior, AAA discount.
Extras Crib.

Eiler's Inn   *Tel: 714–494–3004*
741 South Pacific Coast Highway, 92651

Located in the heart of Laguna Beach, Eiler's Inn, owned by Henk and Annette Wirtz, features a European atmosphere. Breakfast includes fresh-baked breads, fresh fruit and juice, boiled eggs, and hand-ground Viennese coffee.

"The innkeepers provide excellent information about the beaches and shops." *(Lisa Simonetti)* "The rooms encircle a central courtyard, with a balcony providing access on the second floor. (Downstairs rooms are less private and a bit dark when the door is closed and the curtains drawn.) Each is different, some with Victorian antiques, others with Laura Ashley comforters. The plant-filled courtyard is lovely, with a large fountain and plenty of chairs and tables. The suite has a stunning ocean vista from the living room. You can abandon your car and walk to everything—shops, galleries, the beach. Although on the main highway, the rooms are surpris-ingly quiet because they focus on the courtyard not the street." *(SWS)* "The Forest Room is decorated in shades of mauve with flowered wallpa-per, great old furniture, ruffled curtains, and delicious linens." *(Gail Bern-stein)* "Our room, #209, was one of the nicest, opening to the courtyard in front, and an ocean-view deck in back." *(Amy Peritsky)* "Guests gather in the courtyard for breakfast and friendly conversation, afternoon iced tea, and for wine and cheese from 5–7 P.M. Sunday breakfast is highlighted by apple strudel with whipped cream." *(Richard Kobrin, also MP)*

Open All year.
Rooms 1 suite with kitchen, fireplace, TV; 11 doubles—all with private shower, fan.
Facilities Library with classical guitarist Saturday evenings, TV, games; lobby with fireplace; sun deck, garden courtyard with fountain. ½ block from ocean.
Location 60 m S of Los Angeles. Downtown. Five lights south of the Main Beach at the corner of Cleo and Pacific Coast Highway.
Restrictions Children "not encouraged." Parking "tight."
Credit cards Amex, MC, Visa.
Rates B&B, $175 suite, $100–130 double. Extra person, $20. $15 less midweek off-season. 2-night weekend minimum.
Extras Danish, Spanish, French, German spoken.

Inn at Laguna Beach 🏃 ♿   *Tel: 714–497–9722*
211 North Coast Highway, 92651   800–544–4479
                                                Fax: 714–497–9972

The Inn at Laguna Beach is where you'd expect it to be—its white stucco buildings climb the bluff overlooking the main beach and village. Guest rooms have large windows, crisply dressed with wooden blinds, simple furnishings with Spanish-style accents in wrought iron and wood, and soothing colors of gray, blue, and soft peach. Rates include a light break-fast of coffee, juice, and pastry.

"The lovely rooms are large and tastefully appointed, and most face the beach. Many have private patios with table and chairs. The Jacuzzi and swimming pool are on a bluff overlooking the sea. The public rooms are light, airy, and well maintained. Breakfast service starts at 6:30 A.M., so even if you have to catch an early flight you can still get a bite to eat." *(William Frick)* "At sunset, head for the rooftop deck for a drink and a wonderful view." *(MW)* "Great location overlooking the beach, within walking distance of shops and restaurants." *(Alan Barmaper)* "Attentive, knowledgeable staff." *(C. J. Elias-West)*

Open All year.
Rooms 70 doubles—all with private bath and/or shower, telephone, radio, TV, VCR, air-conditioning, mini-bar, refrigerator, hair dryer. Some with desk, balcony.
Facilities Lobby, roof top solarium/sun deck, Jacuzzi. 1 acre with heated swimming pool, hot tub. On ocean beach for water sports. Underground parking. Tennis, golf nearby.
Location 1 block N of town center.
Credit cards Amex, CB, DC, MC, Visa.
Rates B&B, $99–299 double. Extra person, $20. 10% senior, AAA discount. Minimum stay some weekends.
Extras Wheelchair access; rooms equipped for disabled. Crib. French, German, Spanish spoken.

LA JOLLA

La Jolla (pronounced "La Hoya") is a suburb of San Diego, about a 20-minute drive north of downtown. Not just a bedroom community, this sophisticated village on the Pacific Ocean has a number of attractions, including the Museum of Contemporary Art, the Scripps Institute of Oceanography, and U.C. San Diego, along with over 30 restaurants and 120 shops, which range from trendy to traditional. Cove Beach, a marine-life preserve, is a favorite for snorkeling. The Torrey Pines Golf Course and the Del Mar Racetrack are a short drive away to the north.

La Jolla is located 89 miles south of Los Angeles and 12 miles north of San Diego.

Also recommended: In the heart of the village, at the corner of Fay and Silverado, is the **Empress Hotel** (7766 Fay Avenue, 93027; 619–454–3001 or 800–LA–JOLLA), offering a garden patio with fountain, a sundeck, hot tub and exercise room, plus valet parking. B&B rates for the 72 guest rooms range from $90–140, each with private bath, hair dryer, and in-room refrigerator; some have ocean views, kitchenettes, and whirlpool tubs.

Families and sports buffs will enjoy the **La Jolla Beach and Tennis Club** (2000 Spindrift Drive, 92037; 619–454–7126 or 800–624–2582). Set right on the beach, the club's facilities include a dozen tennis courts, a pitch and putt golf course, a swimming pool, a kiddie pool, and two restaurants. Guest accommodations range from basic hotel rooms to three-bedroom apartments with kitchen, living area with fireplace, and multiple baths; most have ocean views.

Information please: We need reports on **The Bed & Breakfast Inn at La Jolla** (7753 Draper Avenue, 92037; 619–456–2066), a beige stucco home built in 1913 and one of the first examples of Irving Gill's "Cubist" architecture. Conveniently located within two blocks of restaurants and shops, it is across a grassy park from the cliffside cove path. Rooms are beautifully decorated in Laura Ashley fabrics, although some are quite small. Rates include a home-baked continental breakfast and afternoon wine tasting. Comments?

About 15 minutes north of La Jolla in the charming coastal town of Del Mar is the **Rock Haus Inn** (410 Fifteenth Street, Del Mar 92014; 619–481–3764), set on a hill overlooking the town and the Pacific Ocean. This renovated Craftsman-style California bungalow was built at the turn of the century. Most of the 10 guest rooms have ocean views, and one has its own fireplace. The inn is an easy walk to good restaurants, shops, and the beach. The $75–135 double rate includes a breakfast of fresh fruit, rolls, muffins, breads, juice, and coffee.

La Valencia Hotel ✕
1132 Prospect Street, 92037

Tel: 619–454–0771
800–451–0772
Fax: 619–456–3921

Built in 1925 of pink stucco and red tile, La Valencia overlooks Cove Beach and is surrounded by some of La Jolla's finest boutiques. Rooms are traditionally decorated, and most have ocean views.

"Careful restoration. The wide oak woodwork was returned to its original beauty, the main lounge—'La Sala'—with its Spanish tile inlays, beamed and painted ceiling, and beautiful view of the ocean, was brightened and up-to-dated. The bedrooms are elegantly appointed with reproduction antique furniture (and an armoire to hide the TV), fine prints, good lighting, and comfortable beds. The sybaritic new bathrooms, done in marble and brass, have good lights, mirrors, fluffy towels, robes, telephones. The Sky Room restaurant is an elegant small dining room atop the hotel with a panoramic view all the way to Santa Catalina." (NB) "Accommodating staff. Good food, especially at the reasonably priced brunch. The immaculate guest rooms overlook the ocean or the well-tended garden. Though compact, ours had water views and was charmingly done in green and soft pastels. The public areas are equally appealing, with relaxing piano." (JL) "In the heart of the village, steps from all attractions." (Sally Ducot) "Beautiful old hotel, location incredible, 1920s–30s atmosphere." (Robert Wolkow)

Open All year.

Rooms 10 suites, 90 doubles—all with private bath and/or shower, telephone, radio, TV. Most with desk. Some with balcony, kitchenette.

Facilities Lobby, 3 restaurants, bar with pianist, library, terrace. Gardens, shuffleboard, heated swimming pool, hot tub. 120 steps to Cove Beach for swimming, snorkeling, scuba diving. Valet parking. Tennis nearby.

Location Downtown. From Torrey Pines Rd., turn N at Prospect to hotel.

Restrictions Traffic noise in street-side rooms.

Credit cards Amex, DC, MC, Visa.

Rates Room only, $325–600 suite, $145–295 double. Extra person, $10. Prix fixe dinner, $40. Alc breakfast, $8–12; alc lunch, $12; alc dinner, $50.

Extras French, Spanish spoken. Member, Preferred Hotels.

Prospect Park Inn   *Tel:* 619–454–0133
1110 Prospect Street, 92037   800–433–1609
                                               Fax: 619–454–2056

Overlooking La Jolla Cove, the Prospect Park Inn was built in 1945.
Purchased in 1985 by Sharon Dunn, it has been managed by Jean Beazley
since 1990.

"An excellent value; run with European efficiency. Great location near
the ocean and steps from stores and scores of restaurants. While not large,
our second story room (#15) had a balcony and a kitchen. It was spacious
enough to accommodate a queen-size bed and still leave room for an arm
chair and space to walk around. The room was tastefully decorated in
beige and peach tones with ample reading lights, closet and drawer space.
You can breakfast in your room or on the sun deck, overlooking the
Pacific. Just call down when you're ready and the tray—complete with
daily newspaper—is delivered promptly. We stayed for a week and found
a different basket of goodies each day—fresh orange juice, croissants, fruit
scones, muffins, or other delicious pastries. The inn is squeaky clean. Our
bathroom was well-lit and we appreciated the oversize bath towels and
extra shelf space to hold toiletries. At the end of the day, guests can relax
with tea and cookies in a small library. Apples and candies are always
available." *(Carolyn Myles & Colburn Aker)* "Cordial staff made every
effort to be helpful." *(ABK, also Elisabeth McLaughlin)*

Open All year.
Rooms 2 suites, 22 doubles—all with full private bath, telephone, radio, clock,
TV, air-conditioning, fan, coffee maker, hair dryer. 8 with refrigerator, 12 with
balcony.
Facilities Library, sun deck. Free indoor parking in garage across street; off-street
parking. 1 block to ocean, park.
Location Center of village.
Restrictions Traffic, restaurant noise in front rooms (until 11 P.M.). No smoking.
Credit cards Amex, DC, Discover, MC, Visa.
Rates B&B, $200–260 suite, $80–120 double. Senior, AAA discount. Weekly,
corporate rates.

LAKE ARROWHEAD

Lake Arrowhead is a popular all-season resort with Los Angelenos, with
lake fishing, the scenic 40-mile Rim-of-the-World drive (at 5,000 plus feet
with spectacular vistas), and nearby San Bernardino National Forest for
winter activities, including downhill and cross-country skiing. It's located
in the San Bernadino Mountains in the Inland Empire region of southwest
California, 90 minutes from Los Angeles. From I-10, go north on I-15E to
Route 30 E to State Highway 18. Go north, then east on Highway 18.

Information please: Lake Arrowhead's first B&B was the **Bluebelle
House** (263 South State Highway 173, P.O. Box 2177, 92352; 909–336–
3292 or 800–429–BLUE), opened in 1983 by Rick and Lila Peiffer. Double
rates for the five guest rooms range from $85–120, and include a full
breakfast and afternoon refreshments. "Warm hospitality, relaxing atmo-

sphere. Every corner is decorated beautifully with florals, plants, and collectibles. Ample breakfast served at the beautifully set dining room table." *(Deborah Jackman)*

For additional area entries, see **Skyforest.**

The Carriage House B&B
Tel: 909–336–1400
472 Emerald Drive, P.O. Box 982, 92352

Tucked in the pines just a stone's throw from Lake Arrowhead, the Carriage House welcomes visitors with its country decor, rich oak woodwork and floors, and leaded glass windows. Lee and Johan Karstens, owners since 1989, invite guests to snuggle under European down comforters at night; the morning brings breakfasts of fresh fruit, baked goods, coffee and tea, and Belgian waffles with raspberry sauce or perhaps eggs Florentine.

"Ideally located next to the lake and a beautiful lakeside path to the village, full of shops and restaurants. From the heart- and potpourri-filled Surrey Room you can step out on your own private balcony for a majestic view of the lake. In the morning, we enjoyed a delicious breakfast with fellow guests; in the evening, a special treat was coming home to a turned-down Victorian featherbed and a homemade treat." *(Reneé & William Fremgen)* "Exceptionally clean; great warmth and hospitality." *(Angela Heidfeld)* "Johan and Lee are excellent hosts, making you feel as if the house were your own. Every day at 5 P.M. we sat in front of the fire with a glass of wine and a snack, chatting with the other guests, sharing the day's events or the plans for the evening ahead. Friendly inn-dog, Deke." *(Haven Show)* "Excellent dining recommendations." *(GH)* "Lee has got it just right, friendly and informative, but not intrusive." *(Ruth Tilsley)*

Open All year.
Rooms 3 doubles—all with private bath and/or shower, radio, clock, TV, fan. 1 with VCR, balcony.
Facilities Dining room, living room with fireplace, stereo, books; sun room with TV/VCR, stereo, games, CD/video library; deck with hammock. Near lake for water sports; lakeside walking path.
Location 2 m from Lake Arrowhead Village. On Emerald Drive, off Rte. 173.
Restrictions No smoking. Children over 13.
Credit cards Discover, MC, Visa.
Rates B&B, $95–120 double. Extra person, $15. 10% discount seniors, also midweek, 2-night stays. 2–3-night weekend, holiday minimum.
Extras Dutch spoken.

Eagle's Landing
Tel: 909–336–2642
27406 Cedarwood, 92317
Mailing address: Box 1510, Blue Jay, 92317

Dorothy and Jack Stone built and operate Eagle's Landing in a spacious contemporary house, nestled into the wooded hillside. Rooms are large, amply lighted, and comfortably furnished with accents from the owners' collection of folk art, antique farm implements, and travel remembrances. Rates include a full breakfast (brunch on Sunday), and afternoon wine hour.

"An attractively designed house with multi-level decks, balconies and tower in a setting of pine and spruce. Our suite had a private balcony and fireplace. Dorothy served us a delicious breakfast in the top of the tower." *(Judith Powell)* "The Lake View suite has over 900 square feet of space with a woodburning fireplace, queen-size bed, huge sofa-bed, refrigerator, and a large covered patio. Delicious 'Eagle's Nest' for breakfast—hot fruit with cinnamon-spiced sauce and topped with vanilla yogurt, accompanied by muffins and cheese." *(Jan Peverill)* "Dorothy and Jack must have written the book on hospitality and graciousness." *(Shirley Barlow)* Reports welcome.

Open All year.
Rooms 1 suite, 3 doubles—all with private bath and/or shower, radio, fan. Suite with fireplace, TV, wet bar, deck.
Facilities Breakfast room, living/family room with TV, games, stereo; decks. ⅓ acre with picnic area, hammock.
Location 20 m N of San Bernardino, 2 m W of Lake Arrowhead. From Hwy. 18, follow signs to Blue Jay. At fork in road in Blue Jay, go left on North Bay Rd. Inn on left at corner of North Bay and Cedarwood Rd.
Restrictions No smoking. "Not appropriate for children."
Credit cards Discover, MC, Visa.
Rates B&B, $185 suite, $95–125 double. Extra person, $20. 10% senior discount midweek. 2-3 night weekend/holiday minimum.

LEGGETT

Bell Glen B&B in the Redwoods   *Tel: 707–925–6425*
70400 Highway 101, 95585

For a truly relaxing getaway, what could be more appealing than to relax on the porch of your own cozy cabin, sipping a glass of wine as you watch the river peacefully flow by? Owned by Gene and Sandy Barnett since 1989, the Bell Glen consists of a restaurant and rathskeller (originally built as a stagecoach stop in the 1800s), a youth hostel, and six secluded cabins overlooking the Eel River. Gene does the cooking, and serves a four-course prix fixe meal at 7:30 P.M. on weekends; a recent menu included vegetable pasta soup, salad, a choice of Dover sole, Peruvian chicken, or herb lemon pasta, and Kahlua chocolate cake.

"The wood-shingled cabins are lovely with painted wood panelling and floral wallpaper, antiques or old wooden furniture. The restored older cabins have wide-board floors, log beams, and exposed wood ceilings. The large wooden bedsteads, some of which have canopies, have bedside tables with reading lamps. A sideboard holds a welcoming bottle of wine and breakfast fixings; before bedtime, a wicker basket is delivered with fresh fruit, cream cheese, and a datenut loaf. The bathrooms are large and modern, with stenciled details. Cottage E has a Jacuzzi tub on the wooden front porch overlooking the wide rocky bed of the Eel River and the cliffs beyond. The 14-foot-deep swimming hole in the crystal clear river has a small rocky beach; free inner tubes are available to shoot down the small rapids about 150 yards further down river. We thoroughly enjoyed dinner in the small pine-panelled rathskeller with bartender Leon, who made enjoyable company as we sipped a locally bottled brew." *Mark Mendenhall)* Additional reports appreciated.

Open Mid-April–Thanksgiving. Dining room open weekends & by reservation; pub open nightly.
Rooms 6 cabins—all with private bath and/or shower, clock/radio, refrigerator, porch. 1 with double Jacuzzi tub, 3 with desk, 2 with air-conditioning, 1 with fireplace.
Facilities Restaurant, pub/bar with TV/VCR, piano, occasional live music; sauna, laundry. 8 acres with gazebo, gardens, duck pond; $1/4$ m riverfront with swimming hole, tubing. Hiking nearby.
Location North Coast. Northern Mendocino Cty. 185 m N of San Francisco; 85 m S of Eureka. 2 m to town.
Restrictions No smoking.
Credit cards Discover, MC, Visa.
Rates B&B, $85–150 double. Extra person, $15. Prix fixe dinner, $20 (reservations required). AAA discount. Extended stay, off-season rates.
Extras Limited wheelchair access. Crib. Spanish spoken.

LITTLE RIVER

Little River is a tiny village located two miles south of the Victorian town of Mendocino. You can easily visit all of Mendocino's boutiques and restaurants during the day and then escape the evening noise and bustle by staying in Little River.

Located on the North Coast, it's 155 miles north of San Francisco. The town was originally settled in the 1850s as a major source of redwood lumber for San Francisco. (Redwood, being pitch-free, was found to be more fire-resistant than other woods.) Logs were floated down the river to the coast, then taken by schooner to San Francisco.

Information please: The **Inn at Schoolhouse Creek** (7051 North Highway One, 95456; or 707–937–5525) consists of an old ranch house, built in 1863; several turn-of-the-century cottages, probably built as housing for mill workers; and a 1930s-era motor court. Rooms are simply furnished, with good lighting, pine- or redwood-paneled walls, and print comforters. You can order breakfast from the menu the night before, then come to the lounge at the time requested to enjoy your meal. Room rates are $60–120.

Reader tip: "Nearly all of Little River's inns are on Highway 1, so be sure to insist on a quiet room if you're a light sleeper."

For additional area entries, see **Mendocino**.

Glendeven   *Tel: 707–937–0083*
8221 North Highway 1, 95456

A Maine-style farmhouse built in 1867, Glendeven has been owned by Jan and Janet deVries since 1977; the decor effectively combines antique quilts and country furnishings with contemporary arts and crafts. Stevenscroft is a relatively new building modeled after the original Victorian one. "The Gallery at Glendeven" occupies the ground floor of the Barn; it features Jan's handmade seating in addition to other fine contemporary art and crafts; the second floor suite is ideal for families.

"A short walk to the ocean and beautiful Van Damme State Park. The inn is surrounded by beautiful gardens for privacy." *(Irene Thomas)* "We stayed in the Stevenscroft annex; it was quiet, private, and romantic. From our table, we watched many birds and a deer enjoy breakfast too." *(Kathleen Owen)* "A nice touch was a cassette player with tapes in our room." *(Joe & Anne Miller)* "I was welcomed with cookies and sherry, and studied the restaurant menus before the fire in the sitting room. Pinewood is a beautiful downstairs suite in Stevenscroft, with knotty-pine walls and a red and blue color scheme. The bedroom had handmade quilts on the walls and a queen-size canopy bed; two wing chairs and a reading lamp are set before the fireplace. The comfortable sitting area had a window overlooking the bay at Van Damme Beach. French doors led onto a shaded redwood deck. Breakfast was delivered to my door in a picnic basket: fresh-squeezed orange juice, still-warm blueberry muffins, a boiled egg, fruit, coffee or tea." *(Linda Goldberg)*

Open All year.
Rooms One 2-bedroom suite, 10 doubles—all with private bath and/or shower. Some with desk, fireplace, deck or balcony. 4 rooms in Stevenscroft; 6 in Farmhouse; suite in Barn.
Facilities Sitting room with fireplace and piano, gallery. 2 acres with brick terrace, flower gardens, picnic area. Fern Canyon nearby for walking, jogging. 1/4 m to Van Damme State Park.
Location On Hwy. 1, 2 m S of Mendocino, 1/4 m N of Van Damme State Park.
Restrictions No smoking. Traffic noise in some rooms.
Credit cards MC, Visa.
Rates B&B, $185–240 suite, $90–160 double, $70–140 single. Extra person, $20. Midweek discount. 2-night weekend minimum. Tipping encouraged.
Extras Dutch, Tagalog spoken.

Heritage House &
5200 North Highway 1, 95456

Tel: 707–937–5885
800–235–5885
Fax: 707–937–0318

With inns typically changing hands every five years, it's unusual to find one that's been owned by the same family since 1949. That was the year that L.D. Dennen bought an 1877 farmhouse, converted it into a restaurant, and began building cottages on the grounds. The inn is owned today by his daughter Gay Dennen Moore and R.J. Moore, and is extremely popular, especially at holidays. Although a few of the units are to the east of Highway 1, most are on the west, with no traffic to mar the water view. In addition to juice, fruit, and cereal, breakfast choices include honey cinnamon waffles, sole with spinach, and eggs Benedict. The dinner menu might offer sea scallops with wild mushrooms, coriander marinated pork, or prime rib.

"Magnificent views, elegant accommodations, beautiful grounds and flowers, and the distinctive scent of the towering eucalyptus trees. Excellent breakfast of fresh fruits, French toast, muffins, eggs and bacon. Wonderful moonlit walk along the cliff path to the oceanside gazebo." *(Tom Wilbanks)* "The ocean is a mighty presence here, almost on one's doorstep." *(Willard Parker)* "Set in the woods, our room was huge, with a double bed, two twin beds, a sofa, and a wood-burning stove." *(Maria eele)* "At the entrance is the dining room, check-in area, and gift shops. The weathered shingled cottages are spread out over the grounds, and most rooms have views of the ocean and bay. Ours, called Same Time, was magnificent, with a good-size room, fireplace stocked with wood, comfy easy chairs, and a spacious bathroom. The restaurant offers an excellent menu, professional and courteous service, plus good water views." *(Bob & Ellie Freidus)*

Open Mid-Feb.–early Jan.
Rooms 13 suites, 64 cottages—all with private bath and/or shower, balcony/deck/patio. Most with desk, fireplace/woodstove. 12 with Jacuzzi tub, 12 with refrigerator. Accommodations are in groups of duplex, triplex, fourplex buildings.
Facilities Restaurant, living room with fireplace, piano, books; deck, gift shop. Lounge with weekend piano player. 37 acres with gazebo, beach. Golf, tennis, fishing nearby.
Location 5 m S of Mendocino.
Restrictions No smoking in dining room, lounge. Jackets, ties at dinner. Traffic noise in some rooms.
Credit cards MC, Visa.
Rates MAP, $223–375 suite, $140–375 double, $120–355 single. Extra person, $75. Minimum stay holidays. Alc lunch, $10; alc dinner, $35. Midweek, off-season rates.
Extras Wheelchair access; some bathrooms specially equipped. Babysitting.

Stevenswood Lodge ♿   *Tel:* 707–937–2810
8211 North Highway 1   800–421–2810
Mailing address: P.O. Box 170, Mendocino, 95460 *Fax:* 707–937–1237

Owned by Robert Zimmer, Stevenswood is a contemporary lodge surrounded by trees and foliage. The second-floor deck is nice for sipping wine or simply watching the birds. Complimentary wine and hors d'oeuvres are served from 5–7 P.M., and a well-stocked wine cellar has some nice vintages for sale. Guest rooms have high, sloping wood ceilings, excellent lighting, and handmade curly maple furniture. Japanese tiles highlight the bathrooms, fully equipped with amenities. After a walk through the forest, Van Damme park, and the beach, we enjoyed wine and cheese, while looking through the menu book, deciding where to have dinner. For breakfast we had banana bran muffins, fresh sliced fruit, and baked eggs with leeks, prosciutto, and Gruyère." *(Linda Goldberg)*

"Remarkable attention to detail was signaled by the solid wooden door to our room, the wooden countertop and luggage stands to facilitate unpacking. Our bathroom was done in dramatic cerulean blue tile, and the bed was outfitted with downy comforters and extra pillows." *(Ann & Del Anorbes)* "Clean, crisp contemporary design with lots of windows for forest and water views, a fireplace ready to light, and the peaceful setting." *(Dee Cumberland)*

Open All year.
Rooms 9 suites, 1 double—all with private bath and/or shower, telephone, TV, fireplace, desk, refrigerator. Two with shared deck. Some with desk.
Facilities Breakfast room, living room, lounge with fireplace; decks. Art gallery, conference room. 6 acres with gardens, woods.
Location Highway One; 2 m S of Mendocino.

135

Restrictions No smoking. "Children welcome with direct parental supervision.
Credit cards Discover, MC, Visa.
Rates B&B, $120–195 suite, $95–115 double. Extra person, $25. Tipping encouraged. Midweek senior discount. 2–3-night weekend, holiday minimum.
Extras Wheelchair access; 4 rooms equipped for disabled. Airport/station pickup. Crib, babysitting.

LOS ANGELES

Larger than Rhode Island and Delaware combined, Los Angeles is both linked and separated by an amazing maze of freeways. In fact, if the people of Detroit could have dreamed up the perfect town, they would have invented Los Angeles, where it is impossible to get anywhere without a car.

Los Angeles is a hodgepodge of different ethnic groups—you can visit different restaurants and shops for a taste of countries from Hungary to Thailand, from Polynesia to Ethiopia. Large Mexican, Japanese, Chinese, and Southeast Asian neighborhoods are intrinsic parts of Los Angeles. There's really a lot to see in Los Angeles—not just the TV and movie industry tours but other kinds of cultural and historic sights as well, including a number of outstanding art museums. Contact the Los Angeles Visitors and Convention Center (505 South Flower Street, 90071; 213-239-0204) for a copy of their "Visitor's Guide."

To make things a little easier, we've grouped most of our listings for the Los Angeles area in this section, so you won't have to check through the whole chapter to find Beverly Hills or North Hollywood. Before you make reservations, it's a good idea to look at a map and identify the area where you'll be spending most of your time; then book your room in that area of the city. Los Angeles is so spread out and the traffic so heavy (the afternoon rush hour starts at 3 P.M.) that you could easily spend your entire day in the car (and a car you must have). If you're traveling with the family and will mainly be doing the theme-park circuit, you'll be better off staying in Orange County to the southeast.

LA is a three area code town: downtown remains 213; to the north it's 818; and the area south and west of downtown has become 310. Los Angeles is located in Southern California, about 400 miles south of San Francisco and 125 miles north of San Diego.

To save money on many Los Angeles area hotels, call **Express Hotel Reservations** at 800–356–1123 or 213–236–9295. They offer discounts of 20–50 percent off rack rates, and since they receive a commission from the hotels, there's no charge to you.

Information please: Built in 1927 in a French Normandy style, complete with Gothic windows and massive beamed ceiling in the living room, the Chateau Marmont (8221 Sunset Boulevard, Hollywood, 90046; 213-655-5311 or 800–CHATEAU) is a historic Los Angeles landmark, famous (and infamous) for the many stars that have stayed here. Surrounded by gardens, the hotel offers sweeping views of the city and Hollywood Hills. Rooms have been refurbished and updated to meet the telephone and electronic requirements of today's Hollywood, without disturbing the 1930s era charm and ambience of Chateau's eclectic furnish-

ings. "A must for movie fans." The rates for the 51 suites and doubles is
$160, with bungalows ranging from $210–750.

Just south of Beverly Hills is the recently built **Carlyle Inn** (1119 South
Robertson Boulevard, 90035; 310–275–4445 or 800–3–CARLYLE). This
32-room hotel includes a buffet breakfast, afternoon tea, and a cocktail
hour in its $115–190 rates. Also offered is a free shuttle service within a
five-mile radius, a health club, sun deck with hot tub, and well-equipped
guest rooms and baths. The Kimco Hotel chain, well-known for its boutique hotels in San Francisco, has opened its first Los Angeles property,
the fully refurbished **The Beverly Prescott Hotel** (1224 South Beverwil
Drive at Pico Boulevard, P.O. Box 3065, Beverly Hills, 90212; 310–277–
2800 or 800–421–3212). Most of the 140 luxurious guest rooms have
balconies, plush overstuffed furnishings in florals and stripes, two telephones, terry robes, and more at rates of $175 double. There's even a
swimming pool for a cooling dip. Ask for a high-floor room facing the hills
to avoid traffic noise.

Another B&B choice in the historic West Adams district is the **Salis-
bury House** (2273 West 20th Street, 90018; 213–737–7817 or 800–373–
1778), two blocks from the Santa Monica Freeway, and minutes from
downtown, USC, the Convention Center, and Beverly Hills. This 1909
California Craftsman house has original wood-beamed ceilings, stained
and leaded glass, and antique-filled rooms. Double B&B rates for the five
guest rooms range from $75–100, and include a full breakfast (mushroom
quiche or apple puffed pancakes) and afternoon tea and shortbread. Just
half a block from the beach and within walking distance of numerous
restaurants is the **Venice Beach House** (15 Thirtieth Avenue, Venice,
90291; 310–823–1966). Double rates for the nine guest rooms range from
$80–150, and include a buffet breakfast of fresh fruit and juice, and
home-baked goods. "Located in a quiet residential area, yet minutes from
Santa Monica, LAX, or downtown LA. Friendly staff." *(Gerry Michael)* The
elegant, Edwardian **Lord Mayor's Inn** (435 Ocean Avenue, Long Beach,
90802; 310–436–0324) was the home of Long Beach's first mayor. Converted into a B&B in 1988, it offers five guest rooms with private baths,
and includes a full breakfast in its $85–95 double rates. "Our room was
spotless, the food was excellent, and the atmosphere relaxing." *(Ruth
Johnson)*

Channel Road Inn ♀ ♿

219 West Channel Road, Santa Monica 90402

Tel: 310–459–1920
Fax: 310–454–9920

A shingle-clad Colonial Revival home, the Channel Road Inn was built for
Thomas McCall in 1910. The house was moved to Santa Monica Canyon
in the 1970s and then abandoned after reconstruction plans fell through;
fortunately, it was rescued from demolition and restored as a B&B in 1988.
During the renovation process the walls were stuffed with insulation and
the windows double-glazed. One guest room has an elaborate Victorian
bedroom set, while another has a pencil-post canopied bed framed with
feather-light sheers; most have ocean views. Rates include a breakfast of
home-baked breads and muffins, an egg dish, and fresh fruit plus afternoon
wine, cheese, and tea.

"Four or five good restaurants are within easy walking distance." *(Sally*

Ducot) "Welcoming owner Susan Zolla and innkeeper Kathy Jensen were helpful with dinner reservations, and were sensitive to our dietary needs." *(Sharene Walsh)* "Exquisite wood panel work; the living room is warm, colorful, spacious, and well appointed. Ample parking, safe location." *(LJ, also Margaret Young)*

"The well-appointed Honeymoon Suite has a sitting room with a French door leading to a porch, as well as a deck spa with Pacific views." *(Sylvia Barkley)* "Right near the beach but accessible to LA. Delicious breakfast." *(Suzanne Harris)* "Kathy assisted with my luggage, and offered me a refreshing drink. Small touches made for a homey feeling—a welcoming note, just-picked roses, freshly baked chocolate chip cookies, plush terry cloth robe, huge bath sheets, a wicker basket filled with toiletries, and a magnifying mirror in the bathroom." *(Gail Davis)* Reports welcome.

Open All year.
Rooms 2 suites, 12 doubles—all with private bath and/or shower, telephone, TV/VCR, radio, fan. 12 with desk.
Facilities Breakfast room, living room with fireplace, library. 1/2 acre with garden, hot tub. Beach towels, bicycles. 1 block to beach. 30-mile bike path parallels beach. Horseback riding, tennis nearby. Fax, secretarial, conference services.
Location Los Angeles area, Santa Monica Canyon. 25 min N of downtown Los Angeles. From Pacific Coast Hwy., exit at W. Channel Rd. From San Diego Freeway (Hwy. 405) take Wilshire W. exit & go to 7th St. (becomes Channel Rd.).
Restrictions Traffic noise in front rooms. No smoking.
Credit cards MC, Visa.
Rates B&B, $95–225 suite or double. Extra person, $10. Crib, $10.
Extras Wheelchair access; 1 room equipped for the disabled. Crib, babysitting. French, Spanish, Italian spoken.

Hotel Bel-Air ✗ ♿

701 Stone Canyon Road
Los Angeles, 90077

Tel: 310–472–1211
800–648–4097
Fax: 310–476–5890

Glowing superlatives seem to be the operative mode when it comes to describing the Bel-Air—it receives top honors in nearly every hotel ranking survey.

"A classic pink stucco building in a spectacular setting—a wooded, secluded canyon close to the Bel-Air Country Club. Beautifully landscaped grounds, with a fabulous swimming pool. The lobby is cozy and well appointed, with a fireplace. The luxurious rooms are individually done in pastel colors with down comforters. The restaurant is excellent, and the bar is the former haunt of Humphrey Bogart and other movie stars of the 1940s." *(Linda & Paul Duttenhaver)* "Discreetly situated in a superrich residential suburb, surrounded by the palaces of movie moguls. In the restaurant, the atmosphere was *soigné* but the service was far from aloof; meals were excellent." *(Hilary Rubinstein)* "Unbelievable service—and everyone greets you by name. My room, 314, had a king-sized bed, fresh fruit and flowers, fireplace, two-line telephone at the desk with extensions by the bed and in the bath, vanity table (with Hollywood lighting, of course), hairdryer, plush robes, slippers, thick bath towels, and a private patio overlooking Shangri-La gardens with the famous swan pond." *(Gail Davis)*

Open All year.
Rooms 39 suites, 52 doubles—all with full private bath, telephone, radio, TV, desk, air-conditioning. Many with Jacuzzi, patio, fireplace, or balcony.
Facilities Restaurant, piano bar with fireplace, 24-hour room service, hairdresser. 1½ acres with heated swimming pool, pond with swans. Valet parking.
Location Turn off Sunset Blvd. onto Stone Canyon Rd. to hotel.
Credit cards Amex, DC, MC, Visa.
Rates Room only, $495–2,000 suite, $265–435 double, $225–395 single. Alc breakfast, $12–22; alc lunch, $25–45; alc dinner, $60–85.
Extras Wheelchair access. Crib, babysitting. Spanish, French, German spoken. Member, Preferred Hotels Worldwide.

Inn at 657 ¢   *Tel:* 213–741–2200
657 West 23rd Street, Los Angeles 90007   800–347–7512

Long-time owner Patsy Carter recently renovated this 1940s apartment house, located in a bustling downtown neighborhood, as a B&B, with the goal of "providing the business traveler with the features of a hotel and the charm of a B&B." The decor is traditional and amenities include fresh flowers, goose-down comforters, and refrigerators stocked with fresh fruit and juice. There's also a garden hot tub, and breakfasts of eggs to order, griddle cakes, and sausage, served at the guest's convenience.

"My room in the main house had a private bath down the hall. I enjoyed a breakfast of pancakes with fresh fruit, with a view of orchids and camellias in the well-tended garden. I was welcome to use the main kitchen for fixing a snack." *(Amy McEwen)* "Bowls of fresh fruit and nuts, and fresh flowers awaited in my two-bedroom suite, complete with kitchen, living room and dining room. Interesting neighborhood with Mount Saint Mary's College (housed in attractive Tudor-style buildings) right across the street. Delightful breakfast with mango juice and exceptional whole grain bread. While never intrusive, Patsy's motherly attentions made me feel right at home." *(Gail Davis)*

Open All year.
Rooms 4 suites, 2 doubles—all with private bath and/or shower, telephone, TV, desk, air-conditioning, fan, refrigerator. Suites with VCR, kitchen, balcony.
Facilities Living room with piano, dining room, porch, deck. Lawn with hot tub, patios. Off-street parking.
Location Downtown LA; N Univ. Park. 1 block W of Figueroa St. On DASH line & USC Tramline. Walking distance to USC, Exposition Park museums.
Restrictions No smoking in suites.
Credit cards None accepted.
Rates B&B, $95–135 suite, $65–125 double. 10% senior, AAA discount.
Extras Spanish spoken.

La Maida House ✕   *Tel:* 818–769–3857
11159 La Maida Street
North Hollywood, 91601

La Maida House is an inn of distinction set in an otherwise undistinguished Los Angeles suburb. Antonio La Maida built this 7,000-square-foot old-world villa in the 1920s using marble, oak, mahogany, and hand-painted tile. The house was stunningly restored by owner Megan

139

Timothy, who created many of its paintings, sculptures, and stained glass. Rates include continental breakfast and afternoon aperitifs. The four course dinners might include Middle Eastern couscous or Italian pasta, but no animal products are served. Many of the fruits and vegetables served come from the inn's gardens.

"Primavera, in one of the bungalows, was done in white wicker and shades of soft dusty pink with touches of apple green. The queen-size bed had a white iron and brass headboard, with reading light and bed table on each side. The color-coordinated bathroom had ample towels, a Jacuzzi tub, hand-stenciled tulips on the wall, and small stained glass window. Across the street at the main house, we saw several rooms—one in Swedish country pine; another with a massive four-poster bed, and a dramatic contemporary quilt canopy; a third in English hunting green with white trim, with a reproduction brass bed. Everywhere are stained glass windows, including a stunning yellow, orange, and red peacock above the main stairway landing." (SWS)

"Landscaping, interior decoration, the cats, Megan—all delightful. Megan's food is so good that I didn't mind the vegetarian menu." (Cynthia Gibat) "Delicious warm cinnamon bread and fresh strawberry and grape juice for breakfast. Bedtime cookies were a treat." (Sharon White) "Megan and her staff were most helpful; pleasant Renaissance music at breakfast. (James C. Owens)

Open All year.
Rooms 4 suites, 8 doubles—all with private bath and/or shower, telephone, radio, TV, desk, air-conditioning, fan. Some with whirlpool bath, fireplace, private patio, refrigerator. 8 rooms in annexes.
Facilities 2 dining rooms, living room, TV room, atrium, patio, conference room, gymnasium. Lily pond, gardens, fountains, gazebo, swimming pool, exercise room. Tennis nearby.
Location 20–30 min. from most attractions; 2 min. to Universal City. Near intersection of Hollywood & Ventura Freeways. Call for directions.
Restrictions No smoking. No animal products served. No fur clothing permitted.
Credit cards MC, Visa.
Rates B&B, $155–210 suite, $85–155 double. Extra person, $25. 2-night minimum stay. Discounts for extended stay (more than 1 week). Prix fixe dinner, $35 plus 20% service.
Extras Spanish spoken.

MENDOCINO

Originally founded by Maine sea captains, Mendocino still looks very much like a New England fishing village—so much so that it has been used many times as a set for movies meant to be taking place on the East Coast.

Aside from looking into the many craft shops and art galleries and discovering the area restaurants and vineyards, take the time to explore the shore and the redwood forests, accessible in the area's five state parks. Canoeing, trail rides along the beach, river and ocean fishing, whale watching, tennis and golf are all favorites. For more information on area

ttractions, please see the "North Coast" section of the chapter introduc-
on, plus the listings for Fort Bragg and Little River.

Mendocino is located about 150 miles north of San Francisco, in the
enter of the Mendocino coast. From San Francisco, take Highway 101
hrough Santa Rosa to Cloverdale. Then take Route 128 to Highway 1
orth to Mendocino. From Eureka, take Highway 101 south to Leggett,
nd follow Highway 1 through Fort Bragg to Mendocino.

Many Mendocino inns maintain the same rates year-round, while oth-
rs offer reductions of about 20 percent in the (winter) off-season. A
wo-night weekend minimum is standard at almost all.

Reader tips: "Although we found the town of Mendocino to have an
verabundance of T-shirt shops, we'd recommend walking its 'Ecological
adder,' and exploring its many trails and beaches. Be aware that the fog
nay not lift until noon—sometimes it stays all day. Excellent dinner at the
Albion River Inn; make reservations for an early dinner so you can get a
vindow seat to appreciate the incredible views." *(EL)* "Be aware that many
f Mendocino's restaurants and shops do not accept credit cards, although
hey will take an in-state check. Fill up your gas tank before you get to
own; the one gas station is very expensive." *(Linda Gold)* "It's a shock to
ay $150 per night instead of the $90 a night for a comparable B&B in
he Gold Country. Maybe they should call it 'Spendocino.'" *(KO)* "Al-
hough many of Mendocino's village inns claim to have water views,
hese are *distant* views of the bay, not the dramatic ocean views found in
earby Little River. Although it's probably lovely in winter, we would not
onsider staying in the village when it's crowded with summer tourists."
SHW)

For additional area entries, see listings for **Little River**, just 2 miles
way, **Elk**, 15 miles south, or **Fort Bragg**, 8 miles north.

Information please: The **Joshua Grindle Inn** (44800 Little Lake Road,
.O. Box 647, 95460; 707–937–4143), a Victorian farmhouse, was built
y Joshua Grindle in 1879, and 100 years later became a country inn.
Rooms are light, airy, and furnished with antiques. The inn offers views
f the village, the bay, and the ocean; all of Mendocino's attractions are
short walk away. The $90–155 double rates include a breakfast of fresh
ruit and juice, homebaked breads and muffins, a hot egg dish or casserole,
offee and tea.

The **Brewery Gulch Inn** (9350 Highway 1, 95460; 707–937–4752)
as a quiet setting just minutes from the village, and offers comfortable
ccommodations in an 1860s farmhouse surrounded by lovely gardens
nd shade trees. The five guest rooms are simply furnished, with soft
omforters, down pillows, country print fabrics, books, and games. The
75–130 rates includes a full breakfast, with fresh eggs from the hen
ouse.

Agate Cove Inn　　　　　　　　　　　　　　*Tel:* 707–937–0551
1201 Lansing Street, P.O. Box 1150　　In No. Calif.: 800–527–3111
95460

The main structure of this 1860s farmhouse was built by Mathias Brinzing,
Mendocino's first brewer. The exterior of the building appears much as it

did at the turn of the century; the candlestick fence still graces the entr
garden. Innkeepers Sallie McConnell and Jake Zahavi have complete
renovated most of the cottages since 1988 when they bought the inn, an
the decor includes handmade quilts, country furniture, and quaint fabri
and wallpapers. The family-style breakfasts, prepared on an antique woo
stove, include Jake's home-baked bread, fresh fruit and juice, jams an
jellies, coffee and tea, plus an entrée of omelets, eggs Benedict or Frenc
toast, with country sausage or baked ham.

"Sits on a bluff overlooking spectacular coastline." *(Diana Halpenn*
"The secluded Topaz cottage features a canopy bed, double shower, larg
deck with sea view, a Franklin fireplace, and a dresser (no closet)." *(Lina
Goldberg)* "Breakfasts are terrific, and the dining room has a spectacul
view. Rooms are clean, individually decorated, comfortable, and quiet
(Suzanne & David Brown) "The innkeepers are always eager to provi
information yet respect guests' privacy." *(Sherry & Ronald Colburn)* "Ou
room was thoroughly cleaned while we had breakfast. Mattresses are firn
the comfortable rocking chairs were ideal for enjoying the sherry left fc
each evening." *(Judy & Dick Falcioni)* Comments welcome.

Open All year.
Rooms 2 doubles in main house, 8 cottages—all with private bath and/or showe
writing table. 9 with TV, fireplace, deck. 1 with radio.
Facilities Dining room, living room with fireplace, games. 1½ acres.
Location Take Lansing St. exit off Hwy. 1. ½ m N of town center.
Restrictions No smoking. No children under 12.
Credit cards Amex, Discover, MC, Visa; $10 cash discount.
Rates B&B, $85–185 double. Extra person, $25. 2-night weekend minimun
Midweek off-season rates.
Extras Airport/station pickup. French spoken.

Headlands Inn &

Tel: 707–937–443

Corner of Howard and Albion Streets
Mailing address: P.O. Box 132, 95460

The Headlands Inn began life in 1868 as a one-story barber shop on Mai
Street; a second story was added in 1873 to provide living quarters fc
the barber's family. In 1893 the house was moved from its origin
location on Main Street to its current one, transported by horses pullin
the house over rolling logs. David and Sharon Hyman, owners since 199
are interior designers, and have added many of their own antiques an
handcrafted furnishings to the decor. Breakfast, served on a tray in eac
guest's room, includes fruit dishes garnished with edible flowers an
perhaps bacon quiche, tomato shells with baked Gruyère-topped eggs, c
peach amaretto crepes.

"Generously sized rooms with comfortable appointments and terr
robes." *(Sharon Martin)* "Inviting common areas. Our room's little sittin
area was the perfect place to enjoy breakfast, delivered directly to th
room at 9 A.M. Our large private deck provided a view of the stars i
night, the village during the day." *(Maria Valls)* "Sharon and Dave we
always available, yet never hovering, assisting us with reservations an

:commendations." *(Ellen Walters)* "Rooms have been lovingly decorated
vith warm soothing colors, and plush beige carpeting. My favorite is the
essie Straus room, with a bay window and a garden and water view."
Linda Goldberg)

Open All year.
Rooms 1 cottage, 4 doubles—4 with full private bath, wood-burning fireplace,
ock. 1 with private shower, parlor stove. 1 with deck.
Facilities 2 parlors, with piano, games, books. Front porch, decks, gardens. 2
locks to Big River Beach.
Location Historic District, 2 blocks from center. Going N on Hwy. 1, turn left
• business district; pass church, then right on Howard St. Inn is 1½ blocks on
ft.
Restrictions No smoking. Street noise in some rooms.
Credit cards None accepted.
Rates B&B, $103–172 double. 2–4-night weekend, holiday minimum. Reserve 1
> 3 months in advance for weekends and in summer.
Extras Cottage has wheelchair access. Free local airport pickup. Limited Spanish
poken.

John Dougherty House   *Tel: 707–937–5266*
71 Ukiah Street, P.O. Box 817, 95460

Marion and David Wells welcome guests to their 1867 farmhouse over-
ooking the bay. Accommodations include a guest suite in a historic water
ower (with an 18-foot beamed ceiling) and a separate cabin, to supple-
ent the "Port" and "Starboard" cottages in the garden.

"We stayed in the Captain's Room, with the private veranda overlook-
ng the village and the water beyond. The bathroom had a fine array of
oaps, perfumes, shampoos, lotions and big, fluffy towels. We also en-
oyed a bountiful breakfast and nice chat in front of the fire with our
osts." *(Joan & Larry Martens)* "The First Mate room, had a view of the
illage, walls stenciled with blue flowers, and a carved headboard depict-
ng a whale swallowing a woman. The local Mendocino chocolates on the
resser, fresh flowers, bottled water dispenser, and complimentary wine
1 the room's small refrigerator added a nice touch. A mellow inn cat
amed Tristan shared my room. David and Marion helped me with dinner
eservations, and provided area pamphlets and magazines. Breakfast was
standout—fresh fruit, hot currant scones, chicken-sausage rolls, banana
ut bread, juice, tea, or coffee." *(LG)* "Beautiful little garden in the back and
leasant hosts." *(Shirley Dittloff)*

Open All year.
Rooms 4 cottages/suites, 2 doubles—all with private bath and/or shower, TV.
Most with veranda, fireplace, refrigerator.
Facilities Living/dining room with fireplace, keeping room, porch, garden.
)cean, boating, horseback riding nearby.
Location Village center.
Restrictions No smoking. Not recommended for children under 13. Sidewalk
lose to some rooms.
Credit cards MC, Visa.

143

Rates B&B, $95–165 cottage/suite, double. Extra person, $15. 2-night weekend minimum. 3 nights for price of 2, midweek, off-season.
Extras Free local airport pickup.

Stanford Inn by the Sea/Big River Lodge 🍴 ♿ *Tel:* 707–937–561!
44850 Comptche-Ukiah Road and Highway 1   800–331–888∢
P.O. Box 487, 95460   *Fax:* 707–937–030.

Originally built as a motel, the Stanford Inn was bought in 1980 by Joa∢ and Jeff Stanford, who have upgraded their property into a quality bed & breakfast inn. Their other endeavors include raising their two children operating a canoe livery service, breeding llamas, and growing organi produce. Breakfast consists of fresh fruits and juices, champagne, coffee tea, hot chocolate, granola, porridge, quiche, and pastries. Afternoon win and hors d'oeuvres are also served in the common room, furnished wit∣ antiques and collectibles.

"On a hillside overlooking the ocean and the town, the inn's ground are beautifully landscaped. Our room was furnished in antiques and qual ity reproductions, with a cozy sitting area, plants, and lovely artwork Plumbing is modern, with good water pressure; quality soaps and toilet ries were supplied. White wine was served in the lobby in the earl∣ evening. We scanned restaurant menus and the staff assisted us wit∣ advice and reservations. Our sleep was undisturbed by noise from traffi or other guests." *(Timothy & Cynthia Egan)*

"My four-poster king-size bed had a cozy white and mauve comforte and pillow shams, great reading lamps, and remote-control TV. The radi∢ was playing, the fireplace was ready to light, there were chocolates crackers with herb cheese dip, a tangerine, fresh flowers, and crysta decanter of red wine and two crystal wineglasses ready on the coffe table." *(Linda Goldberg)* "The enclosed swimming pool is also a gian conservatory with flowering shrubs and trees, and translucent walls. *(Hugh & Marjorie Smith)* "Free bikes and canoes, the heated swimming pool, the view from our balcony, and the videos for our kids." *(EL)*

A word of advice: "The second-floor rooms have a slightly better view plus more privacy, since the balconies are separated while the first-floo porches are not."

Open All year.
Rooms 3 suites, 1 cottage, 22 doubles—all with private bath and/or showe∣ telephone, radio, TV/VCR, desk, wood-burning fireplace, refrigerator, coffe maker, deck.
Facilities Common room with fireplace, deck; videotape library. 10 acres wit∣ greenhouse enclosed heated swimming pool, sauna, hot tub; flower and vegetabl gardens, horses, ducks, llamas. Mountain bicycles, fishing; canoe, kayak, outrigge rentals. Beaches, dock nearby.
Location ¼ m S of village, at corner of Hwy. 1 & Comptche-Ukiah Rd.
Restrictions No smoking in common areas.
Credit cards Amex, CB, DC, Discover, Enroute, MC, Optima, Visa.
Rates B&B, $200–260 suite, $170–190 double. Extra person, $15. 2–3-nigh weekend/holiday minimum. Gardening seminars, March–Oct.
Extras Wheelchair access; bathroom equipped for disabled. Airport/statio pickup. Pets permitted by arrangement. Crib. French, German, Spanish spoken.

Whitegate Inn
499 Howard Street, P.O. Box 150, 95460

Tel: 707–937–4892
800–531–7282
Fax: 707–937–1131

When the Whitegate was built in 1883, a newspaper article described it as "one of the most elegant and best appointed residences in town." Under the ownership of Carol and George Bechtloff, who bought the inn in 1991, this description applies equally today. Rates include a full breakfast, afternoon cookies, pre-dinner refreshments, and bedtime chocolates.

"I was warmly greeted by Carol and George. One of the inn cats has become the official greeter who runs to the door to welcome guests, then 'shows them to their rooms.' The elegant dining and living rooms have coordinating Oriental carpets, hand-painted wallpaper borders, and beautifully upholstered Victorian furniture, in a soothing color scheme of seafoam green and rosy peach. The dining room has collections of cut glass and porcelain figurines, with a crystal chandelier, silver tea service, and Victorian artwork. Rich floral fabrics and wallpaper borders add elegance to the guest rooms without clutter; plush towels and bath rugs, luxurious linens and curtains add comfort. The flower-filled backyard offers a distant view of the sea from the gazebo. Breakfasts include artichoke potatoes, eggs Florentine, shrimp soufflé, caramel-apple French toast, or waffles, with fresh fruit salad or a granola parfait, fresh-squeezed juices, and cinnamon rounds. Light hors d'oeuvres and wine are offered at 5 P.M." *(Linda Goldberg)* "The inn is extremely clean, well maintained, quiet and private with plenty of parking along the street. George and Carol were eager to please and helped us with restaurant reservations." *(Terri Ann Flores)*

Open All year.
Rooms 1 cottage, 5 doubles—all with private bath and/or shower, clock, fireplace/woodstove. 2 with TV, refrigerator, 1 with deck.
Facilities Dining room, living room with piano, deck/gazebo. ½ acre with off-street parking, lawn games. 1 block from ocean.
Location In village historic district. Turn W of Hwy 1 into Mendocino at Little Lake Rd. (only stoplight). Go W 2 blocks, turn left on Howard St., & go S 1 block to inn on corner of Howard & Ukiah.
Restrictions Absolutely no smoking inside. No hard liquor. Children over 12.
Credit cards Amex, MC, Visa.
Rates B&B, $145 cottage, $95–185 double. Extra person, $15. $20 midweek off-season AAA, senior discounts. 2-3 night weekend/holiday minimum.
Extras Airport/station pickups.

MONTARA

The Goose & Turrets B&B ¢
835 George Street, P.O. Box 370937, 94037-0937

Tel: 415–728–5451

The Goose and Turrets is a Northern Italian villa-style home built in 1908, restored as a B&B in 1986 by Raymond and Emily Hoche-Mong. Rooms are eclectically decorated with antique and contemporary furnishings, original paintings, and wood carvings. Breakfast is served at 9 A.M., and might feature smoked salmon and herbed cream cheese on bagels, Tennessee sausages and Southern spoonbread with sourwood honey, or Southwest corn-pepper pancakes served with sour cream and salsa, plus freshly ground coffees, imported teas, and fresh fruits and berries.

"The beds are firm, with down comforters to keep you toasty warm. The immaculate bathrooms have robes and a heated towel rack." *(Michael & Linda Teutscel)* "Lovely garden; quiet street with ample parking." *(Ellen Belliveau)* "Two adorable if pesky 'guard' geese live in the inn's beautiful gardens. Our little room had a dressing room with an armoire, a desk with a welcome note, bottled water, and delectable chocolate truffles with evening turndown service." *(Cindy Banks)* "We met the other guests over afternoon tea, highlighted by a delicious berry tart. Emily and Raymond were always on hand, but did not hover." *(Monique Noah)*

"Hummingbird is the largest room, colored in blue and gray, with a woodburning stove and extra large bathroom. Super lighting for reading in bed and putting on makeup. Responding to my request for a strictly vegetarian meal, I was served a delicious Egyptian dish of fava beans and onions with pita bread, followed by strawberry sorbet. Warm, welcoming, helpful owners. Montara has a lovely little beach, too." *(Gail Davis)*

Open All year.
Rooms 5 doubles—all with private bath and/or shower. All with desk.
Facilities Breakfast area, living room with woodstove, books, audio tapes,games, piano. 1 acre with swing, hammock, bocce ball court, garden, fountain. ½ m to beach for water sports.
Location San Francisco Bay area. 25 m S of S.F; 20 min. to SF airport. 8 m N of Half Moon Bay. Take Hwy. 1 S to Montara.
Restrictions No smoking. Minimal interior soundproofing.
Credit cards Amex, Discover, MC, Visa.
Rates B&B, $93–110 double, including tax. Extra person, $10. Midweek, senior discounts. Weekly rates.
Extras Local airport pickup. Crib. French spoken.

MONTEREY

Originally built up around the sardine fishing and canning business (which collapsed about 40 years ago), Monterey was first made famous by John Steinbeck's novel *Cannery Row*. The old cannery buildings have long been renovated and now house art galleries, antique shops, restaurants, and inns. Its most popular attraction is the Monterey Bay Aquarium, an innovatively designed building, that is now home to over 500 species of ocean life.

For more information on the Monterey peninsula, see the Central Coast section of the introduction to this chapter; for additional area entries, see **Pacific Grove.**

On scenic Highway 1, Monterey is located about 120 miles south of San Francisco and 320 miles north of Los Angeles, on California's central coast. From Los Angeles, drive up Highway 101 to Salinas, then west on Route 66. If you have more time, exit 101 at San Luis Obispo and stay on Highway 1 to Monterey. From San Francisco, take Highway 101 to

Route 156 to Highway 1, or stay on Highway 1 the whole way if you've time.

Reader tips: "Be warned that Cannery Row is wall-to-wall tee-shirt shops and junk food carry-outs. Rock music blares from store fronts, and bumper-to-bumper traffic edges down the street. But go anyway to see the aquarium." *(SHW)* "Try Bradley's for an outstanding dinner." *(Bob Freidus)*

Also recommended: Right on Del Monte Beach is the **Monterey Beach Hotel** (2600 Sand Dunes Drive, 93940; 408–394–3321; 800–242–6627), a 200-room Best Western property with rates ranging from $90–170. Dog-lovers will be glad to know that pets are welcome, and *Peggy Vaughn* recommends it for this reason, as well as for its "nice, clean rooms with fantastic ocean views, swimming pool, and convenient fourth-floor restaurant."

Jabberwock   *Tel: 408–372–4777*
598 Laine Street, 93940

Named after the Lewis Carroll poem, the Jabberwock carries its theme from the names of the rooms to the breakfast creations.

"Great location, very near the aquarium and Cannery Row, but not in the middle of it. Barbara and Jim introduced guests and made sure everyone felt comfortable. Beautiful views from the sundeck; delicious hors d'oeuvres served there in the evening." *(Elizabeth Lamping)* "Delicious homemade cookies and milk were waiting in the living room when we returned after dinner. We pulled out the Scrabble set and got a good game going. Our comfortable room had eyelet and goose-down comforters, cordials, books, mints, and big, soft towels; a delightful fragrance of orange pervaded the house. Parking is good and access to the town was convenient for both walkers and drivers. The Looking Glass theme was intriguing, especially with the custom-made 'backwards' clocks. The Allens helped us plan excursions around town and made dinner reservations." *(Janet Hardee)* "Our spotless room had a clear view of the bay, with a sofa right in front of the fireplace. Thick terry robes hung in the closet." *(Mary Lou & Albert Lautier)* "We went out to dinner together to a place Jim recommended and laughed all night. Perfect for a single traveler." *(Mark Corigliano)*

Open All year.
Rooms 1 suite, 6 doubles—5 with private bath and/or shower, 2 with maximum of 4 people sharing bath. Suite with fireplace.
Facilities Dining room, living room both with fireplace, library, enclosed sun porch. 1/2 acre, garden, waterfall, picnic table. 4 blocks to Monterey Bay. Off-street parking.
Location 4 blocks from Cannery Row and Aquarium. From Hwy. 1 turn W onto Hwy. 68 for 2 1/2 m. Go right on Prescott, right on Pine, left on Hoffman 4 blocks, & turn right at Laine to inn.
Restrictions No smoking. Prefer children over 12.
Credit cards MC, Visa.
Rates B&B, $180 suite, $100–150 double. 2–3-night weekend, holiday minimum.
Extras Spanish, French, Danish spoken.

Old Monterey Inn
500 Martin Street, 93940

Tel: 408–375–828
Fax: 408–375–673

The Old Monterey Inn is a half-timbered Tudor-style residence built i
1929. It was bought in the 1960s by Ann and Gene Swett as their privat
home; as their six children grew up and moved out, their rooms wer
gradually redone as guest rooms. The inn is decorated with stained glas
windows and skylights, period furniture, and family antiques; guests sta
cozy under European goose-down comforters.

"The fountain edged with carnations was a prelude to the beautifu
gardens." *(Tom Wilbanks)* "The lavish breakfasts can be enjoyed outsid
in the garden or packed in a basket for those leaving before 9 A.M." *(Elli
Spitzer)* "The innkeepers prepare helpful newsletters with tips on picnick
ing, restaurants, and shopping." *(Jane & Rick Mattoon)* "The Garden Cot
tage has a sitting room furnished with a white wicker settee and rockin
chair facing a fireplace, a huge skylight, and Dutch door with a staine
glass window. The exquisite bedroom has a king-size bed with a partia
canopy, and bay windows that look out over the stunning rose garden.
(Richard & Sheri DeBro) "Terrific breakfast of homemade granola wit
yogurt and strawberries, Belgian waffles, strawberry muffins, freshl
squeezed orange juice, crescent rolls, and hot chocolate. The guest refrig
erator was stocked with a wide variety of complimentary juices, water
and soft drinks." *(Rick & Cynthia Gould)* "Within walking distance o
everything." *(Ray Farris)* "Enthusiastically confirm existing entry. Fres
flowers enhance every room." *(Marilyn Pegler)* "Lovely furnishings, wit
the feel of a real home. Coffee, tea, and cookies are set out in the afternoo
with sherry served at 5 P.M. in the spacious living room. Lots of big
comfortable seating, plenty of books, magazines, and local restauran
menus." *(Bob & Ellie Freidus)*

Open All year. Closed Dec. 25.
Rooms 1 suite, 8 doubles, 1 cottage—all with private bath and/or shower, radio
1 room in annex with whirlpool tub. 8 with fireplace. Some with refrigerator, deck
Facilities Dining room, living room both with fireplace. 1 acre, flower gardens
sitting areas, hammocks, picnic area. Near Monterey Bay & Aquarium.
Location 4 blocks from center. Take Munras Ave. exit from Hwy. 1, left o
Soledad Dr., right on Pacific St. Go ½ m to Martin St.
Restrictions No smoking.
Credit cards MC, Visa.
Rates B&B, $240 suite & cottage, $170–220 double. Extra person (in suite only
$50. 2–3-night weekend/holiday minimum.

MOSS BEACH

Reader tip: "Dinner at the Moss Beach Distillery is a must!" *(Debbi
Sorich)*.

Seal Cove Inn 🏃 ♿
221 Cypress Avenue, 94038

Tel: 415–728–SEA
Fax: 415–728–411

Guidebook author Karen Brown, along with her husband, Rick Herbert
took their years of travel experience and built an inn of their own

verlooking a field of wildflowers, with the ocean in the distance. Con-
ructed in 1991, the inn has handsomely decorated guest rooms, in a
ariety of styles from English country to French Provençal to American
mish.

"Karen and Rick built the inn with the goal of including all the things
ey like about other inns—fresh flowers everywhere, fruit, refrigerators
ocked with complimentary wine, snacks, and soft drinks, heated towel
cks, even movies and popcorn. The Carl Larsson Room was decorated
ith 18 of his famous illustrations, furniture, and fabrics, in keeping with
e Scandinavian theme. Delicious breakfast of freshly squeezed orange
ice, fruit, waffles or French toast. Wine and appetizers served at 5 P.M."
O) "Karen and Rick went out of their way to make us feel at home. We
reakfasted on Monte Cristo sandwiches with raspberry preserves." (Kim
choknecht) "We enjoyed walking to the beach and its tide pools or up to
e bluff overlooking the ocean for spectacular sunsets." (Cliff & Elizabeth
Vright) "I spent an evening settled in my room, wrapped in a fluffy terry
be, enjoying the fireplace. The next morning I sipped coffee and read
e newspaper waiting outside my door. Over afternoon tea, Karen
hatted with me about the coastal area, giving a personal touch to my day
f touring." (Mary Kathryn Newberry) Comments appreciated.

Open All year.
Rooms 2 suites, 8 doubles—all with full private bath, telephone, radio, TV/VCR,
n, wood-burning fireplace, refrigerator, hair dryer, deck/patio/balcony. Some
ith desk. 2 with whirlpool tub.
Facilities Living room with fireplace, video library, books; dining room, confer-
nce room. 1 1/2 acres adjoining 20 acre marine reserve. 5 min. walk to beach for
hale-watching, fishing, surfing.
Location 17 m S of San Francisco, 6 m N of Half Moon Bay. From Hwy. 1 turn
V on Cypress Ave. to inn on right.
Restrictions No smoking.
Credit cards Amex, Discover, MC, Visa.
Rates B&B, $250 suite, $165–185 double. Extra person, $25. 10% senior, AAA
iscount. 2-night holiday weekend minimum.
Extras Wheelchair access; 1 room equipped for disabled. Crib. French, German,
panish spoken.

MUIR BEACH

Pelican Inn ✕   Tel: 415–383–6000
0 Pacific Way, 94965–9729

When the fog rolls in and you need a cozy haven, consider the Pelican
nn, a Tudor replica built in 1979 and managed by R. Barry Stock since
986. Rates include an English breakfast of bacon, eggs, sausage, grilled
omatoes, toast, marmalade, fruit, orange juice, coffee and tea. Lunch
hoices include traditional favorites like cottage pie, bangers and mash,
nd fish 'n chips, while dinner entrées range from mixed grill to Pacific
napper with basil cream sauce.

"Loved the British atmosphere and English antiques. The Resident's
ounge is a cozy living room reserved for overnight guests. We had lunch
n the attractive patio; the menu was interesting and the food good. We

149

walked to the beach a short way down a country road. Rugged countr
side." *(Eileen O'Reilly, also Joy Sugg)*

Area for improvement: "Brighter authentic bedside lighting."

Open All year. Closed Christmas. Restaurant closed Mon.
Rooms 7 doubles—all with private shower and/or bath, desk. 3 with balcon
deck.
Facilities Restaurant with fireplace, bar, living room with fireplace, patio. 1 ac
with off-street parking. Ocean nearby for fishing, swimming, cliff hikes.
Location Marin Cty, 30 min. N of San Francisco. From Hwy 101 N of S
Francisco take Stinson Beach Hwy 1 turnoff. Left at 1st light onto Hwy 1 & g
5 m to inn.
Restrictions No smoking in restaurant. No hard liquor.
Credit cards MC, Visa.
Rates B&B, $145–160 double. Extra person, $25. Alc lunch, $8; also dinner, $2
Extras Restaurant, downstairs bathrooms wheelchair accessible. Crib. Spani
spoken.

MURPHYS

The sleepy village of Murphys is in the heart of Gold Country's souther
Mother Lode, one of the best preserved of the Calaveras County minin
towns. The town has a community park, swimming pool, and tenn
courts open to visitors. There are state parks nearby for hiking and fishin
and visitors enjoy gold panning and visiting caves and wineries (six maj
ones within two miles), golf and skiing. While here, don't miss th
enormous sequoias at Calaveras Big Trees State Park. Murphys is locate
in the foothills of the Sierras, 2½ hours east of San Francisco, just east
Angel's Camp on State Route 4.

Dunbar House, 1880 *Tel:* 209–728–289
271 Jones Street, P.O. Box 1375, 95247 800–225–376
Fax: 209–728–145

Dunbar House is an Italianate Victorian home, bought by Bob and Barba
Costa in 1987; Felice Cizmick is the manager. From 8:30–9:30 A.M., gues
are served breakfast in the dining room, the garden, or in their rooms;
typical menu might include artichoke bacon frittata, rosemary potatoe
lemon scones, fresh fruit with Amaretto sauce, and orange juice spritzer

"The inn was built in 1880 and has been painstakingly restored an
elaborately furnished with antiques." *(Jim & Sybilla Elrod)* "We we
greeted with an afternoon buffet of fruit, cheese and crackers, then e
corted to our room. Fascinating pictures, books, magazines, and memor
bilia found throughout the inn. The comfortable Ponderosa Room
medium-sized with a sink in the room and a small bath with a claw-foote
shower/tub combination; our refrigerator was stocked with a bottle
local wine. The ample and delicious breakfast was served family style
the large dining room table." *(JTD)* "The cozy parlor fire and gentle mus
or the welcome breeze on the veranda, create a relaxing atmosphere
(Robert Reagan) "The innkeepers ensure that their guests are well fed an

well rested." *(JoAnna Johnson)* "Inviting verandas and tree-shaded grounds." *(L.L. Rowell)* "Delightful small touches—the flowers, the lemon drops, bath amenities, potpourri, magazines." *(Elaine Rex)*

Open All year.
Rooms 2 suites, 2 doubles—all with full private bath, clock/radio, TV, desk, air-conditioning, fan, woodstove/fireplace, refrigerator, hair dryer. 1 with double whirlpool tub.
Facilities Dining room with fireplace, parlor with fireplace, piano, stereo, games, books, VCR/videotape library; veranda. 1 acre with off-street parking, gazebo, gardens, lawn games, hammock.
Location Turn W off Main St. at Monument. 2 blocks from historic district.
Restrictions No smoking. Children over 10.
Credit cards Amex, MC, Visa.
Rates B&B, $145 suite, 105 double, $100 single. Extra person, $20. 2-night weekend minimum. Carriage winery tour/picnics. Ski packages.

Murphys Historic Hotel & Lodge ¢ ✗ ♦   *Tel:* 209–728–3444
457 Main Street, P.O. Box 329, 95247   800–532–7684
                                     Fax: 209–728–1590

Although the wrecking ball may have been the worst enemy of historic buildings in the 20th century, in the 19th century, fire was their chief nemesis. Built in 1855 with thick stone walls and iron shutters, the supposedly "fireproof" Sperry & Percy Hotel lasted three years before flames destroyed the roof and back part of the building. Rebuilt in 1859, it has operated continuously as a hotel, and maintains much of the same character as it did when Ulysses S. Grant, Mark Twain, Horatio Alger, and the infamous bandit Black Bart signed the register. In 1963, a group of local investors took over the ownership, dedicated to the hotel's preservation; they also constructed two modest adjacent motel buildings. Michael Lane is the manager. Rates include a continental breakfast and a complimentary cocktail in the saloon. Typical dinner entrées might be seafood fettuccine, lemon pepper chicken, and prime rib.

"Historic 1860s atmosphere and furnishings, from the creaking floorboards to the decor." *(SC)* "Breakfast buffet of cereal, fruit, and pastry. Excellent dinner featuring fine local wines. Authentic saloon enthusiastically frequented by locals. Friendly, helpful staff. Room #10 at the front of the hotel has French doors which open onto a charming veranda overlooking Main Street. Everything was clean, including the shared baths." *(Stephanie Johnston)* Comments welcome.

Area for improvement: "Better quality breakfast pastries."

Open All year.
Rooms 1 suite, 8 doubles in hotel with shared bath, fan, veranda; 2 suites, 18 doubles in two motel annexes with private shower/bath, telephone, clock, TV, desk, air-conditioning.
Facilities Restaurant, saloon with TV, weekend entertainment, banquet room, veranda. Off-street parking, garden.
Location Center of town.
Restrictions Bar, street noise weekend evenings in front rooms in season. No smoking in dining room.
Credit cards Amex, CB, DC, Discover, MC, Visa.

Rates B&B, $90–105 suite, $70–85 double. Extra person, $6. No charge for children under 12. 10% senior discount. 2-3 night weekend/holiday minimum. Alc lunch, $7.50; alc dinner, $21. Golf, ski, river-rafting packages.
Extras Limited wheelchair access to restaurant. Cribs. Spanish, German, Italian, French spoken.

NAPA

Although Napa's founding about 100 years ago was due to the gold rush, today's gold flows from the wine industry and the extensive tourism industry that has developed along with it. The town is a popular base for wine touring—perhaps overly so during fall harvest weekends. Napa is located in the North Coast region, in Napa Valley Wine Country, just one hour north of San Francisco.

Information please: The **Old World Inn** (1301 Jefferson Street, 94559; 707–257–0112 or 800–966–6624) is a peach-colored Victorian home built in 1906. Owner Diane Dumaine offers a full breakfast with a fresh fruit buffet, croissants, muffins, coffee cake, and asparagus frittata or mushroom crepes. The eight guest rooms are decorated in pastel shades, and the B&B double rate ranges from $105–140.

Beazley House   ♿   *Tel:* 707–257–1649
1910 First Street, 94559   800–559–1649
                                         Fax: 707–257–1518

A Napa landmark since 1902, Beazley House was Napa's first B&B when Carol and Jim Beazley opened it in 1981. Guest rooms are furnished with antiques and country flair; all have queen-size beds. Breakfast consists of freshly baked breads, muffins, fruit, yogurt, granola, and baked egg dishes; low-fat menus a specialty. "Comfortable beds, good food and attentive service. The owners are responsive to guests' suggestions." *(Alexia Martin)* "Bed & Roses is a spacious room with a vaulted ceiling, gorgeous queen-size brass bed, antique dresser with a tray of bottled water and chocolate kisses awaited us on the dresser, desk, and comfortable chairs with a reading lamp. Although somewhat dark, the room had a wonderfully romantic atmosphere; we really enjoyed the whirlpool tub with the fireplace blazing. The bathroom had excellent light for makeup and a shower stall. Upstairs, the West Loft has a huge Palladian window framed with a colorful stained glass design of grape vines. The carriage house rooms are quiet and close to the parking area. Fran was most helpful with dinner suggestions." *(Gail Davis)*

Open All year.
Rooms 2 suites, 9 doubles—all with private bath and/or shower, telephone (on request), clock/radio, air-conditioning. Some with desks, gas fireplace, refrigerator, patio. TV on request. 5 rooms in carriage house. 4 with double whirlpool tubs.
Facilities Dining room, living room, library, porch. 6/10 acre with off-street parking, garden with fountain, swing.
Location Historic district. From Hwy. 29 N, take Central Napa 1st St. Exit & follow around to right until 2nd St. Go right on 2nd, left on Warren to inn at corner of 1st & Warren.

Restrictions No smoking. Children over 10.
Credit cards Amex, MC, Visa.
Rates B&B, $145–210 suite, $75–185 double, $74–170 single. Extra person, $45. 10% senior, AAA discount. 2-night weekend minimum. Off-season midweek rates; ballooning, wine train packages.
Extras Wheelchair access; 2 rooms specially equipped. Babysitting. Spanish, French spoken.

Churchill Manor ♿   *Tel: 707–253–7733*
485 Brown Street, 94559   *Fax: 707–253–8836*

Churchill Manor is a magnificent three-story mansion built in 1889, now listed on the National Register of Historic Places. It and was purchased in 1987 by Joanna Guidotti and Brian Jensen, who report that "Churchill Manor is like the Golden Gate Bridge—it will never be completely finished before you start over again—but that's half the fun." The manor encompasses 10,000 square feet, with seven fireplaces and 12-foot carved redwood ceilings and columns, and is decorated primarily with European antiques, Oriental rugs, and brass and crystal chandeliers. Breakfast includes omelets or perhaps French toast, afternoon fresh-baked cookies, and evening Napa varietal wines and cheeses.

"The huge grounds were lovely, and the common areas were like something out of a different era (which they are)." *(Mark Mendenhall)* "We were welcomed with delicious cookies and cool beverages in the sunroom." *(Pat Malone)* "After one early morning walk, we sat down to relax on one of the pretty wicker settees on the veranda overlooking the beautiful gardens. Brian surprised us with fresh coffee, juice and fruit." *(Wilfred Sweet)* "Victoria's Room is furnished in Art Deco style with a king-size bed, fireplace, clawfoot tub and the tallest shower stall I've ever seen. A beautiful bouquet of roses had been brought in from the garden. The breakfast room is sunny and cheerful with individual tables. We were served fresh fruit, juice, muffins, croissants and a choice of French toast or an omelet." *(DG)* "Friendly cats."

Worth noting: "I would not feel comfortable walking alone after dark in this neighborhood, but the manor's safe and beautiful grounds more than compensated."

Open All year.
Rooms 10 doubles—all with private bath and/or shower, telephone, radio, desk, air-conditioning. 1 with Jacuzzi, 3 with fireplace.
Facilities 3 living rooms with fireplace, games (1 with TV/VCR); music room with grand piano, fireplace; garden breakfast room, veranda. 1 acre near river. Off-street parking. Tandem bicycles, croquet. Tennis, golf, health spa, mud baths, balloon rides nearby.
Location Historic section, 4 blocks from center. From Hwy. 29, take Imola Ave. exit; go E to Jefferson; turn left & go ¾ m to Oak; turn right & go 7 blocks to Brown. Manor on right corner.
Restrictions No smoking. Children over 12. Creaky floor-boards might disturb light sleepers.
Credit cards Amex, Discover, MC, Visa.
Rates B&B, $135–160 suite, $75–160 double. Extra person, $15. 2-night minimum with Sat. stay.
Extras Limited wheelchair access. Local airport pickups.

153

The Napa Inn

Tel: 707–257–1444

1137 Warren Street, 94559

"The Napa Inn is a beautifully restored, Queen Anne–style home, located on a quiet residential street. The spacious parlor is furnished with comfortable chairs, antiques and collectibles; complimentary sherry was set out for guests, and classical music played on a vintage radio. The innkeeper, Carol Morales, has interesting stories to tell about the furnishings and photographs in the inn. The Eastlake Suite has an antique carved bed and dresser, with a comfortable sofa in the sitting area. The bathroom had a claw-foot tub with shower, and was extremely clean. Carol is quite a cook; you help yourself to the ample breakfast and sit with the other guests around the large dining table, sharing stories about the local wineries and restaurants. We had an egg casserole, pastries, fruit, and coffee. In the afternoon, strawberry pie and lemonade were perfect for a hot day in wine country." *(Wendy Kameda)* "Our spacious and charming suite on the third floor had a gas fireplace, built-in bench seats and a king-size brass bed set beside a pretty Palladian window. Angled ceilings created an interesting low entryway for the bathroom, situated inside the house's main turret. We returned after dinner to find a delicious chocolate cake waiting to be devoured in the dining room." *(Gail Davis)*

Open All year.
Rooms 2 suites, 3 doubles—all with private bath and/or shower, fan, air-conditioning. 2 with gas fireplace.
Facilities Parlor with player piano, gas fireplace, books, games; dining room, guest refrigerator. Off-street parking.
Location 3 blocks from center of town. From Hwy. 29, take 1st St. exit, then quick left turn onto California Blvd. Go 1 block to Clay St. & turn right. Turn left on Warren St. to inn on left.
Restrictions No smoking. "Not appropriate for children."
Credit cards MC, Visa.
Rates B&B, $160–170 suite, $120–135 double. Extra person, $25.

NEVADA CITY

Founded in the heat of the gold rush, Nevada City remains one of the most picturesque towns along the Mother Lode. Victorian homes, white frame churches, and covered sidewalks still line the hilly streets, in spite of two fires that ravaged the town in the 1800s; excellent restaurants and charming shops invite strolling and browsing. Nevada City is located in the Sierra foothills, approximately 50 minutes northeast of Sacramento and 3 hours northeast of San Francisco. Nearby are golf, tennis, swimming, hiking, fishing, downhill and cross-country skiing, river rafting, and horseback riding.

Ten miles north of Nevada City are the Malakoff Diggins, the site of the world's largest hydraulic gold mining operation where miners directed high-powered streams of water onto the hillsides. Effective as the practice was, entire mountainsides were washed away before some of the earliest environmental legislation stopped the destruction.

Flume's End
317 South Pine, 95959

Tel: 916–265–9665

Built in 1863, Flume's End B&B was bought by Steve Wilson and Terrianne Straw in 1990. "Flume's End appears to be an unprepossessing Victorian cottage, set right on the street. In back, the inn descends a steep hillside, overlooking spring-fed, fast-flowing Gold Run Creek. Although the common areas are basic, its bedrooms are appealing with country Victorian floral fabrics and wallcoverings, and modern baths. Our favorite was the Creekside Room, cantilevered over the creek—you look through floor-to-ceiling windows to the rushing waters below. Several levels of terraces overlook the stream and shaded hillside. It's hard to believe that town is just a short walk across the scenic Pine Street Bridge." *(SWS)* Breakfasts, served on the terrace deck, might include smoked salmon and dill tart, spicy browned potatoes and locally made sausage. Homemade fudge, brownies, and cookies are put out each evening for guests to savor.

"We enjoyed chatting with Steve and Terrianne about their experiences as innkeepers." *(DCB)* "The Garden Room has its own little deck right above a waterfall. Although both the room and bed were small, we loved it because of the sound of the water, plus the Jacuzzi tub. Outside our room was a little living room with a woodstove and a stocked guest refrigerator. Excellent breakfast of cheese-baked potatoes, homemade granola, baked apple sauce, eggs Florentine, bread, and French roast coffee." *(Lisa Gallagher, also JTD)*

Open All year.
Rooms 1 cottage, 5 doubles—all with private shower and/or bath, radio, air-conditioning. 2 with balcony, Jacuzzi; cottage with kitchenette, stove, deck.
Facilities Dining room, living room with fireplace, piano, banjo, flute. Family room with TV, refrigerator, wet bar. 3½ acres with terraces, creek. 15 min. to cross-country skiing; 45 min. to downhill.
Location 2 blocks from town.
Restrictions No smoking.
Credit cards MC, Visa.
Rates B&B, $75–135. 2-night weekend minimum.

The Red Castle Inn ¢
109 Prospect Street, 95959

Tel: 916–265–5135

On a steep hillside overlooking Nevada City sits this dramatic four-story Gothic Revival red brick mansion, dripping white icicle trim with elaborately carved balconies. Long-time owners Mary Louise and Conley Weaver have decorated the 1860 mansion with a mixture of antiques and period pieces, many with an Oriental accent. A special feature is the horse-drawn carriage ride through the historic district every Saturday morning; guests also take the lighted footpath leading from the inn to the town below.

"We were welcomed by Mary Louise, then shown to our room, with a handsome canopied bed and love seat. Across the hall in the living room, guests gathered for tea, a delicious whipped-cream cake, and chocolate nut cookies; Conley joined us to answer questions about the area. The Weavers had made advance reservations for us at one of Nevada City's many fine restaurants. The lavish breakfast is set out in the front hall: fresh fruit and granola, an egg and cheese bake with pear chutney, apple crêpes, muffins and zucchini bread. We took our tray into the living room and sat on the couch." *(SWS)* "Great barley cereal for breakfast; afternoon lemonade was a welcome break. We took our breakfast trays outside to the chairs and tables on veranda and lingered over the view of Nevada City." *(Kathleen Lowe Owen)* "Plentiful supply of reading material on the Gold Country." *(Marylou Sweeney)*

Open All year.
Rooms 3 suites, 4 doubles—all with private shower and/or bath. 4 with desk, air-conditioning, fan; 2 with radio. Most with private balcony.
Facilities Parlor with pump organ. 1½ acres with terraced gardens, fish pond with fountain, croquet, swing. Swimming, fishing, tennis, winery, brewery nearby. Off-street parking.
Location Walking distance to historic district. From Hwy. 49, take Sacramento St. exit and turn right just past Chevron station. Turn left on Prospect St.
Restrictions No smoking. "Children must be carefully supervised."
Credit cards MC, Visa.
Rates B&B, $100–140 suite, $70–125 double, $65–120 single. Extra person, $20. 2-night holiday/weekend minimum April–Dec. Corporate rates. Christmas dinner with entertainment.
Extras Airport/station pickup.

NEWPORT BEACH

Although a noisy mob scene in spring and summer, Newport's wide beaches are ideal for long quiet walks, jogs, or bike rides off-season; stroll down to Balboa to explore its appealing shops or to catch the hydrofoil to Catalina. Weekend rates here are high; come midweek and ask for a corporate rate.

Information please: The **Doryman's Inn** (2102 West Ocean Front, 92663; 714–675–7300) is located on a busy corner right on the beach with glorious views. On the first floor is a popular seafood restaurant; on the second floor, reached through a separate entrance, is the inn. Rooms are lavishly decorated with European antiques, floral fabrics and lace curtains, reproduction Victorian wallpapers, and sunken marble bathtubs. The buffet breakfast of pastries and breads, brown eggs, cheeses and yogurt, fresh fruit and juices, tea and coffee can be enjoyed in the parlor or on the flower-filled terrace. B&B double rates for the ten guest rooms range from $140–275.

NIPTON

Hotel Nipton   *Tel:* 619–856–2335
72 Nipton Road, HCI Box 357, 92364   *Fax:* 702–896–6846

If you want to get away from it all—really far away—go to the desert town of Nipton, the last stop on I-15 before Nevada. Built between 1904 and 1910, the hotel was restored with southwestern flair in 1986 by owners Gerald and Roxanne Freeman. Experienced desert dwellers, they are pleased to help guests enjoy the East Mojave National Scenic Area, a rugged desert wilderness. Guest rooms have been named for local personalities (silent film star Clara Bow was a frequent guest), and decorated with old photographs, personal mementos, original documents, and antiques.

"Warm, friendly, unpretentious, genuine. The hotel's historical significance is well researched and verified." *(HL)* "The small desert town of Nipton seems like another world, but the owners of the hotel are definitely aware of today's travelers' need for service and privacy. The sitting room has terrific old pictures, and the scenery is astounding, with desert and mountains that seem to go on forever. Breakfast is served in the parlor, and included good coffee, orange juice, fruit and huge blueberry muffins." *(Sherrill Brown)*

Open All year.
Rooms 4 doubles share 2 baths. All with air-conditioning.
Facilities Parlor with books, radio. Cactus garden. Hiking, mt. biking, fishing, boating nearby.
Location East Mojave National Scenic area. 55 m SW of Las Vegas, between Grand Canyon & Death Valley. 10 m off I-15.
Restrictions Smoking OK. Train noise possible.
Credit cards DC, MC, Visa.
Rates B&B, $45 double. Extra person, $8.
Extras Limited wheelchair access.

OJAI

Ojai is set in a lovely valley, surrounded by coastal range mountains; the climate is both dry and moderate. There are numerous art galleries and craft shops here, and the town hosts several music festivals during the year. Ojai is located on the central coast, 40 miles southeast of Santa Barbara and 73 miles northwest of Los Angeles.

Also recommended: Although too large for a full entry, we've had consistently good reports on the **Ojai Valley Inn** (Country Club Road, 93023; 805–646–5511 or 800–422–OJAI). A full-service resort dating back to the 1920s, the original buildings have thick adobe walls, clay-tile roofs, massive fireplaces, and heavy beamed ceilings. A major expansion and renovation was completed in 1988 providing all the facilities one would expect of a luxury resort. The 202 luxurious hotel rooms are equipped with all amenities, and many have beautiful mountain views. The 220 acres have two heated swimming pools, 8 tennis courts, an 18-hole golf course, children's playground and more. Double room rates range from $195–260, and kids stay free; ask about package rates.

Information please: "Set back from the main street, east of the hustle and bustle of downtown, **The Theodore Woolsey House** (1484 East Ojai Avenue, 93023; 805–646–9779) is a stone and clapboard house with a rose-covered trellis, surrounded by gardens and huge oak trees. The property also has an inviting swimming pool framed by palm trees and the mountains. Guests can just watch the sunrise or breakfast on fresh fruit, cereal, muffins, bagels, coffee cake, and fresh-squeezed orange juice on the inviting second-floor sundeck. The six guest rooms have private or shared baths, and are charmingly decorated with antiques and coordinating floral comforters, wallpapers, and curtains." *(GD)* Rates range from $60–110.

The in-town **Ojai Manor Hotel** (210 East Matilija, P.O. Box 608, 93023; 805–646–0961) combines antique charm and modern sculpture. Built in 1874 as a schoolhouse and opened as a B&B in 1984, its six artfully decorated guest rooms share three baths. The $80–90 rates include a breakfast of cereal, fresh fruit and fresh-squeezed orange juice, plus a variety of home-baked muffins, breads, and coffee cakes, as well as evening refreshments. "A charming house with a wrap-around porch and rose garden, with a quiet in-town location, just a block from the main street." *(GD)*

OLEMA

Olema is located 35 miles north of San Francisco, in Marin County, with Point Reyes National Seashore to the west, and Golden Gate National Recreation Area to the east. Giant redwoods can be seen in Samuel Taylor State Park.

Information please: The **Roundstone Farm** (9940 Sir Francis Drake Boulevard, P.O. Box 217, Olema 94950; 415–663–1020), was designed by solar architect Jim Campe to take full advantage of the surrounding natural beauty. "This ten-acre ranch has four guest rooms beautifully decorated with custom-made furniture and antiques, each with its own fireplace and private bath." *(April Burwell)* Breakfast is included in the $115–135 double rates.

For additional area entries, see **Inverness**.

Point Reyes Seashore Lodge   ♿
10021 Coastal Highway One,
P.O. Box 39, 94950

Tel: 415–663–9000
Fax: 415–663–9030

A turn-of-the-century country lodge, the Point Reyes Seashore Lodge offers comfortable accommodations at reasonable rates. Guest rooms have simple but comfortable furnishings. Rooms with whirlpool bathtubs have screens joining the bedroom with the bath, providing a tranquil view of the pastoral surroundings and Mt. Wittenberg. The suites have upstairs sleeping lofts with European feather beds, and a sofa bed sitting area by the fireplace. "Rustic, roadside inn. Once you enter the inn and see the grounds at the back, you forget where you are." *(Joe & Anne Miller)* "Lovely grounds; tasty breakfast of juice, coffee, sweet rolls, muffins, cheeses, cereals. The front desk staff gave us good suggestions for area activities." *(Stephanie Roberts)*

Open All year.
Rooms 3 suites, 18 doubles—all with private bath and/or shower, telephone.

Most with whirlpool tub, some with fireplace. Suites with sleeping lofts, double whirlpool tub, wet bar, refrigerator.

Facilities Common area with games, puzzles, billiards table. Hiking, bicycling, horseback riding, whale-watching, bird-watching, beachcombing, golf nearby.

Location West Marin. On Hwy. 1. From Hwy 101, take Sir Francis Drake Blvd. to Olema.

Credit cards Amex, Discover, MC, Visa.

Rates B&B, $140–185 suite, $75–140 double. Extra person, $15. Weekly rates.

Extras Wheelchair access; facility specially equipped.

ORLAND

The Inn at Shallow Creek Farm ¢   Tel: 916–865–4093
4712 County Road DD, 95963

"A quiet location, close enough to the freeway so as not to get lost, but far enough away not to hear it" *(Norma & Mike McClintock)* summarizes the initial appeal of this inn's location near Interstate 5, roughly a halfway point for those traveling between California and southern Oregon. Kurt and Mary Glaeseman have owned the farm since 1982, and in addition to the care and feeding of their guests, tend to citrus orchards and poultry flock.

"When you turn into the shade of the tree-lined front yard, ducks, geese, and guinea hens will come to greet you. Surrounding the inn are groves of citrus trees, which give the air a glorious scent when in bloom. Breakfast is served family-style around the big oak table, and included eggs from the farmyard, fruit and preserves from their trees." *(Geralynn Myrah)* "Kurt recommended historic sites, a quiet lakeside spot, and a nearby restaurant." *(Collin Batey)* "Spacious guest quarters, countless books, and comfortable sofas and chairs." *(Robin Harris)* "The area is good for long walks, or sitting in the shade of the huge trees. In cool weather, the living room is inviting with comfortable leather furniture and a cozy fire." *(Glen & Mary Hughes)* "Warm, homey, attractive in an undecorated way, which we prefer to places with matching everything." *(Eileen O'Reilly)*

Open All year.

Rooms 1 cottage, 1 suite, 2 doubles—2 with private bath and/or shower, 2 with maximum of 4 sharing bath. All with telephone, air-conditioning. 2 with desk. Cottage with wood-burning stove.

Facilities Dining room, living room with fireplace, piano, TV, stereo. Sun porch with books, games, refrigerator. 3 acres with citrus orchards. 5 m to lake for boating, swimming, fishing, hiking.

Location Central Valley. N. Sacramento Valley, Glenn County. 100 m N of Sacramento, 20 m W of Chico, 2 ½ m W of I-5. Take Black Butte/Orland/Chico exit and go W 2 ½ m on Newville Rd. Turn right at Rd. DD. Go ½ m, cross small concrete bridge, and turn right down the 1st country lane.

Restrictions No smoking.

Credit cards MC, Visa.

Rates B&B, $75 cottage, $65 suite, $55 double. Extra person, $15. Includes tax and service.

Extras Airport/station pickup. French, German, Spanish spoken.

OROVILLE

Jean's Riverside B&B ¢   ♿   *Tel: 916–533–141*
45 Cabana, P.O. Box 2334, 95965

Named for the riches that were once mined here, the "city of gold"
home to Jean's Riverside B&B, overlooking the Feather River. This rust
cedar building was originally constructed in 1936, and has been owned b
Jean Pratt since 1955. In 1978, she expanded and opened her home as a
inn. The simply furnished but comfortable guest rooms have natural ceda
walls and large windows with views of the river, Oroville Dam, and th
Sierras. Nearby are numerous restaurants and over 20 local antique an
craft shops. Local sights include the Chinese Temple, Oroville Dam, an
ghost towns. Every morning the breakfast menu centers on gold miner
sourdough bread, with local fruit and homemade jam. "Homey, comfor
able accommodations, lovely views, peaceful setting, excellent sourdoug
pancakes, gracious and knowledgeable hostess." *(GR)* More commen
welcome.

Open All year.
Rooms 3 suites, 1 cottage, 12 doubles—all with private bath and/or showe
clock, TV, desk, air-conditioning. Some with telephone, fan, woodstove, balcony
patio.
Facilities Dining room, living/family room, deck. 5 acres on Feather River fc
swimming, fishing, gold panning; swimming pool; lawn games. Hiking, bicyclin
golf, tennis nearby.
Location Central Valley/Gold Country. 75 min. N of Sacramento. From I-70, ex
at Oro Dam Blvd. (162), & go W across river, then N on Middlehoff La. to ir
on far right corner of Cabana La. 2 min. from town, I-70.
Restrictions No smoking. Children welcome in cottage.
Credit cards CB, DC, MC, Visa.
Rates B&B, $95–105 suite, $55–88 double. 10% discount on 3-night stay.
Extras Limited wheelchair access. German, French spoken.

PACIFIC GROVE

Set on the Monterey Peninsula, bordering the town of Monterey, Pacifi
Grove begins at the Monterey Bay Aquarium on Cannery Row an
extends along the bay to the beginning of the Seventeen-Mile Driv
Many think this is the peninsula's best town for bicycling and shore
walking. The town was founded by Methodists in 1875 as a "Christia
seaside resort"; most of its Victorian inns were built during this period. I
rather stodgy character lingered on—until the late '60s, liquor could b
bought in Pacific Grove only with a doctor's prescription. The town i
filled with flowers in the spring, but its most famous site is "Butterfly Park
(George Washington Park), where thousands of monarch butterflies wir
ter from October to March.

Pacific Grove is located about 120 miles south of San Francisco. Fc
more information on the Monterey Peninsula, see listings for Montere

nd Carmel (three miles away) as well as the Central Coast section of the introduction to this chapter.

Reader tip: "We visited Pacific Grove during the annual summer celebration, and beach party noise kept us awake until the wee hours; on my next trip, I'll try another weekend." *(EL)*

Also recommended: Although not quite right for a full entry, *Mark Mendenhall* has given us an enthusiastic report on **Asilomar Conference Center** (800 Asilomar Boulevard, P.O. Box 537, 93950; 408–372–8016): Covering over 100 acres, rustic Asilomar is a half-block from the ocean in a peaceful sand dunes environment. Comprised mostly of about 100 small to medium-sized redwood paneled rooms contained in two-story lodges set in clusters on this sand dunes campus, most of the shingled buildings and conference center are historic landmarks designed by California architect Julia Morgan. Our tiny room had craftsman-style bed tables and a desk, an iron rail bedstead, good lighting for reading, and a half-dozen windows that opened to let in the sea air. The renovated bathroom was small but adequate. The full breakfast was served in the cafeteria, and reminded me of college food; you joined your neighbors at shared tables for eight." *(Mark Mendenhall)* Double rates are $114–128.

he Centrella	*Tel:* 408–372–3372
12 Central Avenue,	Outside CA: 800–233–3372
.O. Box 51157, 93950	*Fax:* 408–372–2036

Like many Victorian inns, the Centrella had deteriorated into a decaying rophouse when its current owners purchased it in 1982. Restored to its 1890s glory, the rooms are light and airy, decorated in a country look with lots of wicker, some antiques, and Laura Ashley fabrics. Rates include the morning paper, a breakfast buffet of cereal, fresh fruit and juice, eggs and waffles, yogurt, and breads and pastries, as well as evening sherry and ors d'oeuvres.

"Comfortable king-size bed; the plumbing functions beautifully." *(MAA)* "Service friendly and easygoing. Bath amenities exceptionally nice." *(S. Moeckel)* "Enjoyed the romantic, private Attic Suite; lovely furnishings." *(Sherry Barson)* "Good location; good water pressure, quiet setting, parking no problem." *(DC)*

Minor niggle: "Our cottage seemed slightly musty."

Open All year.
Rooms 3 suites, 18 doubles, 5 cottages—24 with private shower or tub, 2 with maximum of 4 people sharing bath. All rooms with telephone. Some with TV, refrigerator. Cottages with fireplace.
Facilities Living room with fireplace, TV, books, 2 courtyard gardens. Limited off-street parking. 2 blocks to ocean. Jogging/bicycling path nearby.
Location Downtown. Exit Hwy. 1 at Hwy. 68W (Holman Hwy.) to Pacific Grove. Name changes to Forest Ave. in town. Follow Forest to Central Ave. Turn left & go 2 blocks to inn at corner of 17th St. & Central Ave. 1 block to downtown.
Restrictions Traffic noise in some street-side rooms before 10 P.M. No smoking. Children under 12 in cottages only.
Credit cards Amex, MC, Visa.
Rates B&B, $175–185 cottage, $150 suite, $70–125 double. Extra person, $15. 2-night weekend minimum. Midweek, package rates.

Extras Wheelchair access; 1 room specially equipped. Airport/station pickup Italian, Turkish, Spanish spoken.

Gosby House Inn
643 Lighthouse Avenue, 93950

Tel: 408–375–128

Listed on the National Register of Historic Places, the Gosby House is a Queen Anne–style Victorian mansion, built in 1877, and is one of the Four Sisters Inns, owned by the Post family.

"Classical music, a wood-burning fireplace, and the tempting aroma of something baking create a delightful atmosphere, as do the signature stuffed teddy bears. The house sits on the corner of a quiet street lined with boutiques, bookstores, cafés, and a bakery; it's an easy walk to the bay. The friendly staff will secure choice restaurant reservations, a picnic basket for a day of whale watching, or tickets to the aquarium. An ample selection of restaurant menus and past visitor diaries will help you choose both activities and dining spots." *(Diane Wyzga)* "We'd vote for Room 2. as the best room." *(Lisa Berkman)* "At night, a rose was placed on our pillow with two Godiva chocolates." *(Sherri Mandel)* "Delightful, from the black cat draped across the wicker settee on the front porch, to the soft drinks, coffee and tea available round the clock. Our room was beautifully appointed with a yellow and white striped wallpaper with pink cabbage roses, a fireplace, bay window overlooking the garden, Jacuzzi tub and separate shower, and French doors opening to a balcony with a view of Monterey Bay. Balances B&B and small hotel atmosphere." *(Terri Fields)*

Open All year.
Rooms 22 doubles—20 with private bath and/or shower, 2 rooms with 4 people sharing bath. All with telephone. Radio on request. 12 with fireplace, 2 with kitchen.
Facilities Breakfast room, parlor with fireplace, porch with swing. Small garden with seating area; bicycles. 4 blocks to bay. Golf, tennis nearby.
Location Downtown. Exit Hwy. 1 at Rte. 68W (becomes Forest Ave.) to town turn left on Lighthouse, 2 blocks to inn.
Restrictions No smoking. Daytime street noise in some rooms; early morning kitchen/dining noises in two rooms. Least expensive rooms quite small.
Credit cards Amex, MC, Visa.
Rates B&B, $85–150 double. Extra person, $15. Picnic lunches on request. Winter packages.
Extras Crib, babysitting. French spoken. Member, Four Sisters Inns.

The Green Gables Inn
104 Fifth Street, 93950

Tel: 408–375–209

Built in 1888, the Green Gables is a half-timbered, many-gabled Queen Anne Victorian with beautiful stained glass and leaded small-paned windows. Rooms are decorated with antiques, ruffled curtains, and wall-to wall carpets. Rates include a full breakfast, and evening wine and hors d'oeuvres.

"A wonderful 'painted lady' exterior, white with dark green trim, full of towers and turrets. Each room on the second floor has its own tower— which makes for an intriguing space. Decor is high Victorian, with fancy window treatments, lace, and what-nots everywhere. The shared baths are almost as large as some bedrooms and are well equipped with towels and amenities. It's a neat area for climbing on the rocks, as there are no buildings on the ocean side of the street. The view is open and unspoiled." *(SHW)* "Perfect location. Walk to the Aquarium or Lover's Point in minutes or ride the inn's old one-speed bikes along the beautiful ocean-front bike path/walkway. Our large, lovely suite in the Carriage House had a balcony from which we could peek at the ocean. Delicious baked goods at breakfast; equally good were the cookies offered each afternoon and evening." *(EL)*

Open All year.
Rooms 1 suite, 10 doubles—8 with full private bath, 3 with maximum of 4 people sharing bath. Some with radio, TV, fireplace, desk. 5 rooms in carriage house.
Facilities Parlor, dining room with fireplaces. Outdoor garden and sitting area. On water, ½ m to beach.
Location 5 blocks from center. From Hwy. 1, exit at Hwy. 68W, go right on Forest Ave. Turn right on Ocean View Blvd. to Fifth St.
Restrictions No smoking.
Credit cards Amex, MC, Visa.
Rates B&B, $155 suite, $100–160 double. Extra person, $15.
Extras Crib, babysitting. Member, Four Sisters Inns.

The Martine Inn ♿

255 Oceanview Boulevard, 93950

Tel: 408–373–3388
Fax: 408–373–3896

Although built in 1899 as a Victorian cottage, the Martine Inn was remodeled over the years as a pink-stuccoed Mediterranean mansion. The inn was bought by the Martine family in 1972 and was opened as an inn by Marion and Don Martine in 1984. It has been fully restored and decorated in period, from authentic wall coverings to museum-quality antique furnishings.

"Perfect location within walking distance of the aquarium, Cannery Row, and the Wharf. Right on the ocean with a jogging trail that goes along the shore for miles." *(F. T. McQuilkin)* "From the parlor, you get a magnificent view of the rocky coastline, while enjoying wine and hors d'oeuvres. Breakfast included fresh fruit, home-made muffins, a hot entrée, and piping hot coffee." *(Mrs. Donald Hamilton)* "Friendly innkeepers, pleased to help us make dinner plans in Carmel and Monterey." *(Kathryn Chu)*

"Elegant, romantic ambiance. Spectacular oceanfront setting, high above the street below. Don proudly showed us his collection of classic MGs which he restores and races. Incomparable water views. The fireplace was set and awaited only a match to light it. Lace-curtained French doors separated the bedroom and bath. Bedside lights made reading in bed a pleasure. A vase of roses and bowl of fresh fruit was set on our dresser. At night, our bed was turned down, a chocolate placed on each pillow. We fell asleep to the sounds of the gently pounding surf. The large dining room also has picture windows, with binoculars set on the windowsills to enhance viewing." *(Gail Davis)*

Open All year.
Rooms 19 doubles—all with private bath and/or shower, telephone, desk, refrigerator. Many with fireplace.

Facilities Dining room, parlor with fireplace, piano entertainment nightly; library with fireplace, conference room with TV/VCR, game room, 2 sitting rooms. Courtyard with fountain, garden, gazebo, hot tub, and steam room. Fishing, jogging, bicycling, tennis, golf nearby. Limited on-site parking.
Location 3/4 m from center, directly on Monterey Bay. 4 blocks to aquarium.
Restrictions Smoking permitted in guest rooms with fireplace only. "Children discouraged."
Credit cards Amex, MC, Visa.
Rates B&B, $125–230 double. Extra person, $35. 2–3-night weekend/holiday minimum. Picnic lunches on request.
Extras Wheelchair access; 1 room equipped for disabled. Airport/station pickup, $16.

Seven Gables Inn
555 Oceanview Boulevard, 93950   *Tel:* 408–372–4341

Built in 1886, Seven Gables is a grand Victorian home situated on a rocky point at the edge of Monterey Bay. The inn features ocean views from all guest rooms, and contains an exceptional collection of Victorian antiques, including Tiffany stained glass windows, crystal chandeliers, Oriental rugs, inlaid furniture, and queen-size canopy beds. The inn is owned and operated by the Flatley family, who have been in the B&B and antique collecting businesses since 1958. Rates include a full breakfast, served from 8–10 A.M., and afternoon tea at 4 P.M.

"We stayed in the least expensive room, yet still had a fine view and comfortable accommodations. Gorgeous gardens. The tasty breakfast included an egg dish, breads, fresh fruit, yogurt, and fresh-squeezed orange juice." *(James & Janice Utt)* "Meticulously clean; beautiful decor; friendly, efficient staff." *(Adele & Paul Britton)* "Although the location is convenient to everything in Monterey, the inn's best feature is the Flatley family who own and run it." *(Lonnie Felker, also Irene Kolbisen)* Reports welcome.

Open All year.
Rooms 11 doubles, 3 cottages—all with private shower and/or bath, desk.
Facilities Parlor, dining room, family room, breakfast area, porches. Gardens with patios.
Location On ocean, 2 blocks from beach. 1 block to downtown. From Hwy. 1, take Pacific Grove exit (Rte. 68W) to Pacific Grove. Continue on Forest Ave. to Oceanview Blvd., then right 2 blocks to Fountain Ave. & inn.
Restrictions No smoking. "Well-behaved, older children are welcome."
Credit cards MC, Visa.
Rates B&B, $105–205 double. 2-night weekend minimum.
Extras German, Italian, Spanish spoken.

PALM SPRINGS

Located in California's Desert Country, Palm Springs is 115 miles east of Los Angeles, 26 miles east of Joshua Tree National Monument. Palm Springs is famous for its warm and dry winter climate and its championship golf courses. For instant air-conditioning, the tramway to the top of the San Jacinto Mountains is also a favorite; you can even cross-country ski there in winter. Hiking in nearby Palm Canyon, home to trees over a thousand years old, is also popular. Because summer is very definitely off-season here, rates drop considerably during the hottest months.

Reader tips: "Be aware of the college 'spring break;' Palm Springs gets noisy when overrun with students, motorcycles, and police." Also: "Be aware that the desert can be windy." And: "We were disappointed that smog can reach Palm Springs; on our last visit, the air lacked the crystal clarity it once had."

Also recommended: The **Villa Royale** (1620 Indian Trail, 92264; 619–327–2314 or 800–245–2314), a B&B inn with 31 rooms and suites, each decorated with furnishings and art to reflect a different European or Mediterranean country, is spread over three acres with interior courtyards and swimming pools. A continental breakfast is included in the $75–250 rates. "Lovely well kept gardens. The inn has a romantic hideaway feeling to it. The modest price we paid was reflected in little ways—small towels and no one about to carry bags—but was balanced by the inn's charm. Excellent meal in the lovely restaurant with service to match." *(RT)*

L'Horizon ♿

1050 East Palm Canyon Drive, 92264

Tel: 619–323–1858
Fax: 619–327–2933

According to longtime manager Zetta Castle, "L'Horizon was built by Bonita Granville Wrather and her husband, Jack Wrather. Among their many enterprises—the Disneyland Hotel, the Queen Mary, the Spruce Goose, and others—this intimate hideaway was their favorite. Today, the continues to be operated by The Wrather Company in Beverly Hills."

"Our breakfast of oversized muffins and delicious coffee was served on color-coordinated trays and dishes. The signature pale lavender petunias are abundant and add a pretty accent to the desert-colored buildings and mountain backdrop while the mature fruit and palm trees give the feeling of an oasis." *(Howard & Bette Krom)* "The spacious, airy guest rooms are clustered in several small buildings around the inn's swimming pool; I enjoyed the hot tub, with its view of the mountains. My room, furnished with a king-size bed and Southwestern decor, had attractive wooden shutters covering the glass doors for complete privacy. Freshly cut pink tea roses and a wicker basket of Caswell-Massey toiletries were on the bathroom vanity. I found the Sunday *LA Times* outside my door in the morning and read it over breakfast on my private patio. Warm, gracious staff." *(Gail Davis)* "Endorse existing entry." *(GD)*

Open Oct. 1–July 4.
Rooms 22 suites, doubles—all with private bath and/or shower, telephone, radio, TV, air-conditioning, patio.
Facilities Library with games. 2 acres with heated swimming pool, Jacuzzi, lawn games, bicycles. Concierge service.
Location 2 m from town.
Restrictions No children, except Thanksgiving, Christmas holidays.
Credit cards Amex, Discover, MC, Visa.
Rates B&B, $185–225 suite, $85–100 double.

Extras Wheelchair access; some rooms equipped for the disabled. Airport/station pickup.

Sakura B&B ¢
1677 North Via Miraleste, 92262

Tel: 619–327–0705
Fax: 619–327–6847

For a complete change of pace, a Japanese-style B&B awaits your discovery. Guests can relax in Japanese kimonos and slippers; in the morning, you'll have a choice of an American breakfast of fresh bread or croissants, fresh fruit and beverage, or by request, a Japanese breakfast. "American George Cebra and his adorable wife Fumiko have lovingly designed a simple yet elegant Japanese-style B&B. Two large guest rooms are furnished in traditional Japanese decor, complete with tatami mats on the floor, handmade futon beds, rice-paper windows and lamps, sliding shoji doors leading out to the swimming pool, Buddha statues, and other beautiful Japanese decorations. The third guest room is rarely used when the other rooms are full. Fumiko served us her delicious chrysanthemum tea while we listened to the delicate sounds of Japanese music drifting through the air. The Cerbas are warm, gracious and hospitable." *(Gail Davis)*

Open Nov.–May.
Rooms 3 doubles—1 with private bath, 2 with maximum of 4 sharing bath. All with TV.
Facilities Library with VCR/tapes, guest laundry, porch with fireplace, deck. Swimming pool, hot tub, gardens, fruit trees. Shiatsu massage by appointment. Golf, tennis nearby.
Location Close to tramway, bus, airport. At corner of Vista Chino.
Restrictions No smoking.
Credit cards None accepted.
Rates B&B, $55–125 double, $45–65 single. Japanese, vegetarian dinners on request, $10–15.
Extras Airport/station pickup. Japanese spoken.

PALO ALTO

Palo Alto, meaning "tall tree," was named for a landmark redwood tree, which appears today on the seal of Stanford University. You can get an overview of the city, located at the southern end of San Francisco Bay, 30 miles south of San Francisco, from the top of the Hoover Tower, on campus. Also recommended is a visit to the Leland Stanford Museum to see the extensive collection of Rodin sculptures; the museum is also home to the original Golden Spike, driven in 1869 to signal the completion of the transcontinental railroad.

Also recommended: The European-style **Garden Court Hotel** (520 Cowper Street, 94301; 415–322–9000 or 800–824–9028) has 61 spacious, elegant guest rooms, with flower-bedecked balconies overlooking an interior courtyard. The hotel's Northern Italian restaurant, Il Fornaio, serves meats and poultry from the wood-fired rotisserie, and all pasta, bread, and desserts are made on the premises. "Handsome, well-equipped rooms with lots of thoughtful extras. Delicious coffee and muffins delivered to your door. Excellent location within walking distance of numerous restaurants, shops, and the Stanford campus. Friendly atmosphere, fine service." *(Matt Joyce)* B&B double rates range from $175–195, with weekend and corporate rates available.

Alan and Marian Brooks are the hospitable owners of the **Palm House B&B** (1216 Palm Avenue, San Mateo, 94402; 415–573–PALM), a three guest-room homestay B&B located about halfway between Palo Alto and San Francisco. "Guests are pampered with every comfort, from a welcome drink served in fine crystal to healthy breakfasts served on lovely china. They even provide pure cotton, sun-dried sheets and towels. This turn-of-the-century home had leaded windows, dark wood paneling and beams, a huge porch, a balcony, and solarium." *(Katherine Madden)* The B&B double rate is $70, and includes a home-cooked breakfast and afternoon refreshments. More comments welcome.

Information please: Unpretentious and straightforward, **The Hotel California** (2431 Ash Street, 94306; 415–322–7666) offers small but livable guest rooms, some with brass beds, ceiling fans, and armoires, while others feature full closets and air-conditioning. Breakfast is available at the bakery downstairs. The guest rooms ring the perimeter of the building, while inside is a courtyard, perfect for visiting with other guests or for soaking up the sun while reading a good book. Double B&B rates are a $53–60.

POINT SAN PABLO

East Brother Light House   Tel: 510–233–2385
Mailing address: 117 Park Place, Point Richmond, 94801

Just about everyone has a fantasy about sleeping in a lighthouse, and this may be as close as you'll ever get. The East Brother Light station, not far from Point San Pedro, was constructed in 1873, and is the oldest Bay Area lighthouse still in operation. It was manned continuously until 1969, when the Coast Guard automated the light and closed the buildings. In 1979, a nonprofit organization was formed to restore the island's facilities and open them to the public. Guests stay in a Victorian house with gingerbread trim adjacent to the lighthouse. Rooms are furnished with period antiques and reproduction wallpapers, and offer views of San Francisco, the mountains or the bay. Rates include boat transportation from Point San Pablo Yacht harbor, a five-course dinner with wine, plus a breakfast of fresh fruit and a hot entrée, along with a tour of the island. "Accommodating innkeepers, delicious food, wonderful experience." *(Roger Budd)* "Peaceful setting in San Pablo bay—we watched ships go by and baby seagulls hatching." *(Boone Okonek)*

Open All year, Thurs. through Sun.
Rooms 4 doubles share two baths.
Facilities Dining room, living room, family room with woodstove, books. Fishing from pier.
Location 35–40 min. from San Francisco.

167

Restrictions Fog horn. No smoking.
Credit cards None accepted.
Rates MAP, $220–295 double, $220–235 single.

QUINCY

An old gold mining town, Quincy is close to several state and national parks for hiking and fishing, and is set at the eastern end of the stunning and precipitous Feather River Canyon; 25 miles to the east is a ski area situated in the ghost town of Johnsville. Quincy is located in the High Sierras, 75 miles northwest of Reno, Nevada, 146 miles north of Sacramento, and 230 miles northeast of San Francisco via Highway 70.

Reader tip: "The area around Quincy is beautiful in September, with lots of color, warm days, crisp nights." *(SR)*

Information please: Built in 1893 in the Queen Anne style, **The Feather Bed** (542 Jackson Street, P.O. Box 3200, 95971; 916–283–0102), was restored as an inn in 1979. The five guest rooms and two secluded cottages are decorated with antiques and period wallpaper. A continental breakfast is included in the double rates of $70–85 ($100 for the cottages).

New England Ranch ¢   ♿
2571 Quincy Junction Road, 95971

Tel: 916–283–2223
Fax: 916–283–2223

"Every detail of this 1850s farmhouse has been lovingly restored to its original charm; the only modern reminders are the up-to-date plumbing, lighting, and heating. Welcoming owner Barbara Scott offers her guests a walking tour of the ranch, including her delightful menagerie—a llama, a donkey, two beautiful Scottish long-haired cows, and three cats. Guests may roam the grounds, or feed the animals. The comfortable guest rooms are decorated with antiques, old photographs, baskets of dried flowers, books, and have views of the snow-capped peaks. Vincent's Room has an old-fashioned, high bed with a marvelous queen-size mattress and handmade quilt. Terry robes were provided for the large bathroom, equipped with shampoo and bath gel. Coffee and juice are available for early risers. We breakfasted on apple cobbler, herbed scrambled eggs, light chicken-apple sausage, and fresh fruit, plus just-baked breads and muffins." *(Raoul Renaud)* "We enjoyed early morning walks on the quiet country roads, afternoon snoozes in a hammock shaded by old locust trees, and dips in the creek." *(Mrs. & Mrs. Harry Graham)* "Barbara served delicious breakfasts on the finest china and crystal; one day we had a peach smoothie and zucchini walnut pancakes with bacon and melon. Peaceful night-time sounds of cattle lowing, cow bells, frogs. Great hiking in the area." *(Lea Weber)* "Clean air and blue skies in a wonderfully remote, peaceful, rugged setting." *(William Conner)*

Open All year.
Rooms 3 doubles—all with private bath and/or shower, clock, fan.
Facilities Dining room, living room, sitting room with books. 88 acres with gardens, stables, mountain bicycles, hiking, horseback riding trails (no horses for

hire), stream for fishing, swimming; herb/vegetable/preserves shop. Tennis, golf nearby. 20–30 min. to cross-country, downhill skiing. At foot of Plumas National Forest.

Location American Valley. 2 miles to town. 2 m from Hwy 70 turnoff at Chandler Rd. at corner of Chandler & Quincy Junction Rds.

Restrictions No smoking. Children over 5.

Credit cards MC, Visa.

Rates Room only, $65–85 double, $60–80 single. B&B, $75–95 double, $65–85 single. Extra person, $10. Winter discounts midweek. Picnic lunches on request.

Extras Stabling/pasture for horses; pets with approval. Airport pickups. Limited wheelchair access. Airport pickup.

RANCHO SANTA FE

Information please: We need current reports on the well-known **Inn at Rancho Santa Fe** (5951 Linea del Cielo at Paseo Delicias, P.O. Box 869, 92067; 619–756–1131 or 800–654–2928) originally developed by the Santa Fe Railroad, and owned by the Royce family since 1958. "Though the inn is old and the furnishings simple, we found everything to be in perfect working order. Off our room was a private patio for relaxing and sunning." *(RW)* B&B double rates for the 90 guest rooms (most in cottages spread over the 20-acre grounds) range from $80–180; meals are extra. In addition to its beautiful gardens, facilities include a championship croquet course, 3 tennis courts, a heated swimming pool, 20 miles of walking trails, and a beach cottage at Del Mar for ocean swimming. Three 18-hole golf courses are nearby. Reports please.

RED BLUFF

Also recommended: The only accommodations inside Lassen Volcanic National Park are the **Drakesbad Guest Ranch** (mailing address: 2150 North Main Street, Red Bluff 96080; 916–529–1512), about 90 miles east of Red Bluff. Named for the warm water baths and swimming pool filled by the nearby hot springs, the ranch has been providing bed and board for over a century; kerosene lamps are provided to light the rustic cabins. You can hike or take a guided horseback ride to Boiling Springs Lake, the Devil's Kitchen, Terminal Geyser, and other colorfully named geological wonders. The clang of the dinner bell announces each meal; food is simple but ample, and sack lunches are available for day-long hikes or rides. "Simple but comfortable accommodation, tasty food; the staff is pleasant and accommodating, the scenery breathtaking." *(Richard Jones)* Drakesbad is accessible only via the road from Chester; reservations are made through national park concessionaire California Guest Services in Red Bluff. If you want to call the ranch directly, call "916 and ask for Drakesbad 2 via Susanville operator."

The Faulkner House ¢   *Tel: 916–529–0520*
1029 Jefferson Street, 96080

The Queen-Anne style Faulkner House, built in 1890, has been owned since 1984 by Mary and Harvey Klingler. Family heirlooms accent the decor; the Arbor Room has a European-carved bedroom set, and the Rose Room features a brocade-covered fainting couch. "The wide avenues of Red Bluff are lined with shade trees and well-kept Victorian homes. Faulkner House is an oasis for travelers driving the California interstate desert of cement. Our hosts greeted us with tea and nut bread after a long drive, and indulged us with bowls of M&Ms and glasses of port." *(Pam & Gary Medley)* "The cozy Wicker Room has handsome flowered wallpaper, attractive antiques, with a pedestal sink and shower in the room, and the shower in a converted closet. The parlor was comfortable for reading and relaxing. The lovely dining room has a huge hutch; just-picked roses scented the room. We had orange juice, cantaloupe with strawberries, French toast with bacon, and coffee. The innkeepers were friendly but discreet." *(Karl Wiegers & Chris Zambito)*

Open All year.
Rooms 4 doubles—all with private bath and/or shower, air-conditioning.
Facilities Dining room, living room with fireplace, parlor, family room with games, screened porch. Patio, garden. Near Sacramento River for boating, fishing.
Location Central Valley, 30 m S of Redding. From the N, take 1st Red Bluff exit off I-5. Continue S on Main St. to Union St. Turn right, go 2 blocks, turn left on Jefferson St. to inn on right.
Restrictions No smoking. No children under 12. Train whistles will disturb light sleepers.
Credit cards Amex, MC, Visa.
Rates B&B, $55–80 double, $53–78 single.
Extras Airport/station pickup.

REDDING

Palisades Paradise B&B ¢   *Tel: 916–223–5305*
1200 Palisades Avenue, 96003   800–382–4649

A contemporary home built in 1977, the Palisades Paradise was opened as a B&B in 1986 by Gail Goetz. Weekday breakfasts include cereal, fresh fruit, and pastry; on weekends a full breakfast is offered. "Gail had the city's first B&B, and lobbied for a year for permission to open. The view from the deck of the Sacramento River and mountains beyond is outstanding. Wonderful baked pancake topped with gorgeous fresh fruit and whipped cream." *(Shirley Dittloff, and others)* "The hot tub is right on the edge of the bluffs overlooking the river—gorgeous at sunset." *(Patricia Pantaleoni)* "Outstanding personal attention and flexibility regarding guests' needs and schedules. Good information on surrounding area." *(Stephen Aronow)*

Open All year.
Rooms 2 doubles share 1 bath. All with radio, clock, TV, air-conditioning, fan.

acilities Dining room, living room with fireplace, piano, TV/VCR, guest refrig-
rator, balcony, patio. ½ acre with off-street parking, hot tub, tree swing, lawn
ames. River rafting, fishing, boating swimming nearby.
ocation Halfway between Sacramento & OR border. Center of town.
estrictions No smoking. Children over 8 unless both rooms taken.
redit cards Amex, MC, Visa.
ates B&B, $55–75. Extra person, $10. 5% AAA, senior discount.
xtras Crib.

REDLANDS/RIVERSIDE

nformation please: A few miles from I-10 is the **Morey Mansion** (190
erracina Boulevard, Redlands, 92373; 909–793–7970). This striking
Queen Anne Victorian—complete with a Russian onion dome, French
mansard roof lines, and a Chinese-style veranda—was crafted of golden
ak and redwood in 1890 by David Morey, a retired shipbuilder and
abinet maker. "Small orange blossoms are carved all over the exquisite
voodwork, and the original upholstered wall covering is still in place and
till vibrant. We stayed in Sarah's Chamber, a two-room suite with some
original furnishings. The ceilings were high and the colors and ceiling
lesigns were exquisite. Our bathroom—down the hall—also had the
original fixtures with a pull-chain toilet and a large porcelain tub with
ourled maple surround. A tasty breakfast of orange juice, banana bread,
ea, and melon was set up for us by the front room window, which we
oreferred to the formal dining room." *(Rick & Cyndy Gould)* B&B double
ates range from $109–185. Reports welcome.

A few miles west in Riverside is the extraordinary **Mission Inn** (3649
Seventh Street, 92501; 909–784–0300 or 800–843–7755), a famous Cali-
ornia landmark, recently re-opened after a $40 million renovations. Many
of the 240 rooms have such architectural features as domed ceilings,
wrought iron balconies, tiled floors, leaded and stained glass windows,
gargoyles, and carved pillars. The architectural style is Mission Revival,
with touches of Spanish, Moorish, Italian, and Chinese. In Rancho Cucamonga, about 20 miles north of Riverside and east of Redlands is the
Christmas House (9240 Archibald Avenue, Rancho Cucamonga 91730;
909–980–6450), a 1904 Queen Anne Victorian home, named for its long
history of gala Christmas parties, complemented by the red and green
stained glass throughout the house. Now restored as a B&B and furnished
in period, B&B double rates range from $70–170, depending on size, and
include such breakfasts as spiced fruit compote and cheese crepes with
cranberry hazelnut sauce.

SACRAMENTO

Sacramento was founded by John Sutter, who is best known as the man
on whose property gold was discovered in 1848, precipitating the great
California Gold Rush of 1849. The town grew into a key supply source
for the northern Mother Lode country and was named the state capital in

1854. It remains a major transportation hub to this day. It has a few sights of interest—the State Capitol, Sutter's Fort, Old Sacramento, and the California State Railroad Museum—but most Sacramento visitors come for the business of government or the business of business. Those who want to get out of town enjoy swimming, fishing, and rafting in the nearby Sacramento and American rivers.

Sacramento is located in Gold Country, 90 miles northeast of San Francisco and 90 miles southwest of Lake Tahoe. The center city is laid out in a grid pattern of numbered and lettered streets, with the former running east/west and the latter running north/south.

Reader tip: "We had an excellent dinner at Paraguay's." *(Bob Freidus)*

Information please: The **Hartley House** (700 22nd Street, 95816; 916–447–7829 or 800–831–5806) is a handsome a turn-of-the-century mansion with original hardwood floors, dark stained woodwork, leaded and stained glass windows, and brass fixtures converted from gas. Each of the five guest rooms have a private bath, telephone, and air-conditioning. The B&B double rates of $95–135 include a full breakfast, afternoon sherry, an always-full jar of freshly baked cookies, and turndown service with mints. "The Dover Room is the inn's largest with a queen-sized brass bed, a large armoire with a small color TV, and a bathroom with a claw foot tub with shower. The other guest rooms were nice but smaller. For breakfast we had eggs poached in cream on a buttered English muffin, with juice and fresh fruit." *(Karl Wiegers)* More comments appreciated.

Amber House B&B ¢
1315 22nd Street, 95816

Tel: 916–444–8085
800–755–6526
Fax: 916–447–1548

Amber House, a brown Craftsman-style home from the early 1900s, has been owned by Jane and Michael Richardson since 1987. The inn has the original stained glass windows and distinctive woodwork of the period, and is furnished with Oriental rugs, velvet wingback chairs, antiques, and collectibles. Guest rooms have antique beds and washstands; patterned wallpapers and fresh flowers are used to accent the colorful glass in the windows. The renovated 1913 bungalow next door offers marble-tiled Jacuzzi bathrooms. Rates include early morning coffee and a full breakfast served in the dining room, on the veranda, or in your room.

"The library is stocked with books and local restaurant menus, and sherry is always available. At 5 P.M., Michael joined us for wine in the living room and we chatted about area attractions and restaurants." *(JoAnn Davis)* "My first-floor room had a TV/VCR in an armoire, a comfortable queen-size bed with excellent reading lights, and a luxurious bathroom with equally good lighting. Accented by blue stained glass windows, the dining room was a perfect setting for Michael's hearty breakfast of melon with poppy seed dressing, followed by fluffy scrambled eggs with scallions and cheese, spicy home fries, a ham croissant, and flavored coffee. The inn's residential location is quiet and convenient, a medium walk or an easy drive downtown." *(SWS)* "An exceptional example of a Craftsman-style house, with wonderful trim and detailing. We had breakfast in our room; the small table was set with silver, china, and linens." *(RF)* "Endorse existing entry. We stayed in the Lord Bryon Room with a marvelous marble bath and Jacuzzi. Hospitable, genuinely caring hosts, excellent breakfasts." *(Dr. & Mrs. Ethan Ruben)*

Open All year.
Rooms 9 doubles—all with private bath and/or shower, telephone, radio/cassette players. TV/VCR, desk, air-conditioning. 5 with double Jacuzzi. 4 in annex.
Facilities 2 living rooms with fireplace, 2 dining rooms, 2 libraries, veranda, meeting room.
Location Midtown. 7 blocks E of Capitol building, between Capitol Ave. and N St.
Restrictions No smoking.
Credit cards All major.
Rates B&B, $80–195 double, $75–150 single. Extra person, $15. Corporate rates.

Abigail's ¢	*Tel:* 916–441–5007
2120 G Street, 95816	800–858–1568
	Fax: 916–441–0621

Susanne and Ken Ventura, describe their inn as being "especially good for the business traveler. We have all the little things people tend to forget— an iron or hair dryer, aspirin, razors, and so on. Our guests also enjoy the extra touches—beds turned down, evening tea and hot chocolate, a refrigerator stocked with cold drinks, and extra-soft towels. Our building is a 1912 Colonial Revival mansion; the rooms are large and airy, with lots of windows." Breakfast specialties include fresh fruit, zucchini waffles, and home-baked coffee cake.

"An imposing white house with tall columns framing the front door. We were shown to our rooms, given a tour of the house, and were soon relaxing in the outdoor hot tub amid a flower-filled garden." *(Sandy Holmes)* "The well-lit guest rooms are supplied with books and bedtime sherry; the beds were firm and comfortable and the plumbing efficient. The living room is huge with an eclectic assortment of cushy sofas and chairs, perfect for curling up with a good book. Abigail's is located on a tree-lined street in a quiet neighborhood close to shops and good restaurants." *(JoAnn & Richard Mlnarik)* "The light-filled solarium room has a lovely deck and a private bath across the hall. Excellent cookies and hot chocolate awaited us at night; tea and coffee are always available." *(Jennifer Ball)* "Friendly inn cats, Abigail and Sabrina. A fainting couch, plus a desk and chair, provided good spots for reading or working in my room. Fun political chats over breakfast." *(DCB)* "Margaret's Room is spacious, with a king-size poster bed. Suzanne and Ken were helpful and pleasant." *(Les Lewis)*

Open All year.
Rooms 5 doubles—all with private bath and/or shower, radio, desk, air-conditioning. Telephone, TV, refrigerator on request. 1 with deck.
Facilities Living room with fireplace, dining room, sitting room with piano, games; guest refrigerator. Hot tub, garden with patio. Limited off-street parking.
Location Walking distance to downtown. From Business 80 loop, exit at "H" St. (E) or "E" St. (W) to "G" St. at 22nd St. From I-5, take "J" St. exit to 22nd St.

Restrictions Some traffic noise in 2 street-side rooms. No smoking.
Credit cards Amex, DC, MC, Visa.
Rates B&B, $79–150 double. 2–3-night holiday minimum.

ST. HELENA

St. Helena is located 60 miles north of San Francisco, in the Napa Wine Valley region of the North Coast. Although there are many things to do in the area, the main activity is visiting wineries—there are nine in St. Helena alone. Keep in mind that this area is extremely popular from June through October, especially on weekends. Try November, April, and May for good weather and smaller crowds.

Reader tip: Local zoning laws limit B&Bs to three guest rooms and to serving only a continental breakfast; this appears to be observed in the breach—by expanding the morning meal under the heading "gourmet continental" and by expanding suites to become two separate rooms with adjoining facilities, as needed.

Also recommended: The **Wine Country Inn** (1152 Lodi Lane; 707–963–7077) is a small hotel built in 1976. Each of the 25 guest rooms in the main building and the barn annex has its own distinctive colors and furnishings, including handmade quilts, and most have fireplaces. "Clean, attractively decorated, good continental buffet breakfast, nice swimming pool and spa. Close to Berringer and Sterling wineries." *(Joy Sugg)* B&B double rates range from $90–205.

Information please: For an elegant small resort, suitable both for families or romantic escapes, the **Meadowood Resort** (900 Meadowood Lane, 94574; 707–963–3646 or 800–458–8080) may be a good choice. Although reminiscent of an old-style Adirondack lodge or Newport cottage, Meadowood was originally built as a private country club in the 1960s, and was expanded into a full-scale luxury resort in the 1980s. Guest rooms are clustered in lodges scattered around the grounds, while the main lodge is home to the elegant Starmont Restaurant as well as the more casual Fairway Grill. In addition to a heated swimming pool, 6 tennis courts, a 9-hole golf course, and a playground, Meadowood has two championship croquet courts, with a resident teaching pro.

We need reports on the well-known **Auberge du Soleil** (180 Rutherford Hill Road, Rutherford 94573; 707–963–1211 or 800–348–5406), about 5 miles south of St. Helena. Its restaurant is famous for creative California cuisine, and the 48 luxurious guest rooms occupy a series of elegant cottages with stunning views of the Napa Valley, plus such amenities as fridges stocked with champagne and juices, a wet bar with coffeemaker, whirlpool baths, lounging robes, and fireplaces. The 33 acres offer a heated swimming pool, hot tub, 3 tennis courts, health spa, bicycles, and hot air ballooning. Double room rates start at $295 and ascend skyward.

For more information, see the North Coast section of the chapter introduction and the listings for Calistoga.

ST. HELENA

Chestelson House ¢
1417 Kearney Street, 94574

Tel: 707–963–2238
800–959–4505

In a quiet neighborhood just a few blocks from shops and restaurants, Chestelson House offers creative, family-style breakfasts prepared by owner Jackie Sweet. Favorite entrées include rosemary potatoes and peppers with Italian sausage and poached eggs, or sourdough waffles with orange caramel sauce. The guest rooms are individually decorated and named for verses in Robert Louis Stevenson's *A Child's Garden of Verses*.

"Our room had a queen-size bed with brass headboard, armoire with bathrobes, thick carpeting and white-painted shutters. Breakfast was an event, with fresh-baked goodies, fresh-squeezed juice, and friendly company." *(Kathleen & James Conley)* "We learned about restaurant and wine choices, and other local events, while conversing with Jackie over tea and cookies in the afternoon, or during the evening wine and crackers in the cozy parlor." *(Keith & Caren Corbin)* "Heavenly strawberries with whipped cream and homemade biscuits for breakfast. My room was well lit and airy, with lots of windows to open; instant hot water for the old-fashioned clawfoot tub. Parking on the street in front of the inn was never a problem." *(Margie Heldt)* "Our private balcony was shaded by a large tree, perfect for reading or naps." *(Ron & Chris Roberts)* "Our secluded first floor suite was clean and spacious, soothingly decorated in soft pinks, cool greens, and off-white. The bay window near the whirlpool tub displayed seashells and ferns; candles and bubble bath added to the experience." *(Connie Rhodes)* "Home-baked cookies or Jackie's special chocolate truffles are an evening treat." *(Irene Howard)*

Open All year.
Rooms 1 suite, 2 doubles—all with full private bath, desk, air-conditioning. 1 with balcony. 1 with double whirlpool tub.
Facilities Breakfast room, living room with fireplace, TV, stereo; porch with glider. Golf, tennis, bicycle rentals nearby.
Location 2 blocks from downtown. From Hwy. 29 N turn left at 1st light onto Adams. Go 2 blocks, turn right onto Kearney.
Restrictions No smoking.
Credit cards MC, Visa.
Rates B&B, $98–145 suite, double. Extra person, $25. 2-night weekend minimum. Dec.–March off-season rates. Picnic baskets.

Shady Oaks Country Inn
399 Zinfandel Lane, 94574

Tel: 707–963–1190

Owned by John and Lisa Wild-Runnells since 1986, Shady Oaks is set amid oak and walnut trees, surrounded by Napa's vineyards. The 1920s-era main house has guest rooms furnished with antiques; one has lace curtains, antique queen-size bed, oak armoire and the original wallpaper, while another has an ornate Victorian loveseat. The two suites are in the adjacent 1880s winery building; old stone walls are the backdrop for the antique brass and iron beds, accented with pastel colors and wicker. On the patio, where white Roman-style pillars are covered by century-old wisteria, guests can enjoy a champagne breakfast with eggs Benedict or Belgian waffles, fresh fruit, and homebaked breads.

"We compared vineyard and dining experiences with the other guests, during the enjoyable afternoon wine and cheese gathering." *(Jan Carpenter)* "The Winery Retreat was spacious and comfortable with quality linens, fluffy towels, and bedside chocolates." *(Susan Tuttle)* "John and Lisa were helpful in making dinner and winery tour reservations on a busy weekend, and in steering us away from weekend crowds on the Silverado Trial. Delightful breakfast." *(Glenn Roehrig)*

Open All year. Closed Dec. 24, 25.
Rooms 2 1-2 bedroom suites in winery, 2 doubles in main house—all with private bath and/or shower, air-conditioning, fan. 2 with desk, 1 with balcony. 2 with private entrance.
Facilities Breakfast room/parlor with fireplace, sitting room, patio. 2 acres with garden, lawn games. Near Lake Berryessa for water sports.
Location 2 m S of St. Helena. From Hwy 29, go E on Zinfandel Lane to inn on right.
Restrictions No smoking. "Well-behaved children welcome in suites."
Credit cards None accepted.
Rates B&B, $135–175 suite, double. Extra person in room, $25. 2-night weekend, holiday minimum.

SAN DIEGO

San Diego is located in southernmost coastal California, 127 miles south of Los Angeles and about 20 miles north of Tijuana, Mexico. For many years a sleepy coastal town, San Diego didn't really start to grow until World War II, when the U.S. Navy moved its headquarters from Honolulu to San Diego. Since then, the city has grown to become California's second largest. San Diego's climate is arguably one of the best in America—very little rain, with an average winter temperature in the mid-60s and summer in the mid-70s. Major sights of interest include Balboa Park's many museums, the world-famous zoo, Old Town San Diego, Cabrillo National Monument, Sea World, the Maritime Museum, and trips on the Tijuana Trolley to Mexico.

To make sure you're getting the best rate available, it's worth calling **San Diego Hotel Reservations** (619–627–9300 OR 800–SAVE–CASH), offering discounted rates at over 250 hotels throughout San Diego County, including several recommended here; this service is free to travelers.

Also recommended: In Pacific Beach, just a few miles north of downtown, is the **Crystal Pier Hotel** (4500 Ocean Boulevard, San Diego 92109; 619–483–6983 or 800–748–5894) which consists of bungalows built atop the 350-foot pier. "Spacious, light, airy, and delightfully decorated to make you feel at home over the ocean. Each bungalow has a small efficiency kitchen complete with microwave and coffeemaker. The pier is open to the public during daylight hours, so when you make your reservation, decide whether you want the privacy of the new bungalows with private decks, or enjoy the camaraderie of others (the older ones have patio areas along the outer walkway). At the edge of the pier is a breakfast and lunch place called Kono's Surf Club, for an excellent and reasonably priced meal." *(Mary Louise Rogers)* Double rates range from $85–180, with weekly rates available.

Too large for a full entry is the **Rancho Bernardo** (17550 Bernardo Oaks Drive, San Diego 92128; 619–487–1611 or 800–542–6096), a full-service luxury resort ideal for a family getaway, located about 25 miles east of San Diego. Facilities include 45 holes of golf, 12 tennis courts, a health club, and two excellent restaurants. Double rates for the 287 units range from $125–235, with numerous packages available. "The fabulous children's program runs from 9 in the morning to 9 at night during vacations; we couldn't tear our kids away. A wonderful place for R&R." *(EL)*

Information please: Overlooking the northwest corner of Balboa Park are the **Park Manor Suites** (525 Spruce Street, 92103; 619–291–0999 or 800–874–2649), built in 1926 and extensively renovated. Rates include a continental breakfast and range from $60 for a studio to $160 for a two-bedroom suite. Most have kitchens with Louis XIV and Chippendale furnishings. Budget travelers may want to consider **La Pensione Hotel** (1546 Second Avenue, 92101; 619–236–9292), not far from Balboa Park and downtown. Rooms have private baths, kitchenettes, and TVs, and double rates are a modest $50 daily, $160 weekly.

Listed in past editions, we need current reports on the **Horton Grand Hotel** (311 Island Avenue, 92101; 619–544–1886 or 800–542–1886), a 134-room complex of three re-created Victorian-era hotels in the redeveloped Gaslamp district, once San Diego's skid row. The queen-size beds are modern, with draped antique headboards; the marble fireplaces are antique as well, but they frame gas-log fireplaces, and the mirror above each mantel hides a remote control TV. Double rates range from $89–189, with weekend rates starting at $59. For an out-of-town visit, there's **Brookside Farm** (1373 Marron Valley Road, Dulzura 91917; 619–468–3043), a rambling 1920s farmhouse, in a rural mountain town 35 miles southeast of San Diego. Innkeeper Edd Guishard is not only a trained chef, but he also makes the stained glass windows that highlight the decor. The atmosphere is relaxed, friendly, and down-home. A full breakfast is included in the $65–115 double rates.

For more information on San Diego area accommodations, see listings under **La Jolla,** 20 minutes north of the city and **Coronado,** four miles southwest.

Balboa Park Inn ¢ ♿	*Tel:* 619–298–0823
3402 Park Boulevard, 92103	800–938–8181
	Fax: 619–294–8070

Dating back to 1915, The Balboa Park Inn is a complex of four pale pink Spanish Colonial-style buildings with a variety of individually furnished rooms, each with queen-, king-, or twin-size beds and a sitting area. The decor ranges from Spanish to Southwestern, Victorian to country, and the rates include a continental breakfast delivered to your door with the daily paper. In addition to its pleasant ambience and reasonable rates, the inn's key advantage is its convenient location across the street from Balboa Park. Balboa Park is the cultural hub of San Diego and offers a full range of sport and cultural activities, including seven museums, the famous San Diego Zoo, and the Old Globe Theater.

"Comfortable accommodation, great location, reasonable rates." *(Shirley Dittloff)* Reports welcome.

Open All year.
Rooms 19 suites, 7 doubles—all with full private bath, telephone, TV, refrigerator. Some with kitchen, microwave, wet bar, wood-burning fireplace, Jacuzzi, deck/patio.
Facilities Courtyard, terrace, balconies, garden with fountain, guest laundry. Non-restricted street parking; security provided. Balboa Park for golf, tennis, Olympic-size swimming pool.
Location N edge of Balboa Park. Walk to San Diego Zoo, etc. Minutes to downtown via #7 bus. 10 min. to airport, train, bus stations. From I-5, exit at Hwy 163 & go N. Turn right at Richmond, right at Upas to inn at corner of Upas & Park Blvd.
Restrictions No smoking in some rooms.
Credit cards All major.
Rates B&B, $85–190 suite, $80–100 double, $75–95 single. Extra person, $8; children under 12, free. 3 night holiday minimum.
Extras Wheelchair access; bathroom specially equipped. Crib, babysitting. Spanish spoken.

Heritage Park Inn ¢ ♁ ♿
2470 Heritage Park Row, 92110

Tel: 619–299–6832
800–995–2470
Fax: 619–299–9465

Heritage Park is a seven-acre site, home to seven classic period structures from the 1800s. The buildings, originally located on Third Avenue in San Diego, were moved here in 1978. The B&B is a 1889 Queen Anne mansion, adorned with a variety of chimneys, shingles, a corner tower, and encircling veranda. In 1992, the inn was bought by longtime San Diego residents Nancy and Charles Helsper. Rooms are furnished with 19th-century antiques, and rates include a breakfast buffet, an afternoon social hour, and a classic film shown in the parlor, evenings at 7 P.M. Breakfast menus might include Victorian French toast with apple cider syrup and sour cream–peach coffee cake; plus homemade granola, yogurt, fruit, juice, coffee, and herbal teas.

"Hillside setting with a nice view of the city." *(Carla Lund)* "Beautifully coordinated wallpapering and stencilling throughout the house." *(Anne Mietzel)* "Delicious breakfast of fresh fruit and cooked-to-order pancakes served on the porch." *(Robert Wolkow)* "Loved the crab souffle and raspberry almond scones." *(Jeannie Bell)* "You can stroll from a beautiful Victorian village into present-day San Diego a few blocks away." *(Elisa & Marco Gabrielli)* "The Helspars went out of their way to make our stay special." *(Steve Ruderman)* Reports welcome.

Open All year.
Rooms 1 suite, 8 doubles—6 with private bath and/or shower, 2 with a maximum of 4 people sharing bath. All with radio, clock, desk. 3 with fan or fireplace. Telephone on request. Suite in adjacent building with Jacuzzi tub.
Facilities Parlor with fireplace, TV/VCR; dining room, guest refrigerator, veranda. Conference facilities. Croquet. In 7-acre Victorian park. Off-street parking.

Location 1 block to Old Town. 2 m from downtown. Follow I-5 to Old Town Ave. exit. Turn left on San Diego Ave., right on Harney to Heritage Park to inn on right.

Restrictions No smoking.

Credit cards Amex, MC, Visa.

Rates B&B, $200 suite, $85–130 double, single. 15% senior, AAA discounts. 2-night weekend minimum. Candlelight dinner, $105 per couple plus 15% service. Special occasion packages.

Extras First floor wheelchair accessible; bathroom specially equipped. Airport/station pickup. Spanish spoken.

SAN FRANCISCO

Romanticized in song, hyped in commercials, featured in movies and sitcoms, San Francisco is everything promised and more. Compact, ethnically diverse, culturally rich, filled with wonderful stores, cable cars, and restaurants, it's what every city should aspire to be. The weather is best in late summer and early fall, but you don't come here to get a tan, so what does it matter? Bring your walking shoes and a sweater (even summer can be cool), and explore everything. Less well known but worth visiting are the exquisite Japanese Tea Garden and Asian Art Museum in Golden Gate Park and the museums and bookstores at North Beach. Watch the sea lions from Cliff House near Point Lobos Avenue.

For discount rates of 10 to 60 percent at many San Francisco hotels and B&Bs, including several listed here, call **San Francisco Reservations** (22 Second Street, 4th floor, 94105; 415–227–1500 or 800–677–1550) or **Discount Hotel Rates** (3 Sumner Street, 94103; 415–252–1107 or 800–576–0003). If you'd prefer having your own apartment, contact **B&B International** (P.O. Box 282910, 94128-2910; 415–696–1690). "We stayed at **Molly's B&B** on Russian Hill just one block from Lombard and 1/2 block from the cable car. For $175, we had a spacious two-bedroom second-floor apartment for the four of us. The innkeepers live upstairs. Molly's an artist and stencilled all the walls beautifully." *(Penny Poirer)*

Reader tips: "San Francisco has excellent public transportation, even by East Coast standards, and it's a very economical and practical alternative. Valet parking approaches $20 a day, and in some areas, on-street parking requires you to move your car every two hours 8 A.M. to 9 P.M." *(Adam Platt)* Also: "San Francisco is noisy at all hours. If you're a light sleeper, be sure to let the innkeeper know when making reservations!" *(SHW)*

Important note: Space limitations simply do not permit us to include full write-ups on San Francisco's many wonderful hotels and inns. The abbreviated recommendations which follow are no reflection of their quality—we just don't have the room to describe each place in full.

Also recommended—budget: Location and price, combined with a friendly ambiance, are key advantages of **The Andrews Hotel** (624 Post Street, 94109; 415–563–6877 or 800–926–3739). It's just a block or two away from the St. Francis and the Hyatt, yet the prices are about half. The B&B double rates for the 48 guest rooms range from $82–119, including

CALIFORNIA

a breakfast of croissants, jams, fresh fruit, muffins, dark roast coffee, an teas, plus an afternoon glass of wine. Most rooms are small, the furnis ings simple, but the housekeeping is thorough and the staff friendly. T**h Cartwright** (524 Sutter Street, 94102; 415–421–2865 or 800–227–384 a favorite of many readers, is now a Kimco Hotel, but still claims to off friendly, personalized service from long-time employees. Unusual in budget-priced hotel are the triple-sheeted beds, over-sized reading p lows, terry cloth robes, evening mints, and fresh flowers supplied daily guest rooms. Some rooms and baths are small, but the location is exce lent, close to the cable car, buses, and Union Square shops. Double rat for the 110 guest rooms range from $99–119.

Travelers come back to the **Golden Gate** (775 Bush Street, 9410 415–392–3702 or 800–835–1118) for the personal attention its reside owner/operators provide, its pleasant atmosphere and convenient loc tion. Its 23 rooms rent for a reasonable $55–89; while Spartan in size ar decor, the mattresses are top quality, and the hot croissants are outstan ing. "Afternoon tea and cookies are an added plus." *(Dianne Crawfor* "Rooms on the higher floors are brighter, lighter, and quieter. If the sittin room is crowded at breakfast, ask for a tray to take up to your room *(Lynne Derry)* Two blocks from Union Square is the **Hotel Sheehan** (6. Sutter Street, 94102; 415–775–6500 or 800–848–1529), built as YMCA, and renovated as a hotel, with the city's largest heated indo swimming pool. Double rates of $50–100 include continental breakfas "Young, energetic, friendly Irish staff. Great location, delicious h scones." *(Janet Murray)*

Also recommended—moderate: The Inn San Francisco (943 Sou Van Ness Avenue, 94110; 415–641–0188 or 800–359–0913) is an Italia ate Victorian B&B, painted pink, green, and gold, located in a residenti area 12 blocks from the Civic Center. Inside it has marble fireplaces, orna woodwork, and authentic period decor, accented with Oriental rug polished brass fixtures, and fresh flowers. "The rooftop sun deck offers panoramic view of the city, and the garden hot tub is perfect after a da of sightseeing. Excellent breakfast buffet with fruits, eggs, juices, an several different kinds of breads." *(Dale & Virginia Wright)* "Room #4 in the adjacent building had a light and airy country feeling, unlike th darker Victorian-style rooms in the main house. Pluses include the indivi ually controlled heat, marble fireplace, private balcony, skylight, ultr comfortable queen-size featherbed, and bathrobe. Hospitable, graciou innkeepers." *(Gail Davis)* B&B double rates for the 22 guest rooms rang from $75–195.

The **Union Street Inn** (2229 Union Street, 94123; 415–346–042 offers a tranquil, English garden setting complete with the fragrance lilacs and camellias, just a ten-minute walk from Union Square and th Civic Center. "This delightful Victorian home is on one of the lovelie streets in San Francisco, lined with cafés and shops. Our beautifull furnished room was large, comfortable and overlooked the garden. E tremely gracious and friendly staff." *(Gail Davis)* "Lots of charm, especial the carriage house out back." *(Carol Blodgett)* B&B double rates for the si guest rooms range from $125–225.

180

The **Hotel Griffon** (155 Steuart Street, 94105; 415–495–2100 or 00–321–2201) is "a charming European-style rehab by the bay, the mbarcadero, the Financial District, and the South of Market District. Our executive queen' room was small but attractive, with a full bath, queen-ize bed, small couch, desk, and plenty of lighting. There's an excellent estaurant, but avoid the guest rooms just above it. The hotel is central o public transportation, and walking distance from many San Francisco ights. Staff friendly." *(AP)*

"The **Inn at Union Square** (440 Post Street, 94102; 415–397–3510 or 00–AT–THE–INN) is small and secure, with 30 rooms and suites. Among its many positive attributes are its location, half a block from Union Square, the wonderfully furnished and individually decorated ooms; the breakfast of Italian roasted coffee, fresh fruit and juice, crois-ants and muffins; afternoon tea with cucumber sandwiches and other lelectables; evening wine and cheese; and a friendly, welcoming, knowl-dgeable staff." *(Hugh & Marjorie Smith)* B&B double rates are $120–180.

ackson Court (2198 Jackson Street, 94115; 415–929–7670) is a 1901 brownstone located in the elegant residential district of Pacific Heights, with big windows and high ceilings. The decor is a balanced mix of antiques and contemporary furnishings. Rates include a self-serve break-ast of fresh fruit and juice, strong coffee, croissants, bagels, and whole-grain bread, plus afternoon sherry. "Classy home in a lovely residential area. Each room is lovely, clean, and inviting." *(Carol Blodgett, also (Maxine Nickelsberg)* The ten suites and doubles each have a private bath, tele-phone, radio, TV, and desk, and two have a working fireplace; B&B rates ange from $108–150.

An eccentric but entertaining choice is the **Mansion Hotel** (220 Sac-amento Street, 94115; 415–929–9444), decorated with antiques and an extraordinary collection of objets d'art and not so d'art. "Wonderful breakfast; nice, quiet location; with bus stop across the street." *(Carol Blodgett)* Double and suite rates range $90–250, including breakfast, flow-ers, nightly concerts, a performing ghost, a magic parlor, and more. On he Golden Gate Park panhandle, about three blocks from the park itself, s the **Victorian Inn on the Park** (301 Lyon Street, 94117; 415–931–1830 or 800–435–1967), a handsome Victorian mansion, decorated with authentic period furnishings. Double rates for the 12 guest rooms range rom $99–159, and include a breakfast of fruit, juice, croissants, and breads. All guest rooms have a private bath, telephone, and TV, with off-street parking available. The **Monticello Inn** (127 Ellis Street, 94102; 415–392–8800 or 800–669–7777) has patterned its decor after its name-ake, with Colonial reproduction furnishings and Williamsburg colors. In addition to valet parking, the inn offers a free morning limo to the financial district. **Washington Square Inn** (1660 Stockton Street, 94133; 415–981–4220 or 800–388–0220) is located in the Italian District of North Beach, almost midway between Fisherman's Wharf and Union Square. The 16 guest rooms are decorated with English and French antiques, and the easonable rates include continental breakfast.

Also recommended—luxury: The **Archbishop's Mansion Inn** (1000 Fulton Street, 94117; 415–563–7872 or 800–543–5820) was built for the

archbishop of San Francisco in 1904, and has been restored as a sm
luxury hotel. Rooms are formally decorated with an operatic theme, wi
Victorian antiques, flower-painted ceilings, canopy beds, embroider
linens, Oriental rugs, marble fireplaces, and crystal chandeliers. Rat
include a light breakfast of croissants, scones, or pastry, juice, and
beverage of choice, delivered to your room or served in the dining roo
in the afternoon, wine is served in the parlor. B&B double rates for the
rooms range form $$115–195. **Campton Place**, a small luxury hotel ju
off Union Square (340 Stockton Street, 94108; 415–781–5555 or 80(
235–4300), consists of two buildings joined by an atrium, and plush
decorated with marble, brass, and velvet. "Very expensive but luxurio
and well furnished, with the most comfortable bed I've ever slept i
Pleasant staff." *(M. Freedman)* The **Four Seasons Clift Hotel** (495 Gea
Street [at Taylor] 94102; 415–775–4700 or 800–332–3442), built rig
after the 1906 earthquake and fire, offers elegant guest rooms and com
mon areas. Located at the bottom of Nob Hill, its convenience to Unio
Square and the attentiveness of its staff make it most appealing.

If you're ready for that special-occasion splurge of all splurges, Th
Sherman House (2160 Green Street, 94123; 415–563–3600 or 800–424
5777) is probably the place to go. This gleaming white Victorian palazz
built in 1876, is decorated in exquisite detail with period antiques, im
ported chandeliers, Belgian tapestries, and the finest fabrics and furnish
ings; service is equally indulgent. "A jewel. We had one of the lea
expensive rooms, and found it small but lovely, with a draped canopy be
a wood-burning fireplace, comfortable reading chairs, and more. The roo
looked out on the pretty inside courtyard garden. Breakfasts in the sola
ium are wonderful. The windows overlook the Golden Gate Bridge an
San Francisco Bay, and the food is marvelous—delicious muffins an
pastries, perfect fruit, French toast, and other entrées." *(EL)* B&B doub
rates for the 13 guest rooms and suites range from $175–750, and als
include evening hors d'oeuvres and wine.

Information please: We'd like reports on the **The Bed & Breakfa
Inn** (4 Charlton Court, 94123; 415–921–9784) is located on a quiet mew
just off bustling Union Street. The inn is composed of two adjoinin
buildings, furnished with a mixture of contemporary and antique piece
"Interesting location off Union Street; cozy New England feel." *(CB)* If
view of San Francisco Bay is what you must have, the **Harbor Cou
Hotel** (165 Steuart Street, 94105; 415–882–1300 or 800–346–0555) is
recently opened Kimco Hotel on the Embarcadero waterfront in dow
town San Francisco. Ask for a water-view room; it's well worth the sma
extra charge. The 130 rooms are furnished in neo-Victorian style, and th
$140–160 rates include free use of the workout room and indoor swim
ming pool, valet parking, morning coffee and evening wine service.

For a change of pace, consider the **Miyako Hotel** (1625 Post Stree
94115; 415–922–3200 or 800–533–4567), located in the Japan Center,
five-acre complex in the northern part of the city. The hotel offers bot
Western- and Japanese-style accommodations, and rates range fro
$130–189.

For another San Francisco area entry, see **Sausalito.**

Hotel Vintage Court ¢ 🛏 ✕ &.
550 Bush Street, 94108

Tel: 415–392–4666
800–654–1100
Fax: 415–433–4065

"This appealing little hotel is located a few blocks from Union Square, just off the Powell Street cable-car line. The bedrooms feature wainscoting, matching flowered chintz curtains and bedspreads." *(CM)* Included in the rates are a French continental breakfast; coffee and tea service all day; midweek morning limousine service to the Financial District; and afternoon wine-tasting. For dinner, guests may want to try Masa's, one of the city's top French restaurants, with possibly the largest selection of California wines. "Our spacious twin room was decorated in an appealing dark flowered chintz and had good reading lights, a comfortable chair, and ample closet space." *(Carolyn Mathiasen)* "Exceptionally tasty baguette and croissant for breakfast." *(Eileen O'Reilly)* "Pretty lobby with lighted fireplace and gracious staff; quick and courteous checked-in. Our spacious eighth-floor room had a lovely window seat and adequately sized bathroom. We could hear the pleasant, not-too-distant clang of the passing cable cars. I saw a less expensive room which was smaller, but still nice." *(Gail Davis)*

Minor niggles: "When booking, be sure to request a larger room, a bath with both a tub and shower, and a regular-size closet." And: "Us old-fashioned tea drinkers prefer Lipton's or English breakfast."

Worth noting: If you call for reservations and the hotel is full, we have had positive reports on most other hotels in the Kimco group.

Open All year. Restaurant closed Sun., Mon., also Dec. 21 through 2nd week of Jan.
Rooms 1 suite, 105 doubles, singles—all with private bath and/or shower, telephone, clock/radio, TV, desk, air-conditioning, fan, mini-bar. Suite with fireplace, Jacuzzi.
Facilities Lobby with fireplace; restaurant; meeting room. Room service 4 P.M. to midnight. Valet, laundry services. Health club facilities nearby. Parking garage $1/2$ block away, $15.
Location Nob Hill/Union Square. $1 1/2$ blocks N of Union Sq., between Powell & Stockton. 15-min. walk to financial district; 5–10 min. to Chinatown.
Restrictions Smoking in designated areas only. Street noise in some rooms.
Credit cards All major cards.
Rates Room only, $250 suite, $119–149 double. Extra person, $10. AARP discount. Corporate rates. Prix fixe dinner, $68.
Extras Wheelchair access; some rooms equipped for the disabled. Crib, babysitting. Weekday morning limo service to financial district. Spanish, Tagalog, Chinese spoken. Member, Kimco Co.

The Huntington 🛏 ✕
1075 California Street, 94108

Tel: 415–474–5400
800–227–4683
Fax: 415–474–6227

Sitting at the crest of Nob Hill, the Huntington Hotel has two impressive views—Union Square and the Bay Bridge in one direction, and Grace Cathedral and Huntington Park in the other. Built as a residence hotel and family-owned since 1924, the building's generous proportions are en-

CALIFORNIA

hanced by elegant decorations, fine fabrics, and antique furnishings. Al
though menus change frequently, typical entrées in the hotel's restaurar
include rack of lamb with lemon-thyme crust, grilled veal with portobell
mushrooms, and crab and black bean enchiladas.

"An exceptional feeling of spaciousness, and wonderful views from th
higher floors. The hotel's restaurant, The Big Four, is named for railroa
magnates Crocker, Hopkins, Huntington, and Stanford. Banquette seatin;
of dark green leather, mahogany panelling, thick etched glass cockta
tables, and bevelled mirrors give the impression of an exclusive club. Th
spacious guest rooms are handsomely decorated in soft shades of crean
blue, and peach, with accents of Asian art; some have luxurious nev
marble bathrooms. Nightly turndown service included chocolates an
fresh towels, in addition to the terry robes. Our room had a king-size be
and a seating area, with a view past Grace Cathedral and Huntington Par
to the bay and Marin County beyond. The burgundy and pewter sprea
matched the drapes and upholstery. The peachy beige walls comple
mented the extra-clean beige carpet. The bed was triple-sheeted, with fou
down pillows. The white-tiled bathroom had the original massive whit
fixtures plus a selection of toiletries. I was impressed by the caring attitud
of the staff, the subdued elegance of the building, the size of the room:
and the view." (SHW)

Open All year.
Rooms 40 suites, 100 doubles—all with private bath and/or shower, telephon
radio, TV, desk, fan, hair dryer; shoeshine on request. Suites with kitchen or we
bar.
Facilities Restaurant, bar/lounge with piano entertainment nightly, meetin;
rooms. Business services. Concierge service. Health club privileges. Hotel parking
$17 per night.
Location Nob Hill between Taylor & Mason Sts. California St. cable car stops a
front door.
Restrictions Smoking restricted in restaurant. Cable car noise, elevator noise i
some rooms.
Credit cards All major credit cards accepted.
Rates Room only, $250–685 suite, $185–235 double, $165–215 single. Extr
person, $20. Alc lunch, $24; alc dinner, $50.
Extras Crib, babysitting. Complimentary limo service to financial district, Unio
Square. Member, Small Luxury Hotels, Preferred Hotels.

Inn at the Opera 🛏 ✖ ♿
333 Fulton Street, 94102

Tel: 415–863–840
In CA: 800–423–961
Outside CA: 800–325–270
Fax: 415–861–082

Built more than a half century ago to cater to opera stars, the Inn at th
Opera has been transformed into a luxury hotel for artists and fans alike
The European-style rooms are handsomely decorated with muted color
and quality reproductions; amenities include terry robes and night-tim
chocolates. The lounge and restaurant, Act IV, has an "English club" look
with dark wood paneling and leather chairs.

"The friendly, accommodating French owners give this small hotel

184

European atmosphere. Quiet location, convenient to Brooks Hall." *(Peter Francis)* "Attentive service; Act IV is a delightful restaurant, popular with the opera/ballet crowd." *(William Rothe)* "Fresh, lovely decor. The rooms are small; it's worth paying a little extra for a suite. Delicious breakfast of fruits and baked goodies, served in the English pub. Nice amenities in the bathrooms, everything clean and neat. Parking can usually be found on the street." *(Carol Blodgett)* "The desserts were beyond description, service and atmosphere superb." *(Doris Gladstone)* "The Opera Package is a great way to get good opera seats, pleasant accommodations, and a wonderful dinner in one stroke." *(Barbara Mahler)* "The lobby has the ambiance of a friend's parlor. My room was comfortable, with plenty of shelves in both the bath and closet, lots of pillows and towels." *(Cindy Schonhaut)*

Open All year.
Rooms 18 suites, 30 doubles—all with full private bath, telephone, radio, TV, desk, refrigerator, wet bar, microwave.
Facilities Lobby, restaurant, bar/lounge with fireplace, nightly pianist. Concierge, room service. Valet parking, $16.
Location 1 block W of City Hall. On Fulton, between Franklin & Gough Sts.; 1 1/2 blocks from Van Ness. "About 90 feet from the opera hall."
Restrictions Prefer children over 10.
Credit cards Amex, MC, Visa.
Rates B&B, $175–215 suite, $115–165 double. Extra person, $10. Alc lunch, $18–25, alc dinner, $35–60. Special packages.
Extras Wheelchair access; some rooms equipped for disabled. Crib, babysitting. Chinese, Danish, French, Spanish, German spoken.

White Swan Inn 🏨
845 Bush Street, 94108

Tel: 415–775–1755
Fax: 415–775–5717

Built just after the famous 1906 earthquake, the White Swan is a Four Sisters Inn owned by Roger and Sally Post. The architecture is English, and the interior decor complements it with warm woods and English cabbage rose wallpapers. Rates include breakfast, afternoon tea and cookies, wine and hors d'oeuvres. Under the same ownership is the nearby **Petite Auberge** (863 Bush Street, 94108; 415–928–6000), decorated in the style of a French country inn, with soft colors, antiques, French-type wallpapers, and fresh flowers.

"The triple-sheeted king-size bed was wonderfully firm, with white trapunto-stitched spread and lace pillows. At evening turndown, the towels were replaced, and chocolates were left on the pillow with the weather forecast. The bath was fully equipped with amenities like terry robes, cotton balls and swabs, in addition to shampoo and lotion. The breakfast buffet was good, with a different quiche each day, plus Bircher muesli, breads, melon, strawberries, orange or grape juice, and hot beverages." *(SHW)* "Quiet room in the back, with a separate vanity area, a walk-in closet, and a kitchen-like area." *(Carol Blodgett)* "At breakfast I sat next to the windows, overlooking a small patio with flowers in bloom. In the afternoon, we relaxed in the back, on the narrow porch shaded by large trees. The desk staff was helpful with restaurant information and careful with phone messages. I could forgo the teddy bears on the stairs, but after four days of business meetings, I was actually patting a few on the head." *(Natalie Foster)* "Just as lovely as your description. The teddy bears and bedside fireplace switch are the greatest!" *(Alma Derricks)*

Open All year.
Rooms 1 suite, 24 doubles, 1 single—21 with full private bath, 5 with shower only. All with telephone, radio, TV, fireplace, refrigerator.
Facilities Living room, library, both with fireplace; dining room/solarium, conference room. Small garden with fountain, deck. Valet parking, $17.
Location Union Square area. 2½ blocks NW of Union Square, 2 blocks from Nob Hill, 1½ blocks from Powell St. cable car. Street noise in front rooms. No smoking.
Credit cards Amex, MC, Visa.
Rates B&B, $195–250 suite, $145–160 double. Extra person, $15. Romance package.
Extras Crib, babysitting. French spoken. Member, Four Sisters Inns.

SAN GREGORIO

Rancho San Gregorio ¢ 👬   *Tel:* 415–747–0810
5086 LaHonda Rd., Rte. 1 Box 54, 94074   *Fax:* 415–747–0184

Set in the pine-covered hills overlooking San Gregorio Valley, this Spanish Mission-style home has heavy redwood beams, terra cotta floors, and carved oak antiques. Innkeepers Bud and Lee Raynor built the house in 1971 and have been extending their hospitality to B&B guests since 1986. Lee notes that "we grow apples, pears, plums, berries, kiwi, zucchini, artichokes, and more. Depending on the season, our breakfasts might include fresh-squeezed orange juice, baked spiced home-grown pears with cinnamon yogurt, mushroom egg bake, sausages, homemade whole wheat bread with homemade plum jam, and apple cake."

"Bud and Lee provide you with area maps and helpful recommendations." *(Andrew Rateaver)* "This area extends from redwood forests of the Santa Cruz Mountains, down through lush foothills to the coast. The Raynors' property has a history reaching back to the Spanish ranchers, and Bud shares colorful stories of the artifacts he's found." *(Ginny Babbitt)* "The orchards, quiet hills, and creeks were pleasant for private, relaxing walks." *(Charles Moorman)* "The guest refrigerator stocked with drinks and snacks demonstrates the attention paid to guest comfort." *(Douglas Grant)* "Bud and Lee's breakfasts were great fuel for the bicycling we did along quiet roads with views of the ocean beyond." *(Timothy Leermont)* "During breakfast, we were introduced to the other guests and helped with plans for a day of sightseeing along the coast. The inn dog Sancho plays a mean game of ball." *(Alan & Sharon Leaf)*

Open All year.
Rooms 1 suite, 3 doubles—all with private bath and/or shower, radio, desk, deck, 3 with woodburning stove, 2 with refrigerator.
Facilities Dining room with organ, woodstove; living room with woodstove, TV/VCR, videotape library, stereo.
Location San Mateo County. 45 m S of San Francisco; 45 m N of Santa Cruz. 10

m SE of Half Moon Bay; 25 m W of Redwood City/Palo Alto. 5 m inland from coastal Hwy. 1 on Hwy. 84.

Restrictions No smoking.

Credit cards Amex, Discover, MC, Visa.

Rates B&B, $145 suite, $85–105 double. Extra person, $15. 10% midweek discount.

Extras Airport pickup with prior notice. Crib.

SAN JOSE

For an additional area entry, see listing for the **Inn at Saratoga** in **Saratoga**, just 20 minutes north of San Jose.

Information please: About 25 miles south of San Jose and east of Santa Cruz is the **Country Rose Inn** (455 Fitzgerald Avenue #E, San Martin 95046; mailing address, P.O. Box 1804, Gilroy, 95021-1804; 408–842–0441), close to Gilroy, the "Garlic Capitol of the U.S." A renovated 1920s Dutch Colonial home set in a grove of eucalyptus, oak, and pine, the guest rooms of have a rose motif extending from the fresh flowers to the decor, and are comfortably furnished with some antiques and family memorabilia. A typical breakfast includes orange juice, baked apple pancake, fresh fruit, and cream biscuits. B&B double rates for the five guest rooms range from $79–119.

The Hensley House   *Tel:* 408–298–3537
456 North Third Street, 95112   *Fax:* 408–298–4676

"San Jose, the oldest city in the state, has the largest collection of restored Victorian homes outside San Francisco, yet here we sit in the middle of Silicon Valley," report owners Sharon Layne and Bill Priest, "so we have tried to offer the best of both worlds—historic ambiance with business services." A Queen Anne Victorian home built in 1884, a portion of the interior was remodeled in the Craftsman or Tudor style about 1906; most of the original woodwork remains. Painstakingly renovated over a three-year period, Hensley House was opened as a B&B in 1990. Each of the guest rooms is painted in hues of burgundy and blue with coordinating hand-stenciled wallpaper motifs and crystal chandeliers. Rates include breakfast and afternoon refreshments; a typical morning menu includes fresh fruit and juice, cereals, breads, and a hot entrée such as eggs Blackstone or waffles.

"The inn has a good, quiet location downtown near the rail system. Thoughtful touches included the feather bed, good reading lights, plush towels, and nice soaps." *(Dianne Crawford)* "Our romantic evenings ended under a soft down comforter, with glasses of sherry and a late night video chosen from their collection. Excellent breakfast, served in the elegant dining room." *(Mike & Mary Darwin)*

Open All year.

Rooms 1 suite, 4 doubles—all with private bath and/or shower, telephone, radio, TV/VCR, desk, air-conditioning, fan, refrigerator. 2 with whirlpool tub, 1 with fireplace, wet bar.

Facilities Dining room, living room with fireplace, piano, books, videotape library. Fax, PC, business services. Garden, gazebo. Health club for guests, tennis court, park nearby.
Location Bay area, 50 m S of San Francisco. Downtown historic district. From Rte. 101, go SW on Julian St. Turn right on Third St. to inn on corner of Hensley.
Restrictions No smoking. Prefer children over 12. On-street parking.
Credit cards Amex, DC, Discover, MC, Visa.
Rates B&B, $119 suite, $75–125 double. Extra person, $20. AAA, senior discount. Lunch, dinner by prior arrangement.
Extras Airport/station pickup.

SAN LUIS OBISPO

In California's central coast region, San Luis Obispo is 200 miles north of Los Angeles and 200 miles south of San Francisco. Affectionately known as "SLO," this town of 50,000 is surrounded by mountains, and some 35 wineries within an easy drive. Pismo, Avila, and Grover beaches are nearby, as is Hearst Castle.

Also recommended: A bit large for a full entry (67 inn rooms, 34 rooms in the adjacent Trellis Court motel) is the **Apple Farm Inn** (2015 Monterey Street, 93401; 805–544–2040 or 800–374–3705), built in 1988 to provide the ambience of a turn-of-the-century Victorian inn, combined with the convenience of a modern hotel. A re-created water-powered mill grinds corn and presses apples for the inn's cornbread and cider; it even provides the power to make homemade ice cream. The inn's restaurant serves chicken and dumplings and smoked ribs, with hot apple dumplings or strawberry shortcake for dessert. Some readers tell us Apple Farm is their favorite getaway, others noted that it was "too sanitized, stylized, and cutesy for our tastes." Known for being wonderfully tacky, the **Madonna Inn** (100 Madonna Road, 93405; 805–543–3000 or 800–543–9666) has such theme rooms the Cave Man room, carved from solid rock. The Madonna's color scheme is equally memorable—although some rooms are done in lime green or bordello red, what you'll find throughout is bright pink, from the napkins to the toilets, from the matches to the dining room banquettes. Double rates for the 109 guest rooms range from $85–170.

William Frick was pleased with his stay at the 166-room **Cliffs at Shell Beach** (2757 Shell Beach Road, Pismo Beach 93449; 805–773–5000 or 800–826–5838): "Although not an inn, this modern, luxurious beach resort is poised directly above dramatic Shell Beach, about 15 minutes south of San Luis Obispo. The rooms are modern, clean, and well equipped, most with balconies, a separate sitting area, and luxurious marble baths. The large swimming pool and hot tub are attractive, and workout rooms are provided. The staff is efficient and helpful with hints for local attractions and dining. The standards of maintenance and cleanliness are high, and the restaurant is most satisfactory." Double rates are $115–160.

For an additional area entry, see listing for the **Baywood Inn** in **Baywood Park**, 12 miles west of San Luis Obispo.

Garden Street Inn ♿   *Tel:* 805–545–9802
1212 Garden Street, 93401

The Garden Street Inn is an Italianate Queen Anne home built in 1887, and restored as an inn in 1990 by Dan and Kathy Smith. The guest rooms have antique furnishings, queen- or king-size beds, and decorating motifs which range from Irish to Western, butterflies to sports memorabilia. The dining room is highlighted by the original stained glass windows; breakfast is served at individual tables and includes fruit, juice, cereal, an egg entrée, and home-baked bread. Wine and cheese is offered from 5:30–6:30 P.M.

"A meticulously restored two-story home, just two blocks from the Mission and the Thursday night farmer's market, and only six blocks from the best restaurant in town. Our sweet room had light, frilly blue fabrics, with good lighting in the bathroom. The tasty breakfast included a soufflé and fresh fruit. The innkeepers are helpful and friendly, and happily make dinner reservations. The inn's official greeter, Mozart, is a lovable little dog." *(Kathleen Lowe Owen)* "Welcoming innkeepers; quiet, charming atmosphere; excellent service; delicious, ample food; central location." *(Barbara Witt)* "Delightful library for relaxing, reading, or visiting with the other guests." *(Richard Schaublin)*

Area for improvement: "A reading lamp on my side of the bed."

Open All year.
Rooms 4 suites, 9 doubles—all with full private bath, radio, air-conditioning, fan, balcony/deck. 6 with whirlpool tub, 2 with desk, 5 with fireplace. Clock, telephone on request.
Facilities Dining room, library with piano, fireplace; decks. Near ocean for water sports. Swimming, golf, tennis, hiking, horseback riding, bicycling nearby.
Location Downtown. 1 ½ block from historic district.
Restrictions Traffic noise in 4 rooms. No smoking. Children over 16.
Credit cards Amex, MC, Visa.
Rates B&B, $120–160 suite, $81–120 double, $77–120 single. 10% senior, AAA discount. 2-night holiday/special event minimum.
Extras Wheelchair access; bathroom specially equipped. Airport/station pickups.

SANTA BARBARA

With its crystal-clear skies and steady 65-degree temperatures, Santa Barbara has been a popular winter seaside resort for over 50 years. The rest of the year has always been just as nice, with summer temperatures rarely exceeding the 70s, but people have only recently begun to discover Santa Barbara's year-round appeal. Most activities here are connected with the ocean—the beautiful beaches are ideal for swimming, surfing, diving, sailing, as well as whale and seal watching—but the city is also becoming known as an arts center, with several museums and galleries of interest. In addition to lots of lovely shops, Santa Barbara is the place to go for some of California's best food. Of course, there's no shortage of golf courses or tennis courts either.

The city's appearance is strikingly Spanish—adobe walls and red-tiled roofs abound. Part of this is because of the city's Spanish heritage—it was ruled by Spain for over 60 years—but a 1925 earthquake, which leveled much of the town, is also responsible. When rebuilding began, the local Architectural Board determined that Spanish, not Victorian, style would prevail.

Santa Barbara is located at the southern end of California's Central Coast, 91 miles north of Los Angeles, via Highway 101, and 335 miles south of San Francisco. Weekend traffic coming up from LA can be heavy.

Worth noting: Santa Barbara is an expensive town; $100–120 per night gets you adequate, not luxurious, accommodations; we've noticed rate increases of over 10% at several B&Bs since the last edition went to press. If you'll be in Santa Barbara during the week on business, don't make a reservation without inquiring about corporate rates; nearly every establishment offers them. Rates also tend to be 10 to 20 percent lower from October to May.

Also recommended: Five miles south of Santa Barbara is the **Inn on Summer Hill** (2520 Lillie Avenue, Summerland 93067; 805–969–9998 or 800–845–5566), a rambling Craftsman-style bungalow constructed in 1989. Guest rooms are decorated in a fantasy of European country-style fabrics and patterns, billowing curtains and ruffled cushions, most with a king-size canopy bed. Floral paintings and antique trunks provide accents, along with Tiffany-style lamps and fresh flowers; all rooms have ocean views, private baths, telephone, TV/VCR, stereo, air-conditioning, and gas fireplace. Although right on Highway 101, double-glazed windows keeps traffic noise to a minimum. Rates include a creative full breakfast, afternoon tea and cookies, wine and hors d'oeuvres, and after-dinner dessert. Terry robes are supplied to wear en route to the gazebo-covered hot tub. B&B double rates for the 16 guest rooms range from $160–195, with extra charges for breakfast in bed and videotape rentals.

The **Montecito Inn** (1295 Coast Village Road, 93108; 805–969–7854 or 800–843–2017), built in 1928 by Charlie Chaplin and Fatty Arbuckle, was a favorite getaway for the movie stars of the day. It features wrought-iron balconies, white stucco walls, classic red Spanish tiles, and graceful arches. The 53 guest rooms are decorated in lavender florals, others in handsome ivory and browns—with French country furniture, overhead fans, and tiled baths. "Convenient location on Montecito's main street, though some rooms can be noisy. Small but appealing swimming pool and hot tub." *(SWS)* "Spacious, comfortable suite; excellent, reasonably priced restaurant. Used the hotel's free bicycles to ride along the ocean path." *(EL)*

Information please: A Victorian gem, built in 1898, is the **Tiffany Inn** (1323 De la Vina Street, 93101; 805–963–2283 or 800–999–5672). The seven guest rooms, all with queen-sized beds, are furnished with antiques and other period pieces. The Rose Garden and Nichole rooms share a bath, and the $75 rate make them a best buy in pricy Santa Barbara; the other rooms, with private bath, go from $135 to $190. Rates include a full breakfast, served in the dining room or veranda, and evening refreshments.

Five miles south of Santa Barbara is the famous **San Ysidro Ranch** (900 San Ysidro Lane, Montecito 93108; 805–969–5046 or 800–368–6788), a

eautifully groomed and furnished luxury resort. Many famous people
ave stayed here—presidents, kings, and prime ministers—yet the atmo-
phere remains California casual. "All rooms are in separate cottages
cattered around the ranch, located at the foot of a mountain. John F.
.ennedy stayed here on his lengthy honeymoon." *(John & Ivy Shelton)*
ome of the 43 suites and cottages are spacious and elegant, with beautiful
nountain and distant ocean views, others are considerably more modest.
.ates range from $225–750, exclusive of any meals, refreshments, snacks,
nd most activities.

The Bath Street Inn
720 Bath Street, 93101

Tel: 805–682–9680
800–788–BATH

A Queen Anne Victorian built over 100 years ago, the Bath Street Inn has
een owned by Susan Brown since 1981. Rooms are decorated with
eriod wallpapers and highlighted with handmade quilts and English
ntiques, complemented by firm beds, good reading lights, and ample hot
vater.

"Delicious blueberry pancakes, fresh fruit, and good coffee." *(Carol
Morgan)* "The Abigail Room had two twin beds made into a king, two
omfy chairs, a small table, an armoire, good lighting, and a down com-
orter. Small but cozy living room with comfortable couch and chairs.
Breakfast is served between 8–9:30 A.M., and consisted of juice, a baked
apple, granola with yogurt or milk, cheese coddled egg with muffins and
oast. The third floor sitting/TV room has a beautiful mountain view."
SWS) "We had breakfast in the lovely garden almost every morning. The
Garden Room is light and airy, with wall fabrics and white wicker; the sink
nd the claw-footed tub were in the room, the toilet in a former closet."
Carolyn Myles) "The outside of the building is well lighted and safe at
ight." *(MM)*

Open All year.
Rooms 10 doubles—all with full private bath and/or shower. 2 in annex with gas
ireplace, TV, telephone; 1 with Jacuzzi, 1 with double shower.
Facilities Dining room, TV lounge, library, deck. Gardens. Off-street parking.
1½ m to ocean. Bicycles.
Location 6 blocks from shopping area. Exit Hwy. 101 at Carrillo, go E to Bath
St., N 7 blocks to inn between Valerio & Islay.
Restrictions No smoking. Minimal interior soundproofing.
Credit cards Amex, MC, Visa.
Rates B&B, $95–150 double, $90–145 single. Extra person, $20. AAA, senior
liscount; corporate rates midweek. 2-night weekend minimum.

Blue Quail Inn ¢
1908 Bath Street, 93101

Tel: 805–687–2300
In CA: 800–549–1622
Outside CA: 800–676–1622

Picture a California Craftsman-style bungalow and four cottages with a
sunny lawn and shaded patios, and you'll see the Blue Quail Inn. Owner
leanise Suding Eaton has decorated the guest rooms with antiques and
country furnishings, naming each one after a North American bird. Rates
nclude afternoon cider and wine, evening sweets, and breakfast—perhaps

popovers, zucchini-dill quiche, boysenberry coffeecake, and baked apple usually served on the patio. "The gardens were lovely, the cottage charming, clean, quiet, and well maintained." *(Sabella Haverland)* "We wer welcomed with cheese, wine and juice; when we returned from dinne cookies and hot chocolate were waiting." *(Deborah Magee)* "Simple bu charming rooms, a refreshing change from the clutter of many other inns. *(SWS, also Vicki Schulkin)* Comments welcome.

Area for improvement: "My room needed a second bedside light an table."

Open All year.
Rooms 4 suites, 5 doubles—all with private bath and/or shower, radio, fan; som with desk. Rooms in 4 cottages and main house.
Facilities Dining/living room, TV, guest refrigerator. Garden, patio, bicycles.
Location 1 m to downtown. From Hwy. 101, go NE on Mission. Turn right o Castillo St., left onto Pedregosa St., left onto Bath St. to inn.
Restrictions No smoking. Traffic noise in front rooms might disturb light sleep ers. Children welcome in private cottage.
Credit cards Amex, MC, Visa.
Rates B&B, $125–165 suite, $85–95 double. Extra person, $20. 2-night holiday weekend minimum. Off-season, midweek rates. Picnic lunches.
Extras Airport/station pickup by prior arrangement.

The Cheshire Cat Inn   *Tel: 805–569–161*
36 West Valerio Street, 93101   *Fax: 805–682–187*

In 1984 Christine Dunstan restored two of Santa Barbara's oldest adjoin ing homes, opening them as a B&B. Named for characters in *Alice i Wonderland*, most have Laura Ashley-style fabrics and sitting areas high lighted with English antiques. A full breakfast is served in the dining roon or on the shaded patio; locally made chocolates and imported cordials ar placed in each guest room as a welcome gift.

"The Mock Turtle room has four huge windows overlooking the fron garden, and was beautifully decorated, immaculate, and quiet. Th grounds were glorious, with flowers everywhere, and a wonderful Jacuzz in the gazebo, with white lights twinkling in the trees and hanging potte plants and flowers." *(Cynthia Grylov & Thomas Pinto)* "The location is idea for walking to shops and restaurants." *(Mary Ann Dupré & David Jacobs* "Lovely guest rooms, many with beautifully tiled Jacuzzi tubs. Som rooms have a summer look with soft blues, pinks and greens while other have deeper maroons and navy color schemes." *(SWS)* Reports welcome

Open All year.
Rooms 8 suites, 6 doubles—all with private bath and/or shower, telephone, fan Some with TV, fireplace, Jacuzzi, microwave, refrigerator, patio or balcony kitchen. 2 rooms in Coach House.
Facilities Dining room, parlor, lounge, all with fireplace. TV/game room. ½ acr with patio, swing, rose garden, gazebo with hot tub, bicycles. Off-street parking
Location 3 blocks to theater, restaurants, shops. Take State St. to Valerio St.
Restrictions Noise in 3 rooms might disturb light sleepers. No smoking.
Credit cards MC, Visa.
Rates B&B, $169–249 suite, $79–169 double. 2-night weekend minimum. Corpo rate rate midweek, $75 single.

Glenborough Inn ¢
1327 Bath Street, 93101

Tel: 805–966–0589
800–962–0589
Fax: 805–564–2369

Travelers who steer clear of B&Bs because the enforced early-morning camaraderie is not their cup of tea—or coffee—will enjoy the Glenborough. The innkeepers maintain guests' privacy by bringing breakfast to each room between 8:30–9:30 A.M.; the meal includes a hot entrée, freshly baked bread, fresh fruit, and juice. Owned by Michael Diaz, Steve Ryan and Ken Armstrong since 1992, the inn comprises a 1906 Craftsman-style building with beveled glass windows and cross-cut oak beams, plus two Victorian cottages across the street. Guest rooms are simply furnished with some antiques, most with queen-size brass, iron, or canopy beds, and floral fabrics. Guests enjoy gathering for wine and hors d'oeuvres from 5–6 P.M.; tea and cookies are available after dinner.

"Delicious breakfasts, delivered on time." *(Kenneth Vogt)* "Quiet, safe location; short walk to downtown. Unusual privacy for a B&B." *(Gary Kuenzli)* "Plants and a profusion of flowers in the lush garden." *(PH)* "Michael, Steve, and Ken really care about their guests, and keep abreast of restaurants, events, and activities. Excellent value." *(Barbara Harris)* "Close to the shuttle, so you don't need a car." *(Darlene Jordan)*

Open All year.
Rooms 3 suites, 8 doubles in 3 buildings. 5 with private bath and/or shower, 6 with maximum of 4 people sharing bath. All with telephone, radio, clock, fan. Some with desk, fireplace, patio.
Facilities Dining room, parlor with fireplace, games, books; guest refrigerator, porch, bicycles. Gardens, hot tub, lawn games. Off-street parking.
Location Downtown residential area; 3 blocks to restaurants, shops, museums. On Bath St. between Victorian & Sola. From Hwy. 101, go E on Carrillo, N on Bath.
Restrictions No smoking. Children over 6.
Credit cards Amex, DC, Discover, MC, Visa.
Rates B&B, $160–180 suite, $65–75 double. Extra person, $30. Tips appreciated. Senior, AAA, corporate rate midweek, Oct.–May. 2-3 weekend/holiday minimum.
Extras Spanish spoken.

Old Yacht Club Inn
431 Corona Del Mar Drive, 93103

Tel: 805–962–1277
In CA: 800–549–1676
Outside CA: 800–676–1676
Fax: 805–962–3989

A California Craftsman-style home built in 1912, the Old Yacht Club owes its name to the fact that it served as headquarters for Santa Barbara's yacht club in the 1920s. Restored as Santa Barbara's first B&B in 1980 by Nancy Donaldson, Lu Caruso, and Sandy Hunt, the inn is known for old-fashioned hospitality and fine food. A typical breakfast might include piña colada juice, poached pears, regular or low-cholesterol omelets with cheese, salsa, and green chiles, sour cream coffee cake, and lemon bread; rates also include afternoon cookies and evening refreshments. A typical Saturday night dinner menu might include marinated artichokes, sorrel soup, spinach salad, swordfish with tarragon, orzo with red peppers, and Italian swirl cheesecake.

"The cozy living/dining room has several tables, a small sitting area, lots of antiques and knickknacks and a piano for evening sing-alongs." *(Roy & Sari Martens)* "Parking is plentiful, with motion-activated lights." *(Janet Guiscardo)* "Great location on a quiet side street near the beach, pier, shops, and restaurants. Bicycle or take the trolley everywhere else." *(Carol & Lee Agon)* "Oozes warmth and hospitality. My room felt like grandma's guest room—simple but comfortable—with a large deck, window seat and queen-size bed." *(Gail Davis, also SWS)* Reports needed.

Open All year.
Rooms 1 suite, 8 doubles—all with private bath and/or shower. All with telephone; TV upon request. Some with desk, deck, or balcony. 1 with whirlpool tub. 4 rooms in adjacent Hitchcock House.
Facilities Dining room, living room with fireplace, piano, games, stereo, library; deck, porch, off-street parking. Bicycles, beach chairs. Golf privileges at country club. 1 block to beach.
Location 1½ m to town. Exit Hwy. 101 at Cabrillo. Go W on Cabrillo past bird refuge to Corona del Mar, between the Sheraton and Cabrillo Inn. Turn right to #431.
Restrictions No smoking. Children permitted in Hitchcock House.
Credit cards Amex, Discover, MC, Visa.
Rates B&B, $100–150 suite, $80–140 double, $65–145 single. Extra person, $30. Off-season discounts. 2-night weekend minimum. Picnic lunches. Sat. night prix fixe dinner, $25.
Extras Station pickup, free; airport pickup, $8. Some Spanish spoken.

Simpson House Inn &
121 East Arrellega Street, 93101

Tel: 805-963-7067
800-676-1280
Fax: 805-564-4811

Glyn and Linda Davies purchased the Simpson House in 1976, but did not open the doors of their B&B until 1985, after years of restoration work, plus a fight to change the zoning laws. With both battles won, resident innkeeper Gillean Wilson can devote her time to pleasing guests. A typical breakfast might include fresh-squeezed organic orange juice, homemade granola, baked pears with whipped cream, savory eggs, and hot scones, while the evening appetizers might be artichoke dip, tapenade with sourdough toast, and vegetable antipasto.

"Lovely gardens, mature shade trees, and large hedges provide privacy. Breakfast can be taken on a large porch or on your own private balcony with fantastic views of the mountains." *(Vivek Allada)* "Huge living and dining room with beautiful Oriental rugs. Guest rooms in the main house are decorated with lovely antiques; the handsome barn suites have king-sized beds and a rustic country look, accented with antique farm equipment; and the romantic cottages have French antiques." *(SWS)* "At night a turned-down bed, mints, and cream sherry await your return." *(C.C Sinewe)* "Bathrooms combine modern functionality with period charm—brass fixtures and old-fashioned wallpaper." *(Sylvia & Brian Weinberg)* "Though small, my light and airy room had lots of windows, and was done in pinks, greens, and white wicker." *(JL)* "Impeccable service by Gillean Wilson. We visited with the other guests during evening wine and hors d'oeuvres; afternoon hot cider and just-baked cookies were a treat. *(Linda Vause)*

Open All year.
Rooms 3 cottages, 4 suites, 6 doubles—all with private bath and/or shower, desk. Some with air-conditioning, fireplace, deck. 4 suites in restored barn—all with telephone, TV/VCR, fireplace, deck. Cottages with fireplace, Jacuzzi tub, TV/VCR.
Facilities Dining room, living room with fireplace, library; porch. 1 acre, garden, sitting areas, croquet, picnic area. Bicycles, beach equipment. Golf, tennis nearby.
Location 5 blocks from center. From Hwy. 101 N take Santa Barbara St. exit. Go right 13 blocks then left on Arrellega St. From Hwy. 101 S take Mission St. exit. Go left on State St., right on Arrellaga St.
Restrictions No smoking.
Credit cards Amex, Discover, MC, Visa.
Rates B&B, $235–270 cottage, $210 suite, $105–165 double. Extra person, $25. 2-3 night weekend, holiday minimum. 20–30% midweek discount.
Extras Wheelchair access. French, Danish, Spanish spoken.

SANTA CRUZ

Santa Cruz is a classic old beach resort, complete with a boardwalk and amusement park. The area's white sand beaches—fun for both swimming and fishing—have been a playground for San Franciscans for over 100 years. The municipal pier is lined with seafood restaurants and souvenir shops, while the local sea lion population frolics in the water below. Other nearby attractions include the redwood forests, golf, tennis, hiking, fishing, and, of course, shopping. Santa Cruz is also home to 20 wineries, seven with tasting rooms—and no tour buses.

Summer is peak season here; many, although not all, establishments lower their room rates from November through February. Located on Monterey Bay, on the Central Coast, Santa Cruz is 75 miles south of San Francisco, 35 miles south of San Jose, and 40 miles north of Carmel/Monterey.

Reader tips: "The drive to Santa Cruz (Spanish for holy cross) takes about 40 minutes from the San Jose Airport on a winding road over redwood-covered mountains. As you descend, you see the town nestled in the coastal plain with Monterey Bay as a backdrop. The best view is from the University of California Santa Cruz campus in the northwest part of town, and it's just as lovely at night as during the daytime." *(Michael Salkind)* Also: "The best time to visit is in the spring or fall when the days are warm and summer fog and tourists are absent." *(Matt Joyce)*

Information please: A few miles southeast of Santa Cruz is Capitola, a popular beach resort on Monterey Bay. **The Inn at Depot Hill** (250 Monterey Avenue, Capitola 95010; 408–462–DEPO) was built in 1901 as a railroad depot, and has been transformed into a luxurious eight-room inn. B&B double rates range from $165–265. "Good location; formal but pleasant lobby and living room; top-quality fabrics, linens, and furnishings; charming receptionist." *(SD)* Overlooking the Pacific from its blufftop location is century-old **El Salto** (620 El Salto Drive, Capitola 95010; 408–462–6365) with a Victorian manor house and 14 intimate cottages scattered about the flower-filled grounds; double rates range from $125–225 and include a continental breakfast.

For additional area entries, see listings for the **New Davenport B&B**

CALIFORNIA

in **Davenport**, the **Inn at Saratoga** in Saratoga, and the **Blue Spruce**, four miles south in **Soquel**.

Babbling Brook Inn ♿
1025 Laurel Street, 95060

Tel: 408–427–2437
800–866–1131
Fax: 408–427–2457

The site of the Babbling Brook Inn was a favorite fishing spot of the Ohlone Indians. Later it housed a gristmill, then a tannery, and was even used as a set for silent movies. It was converted into a B&B in 1981, and was bought by Helen King in 1986. Four of the guest rooms are in the original historic buildings, with the remainder in chalet-style buildings; the decor is French country.

"The inn's garden is a profusion of calla lilies, pansies, poppies, phlox, hummingbirds, and curios. Eight of the guest rooms are named for post-impressionist artists and are decorated with their works and colors. Tea and wonderful homemade cookies are available all day, and wine and cheese are served in the evening. Guests share their thoughts about the inn and area restaurants in guest books which make entertaining reading." *(Michael Salkind)* "Fires were fed all evening and the rooms were cozy and warm in a cold, rainy week." *(Nancy Coyne)* "The FMRS Garden Room has a comfortable, four-poster king-sized canopy bed, with good reading lights and fresh flowers. The tiled hearth and woodstove were perfect for cool, foggy evenings. An enormous window overlooks the creekside garden. Breakfast included eggs rellenos, croissants, muffins, fruit salad, yogurt, granola, fresh-squeezed orange juice, coffee, and tea, served on English china. Guests have the choice of eating at small tables or taking trays to their rooms." *(Matt & Janet Joyce, also Randy Delucchi)* "The Countess Room is spacious and inviting." *(SD)*

Open All year.
Rooms 1 suite, 11 doubles—all with private bath and/or shower, telephone, radio, TV, desk. Most with fireplace, private entrance, deck. 2 with soaking jet tub, 2 with whirlpool tub. Rooms in 4 separate buildings.
Facilities Living/dining room with fireplace, deck/patio. 1 acre, gardens, brook, waterfall, waterwheel, gazebo. Off-street parking. Swimming, tennis, golf nearby.
Location 7 blocks from downtown. 1½ blocks off Pacific Coast Hwy. 1.
Restrictions Street noise in 2 front rooms until 10:30 P.M. No smoking. Children over 12.
Credit cards Amex, CB, DC, Discover, MC, Visa.
Rates B&B, $85–150 suite, double. Extra person, $15. 2-night weekend minimum. $75 midweek "Getaway Special" package, Sept. 30 to May 1. Corporate rates. Prix fixe lunch, $7.
Extras Wheelchair access; some rooms equipped for the disabled. Some French, Spanish spoken.

SANTA ROSA

Information please: Built in 1877 by a gold miner who did not lose all his money, **The Gables** (4257 Petaluma Hill Road, 95404; 707–585–

7777), sports 15 gables, keyhole-shaped windows, and three marble fire-places shipped around the Horn from Italy. This High Victorian Gothic Revival mansion is decorated with antiques and collectibles. The 3½ acre rural setting has a 150-year-old barn, creamery, stream and the original outhouse—but never fear, each of the seven guest rooms has a private bath. B&B double rates of $95–135 include a full breakfast.

Hotel La Rose ¢ ♀ ✕ &.
305 Wilson Street, 95401

Tel: 707–579–3200
800–527–6738
Fax: 707–579–3247

Although Santa Rosa was settled in the 1850s, its growth accelerated with the arrival of the railroad in 1870, when it became a regional commercial center. A reflection of the town's prosperity was the construction of Railroad Square's handsome stone buildings, built by Italian stone masons. Now listed on the National Register of Historic Places, the Hotel La Rose—its name carved in the hotel's stone facade—was renovated in 1985 and has been owned by Claus and Debbie Neumann since 1990. The buffet breakfast is served from 7:30–11 A.M., with fresh fruit and juice, yogurt, granola, freshly baked muffins, and English muffins. A recent dinner in the hotel's restaurant included mussels in herb garlic sauce; angel hair pasta with smoked chicken; and berries with port wine sauce.

"Hotel convenience, inn atmosphere. Our top-floor suite was spacious and comfortable, with a brass king-size bed, large closet, sitting area with sofa and chairs, writing desk, armoire with TV, and ample reading lights. The bath had contemporary fixtures and excellent lighting. The hotel's restaurant, Josef's, has an inviting and intimate atmosphere with a lovely old oak bar." (Gail Davis) "Comfortable, spotless, well-appointed rooms; excellent coffee." (Marc Bruvry) "Pleasant, quiet sitting room off the lobby, with an equally appealing breakfast room." (James Warnemuende) "Friendly, safe atmosphere; accommodating staff and management." (Suzanne Danielson)

Open All year. Restaurant closed Sun., Mon.
Rooms 12 suites, 37 doubles—all with private bath and/or shower, telephone, radio, clock, TV, table, air-conditioning. 23 with balcony/patio. Refrigerator on request. 20 rooms in Carriage House.
Facilities Restaurant, bar/lounge with fireplace, sitting room, breakfast room, meeting rooms. Garden courtyard, off-street parking. Park across street. Ocean, lake, river, hiking, golf, ballooning nearby.
Location 50 m north of San Francisco. Railroad Square. From Hwy. 101, take downtown Santa Rosa exit. Go W on 4th St. & turn right on Wilson to hotel on right, between 4th & 5th.
Restrictions Traffic noise in some rooms if windows opened. Smoking permitted in Carriage House.
Credit cards Amex, MC, Visa.
Rates B&B, $65–95 suite, $55–85 double, $45–70 single. Extra person, $10. No charge for children under 13. Alc lunch, $12; alc dinner, $25. Corporate rates; golf, balloon packages.
Extras Wheelchair access; 4 rooms specially equipped. Crib. German, Spanish, some French spoken.

SARATOGA

The Inn at Saratoga 🛉 ⚹.
20645 Fourth Street, 95070

Tel: 408–867–5020
In CA: 800–543–5020
Outside CA: 800–338–5020
Fax: 408–741–0981

Named for New York's famed Saratoga Springs, this California village selected its name in 1865 to promote the local hot springs by capitalizing on the fame of its eastern namesake. Today, visitors come to Saratoga because of its proximity to Silicon Valley, to sample its excellent restaurants, visit the local wineries, enjoy the concerts at the Carriage House, and to explore local museums, gardens, and redwood groves.

The Inn at Saratoga opened in 1987, and is designed to provide a relaxing atmosphere for both business and vacation travelers. The guest rooms overlook Saratoga Creek and tree-filled Wildwood Park, and are luxuriously furnished with contemporary decor, a teal, peach, and mauve color scheme, featherbeds and quality linens. Rates include the morning newspaper and breakfast of orange juice, fruit, bakery-fresh pastries with coffee, tea, and decaf, plus afternoon refreshments.

"From my soft perch atop a four-poster featherbed with six pillows, I had a floor-to-ceiling view of the park's trees. At night, the foliage is lit with a soft spotlight to provide a pleasant view. I opened the window slightly to hear the light trickle of the brook. I slept in the next morning, then relaxed in the oversized whirlpool tub, watching CNN on the bathroom TV. I had a delicious dinner at Mia Bella, one of twenty nearby restaurants." *(Alma Derricks)*

Open All year.
Rooms 5 suites, 41 doubles—all with full private bath, telephones (with dataport), radio, TV/VCR, desk, refrigerator, air-conditioning, fan, wet bar, hair dryer, towel warmer. Most with patio/balcony. 7 with double whirlpool tub, bathroom TV.
Facilities Lobby, club room with games, TV/VCR; patio, off-street parking. Health club nearby; membership included. Riding, walking trails nearby.
Location San Francisco Bay Area; foothills of Santa Cruz Mts. 10 min. to Silicon Valley, 20 min. W of San Jose, 20 min. NE of Santa Cruz, 55 min. S of San Francisco. Walking distance to town. $\frac{1}{2}$ block N of Hwy. 9 (Big Basin Way).
Credit cards Amex, DC, MC, Visa.
Rates B&B, $295–440 suite, $145–245 double. Extra person, $15. No charge for children under 18.
Extras Wheelchair access. German, Spanish spoken.

SAUSALITO

Just across the Golden Gate Bridge from San Francisco, Sausalito perches precariously on steep hillsides dropping to the bay below. Originally developed in the mid-1800s with elegant Victorian mansions, its nature became more bawdy and commercial when the town became the railway and ferry terminus at the century's end. Sausalito's waterfront was again active during World War II, when it became a center for Liberty ships, with the shipyards in operation round-the-clock. The town has been known as a center for artists and craftspeople since the '50s and has been popular as a tourist center since ferry service was resumed in 1970.

The Casa Madrona Hotel 🛏 ✕ ♿
801 Bridgeway, 94965

Tel: 415–332–0502
800–288–0502
Fax: 415–332–2537

Owned since 1976 by John Mays, the Casa Madrona consists of an 1885 Victorian mansion with a new section completed in 1983; the two structures are linked by suites and rooms winding down the hillside. The old rooms are furnished with antiques, while many of the newer ones have Mediterranean touches. The restaurant specializes in American cuisine with Pacific Rim accents. "Tucked into the hills above the bay, up a flight of stairs from the main boardwalk. Most rooms have a private deck with a bay view. Several waterside restaurants are within walking distance." (Christine Adkins) "Helpful, congenial staff. Glorious gardens." (Paula Gaskins) "Bathrooms are clean, modern, and well-maintained." (Patrick Aritz) "Breakfast consists of juice, coffee, fruit, and muffins." (AW) "Unusual, interesting accommodations. Fantastic water views in the dining room." (HBS) Reports?

Open All year.
Rooms 3 suites, 24 doubles, 5 cottages—all with full private shower and/or bath, telephone, radio, TV, desk, air-conditioning.
Facilities Parlor, restaurant with piano music 3 nights weekly. Gardens, hot tub. Tennis, golf nearby. Valet parking, $5.
Location San Francisco Bay Area, Marin County. 15 min. drive, 30-min. ferry from San Francisco. On main street. From Hwy. 101, take Sausalito exit onto Bridgeway, follow to 801. 350 yds. to ferry.
Restrictions Smoking restricted.
Credit cards Amex, DC, Discover, MC, Visa.
Rates B&B, $150–300 suite, $105–195 double. Extra person, $20. 2-night weekend minimum. Alc lunch, $15; alc dinner, $30–35. Sunday brunch, theme dinners, tastings.
Extras 1 room wheelchair accessible. Crib, babysitting. German, Spanish, French, Vietnamese, Chinese spoken.

SKYFOREST

For additional area entries, see **Big Bear Lake.**

Skyforest B&B Inn
760 Kuffel Canyon Road, P.O. Box 482, 92385

Tel: 909–337–4680

A contemporary log lodge built by Lawrence Gordon in 1983, Skyforest has been managed by Meta and Tom Morgan since 1989. The inn takes its name from the 24 skylights throughout the inn, which make both the sky and the surrounding forest an intrinsic part of the inn's decor. Weekday rates include a breakfast of fruit, muffins, cereal and oatmeal; a hot entrée is served on weekends, as are evening wine and hors d'oeuvres.

"Lovely modern home in a quiet residential neighborhood just outside of Lake Arrowhead. Guest rooms are spacious, nicely decorated, and comfortable. Breakfast entrées include omelets with herb-fried potatoes, stuffed French toast, or quiches with hash-brown potato crusts. Helpful accommodating innkeepers Meta and Tom, also provide information about local events and menus for nearby restaurants. Guests are welcome to sit by the fire or sample the large selection of videos. Ample parking." *(Ross & Merrie Lyn Shickler)* "In the woods, yet close to restaurants and shops. Enjoyed watching Meta feed the birds, squirrels, and raccoons on the deck." *(Bonnie Stuckey)* "Enjoyed chatting with the other guests over Meta's delicious breakfasts, and hearing about Tom's plans for continued improvements." *(Jessica Golden Tolsky)*

Open All year.
Rooms 1 suite, 4 doubles—3 with private bath and/or shower, 2 with maximum of 4 sharing bath. All with air-conditioning; 2 with desk, 4 with balcony/deck.
Facilities Dining room, living room with fireplace, loft with TV/VCR, stereo, books. Hiking, skiing, 3 lakes for water sports nearby.
Location San Bernardino Mts. Lake Arrowhead/Big Bear. 2 ½ hrs. E of LA. 5 min. from Lake Arrowhead on Hwy. 18.
Restrictions No smoking. Children over 12. Snow chains required Nov.–March.
Credit cards None accepted.
Rates B&B, $125–150 suite, $75–100 double. Extra person, $25. 2-3 night weekend/holiday minimum. Nov.–March ski packages.

SOLVANG

Solvang was founded in 1911 by midwesterners of Danish heritage, who wanted to start a traditional Danish folk school and ended up with an entire Danish-style town. Danish customs still prevail, and many come to Solvang for the European atmosphere, shops, bakeries, and outdoor theater.

Solvang is located in the Central Coast region, 135 miles north of Los Angeles in the Santa Ynez Valley Wine Country. It's 30 miles from Santa Barbara and about 15 minutes from the beach.

Reader tip: "Solvang is tacky! I suppose an insatiable craving for fudge might justify a brief stop, but I can't imagine wanting to spend the night here when there are so many appealing alternatives close by." *(Ralph Miller)*

Information please: Inn at Peterson Village (1576 Mission Drive, 93463; 805–688–3121 or in CA, 800–321–8985) is a modern facility constructed in the style of old Denmark and shares its building with the 24 shops and cafés of Petersen Village. The 42 guest rooms are luxuriously decorated with canopy beds and love seats; TVs are discreetly hidden in armoires. A continental buffet breakfast and afternoon wine is included in the $95–170 double room rates. Also in town is the **Chimney Sweep Inn** (1554 Copenhagen Drive, 93463; 805–688–2111 or 800–824–6444), with country-style rooms, four-poster or canopy beds, a courtyard garden, gazebo-covered hot tub, in-room coffee, and Danish bakery breakfast. Lodge rates range from $70–140, cottage rates from $145–255.

Also recommended: A few miles north of Solvang, the **Grand Hotel** (2860 Grand Avenue, Los Olivos 93441; 805–688–7788 or 800–446–2455) offers 20 guest rooms, gently decorated with country Victorian furnishings, each with floral wallpaper, pine furniture, ceiling fan, electric fireplace, and whirlpool tub. The hotel restaurant serves California cuisine, and guests can relax in the inviting swimming pool or hot tub. Rates for this four-diamond escape range from $160–325, including wine and continental breakfast.

For an additional area entry, see listing for **The Ballard Inn** in **Ballard.**

Alisal Guest Ranch 🏃 ✕ 🔫 ♿
1054 Alisal Road, 93463

Tel: 805–688–6411
800–4–ALISAL

Families who've despaired of ever finding a welcome for their children among California's inns will find an oasis at the Alisal; it's enjoyed equally by adult travelers as well, especially when school is in session. Dating back to an 1803 land grant originally totalling 13,500 acres, Alisal means sycamore in Spanish. The ranch was used primarily for raising cattle until 1946; at that time it was purchased by the Jackson family who started taking in guests. The Jacksons still own the ranch and cattle are still raised here, but the focus has now shifted from four-legged to two-legged inhabitants. Full western activities—trail rides, square dancing, cookouts, and hay rides—await the energetic, but one can just as easily spend the day reading in the library and dozing by the pool. The common rooms are decorated with western flair, highlighted by Indian rugs and wall hangings.

"Beautiful mountain views and scenery. Friendly, competent staff, good food, and lots to do. Wonderful weather, even in winter, when the daytime temperatures are in the 70s." *(Sandy Knox-Johnston)* "Peaceful setting. Our cottage had been recently redone with Navajo-inspired fabrics and bleached wood cathedral ceiling. Though the furnishings are basic, some of the older units are comfortable choices for families; those with young children will prefer rooms close to the swimming pool and playground. Paved paths connect the ranch's many buildings, making walking easy. Generous portions, delicious dinner, accompanied by a fine Cabernet Sauvignon bottled for the ranch by Firestone Vineyards. Service was professional and friendly." *(SWS)*

Open All year.
Rooms 34 suites, 29 doubles, 2 3-bedroom cottages—all with private bath and/or shower, desk, fan, wood-burning fireplace, refrigerator. 2–8 rooms per unit.
Facilities Dining rooms, living room with fireplace, game/TV room, bar/lounge with pianist, library. 10,000 acres with heated swimming pool, hot tub, 7 tennis courts, 18-hole PGA golf course, horseback riding, 100-acre stocked private lake for fishing, boating, fishing, windsurfing, sailing; hiking, bicycling, archery, lawn games; children's craft/activities program during summer months.
Location From Hwy. 101, take Solvang/Lompoc exit on Hwy. 246 and go E. Pass through Buellton and go 3 m to Solvang. Turn right on Alisal Rd. (past golf course) to entrance.
Restrictions No smoking in dining room. Gentleman must wear a jacket at dinner; no jeans, t-shirts or shorts for children at dinner.
Credit cards MC, Visa.
Rates MAP, $305–365 suite, $285 double. Extra person, $65. 12–15% service.

2-night minimum stay; 3–4-night holiday minimum. Midweek off-season (Sept.–mid-June) rates include horseback riding, tennis, golf.
Extras Wheelchair access. Crib, $30; babysitting. Spanish, Italian, Portuguese spoken.

SONOMA

Sonoma is California's oldest mission, founded in 1823. Today people come to Sonoma primarily to visit the area wineries; California's first vineyard was planted here in 1855 by a Hungarian nobleman by the name of Haraszthy. Visitors also enjoy touring its historic buildings, playing golf and tennis, and going horseback riding or ballooning.

Sonoma is located in the North Coast region, in the Sonoma Wine Country, about 40 miles north of San Francisco. From San Francisco, take Highway 101 to 37 east, then 121 north to Highway 12, which runs right through the town.

Reader tip: "For a brilliant meal, try the East Side Oyster Restaurant." *(Bob Freidus)*

Also recommended: On the plaza is the **El Dorado Hotel** (405 First Street West, 95476; 707–996–3030 or 800–289–3031), dating from 1843, with 27 guest rooms redone with elegant simplicity. Rates range from $80–140, including continental breakfast. "Our spacious room overlooked a vine-covered courtyard, and the heated swimming pool was a real plus. Sonoma is a charming old Spanish town, with sights to see if you tire of vineyards. The hotel's Piatti Restaurant has delicious Italian food; also recommended is the dining room of the Sonoma Hotel across the street." *(Joanne Kronauer)*

Victorian Garden Inn ¢
316 East Napa Street, 95476

Tel: 707–996–5339
800–543–5339
Fax: 707–996–1689

A Greek Revival farmhouse built in 1870, the Victorian Garden Inn is furnished with period antiques, surrounded by authentic Victorian gardens, complete with mazes and secret corners. Breakfast can be enjoyed in the dining room or taken on a bed tray to your room; rates also include evening wine or sherry, served by the parlor fireplace or on the creekside patio.

"Set back on a quiet street, surrounded by trees and rose bushes. The Garden Inn Room was decorated in Laura Ashley pink and white, with an elevated white cast iron bed, a sitting area, dressing area with large mirror, and a bathroom with a claw-foot tub, supplied with bubble bath and soaps. Abundant muffins, Danish, fresh fruit and juice at breakfast." *(Lisa & Mark Gallagher)* "Little touches included big terry robes; a rubber ducky in the bathtub; fresh cut flowers everywhere; chairs and benches in the garden for privacy and enjoyment; and a decanter of port in the parlor." *(Sasha Crighton)* "Fully endorse existing entry. Delicious breakfast, served at your convenience." *(Bob Freidus)*

Area for improvement: "We prefer a queen-size bed to a double."

Open All year.
Rooms 1 cottage with fireplace, 3 doubles with private and shared baths. 2 with private entrance.
Facilities Dining room, living room with fireplace. Gardens, swimming pool.
Location Between E. 3rd and E. 4th St. 3 blocks E of Plaza.
Restrictions Smoking restricted.
Credit cards Amex, MC, Visa.
Rates B&B, $139 cottage, $79–129 double. Extra person, $20. 2-3 night weekend, holiday minimum.

SONORA

The seat of Tuolumne County, Sonora was named by Mexican miners after their home state. Sonora's handsome Victorian homes date from gold rush days when it was the site of the richest gold mine in the Mother Lode. Summer activities include sightseeing and spelunking in the nearby caves, along with golf, and several lakes and rivers for water sports. Winter offers skiing at Bear Valley and Dodge Ridge. Sonora is located 120 miles east of San Francisco, 70 miles west of Yosemite.

Information please: Under the new ownership of Jean and Charlie Marinelli is the **Lavender Hill Inn** (683 South Barretta Street, 95370; 209–532–9024), built in 1900 and eclectically furnished with antiques and reproductions. There is a porch swing for relaxing on summer evenings and a fire in the woodstoves for winter chills. B&B rates for the four guest rooms range form $70–80.

Also listed in previous editions is the family-oriented **Lulu Belle's** (85 Gold Street, 95370; 209–533–3455). B&B double rates for the six guest rooms range from $85–95, including a full breakfast. "Homey atmosphere, great for music lovers. Suite Lorraine and the Blue Room, decorated in pastels and country florals, overlook the garden." *(SWS)* "Exceptional hospitality; cheerful, accommodating innkeepers; delicious breakfast, comfortable beds." *(Diane Blas, and others)* Reports needed.

SOQUEL

Blue Spruce Inn
2815 South Main Street, Soquel, 95073

Tel: 408–464–1137
800–559–1137

Soquel makes a fine base for visits to the Santa Cruz mountain wineries, the Capitola and Santa Cruz beaches, and nearby state forests for hiking. The Blue Spruce is composed of two adjacent homes, built in 1875 and 1891, restored by Pat and Tom O'Brien in 1989. Guest rooms are charmingly decorated with brass and iron beds, graced with Amish quilts; walls are hung with original local art. Rates include breakfast (served at guests' convenience) and afternoon cookies; the morning menu might offer raspberries with vanilla yogurt, applesauce cake, granola, mushroom strata, and chicken-apple sausage; or fresh fruit, almond scones with lemon curd, hot oatmeal, and sourdough Belgian waffles.

"Outstanding hospitality, charming atmosphere, immaculate housekeeping. No detail is overlooked at this cozy, comfy inn. Reading in my color-coordinated terry robe (matching the colors of the room, Seascape) on my little patio was delightful. I slept soundly on the queen-size brass featherbed. Pat's warmth and genuine concern for my comfort made me feel truly pampered." *(Gail Davis)* "Delicious breakfasts, good company.' *(Claire Calderon)*

Open All year.
Rooms 6 doubles—all with private bath and/or shower, clock. 5 with balcony/deck, gas fireplace; some with telephone, radio, TV/VCR, desk, double whirlpool tub. 3 guest rooms in carriage house.
Facilities Living/dining room with fireplace, books, guest refrigerator, deck. ⅓ acre with garden hot tub, off-street parking. Swimming, golf, tennis, beaches, boating, fishing, hiking, mountain bicycling nearby.
Location 4 m S of Santa Cruz, 60 m S of San Francisco, 30 m SW of San Jose, 20 m N of Monterery. Historic area, 2 blocks from downtown. 1 m from Capitola beaches. From Hwy. 1, take Capitola/Sequel exit. From N, turn left from exit & go under freeway to 1st stop sign at Main St., then go right to inn on left. From S, turn right at exit & right again onto Main.
Restrictions No smoking.
Credit cards Amex, MC, Visa.
Rates B&B $85–125 double, $80–120 single, Extra person, $20. 10% midweek discount Oct.–April. 2-night weekend minimum. Midweek packages.
Extras Airport/station pickup, $25. Spanish spoken.

SUTTER CREEK

Sutter Creek is located in Gold Country, in Amador County, about 45 minutes west of Stockton and Sacramento and 2½ hours from San Francisco. In addition to gold panning, visitors look for gold of another sort in the liquid found at the many area wineries.

Also recommended: One of California's first B&B inns is the **Sutter Creek Inn** (75 Main Street, Box 385, 95685; 209–267–5606), built in 1859 and opened by Jane Way in 1966. B&B double rates for the 18 guest rooms range from $50–115, although the majority go for $88, including those with the well-known swinging beds. Breakfast is served at 9 A.M., and might include a cheese-egg casserole or pancakes and ham. "The Garden Cottage has a canopy bed, sitting area with overstuffed chairs, and a fireplace. Coffee, cookies, and lemonade were set out on the sideboard, so we could help ourselves. The flower-filled garden has ample seating if you'd like to sit and relax, as does the sitting room. Friendly staff and owner." *(Sharon Bielski)*

About a mile from town is the **Gold Quartz Inn** (15 Bryson Drive, 95685; 209–267–9155 or in CA: 800–752–8738), in a mixed residential/commercial area just off Highway 49. Built in 1988 in a neo-Victorian style, one frequent contributor describes this 24 guest-room inn as being "an elegant small hotel, with extensive, beautifully furnished common areas. Breakfast and afternoon tea are often served on the spacious second-floor deck. The lovely guest rooms are ample in size, furnished in Queen nne reproductions, with well-equipped modern baths." *(JTD)* "Tea time as great with wine and cheese, tea and cookies. Breakfast, served at dividual tables, was different each morning, including muffins, potatoes, acon, pears, sausage, pineapple crepes, a scrambled egg dish with salsa, range and cranberry juices, tea and coffee. Loved the stuffed bunny on ur bed." *(Julie & Doug Phillips)* B&B double rates range from $75–125.

Information please: From Highway 49, all you can see of **Hanford House** (61 Hanford Street, Highway 49, P.O. Box 1450, 95685; 209–67–0747) is an old brick building. The majority of the B&B was added uch more recently to the back, and includes spacious common and guest ooms, with a cheerful, relaxed, largely contemporary decor. The living oom has a cathedral ceiling with exposed rafters, several inhabited by eddy bears, plus three comfortable couches. The dining room walls are overed with the owners' 'guest book' of signatures and sketches by uests, often with a teddy bear motif. Guest rooms are simply furnished, ith floral comforters and good bedside lighting. Rates include the news-aper accompanied by early morning coffee and tea, and a hearty conti-ental breakfast.

he Foxes in Sutter Creek	Tel: 209–267–5882
7 Main Street, P.O. Box 159, 95685	Fax: 209–267–0712

ete and Min Fox purchased this house, dating back to 1857, in 1980; in 986, they constructed a carriage house behind the original Victorian tructure. The spacious guest rooms are luxuriously furnished with an-ques and quality reproductions. Breakfast might include grapefruit juice, arm winter compote of pear and cranberry, Swedish pancakes with fresh erries, and Black Forest ham.

"Each guest room has a table with two chairs, where your breakfast is rought at the time requested on gleaming silver tea service. Our favorite as the Garden Room, on the second floor of the carriage house. Two omfortable upholstered chairs are set before the fireplace, while the reakfast table overlooks the branches of a lovely shade tree. Even the ompact gardens surrounding the house have tables for two, screened ith greenery for privacy, where you can also relax or enjoy breakfast." *SWS)* "Pete and Min were friendly and helpful, and suggested an excel-ent restaurant for dinner. The location was perfect for exploring this elightful Gold Rush town. We wandered around in the evening when the treets were almost deserted, and felt like we had traveled back in time." *TD)*

Worth noting: "The set-up does not encourage guests to gather in the nside common areas."

Open All year.
Rooms 6 doubles—all with private bath and/or shower, radio, air-conditioning. ome with fireplace, TV. 3 rooms in annex.
Facilities Dining room, living room. Gardens with gazebo, patio. Tennis, golf earby.
Location Gold Country. On Main St. (Hwy. 49) in center of town.
Restrictions No smoking. "Inn not appropriate for children."
Credit cards Discover, MC, Visa.

205

CALIFORNIA

Rates B&B, $95–140 double, $90–135 single. 2-night weekend minimum.
Extras Local airport pickup by arrangement.

TAHOE CITY

Chaney House
4725 West Lake Road, P.O. Box 7852, 96145

Tel: 916–525–733
Fax: 916–525–441

Built in 1928 by Italian stone masons, and set amid massive pines, th
Chaney House has 18-inch thick stone walls, Gothic arches, a massiv
stone fireplace in the living room that reaches to the top of the cathedr
ceiling, exposed wooden beams, and pine paneling throughout. Gary ar
Lori Chaney purchased it as a private home in 1974 and opened Chane
House to B&B guests in 1989. Rooms are traditionally furnished wit
some antiques; most have queen- or king-size beds topped with fluff
quilts. Breakfast is served at the dining room table at guests' convenienc
or in good weather, on the patio overlooking the lake. A typical men
might include oven-baked French toast with homemade blackberry sauc
and crème fraiche, fresh fruit parfaits, and homemade coffee cake. "On th
quiet west side of Lake Tahoe. Delicious breakfast served in the attractiv
dining room." *(AS)* "Panoramic view of the lake from the great room
where wine and cheese is served each evening. Lori and Gary create
welcoming atmosphere which encourages full use of their home an
grounds." *(Gretchen & Jim Hinerman)*

Open All year.
Rooms 1 apartment with kitchen over garage; 2 suites, 1 double—2 with privat
bath and/or shower, 2 with private half-bath, maximum of 4 people sharin
shower. All with telephone, clock; 2 with radio, deck, 1 with TV.
Facilities Dining room, living room with fireplace, TV, stereo; patio. 1 acre wit
off-street parking; lakefront with private beach, pier; bicycle, paddle boat rental
Bicycling, hiking, boating, fishing, windsurfing, golf, tennis, downhill/cross-cour
try skiing (18 ski areas) nearby.
Location High Sierras; near CA/NV border. 50 m W of Reno; 5 miles S of towr
West shore. From I-80, go S on Hwy. 89 (Lake Tahoe Blvd.) to Tahoe City. G
right on W Lake Blvd. (Hwy. 89) for 5 m. Inn on left just after Cherry St., N c
Homewood.
Restrictions No smoking. Children over 10.
Credit cards None accepted.
Rates B&B, $95–110. Extra person, $20. 2-night weekend minimum. Weekly rat
in apt.

TEMECULA

Loma Vista B&B
33350 La Serena Way, 92591

Tel: 909–676–704

If you're lamenting the fact that your Southern California trip won't allov
you to visit wine country, just alter your Los Angeles–San Diego routing
slightly and overnight at Loma Vista, with a hilltop setting overlooking

acres of vineyards. Thirteen wineries open for tasting are minutes away. A Mission-style home, Loma Vista's guest rooms are named for locally grown grapes, and are furnished with queen- and king-sized beds in a variety of styles—white wicker, Art Deco, Southwestern, and country oak. A typical breakfast includes strawberries with vanilla yogurt and granola, huevos rancheros with avocado, cornbread muffins, and champagne.

"Betty and Dick Ryan designed and built Loma Vista as a B&B in 1988. The rooms are beautifully decorated and furnished, the atmosphere is restful and quiet, the hilltop view is spectacular, and the food is delicious and abundant. Betty and Dick create a relaxing ambience, demonstrated by the easy camaraderie of the guests who gathered on Saturday evening for the 6 o'clock wine and cheese get-together on the patio, and again the next morning for the delectable breakfast cooked and served by the Ryans. The Sauvignon Blanc room was done in Southwestern style, with a comfortable four-poster peeled pine bed and inviting sitting area. Our balcony offered a lovely view of the valley lights and distant town. We had a wonderful Italian dinner at the Bailey Wine Country Cafe, and a fun taste of country music at the Midnight Roundup in Old Town Temecula." (Toni & Lee Marteney)

Open Closed Jan. 1, Thanksgiving, Dec. 25.
Rooms 6 doubles—all with private bath and/or shower, radio, air-conditioning. 4 with balcony. Some with desk, fan.
Facilities Dining room, living room with fireplace, TV, games, library. Patios with fire pit, hot tub. 5 acres with gardens, vineyards. 5 m to Lake Skinner for boating, fishing. Golf nearby.
Location San Diego area. 61 m N of San Diego, 75 m S of LA, 60 m E of Orange County. 4 m to town. Take I-15 to Rancho California Rd. Go E 4½ m and look for Callaway Winery on left. Inn is located on first dirt road past winery.
Restrictions No smoking. "Only 2 people allowed in a room, so parents must split up to sleep with child in separate room."
Credit cards Discover, MC, Visa.
Rates B&B, $95–125 double. Extra person, $25. 2-night weekend minimum for patio rooms. Midweek rates.
Extras Spanish spoken.

TRINIDAD

Trinidad is a little fishing village located on the North Coast, 25 miles north of Eureka, 300 miles north of San Francisco. Visitors enjoy hunting for agates on the beach at Patrick's Point State Park, hiking in the redwood forests just a short drive to the north, or exploring the waterfalls of Fern Canyon. The town was used as a port by gold miners in the 1850s and was a whaling station in the 1920s. Today's visitors come to view the migrating whales and to enjoy fishing for salmon, cod, crab, and clams.

Reader tip: "Larrupin definitely seems to be the best restaurant in the area, with an accommodating staff and well-prepared grilled items. Redwood National Park is a short drive away, and hikes in Fern Canyon and the Lady Bird Johnson Grove are not to be missed." (EL)

The Lost Whale Inn ⚓

Tel: 707–677–3425

3452 Patrick's Point Drive, 95570

The Lost Whale is a Cape Cod–style B&B, built in 1989 and designed with families in mind; Susanne Lakin and Lee Miller are the innkeepers. The enclosed yard has a playhouse, farm animals, and berry patches. A scenic wooded trail leads to a private beach with tide pools to explore.

"Four of the six guest rooms have beautiful ocean views, complete with the sounds of sea lions barking and waves crashing. Cookies or scones are always available on the side board along with coffee and tea. The cozy sitting area has large ocean-view windows, comfy chairs, and a table with a jigsaw puzzle in progress." *(Dan & Sherry Wentland)* "Guest rooms are immaculate, light and airy, simply furnished with lace curtains billowing in the fresh air, sea shells, and whale artwork." *(Patricia Kuhn)* "The family-style breakfast included delicious eggs scrambled with fresh salmon, potatoes, blackberry coffee cake, or on another occasion, wild rice pancakes and egg frittata. Children of guests were served separately with the children of the hosts' family, and all seemed to appreciate the arrangement." *(Pat Fink)* "Lovely pine furnishings, blue and white color scheme. The bright, attractively furnished great room adjoins a large inviting deck, and one can look out at the woods and ocean below. Our daughter loved the sleeping loft, the friendship she developed with the innkeepers' daughter, the friendly farm animals, and the rugged beach. Susanne and Lee were great." *(EL)*

Open All year.

Rooms 8 suites with private bath and/or shower. 2 with balcony, 3 with sleeping loft.

Facilities Living room with books, games, puzzles, woodstove; dining room, deck with hot tub; 4 acres with gardens, playhouse, farm animals. Trail to private beach. Adjoins Patrick's Point State Park.

Location 1 m from Hwy. 101. Take Seawood Dr. Exit off Hwy. 101 N; go left under highway, right on Patrick's Pt. Dr. 1.8 m N to inn on left. From Hwy. 101 S, take Patrick's Point Dr. Exit S 1 m to inn.

Restrictions No smoking. Strict 7–day cancellation policy.

Credit cards Amex, Discover, MC, Visa with 5% surcharge.

Rates B&B, $95–140 suite, $85–130 single. Extra adult, $15; extra child (age 3–16), $10.

Extras Airport pickup. Crib, highchair.

Trinidad B&B

Tel: 707–677–0840

560 Edwards Street, P.O. Box 849, 95570

A cozy Cape Cod–style home, the Trinidad B&B has been owned by Paul and Carol Kirk since 1984. The house offers lovely views looking southward to the water and the rugged Pacific coast. Breakfast includes homebaked breads and muffins, fresh or baked fruit, local cheese, juices, coffee and tea served family-style; in the suites it is delivered to your door.

"A welcoming fire in the fireplace, cookies in the jar, even a corner table with a jigsaw puzzle in progress. We relaxed on the porch, walked along the beach, and curled up after dinner with a book." *(Linda & Jerry Slater)* "Our clean, comfortable, cozy room overlooked the harbor. Delicious fresh fruit and homemade breads for breakfast." *(Lee Todd)* "An easy walk to shops and restaurants; we enjoyed the local wildlife." *(Elizabeth Stevenson)* "Our favorite room is over the garage, with a wonderful kitchen and dining area." *(Lynn Green)*

Open Closed Mon., Tues., Nov. through Feb.
Rooms 2 suites, 2 doubles—all with private bath and/or shower. 1 suite with fireplace; 2 with refrigerator.
Facility Living room with fireplace, games, library. Near beach and fishing harbor for boating, fishing.
Location From Hwy. 101, take Main St. into town. At end of Main, turn left on Trinity and continue 2 blocks to Edwards St. Turn left to inn.
Restrictions No smoking. "Children over 10 preferred."
Credit cards Discover, MC, Visa.
Rates B&B, $145–155 suite, $105–125 double. Extra person, $15. 2-night weekend, holiday minimum. Midweek rates, off-season.
Extras Airport pickup by prior arrangement.

TUOLUMNE

Oak Hill Ranch ¢   *Tel: 209–928–4717*
18550 Connally Lane, P.O. Box 307, 95379

Set amid stately oak trees and native flowers and shrubs, overlooking the Sierra Nevada foothills, the Oak Hill Ranch is a Victorian-style home, built in 1983 of reconditioned Victorian-era materials and decorated with Eastlake and other period antiques. It's located in a town and county pronounced Twal'-uh-mee.

"Sanford and Jane, dressed in Victorian style, welcomed us to their home, furnished with wonderful antiques. They were knowledgeable about local activities, best routes to Yosemite and helpful with dinner reservations. We stayed in the Cow Palace, a charming and comfortable cottage." *(Mary Pola)* "The drive to the house leads past white fence posts with horses grazing, Jersey cows resting under shade trees, with the hills as a backdrop." *(Patty & Jim McDonald)* "Jane and Sanford made sure we were introduced to other guests as soon as possible." *(Philip Kerr)* "Jane adjusted the breakfast menu to accommodate our dietary needs. The tropical fruit smoothie, fresh pineapple, and waffles with strawberries were delicious." *(Dan & Nancy Grove)* "Gracious hosts, delicious breakfast, clean and well-kept inn." *(Mrs. Lewis Harty)*

Open All year.
Rooms 1 suite, 1 cottage, 4 doubles—3 with private bath, 2 with maximum of 4 people sharing bath; 1 cottage (sleeps 6) with rock fireplace, kitchen. All with air-conditioning, fan.
Facilities Living room with fireplace, games, player piano, pump organ; dining room. 56 wooded acres with gardens, gazebo, pond, badminton. Hiking, horseback riding, golf, skiing, tennis, river and lake rafting, fishing, swimming nearby.
Location Gold Country, 3 hrs. E of San Francisco. 1 m from town. From Sonora, take Tuolumne Rd. 10 m to Tuolumne; in town, go right at Chevron Gas/Frosty Food Stand onto Carter, through town to Elm. Left on Elm 1 block, then right onto Apple Colony Rd. Go left on Connally Lane ¼ m to ranch.

Restrictions No smoking. No children under 15.
Credit cards None accepted.
Rates B&B, $155 suite, $115 cottage (2 persons), $70–85 double. Extra person, $18. 2-night minimum on major holidays, local celebrations.
Extras Limited wheelchair access. Kennel nearby for pets. Local airport pickup. Some Japanese, Spanish spoken.

UKIAH

Vichy Springs Resort &

2605 Vichy Springs Road, 95482

Tel: 707–462–9515
Fax: 707–462–9516

Named for the famous French mineral springs, Vichy Springs' water is naturally warm and effervescent. When bottled mineral water again became popular in the 1980s, Gilbert Ashoff convinced his partners to open a bottling plant in Vichy Springs, and took over the rundown resort in 1989. After rebuilding the lodge, Gilbert furnished it to reflect its period origins. Rates include breakfast and use of the mineral baths and swimming pool.

"In its glory days, visitors included Robert Louis Stevenson, Jack London, Mark Twain and three U.S. presidents. The long redwood building housing most of the guest rooms dates from the 1860s. A comfortable porch runs its length, affording views of the oak-covered hills." *(William MacGowan)* "Guest rooms are small and pleasant, with white walls, clear pine floors and attractive floral print decor; bathrooms were smaller yet. Breakfast was excellent—a buffet of granola, fruits, breads and pastries, juices, coffee, and hard-boiled eggs. Take thongs for the rough stone path to the mineral baths, most of which are in an enclosed shed. The century-old, ochre-colored troughs, when filled to the brim with lukewarm, naturally carbonated mineral water, made for a peaceful soak. We swam in the cold, clear mineral water of the 80-foot-long pool, and took a midnight dip in the Jacuzzi with a view of the starlit sky. Take a hike along the small river into the cool, shaded woods. For wine-tasting and local artwork, the nearby Parducci Winery is worthwhile." *(Mark Mendenhall)* Reports appreciated.

Open All year.
Rooms 2 cottages, 12 doubles—all with private bath, telephone, radio, desk, air-conditioning. Cottages with fireplace, kitchen.
Facilities Dining room, porch, therapeutic massage building, hot tub, indoor/outdoor bathing tubs, mineral swimming pool. 700 acres for hiking, bicycling, children's play equipment. RV parking. Tennis, golf, waterskiing nearby.
Location North Coast/Redwood Empire. 2 hrs. N of San Francisco. Follow Hwy. 101 N to Ukiah. Go E on Vichy Springs Rd. & follow signs approx. 3 m to resort.
Restrictions No smoking. "Soundproofing between guest rooms was minimal."
Credit cards Amex, CB, DC, Discover, JCB, MC, Visa.
Rates B&B, $150–160 cottage (for 2 people), $125 double, $85 single. Extra person, $25. 2-night holiday minimum. Day use rates for mineral baths.
Extras Wheelchair access. Station/airport pickup. Babysitting. Spanish spoken.

VALLEY CENTER

Lake Wohlford B&B ♿
27911 North Lake Wohlford Road, 92082

Tel: 619–749–1911
800–831–8239

While every inn aims to be "guest-friendly," Tatiana Ovanessoff and Nicholas Rottunda, who built the Lake Wohlford B&B in 1993, work hard to be "earth-friendly" as well. Their handsome log and stone home is decorated with comfortable cotton fabrics and twig furniture, and offers wonderful views of the natural high desert terrain, with Mount Palomor in the distance. The spacious living/dining area has oversize windows and skylights, with a natural rock fireplace reaching to the eaves.

Nick is an environmental chemist, while Tatiana, who is Russian Armenian, lived for 18 years in Iran before becoming a management consultant in San Diego. They left the city to raise their children in the country. Breakfast menus change daily; in addition to fresh orange juice and mocha java coffee, you might enjoy baked pears, lemon pancakes with raspberry sauce, Russian cake, grapefruit tart, and buttermilk scones.

"Comfortable rooms, ample breakfast, gracious hosts. Best was Tatiana's guided nature walk about the property, in which I learned much about San Diego County's natural terrain and environment. Delicious homemade doughnuts and lemonade." *(Robert Gerber)* "Exceptional home-baked pastries. In the evening we drove into Escondido for an excellent meal at 150 Grand Cafe." *(Mrs. John Donaldson)* "Spotless and fresh, in a beautiful hilltop setting." *(Barbara Witt)*

Open All year.
Rooms 5 doubles—3 with private whirlpool tub, 2 with maximum of 4 sharing bath. All with radio, clock, desk, air-conditioning, fan. 1 with VCR.
Facilities Living room with fireplace, books; library, decks. 48 acres with creek, hammock, nature trails. Bicycle rentals. 3.5 m to lake for fishing. Golf, horseback riding nearby. 30 min. to beach.
Location San Diego County. 40 m NE of San Diego, 120 m S of Los Angeles. 10 m N of Escondido. 14 m from San Diego Wild Animal Park. Exit I-15 at Valley Pkwy, just N of Escondido. Go E on Pkwy; becomes Valley Center Rd., then Woods Valley Rd. Go left on N Lake Wohlford Rd. to inn on right.
Restrictions No smoking. Children welcome during "Children's Weeks."
Credit cards MC, Visa.
Rates B&B, $88–128 double, $78–118 single. No tipping. 2-night weekend minimum. Picnic baskets.
Extras Wheelchair access; 1 bathroom specially equipped. Bus station pickups, $10. Crib. Spanish, French, Farsi spoken.

VOLCANO

Saint George Hotel ¢ ✗
16104 Volcano-Pine Grove Road, P.O. Box 9, 95689

Tel: 209–296–4458

The Saint George, built in 1862 and listed on the National Register of Historic Places, was once the tallest and most elegant hotel in the Mother Lode. Marlene and Chuck Inman have owned it since 1975. "The rooms

CALIFORNIA

are filled with interesting and unusual antiques; the beds have prett
crocheted spreads. If you like authenticity, choose one of the origina
rooms facing the front in the main hotel. Volcano had 10,000 people i
the 1860s; now the population is 102. Modern life has passed it by—a
the better to wander the tiny streets and have conversations with th
past." (SC) "One can enjoy a 'Moose Milk' or add a business card an
dollar bill to those covering the ceiling. Marlene and Chuck are activ
innkeepers, providing the atmosphere for people to meet one another.
(Ruth Ann & Terry Lane) "Love the out-of-the-way location and ur
changed atmosphere of the hotel. Food is always first rate, and the win
list features local vintages. Rooms are clean and comfortable, if a bi
Spartan." (William Vendice) "Our favorite spot for relaxing is the porch.
(Laura Hartman) Reports?

Open Mid-Feb. through Dec. Closed Mon., Tues.
Rooms 18 doubles, 2 singles—5 with private shower, 1 with full private bath, 1
rooms with 4–8 people sharing bath. 6 rooms in annex.
Facilities Dining room, bar, lounge with fireplace. 1 acre with horseshoes, ham
mock. Fishing, swimming hole 1 block away. Tennis, golf nearby.
Location Gold Country. 61 m E of Sacramento. From Jackson, take Hwy. 88 N
to Pine Grove; from Pine Grove, follow road N to Volcano.
Restrictions No smoking in guest rooms. No children under 12 in main house
OK in annex.
Credit cards MC, Visa.
Rates B&B (Weds.–Thurs.), $71–81 double. MAP (Fri.–Sun.), $112–122, include
tax, service. Prix fixe dinner, $15–20 (by reservation only). 15% service.
Extras Pets permitted in annex by prior arrangement. Babysitting.

WESTPORT

Travelers come to Westport for total "R&R": to hike in the surroundin,
mountains and wander the deserted beaches. "Set on a high bluff over
looking the ocean, Westport is one of the smallest, most peaceful place
we've ever visited. As if time had passed it by, you can walk dow
almost-deserted streets, and in the middle of town horses graze in field
overlooking the ocean. Even in December there were flowers bloomin,
and thousands of crickets chirping. It's a wonderful place for a leisurel
after-dinner walk." (SC)

Westport is located on the North Coast, in the Mendocino area, 18
miles north of San Francisco, 15 miles north of Fort Bragg.

Howard Creek Ranch ¢   Tel: 707–964–672.
40501 North Highway 1, P.O. Box 121, 95488

The Howard Creek Ranch was first settled in the 1860s, when it include
2,000 acres for raising sheep and cattle, plus a sawmill, blacksmith shop
and stagecoach shop. Many of these buildings, all constructed of virgi
redwood, have survived. The inn is the original Howard homestead, an
owners Charles and Sally Grigg have furnished it with collectibles an
antiques. A typical breakfast includes vegetable cheese omelets, plu
banana or blackberry hot cakes, sausage, bacon, fruit, juice, coffee, an
homegrown mint tea.

212

"Fresh flowers from Sally's garden scent the common areas. Our spacious bedroom had skylights for stargazing, a wonderful view of the ocean, and ample fresh towels and bedding." *(Lavon Delp)* "The decor of lace curtains, books, and 'homey' accents creates a relaxing, comfortable atmosphere; evidence of Charles' craftsmanship is everywhere." *(Linda Riley)* "The food was deliciously prepared and served by the proprietors. Sally and 'Sonny' are friendly and interested without being pushy or obtrusive." *(Nancy Follis)* "Hummingbirds sipped from the plentiful flowers, deer came by in the morning, and the friendly cats stopped by our cabin to say hello. The hot tub on the hill (along with the sauna and open-air showers) is unsurpassed. At breakfast, Sally seats people in groups to make for good table conversation. A short walk along the blackberry bushes brings you to a beautiful, desolate stretch of beach." *(Barbara Ochiogrosso)*

Open All year.
Rooms 3 suites, 4 doubles, 3 cottages—all with full private bath. Some with radio, desk, deck.
Facilities Parlor with fireplace, dining room, music room. 40 acres with gardens, hot tub, sauna, swimming pond, massage room. 300 feet to ocean. Hiking, beachcombing, whale watching, horseback riding, deep-sea fishing, bicycling nearby.
Location North Coast. 3 m N of village. From Westport, look on right for a large state sign, "Vista Point/One Mile." Turn into the next driveway after sign (milepost 80.49)—gate is marked. From the N, 2½ m after reaching ocean, cross Howard Creek Bridge and take 1st driveway on left.
Restrictions Smoking restricted. Children by prior arrangement.
Credit cards MC, Visa.
Rates B&B, $55–125 suite, $50–85 double. Extra person, $15. 2-night minimum some weekends.
Extras Spanish, Dutch, Italian, German spoken. Pets by arrangement.

YOSEMITE

Yosemite's proximity to California's major cities makes it one of the country's most popular national parks. Recent statistics indicate that well over 3 million visitors come to Yosemite annually, *with more than 500,000 arriving in July alone.* January visitors number closer to 100,000, most of them day-trippers not competing for scarce beds at prime hotels. So, if you can, go off-season, and bring along snowshoes or cross-country skis, and explore the deserted trails in peace—and remember that Yosemite is far more than congested Yosemite Valley.

Reader tip: "Keep in mind that Yosemite is an extremely large park, and slow-moving traffic makes for sluggish travel. In September, it took us one hour to get from Fish Camp to Yosemite Village, and 2½ hours to reach Tuolumne Meadows at the park's eastern end. Overall, this is a difficult, crowded park to visit in season, with expensive, disappointing accommodations and food—both inside and outside the park boundaries." *(Adam Platt)* "Although car travel in this park can be slow and frustrating, the scenery is unmatched. Park your car (come early to find a space), then take shuttles, ride bikes, and hike around the valley." *(JTD)*

For additional area entries, see **Fish Camp** and **Groveland.**

The Ahwahnee 👤 ✕ 🎿 ♿

Tel: 209–252–4848

Yosemite National Park, 95389
Yosemite Reservations, 5410 East Home Avenue
Fresno, 93727

Given its popularity, you won't be surprised to learn that the Ahwahnee recommends reservations one year ahead for weekends during the summer. Built in 1927, the Ahwahnee is a massive six-story structure with three wings, faced with native granite and concrete stained to look like redwood. The rooms are decorated with American Indian motifs, including original craft and art work; many have been recently renovated. The landscaping was planned by Frederick Law Olmsted, the designer of New York City's Central Park.

"Those fortunate enough to be selected in the Christmas/New Year's lottery enjoy a truly special experience, with the majesty of Yosemite in the snow." *(Hilary Huebsch Cohen)* "Try to book in the off-season, and be sure to see your room first (they vary in upkeep, restoration, size, and views)." *(SC)* "We are pleased and a little astonished to report that our visit was outstanding, including service in the hotel and dining room. We made our reservations a year in advance and were rewarded with a spectacular corner room with a balcony and windows on two sides. At the time of our visit (late March), the hotel was not crowded, and we were able to walk the trails in the Valley alone." *(Duane Roller)* "A fabulous, old-fashioned hotel; the public rooms and restaurant are worth the trip." *(Robert Freidus)*

Areas for improvement: "The dining room looked a lot better than the food tasted. A woman in the room next to us was awake all night coughing—we know because we could hear her clearly through the walls."

Open All year.
Rooms 99 doubles and singles in main hotel, 24 doubles in 7 cottages—all with private bath. Hotel rooms with desk, TV, air-conditioning. Cottage rooms with ceiling fan, heat.
Facilities Restaurant, bar/lounge, lobby with 2 fireplaces, mural room, solarium, club room. Gift shop, game room, heated swimming pool, 2 tennis courts. Horseback riding, bicycling, climbing, hiking, fishing, rafting, photography, nature programs, downhill and cross-country skiing, ice skating, snowshoeing nearby.
Location High Sierras.
Credit cards Amex, MC, Visa.
Rates Room only, $208 double, $202 single. Extra adult, $20; extra child under 12, free. Midweek rates off-season. Midweek ski packages.
Extras Wheelchair access some rooms. Crib, babysitting. Spanish spoken.

Wawona Hotel ¢ ✕ 🎿

Tel: 209–252–4848

State Route 41, 95389

A National Historic Landmark, the Wawona and an earlier inn on this site have accommodated travelers for over 130 years. Surrounded by rolling lawns, this classic Victorian hotel has a double-storied balcony, ideal for relaxing after a day of hiking, and beautifully restored interiors. Guests especially enjoy the period decor and sunset views from the hotel's restaurant.

"We loved everything about this historic old hotel, from our handsome room to the food in its restaurant, to the setting among the big trees." *(Diane Cox)* "The double rooms with private bath are attractively decorated and moderately priced." *(Adam Platt)* "The best place to stay in the southern part of the park. The food is good, solid, and plentiful. Breakfast was best, with long serving hours, and tasty pancakes and waffles." *(Bob Freidus)*

Minor niggles: "The bathless rooms use facilities which can be on another floor, serve several guests at once, and have no privacy. Bring a robe or a coat, since the outside hallways are covered but not enclosed."

Open Weekend before Easter through Thanksgiving; Christmas holidays; Thurs.–Sat. nights Jan.–Easter.
Rooms 104 doubles—50 with private bath and/or shower, 54 with shared bath. Rooms in 6 buildings.
Facilities Restaurant, swimming pool, tennis court, 9-hole golf course, golf shop, guided horseback riding trips. Climbing, hiking, fishing, rafting, photography, nature programs, downhill and cross-country skiing, ice skating, snowshoeing nearby. 1/4 m to Pioneer History Center; 6 m from Mariposa Grove.
Location High Sierras. Approx. 5 m N of S entrance to park. 27 m (approx. 45 min.) S of Yosemite Valley.
Restrictions Noise from other guest rooms may disturb light sleepers.
Credit cards DC, JCB, MC, Visa.
Rates Room only, $64–87 double. Extra person, $10, child under 12, free.

YOUNTVILLE

Yountville is located in the North Coast, Napa Valley Wine Country, 8 miles north of the town of Napa and 55 miles north of San Francisco off Route 29.

Information please: Formerly the Magnolia Hotel, the **Maison Fleurie** (6529 Yount Street, P.O. Drawer M, 94599; 707–944–2056) was bought by Roger and Sally Post of the Four Sisters Inns, in 1994. Constructed of brick and native fieldstone, the Magnolia was originally built as a hotel in 1873. During its checkered past, it served as a bordello, a bootlegging center during Prohibition, and as a 4-H Club meeting place. Now remodeled with French country decor, the $110–190 B&B double rates for the 13 guest rooms include a full breakfast, afternoon wine and hors d'oeuvres, evening turndown, free bicycles, and oversize towels for the swimming pool. Reports please.

Vintage Inn 🛏 ✕ 🛝 ♿
6541 Washington Street (Hwy. 29)
P.O. Box 2536, 94599

Tel: 707–944–1112
800–351–1133
Fax: 707–944–1617

Constructed in the 1970s by Kipp Stewart, designer of the Ventana Inn in Big Sur (see entry), the Vintage Inn is a cluster of small buildings, linked by walkways and a flowing fountain and stream meant to cool the air and camouflage traffic noises. Rooms have natural wood, handcrafted furnishings, and ivory and beige fabrics hand-painted in mauves, plums, and burgundies. Numerous specialty stores and fine restaurants are within walking distance; dozens of wineries are just a short bike ride or drive

"The staff was helpful, patient, and courteous. The lovely lobby has a baby grand piano, plush sofas, huge fireplace, and wooden floors. Our immaculate room had a vaulted ceiling with fan and track lighting, fireplace with logs, king-size bed with accent pillows, French doors opening onto a balcony overlooking the vineyards, terry-cloth robes, and a complimentary bottle of the inn's wine. The delicious breakfast included fresh fruit, cheese, bagels, croissants, sweet rolls, muffins, egg salad, cereal, yogurt, coffee, tea, milk, fresh-squeezed orange juice, and champagne, all beautifully presented on silver serving pieces." *(Karen Gruska)* "Though the inn was full, privacy was maintained. The grounds were meticulously kept, reflecting the lushness of the valley." *(Barbara Hattem)* "Combine hotel convenience with inn charm." *(DD, also Hugh & Marjorie Smith)*

Open All year.

Rooms 80 doubles—all with full private bath, telephone, radio, TV, air-conditioning, fan, fireplace, refrigerator, Jacuzzi, coffee maker, porch or patio. Most with desk. 8 with wet bar. Rooms in clusters of 4 to 12 units; 4 rooms in individual villas.

Facilities Lobby with fireplace, piano, bar; conference rooms. 3 acres with fountain, gardens, heated swimming pool, hot tub, 2 tennis courts, biking, jogging trail, hot air balloon (weather permitting). Bicycle rentals. Concierge, room service. Golf nearby.

Location Center of town.

Restrictions Traffic noise in rooms near Hwy. 29. No smoking in most guest rooms.

Credit cards Amex, CB, DC, Discover, MC, Visa.

Rates B&B, $144–204 double. Extra person, $25. 10% senior discount. Midweek packages off-season. 2-night weekend minimum April 1–Nov. 21.

Extras Wheelchair access; 4 rooms equipped for the disabled. Pets permitted; $2 one-time charge. Crib, babysitting. Spanish spoken.

Free copy of *INNroads* newsletter

Want to stay up-to-date on our latest finds? Send a business-size, self-addressed, stamped envelope with 52 cents postage and we'll send you the latest issue, *free!* While you're at it, why not enclose a report on any inns you've recently visited? Use the forms at the back of the book or your own stationery.

Hawaii

Kilauea Lodge, Volcano Village

Not long ago, a trip to Hawaii meant only Honolulu and the beaches of Waikiki, because that's where all mainland flights arrived. More recently though, the combination of overcrowding in Honolulu and the expansion of direct air service to several other islands has changed the picture substantially, and most other islands have become equally popular. Rent a car to get away from the tour buses; even better is to start hiking and you'll soon leave the crowds behind.

Remember that each island has two weather zones: the leeward side, to the south and west, where the weather is sunny and dry; and the windward side, to the east and north, which is rainier but has the lush vegetation one associates with Hawaii. On the Big Island, for example, monthly precipitation is typically two inches on the leeward side, ten on the windward. Check the map and plan in accordance with your preferences.

Note: A restaurant license is required for B&Bs to serve a hot (or full) breakfast, so most serve expanded continental.

Homestay B&Bs have become quite popular throughout the islands, and are typically booked through a reservation service. If you can't find what you want, consider calling one of the agencies noted below; rates are very reasonable. **Hawaii's Best Bed & Breakfasts** (P.O. Box 563, Kamuela 96743; 808–885–4550 or 800–262–9912) is the brainchild of Barbara Campbell. After years with one of the big resorts, Barbara has not only her own B&B cottage in Kamuela near Parker Ranch, but also represents over a dozen others on the big island of Hawaii and several on the other islands. Hawaii's oldest B&B reservation service is **Bed & Breakfast Hawaii** (P.O. Box 449, Kapaa 96746; 808–822–7771 or 800–733–1632) with numerous B&Bs on every island. International visitors may want to contact **Three Bears Hawaii Reservations** (72–1001 Puukala, Kailua-Kona 96740; 808–325–7563 or 800–765–0480); its owners are fluent in German and French.

Reader tip: "As far as we could tell, a *lanai* (la-NIE) is used interchangeably in Hawaii to mean a balcony, porch, or deck."

Entries are listed alphabetically, first by island, then by town.

HAWAII—THE BIG ISLAND

More than twice the size of any other Hawaiian island, The Big Island offers the greatest variety of scenery, with the drama of active volcanoes, stark lava flows, black sand beaches, and great hiking.

CAPTAIN COOK, HAWAII

Information please: On the slopes of Mauna Loa, 1,400 feet above the Kona Coast, is the **Manago Hotel** (Box 145, 96704; 808–323–2642) owned by the Manago family since its founding in 1917. Most of the newer rooms have spectacular views of Kealakekua Bay and the City of Refuge. Japanese and American food is available three times daily, at reasonable prices; stop for lunch if you're exploring the coast. Double rates range from $25–60; restaurant prices are equally reasonable.

Adrienne's B&B ¢   *Tel:* 808–328–9726
85–4577 Mamalahoa Highway,
R.R. #1, Box 8E, 96704

Adrienne and Reginald Batty invite B&B guests to share their custom contemporary cedar home, with its 180° ocean views. Rates include a breakfast of 100% Kona coffee, Hawaiian teas, locally picked fresh fruits (strawberries, papayas, bananas, pineapples, starfruit, mountain apples, or mangoes), local juice, and such home-baked breads such as coconut macadamia, cheddar cheese, or cinnamon raisin, with local jams and jellies.

"Set in a suburban area on a hillside, this homestay B&B is a peaceful, delightfully decorated home with great views overlooking the ocean in the distance. Our ocean view room had a private lanai where we enjoyed a sunset drink while relaxing on a small homemade hanging swing. The hot tub was equally inviting. Breakfasts are served on the big upstairs deck, complete with a lazy Susan full of delectable goodies, which Reginald (who reminded me of a jovial Colonel Sanders) was pleased to explain. He also asked all guests to introduce themselves, which made for a congenial atmosphere. On each guest's last day, Reggie takes a Polaroid photo for the B&B guest book. Adrienne has added a lot of nice touches to her home, including a free video collection that would put most stores to shame." (*Jill Reeves*)

Open All year.
Rooms 4 doubles—all with private bath and/or shower, refrigerator, ceiling fan. 3 with TV/VCR, 2 with lanai.
Facilities Living room with TV/VCR; video library. Lanai with covered hot tub, covered breakfast area.
Location Kona Coast, 18 m S of Kailua-Kona. Slopes of Mauna Loa, above Place of Refuge & Honaunau Bay. From the Kona Airport, take a right onto Rte. 19 which becomes Rte. 11 at the light. Continue S, look for green mile markers on left. House is 5th on right after MM #103.
Restrictions No smoking. Jacuzzi jet on low only after 9 P.M.

Credit cards MC, Visa.
Rates B&B, $50–80 double. Extra person, $15.

HILO, HAWAII

Information please: A modern home on the bluff facing the ocean, **Hale Kai** (111 Honolii Pali, 96720; 808–935–6330) has four guest rooms with water views and private baths. Guests can relax in the swimming pool, Jacuzzi, or patio, or take advantage of the common rooms. B&B double rates range from $85–103. Reports?

Dolphin Bay Hotel ¢
333 Iliahi Street, 96720

Tel: 808–935–1466

According to longtime owner L. H. Alexander, the Dolphin Bay is not for "people who are interested in a large luxury hotel and all that goes with it. The people who come here go off to see the exotic points of interest by day, and return in the evening. We do our best to map out trips, arrange tours, advise on restaurants, and provide any other service people desire."

"Unpretentious, charming, and absolutely delightful, as is John Alexander, the manager, whose family owns the hotel. He will gladly give directions, recommend restaurants, and help out. The suites are roomy, clean, and pleasantly decorated. Favorite moments are morning coffee on the lanai or relaxing with a cool refreshing drink at sunset. Plan to rent a car; though you can easily walk into town you'll want it for sightseeing. Hilo is a charming town, convenient to Volcanoes National Park and Akaka Falls. Rainbow Falls is just a mile from the hotel. The hotel is within walking distance of Hilo Bay but not on it; there's no restaurant, room service or swimming pool; night-life in Hilo is practically non-existent." *(Gail Boggs)*

"The hotel is surrounded by fruit trees, orchids and other colorful flowers, birds, and a small stream. Papayas, bananas, starfruit and others are there for the taking." *(Vera & Vince Ives)* "Friendly staff, with owners who are always willing to remedy a complaint. The rooms are clean, the lighting good, the plumbing efficient, and the parking well lighted." *(Harrison & Roma Correll)* "Homey and relaxing." *(April Burwell)* Comments welcome.

Open All year.
Rooms 5 1- and 2-bedroom suites, 13 doubles—all with private bath and/or shower, TV, desk, fan, kitchen. Some with deck.
Facilities 2-acre garden. Off-street parking. 5 m to swimming, snorkeling.
Location Pu'ueo residential area, 4 blocks N of downtown. 2 blocks from bay. 30 min. from Volcanoes Nat'l. Park, 2 hrs. from Kona.
Credit cards MC, Visa.
Rates Room only, $82 suite, $52–72 double, $42–72 single. Extra person, $10. Weekly rates.
Extras Crib. Japanese spoken.

HOLUALOA, HAWAII

Holualoa Inn
P.O. Box 222, 96725

Tel: 808–324–1121
800–392–1812
Fax: 808–322–2472

Set among the pastures and coffee groves of a private estate, the Holualoa Inn overlooks the ocean 1200 feet below. A refreshing change from the frills and furbelows of Victorian B&Bs, the inn's decor is spare and elegant, primarily contemporary Scandinavian furnishings highlighted by Hawaiian and Indonesian art. Built of imported cedar in 1979, the inn is managed by Desmond Twigg-Smith. Breakfast includes home-grown fruit and Kona coffee, accompanied by breads, pastries and occasional hot entrées. At sunset, guests adjourn to the poolside or rooftop gazebos for wine, cheese, crackers, and views of Kailua Bay and the Pacific.

"One's first impression is of the beautiful eucalyptus floors, the breezy open structure, and the view of the Kona coast. Food is well served and healthy, with delicious home-grown papayas, incredibly light pancakes made with hand-ground grains, and Portuguese sausage." *(Barbara & John Richards)* "The guest rooms are spacious, airy, private, and tastefully decorated in various South Pacific themes, with outstanding views. The inn is located in a tropical garden which produces the fruits and coffee served for breakfasts." *(Norman Collingwood)* "Polite, interesting, unobtrusive, conscientious staff." *(Clint MacKinney)*

"Lots of fresh towels and Crabtree & Evelyn soaps and milk bath. There were coolers, ice, towels and mats to take to the beach. Holualoa is a haven for local artists, selling art and craft work at reasonable prices." *(Mr. & Mrs. Michael Bate)* "Walking distance to the charming little village." *(Nancy & Michael Sketch)* "In March, it was cool with brief afternoon showers, a wonderful respite from touring warmer areas or spending time at the beach." *(Paul & Jan Wrotenbery)*

Open All year.
Rooms 1 cabin, 1 suite, 3 doubles—all with private bath and/or shower, radio, desk. Suite with whirlpool tub. 2 with balcony.
Facilities Dining room, living room with fireplace, piano, pool table; common room with TV, library, guest refrigerator/microwave. 40 acres with swimming pool, 2 gazebos, gas grill, gardens. Golf, tennis, horseback riding, water sports nearby.
Location Kona Coast. 4 m from Kailua-Kona. 150 yds. to Holualoa.
Restrictions No smoking. No children under 12.
Credit cards Amex, MC, Visa.
Rates B&B, $150 cabin, suite; $100–150 double. Extra person, $15. Tips welcome. 2-night minimum.

HONOKAA, HAWAII

Information please: With ocean views on three sides, the **Paauhau Plantation House** (P.O. Box 1375, Honokaa, 96727; 808–775–7222) is built on an ocean point at the 1,200 foot level. Three guest rooms and two cottages are available at B&B double rates of $105–140, including use of the tennis court.

Waipio Wayside B&B ¢
P.O. Box 840, 96727

Tel: 808–775–0275
800–833–8849

Owned by Jacqueline Horne, Waipio Wayside was built in 1938 as a sugar cane plantation home, and has been furnished in old Hawaiian motifs with antiques, Chinese rugs, and rattan and wicker furnishings. Breakfasts are highlighted by locally grown fruit and pure Hamakua coast coffee—a blend of Kona and Jamaican Blue beans. A short drive away is the Waipio Valley, known for its black sand beach and beautiful waterfalls.

"An antique-filled yet spacious New Age home, classy and comfortable. The hardwood floors and muted colors complement the lush gardens that surround the house. Special memories include soaking in the original oversize bathtub, surrounded by wonderful scented oils, salts, and lotions; coming back to a hot cup of tea after a long hike down into the magical Waipio Valley; having a glass of wine out on the enormous deck and talking with Jackie about the area and her concern for the environment; and the area's natural beauty. A truly homey place." *(Jill Reeves)*

Open All year.
Rooms 5 doubles—2 with private full bath, 1 with half-bath, 2 with maximum of 4 sharing bath.
Facilities Dining room, living room with TV. Deck with hammocks, gazebo, gardens, fruit trees, sugar cane fields.
Location NE coast, Big Island. 20 min. E of Waimea (Parker Ranch), 1 hr. NW of Hilo, 75 min. E of Kona. 10 min. E of Waipio Valley. 2 m W of Honokaa Post Office, on Hwy 240 going toward Waipio Valley, on ocean side. After white picket fence, take 2nd driveway to parking lot.
Restrictions No smoking.
Credit cards MC, Visa.
Rates B&B, $55–95 double, $50–90 single. Extra person, $15.

KAILUA-KONA, HAWAII

Also recommended: Although too big for a full write-up with 318 rooms, *Nanci & Norm Cairns* were delighted with their stay at the **Keauhou Beach Hotel** (78-6740 Alii Drive, 96740; 808–322–3441 or 800–367–6025). Although the hotel itself is large and modern, with spacious contemporary ocean- and garden-view rooms, the lush grounds are rich with history—King David Kalakaua retreated here from the summer court at Kailua, and petroglyphs and temple ruins await your exploration. "We were treated to fresh fruit and toiletries in the room. Fabulous Chinese buffet in the Kuakini Terrace restaurant, with a plantation atmosphere. Lovely beach area to the hotel." Double rates range from $100–165, with packages available; children under 18 are free in parents' room.

About 15 miles north of Kailua-Kona via Highway 19 is the well-known **Kona Village Resort** (P.O. Box 1299, Kaupulehu-Kona 96745;

808–325–5555 or 800–367–5290) built on the site of the ancient Hawaiian village of Kaupulehu. In 1801, when Mt. Hualalai erupted, this cove was the only one spared the massive lava flows that devastated the area. The village's 125 thatched *hales* (Polynesian-style bungalows) have been built among the actual stone platforms of the ancient Hawaiians, and are located around the lagoon, along the beach, and in a lava field along the ocean. Although a few "minor niggles" are on file, many feel that Kona Village Resort is still the best Polynesian resort on the island, and one of the finest tropical resorts in the world. Popular with both couples (excepting school vacations) and families alike, activities include pool and ocean swimming, tennis, snorkeling, sunfish sailing, canoeing, boat excursions, and a children's program. All this does not come cheap; all-inclusive double rates start at $390 off-season, and ascend past $600; service is 15% additional.

Information please: Listed in previous editions, we need current reports on the **Kailua Plantation House** (75–5948 Alii Drive, 96740; 808–329–3727), offering superb ocean views and relaxing accommodations. Built as a B&B, it faces the Pacific from atop a promontory of black rocks formed by ancient lava flows. Most rooms have tiled floors and sliding glass doors that lead out to balconies; furnishings are spare but elegant, mostly bamboo with soft Hawaiian print fabrics. Double rates for the five guest rooms range from $135–185, including a breakfast of breads, muffins, Hawaiian fruits, Kona coffee, tea, and juice, plus a hot entrée such as Belgian waffles, French toast, or quiche, served from 7:30–9:30 A.M.

Under the same ownership as Adrienne's B&B (see entry under Captain Cook) is **Adrienne's Casa del Sol B&B** (77–6335 Alii Drive, 96704; 808–328–9726 or 800–328–9726), offering five luxurious suites and doubles, at rates of $90–200, with a breakfast of fresh local fruit and home-baked bread. This tile-roofed Spanish-style home has both antique and contemporary furnishings, and offers magnificent ocean views, and use of the hot tub and heated swimming pool.

In a peaceful setting ten minutes from Kailua Village is **Hale Maluhia B&B** (76-770 Hualalai road, 96740; 808–329–5773 or 800–550–9927), the rambling shingled home of Ken and Anne Smith, built on old coffee plantation land at an elevation of 900 feet. The interior combines open-beamed ceilings and natural woods with Hawaiian and Victorian furnishings. Breakfast is served on the lanai, and double rates range from $55–110.

KAMUELA, HAWAII

Also recommended: About an hour's drive inland from either Kailua-Kona or Hilo is Kamuela, a small country town and the center of the famous Parker Ranch. *Phyllis Gocke* recommends the **Parker Ranch Lodge** (P.O. Box 458, Kamuela 96743; 808–885–4100). The 20 rooms of this motel (5 with kitchenette) have two queens or a king-size bed, rent for $68–80 double, and look out to the Kohala Mountains. "Meticulously maintained by resident managers Joshua and Janice Akana; the knowl-edgeable Akanas are exceptional sources of information on the many area explorations and activities. The ranch-style furnishings are enhanced with thoughtful amenities and bouquets of Kamuela roses. A few steps away is the Paniolo Country Inn, providing excellent meals with fresh ranch eggs." For another alternative, contact Barbara Campbell at the **Waimea Gardens Cottage** (P.O. Box 563, Kamuela 96743; 808–885–4550 or 800–262–9912). Two charming cottages are available, at B&B double rates of $110–120. For information on Barbara's reservation service, see the chapter introduction.

VOLCANO, HAWAII

Try to spend a couple of days exploring Hawaii Volcanoes National Park, one of only two national parks devoted to active volcanoes; the park is bigger than the island of Oahu, so allow ample time. The summit areas are in a sub-alpine tropical rain forest zone, with about 125 inches of rain annually, making for lush green forests. At an elevation over 3,500 feet, the weather is typically cool and rainy, so come prepared with warm, comfortable clothes, sturdy hiking shoes (an extra pair is good when the first pair gets wet), and rain gear; binoculars are recommended for bird-watching. Stop at the visitors' center for details on the drives around the Kilauea caldera or down the Chain of Craters road, and maps for the many exciting hiking trails; heli-tours are also a thrilling option. Area restaurant options are extremely limited, so ask your innkeeper about advance reservations. The park is about 25 miles southwest of Hilo on the "Big Island" of Hawaii.

Information please: If proximity to the Kilauea caldera is your para-mount concern, make advance reservations for a crater-view room at the **Volcano House** (Box 53, Hawaii Volcanoes National Park, 96718; 808–967–7321). When Mark Twain stayed at the Volcano House in 1866, the building was made of grass and ohia poles; he thought the $5 nightly charge for room and board was a fair deal. Guests have been coming ever since, although the main building of today's Volcano House was built in 1941, with a wing added in 1963. Rooms have standard hotel layouts; all were refurbished with handsome Koa wood furnishings in 1991. Be aware that the lobby and restaurant can be busy with tourist throngs; guest rooms facing the parking lot can be noisy with car and bus traffic. Comments welcome.

Carson's Volcano Cottage (P.O.Box 503, 96785; 808–967–7683 or 800–845–LAVA) has three guest rooms and a cottage, each with individ-ual decor. "Our room had pictures of old Hawaii, a flower-carved head-board on the bed, high sloping ceiling with wood beams, wicker chairs, and lace-draped windows overlooking the lush surroundings. Freshly cut tropical flowers were in vases all around. The refrigerator was stocked with do-it-yourself breakfast makings—fruit plate, bagels, cream cheese, and delicious home-smoked salmon. The innkeepers live on the property in their own separate home, and the pets running around are friendly—

223

chickens, a dog, and three Persian cats." *(Wendy Kameda)* The one-acr grounds have gardens and a hot tub; B&B double rates range fror $65–85.

Chalet Kilauea—The Inn at Volcano ¢
Wright Road, Box 998, 96785

Tel: 808–967–778
800–937–778
Fax: 808–967–866

The Chalet Kilauea, owned by Lisha and Brian Crawford since 1990, is contemporary home renovated and expanded to accommodate overnigh guests. Each room in the main house is decorated in a different intern. tional theme: African safari, Continental lace, and Oriental.

"A charming home in a residential area of Volcano, close to the gate of Volcanoes National Park. We stayed in the two-level Treehouse Suit with natural wood paneling and contemporary decor, separated from th main house by a deck. The 'no shoes in the house' rule is easy to abid by when you find comfortable Japanese-style cloth slippers in your roon along with fluffy white robes. Our window looked out into a fern fores and our comfortable room had a sitting area and a modest but function. bathroom. Brian and Lisha were friendly, helpful, and unobtrusive host Breakfast—served from 8–9 A.M.—was prepared by Brian, and include fresh papaya with Tahitian lime, waffles with fruit, and fresh juice." *(DCI* "Lush setting, careful attention to detail. Brian and Lisha Crawford ar widely travelled, and have furnished their home with ebony sculpture from Africa, Art Deco from Northern Europe, and more. Breakfast ir cluded Alaskan smoked salmon. I lounged in the Jacuzzi, browsed throug the extensive library, and dozed contentedly by the open fire." *(Sai Rollason)*

Open All year.
Rooms 4 vacation homes, 1 suite, 3 doubles—all with private bath and/c shower. Some with whirlpool tubs, telephone, stereo, TV, fan, fireplace, refrigera tor, deck. Suite with refrigerator, microwave, coffee maker. 4 rooms in separat buildings.
Facilities Dining room, living room with fireplace, library, stereo. Deck, hot tub laundry facility. Hiking, bicycling, golf, swimming, bird watching.
Location In village. From Rte. 11 turn on Wright Rd. (Rte. 148). Go 3/4 m t Chalet Kilauea sign on right.
Restrictions No smoking. No shoes in house. Children welcome in cottages.
Credit cards Discover, MC, Visa.
Rates B&B, $75–175 cottage, $125 suite, $95 double, $75 single. Extra persor $15. 3-night minimum in vacation homes.
Extras French, Dutch, Spanish, Portuguese spoken.

Hale Ohia Cottages ¢ ♦ ઙ
Highway 11, P.O. Box 758, 96785

Tel: 808–967–798(
800–455–380

The historic Dillingham summer estate, Hale Ohia was built in 1931, an includes the main residence and several cottages. The gardens were devel oped over 30 years by a resident Japanese gardener; the natural volcani terrain was gently groomed into a beautiful botanical garden.

"Beautiful landscaping around the main house and cottages, tucke

ack among many trees and beautiful flowers. Owner Michael Tuttle went
out of his way to advise us on what to see and do; he takes pride in
everything he does. Attractive, comfortable accommodations. Beautifully
prepared continental breakfast. Great for couples or families." *(Brenda
Stanko)*

Open All year.
Rooms 3 cottages, 2 suites—all with private bath and/or shower, lanai. 1 with
fireplace, 2 with kitchenette.
Facilities 3 acres with gardens, gazebo, Japanese soaking tub.
Location 26 m from Hilo, 11 m from Volcano Village, 1 m from HI Volcanoes
Nat'l. Park. From Hilo, take Hwy. 11 to Volcano. After passing Rte. 148 on right,
watch for driveway for Hale Ohia on left.
Credit cards MC, Visa.
Rates B&B, $85–95 cottage, $65–85 double. Extra person, $15. Weekly rates.
Cleaning, laundry service extra.
Extras Wheelchair access.

Kilauea Lodge ♦ ✕ ⭐

P.O.Box 116, 96785

Tel: 808–967–7366
Fax: 808–967–7367

Hawaii may not be the first place that comes to mind when "mountain
country inns" are mentioned, but that's just what Kilauea Lodge is. Built
in 1938 as a YMCA lodge, it was converted into an inn in 1987 by Albert
and Lorna Jeyte. Lorna notes that "I was raised on the Big Island, and have
decorated our inn with original Hawaiian art and furnishings made from
local woods. Our menu combines local specialties with dishes reflecting
Albert's European background." The inviting guest rooms are country
comfortable with patchwork quilts, and breakfast is a hearty meal of bacon
and eggs to order, pancakes, or Hawaiian-style French toast with fresh
fruit.

"The comfortable common room is filled with games and books on
Hawaiian history and lore. All the rooms have polished hardwood floors
and some have wooden cathedral ceilings. The food is excellent—favorite
entrées included the seafood with fettuccine, the prawns, and the pau-
piettes of beef." *(FM)* "Lots of menu choices, delicious food, and a warm
atmosphere with candlelight and a crackling wood fire in the big stone
fireplace. The waitress and the host were most helpful; great service."
(Wendy Kameda) "Friendly, happy staff; delicious food." *(Ruth Streveler)*

"Peaceful, secluded location; welcoming buildings, attractively designed. Spacious guest rooms are beautifully appointed with carefully
chosen furnishings, large and comfortable beds, pleasing art work, exceptionally luxurious bath sheets and towels. All is kept in immaculate
condition by a dedicated staff who take a personal interest in guests'
comfort. Fresh bouquets of colorful flowers grace every room. Parking is
reserved for guests within steps of their rooms in an area surrounded by
beautiful plantings of orchids, camellias, and gardenias. The lodge dining
room provides excellent breakfast selections, beginning with Puna papaya
and Kona coffee. Although lunch is not served, there are interesting local
stores where an amazing variety of local favorites are available. Chef
Albert offers a tantalizing dishes along with the customary entrées. Homemade soups and desserts are appealing, as are some locally made wines.

Overall, there's nothing to improve except the weather which can turn cranky at times—a book and a fireplace quickly cure that." *(Wayne & Phyllis Gocke, and others)*

Open All year.
Rooms 3 cottages, 11 doubles—all with private bath and/or shower, clock. Some with fireplace, desk, balcony. Rooms in several buildings.
Facilities Restaurant with bar, books, fireplace; common area with games, books, fireplace; screened porch. 10 acres with off-street parking, croquet, hiking trails.
Location From Hwy 11 S, exit at Wright Road & bear left on Old Volcano Hwy to lodge on right. From Hwy 11 N, bear left after Visitors' Center to village. Approx. 1 m from park entrance.
Restrictions Smoking only in fireplace rooms.
Credit cards MC, Visa.
Rates B&B, $105–135 cottage $85–105 double, $80–100 single. Extra person $15. No charge for children under 2. Tips welcome. Alc dinner $35.
Extras Wheelchair access. Cribs, babysitting. German, Spanish spoken.

My Island B&B ¢ ♟

P.O. Box 100, 96785

Tel: 808–967–7216
Fax: 808–967–7719

Built around 1886 by the Lyman missionary family, My Island B&B is the oldest house in the Volcano community. Originally a two-story building, it was later raised so that the existing living room and kitchen could be built underneath. The Lyman family lived here until 1941; the house was then used for storage until it was acquired by the Gordon and Joann Morse family in 1972, with their daughter Kii acting as the manager of their B&B. Rooms are decorated with Koa wood furniture, hand-crafted quilts from Maine, and Joann's paintings; the guest rooms have no closets, the Morses note, because during the 1800s there was no need; people had so few clothes that a few hooks would suffice.

"This eclectic old missionary's house has almost as much character and history as its hosts—Joann, a local artist, and Gordon, a great storyteller who was born on Molokai. Ceilings are low, some floors are slightly slanted, and the fireplace has a fire going continuously, adding to the inviting 'back in time feeling.' Guests gather around the big dining room table for breakfast, and share their experiences. Gordon and Joann pride themselves on having different hot breakfast selections each morning, including waffles and French toast, as well as papaya, guava juice, and coffee (ready at 7 A.M. for early risers). Thanks to Gordon's suggestion, a real highlight (literally) for us included a hike at dusk to view the bubbling lava erupting into the ocean at the end of the Chain of Crater Road. Gordon provided us with a special map and flashlights that made the hike back after dark safe and easy." *(Jill Reeves)*

Open All year.
Rooms 3 vacation homes, 3 apartments with private entrances, private baths, kitchen, TV; 3 doubles—4 with private bath, 2 with maximum of 4 sharing bath.
Facilities Dining room, living room with TV, library. Gardens.
Location In Village. From Hwy 11., turn onto Wright Rd., (Rte. 148). Take 1s right to inn on left.
Credit cards None accepted.
Rates Room only, $100 vacation house. B&B, $55–709 double, $35–65 single. Extra adult, $20; child 3–16, $10; under 3, $5.

KAUAI

Although hardly undiscovered (it's third among total visitors), Kauai has maintained its relaxed island pace despite increased traffic. Visitors will especially enjoy its challenging golf courses and spectacular scenery. Tropical vegetation doesn't last long without ample rain, so try the Poipu area for the best chances for sun.

Reader tips: "A drive to the north shore is a must, as it is the most picturesque and peaceful part of the island, with many beautiful white-sand beaches, high cliffs, lush foliage, and natural, rugged beauty. This side is the least crowded, with less traffic and many tiny villages. There are many interesting things to do on Kauai, other than lounge on the beach. Try a drive to Waimea Canyon, where you can also hike, or a helicopter tour, or an exciting boat trip to view the humpback whales and the impressive Na Pali cliffs." *(Linda Goldberg)* And: "Kauai's red earth stains shoes, clothes, carpets, and more. Many B&Bs ask that you leave your shoes outside, and provide slippers." *(JR)*

KAPAA, KAUAI

Also recommended: Three miles north of Wailua is the **Islander on the Beach** (484 Kuhio Highway, Kapaa, 96746; 808–822–7417 or 800–847–7417), a two-story, 200-room hotel directly on the beach. "Lovely setting. Our window and patio area looked out to the ocean. The staff had placed a fruit basket and fresh coffee in our room. No restaurant but plenty of eating places nearby." *(Nanci & Norm Cairns)* Rates range from $95–195 and include a car or breakfast for two.

LAWAI, KAUAI

Victoria Place ¢ ♿   *Tel: 808–332–9300*
3459 Lawai Loa Lane, P.O. Box 930, 96765

Edee Seymour is a Michigan native who adopted Kauai as a personal paradise, and enjoys sharing its beauty with her guests. Victoria Place is set high in lush hills, overlooking dense jungle, cane fields, and the Pacific. Three of the guest rooms have glass doors that open directly onto a swimming pool surrounded by flowers. Rates include a breakfast of Hawaiian coffee, homemade breads and muffins, and fresh fruit, usually served at poolside.

"You enter the house, set in a cul-de-sac in a small village, through a gate that leads you into a swimming pool area surrounded by flowering bushes and trees. Edee, a wonderful hostess with a great sense of humor, mixed with a dose of Norwegian good taste and practicality, provides guests with every amenity an eager visitor might need. Some appealing touches include the veranda with a great view—a reflective place for a

227

delicious breakfast with local papayas and pineapples, an old-fashioned popcorn machine ready for guests' use, a rack of snorkeling gear, extra towels, and even extra shoes for guests to use when hiking, because of the intensely staining red soil. Our room was clean, comfortable, and tastefully decorated. Edee treats her guests well; she has a strong commitment to promoting the beauty of Kauai. Two nights were not enough." (Jill Reeves)

Open All year.
Rooms 1 apt., 3 doubles—all with private bath and/or shower. Cottage with kitchen, laundry.
Facilities Living room with TV, books; balcony, deck, guest refrigerator/microwave. Swimming pool, garden with fountain. Beaches, golf, tennis nearby.
Location S Kauai, 2 min. from Hwy. 50. 20 min. from Lihue; 10 min. NW of Poipu. From Lihue airport, go straight through light to 2nd light & turn left. At next light, turn right on Hwy 50. Take Hwy 50 past Junction 520, approx. $10^{1}/2$ m from Lihue. Continue $3^{1}/2$ m to Junction 530 (Koloa Rd.). Turn left & continue for 1.2 m. Look for green & white striped pole on left across from Lanai Loa Lane. On right is bus stop sign and dead end sign, marking Lawai Loa Lane. Turn right & go to #3459. At night, watch for Lawai Loa between 2nd & 3rd street lights after 1 mile marker on Koloa Rd.
Restrictions No smoking. Children over 14.
Credit cards None accepted.
Rates B&B, $95–105 apt., $65–85 double, $55–65 single. Extra person, $10. $10 additional 1-night stay.
Extras Wheelchair access; 1 bathroom specially equipped.

POIPU BEACH, KAUAI

Also recommended: The **Poipu Plantation,** (1792 Pee Road, 96756; 808–742–6757 or 800–733–1632), offers seven units beautifully furnished in rattan. Each unit is a one- or two-bedroom apartment complete with kitchen, bathroom, dining area, living room and bedroom. Amenities abound. "All units overlook the ocean and the mountains, offering a breathtaking panorama. Guests can use the hot tub and barbecue, and help themselves to the fruit growing on the plantation's trees. The beach is only a short walk away, and Debbie is happy to offer helpful suggestions for restaurants, beaches and adventures. Be sure to ask for an upstairs apartment to get the best view. An excellent value." (Christie Ray)

Poipu Bed & Breakfast Inn   Tel: 808–742–1146
2720 Hoonani Road, Poipu Beach 96756   800–22–POIPU
               Fax: 800–742–6843

The Poipu B&B Inn occupies a restored 1933 plantation house and has been owned by Dotti Cichon since 1987; Dotti has also built the nearby Oceanfront Inn; most of the five units have king-size beds and double whirlpool baths, and rent for B&B double rates of $125–185. Breakfast includes mangoes, papayas, pomegranates, and other edibles grown in the yard, plus local breads and pastries; rates also include afternoon tea. Snorkel and scuba access is right across the small road; it's a 2–3 city block walk to Poipu Beach.

"This B&B is located just off the main intersection at the turn to Poipu Beach, on a side road leading to the Spouting Horn. This small pink house is right on the road, with a tiny front yard, but the street is not busy. The guest rooms are similar in size and decor, with unpainted fir walls, hardwood floors, and reproduction wicker furnishings; most guest rooms have king-size beds and lavish bathrooms. We stayed in the Bougainvillea room, a corner room with rose wall-to-wall carpeting, a king-size bed, curtains and spread in a coordinating floral print, louvered windows, and an antique dresser. The spectacular bathroom had pink tile and a green Jacuzzi tub, recessed into a windowed alcove surrounded by the garden." *(SHW)* "An added touch in each room is the antique carousel horse. The tropical breakfast is served on a tray in the room or on the lanai." *(Linda Goldberg)* "Rooms have luxurious bedding, thick towels, and soft carpeting." *(Don & Betty Berard)* "The nearby beaches are nice for swimming, snorkeling and surfing." *(Gary & Carolyn Lerch)* "We were made to feel at home and given plenty of advice on what to see and do." *(David & Sharon Michael)*

Minor niggle: "More variety at breakfast."

Open All year.

Rooms 4 doubles—all with full private bath, radio, TV/VCR, ceiling fan. Some with whirlpool tub. Poipu Oceanfront: 4 suites—all with full private bath, clock radio, TV/VCR, desk, ceiling fan, kitchenette with microwave. Some with double whirlpool tub, air-conditioning, wet bar. Off-premises budget cottages available.

Facilities Living room with books, video library; breakfast room, lanai, guest laundry, kitchenette. 1/3 acre with fruit trees. Poipu Oceanfront: common room with video library; guest laundry. 1/2 acre with exotic gardens. Both: beach towels, mats, robes, coolers on by request. Swim, tennis club privileges nearby. 2-3 blocks to beach.

Location S Kauai. From Koloa go 1.4 m on Poipu Rd. At lava rock wall marked "Welcome to Poipu Beach" turn right on Lawai Rd. Go 1 block then bear left on Hoonani Rd. Cross white wood bridge. Inn is 1st house on left. 1/2 m to Kiahuna shopping center, Poipu Beach. 1.4 m from Koloa.

Restrictions No smoking.

Credit cards Amex, CB, DC, Discover, MC, Visa.

Rates B&B, $110–140 double, $100–130 single. Extra person, $20. $10 surcharge for 1-night stay. Senior, weekly, military, car rental discounts. Minimum stay Christmas.

Extras 1 suite wheelchair accessible; bathroom equipped for disabled. Crib, highchair. French, German spoken by owner.

PRINCEVILLE, KAUAI

Hale 'Aha B&B
P.O. Box 3370, 96722

Tel: 808–826–6733
800–826–6733

Princeville is a planned recreational community on the north coast of Kauai, consisting of championship golf courses, the Hanalei Athletic Club, many beautiful condominium projects, exclusive homes, and the Hanalei Bay Resort. A 20-minute scenic drive will take you to the start of the Na Pali hiking trails, and some of the most beautiful beaches on the island are just a short car ride away.

"Hale 'Aha, meaning 'house of meeting,' is a new home, lovingly run by Herb and Ruth Bockelman. The house overlooks the golf course, with distant sea and mountain views. The decor is soothing, in shades of peach, blue, and beige, with houseplants and flowers, and beautiful tile work in the bathrooms. The penthouse suite has open-beamed ceilings, and a deck with views of Bali Hai and the Kilauea lighthouse. Breakfast consists of muffins, breads, cereal, and juice; early morning coffee is available. I felt like a personal guest in a friend's house, because of the inn's warm, homey, comfortable feel." *(Linda Goldberg)* "I felt comfortable enough to stretch out on the couch with one of their delightful books on Kauai. We stayed in the least expensive room with a view of the mountains; it was sizable with a large closet and bathroom, and separate entrance. We enjoyed talking with Herb and Ruth each morning after breakfast, discussing a variety of local and world issues. They are knowledgeable about the island's many attractions and helped us plan our activities." *(John Dearborn)*

Open All year.

Rooms 1 suite, 3 doubles—all with full private bath, private entrance, radio, TV, desk/table, deck, fan, refrigerator. 2 with whirlpool tub, air-conditioning. Suite with kitchenette, laundry, deck.

Facilities Dining room, living room with fireplace, balconies. 1½ acres with off-street parking. Path to secret beach. 7/10 m from golf, swimming, tennis, fitness center. Horseback riding nearby.

Location N coast. 40 min. from airport. From Lihue airport take main road N past Kapaa to Princeville. Turn right on Ka Haku at main entrance to Hanalei. Go past golf course, turn right on Kamehameha Rd. to inn on right.

Restrictions No smoking. No children. Sunday check-ins discouraged; by special arrangement only.

Credit cards MC, Visa.

Rates B&B, $140–190 suite, $80–85 double. Weekly discount. Extra person, $20. 3-night minimum.

WAIMEA, KAUAI

Also recommended: If you don't mind roughing it, **Kokee Lodge** (P.O. Box 819, Waimea 96796; 808–335–6061) offers a thrifty alternative in beautiful Kokee State Park. The air is cool and crisp at 3600 feet, ideal for hiking and fishing. Twelve rustic cabins are furnished with refrigerators, stoves, hot showers, basic eating and cooking utensils, linens, towels, blankets and pillows. Wood for the woodstove is available, and rates are $45 double.

Waimea Plantation Cottages ¢ ✕ ☂ ⅄.   *Tel:* 808–338–1625
9600 Kaumualii Highway, #367, 96796   800–9–WAIMEA
                                          Fax: 808–338–2338

If you'd like the historic charm of old Hawaii, but are reluctant to forgo the convenience of condo-style comfort, Waimea Plantation Cottages may offer the best of both. In 1778, Captain James Cook greeted Kauai's king at Waimea, and later, King Kaumuali'i welcomed the first American missionaries here. In 1884, the Waimea Sugar Mill Company built housing or its employees and their families; in 1934, Port Allen replaced Waimea as a major port, and development slowed to a standstill. Waimea Plantation Cottages consist primarily of early 1900s homes original to the property or brought here from other island plantations, restored to combine simple period charm and modern amenities. The resort is owned by Kikiaola Land Company, and is managed by Raymond Blouin.

Although guests may have a hard time leaving the resort's relaxing grounds, nearby activities include a walking tour of the historic village; to the northwest, the sandy beaches of Polihale at the road's end; and to the north, Waimea Canyon State Park, with magnificent vistas, beautiful hiking trails, and a 3,000-foot deep gorge, dubbed the "Grand Canyon of the Pacific" by Mark Twain. Those looking for more action can head south to the restaurants and night life at Poipu Beach.

"The cottages, spread throughout a century-old coconut grove, create a neighborhood feeling, much like the plantation village it recreates." (George & Nancy Wofford) "The entire staff goes out of their way to make your stay as pleasing an experience as possible. The grounds and cottages are well maintained." (Warren K. Kirk) "If you want glitz and bright lights, this is not for you. It's comfortably unpretentious. Close enough to town to walk in before breakfast for the paper and to check out the local folks' luck, fishing from the pier." (Helen Finney) "A piece of old Hawaii that is still affordable." (Zan Zack) "We like it for the friendly staff and guests, mostly always sunny days (some rain in February), and the peacefulness." (Sheldon Sampson) Comments appreciated.

Minor niggle: "The ocean here is discolored by the Waimea River, so for swimming, we use the pool or go to a nearby beach."

Open All year.
Rooms 50 1-6 bedroom cottages—all with private bath and/or shower, telephone, radio, TV, desk, ceiling fan, refrigerator, balcony/deck, stereo.
Facilities Dining room, coin laundry, microwave. Swimming pool, tennis court, lawn games. Ocean beach, pier for swimming, fishing.
Location SW Kauai. 30 m W of Lihue/Poipu Beach. 10 min. walk to town. Go ½ m W past Waimea Canyon Dr., turn left to inn.
Credit cards DC, MC, Visa.
Rates Room only, $75–325. 3-8 night minimum stay. Weekly rates. Alc breakfast, $5–8; alc dinner, $25.
Extras Wheelchair access. Airport pickups by arrangement. Crib, babysitting. Tagalog spoken.

LANAI

Once known for its pineapple—not its tourist—crop, Lana'i offers a minimum of crowds and beautiful beaches. Until recently, there's been little commercial development, though this has recently changed. The Castle & Cooke company owns 98% of the island and its hotels; Dole Pineapple is one of their subsidiaries, but the pineapple plantations are no longer under cultivation. Plan to rent a car to get around on Lana'i; it may be worth it to pay the extra for four-wheel drive, since there are only 30 miles of paved road. Island activities include swimming in Hulopoe Bay (sometimes with spinner dolphins), scuba diving, and inland explorations by jeep, mountain bicycle, or hikes to the top of Lanai Hale.

Reader tip: "To get to Lana'i, try the ferry from Lahaina, Maui. It's cheaper than the plane, more reliable in poor weather, fun and a pretty ride, and you will likely see humpback whales." *(Carol Blodgett)* (Call 808–661–3756 for information; one-way fare is $25).

Information please: Originally built as a guest house for the Hawaiian Pineapple Company in the 1920s, you can still find a taste of old Hawaii (along with your fresh pineapple juice) on the **Hotel Lanai's** (P.O. Box A-119, Lanai 96763; 808–565–7211 or 800–327–4666) verandas, shaded by towering pines. Each of the 10 guest rooms in this old-fashioned one-story building are similarly furnished with a king-size four poster bed, dresser, desk, and night tables in natural wood, with a braided patchwork quilt, and water color scenes of Lanai. Rates are a reasonable $95 double, plus $5–8 for breakfast.

At the opposite end of the spectrum is the **Manele Bay Hotel**, also managed by Rockresorts. Opened in 1991, the 250-room Manele Bay sits overlooking the beach on Hulopoe Bay; while luxurious and expensive, the ambiance is somewhat different from most Hawaiian resorts, since the rooms have neither air-conditioning nor television. (P.O. Box 774, Lanai City, 96763; 808–565–7700 or 800–321–4666). "A lovely beach resort. More lively atmosphere than sedate Koele, and more children." *(CB)*

LANAI CITY, LANAI

Information please: Dreams Come True on Lana'i (547 12th Street, P.O. Box 525, 96763; 808–565–6961) is a simple B&B furnished with treasures from Bali and Sri Lanka, and surrounded by banana, papaya, and passionfruit trees. Double rates are $75, and include homemade bread and fruit fresh from the trees. Comments appreciated.

Lodge at Koele ♔ ✕ ♯   *Tel:* 808–565–7300
P.O. Box 774, 96763   800–321–4666
                              Fax: 808–545–4561

Lanai's dusty airport and the don't-blink-or-you'll-miss-it town of Lanai City will leave you totally unprepared for the luxurious experience offered by the Lodge at Koele. The Lodge sits on a 59,000-acre up-country estate, and both its architecture and decor evoke turn-of-the-century English manor elegance, from the grand hall with two stone fireplaces to the Library and Trophy rooms, and outside to the croquet lawns and Orchid House. What might otherwise have been a pompous decor is lightened with a mix of country antiques, folk art by local Lana'i artists, and Asian accent pieces. Guest rooms have dark bamboo furnishings and four-poster beds with pineapple finials, and luxuriously equipped bathrooms. Castle & Cooke owns the hotel; Rockresorts manages it. The lodge's restaurant offers an imaginative menu featuring locally grown produce and game; a recent menu included marble of ahi and snapper with radish, fennel and mustard seed, Japanese eggplant terrine with toasted goat cheese and plum tomatoes, and roast Lana'i venison with Molokai sweet potato puree and sage chips.

"Because of its 1,700-foot hillside elevation, the Lodge is sometimes shrouded in mist from nearby Lana'i Hale, the highest point on the island, but that only adds to its step-back-in-time appeal. While definitely upscale in all the public and private rooms, the service is generally low-key and easy to live with." *(BN)* "Beautiful grounds, outstanding decor. Service is professional and helpful. The hors d'oeuvres at tea time are practically a meal. Make reservations for the restaurant well in advance as it is very popular—and very expensive. You can use all the beach facilities at the sister resort, Manele Bay, where sometimes you can see spinner dolphins playing in Hulopoe Bay; there's free shuttle service for the 20-minute drive. Lanai is not beautiful, but fascinating in a stark way. You really feel the old Hawaii on this island, with long stretches of uninhabited beaches." *(Carol Blodgett)* Reports appreciated.

Open All year.
Rooms 102 suites, doubles—all with private bath and/or shower.
Facilities Restaurants, lounge, lobby, gift shops. Orchid house, swimming pool, Jacuzzi, tennis, croquet, lawn bowling, horseback riding, mountain biking, 2 golf courses. At Manele Bay: spa, beach, snorkeling. Scuba diving, sailing, fishing nearby.
Location Lana'i City.
Credit cards Amex, CB, DC, JCB, MC, Visa.
Rates Room only, $550–975 suite, $295–395 double. Extra person, $30; no charge for child under 8. MAP, add $90 per person. Full board, add $115 per person. 3-night minimum Dec. 20–Jan. 2. Package rates. Picnic lunches by arrangement.
Extras Airport pickups by arrangement. Shuttle van between Koele, Manele Bay, Hulopoe Beach, Lana'i City.

MAUI

Years ago, we saw a corny bumper sticker which proclaimed: "Here today, gone to Maui." Unfortunately, millions of others have been so inspired, making Maui second only to Oahu in popularity. Don't expect isolation here, although you will find the full spectrum of accommodations, shopping, night life, water sports, beautiful beaches, and dramatic scenery.

HAIKU, MAUI

Haikuleana ₵   *Tel: 808–575–2890*
555 Haiku Road, 96708

Set among the pineapple fields and pine trees, Haikuleana is owned by Fred Fox. "This B&B is located in the quiet countryside, near Mt. Haleakala National Park, with nightly showers, evening rainbows, and clear, pleasant, tropical days." *(Mr. & Mrs. Wallace McTammany)* "This old Hawaiian plantation house, dating back to 1850, sits back on a spacious lawn surrounded by banana, poinciana, and mango trees. From the front porch, you step into a large, gracious room, where a table is set for breakfast, and the smell of Kona coffee is in the air. To the right is the bright, cheerful living room, with cozy chairs and couch and lots of windows and greenery. The area is full of good and inexpensive restaurants, and Hookipa Beach is great beach for swimming and surfing." *(Doris Evans)* "A simple B&B, yet neat and warmly furnished. Fred Fox is friendly, kind, funny, and accommodating to my schedule. Delicious breakfast of fresh papaya, guava juice, macadamia pancakes topped with toasted coconut and strawberry syrup. Most evenings, we sat on the front porch or in the living room with Fred and the other guests, enjoying a glass of wine or beer and lively conversation, but privacy was easily available if preferred. A tranquil, non-touristy area, yet convenient to many activities." *(Diana Chang)*

Open All year.
Rooms 3 doubles—all with private bath and/or shower.
Facilities Dining room, living room, porch. 1½ acres with gardens. Beach, golf, tennis nearby.
Location N central coast. 12 m from town. From airport follow signs to Hana Hwy, Rte. 36. Pass through Paia along coast, past Hookipa Beach. Turn right at mile marker 11, onto Haiku Rd. Go 1 m to inn.
Restrictions No smoking. Children over 7.
Credit cards None accepted.
Rates B&B, $80 double, $65 single. 2-night minimum. 20% discount 5-night stay.

HANA, MAUI

Reader tip: "Having heard horror stories about traffic on the infamous road to Hana, I opted for a brief plane ride from Kahilui Airport." *(MA)*

Information please: A somewhat more affordable way to experience Hana is at the **Heavenly Hana Inn** (P.O. Box 790, 96713; 808–248–8442), a Japanese-style inn with four simply furnished units opening onto a central lobby and lounge. Each unit has two bedrooms, bath, screened lanai, and dining porch with refrigerator and light cooking facilities; rates are $175 for two, $235 for four. Surrounded by two acres of lawns and gardens, the inn is ½ mile from the coast. Comments?

Hotel Hana-Maui 🛉 ✕ 🐾
P.O. Box 8, 96713

Tel: 808–248–8211
800–321–HANA
Fax: 808–248–7202

One of Hawaii's oldest luxury hotels, the Hotel Hana-Maui underwent a $25 million renovation in 1984 to improve the property, upgrade the food, and refurbish the rooms, which feature oversize rattan furniture, Hawaiian quilts, and lots of wood and plants. The Hawaiian-American cuisine, served in the poolside pavilion or the restaurant, is supplemented by cookouts, clambakes, and luaus. Although many guests choose to relax and do nothing, others prefer to sign up for daily activities ranging from beachside cookouts to guided nature hikes, aqua-aerobics to jeep tours.

"The Hana-Maui, part of a 4,500-acre working ranch, offers total rest nd relaxation. Getting there means taking either a beautiful but nerve-nattering three-hour drive over narrow curving mountain roads or a reathtaking small-plane or helicopter ride. Our room was filled with owers and plants, and had a coffee maker for us to brew our own Kona iold coffee. The food was delicious, with creative use made of Hawaii's opical fruits and fishes." *(MW)* "The staff is glad you've come, and velcome you as if you were coming home. The rooms are light and airy, ach with a ginger tree. The vista from the pool is incredible." *(Toni & Lee Aarteney)* "Our Sea Ranch cottage had a hot tub overlooking the crashing cean, an enormous bathroom, and even an ice-maker in the refrigerator. he luau was good fun, with a real native feeling. Food is also very xpensive, but nearby Hana Ranch has decent food for breakfast, and erves dinner on weekends." *(Carol Blodgett)* Reports appreciated.

)pen All year.

,ooms 40 cottages, 38 suites, 18 doubles—all with full private bath, desk, ceiling an, refrigerator, patio, coffee grinder, coffee maker. 40 with Jacuzzi, soaking tub, vet bar. All in separate buildings.

acilities Restaurants, bar/lounge with fireplace, club room with TV, games, brary; gift shop, boutique, beauty salon. Nightly entertainment. 66-acre grounds vith 2 heated swimming pools, hot tub, tennis courts, 3-hole practice golf course, roquet, bicycling, children's play equipment, horseback riding, hiking trails, hula c ukulele lessons, snorkeling, fishing, fitness center. Laundry service. Seasonal hildren's program. Executive meeting center. Car rentals. Free shuttle bus to earby beach.

ocation E coast of Maui. 40 m E of Kahalui City. Take Hwy. 36 to Hana. Hotel close to intersection of Uakea Rd. and Hana Hwy.

estrictions No smoking in some rooms.

:redit cards All major credit cards accepted.

tates Room only, $435 cottage, $375–795 suite, $305 double. B&B, $443 cott-age, $383–813 suite, $323 double. Full board, $85 extra daily per person; extra hild 4–12, $25; child under 4, free. 15% plus $10 per day service. Rollaway, crib, .20. 4-night minimum, Dec. 20–Jan. 1. Honeymoon, anniversary, family plans. Alc reakfast, $14–18; alc dinner, $120. Prix fixe lunch, $22; dinner, $55. AAA dis-ount.

.xtras Limited wheelchair access. Hana Airport pickups. Crib, babysitting.

KULA, MAUI

nformation please: If congested condomania makes you itch, head nland to the peaceful mountain quiet of Maui's upcountry, just 35 minutes rom the Kahului Airport. About 3000 feet above sea level is the sleepy own of Kula, with views of the ocean below and Mount Haleakala above. Make Kula your base for hikes on Haleakala's trails, and visits to the botanical gardens and the Tedeschi Winery. The **Silver Cloud Ranch** Thompson Road, RR2, Box 201, Kula 96790; 808–878–6101) offers 12 loubles, suites, apartments, and a cottage in buildings dating back to the arly 1900s. Double rates range from $75–140 and include a full breakfast, erved in the garden sunroom. Another option is the **Kula Lodge** (Route 77, RR 1, Box 475, Kula 96790; 808–878–1535 or 800–233–1535)

offering five attached chalet-like cabins with views of the West Maui
mountains; rates range from $120–150. Breakfast, lunch and dinner are
available in the Kula Lodge Restaurant.

LAHAINA, MAUI

Old Lahaina Town plays a distinguished part in the history of Hawaii; as
the first capital of the Hawaiian Kingdom, it was the center of Maui's
cultural and social life. Later it became the whaling capital of the Pacific
in the 1860s, with all the diverse personalities of that era.

Reader tips: "Lahaina reminds me of Monterey, California, and the
crowds on Cannery Row. It is headquarters for whale-watching cruises,
snorkeling tours, shopping, and nightlife, and it strikes me that there are
many similar areas on the mainland." *(SHW)* Similarly: "Though a beautiful location, this congested resort area has little feeling of Hawaii." *(CB)*
But: "Although Lahaina is quite tourist-tacky, it's not hard to look beyond
and find surviving landmarks from the days of whalers and missionaries."
(PG)

Information please: Lahaina Hotel (127 Lahainaluna Road, 96761
808–661–0577 or 800–669–3444) is a re-creation of a Hawaiian Victorian
hotel, with walnut banisters, cast-iron chandeliers, and period antiques.
The guest room furnishings include antique brass, iron, and carved walnut
beds, Laura Ashley and Ralph Lauren fabrics, and lace curtains. The hotel
is connected to David Paul's Lahaina Grill, specializing in New American
cuisine, and is located in a neighborhood of art galleries and restaurants.

The GuestHouse　　　　　　　　　　　*Tel:* 808–661–808!
1620 Ainakea Road, 96761　　　　　　　　　　800–621–894.
　　　　　　　　　　　　　　　　　　　　　Fax: 808–661–1890

Although clean comfortable rooms and good food are important in any
B&B, the GuestHouse also offers another essential ingredient—hospitable
innkeepers who really enjoy their guests. As owners Tanna and Fred
Branum note: "Because we are a very small business, it doesn't take long
to establish a personal relationship with our guests." She goes on to
explain that "when we have a group of scuba divers, we pack a big picnic
and our gear and head out to catch our dinner. I usually videotape all the
above- and below-water action. In the evening, we edit the dive videos
while eating fresh-caught lobster." The GuestHouse was built in 1964, and
has been owned by the Branums since 1988. Rooms have contemporary
decor, and the rates include a family-style breakfast of Hawaiian coffee,
tropical juice, fruit platter, pancakes or French toast, hot and cold cereals,
muffins, and bagels.

"Lovely rooms, welcoming hosts. The Branums encourage questions
and offer ideas on all activities. Fresh-made bread daily; we used the
kitchen to prepare dinner several nights." *(Helen Pelikan)* "This B&B's best
feature is its warm and friendly owners." *(Rick Young)* "Delightful guests
from all over the world." *(Charles Leonard)* "Clean, well-equipped rooms,
plentiful breakfast." *(R. Djoa)*

Open All year.
Rooms 4 doubles—all with full private Jacuzzi bath, clock, TV, air-conditioning, ceiling fan, refrigerator, screened patio. 1 with desk.
Facilities Dining room, living room with books, family room with TV/VCR, kitchen/laundry privileges; beach mats, coolers, towels, boogie boards. Limited off-street parking, swimming pool. 1½ blocks from beach.
Location 1½ m N of town, 1 ½ m S of Kaanapali Beach. From Lahaina town, take Honoapiilania Hwy N to Charthouse restaurant. Go right on Fleming Rd., left on Ainakea Rd to inn 2 ½ blocks on right.
Restrictions No smoking. Prefer children over 12.
Credit cards Amex, MC, Visa.
Rates B&B, $95 double, $85 single. Extra person, $15. AAA, senior discount. Picnic lunch, $10. Honeymoon, scuba packages.
Extras Airport, bus station pickup. German, French, Dutch, Indonesian spoken.

Old Lahaina House ¢
P.O. Box 10355, 96761

Tel: 808–667–4663
800–847–0761
Fax: 808–667–5615

A contemporary home built in 1978, the Old Lahaina was renovated as an inn by John and Sherry Barbier in 1992. Breakfast is served poolside daily at 8:30, and includes French pastries and breads fresh from a local French bakery, fresh fruit, juice, coffee, tea, and locally made jams and jellies.

"John and Sherry are friendly, knowledgeable about Hawaii, and delighted to share their experiences with guests. The rooms are all decorated Hawaiian style, with bright tropical colors and wicker furniture, and are kept clean and neat; two have king-size beds, two have twins. Best are the mountain and ocean views. It's just a five-minute walk to the historic whaling town of Lahaina, which has plenty of shopping, art galleries, and restaurants. Right across the street is the beach, where guest go to snorkel, swim, and soak up the sun. Fresh island fruits—mangoes, papayas, kiwi, local pineapple, bananas—are a breakfast highlight. Some mornings you hate to leave the backyard—it's so pleasant to relax in the pool, meeting people from all over the world. One night we went to a local restaurant to see John perform—he's a singer and performs locally; another evening they prepared a fish barbecue for all the guests." *(Julie Lambert, also Susan Stevenson)* "I awakened early, walked to the beach for an early morning swim, then returned for a dip in the swimming pool, and was ready for breakfast." *(Steve Dutton)*

Open All year.
Rooms 2 suites, 3 doubles—2 with private bath and/or shower, 3 with maximum of 4 people sharing bath. All with telephone, radio, clock, TV, air-conditioning, fan. 2 with refrigerator, 1 with balcony.
Facilities Common room with TV/VCR, stereo, books. Garden courtyard with swimming pool. Private neighborhood beach across st. for swimming, snorkeling, whale-watching. Walk to harbor, town.
Location 7 blocks from center. Directions with confirmed reservations.
Restrictions No smoking in guest rooms.
Credit cards Amex, DC, Eurocard, MC, Visa.
Rates B&B, $79–95 suite, $60 double, $45 single. Extra person, $10. 2-night minimum.
Extras Bus station pickups.

The Plantation Inn ✕
174 Lahainaluna Road, 96761

Tel: 808–667–922?
800–433–681?
Fax: 808–667–929?

An elegant gray and white woodframe building, the Plantation Inn looks as if it dates from 1890, though it was actually completed in 1987, with an addition in 1991. The Victorian theme is carried throughout with stained glass windows, brass and four-poster beds, country pine, wicker, and bamboo furnishings, flowered fabrics and wallpapers, and oak flooring; the baths have Victorian pedestal sinks and chain-pull toilets. The inn's restaurant, Gerard's, is well established and reputed to be one of Maui's best specializing in French cuisine. Rates include early morning coffee and a breakfast of fresh fruit, French toast, Kona coffee, and hot chocolate.

"We stayed in the addition, which was lovely, with a stunning decor attractive baths, and a nice lanai." *(Caroline & Jim Lloyd)* "At the rear of the main building is a lovely guest lounge, highlighted by a carousel horse. The main building contains the basic rooms: #1 has a white iron and brass queen-size bed and white wicker furniture; floral spreads match the wallpaper, and a green room-size carpet covers the floor. The deluxe rooms are in the new building at the back of the property, and have double-paned glass and extra soundproofing; #10 is exquisite, with an Oriental motif, custom-made furniture stained dark red, Oriental screens light hardwood floors, and a dark green bedspread. The small swimming pool is surrounded with brick patios, palm trees, white wicker furniture and attractive landscaping; a poolside pavilion provides shade." *(SHW)* "Fully endorse existing entry. Spacious room with generous sitting area and private veranda; friendly, helpful staff." *(PG)*

Minor niggles: "Our room needed reading lights in the sitting area; we couldn't find the luggage racks; we would have preferred glasses to disposable plastic for drinking."

Open All year.
Rooms 5 suites, 15 doubles—all with private bath and/or shower, telephone radio, TV/VCR, air-conditioning, ceiling fan. Most with desk, refrigerator, balcony/patio; some with kitchenette, Jacuzzi.
Facilities Restaurant, bar, verandas, safe deposit. Videotapes, snorkeling gear laundry machines. Deck, gardens, gazebo, heated swimming pool, hot tub. On-site parking. 1½ blocks from beach, harbor. Tennis, golf nearby.
Location Historic Lahaina Town. From airport, take Rte. 30 (Honoapilani Hwy. into Lahaina. Turn right at Texaco/Union 76 gas stations onto Lahainaluna Rd. to inn 1½ blocks down on left. 2 blocks from Front St.
Restrictions No children under 10 in main building.
Credit cards Amex, Discover, MC, Visa.
Rates B&B, $180 suite, $99–150 double. Extra person, $10–25. $20 car rental. Alc breakfast, $6; alc lunch, $8; alc dinner, $40; 20% guest discount. $25 prix fixe dinner (overnight guests only). Dive, honeymoon packages.
Extras French spoken.

MOLOKAI

Diehard get-away-from-the-crowd types head directly for Molokai, once known as the Forgotten Isle, for empty beaches and hiking trails, deep-sea fishing, hidden coves, and dramatic sea cliffs and waterfalls. Molokai has a limited number of beaches; several are too rough for swimming in the winter months; another, at Kaunakakai, is just mud and rocks.

Reader tip: "Molokai is an intriguing place to visit, and still relatively untouristed. Exciting opportunities for the adventurous, include the mule ride down to the leper colony at Kalaupapa and the Molokai Ranch Wildlife Park. The lack of crowds means a lack of basic visitor services, especially in regard to food. Although restaurant prices are reasonable, selection is minimal and service is slow. A condo unit with a kitchen that lets you do some of the cooking is probably your best bet. We were pleased with **Paniolo Hale** condos at the **Kaluakoi Resort**, managed by Colony Resorts. The screened lanais were delightful for outside sleeping, and it's close to the beach and golf course (P.O. Box 146, Maunaloa 96770; 800–367–2984 or 808–552–2731)." *(SHW)*

OAHU

Hawaii's most crowded island, Oahu is still a must-see for first-time visitors. Explore Waikiki and climb up Diamond Head for a fabulous view, then visit Honolulu's downtown, with its fine museums (especially the Bishop Museum), aquarium, and Chinatown markets and galleries (the Chinatown Historical Society offers walking tours on weekdays). Get a car and discover Oahu's magnificent beaches, many ideal for mile-long walks, unspoiled by development.

HALEIWA, OAHU

Information please: Limiting your Oahu visit to Honolulu gives an incomplete impression of this lovely island. A 90-minute drive from the Honolulu airport will bring you to the lovely North Shore. There's the famous Banzai Pipeline for surfers, Waimea Bay, and shellhunting at Ke Iki Beach. Try overnighting at Alice Tracy's basic but comfortable oceanfront cottages: **Ke Iki Hale** (59–579 Ke Iki Road, Haleiwa 96712; 808–638–8229 or 800–377–4030). The 12 2- and 3-bedroom units are tailored to outdoor living; in addition to a kitchen and private bath, each has a Weber grill, a hammock, and an outdoor shower hanging from a coconut tree. Glorious sunsets year-round; in winter, wave heights on the beach reach 10–20 feet. Double rates range from $75–145 (2-night minimum), with weekly discounts available. Reports appreciated.

HONOLULU, OAHU

Overcrowded, overbuilt, overwhelming, Honolulu is both a big city and a major resort area—an unusual combination. It is perhaps the one place in Hawaii where man-made attractions outnumber those of nature. Go to spiffed-up Waikiki to do your souvenir shopping, then to Diamond Head and Ala Moana Beach Park to clear your head. Visit Iolani Palace to understand a bit about Hawaii's monarchy and the Bishop Museum for a look at the islands' Polynesian heritage. Chinatown will give you a taste of the East, and Pearl Harbor's Arizona Memorial pays homage to America's entry into World War II.

Also recommended: Although it is too big at 456 rooms, the **Halekulani** (2199 Kalia Road, Honolulu 96815; 808–923–2311 or 800–323–7500) is worth mentioning: "Built in 1917, this institution is a sanctuary amid Waikiki's high-rises. A tropical paradise of palms, fountain pools, flowing water and marble. Every detail—valet parking, shoe-polishing, bathroom amenities, evening turndown, morning paper—was accomplished without fail. Highlights of the lavish breakfast buffet in the poolside restaurant included custom omelets, poi pancakes with coconut syrup, endless fruit, almond croissants, and macadamia muffins. Our room and bath were lovely and completely quiet. The swimming pool floor has a enormous blue orchid, made up of 1 million mosaic tiles." *(SHW)*

Although far from "little" at nearly 800 rooms, *Debbie & Michael Swiatek* found Waikiki's **Sheraton Moana Surfrider** (2365 Kalakaua Avenue, 96815–2943; 808–922–3111 or 800–STAY–ITT) to be wonderful indeed. "The original turn-of-the century portion of the hotel (not the tower) has been completely renovated and restored to its former elegance. Rooms have hardwood floors, mahogany furnishings, and ocean views. We were welcomed with fresh flowers and pineapple juice. Sitting on the front veranda of the hotel in antique rocking chairs was a wonderful way to unwind."

Information please: Listed in past editions, we need current reports on the **Manoa Valley Inn**, (2001 Vancouver Drive, 96822; 808–947–6019 or 800–634–5115), a Victorian-style cottage dating back to 1919. Listed on the National Register of Historic Places, this beige-and-white structure has numerous gables and elaborate corbels under the eaves. "Tucked away in the cool Manoa hills yet just a short drive to beaches and shopping. Breakfast is served on the large lanai complete with linens, crystal, and silver. Returning in the evening you can have complimentary wine and look out over the lights of Waikiki." *(Patricia Couch)*

One of Waikiki's boutique hotels, the **Waikiki Joy Hotel** (320 Lewers Street, 96815; 808–923–2300 or 800–733–5569), is convenient to the Royal Hawaiian shopping complex and Waikiki Beach. "The lobby is open and airy, done in Italian marble and glass brick, with beautiful floral arrangements everywhere. The staff is very friendly and enthusiastic and the decor is both contemporary and soothing; colors throughout were mauves, blues, grays, and whites. All rooms have a marble entryway, whirlpool tub, state-of-the-art stereo equipment, and big, luxurious bath towels." *(Cheryl Olofson)*

For a low-rise setting of tropical flora and old-style atmosphere about a block from the beach try the reasonably priced **Breakers** (250 Beach Walk, 96815; 808–923–3181 or 800–426–0494). Double rates range $88–97, and every unit has a fully equipped kitchenette. Reports welcome.

Coconut Plaza ¢ ✕
2171 Ala Wai Boulevard, 96815

Tel: 808–923–8828
800–882–9696
Fax: 808–923–8828

The Coconut Plaza offers comfortable accommodations in a quiet location just a short walk from Waikiki action. The airy rooms have kitchenettes and balconies, tiled floors, soft pastel floral fabrics, coconut wall mattings, and simple wicker furnishings. "My room and balcony were lovely in a casual way, spotless and well appointed. Reading lights were recessed above the bed with dimmer switches everywhere. The room had pretty wicker chairs and a mirrored wall reflecting the view of the Ala Wai canal, golf course, and the hills beyond. Fresh fruit and rolls are served at the buffet breakfast in the open air lobby beside the little swimming pool, with additional seating in the garden terrace. Warm, friendly staff." *(Connie Marks, also SF)* Reports welcome.

Open All year.
Rooms 80 suites & doubles—all with full private bath, telephone, TV, air-conditioning, refrigerator, microwave, balcony. 72 with kitchenettes.
Facilities Lobby, bar/lounge, restaurant, laundromat, swimming pool.
Location 2 blocks from Waikiki Beach, at corner of Ala Wai Blvd. & Lewers St.
Credit cards All major cards.
Rates B&B, $150 suite, $85–120 double. Extra person, $8–15. Corporate rate. 7th night free April–early Dec.
Extras Crib.

New Otani Kaimana Beach Hotel ♟ ✕
2863 Kalakaua Avenue, 96815

Tel: 808–923–1555
800–35–OTANI
Fax: 808–922–9404

The Kaimana—as it is usually called—was built in 1963, and is ideally located in the center of Kapiolani Park, adjacent to Waikiki's central hotel and shopping area. It overlooks Sans Souci beach, one of the best swimming beaches on Oahu, according to long-time general manager Stephen Boyle; it's not bad for people-watching either, judging by its nickname—"Dig Me Beach."

"A favorite haunt of Robert Louis Stevenson, who passed the time relaxing under the large Hau trees. Today the area includes the hotel, the beach and ocean, 500-acre Kapiolani Park, and Diamond Head. The hotel has one of the few outdoor restaurants in Waikiki, the Hau Tree Lanai, and plus an excellent Japanese restaurant, Miyako. It's a 10-minute walk past the beach to the main Waikiki strip. Less than five minutes away are 13 tennis courts, a golfing range, archery, and jogging paths with exercise stations. A short walk away are the Honolulu Zoo, Honolulu Aquarium, the Waikiki Shell, and bus and trolley stops." *(Michael Virgintino)*

"The hotel sits in the shadow of Diamond Head, yet feels light-years away from Waikiki. Decorated in restful pastels, it's a typical nine-story high-rise on the outside, but inside the decor, airy lobby and friendly staff lend it charm. We breakfasted each morning at the beachside Hau Tree Lanai restaurant." *(Debbie Joost)* "The Kaimana has a wonderful open-air tiled lobby with flowers, ferns, and mosaic paintings. We had an excellent dinner of papaya mint soup, followed by shrimp stuffed with eggplant

241

curry, with Midori cheesecake for dessert, at the Hau Tree Lanai dining room. Standard guest rooms are on the small side, but all rooms are pleasantly decorated in pastel shades of lavender, aqua, and beige; most popular are the ocean-view studios. The suites in the Diamond Head wing are very livable, though they lack a view. Avoid the rooms on the corner of the hotel next to the Sans Souci condominium; you can practically touch their balcony from the room lanai." *(SHW)* "We were pleased with our remodeled Park View studio, with views through the palm trees to the beach." *(MA, also Heather Beadle)* Reports appreciated.

Open All year.
Rooms 31 suites, 94 doubles—all with full private bath, TV, telephone, radio, desk, air-conditioning, balcony, mini-bar. Some with kitchenette, hair dryer, coffee maker, microwave, large-screen TV.
Facilities 2 restaurants, 1 with classical guitarist nightly. Room service, beach. Concierge service. Swimming, windsurfing, golf, tennis, hiking, jogging, bicycling nearby.
Location 1 m S of Waikiki, at Diamond Head.
Credit cards Amex, CB, DC, JCB, MC, Visa.
Rates Room only, $170–575 suite, $99–225 double. Extra person, $15; no charge for children under 12. 10% AARP, NARFE discount. "Room & Car," B&B packages. 5-night minimum stay, Dec. 20–Jan. 5.
Extras Crib, babysitting. Japanese, Korean, Spanish, German, Tagalog, Ilokano spoken.

We Want to Hear from You!

As you know, this book is effective only with your help. We really need to know about your experiences and discoveries. If you stayed at an inn or hotel listed here, we want to know how it was. Did it live up to our description? Exceed it? Was it what you expected? Did you like it? Were you disappointed? Delighted? Have you discovered new establishments that we should add to the next edition?

Tear out one of the report forms at the back of this book (or use your own stationery if you prefer) and write today. *Even if you write only "Fully endorse existing entry" you will have been most helpful.*

Thank You!

Oregon

Cowslip's Belle, Ashland

Oregon has incorporated the best of the late 1960s, making it the most mellow and relaxing state in the country. Along with a less hurried pace and spectacular scenery, you will find a variety of cottage industries, aging hippies, and a legislature that takes social concern and the environment seriously.

Coastal Oregon: Rich coastal diversity can be sampled by visiting some of the 66 state parks that provide virtually unlimited access to the shore. The southern coast, from the California border to Bandon, has few visitors. It features quiet beaches and cranberry fields and the wild Rogue River. The midcoast area, from Coos Bay to Lincoln City, can get crowded, especially in summer; but there is good reason—here are beaches up to 500 feet wide and 10 miles long, 300-foot sand dunes, sea lion caves, high bluffs with exquisite views (Otter Crest), and inviting rocky shores. Don't miss Devil's Punchbowl, north of Newport, where the ocean bursts through the rock in "spouting horns." The northern coast, from Lincoln City to the Columbia River, boasts summer sand castle contests, Tillamook's renowned cheddar cheese factory, forested headlands, and Cannon Beach's famous monolith, Haystack Rock. A visit to the coast during winter can be particularly romantic with its misty fog, huge storms, totally isolated beaches, and migrating whales.

Central Oregon: Leaving the coast, you'll find the gentle Coast Range mountains and the fertile southwestern area, with its famous wineries and Shakespeare festival at Ashland. More centrally, the lush Willamette River Valley holds most of the state's population from Eugene to Portland, while still retaining large expanses of rich farmland and forest. East of the Willamette are the Cascades, with 10,000-foot-high mountains. A recommended introduction to this part of the state is Route 126, east of Eugene up the rambling McKenzie River Valley, then Route 242 through one of

243

the most bleak, unusual, and unvisited lava areas in the country. Nearb
Bend provides excellent skiing and more unusual sites: Lava River Caves
Lava Coast Forest, and, 90 miles south, Crater Lake National Park.

Eastern Oregon: Sparsely populated, the southeastern part is domi
nated by the dramatic Steen Mountains, wide expanses of desert and dry
lakes that still display the wheel ruts of the pioneer wagons. By contrast
the northwestern corner has the heavily forested Blue and Wallow
mountains, a destination for gold miners in the 1860s and for backpacker
today. The Columbia River divides the states of Oregon and Washington
descending past dry, striped cliffs, the narrow Columbia River Gorge
Portland, and Astoria, to the Pacific. While the trip down I-84 along the
Columbia is attractive, we recommend driving on the Washington side fo
better views and a more leisurely pace.

A word on the weather: It doesn't rain as much as you have heard. Th
winters are mild and although west of the Cascades it does often rain from
November to mid-April, there are few downpours—just a goodly amoun
of the (in)famous "Oregon mist."

Rates are generally lowest midweek, from October to May.

ASHLAND

Ashland is a small mountain town, set in the foothills of the Siskiyou
Mountains near the Oregon/California border. It is particularly wel
known as the home of the 50-year-old Oregon Shakespeare Festival, held
annually from late February through October. Over 350,000 people come
from all over the Northwest every year to watch first-class professiona
repertory performances of Shakespeare and other classic and contempo
rary playwrights, performed in three different indoor and outdoor thea
ters. (Call 503–482–4331 for ticket information; July and August
performances usually sell out soon after the tickets go on sale in the
winter.)

To accommodate and entertain all these theatergoers, Ashland offers
wide variety of boutiques and galleries, concerts and ballets, restaurant
for every taste, and dozen of B&Bs, yet remains an attractive small town
It's full of visitors in July and August, so make your reservations early, o
visit during June or September. Rates tend to be highest on summe
weekends and lowest midweek in winter, and do not include city tax
Outdoor activities include hiking in Lithia Park or along the Pacific Cres
Trail, rafting, windsurfing, waterskiing, and sailing on nearby rivers and
lakes; and skiing ½ hour away at Mt. Ashland. Crater Lake is a reasonabl
drive, and the area also has several wineries worth visiting.

Ashland is in southwestern Oregon, in the Rogue Valley, 350 mile
north of San Francisco and 290 miles south of Portland. From the north
take I-5 to Ashland; from San Francisco, take I-80 east to I-505, then nort
on I-5.

Reader tips: "Literally steps away from the theater complex is the

Chateaulin Restaurant, where we enjoyed an exceptional meal of salmon with dill and lamb with red peppers, accompanied by a fine wine. Service was well paced, so that we were in our theater seats by curtain time." (MM) Also suggested is Chata for Eastern European fare, in the nearby town of Talent. (Pat Fink)

Information please: An 1896 farmhouse, the **Country Willows B&B** (1313 Clay Street, 97520; 503–488–1590 or 800–WILLOWS) provides a peaceful rural setting two miles from town. Each guest room has a view of the surrounding mountains, a private bath, and air-conditioning. The 90–155 double rates include a full breakfast—perhaps ricotta cheese blintzes with plum sauce or sundried tomato quiche—served on the porch or sunroom, overlooking the willows and the brook. Guests can relax in the swimming pool or hot tub, or go for a spin on the inn's bicycles. Built as a boarding house in 1908, the **Edinburgh Lodge** (586 East Main Street, 97520-2114; 503–488–1050 or 800–643–4434) offers six guest rooms, each with a private bath, at B&B double rates of $85 in peak season. Breakfast might include peaches and cream French toast or fresh berry crepes; scones and tea are served in the afternoon. "Rooms are small, comfortable, and clean rooms; excellent breakfast; convenient to downtown and theaters." (Judith Brown)

On a quiet street a mile from the theaters is the **Romeo Inn** (295 Idaho Street, 97520; 503–488–0884), built in the 1930s. This Cape Cod house is surrounded by 300-year-old Ponderosa pines and furnished with both antique and traditional furnishings, highlighted with Amish quilts or Oriental rugs. There are two suites and four doubles, all with private bath and king-size bed. The B&B double rates of $125–160 include breakfasts of Belgian waffles with fresh fruit and whipped cream, or perhaps a baked chili rellenos casserole. Also included are a separate fresh fruit course, home-baked breads, fresh-squeezed orange juice, coffee and tea. Reports welcome.

Cowslip's Belle Bed & Breakfast ¢   Tel: 503–488–2901
159 North Main Street, 97520   800–888–6819

Carmen and Jon Reinhardt describe their B&B as "a 1913 Craftsman home, with down comforters, fresh flowers, antiques, stained glass, Maxfield Parrish prints, and a rose garden." Goodies such as sour cream Belgian waffles with walnut maple cream or vegetable and cheese strata might be the breakfast entrée. A chocolate delight—mocha pastilles or chocolate ruffles—are left on the pillow every night.

"Close to the Festival theaters and downtown, so it's easy to leave the car and walk. Although on a main street, noise level is minimal. Even the front suite is surprisingly quiet and the rest of the rooms face the garden. The Reinhardts are an encyclopedia of information about Ashland and the Festival." (Jean Kavanagh) "Rooms are simply decorated in Victorian style, meticulously clean, individually temperature-controlled, with ample closet space." (Karen Kennedy) "Carmen and Jon are entertaining hosts, happy to chat when the inn isn't busy. Tasty breakfast of grapefruit and kiwi followed by German pancakes with preserves." (Deborah Brockman) "Jon and Carmen will tempt you with freshly baked biscotti, macaroons, and

more. Our quiet room in the carriage house had a bouquet of fresh flowe
and a super-comfortable willow canopy bed with great bedside readi
lights. We enjoyed the garden with willow swing, and their cute little do
Jon and Carmen prepared a delightful vegetarian breakfast of fresh stra
berries, blueberry muffins, and buckwheat pancakes with blackber
sauce." *(Gail Davis)*

Open All year. Closed Dec. 24, 25.
Rooms 1 suite, 3 doubles—all with full private bath, deck, air-conditioni
refrigerator. 3 with private entrance. 2 rooms in main house, 2 in carriage hou
Facilities Dining room, living room with library, fireplace; porch. Rose gard
patio, deck, willow swing. Paved off-street parking. Tennis, golf, swimming, wa
skiing, boating, fishing, downhill, cross-country skiing nearby.
Location 3 blocks to theater and plaza. On North Main St. between Laurel a
Bush.
Restrictions No smoking. No children under 12.
Credit cards MC, Visa.
Rates B&B, $75–117 suite or double, $70–112 single. Extra person, $30. 2-nig
weekend minimum March–Oct.
Extras Free airport/station pickup. Babysitting.

Hersey House   *Tel: 503–482–45*
451 North Main Street, 97520

A turn-of-the-century home surrounded by beautiful flower beds, t
Hersey House is an easy walk to downtown. Each guest room has
different flavor, from country French to Eastlake, with period and repr
duction furnishings. Innkeepers Gail Orell and Lynn Savage report th
"we offer breakfasts of homemade bread, freshly squeezed orange jui
fruit, coffee, and a hot entrée, served in a relaxed and congenial atm
sphere, encouraging all to linger at the table."

"Little bouquets of fresh flowers are placed in your room daily. T
delicious breakfasts rate equally high in presentation and taste, and a
garnished with edible flowers." *(Joy Durighello)* "Immaculate and qui
While never intrusive, Gail and Lynn are bright and charming, makin
your stay relaxing and informative." *(Lara Bronstone)* "The front porch
perfect with a good book and a glass of iced tea. Moderately sized gue
rooms, nicely appointed with antiques, down comforters and pillow
Since the innkeepers' quarters are separate, you feel as if you have t
house to yourself." *(Carl & Jo Meisel)* "Breakfast is a two-hour affair
beautifully presented fruit, wonderful eggs or perhaps lemon pancak
with raspberry sauce, breads, 9-grain hot cereal, and even a tea men
Hershey kisses on the pillow when your bed is turned down at nigh
(Ellen Dale) "Excellent advice on local restaurants and entertainmen
(Nancy & Dennis Swanson)

Area for improvement: "An in-room thermostat."

Open Late May–late Nov.
Rooms 4 doubles—all with private bath and/or shower, air-conditioning. 1 wi
desk, balcony. 2-bedroom cottage with kitchen.
Facilities Dining room, living room with player piano, Victrola, books, gam
Unscreened porch, deck. Swimming, whitewater rafting, fishing nearby. 15 m
cross-country, downhill skiing.

Location 15 m from Medford Airport. 6/10 m from center. From I-5 S take Exit 19 to inn at corner of N. Main and Nursery Sts. From I-5 N, take Exit 11. Proceed along Siskiyou and Lithia Way to N. Main.
Restrictions Traffic noise in front rooms. No smoking. No children under 12.
Credit cards MC, Visa for payment only.
Rates B&B, $100–110 double, $90–100 single. Extra person, $15. 2-night minimum some weekends.
Extras Free local airport/station pickup.

The Morical House ¢   *Tel: 503–482–2254*
568 North Main Street, 97520

The Morical House was built in the 1880s and was restored 100 years later with particular care given to its stained glass windows and detailed woodwork. Guest rooms are decorated with antiques and homemade comforters, and all have mountain views. Owners Pat and Peter Dahl report that "our commitment is to make our guests' stay as comfortable, relaxing and enjoyable as possible."

"Lovely, restful decor—stuffed animals are a nice, cuddly touch. We enjoyed coming home at night to freshly baked chocolate chip cookies and a relaxing glass of sherry." *(Jeanette Hasty)* "Food was exquisite and tasty: salmon paté and local cheeses at the cocktail hour; eggs Florentine with sausage our first morning and fruited French toast and thick bacon on the second." *(Walter Bankovitch)* "Hosts Pat and Pete are warm and unobtrusive. The sunny dining room overlooks the carefully groomed backyard and rose garden. Guests share their comments on local restaurants in an entertaining journal." *(Peggy Nitschke)* "Decorated with a keen sense of color, creating a serene ambiance. Every inch is sparkling clean and fresh. Water pressure is excellent, and sink and tub fittings are reproduction brass. Towels are plentiful and soft. Abundant down-filled pillows; cheerful spreads and coverlets cover comfortable mattresses." *(Christy Laird)* "Extra raincoats and umbrellas are a typically thoughtful touch." *(Diane Farley)*

Open All year. Closed last 2 weeks in Jan.
Rooms 5 doubles—all with full private bath, air-conditioning.
Facilities Dining room, lobby, parlor with library, guest refreshment area, sun porch. 1½ acres with gardens, croquet, putting green, off-street parking. 1 m to Lithia Park.
Location 1 m from center of town. From I-5 take Exit 19 to town. Inn is 4th building on left after entering city limits.
Restrictions Traffic noise in front rooms if windows opened. No smoking. No children under 12.
Credit cards MC, Visa.
Rates B&B, $70–115 double, $63–94 single. Extra person, $25. 2-night weekend minimum Memorial Day through Sept.

Mt. Ashland Inn   *Tel: 503–482–8707*
550 Mt. Ashland Road; 97520

If you'd like to combine the cozy comfort of a rustic mountain lodge with today's amenities, the excitement of a major cultural center with an isolated mountain retreat, then the Mt. Ashland is just for you. Built by

Elaine and Jerry Shanafelt in 1987, the Mt. Ashland Inn has such distinc
tive touches as log arched doorways, a log slab circular staircase, and bed
made from black oak and madrona wood.

"Jerry cut and milled the logs for this three-story structure from tree
on their land. He is a true craftsman, having made the cherry Windso
dining chairs, the stained glass designs, and the wood carvings; Elain
stitched the beautiful quilts. Peaceful, quiet setting, with excellent hiking
including the Pacific Crest Trail, which passes through the parking lo
Beautiful views of Mt. McLoughlin, Pilot Rock, Mt. Shasta, and th
valleys of southern Oregon." *(Pat Hill, also Pam Phillips)* "While the tem
perature was a balmy 80° in downtown Ashland, we enjoyed the snow
covered scenery of the pine forest just outside our door. The Sky Lake
Suite has spectacular views of Mt. McLoughlin; its refrigerator wa
stocked with assorted juices and soft drinks. The hospitality basket in th
bathroom contained everything you might have forgotten, and the whirl
pool tub had a gently flowing rock waterfall. We requested a stric
vegetarian breakfast, and were delighted with the tofu Florentine wit
salsa, fresh baked banana bread, muffins with tasty preserves, and bake
apples with molasses and wheat germ." *(Gail Davis)*

Open All year.
Rooms 5 doubles—all with private bath and/or shower, fan. 2 with desk. 1 wit
whirlpool tub, refrigerator, microwave, coffee maker.
Facilities Dining room, living room with game table, fireplace, stereo; library wit
TV/VCR, books, videotapes; meeting room, guest phone, refrigerator; deck. 4
acres with forest, hiking and cross-country ski trails. 3 m to downhill skiing.
Location Southern OR. 16 m S of Ashland. From I-5, take Exit 6 (Mt. Ashland
and follow signs to ski area. Turn right on Mt. Ashland Rd. and go 5¼ m to inn
Restrictions No smoking. No children under 10.
Credit cards MC, Visa.
Rates B&B, $85–130 double, $80–125 single. Extra person, $20. 2-night mini
mum, weekends (June–Sept.) & holidays. Sport, ski, mystery packages. Off-seaso
discounts.

Oak Hill Country B&B ¢
2190 Siskiyou Boulevard, 97520

Tel: 503–482–155
800–888–743

This Craftsman-style home was built in 1910 and converted to an inn ir
1987; Tracy and Ron Bass purchased it in 1992.

"Quiet and peaceful. While most guest rooms have a view of th
mountains, it is breakfast that makes a stay so special. After fresh juice o
fruit smoothies, homemade specialties include a vegetable frittata o
Dutch babies with spiced apples, as well as potatoes, fresh or baked fruit
and homemade breads. Tracy even makes bagels, a feat which few hav
tried, let alone mastered. It's served at 8:30 A.M. around the big oak table
enabling all the guests to get acquainted; Tracy and Ron even found tim
to join us and the other guests." *(Stu & Gerry Ganson)* "Excellent servic
and friendly conversation made our stay special. Our large, luxuriou
room had one wall of windows that looked out to the snow-cappe
mountain range. Nice touches included chocolates on our turned-dow
bed, and edible flowers garnishing our breakfast plates." *(Christy Corzine
"Guest rooms are named and decorated for different flowers. Immaculate

with fresh linens daily. Tracy and Ron welcome guests with refreshments, and share solid information on restaurants, plays, and outdoor activities." *(Lori Larson)*

Open All year.
Rooms 5 doubles—all with private shower and/or bath, radio, clock, air-conditioning. 2 with fan.
Facilities Dining room, living room with fireplace, TV/VCR, books, games, deck. ⅓ acre with off-street parking, croquet. Bicycles.
Location 2 m from downtown. From Rte. 5, take Exit 14 & go W on Hwy. 66. Turn left on Tolman Creek Rd., then right on Siskiyou Blvd. to inn on left.
Restrictions No smoking. Children over 8 preferred.
Credit cards MC, Visa.
Rates B&B, $60–90 double, $50–80 single. Extra person, $25.
Extras Local airport pickup. Babysitting.

The Woods House ¢

333 North Main Street, 97520

Tel: 503–488–1598
800–435–8260
Fax: 503–482–7912

This 1908 Craftsman-style home was built by Dr. Woods, a prominent Ashland physician; the Woods family lived here through the 1950s; Françoise and Lester Roddy bought this B&B in 1991. Using old photographs, the terraced backyard was restored to its original design; the gardens feature almost 90 rose bushes, a white and black Concord grape arbor, and various fruit and nut trees. The Roddy's lovable Newfoundland, Jasmine, lives in the backyard as well, (she's not allowed in the house) and is the favorite of many guests. The guest rooms are simply furnished with antiques and period pieces, lace and floral fabrics, original watercolors, and good bedside lamps and tables. A thoughtful approach is taken to breakfast; by 8 P.M. the night before, guests are asked to give their preferences—either a full or "heart healthy" meal in the dining room at 9 A.M.; or a light breakfast brought to the room between 7:45 and 8:30 A.M. A typical menu might include fresh fruit, buttermilk scones or cinnamon-cranberry biscuits, blueberry oatmeal pancakes with turkey ham, or tomato asparagus pie with bacon; each dish is garnished with garden-fresh flowers and herbs and served on fine china, crystal, and linens.

"Thoughtful touches included sherry for two, chocolates, and a teddy bear." *(Carol & John Bodeau)* "The large private garden offers sunshine or a cool place to enjoy a good book. Guests enjoy swapping tips while lingering over coffee in the beautiful dining room." *(Seymour & Eileen Polk)* "Delightful hostess; spotless, comfortable, pretty room; big, thick towels; sherry in the living room; coffee and cookies in the dining room." *(Lindy McLeod)* "Françoise purchased our theater tickets in advance, taking advantage of her seating privileges. The oatmeal was delicious and our room had been cleaned when we returned from breakfast." *(Kristine Ireland)* "We loved the cheese blintzes with raspberry coulis, garnished with lavender blossoms." *(Mary & Scott Saylor)* "Fully endorse existing entry. Our lovely room beyond the parlor at the rear of the house, was surprisingly quiet. The lovely brass canopy bed made me feel like a princess, with pretty, freshly cut flowers and chocolate mints at bedside." *(Gail Davis)*

Open All year.
Rooms 6 doubles—all with private bath, air-conditioning. 1 with desk, fan. 2 share balcony. 2 rooms in carriage house.
Facilities Dining room, living room with fireplace, stereo, books. Porch with swing. 1/2 acre with gardens, gazebo, picnic area. 30 min. to skiing.
Location 4 blocks to downtown. From I-5, take Exit 19, go W on Valley View Rd. Follow signs to downtown. At 1st traffic light, go left on N. Main St. Watch for signs to Shakespeare Information Center. Inn is 1 m S, on right.
Restrictions No smoking. Street noise on front porch.
Credit cards MC, Visa.
Rates B&B, $65–110 double, $65–105 single. 2-night minimum weekends.

ASTORIA

About 15 miles north of Seaside, on the Columbia River, is the town of **Astoria**, with beautiful Victorian mansions, and an outstanding maritime museum.

Also recommended: The **Grandview B&B** (1574 Grand Avenue, 97103; 503–325–5555 or 800–488–3250) offers ten guest rooms with views of mountains and the river from the bay windows and the balcony of this turreted Victorian homes. A full breakfast is included in the double rates of $39–92. "Gracious welcome from innkeeper Charleen Maxwell. The Garden Room has big bay windows and plenty of light. It's an easy four-block downhill walk to the maritime museum, but a bit steep on the way back up. Our breakfast included fresh fruit and omelets." *(William Novack)*

BANDON

Also recommended: Too small for a full entry, **The Highlands Bed & Breakfast** (608 Ridge Road, North Bend 97459; 503–756–0300) sits high above the coastal fog, about 20 miles north of Bandon. This contemporary cedar home offers beautiful views of the coastal range from its wide expanses of glass and a wraparound deck; the decor is traditional, with some antiques. "Secluded hideaway with fabulous views. In addition to the deck and hot tub, guests have use of the entire downstairs living room and kitchen. Marilyn and Jim Dow made us feel right at home; wonderful breakfast of decadent French toast." *(Christine & Walter Boyd, also John Schettler)* Double rates for the two guest rooms range from $65–75.

Lighthouse B&B   *Tel: 503–347–9316*
650 Jetty Road, P.O. Box 24, 97411

Just across the Coquille River from the Lighthouse B&B is the real thing, standing sentinel duty, just as it has for the past century. The inn is a spacious contemporary home with large windows and long decks for watching sunsets or sternwheeler cruises on the river. Innkeepers Bruce and Linda Sisson have furnished their home with contemporary pieces, accented with brass and plants. Breakfast is a simple buffet of fruit, breads or muffins, cheese, cereals, juice, and coffee.

"Great place for walking to build up an appetite for dinner at one of the several good restaurants which Bruce and Linda recommend. The rooms, all on the second floor, are clean, with comfortable beds, modern baths, and all the amenities. The first-floor apartment is occupied by the resident manager, as the Sissons live in town. The lighthouse is nonfunctional, so you don't have a blinding beam in the windows, but a soulful foghorn completes the ambience." *(Don Marioni)* "We'd return for the view and the little town of Bandon. When the tide is out, people go out looking for agates." *(LSW)* "Our greenhouse room was pleasant, and Bandon and its environment provide happy exploring." *(Lee Todd)*

Open All year.
Rooms 4 doubles—all with private bath and/or shower, telephone. 1 with hot tub. Some with TV, desk, fireplace, deck.
Facilities Dining room, living room with woodstove, stereo, TV/VCR. Unscreened porch, deck. On the beach with picnic area. Tennis, golf, fishing, boating, crabbing, clamming nearby.
Location Coos County, 25 m S of Coos Bay on Oregon Coast. Walking distance to "Old Town."
Restrictions Summer foghorn might disturb light sleepers in west rooms. No smoking. No children under 12.
Credit cards MC, Visa.
Rates B&B, $75–100 double, $65–90 single. Extra person, $15. 2-night discount in winter.
Extras Free airport pickup.

BEND

On the eastern edge of the Oregon Cascade Mountains in central Oregon, Bend is host to many sporting and cultural events throughout the year. Visitors enjoy strolling through the downtown area and visiting the many ducks, geese, and swans in Drake Park. The Deschutes River runs through town and is noted for its fly-fishing and white-water rafting. Golf courses, picnic and boating areas, and hiking trails can all be found nearby; downhill skiing is only 20 minutes away at Mt. Bachelor.

Also recommended: For a private and peaceful get-a-way, *Phyllis Morris* recommends **The Guest House** (20020 Glen Vista, 97701; 503–382–8565), a luxury log cabin with great views of the mountains, furnished with American country antiques. A fully equipped kitchen is supplied with farm fresh eggs, homemade bread and jam for a fix-it-yourself breakfast. The B&B double rate is $85; extended stay discounts.

Information please: Six miles northwest of Bend is the recently opened **Three Sisters B&B** (20150 Tumalo Road, 97701; 503–382–5884), a hand-built log home on five acres in a scenic setting with access to the Deschutes River for hiking, swimming, and sunning. Owner Julia Supanich reports that "we cater to families with casual country hospitality." Accommodations are offered in a suite in the main lodge, and in several bunkhouses; B&B rates of $60–75 include breakfasts of German apple pancakes and blueberry scones, and families are welcome. Comments?

Juniper Acres (65220 Highway 20 West, 97701; 503–389–2193) is a log home, set in the woods, and built in 1991; guests will enjoy the abundant wildlife and mountain views at this homestay B&B. "Incredibly clean. Gorgeous setting with not another neighbor in sight, and an awesome view of the snow-capped Cascades. The Bjerks' warm hospitality was combined with their sensitivity to our privacy. Marvelous food, generous portions, served on the deck." *(Jim & Karen Anderson, and others)* Three guest rooms are available, at B&B double rates of $65–90. The Bjerks build log homes as a business, so contacting them is not always easy.

BLY

Aspen Ridge Resort ¢ 🏃 ✕ 🏹

P. O. Box 2, 97622

Tel: 503–884–8685

"Aspen Ridge Resort sits among towering ponderosa pines on a portion of the 14,000-acre Fishhole Creek Ranch, surrounded by the Fremont National Forest. The buildings are constructed of peeled Montana lodgepole pine with blue metal roofs, and overlook a high mountain meadow where cattle and buffalo graze. The impressive lobby has a huge antler chandelier, high peaked ceiling, a massive fieldstone fireplace with mounted buffalo and elk trophies, and comfortable seating. The Western-style bar has an old player piano, a mirrored horse collar, buffalo skull, an old rifle, and bandanna-style curtains. A deck stretches the length of the lodge, with sitting areas to enjoy the sunsets. The food is quite good, and the steaks were perfect.

"The cabins are reached by a walk along split rail fences and wildflowers. Our cabin was large and attractive with front and side porches, wall-to-wall carpeting and cozy seating before the woodstove. There was a modern, well-equipped kitchen, dining area with pine trestle table, a bedroom with a high four-poster bed, and a good-sized bathroom. We also stayed in the lodge in a large, simply furnished room with a queen-size and a double bed. There's much at this top-notch four-season resort." *(Suzanne Carmichael)*

Suggestions for improvement: "Better bedside lighting."

Open All year.
Rooms 5 2-bedroom cabins with private bath, fully equipped kitchen, living room with woodstove. 4 doubles in lodge with private bath; some with balcony.
Facilities Restaurant, bar/lounge with fireplace, TV; lobby with fireplace, gift shop, game room with TV/VCR, Ping-pong; porch, deck. Meeting rooms. 160 acres with horseback riding, hiking, unfenced tennis court, cross-country skiing, snowmobiling. Cattle roundups, rodeos.
Location S central OR. 55 m NE of Klamath Falls, 30 m W of Lakeview. 18 m from town. Take Hwy. 140 to Bly. Go 1 m past Bly & turn on Fishhole Creek Road (#3790) to ranch.
Restrictions Smoking in lounge; 1 cabin only.
Credit cards None accepted.

Rates Room only, $120 cabin, $65–85 double. 2-night minimum in cabin. Alc breakfast, $3–8; alc lunch, $5–11; alc dinner, $16–30. Children's menu.
Extras Local airport pickups.

CANNON BEACH

Cannon Beach is a very popular Oregon beach resort, named for the cannon that washed ashore here in 1846. It's also known for Haystack Rock, which sits just offshore at 235 feet, and is the world's third largest monolith. With seven miles of beach, ideal for beachcombing, swimming, surfing, and surf casting, and a location just a 1½-hour drive west of Portland, finding a room here in peak season can be very difficult; early bookings are strongly advised.

Also recommended: The **Viking Motel** (P.O. Box 219, 97110; 503–436–2269), is a six-room condo/motel managed by Best Western, with a fabulous view of Haystack Rock. "For folks who want oceanfront rooms, comfort, and the amenities of an apartment, the Viking is a choice with rates of $129–155. Comfortable furnishings; unpretentious and homey atmosphere. The gas fireplace took off the chill, the kitchen-dinette setup was convenient, the bedroom was large and comfortable. The location is quiet, off the main road. It's within walking distance of the beach or downtown for a serious walker, but most people take the car." (LNT, also KC)

Near the beach, the **Grey Whale Inn** (164 Kenai, 97110; 503–436–2848) is a Cape Cod-style motel with five suites appointed with original art, fresh flowers, down comforter and a TV/VCR. "Nothing but praise for the decoration and cleanliness of our room. Good, quiet location only a short walk to the beach, but away from the tourist part of Cannon Beach. Owners were charming. Breakfast was a loaf of homemade bread and coffee available in the room." (Joan Ryan) About 25 miles south, **Hill Top House** (617 Holly Avenue, P.O. Box 145, Garibaldi 97118; 503–322–3221) is a small B&B with three guest rooms ($70–90), all with a private bath, set high on a wooded hill overlooking the town and ocean. "Innkeepers Don and Shuzz Hedrick are retired educators. Their home is full of books, flowers, warmth and friendship. Gorgeous views from the hot tub; delicious breakfast." (Susan Tinkle)

Information please: The **Cannon Beach Hotel and Restaurant** (1116 South Hemlock, 97110; 503–436–1392), originally a turn-of-the-century boarding house for loggers, has been extensively renovated and now offers nine guest rooms, some with fireplace and whirlpool tub. The double $50–120 rate includes a continental breakfast. The restaurant specializes in seafood and pasta.

Stephanie Inn
2740 South Pacific, P.O. Box 219, 97110

Tel: 503–436–2221
800–633–3466
Fax: 503–436–9711

In 1993, owners Steve and Jan Martin finished building their oceanfront inn and began the decorating process; massive pine beams frame the rock fireplaces, large windows open to the views of Haystack Rock, and wicker and leather seating areas provide spots for reading or watching the fog roll in. Guest rooms have country and wicker furniture, lush fabrics and patterns, and simple window treatments to give unobstructed views of the ocean and mountains. Breakfast is served from 7:30–10:30 A.M. at individual tables; the menu includes freshly squeezed orange juice, muffins, fruit, granola, Starbucks coffee, and assorted Stash teas plus such entrées as Grand Marnier French toast with smoked ham. Dinner is served at 7 P.M., and a recent menu offered phyllo triangles with sauteed mushrooms; spinach salad with warm bacon vinaigrette; pan-fried catfish with ratatouille or roast pork with apple dressing; and cranberry cheesecake or a fresh berry trifle.

"Country elegant decor, with overstuffed chairs by a river rock fireplace; friendly touches are the coffee and tea out in the lobby, along with a cookie jar of fresh baked cookies, and the wine gathering every afternoon. Terrific views from the ocean front rooms; the mountain view rooms are nice too, at a lower rate. Amenities include terry robes and the morning newspaper, turndown service with chocolates and rose petals scattered over the bed. Excellent dinner followed by a relaxing evening by the fire. Exceptional personal service, comfort and charm." *(Pam Phillips)* "We were there on a stormy day and enjoyed gazing out from our beautiful, well-equipped room." *(Lee Todd)* "First-rate manager Sharon Major offers guests the option of having breakfast served in their guest room, the dining room or the lounge." *(Ernest Harmon)*

Open All year.
Rooms 4 suites, 42 doubles—all with full private bath, whirlpool tub, telephone, radio, clock, TV, fan, fireplace. Most with refrigerator, wet bar, balcony. 1 with desk.
Facilities Dining room with fireplace, library with fireplace, piano, games. Off-street parking. On beach.
Location 1 1/2 m from downtown. From Hwy. 101, take 3rd exit & go N to inn.
Restrictions No smoking. Children over 12.
Credit cards Amex, CB, DC, Discover, MC, Visa.
Rates B&B, $250–360 suite, $189–239 double, $119–239 single. Extra person, $25. 2-night minimum July–Sept. 15th, special events, holidays. Prix fixe dinner, $30–35. $10 for room service.
Extras Wheelchair access; some rooms equipped for disabled. Airport pickup. Spanish spoken.

The Waves ¢ 🏃 ♿   *Tel: 503–436–2205*
224 North Larch Street, P.O. Box 3, 97110

Right on the Seawall, The Waves includes both modern condo-style units with enormous windows and old-fashioned beach cottages. The shops, restaurants, and galleries of Cannon Beach are an easy walk away. Owner Frank Swedenborg reports that they also operate the **White Heron Lodge**—on the water about two blocks away from the Waves office, offering a contemporary-style duplex and a Victorian-style fourplex.

"The word 'motel' is sort of misleading here, because that conjures up images of something tacky and garish, but The Waves has no common lobby and one parks right outside the room, so I guess that will have to do. Our room was beautifully decorated, with blond wood, handsome contemporary prints, skylights, and stone fireplace, with a deck overlooking the fabulous beach. There was even a handwoven throw on the bed. Our room had a full kitchen and a supply of firewood. The building is shingled with cedar, nicely weathered." *(Rachel Gorlin)* And about the White Heron: "At the quiet, north end of town, our unit in the lodge had a kitchen, separate bedroom, living room with fireplace and Murphy bed, bath, and deck overlooking the river and beach. The views are terrific, and the location is away from the chaos of Cannon Beach on a summer weekend." *(Pam Phillips)* Reports needed.

Open All year.
Rooms 4 suites, 31 doubles—all with private bath. Most with kitchen, fireplace, deck.
Facilities Oceanfront spa, beach.
Location Center of town, on beach. Take Second St. toward beach, entrance to motel just before Larch St.
Restrictions No smoking in some guest rooms.
Credit cards MC, Visa.
Rates Room only, $150–250 suite, $75–125 double. 3–7-night minimum July, Aug. 2–3-night weekend/holiday minimum Sept.–June.
Extras Wheelchair access; 2 rooms equipped for disabled. Airport/station pickup by prior arrangement. Crib, babysitting.

CLOVERDALE

Cloverdale is located in Tillamook County, in northwestern Oregon, two hours west of Portland. Cloverdale offers easy access to bay and ocean beaches, lots of flat roads for bicycling, a pioneer museum, and several cheese factories to visit.

Sandlake Country Inn ¢ &.   *Tel: 503–965–6745*
8505 Galloway Road, 97112

On Christmas morning 1890, Ezra Chamberlain received an unusual gift—1 million board feet of red fir timbers dumped onto his beach by a storm-wrecked ship. His neighbor soon dragged some of it to his homestead to build a sturdy farmhouse. Margo and Charles Underwood bought that farmhouse—owned for 80 years by the Allen family—in 1988 and converted it into a small but luxurious inn. The Rose Garden room has a canopied queen-size bed and is done in summery shades of evergreen, wild rose, and alabaster; the Timbers is a large room at the back of the original 1894 farmhouse, with three by twelve-foot exposed bridge timbers, and deep green and burgundy plaid wallpaper. A breakfast might include orange juice, baked apple oatmeal, fresh fruit granola parfaits, coddled eggs, lemon tea bread, dill toast, coffee or tea.

"Private country gardens, fabulous hiking nearby." *(Stephanie Bric)* "While Chuck is a sculptor, his role as all-around farm hand with a wheelbarrow of freshly dug potatoes, trailed by the couple's Westie, lends an aura of unhurried country life. An expansive cedar deck overlooked a rose garden and apple trees where whitetail deer come to eat. Every morning at 7:30, Margo placed a tray with carafe of coffee and just squeezed orange juice on my landing: 30 minutes later, she returned with eggs Florentine, fresh melon, enormous cinnamon rolls and herb toast." *(Bill Norman)* "Cookies and welcome basket upon arrival, homemade bath oils and soaps, fresh flowers, and music. A nice drive here past forests coastal views, and winding roads." *(John McLean)* "Functional antique. which do not clutter up the decor." *(Ruth Miles)* "Margo was always a hand when needed, but respected our desire for privacy." *(Pamela Blikstad)* "Thick terry robes will keep you warm en route to the very private hot tub." *(Sharyn Smith)*

Open All year.
Rooms 1 suite, 2 doubles, 1 cottage—all with private bath and/or shower, radio TV, mini-refrigerator, deck. 2 with fireplace, whirlpool tub, TV/VCR.
Facilities Dining room, living room with fireplace, library, games, guest tele- phone. 2⅓ acres with hot tub, croquet, hammock, clamming equipment, bicycles 1 m to beach.
Location 9 m N of Pacific City. From Pacific City turn left over bridge and continue 8½ m N on Scenic Loop to Sandlake Grocery. Turn left on Galloway Rd. to inn on left ½ m.
Restrictions No smoking. No children under 15 in main house.
Credit cards Discover, MC, Visa.
Rates B&B, $85 suite, $70–100 double, $65–95 single. Cottage, $115. Extra person, $10. 2-night weekend minimum. Gourmet picnic basket, $25 for 2.
Extras Wheelchair access; 1 room equipped for disabled. Station pickup.

DAYTON

Wine Country Farm ¢   *Tel: 503–864–3446*
6855 Breyman Orchards Road, 97114

Simple, traditional decor occupies the inside of this restored 1910 farm- house; what the original builders never expected on the outside are the miles of vineyards that form the heart of the Oregon wine industry. Joan Davenport bought the house in 1990 and opened it as an inn in 1991; the inn's first crush was in 1994. She also raises Arabian horses, one of whom struts its stuff pulling a buggy for picnics.

"Surrounded by vineyards—Perrier, Domaine Drouhin, Trappist Abbey—and hazelnut orchards. The inn sits atop a hill with magnificent views of Mount Hood and Mount Rainer and the adjacent fog-shrouded lowlands. When I returned from an early-morning walk, Joan was emerg- ing from the barn, carrying a basket of large brown eggs. Breakfast consisted fresh-ground coffee, blackberries and cream; an egg casserole with mushrooms and sliced black olives; Mexican salsa; scones; jam from Joan's own Pinot Noir grapes; bacon and homemade sausage; sautéed potato chunks; and blended orange/banana juice. She is urbane, yet con- versational, a businesswoman and an attentive, unobtrusive innkeeper. The lawns, woods, and vineyards are immaculately manicured. One lov- able dog and cat complete the domestic mix." *(Bill Norman)*

Open All year.
Rooms 1 suite, 4 doubles—all with full private bath, clock, fan. 3 with desk, 1 with telephone, fireplace.
Facilities Dining room, living room with fireplace, organ, TV/VCR; family room with fireplace, porch. 13 acres with gazebo, lawn games, carriage rides, trails for hiking, biking. Golf, river nearby. 1 hr. to skiing, ocean.
Location N OR. 30 m SW of Portland. 9 m from town. From Rte. 18N, go left onto Breyman Orchards Rd.
Restrictions No smoking. Children over 12 preferred.
Credit cards None accepted.
Rates B&B, $110 suite, $65–95 double. Extra person, $20.
Extras Airport/station pickup. Horse boarding.

DEPOE BAY

Gracie's Landing ♿   *Tel: 503–765–2322*
235 SE Bay View Ave., P.O. Box 29, 97341   800–228–0448

With a Cape Cod exterior and a traditional interior, Gracie's Landing opened in 1989 and is managed by Dale and LaRona Hoehne. Every room has a view of Depoe Bay, known as "the world's smallest harbor," and all are decorated with a nautical flair. A typical breakfast might include fresh melon wedges, eggs Jonah (an English muffin topped with fresh baby shrimp, poached egg, and Hollandaise sauce), and sweet buns or rolls, finished off with a special "dessert"; special diets are gladly accommodated, with notice.

"The inn is located on the inside edge of the bay, with a narrow, dramatic opening to the Pacific. Although not on the beach, lovely state parks with beach access are within a few miles' drive and are free to the public. The same partnership also owns and operates a delightful restaurant called The Sea Hag; with its piano bar, it has become a favorite gathering place for locals and visitors alike." *(Marguerite Higham)* "Our room was spotless, breakfast was excellent, and LaRona is a gracious hostess." *(Mr.& Mrs. Dick Prater)* "A 5 P.M. hospitality hour gave us a chance to meet the other guests." *(Nancy Goodfellow)* "Color coordinated, well chosen furnishings. Breakfast is nicely presented and delicious; gracious waitresses." *(Mr. & Mrs. William Hilbish)*

Open All year.
Rooms 13 doubles—all with full private bath, telephone, TV/VCR, desk, fireplace, balcony/deck. Some with Jacuzzi.
Facilities Dining room, living room with piano. Library/gameroom with fireplace, books, games, movies. Golf, fishing, whale watching nearby.
Location W OR. 2 hrs. SW of Portland. 3 blocks from town center. Turn E onto Bay View Ave. at only traffic light; inn at end of road.
Restrictions No smoking in some guest rooms and some public areas. No children.
Credit cards Amex, CB, DC, Discover, MC, Visa.
Rates B&B, $75–100 double, $70–95 single. Breakfast in bed, $7 extra. 2-night

minimum weekends/holidays in season. Off-season, midweek, Thanksgiving, Christmas packages available.
Extras Wheelchair access. Station pickup.

DIAMOND

"Located in Oregon's high desert, the town of Diamond peaked with a population of 50 people; now the stone ruins of the original store and some stately poplars are all that's left. From here you can visit Malheur National Wildlife Refuge, where millions of birds—pelicans, trumpeter swans, Canada geese, game and song birds—rest in their annual migration." *(SC)*

Also recommended: "The **Hotel Diamond** (Box 10, 97722; 503–493–1898), built in 1898, has five guest rooms with shared baths ($45–55 double). There's a large screened porch with comfortable, brightly colored furniture, old horse collars on the walls, and baskets of dried flowers. Inside are sitting areas on the first and second floors, a deli/wine shop; and the local post office. Meals are served family-style at long tables in the dining room and include generous choices of homemade fare. Outside is a fenced area for croquet, trees hung with sweet little birdhouses, and flower gardens. Our air-conditioned little room had a comfortable double bed in a white-painted iron bedstead. The innkeepers were friendly and informative." *(Suzanne Carmichael)*

Information please: About 25 miles to the southwest, set along Donner and Blitzen Creek (yes, that's really the name) is the **Frenchglen Hotel** (Highway 205, Frenchglen 97736; 503–493–2825) on the other side of the Malheur National Wildlife Refuge. This small white-frame building is owned by the Oregon State Parks system and has been operated by John Ross since 1991. Rooms are small and simply furnished with double beds; rates range from $42–48. The restaurant is open for three meals a day, with hearty meats, fresh vegetables, and fruit pies as specialties. Dinner is served family-style at 6:30 P.M. sharp, by advance reservation.

McCoy Creek Inn ¢ ♦ ✕ ♿   *Tel:* 503–493–2131
HC 72, Box 11, 97722   *Fax:* 503–493–2131

McCoy Creek Ranch is a fifth-generation working ranch; built in 1918, the ranchhouse was renovated in 1990 by Gretchen Nichols, and Shirley and David Thompson. A sample dinner might include homemade mushroom soup; spinach strawberry salad; lemon sorbet; game hen with currant-raisin sauce and almond wild rice; stir-fry pea pods and peppers; and gingerbread with honey whipped cream. A typical breakfast consists of a fresh fruit plate, link sausage, shirred eggs with basil-tomato sauce or stuffed French toast with apricots, plus coffee and tea.

"Peaceful setting with cows grazing nearby, and dogs, cats, and peacocks wandering the grounds. Our room had dark blue wallpaper, a sloped ceiling, an armoire, queen-size bed with carved headboard, marble-top side table, two comfortable wicker chairs and table, and an Oriental rug

The good-size bath had attractive wallpaper and brass fixtures. From our porch we watched children floating down the creek in rubber tubes. Pleasant dinner, with a fish chowder, salad with tarragon dressing, and a game hen with raspberry sauce. Afterwards, we sat together on the ranchhouse porch, and one of the cowboys joined us and shared his thoughts about cattle and the cowboy life." *(Suzanne Carmichael)*

Open Open April 1st–Oct. 15th.
Rooms 1 cabin, 3 doubles—all with private bath, fan. 3 with porch.
Facilities Restaurant, living room with fireplace, books; porch. Hot tub in separate screened building. On cattle ranch with lawn games, hiking, creek with swimming, tubing. Fishing nearby.
Location SE OR. 190 m E of Bend, 200 m W of Boise, ID. From Hwy. 205, take Diamond Jct. turnoff & go E. Continue past Diamond Jct. for 3 m to sign for inn on right.
Restrictions No smoking. Children welcome by arrangement. Peacocks might disturb light sleepers. Shared ranch access road; give right-of-way to tractors, trucks, pickups.
Credit cards MC, Visa.
Rates B&B, $75 double, $60 single. Extra person, $10. Prix fixe dinner, $15–20. Picnic lunches.
Extras Wheelchair accessible. Airport pickup by prior arrangement. Crib.

EUGENE

Located located halfway between Seattle, Washington, and San Francisco, California, in west central Oregon, Eugene is the home of the University of Oregon and a major center for lumber and wood products.

Also recommended: About 20 miles south off I-5 in Cottage Grove is **The River Country Inn** (71864 London Road, Cottage Grove 97424; 503–942–9334), a Southern-style farmhouse with two guest rooms sharing a large bath. There's a woodstove to keep the common room cozy, rockers on the covered porches and a plate of homemade cookies on the sideboard. The Coast Fork of the Willamette River flows the entire length of the farm. The double rate of $65 includes a full breakfast. "Located at the end of a pretty country road in pastoral farmland." *(Judith Craig)* "My favorite breakfast included Carol's own raspberry jam and biscuits. The extensive gardens produce fresh flowers for every room." *(Jim & Chirs Keener)* "Owner Carol Pryor has created a welcoming, relaxing atmosphere; she is a talented decorator and cook." *(Carrie Campbell)*

Campbell House, A City Inn 🏃 ✕ ♿
252 Pearl Street, 97401

Tel: 503–343–1119
Fax: 503–343–2258

After many tries, Myra Plant succeeded in buying this ramshackle and overgrown 1892 mansion; after a year-long restoration, her B&B opened in 1993. The plumbing and wiring are new, the woodwork gleams, the comfortable seating areas have big sunny windows, upholstered couches, and Queen Anne reproduction chairs. Sonja Cruthers is the manager; breakfast is available from 6:30 A.M. until 10:30 A.M. Favorite entrées include malted mini-waffles (hazelnut-apple, chocolate chip or plain), eggs

Benedict, crepes, or casseroles; specially blended granola and porridge is served with a variety of toppings.

"Excellent food in generous portions. Thoughtful touches included chocolates, early morning coffee at your door, extra pillows, soothing music, clean and fluffy white robes." *(Clare Ellis & Kip Webb)* "Updated Victorian home in the nicest part of Eugene—overlooking the city, its parks and the river bike/hike system." *(James Powell & Joan Procter)* "Lovely Waverly comforters and curtains; old-fashioned clawfoot tubs. Downtown shops and restaurants are just a few blocks away. Fascinating photo albums of the restoration." *(Margala Woods)* "Gracious service at both breakfast and afternoon tea." *(Debbie Forbes)* "Graham crackers tied with a ribbon were left on our child's pillow." *(Mrs. Cal Morris)* "Spiced iced tea with delicate butter cookies, perfumed candles all around. We sat in our room watching great classic videos and had a picnic in the garden." *(Lynne Cannon)*

Open All year.
Rooms 14 doubles—all with private bath and/or shower, telephone, TV/VCR, refrigerator. 3 with fan, 2 with fireplace, 1 with whirlpool tub.
Facilities Dining room, living room with fireplace, library with books, video collection, piano; laundry facilities. 1½ acres with gazebo, lawn games.
Location Skinner Butte historic district, 4 blocks to city center. From I-5, take I-105W. Follow Eugene City Ctr. Mall signs to East Third to Pearl St.
Restrictions Train noise might disturb light sleepers. No smoking. No alcohol.
Credit cards Amex, MC, Visa.
Rates B&B, $175 suite, $105–150 double, $70–145 single. Extra person, $15. 2-night holiday, weekend minimum.
Extras Wheelchair access; 1 room equipped for disabled. Crib, babysitting.

Duckworth B&B ¢
987 East 19th Avenue, 97403

Tel: 503–686–2451

Decorated with antiques, lace curtains, old prints and wicker, this English Tudor inn is located within walking distance of the University of Oregon. Innkeepers Peggy and Fred Ward serve a traditional American breakfast of fresh coffee, tea, and juice with a baked egg dish or hot cakes, waffles, or French toast. Peggy reports that "our guests are welcome to join us for afternoon tea in the parlor, or we'd be happy to serve them in their room."

"We were pampered and comfortable in our large, immaculate room, with a queen-sized bed and cozy flannel sheets. Bubble bath and lovely soaps were a thoughtful touch. A cheery fire in the living room fireplace, and a homey snack of bedtime milk and cookies." *(Carolyn Barnard)* "Victorian or country antiques in every room. Wonderful variety of reading material, including current information on restaurants and activities; also a great videotape selection." *(Phyllis Morris)* "Delicious hearty breakfast—Fred's milkshakes are great." *(Susan Seiler)*

Open All year.
Rooms 3 doubles—1 with private shower, 2 with a maximum of 4 people sharing bath. All with TV/VCR, desk, fan.
Facilities Living room with fireplace, player piano, TV/VCR, videotape library, stereo; garden room with books. Gardens with rock paths, off-street parking, bicycles. River swimming and fishing nearby.

Location Off I-5. 1 m from downtown Eugene. 1 block from University of Oregon.
Restrictions No smoking. No alcohol. No children under 14.
Credit cards None accepted.
Rates B&B, $60–85 double. Discount for extended stay, University parents.
Extras Free airport/station pickup.

The Oval Door ¢
988 Lawrence Street, 97401

Tel: 503–683–3160
Fax: 503–485–5339

A 1920s Craftsman-style home, the Oval Door was built as a B&B in 1990, and was purchased by Judith McLane and Dianne Feist in 1993. Breakfast, served over a two-hour period, includes a choice of juices, home-baked breads, baked pears with yogurt or perhaps blueberry-nectarine crumble; and "Popeye's morning" or maybe zucchini hazelnut waffles.

"Spacious, well furnished rooms. Judy is friendly and helpful." *(Mr. & Mrs. H. Schuyten)* "The house sits on a corner on a quiet, residential street." *(Eileen O'Reilly)* "Thick terry robes were among the amenities of our large, bright and immaculate room. The breakfast included such treats as baked potato boats stuffed with scrambled eggs and topped with salsa, turkey sausage, zucchini muffins and freshly squeezed orange juice." *(EL)* "Live plants and flowers everywhere." *(Joyanne Barret & Helmut Scholz)* "A wonderful in-city inn. Best of all is innkeeper Judy." *(Richard & Mary Ann Setton)* "The double Jacuzzi was romantic with scented bath bubbles and candles." *(Margaret & John Leverett)* "There's an intimate library complete with a rolling ladder to reach the ceiling-high shelves. Outside beautiful trees shade the front porch." *(Janis Baker)*

Open All year.
Rooms 4 doubles—all with private shower, radio, clock, fan, hair dryer. 2 with desk, 1 with whirlpool tub. Telephone on request.
Facilities Dining room with stereo, living room with fireplace, stereo, library with books, fireplace, TV/VCR, unscreened porch. Off-street parking.
Location 2 blocks to center. From I-5, take exit 194B W to end of freeway (Jefferson St.). Go straight, through traffic light, for 3 blocks. Turn left on 10th. Go 1¾ blocks. Inn on left.
Restrictions May be light traffic noise on one side. No smoking. Children by arrangement.
Credit cards MC, Visa.
Rates B&B, $70–88 double, $65–83 single. Extra person, $10. 2-night minimum special events, University functions. 10% discount for 5-night stay.
Extras Airport ($10)/station pickup. Port-a-crib.

FLORENCE

Information please: The **Edwin K B&B** (1155 Bay Street, P.O. Box 2687, 97439; 503–997–8360), built in 1914, offers four guest rooms named and decorated for the seasons. Each has a queen-size bed, and a private bath with clawfoot tub, double shower, or whirlpool bath. Breakfast, included in the $75–105 rate, is served in the dining room in a formal setting with fine china, crystal, and flatware.

Johnson House B&B Inn &.
216 Maple Street, P.O. Box 1892, 97439

Tel: 503–997–8000
Fax: 503–997–8000

Ron and Jayne Fraese restored this 1892 Italianate Victorian (the oldest house in Florence) in 1982 and have decorated it in light, airy shades of blue and ivory, with period furniture, prints, and photographs. Early morning coffee is available at 7 A.M., and breakfast is served at individual tables at 8:30. A typical menu includes fresh-squeezed orange juice, fresh fruit compote, home-baked muffins and breads, wild mushroom soufflé with lox, and sorbet.

"Old-fashioned featherbeds with down comforters and pillows; large and thick bath towels, plenty of hot water; and a magnificent herb garden. The house sits on a corner, one block from Florence's Old Town shops. We enjoyed delightful conversations with other guests, sparked by Jayne's and Ron's wit and personality. Excellent breakfasts with fresh-ground coffee." *(Philip & Susan Anderson)* "The Moonset cabin is darling and well-equipped." *(Lee Todd)* "Terrific suggestions for places to hike along the coast were great." *(Lynn & Shelley Taylor)*

Open All year.
Rooms 1 cottage, 5 doubles—3 with private bath and/or shower, 3 sharing with a maximum of 4 people sharing bath. All with clock, 1 with radio, balcony/deck.
Facilities Dining room, living room with organ, sitting room, porch. 2 off-street, ample on-street parking. Garden. River, ocean nearby with fishing, boating, swimming.
Location Central OR coast. 162 m SW of Portland, 60 m W of Eugene. In historic district. 2 blocks E of Hwy. 101.
Restrictions No smoking. Children over 12 preferred.
Credit cards MC, Visa.
Rates B&B, $75–105 double, $65–95 single. 10% senior, AAA discount Nov.–Mar. Room only in cabin.
Extras Wheelchair access; 1 room equipped for disabled. Florence airport pickup. French spoken.

GLENEDEN BEACH

Salishan Lodge ♦ ✕ ✿ &.
Highway 101, 97388

Tel: 503–764–3600
800–452–2300

Set on a bluff overlooking Siletz Bay, Salishan is a spread-out complex of two-story contemporary buildings, finished in natural wood and connected by covered bridges and walkways. The guest rooms and public rooms are decorated with original art by Northwestern artists. The lodge's three restaurants offer everything from casual to elegant dining, and its wine cellar houses over 21,000 bottles. Although many guests find it hard to tear themselves away from this luxury resort's complete facilities, nearby attractions include the coastal state parks, whale watching in winter, and Oregon's Wine Country.

"A superior, well-run resort. The big dining room was everything an expensive hotel should be. Room service was best with traditional club sandwiches, hot soup and hot pie with no pretense in presentation." *(W.A.*

Grant) "Superb room; service was good—I asked for an iron and it arrived within minutes. The lodge is separated from the beach by U.S. Hwy. 101, but it is a pleasant walk. At the nearly deserted beach we watched a sea lion playing in the surf." *(P. Bottomley)* "Well laid out and attractive for a place that attracts so many conventions." *(John Worsley)*

Less positively: "Perhaps it was the timing of our August visit, but we were disturbed by noisy children next door. Service at dinner was disappointing."

Open All year.
Rooms 3 suites, 197 doubles—all with full private bath, telephone, radio, TV, desk, carport, balcony, mini-bar, fireplace. Rooms in 19 buildings.
Facilities 3 restaurants, library, lounge with piano bar, dancing; art gallery, game room. 700 acres with fitness center, nature paths, heated and covered swimming pool, hot tub, beaches, indoor and outdoor tennis courts, playground, gift shops, children's play equipment, 18-hole golf course. Charter deep-sea fishing, crabbing, clamming.
Location Central coastal OR. 90 m SW of Portland, 675 m N of San Francisco, CA. On Hwy. 101 between Newport and Lincoln City.
Credit cards Amex, DC, Discover, MC, Visa.
Rates Room only, $109–236 double. Extra person, $15; children under 12 free. 2-night weekend minimum, July–Sept. Sport, romance, winter, holiday packages. Alc lunch, $10; alc dinner in the lodge's most expensive restaurant, $44. Children's menu.
Extras Wheelchair access. Pets, $10 per night. Crib, $10 per night; babysitting. French, Spanish spoken.

GOLD BEACH

Set on the southern coast, Gold Beach was named for the deposits obtained by placer mining, which lasted until the 1860s when a flood washed all the remaining gold out to sea. It's a popular resort area, and visitors enjoy exploring the beaches and hiking trails as well as the highly recommended jet boat trips up the Rogue River. Fishing, golf, and horseback riding are other favorite diversions. Gold Beach is on Highway 101 in southeastern Oregon, 35 miles from the California border.

Information please: Thirty miles south of Gold Beach is the **Chetco River Inn** (21202 High Prairie Road, Brookings 97415; 503–469–8128 or 800–327–2688), a contemporary log home, bordered by forest and the Chetco River. Off the paved road and beyond the electric company, the inn operates with the most modern conveniences thanks to alternative energy sources—solar and propane generators. The decor includes Oriental rugs, leather and antique furniture, and brass beds in the four guest rooms. The $85 double rate includes a full breakfast served family style; coffee, tea, and cookies are available all day.

Tu Tu' Tun Lodge ✕ ♿   *Tel:* 503–247–6664
96550 North Bank Rogue, Route 1, Box 365   *Fax:* 503–247–0672

This lodge takes its name from the Tu Tu' Tun Indians, whose name means the "people close to the river." Designed by owner Dirk Van

Zante's architect parents, the Tu Tu' Tun Lodge is built in a rustic bu contemporary style, overlooking the Rogue River. A typical dinner from the set menu might include scallop soup; blue cheese and apple salad smoked turkey with sage, roasted potatoes with onion rings, popovers steamed asparagus with mustard; and apple cranberry pie with ice cream

"Furnishings are simply comfortable, but all is secondary to the gloriou setting provided by the Rogue River. Small amenities are everywhere— fresh flowers, good soaps, wonderful reading material." *(Jack & Harrie Oppenheimer)* "Before dinner we joined the other guests in the main lodge for cocktails, hors d'oeuvres, and good conversation." *(Ginny & Jac Severs)* "I loved its informality (no dress code at dinner) and the real fire. that were lit every evening. The 104-mile jet boat trip up the Rogue Rive was a highlights." *(MS)* "Every thoughtful touch one could wish for from morning newspapers to magnifying mirrors in the bathrooms. Communa dining, to our surprise, turned out to be a plus, due in part to the thoughtful placement of guests by Dirk and Laurie. The food is fresh and beautifully prepared—if one didn't like the posted menu other choices were easily arranged. I don't know when, if ever, we stayed at an inn where so much intelligent thought has gone into the caring of guests.' *(Ruth & Derek Tilsley, also Ginny & Don Breismeister)*

Open April 29–Oct. 30. Suites/cottage open all year.
Rooms 1 cottage, 2 suites, 16 doubles—all with private bath, balcony, or patio. Suites with air-conditioning.
Facilities Restaurant, bar, lounge with fireplace, player piano, billiards; library, gift shop. Heated swimming pool, boat dock and ramp, fishing, horseshoes, pitch and putt, children's play equipment. Hiking, golf, horseback riding nearby. Jet boat rides nearby.
Location 7 m E of town on N bank of Rogue River. From Hwy. 101, at N end of bridge, follow North Bank Rd. to inn. 7 m from ocean.
Restrictions Smoking in guest rooms only.
Credit cards MC, Visa.
Rates Room only, $120–150 suite, $159–195 river house. Extra person, $10. MAP, $195–265 suite/cottage, double. Prix fixe breakfast, $10; lunch, $10; dinner, $33. Box lunch, $9.50.
Extras Wheelchair access. Airport, excursion boat pickup. Some pets by prior arrangement. Crib, babysitting. Spanish spoken.

GOVERNMENT CAMP

For an additional area entry, see listing for **Timberline Lodge** in **Timberline**.

Falcon's Crest Country Inn   *Tel: 503–272–3403*
87287 Gov't Camp Loop Highway   800–624–7384
P.O. Box 185, 97028

From quarrying the rock for the woodstove hearth and exercise room floor to the installation of the cedar ceilings and walls, Melody and Bob Johnson had their hands full with the design and construction of this chalet-style inn. Their work has paid off: the home fits in perfectly with the natural surroundings of the Cascades. Guest rooms are individually decorated around a theme—the Cat Ballou has a satin and lace comforter and brass bed, the Safari has wicker pieces accented with animal-print fabrics, and the Master Suite is outfitted with an antique four-poster bed and a Victorian settee.

"The owners were kind, friendly, hospitable and gracious. Rooms are beautifully maintained with antique and reproduction furnishings, and are extremely clean with quality soaps and lotions. Guests are awakened at the requested time with a choice of juice and muffins, followed by a delicious full breakfast." *(Linda Gorrill)* "B.J. is a chef who obviously enjoys his work and is a great storyteller." *(Frederick Teed)* "Prompt response to all requests. A serene atmosphere in the woods." *(Mark Nugen)* "Located on Mt. Hood and surrounded by national forest. The inn itself has wildlife of several kinds eating bread off the decks." *(Linda Hunter)* "For dinner we had shrimp in dill sauce; tomato bisque soup; pot roast with potatoes, carrots, celery, and mushroom gravy. To top it all off—chocolate cheese-cake." *(Mary Yegge, and others)*

From the "Nothing's Perfect" department: "Parking can sometimes be tricky; we played musical cars in the morning. A regulator would be nice to keep water temperatures from fluctuating during a shower. I would love to be able to make a cup of coffee, tea or cocoa during the day."

Open All year.
Rooms 2 suites, 3 doubles—all with private bath and/or shower, telephone, desk, balcony/deck.
Facilities Dining room, breakfast room, living room with woodstove, TV/VCR, books; hot tub. Parking for 5 cars. Downhill, cross-country skiing nearby.
Location 54 m E of Portland. Take Hwy 26 E to town.
Restrictions No smoking. Older children welcomed, toddlers discouraged.
Credit cards Amex, Discover, MC, Visa.
Rates B&B, $85–169 suite, double. Extra child, $15. 2–3-night weekend/holiday minimum. Prix fixe dinner, by reservation, $7–22. Ski, holiday packages. Multiple night discount.
Extras Station pickup. Limited babysitting.

GRANTS PASS

Grants Pass is located in southwestern Oregon, three hours south of Eugene, and a departure point for many raft trips on the Rogue River. Other activities include hiking, fishing, and jet boat rides.

For an additional area entry, see **Merlin**, 10 miles to the north.

Ahlf House Inn B&B ¢   *Tel:* 503–474–1374
762 N.W. Sixth Street, 97526   800–863–1374

Built by Johan Ahlf in 1898, this Victorian home was restored as a B&B in 1987. Ken and Cathy Neuschafer purchased it in 1993 and have decorated with period antiques and reproductions, with a soft floral theme in many of the wallcoverings and fabrics. Possible morning entrée include stuffed French toast with ham, baked eggs, frittatas, and Belgian waffles with sausage; fruit, muffins, scones, homemade cinnamon rolls, juice and coffee complete the daily menu.

"Ken and Cathy are warm and gracious, making you feel right at home. We appreciated Cathy joining us for breakfast. Spotlessly clean; careful attention to detail." *(Mark Durstenfeld)* "Great breakfast of orange French toast, ginger muffins, fresh fruit, and enjoyable conversation." *(Lisa Gallagher)* "Excellent service, cleanliness, plumbing, and convenience." *(Marcia Lembcke)* "Our hosts were helpful with area activities and entertainment. Convenient parking. Robes in our room were a nice touch." *(David & Kathy Himelrick)*

Area for improvement: "Better bedside lighting."

Open All year.
Rooms 1 suite, 4 doubles—all with private bath and/or shower, radio, clock, air-conditioning. Most with TV. 1 with Jacuzzi, refrigerator, balcony.
Facilities Dining room, living room, family room with TV, games, books; laundry facilities, balcony; gift shop. 1/3 acre with off-street parking.
Location 2 blocks from historic district. From I-5, take exit 58. Turn on Sixth St. Inn on right.
Restrictions Some street noise in front room. No smoking. Children over 10 preferred.
Credit cards MC, Visa.
Rates B&B, $50–65 suite, $55–85 double, $50–80 single. Extra person, $10. Senior, AAA discount.

Home Farm ¢ &.

157 Savage Creek Road, 97527

Tel: 503–582–0980

A tree-lined, white-fenced drive leads to the small farm where Cheri and Bill Murray have created a homey, comfortable B&B within walking distance of the Savage Rapids Park and the Rogue River. Furnishings include hand-stitched quilts and a considerable collection of country crafts and collectibles. Shady trees, porches and decks provide quiet spots for relaxing; a horseshoe game is set up in the pasture. A hearty breakfast with fresh eggs from the hen house is served family style around the handmade trestle table in the breakfast room. Included on the menu are biscuits and gravy, Murray's French toast, quiche and sticky rolls, served with melon or berries from the garden, with juice, coffee and tea.

"Cheri gave us a warm welcome and a tour of the house. The Green Apple room was comfortable, spotless and airy with an adjoining bathroom, supplied with fresh towels daily. Breakfasts were delicious with fresh raspberries and cherries from the farm. The swing on the porch was the perfect place to relax and enjoy the mountain view." *(Theodore & Geraldine Dilts)* Comments welcome.

Minor niggle: "I hated to move Cheri's darling decorations, but needed room for my toiletries."

Open All year.
Rooms 1 suite, 3 doubles—all with private bath and/or shower, radio, clock. 2 with desk, porch; 1 with fan. 2 rooms in bunkhouse.

Facilities Breakfast room, living room with fireplace, TV/VCR, stereo, books; screened porch with swing, deck. 4½ acres with barn, garden, horseshoes, pastures. Walk to Savage Rapids Park and Rogue River for water sports. Golf nearby.
Location From I-5, take Exit 48 W over Rogue River to Hwy. 99. Turn right (N), go 2.7 m to Savage Creek Rd. Turn left, go .1 m to inn on left.
Restrictions No smoking. No children under 10.
Credit cards None accepted.
Rates B&B, $65–70 suite, $50–70 double. Extra person, $10. Corporate rate.
Extras Wheelchair access, bathroom equipped for disabled. Crib.

HALFWAY

Birch Leaf Farm ¢ ♙
RR #1, Box 91, 97834

Tel: 503–742–2990

In case it's not immediately apparent to you—it certainly wasn't to us—Halfway is roughly equidistant from the Hells Canyon and Eagle Cap Wilderness National Recreation Areas. Representing over 3,000,000 undeveloped acres, you might well call it halfway to nowhere, perhaps one of its greatest charms. Birch Leaf Farm is an 1896 farmhouse owned by Maryellen and Dave Olson since 1978. They've updated their home with modern insulation, wiring, and outdoor decks, while preserving the original wainscoting, banisters, and pine flooring. Maryellen notes that "birdwatchers find this transitional area—between the Pacific and the Rockies—to be particularly fascinating." Breakfast includes homemade breads, whole wheat biscuits, eggs "from our own free-range organic chickens," fresh fruit, and yogurt.

"Dave and Maryellen know and love the area, and share it with their guests." (E. Abernathy) "Beautiful natural surroundings with a long list of activities. Wonderful homemade bread and jams, fresh-picked fruits, and superb coffee. Excellent information about the best fishing holes, local eateries, and river-rafting trips." (Dalia Bryant) "Maryellen greeted us with a pitcher of cold lemonade and freshly baked cookies. Rooms are clean, comfortable, with plenty of space and light." (Susan Caldwell) "A day's hike down to Hell's Canyon is a must." (Amali Dissanayake)

Open All year.
Rooms 4 doubles share 2 baths. Separate studio sleeps 4, private bath. All with radio, desk.
Facilities Dining room, breakfast room, living room with piano, TV, library. 42 acres with ponds, orchard. Cross-country skiing from door; 5 m to groomed trails. Wilderness llama tours, pack trips, horseback riding, white-water rafting, canoeing, hiking, bicycling, hunting, fishing nearby.
Location NE OR. 50 m E of Baker. 5 m from town. From Hwy. 86, turn N to go through town 2.5 m to Jimtown store. Bear right past store onto gravel road and go 2 m to inn.
Restrictions No smoking.
Credit cards MC, Visa.
Rates B&B, $50–65 double, $40–50 single. Extra person in room, $15. No tipping. Senior, family, AAA discounts.
Extras Horses boarded.

HOOD RIVER

Reader tips:"Hood River is a world class center for wind surfing, and several shops in town rent and sell boards. A drive up Mt. Hood to the Timberline Lodge makes a nice trip, with plenty of places along the way to stop for day hikes. My favorite was the day trip on the Hood River Railroad in an open-air railroad car up through orchards of the Hood River valley to the base of Mt. Hood. Day trips to the Bonneville Dam, the Maryhill Museum (on the Washington side of the gorge), and drives, walks, or bicycle rides up the Columbia Gorge Highway will keep you fully occupied." *(Allen Dietz)*

Information please: Overlooking the river, the **Hood River Hotel** (102 Oak Street, 97031; 503–386–1900) is a restored turn-of-the-century hotel with 41 suites and doubles, each individually decorated and furnished with reproduction four-poster beds. The hotel has a popular lobby bar and a restaurant which serves traditional and Mediterranean-style meals. Double rates range from $55–95. More comments welcome.

Also recommended: About 20 miles upriver is the **Williams House**, (608 West Sixth Street, The Dalles, 97058; 503–296–2889), an elaborate Victorian home built in 1899 and listed on the National Register of Historic Places. Just a short drive from I-84, its three air-conditioned guest rooms are furnished with Victorian and Georgian antiques, and B&B double rates range from $55–75. "A peaceful house on a grassy hill surrounded by big trees, just a short drive to town." *(JR)* "The Dalles is the cherry capital of the U. S. and not far from the Maryhill Museum. Gracious and informative hosts; breakfast was delicious and beautifully served on the veranda." *(Paul Rothman)* "The master suite has a small bedroom with four-poster bed and a larger sitting room with fresh cut flowers and a beautiful view of the grounds. The bathroom has the original marble, an oversized Victorian bath tub, and plenty of fluffy towels." *(Jennifer O'Neill)*

Columbia Gorge Hotel 🛏 ✕ ♿
4000 West Cliff Drive, 97031

Tel: 503–386–5566
800–345–1921
Fax: 503–386–3359

A hotel was first built on this site in 1903 when guests arrived from Portland via steamers traveling the Hood River. In 1920 Oregon lumber magnate Simon Benson was instrumental in having the dirt road to Portland paved and developed into a scenic highway. He purchased the old hotel, tore it down, and completed the Columbia Gorge Hotel in 1921. Dubbed the "Waldorf of the West," it boasted indoor plumbing for every room, manicured grounds, and excellent cuisine. Fully renovated in 1989, the hotel is now listed on the National Register of Historic Places. Its dining room has a good reputation and features food of the Pacific Northwest—salmon and sturgeon, venison and pheasant.

"Perched at the edge of a cliff 200 feet above the Columbia River Gorge, with Washington on one side, and Mt. Hood towering over the hotel on the Oregon side, this hotel has been beautifully restored with

rniture and decorations of the Jazz era. A creek meanders through the
eautifully landscaped grounds and tumbles over Wah-Gwin-Gwin falls
ext to the hotel. Our attractive room was spacious and airy. The classic
lorthwest dining was excellent; our favorites were the salmon and the
ame dishes; the apple torte is a must. The trademarked 'World Famous
arm Breakfast' took us an average of two hours to complete, and included
ll of the following: huge platters with 30 kinds of fruit; juice; apple
ritters; oatmeal with brown sugar and cream; three eggs cooked to order;
rispy bacon, smoked pork chop, apple and maple pork sausage; golden
ash browned potatoes; homestyle baking powder biscuits with honey;
uttermilk pancakes with hot maple syrup; and freshly brewed coffee."
Allen Dietz) "Our table had a beautiful view of the falls. The food was
xcellent and the presentation superb." *(Joy Sugg)*

"The lounge, named for Rudolph Valentino, a frequent guest in the
otel's early days, is decorated with lovely 1921-era furniture." *(John
McGary)* "A few super rooms—the corner room near the waterfall is the
est in the house." *(Laura Scott)* "Highlights of this hotel are its grounds,
he library/bar, and the fantastic restaurant." *(LNT)* "This area is tremen-
ously busy in summer, especially with rafters, so advance bookings are
dvised." *(Sally Ducot)*

Areas for improvement: "Our mattress was creaky and should have
een replaced." And: "Disinterested young desk personnel."

Open All year.
Rooms 4 suites, 42 doubles—42 with full private bath, telephone, TV, desk, fan.
with a maximum of 6 sharing bath. 2 with fireplace.
Facilities Restaurant, lounge with fireplace, piano music nightly in season, ball-
oom. 5.5 acres with formal gardens, waterfall, bicycles. Hiking, fishing, river
afting, tennis, golf, sailing, windsurfing nearby. 35 m to downhill, cross-country
kiing.
Location N central OR, at the WA border. 60 m E of Portland. 1 m from Hood
iver. From Portland, take I-84E to exit 62, Hood River.
Restrictions Traffic noise from interstate in some rooms. No smoking in dining
oom.
Credit cards Amex, DC, Discover, MC, Visa.
Rates B&B, $210–345 suite, $150–195 double. Extra person, $45. Prix fixe lunch,
15; alc dinner, $45. Full breakfast (for nonresident guests), $23.
Extras Wheelchair access. Airport/station pickup, fee charged. Pets by prior ar-
angement. Crib, babysitting. Spanish spoken.

JACKSONVILLE

acksonville was founded in 1851, following the discovery of gold in Rich
Gulch. Today the town is a National Historic Landmark, with over 75
estored pioneer buildings to see and visit. Music also lures people to
acksonville for the Peter Britt Festivals held every summer, featuring a
vide variety of music and dance, from classical to bluegrass. Jacksonville
s located in southwestern Oregon, 5 miles north of Medford and 21 miles
orthwest of Ashland.

Reader tip: "Pick up a copy of a 'Walk through Time' from the gift

shop at the Jacksonville Inn, thoroughly describing the important hom
and commercial buildings of the town. The Bella Union restaurant, house
in an 1870s building, is excellent for lunch or dinner, with an inform
atmosphere, good desserts and a full bar." *(William Novack)* Several rea
ers commented on the fine meals at the **McCully House Inn**, open dai
for dinner in summer and brunch on Sunday. This restored 1861 mansic
is located on the edge of the shopping and restaurant district.

Also recommended: Just north of town, the **Colonial House** (184
Old Stage Road, P.O. Box 1298, 97530; 503–770–2783 is set on five acr
and flanked by spreading oak trees; the two large suites have peric
furnishings and private bath. A breakfast of omelets, homemade muffir
and local fruits, as well as tea at 4 P.M. is included in the $95–110 rate
"We stayed in the spacious Bridal Suite with a four-poster queen-size be
and a large sitting area. Phil and Arlene Sadler were friendly and helpful.
(Stephanie Roberts)

A mile north of town is the **Old Stage Inn** (883 Old Stage Road, P.C
Box 579, 97530; 503–899–1776 or 800–US–STAGE), a Greek Reviv
farmhouse built around 1857 with 11-foot ceilings and elaborate plast
moldings. The two parlors and four guest rooms are beautifully decorate
with formal Victorian furnishings. A three-course breakfast featuring far
fresh produce and freshly baked breads, and evening turndown servic
with bedside chocolates are included in the double rates of $75–11
Comments?

Jacksonville Inn ✕

175 East California Street, P.O. Box 359, 97530

Tel: 503–899–190
800–321–934

The Jacksonville Inn, owned by Jerry and Linda Evans since 1979,
housed in one of Jacksonville's earliest permanent structures. Built in 186
the walls of the dining area and lounge were built of sandstone quarrie
locally, and specks of gold are scattered throughout the mortar. Favorit
dinner entrées include chicken in phyllo pastry with mushrooms, prim
rib, and seafood fettuccine. The breakfast menu offers such choices ᴀ
scrambled eggs with vegetables and cheese, accompanied by poache
pears, brioche, and sauteed red potatoes; or Belgian waffles with fres
berries and whipped cream.

"Our room was quiet and clean, with a firm, comfortable bed. Lovel
quilts and pillow shams, with in-room coffee and tea. Excellent food, wit
friendly, helpful staff." *(Laura Scott)* "The eight rooms upstairs are done i
casual frontier style with exposed brick walls and country antiques. Roor
#1 has a four-poster canopy bed, and is more spacious than the other
Great fun to enjoy a wonderful dinner and then just retreat upstairs to
cozy room." *(Pam Phillips)* "Fully endorse existing entry." *(William Nc
vack)*

Open All year.
Rooms 1 cottage, 8 doubles—all with private bath and/or shower, TV, radic
air-conditioning, refrigerator. 1 double with Jacuzzi. Cottage with Jacuzzi, stear
shower, sauna, TV/VCR/stereo, fireplace.
Facilities Lobby, dining room, breakfast room, bar/lounge with guitar musi
weekends. Off-street parking.

Location In center of town at intersection of Applegate Road.

Restrictions No smoking in guest rooms. Fire engines might disturb light sleepers.

Credit cards Amex, DC, Discover, MC, Visa.

Rates B&B, $175 cottage, $90–125 double, $60–100 single. Extra person, $10. Alc breakfast $6–9; alc dinner, $20. Children's menu.

Extras Airport/station pickup.

MCMINNVILLE

Information please: The **Mattey House** (10221 N.E. Mattey Lane, 97128; 503–434–5058) is an 1892 Queen Anne Victorian home, set behind its own small vineyard, with four guest rooms appropriately named after wine grapes. Breakfast includes homemade breads, fresh fruits and egg specialties. Oregon wines and appetizers are served in the evening. "Antiques, fresh flowers, and plush bathrobes added charm and comfort. Great location for country walks and wine tasting at local wineries." *(BNP)*

Youngberg Hill Farm Inn
10660 Youngberg Hill Road, 97128

Tel: 503–472–2727
Fax: 503–472–2727

A contemporary farmhouse built in 1989, the Youngberg Hill Farm Inn is owned by Eve and Norm Barnett. A working farm and vineyard, the activities flow with the seasons—lambing in March, blackberry picking in August and September, the grape harvest in October—but all year long guests can enjoy the beauty of the Willamette Valley. A country breakfast is served from 8:30–9:30 A.M. at the large dining room table; lunches and dinners are available by prior arrangement.

"Heading up a large hill to the farmhouse, a field of lambs was on the right and vineyards spread before us. In the evening cheese and crackers or fruit is laid out. A small refrigerator in the dining room offers iced tea, lemonade and an honor bar with wine. Guest rooms have beautiful replica antique beds and bureaus; a hall closet is filled with amenities often forgotten—shampoo, iron, rubbing alcohol, and more. Our corner room had large windows that opened to pleasant country sounds, and comfy swivel chairs. Breakfasts were a delight: the first morning baked apples were wrapped in puff pastry, followed by waffles with walnuts and fresh strawberries. The next day, the meal started with yogurt and granola; then came one strudel filled with meats, onions, and potatoes, and a second stuffed with berries. We walked the logging trails behind the inn, watched the sunset through the woods, and peeked into the barn to see baby chicks, and two little lambs who were being bottle fed. Norm and Eve were helpful with area activities. Dinner at Nick's Cafe in town is a must." *(Lynne Derry)* "Beautiful setting, great breakfast. Five-star dinner nearby at Nick's." *(Lois Mateus)*

Open All year.

Rooms 1 suite, 4 doubles—all with private bath and/or shower, clock, air-conditioning. 2 with fireplace.

Facilities Dining room with refrigerator, living room with fireplace, family room with TV/VCR, porch. 50 acres with parking, hiking trails. Golf nearby.

Location NW OR. 40 m SW of Portland. 10 m from town. From Rte. 18, take second McMinnville exit, marked 99W McMinnville, Corvallis. Go right, past Texaco station, then bear left to stop sign. Go straight onto Old Sheridan Rd. for 1 m to Peavine Rd. Turn right, then go 2 m to Youngberg Hill Rd. Turn left & go 1 m to inn's sign & entry. Wherever a choice, go up hill. Enter through gate & close behind you.

Restrictions No smoking. Children over 10 preferred because of machinery & electric farm fence.

Credit cards Discover, MC, Visa.

Rates B&B, $125 suite, $100–125 double, $95–120 single. Extra person, $25. 2-night special event minimum. Massage, cooking, birding weekends. Prix fixe lunch, $12–15; dinner, $25–37.

Extras Crib. Limited German spoken.

MERLIN

Pine Meadows Inn
1000 Crow Road, 97532

Tel: 503–471–6277
Fax: 503–471–6277

Former San Francisco residents Maloy and Nancy Murdock report that "after a long search, we built this inn in 1991, working alongside our crew, doing the landscaping and decorating ourselves." Breakfast is served at the lace-draped dining table, using organic, natural, and cholesterol-free ingredients as much as possible. Entrées range from oatmeal spice waffles with apricot syrup, to vegetable frittata with mushrooms, asparagus, and onions; guests who prefer a light meal can enjoy a parfait of yogurt, fresh fruit, and granola served with muffins or breads. Guest rooms are charmingly decorated with country Victorian pieces, soft florals, and quilts in a color scheme of white, pink, and blue or green.

"Comfortable beds and spacious bathrooms. Spotlessly maintained with state-of-the-art plumbing and lighting." *(Donn & Margaret Wells)* "Gracious hospitality—friendly, caring, and efficient hosts, dedicated to having their guests relax, enjoy, and be comfortable." *(Richard Starr)* "Our room was light and airy with comfortable chairs and bed, with good lighting for reading. Rooms are quiet; we could not hear other guests. The porch with wicker rockers was a favorite." *(Cheryl Clark)* "The outstanding feature was the peace, beauty and serenity of the woods." *(Robert & Catherine Fox)*

Open All year.

Rooms 3 doubles—all with full private bath, telephone, clock, air-conditioning, fan. 1 with desk.

Facilities Dining room, living room with fireplace, stereo, books; wrap-around porch. 9 acres with hot tub, koi pond, hiking. 1 m to Rogue River rafting, fishing, boating. 1 hour to downhill skiing.

Location SW OR. 45 m N of Ashland, 10 m N of Grants Pass. 2 m from town. From I-5, take Exit 61. Go W on Merlin/Galice Rd. for 5 m & turn right on Crow Rd. Go 1 m to inn on left.

Restrictions No smoking. Children over 8 preferred.

Credit cards None accepted.

Rates B&B, $95–110 double.

NEWPORT

Newport, on the central Oregon coast about 120 miles southwest of Portland, has been a popular resort and fishing town for over 100 years. Visitor attractions include the Devil's Punchbowl, a rock formation that fills with a roar at high tide; the OSU Science Center and Aquarium; and the restored Yaquina Bay lighthouse.

Ocean House B&B   *Tel:* 503–265–6158
4920 N.W. Woody Way, 97365   800–562–2632

Overlooking the surf at Agate Beach is the Ocean House B&B, long-time home of Bob and Bette Garrard. The guest rooms look toward the sea, and the owners will show you the short private trail leading to the beach and tidal pools. Garden decks offer additional views and a relaxing spot for reading or picnicking. Coffee awaits early risers and a full breakfast is served at 9 A.M. in the sunny breakfast room.

"The focal point of the living room is the colorful coastal garden and the Pacific Ocean with its spectacular sunsets. Comfort prevailed in our first-floor room, with good lighting, comfortable chairs, and ample storage space." *(Betty Norman)* "Perched on a spectacular Oregon coastal bluff, steps from a mile-long sandy beach. You can gaze for hours at the windsurfers, fishing boats, and migrating whales in season. Bob is an inveterate gardener, while Betty is a serious artist whose works are on display in the house." *(Jack & Irene Kavanagh)* "Bob is a kind, humorous man who is a wonderful conversationalist and storyteller." *(Marlene Carlan)* "Comfortable rooms, good breakfast, stunning views." *(William Mac-Gowan)*

Open All year.
Rooms 4 doubles—all with private bath and/or shower.
Facilities Living room, breakfast room, porch, decks. 1 acre with flower gardens. Golf, fishing, surfing nearby.
Location 3 m N of center of town, S of Yaquina Head lighthouse.
Restrictions No smoking. No children.
Credit cards MC, Visa.
Rates B&B, $75–115 double.

Sylvia Beach Hotel ¢ ✕ &.   *Tel:* 503–265–5428
267 N.W. Cliff Street, 97365

Newport has many beaches, but you will search in vain for one called Sylvia. This beachfront hotel, aptly described as a cliffhanger by its literary owners, is named for Sylvia Beach, owner of the legendary Paris bookstore Shakespeare and Company, and first publisher of James Joyce's *Ulysses*. The inn was built between 1910 and 1913 as the New Cliff House and has National Landmark status. Rooms, named for different authors, are decorated either in period style or based on the author's books. Tea, coffee, and wine are served in the library at 10 P.M. Breakfast, served buffet-sytle from 8:30–10 A.M. includes a variety of juice and fruit, cereal, fresh-baked cinnamon rolls, plus a hot entrée to order: eggs, quiche, *huevos rancheros,* German or poppy seed pancakes, or French toast. Dinners are served family style at tables of eight, with one seating at 7 P.M. Sunday through Thursday and two (at 6 and 8:30 P.M.) on weekends. A recent dinner included herbed cheese tarts, salad, rosemary blue cheese bread, halibut with cilantro ginger sauce, and Black Forest cake. Many of the guest rooms have queen-sized beds and ocean views.

"You can talk books at meals, outwit other guests at games in the lobby, or read quietly in the third-floor library. If you get there early you can tour the rooms; if not, friendly fellow guests will probably trade you a tour of their 'Oscar Wilde' for your 'Mark Twain.' " *(Kathryn & Bob Gearheard)* "At meals guests sit wherever space is available, so you are usually with different people each time—everyone talks to everyone else. I enjoyed the book-lined attic lounge looking out to the beach and the Pacific." *(Eileen O'Reilly)* "Delicious sea scallops in onion sauce highlighted our wonderful dinner." *(Deborah Brockman)* "The Agatha Christie was very English country, the Jane Austen somewhat austere, and the Melville was, of course, nautical. The Poe room even has a raven." *(DCB)* "The Oscar Wilde room is quite small with a single bed, and a pull-out trundle bed underneath." *(EOR)*

Area for improvement: "Our room was ready for sprucing up."

Open All year. Closed 1st two weeks of Dec.
Rooms 3 suites, 17 doubles—all with private bath and/or shower. 11 with desk. 3 with fireplace, balcony.
Facilities Dining room, library with fireplace, music occasionally; gift shop, lobby with puzzles, deck. ½ acre on 4 m of beach for fishing, hiking, whale watching, bicycling. Swimming, tennis nearby.
Location ½ m from center. From Hwy. 101, turn W on NW 3rd and follow it down to beach where it meets Cliff St.
Restrictions No smoking. "Not suitable for young children."
Credit cards Amex, MC, Visa.
Rates B&B, $125 suite, $55–87 double, $45–77 single. Extra person, $15. 2-night weekend minimum. Prix fixe dinner, $15–25.
Extras 1 room has wheelchair access; bathroom equipped for disabled. Crib.

PORTLAND

Oregon's largest city, Portland straddles both sides of the Willamette River near its confluence with the Columbia. A friendly, manageable city, Portland is known for its parks and its lively arts scene. Over 160 parks and public gardens dot the area, including the 5,000-acre Forest Park, the largest wilderness preserve located within the limits of any U.S. city. Portland's vigorous public arts program includes the Saturday market that brings over 300 quality craftsmen and performers together every weekend from April through Christmas. In September you can visit "Artquake," when downtown streets are closed for lively displays by artists and entertainers. Don't miss the March kite-flying contest, the antique shops lining N.E. 13th Avenue in Old Sellwood, or the Skidmore/Old Town Historical District with its mix of people, ethnic restaurants, and funky shops.

Although city regulations limit Portland's B&B inns to three guest rooms, the ones listed here are in fact much more spacious than the room count would normally suggest. From Portland, it's about a 1 1/2-hour drive west to the ocean and a 1-hour drive to the east for skiing. The Columbia and Willamette River recreation areas are about 15 minutes away for swimming, fishing, sailboarding, and tennis courts and golf courses are in ample supply.

Reader tips: "A Portland institution since 1862, Jake's offers old-fashioned atmosphere, rich mahogany paneling, delicious seafood, and don't-miss hot three-berry cobblers, topped with ice cream (401 S.W. 12th Street; 503–226–1419)." *(RSS)* Also: "Dan & Louis Oyster Bar serves succulent Yaquina Bay oysters, crab Louis, and fried seafood platters. Attentive homey service, reasonable prices. After dinner, visit Powell's City of Books, covering an entire city block; it's open until 11 P.M." *(Mark Mendenhall)* "Portland is loaded with coffee bars; we enjoyed the Three Lions which tempts patrons with wonderful whole wheat scones with raspberries or apricots. Also the Red Wagon." *(Carolyn Myles)*

Also recommended: The **Heron Haus B&B**, (2545 N.W. Westover Road, 97210; 503–274–1846), has a quiet hilltop location, yet is only blocks from the restaurants and shops of northwest Portland. The common rooms of this English Tudor built in 1904 are ample and spacious, most done with contemporary flair. The guest rooms have Hawaiian names and decorative touches, and the suite with private inside hot tub has fabulous views of the city below and Mt. Hood in the distance. Outside, guests may enjoy a swim in the pool. Both the local paper and the *New York Times* arrive every morning with a continental breakfast included in the rates. "We had a large room with two sitting areas and a huge bathroom-dressing area. Julie Keppeler is a charming and accommodating innkeeper. Great location for the best Portland shops and restaurants." *(Margaret Sievers)*

The recently renovated **Imperial Hotel** (400 Southwest Broadway at Stark, 97205; 503–223–7221 or 800–452–2323) has state-of-the-art amenities including refrigerators, computer/modem hook-ups and a daily newspaper at your door, plus vanity mirror/hairdryers and fluffy thick towels. B&B double rates for the 136 rooms range from $65–80.

Information please—hotels: Although it led the way in Portland's historic hotel "boom," we need current reports on elegant **The Heathman Hotel** (S.W. Broadway at Salmon Street, 97205; 503–241–4100 or 800–551–0011), built in the late 1920s and listed on the National Register of Historic Places. It was almost completely gutted and rebuilt in 1984. Now a full-service luxury hotel, its amenities include terry bathrobes and thrice daily maid service; the 151 rooms are furnished in warm earth tones, many with an Oriental motif, and highlighted by original artwork. Its highly acclaimed restaurant serves three meals daily, specializing in northwestern cuisine.

Another restored historic hotel of note is **The Benson** (309 Southwest Broadway, 97205; 503–228–2000 or 800–426–0670), built in 1913 in the French Baroque style. Observing the maxim, "if it's not baroque, don't fix it," the hotel was renovated in 1993 at a cost of $20 million. The common areas are elegant once again, and the 290 suites and doubles comfortable with traditional decor. Double rates range from $140–205.

An elegantly furnished luxury hotel with 35 suites and 39 doubles,

Riverplace (1510 S.W. Harbor Way, 97201; 503–228–3233 or 800–227–1333) is part of Portland's Riverplace Esplanade. Hotel amenities include continental breakfast, terry bathrobes, overnight shoe shine, and morning newspapers.

Information please—B&Bs: The **Georgian House B&B** (1828 N.E. Siskiyou, 97212; 503–281–2250) was built in 1922 and restored in 1987; the inn features leaded windows, a winding staircase, built-in china cabinets, oak floors, sunporch, and fireplace. There are three guest rooms, children are welcome, and the rates of $65–85 include a full breakfast. In the historic Irvington district is the **The Lion and The Rose** (1810 Northeast 15th Street, 97212; 503–287–9245 or 800–955–1647), a renovated 1906 Queen Anne Victorian home with six guest rooms. Guest rooms have private and shared baths, period furnishings, and the rates of $70–110 include a full breakfast served between 7:30–9:30 A.M., with coffee available at 6:30 A.M.

The Governor Hotel ♦ ✕ ♿.
611 S.W. Tenth at Alder, 97205

Tel: 503–224–3400
800–554–3456
Fax: 503–241–2122

Listed on the National Register of Historic Places, the Seward Hotel was built in 1909 at the height of the Arts and Crafts movement; resulting public rooms have lavish architectural detail and fascinating painted surfaces. After a $15 million renovation joined it with the equally historic Princeton Building next door, the hotel re-opened in 1992 as the Governor; George Forbes is the manager. Decor incorporates original details with newer Art Deco and Art Modern flourishes; wall sconces are replicas of a 1940s mica-and-bronze light fixture. Furnishings have a definite 1920s-ish appearance—overstuffed chairs combined with streamlined wooden pieces.

"A wonderfully, elegant hotel. Our sixth floor corner room in the west wing, although not large, was beautifully furnished in soft greens and had a large deck with an incredible view of the city and Mt. Hood. Excellent ventilation, plus electronic thermostats temperature control; comfortable bed, with excellent lighting for reading. The hotel restaurant, Celilo's, served outstanding Northwest cuisine in innovative and creative manner. Wonderful 'Jazz Age' lobby with a large mural depicting the Lewis & Clark expedition; high ceilings and burnished wood add to the luxurious atmosphere." *(Carolyn Myles)* "My standard double room was sparely furnished with a wood-framed bed, night stands on each side, a contemporary desk in the corner, a chaise lounge and a floor lamp by the door; the atmosphere was comfortable and relaxing, and a newspaper was left outside the door early each morning. Courteous, efficient staff. Dinner was well prepared, the service good." *(William Novack)*

Area for improvement: "The large closet served as a bureau, but it needed a light." Also: "Valet parking wasn't always prompt."

Open All year.
Rooms 32 suites, 68 doubles—all with full private bath, telephone, radio, clock, TV, desk, air-conditioning, fan, mini-bar, fax/modem hookups. 23 with fireplace, 8 with balcony/deck, 7 with whirlpool tub.

acilities Restaurant, dining room, living room/lobby with fireplace, porch.
Meeting room, business services. Thurs.–Sat. classical guitar, jazz entertainment.
alet parking, athletic club with indoor heated swimming pool.
ocation Downtown Portland in historic district. Between S.W. Alder & S.W.
Morrison Sts.
estrictions Possible traffic noise. No smoking in restaurant, 50% of guest rooms.
hildren under 10 not permitted access to health club, swimming pool.
redit cards All major cards.
ates Room only, $175–500 suite, $165–275 double, $145–275 single. Extra
erson, $20; children under 7, free in parents room. Senior, AAA discount. Alc
inch, $12; alc dinner, $30.
xtras Full handicap accessibility; some rooms equipped for hearing impaired.
rib, babysitting. German, French, Japanese, Chinese, Russian, Filipino spoken.
Vestin Hotels/Resorts.

Iotel Vintage Plaza ✗ &.
22 S.W. Broadway, 97205

Tel: 503–228–1212
800–243–0555
Fax: 503–228–3598

Moving north from his San Francisco base, hotelier Bill Kimpton has
cored once again with a boutique luxury hotel. In 1991, he purchased the
mperial Hotel, a red-brick Renaissance-style building built in 1894; al-
hough the exterior was left unchanged, the interior was fully restored.
"ypical of his California hotels, the Vintage Plaza has about 100 rooms,
 fine restaurant, and a theme: rooms are named for Oregon vineyards,
nd a wine-tasting is held nightly. Standard doubles are on the small side,
ut most are decorated in burgundy and dark green with gold highlights;
ther rooms are done in pastels. Rates include wine-tasting each evening,
vernight shoe shine, nightly turndown service, morning coffee, muffins
nd orange juice, and the daily newspaper; the Concierge Level rooms
ave soaking tubs, conservatory windows for stargazing, and a private
ounge for evening cocktails and hors d'oeuvres. The hotel restaurant,
'azzo, serves Northern Italian cuisine; possible entrées include grilled
hicken with arugula; pasta with lamb sausage, and lamb chops with
sparagus and fennel risotto.

"Within walking distance of many shops and restaurants; also a good
ocation for business travelers. Service is excellent—when the room I had
eserved was taken, I was switched to a suite with three large rooms, full
ar, a huge Jacuzzi, lots of towels and robes, elegant furnishings and
eriod engravings on the wall." *(KMC)* "A gem—elegant, wonderfully
omfortable, with warm, friendly hospitality. You are pampered, espe-
ially on the floors with a private concierge; exceptional Northern Italian
uisine." *(EB)*

Open All year.
Rooms 107 suites & doubles—all with full private bath, telephone, TV, mini-bar.
acilities Restaurant, lobby with fireplace, bar/lounge with pianist, atrium, con-
ierge level living room, gym and business center. Off-street parking, $9.
ocation Downtown. From airport, take Hwy 205 S to Hwy 84 W. Follow signs
narked "City Center" to Morrison Bridge to Washington St. Go 7½ blocks to
ark Ave. & turn right. Go 1 block to Stark & turn right. Go 1 block to Broadway
k turn right to hotel on left.
Restrictions Some no-smoking rooms.

Credit cards All major cards.
Rates Room only, $190–205 suite, $120–175 double. Alc dinner, $25–30.
Extras Member, Kimco Hotels.

MacMaster House ¢

1041 S.W. Vista Avenue, 97205

Tel: 503–223–736
Fax: 503–224–880

Located in the historic King's Hill neighborhood—one of Portland
wealthiest at the turn of the century—the MacMaster House was built
the 1880s in the Queen Anne style. Some 20 years later the house w
remodeled as a Colonial Revival, with the addition of a colossal portic
with Doric columns and Palladian windows with leaded glass. Owne
Cecilia Murphy has furnished her B&B with an unusual mix of Europea
antiques, African furnishings, Asian wicker, and works by Oregon artist
Sourdough French toast with powdered sugar and fresh blueberries a
among the many breakfast specialties.

"Calming and comfortable from the beautiful bed linens, the speci
arrangements of antiques to the large, soft bath towels. Close to a wo
derful walking path and great shopping; the bus stops right in front." *(Ga
Pearson)* "The ever-changing breakfasts feature wonderful local fruits, nu
and berries. A friendly and casual place." *(Debbie Chung)* "Cecilia is accom
modating and gregarious, creating a convivial atmosphere." *(Adam Plat*
"Eclectic is the best way to describe the decor of the main sitting room
which has an animal skin rug under a desk, chairs with faux fur covers, a
old settee and chairs with black on black fabric, and a little table and cha
set that looks like it belongs in an ice cream parlor." *(SC)* "An enthusiast
cook came up with different delicious breakfast menus each morning
(Daniel Kane)

Open All year.
Rooms 2 suites, 3 doubles, 2 singles—2 with full private bath, 5 with maximu
of 4 people sharing bath. All with TV, air-conditioning; some with fireplace, des
balcony.
Facilities Living room, dining room, library, guest refrigerator, veranda, patio.
blocks from Washington Park for jogging, tennis.
Location King's Hill. 16 blocks from center.
Restrictions No smoking. No children under 14.
Credit cards Amex, MC, Visa.
Rates B&B, $115 suite, $80 double, $65 single (midweek). Extra person, $2
Monthly rates.

Mallory Hotel ¢ 🛏 ✕

729 S.W. 15th Avenue at Yamhill,
97205

Tel: 503–223–631
800–228–865
Fax: 503–223–052

"Regulars" love the Mallory for its old-fashioned, unglitzy charm an
excellent rates. A comfortable older hotel, its rooms are adequately deco
rated; one correspondent suggested better lighting and more variety t
the food, but found it her favorite on all other counts.

"The staff has been there since time immemorial and leave only whe
it's time to retire." *(Victor Christensen)* "I've been traveling on business fo
many years and have never felt comfortable in any other hotel's cockta
lounge; the Mallory's warm and gracious atmosphere puts me at ease.

(Carole Moscari) "The lobby is quite attractive with deep greens predominating, glass, gilt, and cream." *(SC)* "The check-out time of 2 P.M. is extremely generous." *(Mark Mendenhall)* "Appreciated the pull-out clothesline over the bathtub and newspaper at the door." *(Betty Norman)* "The living room furnishings in our suite looked handed down from Grandmother. Our corner bedroom had great ventilation; loads of closet space; a comfortable king-size bed with good reading lights; shower with reliable water pressure; lots of shelf space and good lighting in the modernized bath. Room service delivered our coffee promptly. Nat and Dell's is a little diner one block away, serving tasty waffles and a bracing cappucino." *(Carolyn Myles)* "The staff remembers 'regulars' and makes one feel welcome. An excellent value." *(Stephen Holman)*

Minor niggles: "The sofa bed in our sitting room listed to port and the carpet was a worn shag." And: "The restaurant seemed large and hushed with dim lighting, even in the morning." Also: "Some doubles are quite cramped."

Open All year.
Rooms 13 suites, 131 doubles—all with full private bath, telephone, radio, TV with cable, desk, air-conditioning, fan. Some with refrigerator.
Facilities Restaurant, lounge, 2 parking lots.
Location 5 blocks from downtown. 2 blocks W of I-405.
Credit cards Amex, CB, DC, MC, Visa.
Rates Room only, $100 suite, $60–100 double, $55–70 single. Extra person, $5. 1 child under 12 free in parents' room. Alc breakfast, $3–5; alc lunch, $5–7; alc dinner, $16–18.
Extras Crib. Spanish spoken.

SEASIDE

Oregon's largest and oldest ocean resort, Seaside offers numerous activities, including beachcombing; deep-sea, stream, and lake fishing; clamming and crabbing; plus tennis, golf, bicycling, and horseback riding. Seaside is on Oregon's north coast about 80 miles northwest of Portland (via Route 26) and 17 miles south of the Columbia River. Seattle lies 170 miles to the northeast.

Reader tip: "Bicycle, rollerblade, or stroll all along the Prom for breathtaking views." *(EVL)*

Also recommended: Although a bit small for a full entry, the three-guest room **Beachwood B&B** (671 Beach Drive, 97138; 503–738–9585) is enthusiastically recommended by *Pam Phillips*: "Lovely accommodations and friendly innkeepers, Paul and Susie Nass. Their restored 1910 craftsman bungalow is beautifully done. The Arbor Room in front features green print chintz, lots of pillows, and a window seat with views. The Holladay Suite is great, especially for winter visits, with a canopy bed, sitting room, and double Jacuzzi." The inn is one block from the South Prom and beach, and the $60–110 B&B double rates are reasonable for quality accommodation.

Ellin Van Leeuwen recommends the **Seaside Inn** (581 South Promenade, 97138; 503–738–6403 or 800–772–PROM) on the southern, quieter end of the promenade, two blocks from the Turnaround, and with beautiful

OREGON

views from the front rooms. Each room is decorated with a different theme and has a fireplace, TV, telephone, air-conditioning and most with a whirlpool tub. Double rates of $90–175 include a full breakfast.

Information please: Built in 1898, **The Boarding House B&B** (208 North Holladay Drive, 97138; 503–738–9055) was one of a handful of buildings that escaped the fire of 1912. Restored as a B&B in 1983 by Barb Edwards, modern insulation, plumbing, and wiring add modern comfort; lots of white gingerbread trim and an inviting wraparound porch add a touch of yesterday. A typical breakfast might include orange juice, fresh strawberries with mint, pecan cinnamon coffee cake, egg strata with sausage. "Close to Seaside's attractions, yet quiet and peaceful." *(Mary Kay Santore)*

Two blocks from the beach, overlooking the Necanicum River, **Rita Mae's** (486 Necanicum Drive, 97138; 503–738–8800), is a spacious, modern home with four guest rooms, two with a private bath. Rita Mae handcrafts large porcelain dolls which are displayed around the house. A full breakfast and evening tea or hot chocolate are included in the double rates of $65–79. A few miles north off Route 101, the **Gearhart Ocean Inn** (67 N. Cottage, Gearhart, 97138; 503–738–7373) is a short walk to the beach and offers eleven units, most with kitchens, at double rates of $49–65. "Quiet, clean, simply furnished rooms in a good location away from the tourist areas. Great for families." *(Diane Crawford)*

Gilbert Inn ¢ 👫   Tel: 503–738–9770
341 Beach Drive, 97138

Alexander Gilbert, one of Seaside's founding fathers, donated land for the first South Promenade and built several buildings on Broadway including this Queen Anne-style home. Owners Carole and Dick Rees have put in a lot of work—painting, redoing the bathrooms, adding queen-sized beds, and sprucing up the decor throughout. Adjacent to the inn are four luxury condo units, called Arindale's Accommodations.

"Beautiful 1880s Victorian with the original tongue-in-groove paneling. The inn has a wood-paneled sitting room; an airy plant-filled sun porch; and a parlor with full-length lace curtains, country French furnishings, and a fireplace." *(Mary Robinson)* "Though Emma's Room is the smallest, it was comfortable, with a glimpse of the ocean. The home is elaborately decorated with antiques and a very large cat, named Gilbert, usually adorns the couch." *(Deborah Brockman)* "Wonderful full breakfast with hosts careful to include all guests in conversation while respecting their need for privacy. Superior cleanliness. Seaside is a noisy beach town but the inn's setting is such that a quiet night's sleep is easy. Great location for walking or bicycling on the promenade. Beautiful Victorian landscaping." *(Ann Brookshe)*

Open Feb. 1–Dec. 31.
Rooms 4 2-bedroom condos, 2 suites, 8 doubles—all with full private bath, radio, TV. 3 with desk.
Facilities Breakfast room, parlor with fireplace, sitting room with organ, sun porch. Off-street parking. Beach with 3 m promenade for skating, bicycles, surreys nearby.
Location 1 block from ocean. From S, on Hwy. 101, turn left at "City Center"

sign, left at "A" St. to inn on left. From N on Hwy. 101, turn right on Ave. "B" (2 blocks S of light), go straight to ocean, inn on left.
Restrictions No smoking. "We ask Mom and Dad to decide if children will fit in our setting."
Credit cards Discover, MC, Visa.
Rates B&B, $110 condo, $85 suite, $69–79 double, $64–80 single. Extra person, $10. 2–3-night weekend/holiday summer minimum. Weekly rates.
Extras Local airport/station pickup. Crib, babysitting.

Riverside Inn ¢ 🚶 ♿

430 South Holladay Drive, 97138

Tel: 503–738–8254
800–826–6151

The Riverside Inn was built in 1907 and was restored as a B&B in in 1982. Ken and Sharon Ward are the long-time owners. Rooms are decorated with original art, lace curtains, flowers, and quilts. Breakfast is served in the dining area, on the deck, or in the guest's room. "Private baths and a separate entrance provide privacy and seclusion. Our room had a supply of salt-water taffy, fresh flowers and amazingly comfortable beds. Breakfast masterpieces included banana and toasted pecan pancakes, fresh strawberry French toast, smoked salmon quiche and home-made roast beef hash with eggs, all served with freshly squeezed orange juice, seasonal fruit, home-baked breads and muffins, and delicious coffee." *(Ann Pritchard)* "Sharon and Ken went out of their way to make our stay pleasant." *(Dean Wells)* "Comfortable and friendly; prices are excellent; excellent area information." *(Margaret Young)* "Each room has a special theme, especially in the main house, and the linens and furnishings add to the warm, comfortable feel." *(Debra Huff)*

Open All year.
Rooms 4 suites, 7 doubles—all with private bath and/or shower; radio, TV, fan. Some with desk. 7 with kitchen or kitchenette. 4 rooms in annex, 3 in attached cottages.
Facilities Dining/library/game room. ½ acre with riverfront deck, off-street parking. 3 blocks from Pacific Ocean.
Location 2 blocks to downtown. From N, turn right (W) off Hwy. 101 on Broadway, turn left at Holladay, go 2 blocks to inn on right. From S bear left off Hwy. 101 onto Holladay.
Restrictions No smoking.
Credit cards Discover, MC, Visa.
Rates B&B, $70–85 suite, $49–70 double. Extra person, $10; children under 3 free in parents' room. 2–3-night weekend/holiday minimum. Midweek, off-season packages.
Extras Several rooms with wheelchair access. Airport/station pickup. Crib, babysitting.

SHANIKO

Shaniko Historic Hotel ¢ 🚶 🍴

4th & E Street, 97057

Tel: 503–489–3441

The Shaniko Hotel opened in 1902 during some of the last range wars between cowboys and sheepmen; the two-story building was constructed of handmade brick with walls 18 inches thick. Trade boomed when

Shaniko was the largest wool shipping center in the U. S.; business died when the railroad arrived in Bend—not Shaniko. Today the town stands nearly empty with abandoned buildings and only a handful of full-time residents. The hotel was bought by Dorothy and Jean Farrell in 1985, and was restored as a B&B and restaurant. The restaurant is open for three squares a day; burgers, salads, and sandwiches make up the lunch menu dinner includes such roadhouse classics as turkey with dressing, pork chops, and chicken-fried steak. Homemade pies are a specialty.

"The rooms have been modernized, but the lobby still has its old charm. The restaurant serves good, substantial food." *(Sherrill Brown)* "The town is great fun, old and ghost-townish; the hotel is a no-nonsense restored period piece. At check-in, you get little wood tokens to use in paying for your breakfast of eggs, pancakes or French toast. The spacious lobby has a big ceiling fan, life-size carved sculptures of an Indian and a cowboy, and an upright piano. Rooms are simple but clean, with reproduction antique chairs, and oak iceboxes used as night stands. After dinner, we relaxed in rockers on the front porch." *(Suzanne Carmichael)*

Open All year.
Rooms 1 suite, 16 doubles—all with private bath, fan. Suite with Jacuzzi.
Facilities Restaurant, lobby, porch. Rafting, hiking, rockhounding nearby.
Location N Central OR. 75 m N of Bend, 60 m S of The Dallas, 50 m S of Wasco On Hwy. 97.
Restrictions No smoking.
Credit cards MC, Visa.
Rates B&B, $86 suite, $56 double, $46 single.
Extras Crib.

STEAMBOAT

Steamboat Inn ✗ ♿
Highway 138, 97447-9703

Tel: 503–498–2411
503–498–2411*2
Fax: 503–498–2411

The Steamboat Inn offers fine cuisine, elegantly rustic accommodations and world-famous steelhead trout fly-fishing. This section of the North Umpqua River has long been the favorite fishing spot of such notable sportsmen as Zane Grey and Jack Hemingway. Owners Jim and Sharon Van Loan note that "while many of our guests do come for the challenging fishing, others enjoy the wilderness beauty, comfortable accommodations, and the inn's acclaimed food." Waiting until one half hour after sundown so that anglers can make that last cast, the late evening dinner is served family-style. A recent meal began with an aperitif and spicy chicken wings, followed by red snapper with lime marinade, tomato salad with basil vinaigrette, green chili and corn soufflé, broccoli with sesame butter, herb cheese bread, and ended with rhubarb upside-down cake. Accommodations range from the pine-paneled cabins with original artwork sharing a common veranda to the "hideaway" cottages located ½ mile upstream from the lodge, to more luxurious River Suites which have soaking tubs "with a wilderness view."

282

"Beautiful stretch of river, with steep, rocky, and forested slopes. Our private, attractive cabin had a wood-paneled bathroom with soaking tub and a skylight to let you see the rain and stars, and a well-stocked fireplace. It is better to drive the ½ mile distance to the inn than walk because there's no shoulder on this logging road. The cabins have the advantage of being on the river with its constant roar, so you don't hear the trucks going by. We never fished and found the beauty, quiet, and food, pleasure enough." *(Bill & Amy Barnett)* "The communal seating encourages socializing." *(Donna Brown)* "Good lighting for reading." *(Jack & Priscilla Weaver)* "All details were perfectly executed. Fabulous food and excellent Oregon wine." *(Lois Mateus)* "The Falls Room is our favorite." *(J. Spencer)*

Suggested improvement: "Break the ice by serving appetizers and wine in the library while guests are waiting for dinner to start. Eating at 9:30 P.M. was a bit hard on eastern-time-zone tummies."

Open Mar. 1–Dec. 31. Restaurant closed midweek in winter.
Rooms 2 suites, 8 cabins, 5 cottages—all with private bath and/or shower, deck. Some with fan. Suites, cottages with fireplace, soaking tub, kitchenette.
Facilities Dining room with fireplace, sun room with games, library with TV, porch. 2 acres on North Umpqua River for fishing. Fly-fishing equipment shop, guided fishing excursions. Hiking, creeks for swimming, winery tours nearby.
Location SW OR, Umpqua National Forest, foothills of Cascade Mts. 105 S of Eugene, 38 m E of Roseburg, 70 m NW of Crater Lake. From Roseburg take Hwy. 138 E 38 m to inn.
Restrictions No smoking in public rooms, some guest rooms. Traffic noise in some rooms.
Credit cards MC, Visa.
Rates Room only, $210 suite, $135 cottage, $95 cabin. Extra person, $20. Prix fixe dinner, $30 (with wine).
Extras Limited wheelchair access. Crib, babysitting.

TIMBERLINE

For an additional area entry, see listing for **Falcon's Crest** in Government Camp.

Reader tip: "Mt. Hood could be a great place to hike but the trails were not well marked and the trail maps inadequate."

Information please: The **Timberline Lodge** (Timberline Ski Area, 97028; 503–272–3311 or in OR, 800–452–1335 or in western US 800–547–1406) is a famous historic lodge dating back to the 1930s. Set at an altitude of 6,000 feet, it sits in the shadow of Mt. Hood, Oregon's tallest peak (11,235 feet). A WPA project, it provided jobs for dozens of unemployed janitors, blacksmiths, and carpenters. Although most of them had no training as craftsmen, the hand-forged iron chandeliers and gates, hooked rugs and draperies, hand-carved wooden newel posts, and stained glass windows remain as an impressive testimony to their skills. Built on a massive scale, its main lobby is highlighted by a stone chimney over 100 feet high. After considerable restoration work and renovation of both the guest rooms and common areas, the lodge appears today much as it was when Franklin Delano Roosevelt dedicated it in 1937. Double rates range from $90–160 for the 60 suites and doubles. Facilities range skiing in winter to hiking and water sports in summer. Some recent comments on the food and service have varied. Most recently: "All the grandeur of the Ahwahnee or El Tovar but on a more intimate scale and much better run, too. The dining room was excellent." *(Gene & Roberta Altshuler).* Other recent comments on the food and service have varied.

YACHATS

Pronounced "YAH-hots," this central Oregon coast resort village (140 miles southwest of Portland and halfway between Newport and Florence) offers miles of rocky shoreline and dense forest. Its uncrowded beaches are a favorite with rockhounds (looking for agates, jasper, and petrified wood), beachcombers, fishermen, and clamdiggers. Perhaps best of all is watching the surf pound against the rocky cliffs, especially dramatic during winter storms. South of town, walk to the stone lookout on Cape Perpetua, highest point on the Oregon coast, or follow the hiking trails into the rain forest or along the coast to the sea lion caves, 13 miles to the south.

Also recommended: The **Adobe Resort Motel** (1555 Highway 101 North, P.O. Box 219, 97498; 503–547–3141 or 800–522–3623) offers rooms done in the original adobe as well as more modern ones, plus a handsome restaurant of adobe brick and rough-hewn cedar beams, known for its romantic setting and excellent seafood. Rooms have picture windows to take in the gorgeous ocean views, perfect for whale and storm watching. "A clean, neat motel in a great location with friendly service, excellent catch-of-the-day fish dinner." *(Ruth Tilsley)* The **Shamrock Lodgettes** (P.O. Box 346, 97498; 503–547–3312 or 800–845–5028) has well-equipped motel units with standard modern decor and sliding glass doors, plus rustic log cabins, with stone fireplaces, pine furniture, and fully equipped kitchens. Cabin rates range from $86–106, while motel rooms run $67–90.

Fireside Motel ¢ 🏃 ♿   *Tel:* 503–547–3636
1881 Highway 101 North, P.O. Box 313, 97498   800–336–3573

Managers Bob and Jane Nores explain that the Fireside has two wings: Oceanview rooms face out to the ocean, with direct views of the surf crashing on the basalt ledge 80 feet away; second-floor Northview rooms look up the coastline; and the downstairs units have little or no view. The Fireside is a great choice for dog lovers, since pets are permitted. "Plain and simple with privacy, ocean views, terrific walks, fireplaces, comfortable beds, and friendly staff." *(David Ryan)* "Clean, spacious, well-furnished room (our dogs were equally clean and well-groomed)." *(Samantha & Doug Hickman)* "During whale season, the motel loans binoculars. They also have books, games and puzzles for family fun. The office keeps menus and phone numbers of nearby restaurants." *(Leah Mattison)* "Room 40 was large enough for a sitting area facing the wonderful rocky coast." *(Betty*

Norman) "The distance from the highway eliminates traffic noise, and we heard no noise from other units." *(Ellen & Herbert Schweizer)* "Wonderful walking paths above the beach with comfortable glider-type chairs to sit on." *(Mr. & Mrs. Arthur Sautter, and others)*

Area for improvement: "A dog was barking for hours; we got flea bites in our room."

Open All year.
Rooms 2 suites, 42 doubles, 3 cabins—all with full private bath, telephone, TV, desk, refrigerator, coffee maker; some with fireplace. 1 with jacuzzi.
Facilities 7 acres on beach for fishing, boating, birding.
Location 1 m from center, on Hwy. 101 N.
Restrictions No smoking in some guest rooms.
Credit cards Discover, MC, Visa.
Rates Room only, $95–125 suite, $57–79 double. Extra person, $5. Senior, AAA discount Oct.–mid-May. 2-night holiday minimum. Discount for 7-night stay.
Extras Limited wheelchair access. Pets permitted, $4. Crib, $4.

The Oregon House ¢ 🏃 ♿   Tel: 503–547–3329
94288 Highway 101, 97498

Owners Joyce and Bob Freeman joined the migration north from California in 1987 and bought the Oregon House, salvaging it from years of misuse as a hippie "crash pad." One major restoration later, guest rooms, some with brass and iron beds (all queen- or king-size), have a country decor, accented with wicker and collectibles. The little cottages scattered about the grounds have full kitchen facilities.

"The isolated beach provides a background for glorious, romantic sunsets." *(Jean Rees)* "Warm hospitality from every member of the Freeman family." *(Bernice Malnati & Lucille Dupuis)* "Joyce and Bob were helpful with suggestions for interesting activities. Our kids loved the inn's friendly cats." *(Dawn Hayden)* "Cottages are quiet, private, and attractive, with a beautiful oceanside setting." *(Timothy Scot Peterson)* "The owners are friendly, hospitable, and accommodating." *(Annette & René Miranda)* "The main building and some of the cottages are constructed of white painted concrete block; others are wood framed. The cliff is dotted with windswept cedars; on one side a creek tumbles down a rock path toward the ocean. A lighted path leads down the bank to a beach studded with driftwood and rocks." *(SC)*

Open All year.
Rooms 5 buildings, each with 1–3 housekeeping suites or doubles—all with private bath and/or shower, ceiling fan. Most with kitchen, deck, barbecue grill. 5 with fireplace, 3 with Jacuzzi tub. 1 B&B double with Jacuzzi bath, balcony, use of living room with fireplace.
Facilities 3 1/2 acres with children's play equipment, picnic area. 1 1/2 m of private ocean beach with tidepools, caves. Tennis, golf, fishing nearby.
Location 8 m S of Yachats. 15 m N of Florence.
Restrictions No smoking. Well-behaved children of any age permitted in some cottages; under age 12 must be supervised at all times while outdoors.
Credit cards Discover, MC, Visa.
Rates Room only, $70–110 suite, $45–71 double. B&B, $85 double. 2–3-night minimum weekends/holidays. Outside guests, $4 per person daily.
Extras Limited wheelchair access.

Sea Quest B&B
95354 Highway 101, P.O. Box 448, 97498

Tel: 503–547–3782

Elaine and George Ireland bought this contemporary, weathered cedar house in 1990 and renovated it to provide comfortable guest rooms with unobstructed views of the crashing surf. An eclectic decor fills the house—antiques, comfy sofas and chairs, leafy plants. Breakfast is served buffet-style at a choice of tables, and usually two hot entreés are offered along with homemade granola, large platters of fruit, coffee cakes, muffins, juices and coffee.

"The second floor living room has a fireplace covering an entire wall, and games, books, and collectibles from around the world to explore. Soft music played and we were always welcome to sit and read or talk. Our downstairs room was cozy yet roomy; we melted into our comfortable bed, and a toasty comforter kept us warm as we listened to the crashing surf through the open sliding glass door. Elaine put coffee on at 6 A.M. for early risers; breakfast was delicious. George and Elaine made us feel right at home; terrific restaurant recommendations and suggestions for shopping and sightseeing." *(Rebecca Pfeifer & Bill Gibson)* "Country-style furnishings, with a comfortable homey feel. Bathrooms display George's wonderful, colorful tilework. The location is convenient to hiking trails, sea lion caves, parks, and miles of ocean sand." *(Cheri Larson)*

Open All year.
Rooms 5 doubles—all with private bath and/or shower, private entrance. 4 with whirlpool tub.
Facilities Dining room, living room with fireplace, stereo, games, books; deck. 2½ acres with lawn games. On bluff above beach.
Location 6 m S of Yachats. On Hwy. 101 between mile markers 171–172.
Restrictions No smoking. Children over 14 preferred.
Credit cards MC, Visa.
Rates B&B, $105–245 double. 2–3 night weekend, holiday minimum.

Free copy of *INNroads* newsletter

Want to stay up-to-date on our latest finds? Send a business-size, self-addressed, stamped envelope with 52 cents postage and we'll send you the latest issue, *free!* While you're at it, why not enclose a report on any inns you've recently visited? Use the forms at the back of the book or your own stationery.

Washington

Log Castle B&B, Whidbey Island

About the only things eastern and western Washington have in common are a governor and a shared border, the Cascade mountain range. Western Washington, dominated by water and mountains, includes most of the state's population and scenic highlights: the Olympic Peninsula, Puget Sound, the San Juan Islands, and the Cascade Mountains and volcanoes.

The Olympic Peninsula The large central core of this peninsula is a vast wilderness incorporating the world's only temperate rain forest and the glaciers, peaks, and rugged terrain of the Olympic Mountains. Going west toward the Pacific Ocean, a national wildlife refuge, four Indian reservations, and delicate archaeological digs make public access to the ocean difficult. The north side of the peninsula faces the Strait of Juan de Fuca and is known for Victorian Port Townsend, the Manis Mastodon Site, and 6 mile Dungeness Sandspit, home to over 250 species of birds. Hood Canal and its nearby parks form the eastern edge of this varied peninsula. Access to the Pacific is found southeast of the peninsula between Ilwaco and Pacific Beach. Here you can walk the 28-mile Long Beach, dig for clams, go deep-sea fishing, or fly kites. Virtually the only road on the peninsula is Route 101, often referred to as the Olympic Loop.

Puget Sound Puget Sound extends like a giant thumb into the center of western Washington. Most of the state's population lives along its eastern shore, from Olympia north to Seattle and Everett. In Tacoma, visit 698-acre Point Defiance Park to survey its extensive flower gardens, forest roads, and outstanding views. Scuba divers can don their gear to visit the extensive network of underwater parks.

In the spring be sure to see the acres of blooming daffodils and tulips in Skagit Valley north of Everett. If you're heading up to British Columbia, get off the freeway at Burlington and take scenic Route 11, which hugs the coast and provides gorgeous views of the San Juan Islands.

The Islands of Puget Sound   You can't get the real flavor of Puget Sound until you get out on the water and explore some of the islands. An easy afternoon's outing from Seattle is a round trip on one of the ferries linking urban Washington to nearby commuter islands (Vashon or Bainbridge).

Or board the Mukilteo-Clinton ferry to Whidbey Island and then drive north through rolling farmlands, past sandy beaches, to impressive Deception Pass. For another glimpse of lazy island living, hop on a small ferry west of Bellingham and stay overnight on Lummi Island. For a full-fledged island experience, head up to the San Juan Islands. Poking their pine-ridged noses above water between the Washington mainland and Canada's Vancouver Island, the San Juans can fulfill almost any vacation fantasy from remote hideaways to snazzy spa resorts, from beachcombing and whale watching to browsing in art galleries.

The Cascades and Volcanoes   Every bit the equal of the Colorado Rockies, the rugged, snowcapped Northern Cascade Mountains (Route 20 from Marblemount to Winthrop) are at their best during the fall, when the leaves change color. In the central Cascades you can ski, hike, fish, see 268-foot high Snoqualmie Falls, and visit Leavenworth, a "Bavarian" village. To the south the Cascades are interrupted by 14,410-foot Mt. Rainier, offering rock and glacier climbing, cross-country skiing, spring wildflower bonanzas, and summer hiking. Also plan to visit Mt. St. Helens National Volcanic Monument to witness the devastation that occurred there on May 18, 1980. Call 360–274–2103 for a recorded message about days/hours the Monument is open; or call 360–247–5473 to speak to the Forest Service for additional information.

Eastern Washington   Although it includes two-thirds of the state, most of eastern Washington offers little to tourists. The exceptions are the Yakima Valley, center of Washington's Wine Country; Spokane, a lively city centered around a refurbished riverfront park; the resort areas surrounding 55-mile-long Lake Chelan; and rolling hills and lush vegetation of the Palouse country along Route 195 between Spokane and Colfax. In between these points, visitors will find miles of apple orchards, wheat farms, and desert. Worth stopping to see are the waterfalls in Palouse Falls State Park located south of Washtucna; Okanogan Valley ghost towns; the Ginkgo Petrified Forest east of Ellensburg; and, near Coulee City, the unusual Dry Falls that, in prehistoric times, was the site of a 3½-mile-wide, 400-foot waterfall. More recommendations for this area would be especially welcome.

Note: Summer is very much peak season in western Washington, especially in the San Juans; make reservations two to three months ahead to avoid disappointment, and don't expect to catch the first ferry that comes along.

ANACORTES

Anacortes is on Fidalgo Island, 2 hours south of Vancouver, British Columbia and 1½ hours north of Seattle via I-5 and Highway 20. From I-5 take Exit 230 to Anacortes and San Juan Ferry.

Albatross Bed and Breakfast ¢   *Tel: 360–293–0677*
5708 Kingsway West, 98221   800–484–9507, ext. 5840

People who like boats will especially enjoy the Albatross; just across the street is a marina and a charter boat company. A 1927 Cape Cod-style home with views south to Whidbey Island, the inn still has some of its original cedar walls and woodwork, accented with simple furnishings. Ken Arasim and Barbie Guay have owned the inn since 1992, and serve a hearty breakfast of Belgian waffles or omelets, accompanied with bacon or sausage, juice, and fresh fruit.

"A large home at the commercial edge of a quiet, pleasant neighborhood. Our large room had plenty of lighting, a king-size bed and a sparkling clean bathroom tucked into the original large closets; space to hang clothes and store luggage fit neatly along the wall. In the evening Barbie asked about any dietary restrictions, and took them into account when preparing breakfast. After touring Ken's garage of classic cars, and Barbie's collection of—you guessed it—Barbie dolls—we found that Ken had slipped out and wiped the morning dew off our car windows. They are warm, friendly people who make you feel instantly at ease." *(Dale Johnson)* "We stayed in the Scarlett O'Hara room with an 1860 southern-style canopy bed, and enjoyed a scenic cruise on their sailboat." *(Angele Schunken & Brian Vandenberg)* "Our attractive room had a view of the deer grazing outside." *(Don & Dolores Coleman)*

Open All year.
Rooms 4 doubles—all with private shower, radio, clock. TV available.
Facilities Living room with fireplace, TV/VCR, stereo; dining room, library, guest refrigerator, porch. ¼ acre with off-street parking, lawn games. 46' sailboat for sightseeing, crabbing; bicycle rentals. Tennis, hiking, golf, fishing, boating, scuba diving, beach for swimming nearby.
Location NW WA. 2 m from International Ferry Landing. Enter Anacortes, turn left onto 12th St. Go past Washington State Ferry Terminal (to San Juan Is.). Turn left on Skyline Way. Turn left again onto Kingsway to inn on left.
Restrictions No smoking. Children over 4 preferred.
Credit cards MC, Visa.
Rates B&B, $65–85 double, $60–80 single. Extra person, $15. Senior, AAA discount.
Extras Limited wheelchair access. Ferry/airport/bus station pickup. Pets by prior arrangement.

The Channel House ₵   Tel: 360–293–9382
2902 Oakes Avenue, 98221   800–238–4353

A Victorian home built for an Italian count in 1902, The Channel House is set on the Guemes Channel, and was purchased by Dennis and Pat McIntyre in 1986. An early morning coffee basket is delivered to your door, and breakfast is served in the dining room. In the evening, guests enjoy soaking in the outdoor hot tub, watching the boats and the sunset over Puget Sound.

"The first floor living room has old-fashioned, well-used, comfortable furniture; the library has a fainting couch, books, and games. Our spacious third-floor room had a sloping attic ceiling, a comfortable king-size bed covered with a great puffy comforter, a large bath with clawfoot tub and a gorgeous view of the San Juans; a silver tray stood ready with two champagne glasses. On the landing was a charming sitting area with a wheelbarrow filled with teddy bears, an old-fashioned dollhouse and a baby buggy. Breakfast included fresh melon with grapes, waffles topped with peaches and walnuts, and good homemade bread." *(Suzanne Carmichael)*

"Clean, quiet, and comfortable, despite fronting on the main road to the island ferries." *(Jim Bernat)* "Grandma's room is adjacent to the library; its antique brass bed had a log cabin quilt that belonged to Grandma McIntyre; the bath was tiny but adequate." *(BA)* "Great attention to detail, with a sewing kit, potpourri, bubble bath, extra lavender-scented towels, and robes to wear to the hot tub." *(Susan & Mary Kelly)* "Irish cream coffee and oatmeal raisin cookies were the perfect after-dinner snack." *(Chrys Bolk)* "It is hard to believe that two people can be a continuously cheerful as Dennis and Pat in a job that is so difficult." *(Gene & Roberta Altshuler)*

Open All year.
Rooms 6 doubles—all with private bath and/or shower, clock/radio. 2 doubles in cottage have fireplace, whirlpool tub; 1 with deck.
Facilities Living room, library, dining room, all with fireplace. Hot tub. Boating, fishing, hiking, golf, swimming beaches nearby.
Location NW WA. Enter Anacortes, continue right on Commercial Ave. to 12th St. (Chevron station on corner). Turn left to inn 1½ m on the right.
Restrictions Light sleepers may be disturbed by early ferry traffic. No smoking. Resident cat.
Credit cards Discover, MC, Visa.
Rates B&B, $69–95 double, $59–89 single. Extra person, $20. Off-season rates.
Extras Local airport/station pickups.

The Majestic Hotel 🛏 ✕ ♿   Tel: 360–293–3355
419 Commercial Avenue, 98221   Fax: 360–293–5214

This 1889 French Colonial-style building, originally housing mercantile shops and professional offices, was moved ½ mile in 1907 when it became apparent that the community's "downtown" was developing elsewhere. Virginia and Jeffery Wetmore bought the building in 1984; after stripping it to the framework, they spent the next six years developing The Majestic into an elegant English-style inn. The two-story open lobby features a grand chandelier and fine 19th-century English furniture.

The pub has a white marble bar that once served as a pharmacy soda fountain counter; the 200-year-old dark wood wainscoting and stained glass doors come from an old London pub.

"Our fourth-floor room opened to a large porch overlooking the harbor. It was well decorated in Ralph Lauren style, with well-maintained antiques and carefully chosen modern features. The bathroom was a delight: large vanity area, built-in magnifying mirror, and oversized tub. We enjoyed a breakfast of hot and cold cereal, fresh-squeezed orange juice, and warm croissants." *(Audrey Williams)* "Meticulous attention to detail; professional, friendly staff." *(Jodi Holihan)* "Our room had a distinct Japanese flavor, with rich dark woods and a red and black color scheme; the bathroom was done in jade green marble." *(Dallas Wolkenhauer)*

Open All year. Pub closed Mon., Tues.
Rooms 23 doubles—all with private bath and/or shower, telephone, radio, TV, ceiling fan. Most with refrigerator; some with balcony, soaking tub, desk.
Facilities Dining room, living room, library, pub. Enclosed English gardens, gazebo. Playground, ferry terminal, health club nearby.
Location NW WA. In town center.
Restrictions No smoking in public areas and non-smoking rooms.
Credit cards Amex, Discover, MC, Visa.
Rates B&B, $89–177 double. Extra person, $15. Children under 4 free in parents' room. 10% senior discount. Alc lunch, $10; dinner, $18.50.
Extras Wheelchair access; some rooms equipped for disabled. Local airport/station pickups. Babysitting, massages with advance notice.

ASHFORD

Also recommended: Within Mount Rainier National Park (approximately 20 miles east of Ashford), at an elevation of 5,000 feet, is the **Paradise Inn** (c/o Mount Rainier Guest Services, P.O. Box 108, Ashford 98304; 360–569–2275). *Duane Roller* reports that "it is one of the great, old railroad lodges built at the turn-of-the-century in rustic construction. While it has drawbacks (inundated with skiers, difficult parking, small rooms, overpriced dining room, with a pretentious but limited menu), for location it cannot be paralleled. The great mountain is just outside your window, everchanging in the daylight. It's just a few minutes walk to snow and glaciers." An expansive Sunday brunch is served in the enormous dining room in summer. The lodge is open from late May to early October, and the 126 simply furnished guest rooms, some with private bath, cost $60–115.

Dating back to 1912, **Alexander's Country Inn** (37515 State Road 706 East, Ashford 98304; 360–569–2300 or 800–654–7615) is the oldest structure in the Mt. Rainier area; the 13-foot waterwheel out front is a local landmark. The restaurant specializes in salmon fresh from the Tacoma docks, rainbow trout from the inn's ponds, homemade breads, and wild blackberry pies. The fourteen guest rooms have private and shared baths. "Our room was very comfortable, and breakfast was delicious. The kids enjoyed the hot tub. The desk clerk provided helpful area information." *(Robert Boas)*

Mountain Meadows Inn ¢   *Tel:* 360–569–2788
28912 State Route 706 East, 98304

When we call Chad Darrah's collection of railroading memorabilia "extensive" we really mean it. He has his own caboose and will arrange charters on it or in the cab of the steam train that travels the Mt. Rainier scenic railway between Elbe and Mineral Lake. The Mountain Meadows Inn is a comfortable 1910 farmhouse among the fir and cedar trees, overlooking a small trout pond. This area was once the company-owned town of National, operators of the largest sawmill west of the Mississippi. The mill closed about 50 years ago, and nature again has the upper hand. Today, guests can walk the trails through the town's remains. He cooks breakfast each morning on an 1889 vintage woodstove; home-grown eggs and pork are featured along with freshly ground coffee.

"Breakfasts of homemade muffins, fresh blueberry and banana pancakes, fruit, juice, and chemical-free sausage. Chad is a charming host always ready with a story from his days of logging, railroading, and fishing in Alaska." *(Dee Montpetit)* "Train buffs will love this place." *(Donn & Janet Franklin)* "Comfort and privacy, reservations for restaurants and the local masseuse." *(Jeannamarie & Geoffrey Luce)* "Simply furnished rooms, with some interesting antiques and collectibles. One is drawn to the pondside campfire or the porch, joining lively conversations with the owner, staff, and other guests." *(Stefanie Seltzer)*

Area for improvement: "Updated carpeting, brighter lights for reading."

Open All year.
Rooms 2 suites, 5 doubles—5 with private bath and/or shower—2 with a maximum of 4 people sharing bath. All with radio. 2 with desk, refrigerator, or deck. 4 rooms in annex.
Facilities Dining room with player piano, living room with TV/VCR, veranda. Live music some evenings. 14 acres with trout pond for fishing. Cross-country skiing on site. Rainier National Park nearby.
Location W WA, 50 m SE of Tacoma. 1/4 m from town.
Restrictions Smoking in common areas only. No children under 11.
Credit cards MC, Visa.
Rates B&B, $55–95 suite, double; $50–60 single. Extra person, $15. 10% senior, AAA discount. 2-day holiday/weekend minimum.

BAINBRIDGE ISLAND

Bombay House ¢   *Tel:* 206–842–3926
8490 Beck Road, 98110   800–598–3926

Overlooking Rich Passage, Bombay House is a turn-of-the-century home, set high on sloping lawns and encircled with porches and flowers; Bunny Cameron and Roger Kanchuk are the owners. "The aroma of brewing coffee and muffins baking is followed by a breakfast with whole grain cereals, just-baked goods, fresh fruit, juices and jellies. We watched the birds, and glimpsed the ferry as it winds through nearby Rich Passage. The rooms are neat, clean, and comfortably furnished. Bunny, Roger, and their daughter, Cameron, were friendly, polite, and helpful in guiding us to great local restaurants, activities, and the charming shops in the little town of Winslow." *(Johnnie & Donna Schell)*

"Perched on a hill on this slow-paced country island with forests and open spaces—seemingly a million miles away from Seattle's hubbub. Our spacious second-floor suite, with woodstove, claw-foot tub, and comfortable sitting areas, covered the whole front of the house." *(MB)* "Despite terrible weather, power failures, and phone outages we had a wonderful stay." *(Mr. & Mrs. Norman Rice)*

Open All year.
Rooms 1 suite; 4 doubles—3 with private bath and/or shower, 2 with maximum of 4 sharing bath. All with desk, air-conditioning; 1 with fan, fireplace.
Facilities Living room with fireplace, piano; kitchen/breakfast room, porches. ½ acre with flower gardens. Swimming, fishing, boating, clamming, hiking, tennis, golf, bicycling nearby.
Location W WA. Puget Sound, 35 min ferry ride W of Seattle. 4 m SW of Winslow. From downtown Seattle, take Winslow ferry. Go left on Winslow Way, right on Madison, left on Wyatt, right at the "Y" in the rd., 0.4 m past elementary school, take sharp right on W. Blakely & go right on Beck. Inn at corner of Beck and West Blakely. Agate Pass Bridge (Rte. 305) links island to Poulsbo, Bremerton, Olympic Peninsula.
Restrictions No smoking. No children under 9.
Credit cards Amex, MC, Visa.
Rates B&B, $125 suite, $55–85 double, $50–80 single. Extra person, $15.

BELLINGHAM

Snuggled along the northwest shore of Puget Sound, Bellingham is definitely worth a stop on the way from Seattle to Vancouver. Getting to this midsize town with a Victorian flavor and a smattering of counterculture shops and eateries is half the fun: Route 11 between Burlington and Bellingham winds prettily along the wooded shore, providing outstanding views of the San Juan Islands. The town is home to Western Washington State University. Recommended stops include a stroll among the contemporary sculptures scattered about the University campus, a self-guided tour of its Victorian homes (call 360–733–2900 for a brochure), and a browse through the Old Town antique shops.

Bellingham is located in the northwest corner of Washington, 40 miles south of Vancouver, BC, and 90 miles north of Seattle, easily accessible via Interstate 95.

Information please: Overlooking Lake Whatcom, **Schnauzer Crossing** (4421 Lakeway Drive, 98226; 360–733–0055 or 800–562–2808), offers a cottage, a suite, and a double room for two-legged visitors, in addition to a private tennis court, hot tub, and use of the canoe. "Our suite was decorated in Danish modern furnishings, and had a mini-kitchen with a microwave, refrigerator, coffee maker and a nice selection of snacks. There was a goosedown comforter on the bed, and terry robes to wear to the hot tub. Owner Donna McAllister served a wonderful breakfast with fresh blueberry cobbler, bran muffins, fruit parfaits, and bagels. The two schnauzers were lots of fun." *(Georgia & William Hoover)* B&B rates from $110–185.

North Garden Inn ¢
1014 North Garden Street, 98225

Tel: 360–671–7828
800–922–6414
In Canada: 800–367–1676

To a handsome 1897 Queen Anne Victorian home with comfortable guest rooms—some with superb views of Bellingham Bay—the North Garden Inn adds another ingredient, music. Barbara and Frank DeFreytas, who restored the inn in 1986, offer guests the chance to listen to, sing along with, or play one of the two grand pianos in the house or in Frank's teaching studio. Barbara orchestrates events in the kitchen, and even grinds her own flour for specialty breads and coffee cakes, scones and muffins; other treats at breakfast are croissants with chocolate cream cheese, curried rice with sausage and scrambled eggs, and fresh fruit with yogurt. "Full of music, from the rooms named for instruments to the impromptu musical entertainment liable to break out any time. The De-Freytas's are gracious and ready with ideas on where to eat and what to do. Mrs. DeFreytas is a whiz at homemade baked goods." *(Steve Denzel)* Comments please.

Open All year.
Rooms 8 doubles—all with private bath and/or shower, radio. Some with desk, deck.
Facilities Dining room, sitting room with games, living room with grand piano, library, stereo, fireplace. Rose garden and fountain. Music entertainment occasionally. Lake nearby for water sports. 1 hr to downhill, cross-country skiing.
Location 7 blocks from downtown. From I-5 take exit 253 to Lakeway Rd. Go W to stop at 3-way intersection of Ellis and Holly Sts. Bear right on Holly. Continue to North Garden St. Go left 3 blocks and left again. Parking for inn in alley on right.
Restrictions No smoking. No children under 11.
Credit cards MC, Visa.
Rates B&B, $54–69 double; $49–59 single. Extra person, $10. Christmas packages.
Extras Airport/station pickup. Some French spoken. Member, WBBG.

BLAINE

The Inn at Semi-Ah-Moo 🏃 ✕ ✈ ♿
9565 Semiahmoo Parkway, 98230

Tel: 360–371–2000
U.S.: 800–770–7992
CA: 800–542–6082
Canada: 800–631–4200

Set on a spit of land surrounded by water on three sides, the Inn at Semi-Ah-Moo is a resort hotel, opened in 1987 on the site of the Alaska Packers Association's Semiahmoo Cannery. The simple four-story buildings are reminiscent of the straightforward style of the original cannery, a theme continued inside with the pine floors and exposed beams. Semi-

294

Ah-Moo means either "half-moon bay" or "he who sits beside the shore eating oysters." Seafood is a specialty, from the local oysters, to the salmon, shrimp, and swordfish served in the dining room. Star, the restaurant's name, derives from the original tall ships of the Star Fleet, which sailed the Pacific coast from the 1860s to the 1920s. Packer's Oyster Bar offers local seafood at lunch and dinner, while the R&R restaurant serves a simple broiler menu at dinner and a popular Sunday Champagne brunch.

"The main dining room served excellent oysters, duck and game hen. Dinner in the Oyster bar consisted of steamed clams, a raw vegetable platter, and grilled hamburgers—all with close-up views of the fishing boats returning to the harbor. Reception, room service, dining room staffing and grounds upkeep were all excellent." *(W.A. Grant)* "Staff was like family—friendly and helpful. Housekeeping was excellent." *(Calvin Clemons)*

Open All year.

Rooms 12 suites, 184 doubles—all with full private bath, telephone, radio, TV, desk. Some with fireplace, VCR, balcony.

Facilities 2 restaurants, oyster bar/lounge with entertainment, meeting rooms. 800 acres with indoor tennis, racquetball, squash courts, health club, running track. Indoor/outdoor swimming pool, golf, marina, bicycle path. Boat tours of San Juan Islands, saltwater sport fishing trips.

Location NW WA, on Puget Sound. 100 m N of Seattle, WA. 50 m S of Vancouver, BC. 25 m N of Bellingham, WA. From Seattle or Vancouver, take I-5 to exit 270, turn west on Birch Bay-Lynden Road. Go 3 m to Harbor View Rd., turn right. Continue 1 m to Lincoln Rd. & turn left, follow signs to inn.

Restrictions Smoking in specified rooms only.

Credit cards Amex, CB, Discover, MC, Visa.

Rates Room only, $190–260 suite, $115–240 double. Extra person, $20. Family rate. 25% AARP discount. Romance packages. 2-night weekend minimum May–Oct. Alc breakfast, $4–10, alc lunch $12, alc dinner, $15–35.

Extras Wheelchair access. Bus service from Seattle, Vancouver hotels. Crib. Spanish, German spoken.

BREMERTON

Bremerton, the northern home of the U.S. Navy Pacific fleet, is a hilly peninsula formed by Puget Sound to the east and the Hood Canal to the west. It's a ferry ride west of Seattle, and the local naval museum offers interesting displays.

Information please: The **Willcox House** (2390 Tekiu Road NW, Bremerton, 98312; 360–830–4492), is a handsomely restored 1930s Art Deco mansion overlooking the Hood Canal. The 10,000-square-foot inn, with copper roof and brick-colored slate siding, offers five well-furnished guest rooms, each with its own bath. B&B double rates of $110–185 include a full breakfast, and evening wine and cheese. The ample common areas include a handsome great room, a cozy library, and an inviting game room. The grounds offer a private dock, swimming pool, lush gardens, and wooded hiking trails.

CATHLAMET

Cathlamet is located in the southwest corner of Washington, across th Columbia River from Oregon, 80 miles northwest of Portland and abou 150 miles southwest of Seattle. Its riverside location makes it attractive t birds of all types. From Cathlamet, take the bridge to Puget Island, hom to a wildlife refuge for white-tailed deer and known as Little Norway Area activities include golf, tennis, windsurfing, fishing, canoeing, an bicycling.

From I-5, exit west onto the Ocean Beach Highway (SR 4) and go 2 miles to Cathlamet. From Oregon, take the ferry from Westport to Puge Island and Cathlamet.

The Gallery B&B ¢   *Tel: 360–425–739*
4 Little Cape Horn, 98612   *Fax: 360–425–135*

Carolyn and Eric Feasey welcome guests to their natural wood-shingle and wood-sided home, with spacious decks and floor-to-ceiling window overlooking the Columbia River. Guests enjoy relaxing on the decks watching everything from hummingbirds to bald eagles, tug boats t tankers. Carolyn offers guests the option of a continental or a full break-fast: the former includes a fruit frappé, home-baked muffins, and coffee o tea, while the latter includes eggs Benedict in puff pastry, omelets, o abelskiver pancakes.

"The guest rooms are small but attractive, and Carolyn has thought o almost every imaginable extra to make you comfortable." *(SC)* "Hum-mingbirds and finches, squirrels and chipmunks are welcomed daily wit fresh food; an eagle keeps watch from a tree by the river—this is the scene we enjoyed as we relaxed over a fruit cup filled with melons cut into hear shapes, followed by pastries and breakfast meats. Tables were set with elegant china, crystal, and fresh flowers. Carolyn's artistic talents were evident throughout this peaceful forest hideaway." *(David & Andrea Ar-lington)*

Open All year.
Rooms 3 doubles, 1 single—2 with private bath and/or shower, 2 with private half-bath, shared shower.
Facilities Dining room, living room with fireplace, TV/VCR; art, crafts gallery; balcony sitting area. 2 acres with hot tub. Beach for fishing, swimming, windsurf-ing, hiking, walking, bicycling.
Location From I-5, go W at Longview-Kelso onto the Ocean Beach Hwy. 15 m W of Longview you pass Cowlitz/Wahkiakum Park; inn is 4 m past park & ½ m past milepost 42. From Hwy. 101, inn is 5 m E of Cathlamet on SR 4.
Restrictions No smoking. Children welcome with advance notice. Circular stair-case might be difficult for older travelers.
Credit cards None accepted.
Rates B&B, $60–90 double. Extended-stay rates on request.
Extras Free marina pickup. Pets by prior arrangement. Playpen. Member, WBBG.

CONCRETE–BIRDSVIEW

Also recommended: Close to the Skagit River, Baker Lake and North Cascades National Park is the **Cascade Mountain Inn** (3840 Pioneer Lane, Concrete-Birdsview, 98237; 360–826–4333 or 800–826–0015). "Ingrid and Gerhard Meyers are interesting and welcoming hosts. Because they vacationed in the Cascade Mountain area for many years before building their B&B, they know its mountain hiking trails intimately. We hiked even though it rained, (they loaned us a slicker), and returned to wine and cheese under the porch awning. Hearty breakfasts of fruit, muffins, granola, and eggs. The decor of each room reflects a country in which the Meyers have lived. We were in the Bremen (Germany), where they were born and raised; it had a comfortable bed and a kitchen with microwave." *(Todd Miller & Marsi Fein)* Each of the six guest rooms have a private bath, and most have views of Sauk Mountain; B&B double rates range from $89–110.

EVERETT

Information please: Approximately 20 miles south of Everett is the **Aardvark House** (7219 Lake Ballinger Way, Edmonds, 98026, 206–778–7866). Jim and Arlene Fahey welcome you to climb aboard the *Aardvark*, a paddle wheel barge, for a relaxing cruise around Lake Ballinger. On land they offer three bedrooms, one with crib, at double rates of $45. Breakfast includes home-grown raspberries, blueberries or plums; coddled eggs, omelets, or sourdough waffles cooked over a wood fire—a house specialty. Comments welcome.

Marina Village Inn ✕ ਠ.   Tel: 206–259–4040
1728 West Marine View Drive, 98201   Fax: 206–252–8419

Part of the Northwest's largest marina, the Marina Village is a collection of shops, restaurants, charter boat shops, and an inn, all built in a turn-of-the-century maritime setting. The buffet breakfast includes fruit, cereal, juice, milk, and coffee.

"Cheerful and luxurious rooms, with contemporary oak furniture, original watercolors, and decorator touches; the well-lit bathrooms have handmade pottery sinks. When you're there, be sure to take the passenger-only ferry from Marina Village to Jetty Island for a nice walk along the beach." *(Susan Anderson)* "Bay view rooms are exceptionally nice, with a sunken living room, and telescope to watch the sea lions and passing boats." *(Pat Gilliam)* "Peace, quiet, and privacy. Double-headed showers, luxury linens, and wonderful beds." *(Cristy Gookin)* "Beautiful setting on the bay, with views of the sunrise and the boats leaving the harbor." *(Jim Plummer)* "Caring and friendly staff." *(Dick & Sibyl Ervin)* "Outstanding dinner at Anthony's included great oysters and superb wild Chinook salmon cooked on an alder wood plank. Confetti is also excellent with local draft beer and roast chicken." *(W.A. Grant)*

Open All year.
Rooms 2 suites, 26 doubles—all with full private bath, telephone, radio, TV, desk, air-conditioning, wet bar, refrigerator, coffee maker, pants presser. 15 with double Jacuzzi.
Facilities Library with fireplace, 4 restaurants adjacent. On bay for fishing, boating. Swimming, golf nearby. 1 hr to downhill, cross-country skiing.
Location NW WA. 30 m N of Seattle, on Port Gardener Bay. From Seattle, take I-5 N to exit 193 onto Pacific Ave; proceed W to Marine View Dr. Go right, continue 1 m N to Marina Village.
Credit cards Amex, DC, Discover, MC, Visa.
Rates B&B, $140–225 suite, $82–119 double. Extra person, $20. 10% senior. Corporate rates.
Extras Limited wheelchair access, elevator. Crib. Free overnight moorage.

GIG HARBOR

Gig Harbor is a quiet fishing and boating town, with plenty of shops, galleries, and waterside restaurants offering views of Mt. Rainier. It's located in northwest Washington, approximately 10 miles north of Tacoma, on the west side of upper Puget Sound.

Information please: Originally built as the parsonage of the Methodist Episcopal Church in 1901, **The Parsonage** (4107 Burnham Drive, 98332; 206–851–8654) was a private home before being converted into a B&B in 1985 by Sheila and Edward Koscik. The two guest rooms (sharing a bath) are simply done in blue and white decor. Sheila notes that "from June to October, guests are welcome to pick berries for their breakfast." Breakfasts might also include homemade muffins and jams, and raisin French toast or Dutch baby pancakes. "Spontaneous, warm hospitality; cheery rooms overlooking an inlet with boats of every description; magnificent fruit complements delicious breakfast." *(Katherine Lewis)* B&B double rates are $60–75.

No Cabbages ¢   Tel: 206–858–7797
7712 Goodman Dr. NW, 98335

Jamee Holder, owner of this B&B homestay, notes, "We are relaxed, comfortable, and generous human beings, and that is the kind of person we would like to host."

"Terraced herb gardens line the path down to the rooms, which look out onto a lovely patio shielded by abundant foliage and beautiful madrona trees. Our bed was canopied, comfortable with an abundance of pillows, and pushed right up to the window for easy water views. The wonderful breakfast included fresh fruit topped with pureed strawberries, homemade popovers, spinach and feta cheese omelets. The breakfast room was upstairs and afforded harbor views. We hiked a trail that winds out of the protected harbor to larger waters where we spotted a family of eagles." *(Patrick Walsh)* "Modest-sized rooms with eclectic and interest-

ing decor. The harbor is reached via a long staircase." *(Tom Chang)*
"Outstanding breakfast and wonderful conversation. Mellow, laid-back
place." *(Anne Diemer)*

Open All year.
Rooms 2 doubles share 1 bath. Private entrance.
Facilities Dining/living room, porch, deck. On Puget Sound for water sports.
Location From Rte. 5, take Bremerton-Gig Harbor Exit; go N 10 m on Rte. 16 to
Gig Harbor/City Center Exit. Turn right on Pioneer Way. Turn left onto Harbor-
view and continue to opposite side of harbor. Turn right at Union 76 station; turn
right onto Crescent Valley Rd. Go 1 1/2 m to inn on right.
Restrictions Minimal interior soundproofing. No smoking.
Credit cards None accepted.
Rates B&B, $50 double. Extra person, $7.
Extras Airport/station pickup. Pets by prior arrangement.

GLENWOOD

Flying L Ranch Country Inn ¢ 🏃 ♿
25 Flying L Lane, 98619

Tel: 509–364–3488

Owned by the Lloyd family since 1945, and open to paying guests since
1960, the Flying L Ranch is a relaxing base for an outdoor vacation.
Darvel (who was joined in 1992 by his twin brother, Darryl, as co-
innkeeper) notes that "our favorite guests are naturalists, artists, photographers, and non-motorized outdoors people—hikers, bicyclists, skiers, and
so on—and those who like unpretentious, simple furnishings (accented
with Indian rugs, books, and original art)." Both Darvel and Darryl are
excellent sources of information on area activities and explorations; they
have climbed to the summit of 12,276-foot Mt. Adams many times.
Darvel describes this area of the Cascades as being "like Mt. Rainier
National Park without the people." Breakfast might include huckleberry
pancakes or egg soufflé, pure fruit spread, home-baked bran muffins, fresh
fruit salad with yogurt topping, and ham slices.

"The beauty, the authenticity of the lodgings and the friendliness of
both hosts and guests bring us back." *(Barbara & Max Rutzer)* "Interesting,
appetizing menus. Unspoiled region." *(David Beyl)* "The location is ideal,
between the lush beautiful climate of western Washington, and the dry
climate of eastern Washington." *(Linda Todd)* "Rooms are clean and cozy
with lots of beautiful wood and stone construction." *(JH)* "Darvel sees that
needs are met without intruding. He and his staff provide tasty and ample
breakfasts, accompanied by conversation that puts guests at ease." *(Mar-
tha Westgate)* "Good mattresses and soft pillows." *(Jay Brueggeman)*

Open All year.
Rooms 1 suite, 10 doubles—8 with private bath/and or shower, 3 share 1 1/2
baths. 2 2-bedroom cabins with bath and kitchen. 5 with desk, 3 with fireplace.
Rooms, facilities in 3 buildings.
Facilities 2 equipped common kitchens, dining room, living room with fireplace,
books, piano, stereo; porch, observation deck. Occasional musical entertainment.
160 acres with hot tub, barbecue, picnic tables, campfire circle, lawn games, pond

for swimming, ice skating. Bicycles, ski gear. 3 m trail for hiking, cross-country skiing. Rafting, kayaking, hiking, cross-country skiing nearby. Adjacent to Mt Adams Park/Wilderness, Conboy National Wildlife Refuge.

Location S central WA. 95 m E of Portland, 35 m N of Hood River. From Hood River cross to WA, go 12 m N on Rte. 141 to BZ Corners. Turn right, continue 18 m N on Rte. 141 to Glenwood. Turn right, go E through town $\frac{1}{2}$ m; turn left go N $\frac{1}{2}$ m to inn on right.

Restrictions No smoking.

Credit cards Amex, CB, DC, MC, Visa.

Rates B&B, $90 suite, $65–90 double, $55–80 single. Extra person, $5–15. Cabins, $95–100. Family rate. 2-night weekend/holiday minimum. Prix fixe lunch, $7; dinner $12–15.

Extras Wheelchair access. Station pickup. Horses by prior arrangement. Crib, high chair, babysitting.

HOQUIAM

Lytle House B&B ¢
509 Chenault Avenue, 98550

Tel: 360–533–2320
800–677–2320
Fax: 360–533–4025

Lumber baron Joseph Lytle built his family a grand home in 1899, over-looking Grays Harbor. Today this Queen Anne mansion is owned by Robert and Dayna Bencala, who have furnished it with period antiques and queen-size beds. They report that "with four parlors, the Lytle House is large enough to satisfy anyone's idea of a quiet evening away from home. Bathing arrangements sometimes require a short walk down the hall, so each room has a wicker basket filled with luxuries, and in the baths, clawfoot tubs, heated towel racks, and stacks of thick towels. Fresh-brewed coffee is available for early risers. Breakfast awaits downstairs, served at guests' convenience between 7:30 and 9 A.M. Guests receive menus to indicate their choices the night before: French toast; omelets to order; English shirred eggs with ham and cheese; or Dutch baby pancakes, plus a buffet of yogurt, granola; fruit, juice, coffee, tea, and muffins." "The young owners are friendly and talented. Exquisite antiques; each room is like living in the 1800s." *(Nancy Goodfellow)* "Everything was pleasant, even the dog, who's in charge of napping." *(Roger Newcome)*

Open All year.

Rooms 2 suites, 6 doubles—2 with full private bath, 6 with maximum of 4 people sharing bath. All with clock, 3 with radio, 2 with balcony, desk. 1 suite with kitchen.

Facilities Dining room, living room, parlor with TV/VCR; library with books, stereo, TV/VCR; gift shop, porches. $\frac{1}{2}$ acre with off-street parking, lawn games.

Location 60 m W of Olympia. $\frac{1}{2}$ m to town. From Olympia go W on Hwy. 101, becomes Hwy. 8, then Hwy. 12, then Hwy. 101 again. At end go right onto Hwy. 109. Go right onto Garfield Rd. Go left onto Chenault Ave.

Restrictions No smoking. Any age children with advance notice.

Credit cards Amex, MC, Visa.

Rates B&B, $75–95 suite, $65–75 double, $50–65 single. Extra person, $15. No tipping. 10% AAA discount.

Extras Airport pickup. Crib.

A CONNER

a Conner is a picturesque fishing town with many historic homes, set on
kagit Bay at the Swinomish Channel. The area is particularly popular in
April, when thousands of tulips are in bloom in the nearby fields, and also
om July to September. Some feel that La Conner's historic qualities have
een overwhelmed by the number of tourists visiting during these peak
mes; as usual, we recommend an off-season visit if possible.

La Conner is located in northwestern Washington, about 60 miles north
f Seattle, and 80 miles south of Vancouver.

Also recommended: A Victorian-style contemporary building, **The
Heron** (117 Maple Avenue, 98257; 360–466–4626) has twelve guest
ooms, all with private bath, telephone, and TV; there's a hot tub in the
ackyard and the honeymoon suite has a Jacuzzi tub. Rates of $65–120
aclude a continental breakfast. "Our room was furnished in antiques with
wonderful queen-sized brass bed, two comfortable wing chairs, and
ovely thick towels in the bathroom. Pleasant, helpful staff." *(Barbara &
Jeal Porter)*

The **Rainbow Inn** (1075 Chilberg Road, P.O. Box 15, 98257; 360–
66–4578), a turn-of-the-century farmhouse, has a secluded setting just a
½ mile from town. The eight guest rooms, with private and shared baths,
ave period furnishings, queen-sized beds, and antique-patterned wallpa-
ers. The hot tub is tucked in a gazebo on the back deck with a view of
armlands and Mt. Baker. Rates of $75–95 include a wholesome breakfast
f local fruits, freshly baked breads and muffins, an egg or griddle dish.
Spacious and immaculate room, outstanding breakfast; Sharon Briggs and
on Johnson are friendly and helpful innkeepers who take time to get to
now their guests. There's an extensive library in the parlor; if a guest
oesn't finish a book, they may take it home and mail it back later. They
ave not lost a book yet." *(Pat Borysiewisz)*

For an additional area entry, see listing for **White Swan Guest House
1 Mt. Vernon.**

Iotel Planter ¢   *Tel:* 360–466–4710
15 First Street, 98257   800–488–5409
                                          Fax: 360–466–1320

he Hotel Planter, built in 1907 of solid concrete blocks made on the site,
s a landmark not only for its construction but also for the many years that
provided housing for artists and writers working in La Conner. By the
980s the building had seen better days and was condemned. Local
esidents Donald and Cynthia Hoskins, credited with much of La Conner's
istoric revival, purchased it in 1987. They spent more than two years
dding central heating, electrical systems, insulation, and more bathrooms;
ney re-installed original doors, windows, and wood trim, and rewired
nany of the old light fixtures. The hotel is now listed on the National
egister of Historic Places. A gallery, Earthenworks, occupies a section of
ne first floor; coffee is available every morning near the front desk.

"Good-sized rooms with floral fabrics and pastel colors; tile bathrooms.

Although on the main street, there is an attractive courtyard in the bac
with a gazebo-covered hot tub." *(Sue & Jack Lane)* "Rooms have pir
furniture and designer touches; those at the front and rear corners a
larger. The hotel is right across from the Calico Cupboard, a great plac
for breakfast and lunch." *(Pam Phillips)* Comments appreciated.

Open All year.
Rooms 12 doubles—all with private shower, telephone, radio, TV, ceiling fan.
with Jacuzzi.
Facilities Garden courtyard, hot tub in gazebo. Meeting room, retail shop
gallery, off-street parking.
Location Downtown, at 1st & Morris.
Restrictions No smoking. Traffic noise in some rooms.
Credit cards Amex, MC, Visa.
Rates Room only, $70–110 double. Off-season rates.

Ridgeway Bed & Breakfast
1292 McLean Road, P.O. Box 475, 98273

Tel: 360–428–806
800–428–806

"A large Dutch Colonial brick home, built in 1928, with lace-covere
windows in the comfortably furnished living room. Magazines and book
line the shelves; menus from local restaurants helped us decide where
eat. Our hosts, John and Louise Kelly, were there when we needed the
and disappeared when privacy was appreciated. John can even take yo
on a scenic plane ride. Flowers were in every room as were temptin
chocolate truffles; stuffed bunnies and kittens accented the decor, inclu
ing a real live feline who remained downstairs. Guest rooms are name
for the Kellys' daughters and granddaughters—the Nicole was spaciou
with comfy bed, floral down comforter, matching drapes and an in-roo
clawfoot tub. Breakfast, at the lovely dining room table, included choi
of juices, baked apples, bacon, link sausage, omelets, fresh muffins an
homemade jam, warm fruit compote, and light-as-a-feather oatmeal pa
cakes. In the evening Louise served a lightly warmed, cherry-filled choc
late cake." *(Nancy & Robert Andes)* "Louise and John suggested interestin
adventures—a walk on the dike, cycling the islands, hiking at Deceptio
Pass, or in April, the tulip festival." *(Sharon Weibe)*

Open All year.
Rooms 5 doubles—2 with private bath and/or shower, 3 with a maximum of
sharing bath. All rooms with sink.
Facilities Dining room, living room with fireplace, piano, TV/VCR, stereo, book
porches. 2½ acres with croquet.
Location 4 m E of La Conner, 4 m W of Mt. Vernon.
Restrictions No smoking. Children over 11 preferred.
Credit cards Amex, Discover, MC, Visa.
Rates B&B, $75–95 double, $70–90 single. 2-day minimum stay during Tul
Festival.

Wild Iris
121 Maple Avenue, P.O. Box 696, 98257

Tel: 360–466–140
Fax: 360–466–122

Built in 1991 to resemble an expanded Victorian farmhouse, The Wild Ir
offers individually decorated guest rooms, each with a theme and mo.

with mountain views. Wraparound porches offer inviting spots to sit, and the cozy living room has a stone fireplace and Queen Anne reproduction wing chairs and sofa. A breakfast buffet is served in the dining room, and includes freshly baked pastry, brioche, muffins, cheeses, herbed eggs, fresh orange juice, fruit, and beverages. Dinner is offered on Friday and Saturday night; menus feature sockeye salmon, plus scallops, quail, lamb chops, and pasta dishes. "Quiet location; private, great for a romantic getaway." *(Pam Phillips also James Burr)*

Open All year.
Rooms 12 suites, 8 doubles—all with private bath and/or shower, telephone, TV, fan. 13 with fireplace, 12 with deck, 5 with desk. Radio, clock available. Suites with double Jacuzzi, coffee maker.
Facilities Dining room, living room with fireplace, piano, books; porch. Occasional musical entertainment on weekends. Meeting facilities. Off-street parking. 3 blocks from marina, saltwater channel.
Location 2 blocks from center. Entering town, take 1st left, go 1 block S to inn.
Restrictions No smoking. Children over 12 preferred.
Credit cards MC, Visa.
Rates B&B, $100–130 suite, double. MAP, $195 suite, double. Alc dinner on weekends, $35. Corporate rates.
Extras Wheelchair access; 1 room equipped for disabled. Limited French, Spanish spoken.

LEAVENWORTH

Surrounded by the Cascade Mountains, Leavenworth is a Bavarian-style village offering outdoor recreation in all seasons—fishing, hiking, and rafting, and golf in the warmer months; downhill and cross-country skiing, sleigh rides, sledding, and snowshoeing in the colder months.

Reader tip: "An old mining town fallen on hard times, Leavenworth re-invented itself as an ersatz Bavarian village. Most appealing is the lovely riverside park and promenade; it's clean, graffiti free, and very European with meandering paths, and lots of benches to sit and enjoy the views. Don't come here to shop—the town stores sell what appears to be wall-to-wall kitsch." *(SC)*

Leavenworth is in central Washington, 120 miles east of Seattle and 150 miles west of Spokane. Take I-90 to Ellensburg, go north on Route 97 to Route 2, then east on Route 2 to Leavenworth.

Information please: About 11 miles southeast of Leavenworth, off Route 2/97, is the **Cashmere Inn** (5801 Pioneer Avenue, Cashmere, 98815; 509–782–4212) with five guest rooms (all with private bath), a swimming pool, and hot tub. It's surrounded by flowers, herbs, and orchards—the passion of owners Patti and Dale Swanson. The reasonable rates include a full breakfast and afternoon beverage. "The cozy living room with a fireplace and lots of comfortable chairs is an inviting place to relax and read. We enjoyed a delicious breakfast as well as great scenery in the dining room with its wall of windows." *(Susan DeGaetani)*

The Cougar Inn (23379 Highway 207, Lake Wenatchee, 98826; 509–763–3354), located 20 miles north of Leavenworth, is an old-fashioned country hotel, built in 1890. "Our lovely suite was decorated in white wicker, with a bathroom tiled in green. Beautiful views overlooking the lake with high mountain peaks beyond, and an interesting dinner menu." *(SC)* Rates range from $40–50 double to $70–80 for a cabin.

All Seasons River Inn
8751 Icicle Road, 98826

Tel: 509–548–1425
800–254–0555

After searching in vain for the perfect house to accommodate their bed and breakfast, Kathy and Jeff Falconer decided to build it themselves. An inviting living room offers bay windows overlooking the Wenatchee River and the warmth of a fireplace; guests can gather in the game room to socialize or take in the mountain views. A favorite breakfast features a kiwi and peanut butter parfait; pumpkin bread; Mexican tamale pancakes; sausage and apples; and German potato slices; plus coffee and tea.

"Food was delicious and different." *(Mary Ann Smith & Shirm Stapleton)* "Our bedroom had an antique dresser, a wooden rocker, and high bed— the decorative coverlet exchanged for a down comforter at night. It was like a visit to Grandma's house: wonderful smells coming from the kitchen; cookies in the jar; Kathy waiting on your every need; antiques every- where; the river flowing peacefully by." *(Sheila Cass)* "Bedrooms warmly decorated; little bears abound." *(Arleen Michael)* "Greeted by the aroma of hot apple pie, which we enjoyed later by the fire." *(Ann & Rob Gascoigne)* "Extremely clean. Kathy was friendly and welcoming, without intruding on our privacy. Superb views, the area quiet and restful." *(Shirley Andrews)*

Open All year.
Rooms 1 suite, 3 doubles—all with private bath and/or shower, radio, air-condi- tioning, deck. 3 with whirlpool tub, desk or fireplace.
Facilities Dining room with fireplace, living room with deck, game room, TV room with guest refrigerator, VCR. ½ acre along Wenatchee River rapids, beach. Golf, hiking nearby. Cross-country skis, bikes available.
Location 1 m from downtown. From Hwy. 2, turn S onto Icicle Rd. Go 1 m to inn, 2nd house on left after bridge.
Restrictions No smoking. No children.
Credit cards MC, Visa.
Rates B&B, $120–135 suite, $100–125 double. Extra person, $15. 2-night week- end, holiday, festival minimum.

Mountain Home Lodge
Mountain Home Road, P.O. Box 687, 98826

Tel: 509–548–7077

If you've longed to find a country inn truly free of traffic noise, then head straight for the Mountain Home Lodge. In summer cars can reach it only via a 2½-mile dirt road; in winter it's accessible only via the lodge's heated Sno-Cat. Despite the isolation, the lodge is far from primitive— modern amenities range from the VCR to the outdoor hot tub. Winter rates include all meals, from the hearty mountain breakfast to the fix-it- yourself soup, salad, and sandwich lunch, to the evening fireside hors d'oeuvres and tasty dinners. Meals are served but not included in the summer rates, since guests have the option of going elsewhere. Dinner favorites include crab-stuffed chicken, London broil Oscar, salmon steaks, and shrimp stirfry; breakfast entrées include crustless quiche, leek frittata, and pumpkin pancakes with apple cider syrup.

"Chris, Charlie and the entire staff are congenial hosts, and yet allow ample opportunity for privacy." *(George & Susan Soltman)* "Rooms are comfortable, and well lit for reading. Always clean; the staff does a nice job of tidying up the rooms. Generous portions of good, wholesome food." *(Allan Wyemura)* "Charlie even found a small radio so Jim wouldn't have to miss the Washington/Nebraska football game." *(Lee & Jim Todd)* "Stunning mountain views, lovely deck, cozy living room." *(SC)*

Open All year.
Rooms 1 suite, 8 doubles—all with full bath and/or shower, air-conditioning, fan.
Facilities Dining room, family room with fireplace. TV room with VCR, movies. 20 acres with heated swimming pool, hot tub, tennis court, walking trails, sledding; 30 km of cross-country ski trails, ski rentals, free snowmobile tours.
Location From Leavenworth, go E on Rte. 2 to Duncan Rd. & turn right (S). Take Duncan to Mt. Home Rd. & left to inn. In winter leave car in parking lot at corner of Rte. 2 & Duncan.
Restrictions No smoking. No children.
Credit cards Amex, MC, Visa.
Rates Room only (summer only), $158–208 suite or double. Extra person, $15. Full board (winter only), $158–208 suite or double. Extra person, $45. 2-night minimum Dec. 1 through Mar. 30. In summer, with 24-hr. notice, prix fixe breakfast, $4–9; prix fixe lunch, $7; prix fixe dinner (including house wine & beer), $19.
Extras Station pickup; pickup by lodge Sno-Cat, $10 per person round-trip.

Run of the River B&B
9308 East Leavenworth Road, P.O. Box 285, 98826

Tel: 509–548–7171
800–288–6491

"The name Run of the River comes from a John McPhee short story about small water turbines and reflects owners Monty and Karen Turner's intention to adjust to the flow of life's events. I would say that the effect of the Turners' wonderful place is to smooth the torrents of the outside world to a gentle, vibrant flow to which no adjustment is necessary. This feeling stems as much from their unobtrusive, friendly nature as the rustic charm of the log building, itself something of a work of art with extensive details added by a local craftsman." *(John Morgan & Barbara House)*

Karen and Monty Turner, who built the inn in 1986, offer hot beverages in the lounge each afternoon, and serve a family-style breakfast of juice, yogurt with fruit, and a hot entrée—maybe a ham-mushroom frittata or French toast, concluded with apple cobbler. Typical of their thoughtfulness and thoroughness are their helpful hiking, bicycling, and motoring guides to assist guests in area explorations.

"Impeccably maintained. Monty is approachable, friendly, helpful, and a great cook." *(Dr. A. Alexiadis)* "At the top of the stairs is a basket of toiletries, in case you've forgotten something." *(Karin & Jack Armstrong)* "The Tumwater suite has two woodstoves, double Jacuzzi, comfortable bed with crisp linens, down comforters and a loft." *(Nancy Blatt)* "Rooms have beautifully crafted log beds, and in the common area, the woodstove is backed by a river rock wall and hearth. The delicious breakfast is served at the long oak table, on fine china and silver." *(Paul Stackhouse)* "Calm, cordial innkeepers. Appreciated the designer robes for trips to the hot tub." *(Beth Yedlowski Oziel)* "Outstanding location at the foot of a scenic set of ridges. Unobstructed view of the river—no human habitation in sight—just a natural refuge area for wildlife. Inviting interior with rocking chairs, books, and a friendly cat who enjoys the warmth of the wood stove." *(Lyle & Margaret Neighbors)*

Open All year.
Rooms 2 suites, 4 doubles—all with private bath and/or shower. All with TV, fan, deck. 2 with telephone, fireplace. Suite with 2 woodstoves.
Facilities Breakfast room with stereo, library with TV, phone; deck. 2 acres with hot tub, picnic area, mountain bikes, fishing, hiking trails, bocci.
Location 1 m E of Leavenworth. From Hwy. 2, go 1 m E on E. Leavenworth Rd to inn on right.
Restrictions Absolutely no smoking. No children.
Credit cards Amex, MC, Visa.
Rates B&B, $105–140 suite, $90–125 double, $80–115 single. 2-night weekend, holiday minimum.
Extras Station pickup. Spanish spoken.

LONG BEACH

For additional area entries, see **Seaview.**

Boreas Bed & Breakfast ¢   *Tel:* 360–642–8069
607 North Boulevard, P.O. Box 1344, 98631

Boreas, in Greek mythology, was god of the north wind, which brings crisp clear weather. That's the favorite climate of Sally Davis and Coleman White, who bought this 1920s beach house in 1991 and remodeled it in an eclectic style, mixing art and 1930s furnishings with casual comfort. Nothing obstructs the view of the Pacific except an expanse of sand and seagrass; they report "instead of TV, we offer tape players and a library of books on tape—from humor to mystery." Breakfast can be had at a large table or individual ones; original egg dishes and griddle items are favorites.

"Scrupulously clean, well-maintained, and quiet." *(David Yett)* "Intelligent, creative, considerate innkeepers." *(Walter & Eleanor Glickman)* "Period decor, comfortable bed with quilt, pretty water pitchers, homey stuffed animal, and updated bathrooms. I especially liked the fresh seafood used in the omelets, crepes, and delicious soufflé." *(Bill Strauss)* "The tempting aromas from the kitchen combined with the endless views of the dunes and ocean are my idea of paradise. I borrowed their dog Mollie and went for a long walk on the beach, with a mug of fresh- brewed coffee in hand, returning for a breakfast feast." *(Ali Gill-O'Hara)*

Open All year.
Rooms 1 suite, 3 doubles—2 with private bath and/or shower, 2 with maximum of 4 people sharing bath. All with radio, clock, cassette player. 2 with desk, 1 with balcony.
Facilities Dining room, living room with fireplace, family room with games, piano, stereo, books, audio library. 1 acre with hot tub, lawn games. Golf, fishing nearby. 5-minute walk to beach. 9 miles to kayaking on bay.

ocation 90 m W of Portland, 130 m SW of Seattle. 6 blocks from downtown.
estrictions No smoking. Children over 6 preferred.
redit cards MC, Visa.
ates B&B, $85–95 suite, $65–95 double, $55–85 single. Extra person, $10. 2–3
ght weekend, holiday minimum.
xtras Local airport/station pickup.

UMMI ISLAND

ummi Island is a small strip of land, a short ferry ride west of the
ainland near Bellingham; it's 100 miles north of Seattle, and 50 miles
outh of Vancouver. Owned originally by the Lummi Indians, the island
as a forested ridge at the south end and a rim of houses along the shore
n three sides.

oganita, A Villa by the Sea   *Tel: 360–758–2651*
825 West Shore Drive, 98262

turn-of-the-century home purchased by Ann and Glen Gossage in 1976,
e Loganita has been a B&B since 1990. Set on a grassy hill, the inn's
reat room has large windows offering views of the Strait of Georgia and
e islands beyond, deep leather couches, and a stone fireplace. The
ossages collect art of all kinds, but their favorite is Northwest; music
atures prominently at the inn, impromptu concerts can occur. Guest
ooms have light, airy colors, puffy comforters, and traditional furniture.
reakfast includes fresh fruit, toast and muffins, an egg dish with meat, and
offee or tea; on Sundays, salmon highlights the menu.

"Relaxing home, welcoming hostess; elegant yet comfortable. Com-
ortable rooms, beautiful beach, and good company (or solitude if you
efer)." *(Joanne VanWyck)* "Stunning location. Fabulous sunsets from the
ont deck, where Glen played the guitar and sang one evening. Totally
rivate carriage house in back." *(Pam Phillips)*

pen All year.
ooms 1 3-bedroom cottage (sleeps 4), 3 suites, 2 doubles—all with private bath
nd/or shower, radio, clock. 5 with desk, 1 with deck. 1 suite with fireplace, deck,
lephone. Cottage with telephone, TV/VCR, woodstove, kitchen, laundry, deck.
acilities 2 living rooms with fireplace, piano, TV/VCR, stereo, books; family
oom, deck. 2 acres with hot tub, lawn games, beach.
ocation From ferry, turn right on Nugent Rd. Go 3 m to West Shore Dr. & turn
ft to inn on left.
estrictions No smoking. Children 10 or over, in cottage only.
redit cards MC, Visa.
ates B&B, $95–185 cottage, suite, double. Extra person, $20. 2-night weekend
inimum.
xtras Airport pickup.

Vest Shore Farm ¢ &   *Tel: 360–758–2600*
781 West Shore Drive, 98262

arl Hanson, a retired Boeing engineer, built this unusual octagonal
ome—as well as the greenhouse that supplies their farm with fresh
rganic fruits and vegetables. His wife, Polly, a retired librarian, is chief

cook and gardener. She reports that "we enjoy attracting people wh share our interests: libraries, bag pipers, private pilots, participants in th literary arts and opera. And Carl plays his bagpipes at any excuse or non at all." "Friendly hosts who taught me a lot about the region's flora an fauna—saw lots of bald eagles." *(Jennifer Allen)* "Come here for the slov peaceful pace of island life, the incredible water and island views, and th Hansons' excellent food. Breakfast included fresh fruit with yogurt, juic huge pancakes with homemade berry sauce, bacon and coffee." *(SC)*

Open All year.
Rooms 2 doubles—both with private bath, telephone.
Facilities Dining/breakfast room with fireplace, common area with books, game deck. 21 acres with greenhouse, orchard, gardens, farm animals, lawn game bicycles. Beach across street. Charter fishing nearby.
Location On NW side of island. 1 m ferry ride to mainland. From I-5, take ex 260 to Slater Road. Go W 3.7 m to Haxton Way. Go left 6.7 m to end at ferr landing. Take ferry to island; take road on right 3 m to farm.
Restrictions No smoking.
Credit cards MC, Visa. "Not a child-proof environment."
Rates B&B, $85 double, $75 single. Prix fixe meals by reservation.
Extras Limited wheelchair access. Free ferry pickup. Airport/station pickup, $2 Crib, highchair.

The Willows Inn
2579 West Shore Drive, 98262

Tel: 360–758–262

A West Shore landmark dating to 1910, "Taft's The Willows" was summer resort until the 1950s when became a private residence. In 198 the house was purchased by Victoria and Gary Flynn (she's the grand daughter of the original innkeeper). Now restored, The Willows has light and airy decor incorporating heirloom furniture, fine old linens, an bouquets of fresh flowers. On weekends, a wake-up basket with coffe tea, and Irish soda bread comes to your door at 8 A.M., followed by generous country breakfast at 9 A.M. served at individual tables in th elegant dining room. Tea is offered at 3:30 P.M., and fine dining is accon panied by Northwest wines.

"The many windows in the dining and living rooms offer panoram island views. The cottage on the hill is encircled by flowers and trees, wit Victoria's vegetable and herb garden nearby. From the French doors yo see the islands; we spent afternoons on the large deck, sipping wine an listening to the waves. There's a skylight over the bed, an antique-styl radio with cassette player (tapes provided); the bathroom had a pedest sink and clawfoot tub. Breakfast includes fresh fruit, a hearty bowl Scottish oats, and a filling entree. Our Saturday night dinner started wit hors d'oeuvres and sherry on the veranda; two musicians on harp an guitar serenaded the glorious sunset. Gary is a wine expert, explaining th menu and its selected vintages before escorting you to your table wit hand-written place card. Victoria's five-course dinners are varied an interesting as well as delicious." *(Marge & Robert Zacharczyk)* "Warn gracious hosts who give the gift of privacy. The food is outstanding, th service exceptional." *(John & Camilla Lee)* "Spotless, uncluttered room Wonderful linens, generous meals, out-of-this-world desserts." *(Nanc Huot)*

Open Open mid-Feb.–Nov.

Rooms 2 1–2 bedroom cottages, 4 doubles—all with private bath and/or shower, radio, clock. Some with telephone, desk, fan. Cottages with deck, kitchenette; 1 cottage with whirlpool tub, TV/VCR, stereo, fireplace.

Facilities Dining room, living room with fireplace, stereo, books, games; pub with billiards, darts, stereo, TV; deck. 1 acre with private beach.

Location From ferry landing, go left on Nugent Rd. Go $4/10$ m up hill. Go right on Legoe Bay Rd., follow to inn on W side of island.

Restrictions No smoking. Children over 16 preferred.

Credit cards MC, Visa.

Rates Room only (B&B on weekends), $135–285 cottage, $195–210 suite, $95–210 double. 10% discount for 4-night stay. 2-night minimum, Memorial Day–Labor Day. Alc dinner, $25–40, plus 15% service; advance reservation required. Breakfast for non-guests, $12 plus service.

Extras Wheelchair access; in 1 cottage room.

MAZAMA

Mazama Country Inn ¢ ✕ ♿
P.O. Box 223, 98833

Tel: 509–996–2681
In WA: 800–843–7951
Fax: 509–996–2646

"The North Cascades National Park is a wonderful area for hiking, but there aren't many places to stay unless you're camping. Particularly welcome, is the Mazama Country Inn, on the eastern side of the Cascades, where one can settle in and drive back into the park for day hikes. The well-designed inn was built in the 1980s; there is a horse corral and a wide bubbly river, lots of fir trees and mountain views. Our duplex room had a single bed, bath, and sitting area below, and a double bed in a sleeping loft above; also a little porch. Partly paneled, it was simply but tastefully decorated with a frieze of game birds. The handsome dining room is two stories high with a huge stone fireplace; there's a patio where one can eat breakfast in the sun." *(Carolyn Mathiasen)* "Deer herds feed in the fields behind the ranch." *(Lon Bailey)* "Friendly, warm atmosphere." *(Laura Roman)* "Our room was small but clean. Hearty breakfasts and dinners in the pleasant dining room; menu somewhat limited. For variety in food and venue, Winthrop, a quasi-reconstructed Western town is 16 miles away." (GRA)

Area for improvement: "Bedside reading lights."

Open All year.

Rooms 3 1–3 bedroom cabins, 4 suites, 10 doubles—all with private bath and/or shower. 3 with porch. Suites in annex. Cabins with kitchen, woodstove; 1 with laundry, TV, stereo.

Facilities Restaurant, living room with fireplace, game room with piano, patio. Hot tub, sauna, lawn games, mountain bike rentals, horseback riding, fishing. 35 m cross-country ski trails, ski rentals, lessons. Adjacent to Pasayten Wilderness for hiking, fishing.

Location N central WA, 14 m N of Winthrop on Hwy 20.

Restrictions No smoking. No children under 13 in inn; OK in cabins.

Credit cards MC, Visa.

Rates Room only, $95–240 cabin (for up to 8 people), $75 double. Extra person, $20–25. Packages available. Midweek, off-season specials.

Extras Wheelchair access.

MOUNT VERNON

The White Swan Guest House ¢   *Tel: 360–445–680*
1388 Moore Road, 98273

The White Swan, on Fir Island overlooking the Skagit River, was built in 1898 by a Norwegian ferryboat captain who used the turret to observe the river traffic (including swans—hence the inn's name). Today's crowd come to see the magnificent 1,500 acres of tulips, daffodils, and iris that bloom in the valley, celebrated by the town of Mount Vernon each April during the Tulip Festival; in other seasons, visitors can tour the neighboring village of La Conner. Restored in 1986 by innkeeper Peter Goldfarb the White Swan's clear, sunny color scheme and tasteful country-style floral fabrics reflect his years in Manhattan as an interior designer; the queen- and king-size beds ensure guest comfort. Peter reports that "the White Swan is a small, one-person operation; nothing grand or pretentious, just like 'Granny's' house. Guests are encouraged to enter through the kitchen door, where they'll find freshly baked cookies and lively conversation." Breakfast includes homemade muffins, fruit, juice, coffee and tea.

"Delightful cottage perfect for us and our baby. Wonderful countryside alive with the music of frogs, birds, and cows, enhanced by mountain views. Lovely rooms in the main house." *(Susan Stover-Dalton)*

Open All year.
Rooms 3 doubles in main house share 2 baths. 1 cottage with private bath, kitchen, deck.
Facilities Dining room, parlor with woodstove, porch. 1 acre with patio, English gardens.
Location NW WA, 60 m N of Seattle, 6 m S of La Conner. From I-5, take Exit 221 to Fir Island Rd. Go to yellow blinking light, straight to Moore Rd.
Restrictions No smoking. Children in cottage only.
Credit cards MC, Visa.
Rates B&B. Double $75, single $65. Cottage, $125. Extra person in cottage, $20.
Extras Member, WBBG.

PORT ANGELES

Port Angeles is located in northwestern Washington, midway up the northern end of the Olympic Peninsula, along the Strait of Juan de Fuca 80 miles from Seattle. It's a popular place to overnight for those traveling the Olympic Loop Highway (Rte. 101) and for those taking the ferry to or from Victoria, on Vancouver Island, British Columbia.

Nearby attractions include Hurricane Ridge, just 17 miles from town. At 5,000 feet, it offers a beautiful view of the surrounding valleys, mountains, and sea. Other area attractions include Lake Crescent, the Dungeness Spit Wildlife Refuge, the Sole Duc Hot Springs, charter fishing and boating in the straits or the Pacific, hiking and backpacking, and cross-country skiing in the winter.

For additional area accommodations, see **Sequim.**

Domaine Madeleine B&B, on Finn Hall Road   *Tel: 360–457–4174*
146 Wildflower Lane, 98362

Innkeepers Madeleine Lanham and John Chambers welcome those who like books, gardens, wildlife, spectacular views of water and mountains, and stimulating conversation. But if quiet is your desire, they will "provide a sound level in which you could hear an oyster yawn!"

"From the back this contemporary house has a view of Victoria, British Columbia, and the Strait; to the front are the Olympia Mountains. We even saw whales spouting." *(Elizabeth Baxin)* "Furnished with Asian and European antiques. Both downstairs rooms, the Monet (complete with replica garden) and the Renior have beautiful views. The Ming, upstairs, has a 30-foot balcony, tiled Jacuzzi, and mirrored bath with designer robes and French perfumes. Breakfast included fresh fruit, homemade bread, and a choice of shrimp quiche or strawberry crepes, beautifully served on fine china." *(Marie Harris)* "Welcoming touches included a filled ice bucket, fresh fruit, current magazines, and intriguing books." *(Shale Baskin)* "Every comfort including featherbeds, cassette player and tapes. Impeccably clean. John and Madeleine are both genuinely warm and caring." *(Denise Brown, and others)* "The morning's fresh fruit, homemade bread, salmon and scallop Newburg, and chocolate mousse rivaled any dinner." *(Judy & Allen Rachap)* "Spectacular breakfast served with everybody together, one course at a time, from 9:00–10:30 A.M. Helpful hosts; they do everything and want it to be perfect." *(Betsy Immergut)*

Open All year.
Rooms 1 suite, 2 doubles—all with private bath and/or shower, telephone, radio, TV/VCR, air-conditioning, deck. 3 with fireplace, 2 with Jacuzzi tub.
Facilities Dining room with fireplace; living room with TV/VCR, video library, stereo, books, harpsichord, games; porch, deck, laundry facilities. 5 acres with gardens, badminton, croquet, volleyball. Nature tours.
Location NW WA. 7 m E of town center. Left onto Old Olympic Hwy, 1.4 m; left onto Gherke, 0.3 m; right onto Finn Hall.
Restrictions No smoking. Children over 12 welcome.
Credit cards MC, Visa.
Rates B&B, $145–155 suite, $89–145 double, $69–79 single. Extra person, $25.
Extras Local airport pickup. French, Spanish, German, Farsi spoken.

Lake Crescent Lodge ¢ ♠ ✗ ♿   *Tel: 360–928–3211*
Star Route 1, Box 11, 98362

"Operated by National Park Concessions, Inc., the Lake Crescent Lodge is spread out on the south bank of Lake Crescent, at the base of Storm King Mountain; it's set between the rain forest to the south and the Strait of Juan de Fuca to the north. The buildings include the early 1900s-era wooden main lodge, with its huge wraparound porch and fireplace; the new Pyramid Mountain Lodge, with lake and mountain views; 17 cabins; and two motel-type buildings. The best rooms are in the four large cabins with fireplaces; book early, everybody wants them. The rooms in the lodge on the north side are worth the view over the lake, even with shared baths. The dining room serves large portions of simple food, with friendly college students waiting on tables. Lots of wonderful outdoor activities, plus evening nature programs and many impromptu games or cards or

311

Frisbee." *(Suzanne Carmichael)* "Excellent food, friendly staff. Pyramid Mountain is my first choice of accommodations." *(Shirley Lieb)* "Breathtaking vistas of the lake and sky-high mountains beyond. Good food." *(William McGowan)*

Open Late April through Oct.
Rooms 17 cabins, 35 doubles—47 with full private bath, 5 with maximum of 10 people sharing separate men's and women's bath. Most with desk.
Facilities Lobby/lounge, sun porch, dining room, gift shop, covered porches. 35 acres with lakefront dock, walking trails. Downhill skiing nearby. Rowboat rentals.
Location NW WA, Olympic National Park. On Hwy. 101, 20 m W of Port Angeles. ¼ m from park entrance.
Credit cards Amex, CB, DC, MC, Visa.
Rates Room only, $75–127 cottage (sleeps 2–4), $65–96 double. Extra person, $10. Alc breakfast, $3–8; alc lunch, $8–12; alc dinner, $11–16.
Extras Pets by arrangement, $5. Crib, $10.

Sol Duc Hot Springs Resort ¢ 👫 ✕ ♿ *Tel: 360–327–3583*
Olympic National Park, P.O. Box 2169, 98362

A famous resort at the turn of the century, Teddy Roosevelt was among Sol Duc's many prominent visitors. The hotel burned down in 1916, and it wasn't until fairly recently that the National Park Service successfully rebuilt the resort; Steve Olson took over the lease in 1987. Where once only greasy hamburgers prevailed, visitors can now choose from such entrées as chicken in hoisin sauce; cod in a spicy Caribbean sauce; Dungeness crab with fresh mushrooms; and broiled salmon with lemon butter. Sol Duc is located in the interior of Olympic National Park, at one of the best trail heads. It is the only developed hot springs on the Olympic Peninsula, with three hot spring pools and one freshwater swimming pool.

"The hot springs are outstanding; the employees are friendly and attentive; the area is attractive and peaceful with excellent hiking; and the food is good." *(Philip Puglisi)* "The swimming pools are well designed and comfortable. We hiked to Mink Lake, a rocky but beautiful climb." *(Donna Walmach)* "Our well constructed rustic cabin overlooked the river. Spotless, large, and well lit, with a good bed and heater. Good food; dinner reservations are a must. The trail to Sol Duc waterfall is both easy and breathtaking. Even the trails are litter-free, the product of thoughtful visitors as much as good staff." *(Audrey Williams)* "The real drawing card here is the chef, Lonny Ritter, who prepared some of the best meals I've ever eaten." *(Molly Knox, and others)*

Open Mid-May–Sept 30.
Rooms 32 cabins—all with private bath, porch. 26 single cabins, 6 duplex units with kitchens.
Facilities Dining room, bar/lounge, poolside deli, gift shop, grocery store, massage therapy. Occasional music entertainment. 320 acres with heated swimming pool, 3 hot spring pools, lawn games, hiking, river for fishing.
Location Olympic National Park. 42 m SW of Port Angeles. Go W on 101 30 m, turn left onto Sole Duc Rd. Go S 12 m to resort.
Restrictions No smoking in main lodge, pools.
Credit cards Amex, Discover, MC, Visa.
Rates Room only, $75–85 cabin (double). Extra person, $10. Child under 4, free.

Cooking equipment, $20 deposit. 2-night holiday minimum. Alc breakfast, $3.50–6; lunch, $5–7; dinner, $25. Children's menu. Day use for hot springs/pool, $5.50 per person; over 65, $4.50; children under 4 in chlorinated pools only, free. RV hookup, $15.

Extras Wheelchair access. Pets by prior arrangement, $2. Crib.

PORT TOWNSEND

Port Townsend has been designated a National Historic District and is considered to be the best example of a Victorian seacoast town north of San Francisco. Nearly 70 Victorian buildings can be seen, along with the town's many appealing craft shops, art galleries, and restaurants. Good salmon fishing is available, along with beaches for crabbing, clamming, and oystering. The town offers public golf courses and tennis courts and is within a short drive of the Olympic National Park. Because of the protection of the Olympic Mountains, the climate is fairly mild, with more than 200 sunny days a year and about 20 inches of rainfall (less than half of Seattle's).

Port Townsend is located on northwest Washington's Olympic Peninsula, on Puget Sound. It's less than 60 miles from both Seattle and Victoria and is 13 miles north, via Route 20, off the scenic Olympic Loop, Highway 101.

For additional area accommodations, see **Sequim.**

The English Inn
718 'F' Street, 98368

Tel: 360–385–5302
Fax: 360–385–5302

Built on a hill overlooking a valley with the Olympic range in the distance, the English Inn is an Italianate Victorian home built in 1885, and purchased by Juliette Swenson in 1993. Juliette's experience in the hospitality business goes way back; when she was a child in Bath, England, her parents operated a 20-room hotel. In addition to the original cast hardware and ceiling moldings, the inn is decorated with a rich color palette, complementing the antiques and period furnishings. Guest rooms are named for English poets, and one handsome room has a king-size bed, terracotta walls, and matching comforter, drapes, and wallpaper border in coordinating terracotta florals and dark green, while another is more feminine in pink and blue with wicker furnishings and a quilt-topped queen-size bed. Breakfast includes cereals, fruit, quiche or frittata, homemade fruit bread, scones and jam.

"From my first phone call to the end of my stay, Juliette was pleasant and accommodating. She enjoys what she does and it shows in the care put into this B&B and its atmosphere. Delicious breakfasts." *(Jill Recchi)* "Careful restoration and attention to detail." *(Joe Betts)* Reports welcome.

Open All year.
Rooms 5 doubles—all with private bath and/or shower. 2 with clock, desk, 1 with radio.
Facilities Dining room, living room with VCR. Off-street parking, garden, patio, hot tub, gazebo, bicycles. Golf, ocean nearby.

Location 10-min. walk to Uptown district; 5 min. drive to historic downtown. From Hwy. 20 (Sims Way), go through light at Kearney. Half-left up hill on Washington. Go 2 blocks. Go left onto Walker (becomes Cherry). Go right onto 'F' St. Go 2 blocks.
Restrictions No smoking. Children over 10.
Credit cards MC, Visa.
Rates B&B, $75–110 double. Extra person, $25. Senior discount.
Extras Local airport pickup. Limited French, German spoken.

The James House ¢
1238 Washington Street, 98368

Tel: 360–385–1238
800–385–1238

Built in 1891 and listed on the National Register of Historic Places, The James House is set on a bluff with a sweeping view of Port Townsend, the Olympic and Cascade ranges, and Puget Sound and was purchased by Carol McGough and Anne Tiernan in 1990. Breakfast includes orange juice, freshly ground coffee, fresh fruit with homemade sauces, a quiche or perhaps a soufflé, and freshly baked goodies. Rates also include afternoon tea and cookies, and evening sherry.

"Public rooms are quite grand, with a beautiful three-color parquet floor, an elegant carved banister, plaster work ceilings, and comfortable period furniture. Our two large rooms on the second floor, linked by a nicely refurbished bath, had pretty period wallpaper and unusual matching Victorian beds and dressers." *(Carolyn Mathiasen)* "Our ground floor two-bedroom suite was squeaky clean, and decorated with antiques and little stuffed animals. Beds had floral quilts, color-coordinated linens, and good reading lights." *(Carolyn Myles)* "The innkeepers welcomed us, shared the history of the house and area, made dinner recommendations, and chatted with us during the delicious breakfast." *(Sarah Ducich)* "Shared baths are large and conveniently arranged with shelves for toiletries and covered baskets for dirty towels; plenty of hot water. Anne and Carol combine a balanced mixture of friendliness and helpfulness with a tactful regard for guests' privacy." *(Krasna Svoboda)* "The bridal suite has a clawfoot tub, fireplace, sitting areas, and balcony overlooking the city and bay." *(Timothy Davis)*

Open All year.
Rooms 3 suites with private bath; 8 doubles share 4 baths. All with desk, fan. 2 suites with fireplace, 1 suite with antique parlor stove. 1 cottage with patio.
Facilities Dining room with fireplace, kitchen, parlor with fireplace, piano; library with fireplace. Gardens, lawn games. On-street parking.
Location 1 block from town center.
Restrictions Limited street noise in some rooms. No smoking. No children under 12.
Credit cards MC, Visa.
Rates B&B, $100–145 suite, $65–85 double, $55–65 single, $100 cottage.
Extras Local airport/station pickup.

Lizzie's ¢
731 Pierce Street, 98368

Tel: 360–385–4168

Built by Lizzie Grant in 1887, this Victorian has been beautifully restored and furnished in period; it is owned by Patti and Bill Wickline. Although each room has its charms, guests are particularly fond of Sarah's Room, because of its beautiful view and lovely furnishings, and Lizzie's Room, which has an ingenious canopy, a faux marble fireplace, and a super bath. Breakfast includes fresh fruit in season, eggs, dried fruit compote, yogurt, scones or muffins, juice, and coffee or tea.

"Exquisite vegetarian breakfast, served around huge table that seats sixteen." *(Oren Leong)* "Hope's Room is small, but comfy with poster bed, antique chest and wardrobe, fresh flowers, and stuffed teddy bears. I had a choice of two bathrooms, with lots of towels and wooden pitchers for rinsing. Food was delicious and varied—especially the oatmeal porridge with a honey banana sauce." *(AD)* "Jessie's Room had a private half-bath, a large sitting area, and a view of a beautiful plum tree brought over from the Orient almost a century ago. The living room has an antique Parisian wallpaper made with gold leaf." *(Suzanne Carmichael)* "The backyard has a doghouse replica of the big house. Come in August to get big yellow plums off the tree in the side yard." *(Pat Spaeth)* "The roaring fire in our room provided a cozy retreat from cold rainy weather. Breakfast in the kitchen was as delightful with three guests as it was with a full house, thanks to Patti and Bill's warm, easy personalities. Terrific sightseeing and restaurant recommendations." *(Caroline & Jim Lloyd)*

Area for improvement: "Showers in the shared baths."

Open All year.
Rooms 8 doubles—5 with private bath and/or shower, 3 with shared bath. 1 with fireplace.
Facilities 2 sitting rooms with fireplace, library, piano. Garden. Beach for walking, swimming.
Location 10 min walk to historic downtown. From Hwy. 20, turn left at 1st stop light, right on Lawrence, left on Pierce.
Restrictions No smoking. No children under 10. No check-in before 4 P.M.
Credit cards Discover, MC, Visa.
Rates B&B, $58–105 double. Extra person, $10. 2-night holiday/weekend minimum.
Extras Free ferry/local airport pickup. Member, WBBG.

Old Consulate Inn   *Tel: 360–385–6753*
(F.W. Hastings House)   *Fax: 360–385–2097*
313 Walker at Washington, 98368

A red Queen Anne Victorian home built in 1889, the Old Consulate has been owned by Joanna and Rob Jackson since 1987. They note that "we offer total privacy for our guests. The mansion belongs to them alone—no closed areas, no tours. Guests can relax in five common rooms, offering quiet areas for those who prefer privacy, and the billiard and game rooms when one is in the mood to socialize."

"Set under the eaves, the Village Room was blue and peaceful, spacious and lovely. The Parkside Room was awash with violets and greenery, with coordinated linens, wallpaper and drapes. The Tower Room is decorated in peach and cream, with a clawfoot tub, and a wonderful sitting room in the turret. A different breakfast each day, with wonderful egg dishes, fruit starters, sausages, biscuits with apricot-cream cheese spread, even a cake made with liqueurs and topped with edible flowers. Rob's construction background was apparent in the good heating, plumbing, and maintenance." *(Christine Hecox & Janet Bruce)* "Beautifully refurbished with period antiques. We especially enjoyed the living room and library, each with comfy chairs and working fireplace. The Jacksons are a wonderful, friendly couple; they have collected local restaurant menus and added the candid comments of guests." *(Susan Jones Moses)*

Open All year.
Rooms 3 suites, 5 doubles—all with private bath and/or shower, fan; some with desk, air-conditioning, fireplace.
Facilities Dining room, living room with fireplace, piano; study with books, TV; game room with TV/VCR, fireplace; billiard room. Gazebo, lawn games.
Location 8 blocks from town center. Go past 1st stoplight at Kearney, turn left on Washington St. to inn at corner of Walker St.
Restrictions No smoking. Children over age 12 preferred.
Credit cards Amex, MC, Visa.
Rates B&B, $95–145 suite, $69–145 double, $69–140 single. Extra person, $30–45. 2-night festival minimum.
Extras Local airport/station pickup. French, Spanish spoken.

Ravenscroft Inn

533 Quincy Street, 98368

Tel: 360–385–2784
Fax: 360–385–6724

Not everyone cares for the Victoriana prevalent at most Port Townsend inns. If this includes you, contact the Ravenscroft, a Colonial-style inn built in 1987, and purchased by Leah and John Hammer in 1990. Set on a bluff overlooking Admiralty Inlet, Ravenscroft is a re-creation of an early American seaport inn. Some guest rooms have beamed ceilings, French doors opening to the balconies, floral comforters, and period furniture. A typical breakfast might include a fruit frappe, fresh baked breads or muffins, a hot entrée such as salmon flan, freshly ground coffee and tea. It's served on Leah's extensive collection of fine china and crystal, with John's accompaniment of classical music on the Steinway piano.

"The layout of the house gives maximum privacy to guests; spacious living and dining areas." *(Steven Li)* "The brightly colored Garden Room has paintings of flowers, soft pillows, and excellent shower. It's a ground-level room without a great view, but the breeze cooled it off well. Breakfasts were delicious; my favorite was the phyllo dough filled with spinach and feta cheese, and asparagus with dried fruit." *(Jennifer Neill)* "Warm and cozy fires in both our room and the common areas." *(Jeanne & Robert Case)* "Genuine hospitality, plus another important asset, the cat, Claude dePussy, named for John's favorite French composer." *(Camilla Sparkin)* "You can park your car and walk everywhere. Leah gave us friendly advice on local sights." *(David Brett)* "Fresh coffee and cookies were waiting for us." *(Geraldine & Daniel Morrill)*

Open All year.
Rooms 1 suite, 8 doubles—all with shower and/or bath, telephone, balcony. Some with desk, fireplace, deck. Suite with double soaking tub. TV on request.
Facilities Great room with fireplace, piano; library/TV room. ¼ acre with gardens, fruit trees.
Location In historic district, 3 blocks from downtown. 5 blocks from Puget Sound.

Restrictions No smoking. No children under 12. Ringing telephone can be heard in one room.
Credit cards MC, Visa.
Rates B&B, $140–165 suite, $65–150 double, $58–143 single. Extra person, $20. 2-night holiday/weekend minimum.
Extras Airport pickup with prior arrangement, $35.

POULSBO

The Manor Farm Inn ✕
26069 Big Valley Road N.E., 98370

Tel: 360–779–4628
Fax: 360–779–4876

Owner Jill Hughes has made personal service a focal point at the Manor Farm Inn and goes out of her way to accommodate her guests. Since purchasing the century-old farmhouse and turning it into an inn in 1984, two wings have been added, creating a handsome courtyard. The light and airy decor has antique French country furnishings in both the common and guest rooms. Plenty of space between the dining room tables allows for privacy, and the inviting living room is well supplied with soft contemporary couches. The guest rooms vary in size, but all have cozy eiderdowns, and chocolates at bedtime.

Guests are welcomed with afternoon tea, served at 3:30 P.M. in the drawing room. A basket of scones, homemade raspberry jam, and fresh orange juice is delivered to your door at 8 A.M.; also included is a breakfast of fruit, English porridge and an entrée, perhaps omelets or crepes, served at 9 A.M. in the dining room. The well-regarded restaurant offers a five-course dinner, starting with hors d'oeuvres and sherry in the drawing room; entrées might be roast lamb with mint, braised rabbit with currants, and herbed monk fish on couscous.

"We succumbed to the lovely setting, our special cottage, and the absolutely wonderful food." *(Ruth Tilsley)* "Staff were warm, helpful, creative, but not intrusive. Delicious vegetarian meals (at my request), especially the tomato bisque soup." *(Marianne Lynn Makepeace)* "Tea-time—in the beautiful library, with a warm fire and classical music—was a good opportunity to meet other guests. Our large, airy, immaculate suite was done in colors of cream, white and beige with pine antiques; the sitting room had great overstuffed recliner chairs—great for reading. We caught a rainbow trout which they prepared for our breakfast. Delicious dinner of pasta with vegetables and shrimp, marvelous green salad, homemade bread, and a decadent dessert. We took walks after dinner to check on the lambs and returned to take a luxurious bath with their private label herbal bath salts, herbal and glycerin soap." *(Mr. & Mrs. Lyle Romack)* "Fronting on an inlet with a pretty promenade area along the water, Poulsbo is one of Washington's many Scandinavian communities with shops selling Scandinavian items, candy, and baked goods." *(SC)*

Open All year. Closed Mon., Tues. in Nov., Jan.–April; also Thanksgiving eve and day, Dec. 24–28.
Rooms 2 2-bedroom cottages; 7 doubles—all with full private bath, instant hot tap with supplies for coffee, tea. 2 with fireplace, deck. Cottages with telephone,

TV, kitchen, fireplace, hot tub; 1 with private beach. Beach house cottage several minutes away.

Facilities Dining room with fireplace, living room with fireplace, gift shop, veranda, courtyard. 25 acres with lawn games, orchards, garden, mountain bikes, stocked trout pond (equipment supplied).

Location NW WA. N. Kitsap Peninsula. 20 m NW of Seattle, across Puget Sound. 4 m N of Poulsbo, 4 m S of Hood Canal Bridge. From Seattle, take ferry to Winslow, drive W to Poulsbo. Go N 4 m on Hwy. 3 to Big Valley Rd. & turn right at sign; go 1 m E to inn.

Restrictions No smoking. No children under 16.

Credit cards MC, Visa.

Rates B&B, $205–225 beach house, $175–195 cottage, $115–175 double. Extra person in cottage/beach house, $35. 10% discount for 5-night stay in beach cottage. Prix fixe dinner, $30–40; 20% gratuity. Full breakfast (non-resident guests), $12–14.

PROSSER

Wine Country Inn ¢ ✕ ♿   *Tel:* 509–786–2855
1106 Wine Country Road, 99350   *Fax:* 509–786–7414

Although a "jug of wine, a loaf of bread and thou" may be all you need in the wilderness, we prefer a more extensive menu and more comfortable accommodations when we're on the road. In Washington's wine country, you'll find that the Wine Country Inn offers a pleasant guest rooms, good food, and a pleasant location on the banks of the Yakima River. Built in 1898, the inn has been owned by Christine Flodin and Audrey Zuniga since 1989. Breakfast is served between 8:00 and 9:00A.M. (earlier for business travelers) and the menu includes such dishes as scrambled eggs with red and green peppers, green onions, and cheddar cheese, with apple sausage, or Swedish pancakes with bacon. The dinner menu lists such entrées as rack of lamb with a herb mustard crust, duck with ginger and blackberries, and halibut with wild rice.

"The first floor has a pleasant little restaurant serving three meals a day, with innovative, fresh items on the menu. We were delighted with our lunch of chicken avocado salad and angel hair pasta with a homemade Italian sauce. Outside is a deck where guests can sit and eat or just read while watching the river. The rooms are charming, moderate in size; one has wicker furnishings with a little window seat with river views." *(Suzanne Carmichael)*

Open All year. Closed Dec. 25th.–Jan 3rd. Restaurant closed Mon., Tues.

Rooms 4 doubles—2 with private bath and/or shower, 2 with maximum of 4 sharing bath. All with radio, clock, fan. 1 with desk. TV on request.

Facilities Restaurant, porch. Off-street parking, gazebo. Boat docks, swimming, fishing, 2 blocks away.

Location Benton County. 47 m E of Yakima. From I-82, take Exit 80 (Gap Rd.–Prosser). Follow signs to Prosser. Go 1 m S on Wine Country Rd. to inn on S side of bridge.

Restrictions No smoking. Children over 3.
Credit cards Amex, MC, Visa.
Rates B&B, $50–70 double, $45–70 single. Extra person, $20. Midweek state/business rate, $45. Alc lunch, $6.50, alc dinner, $20. Winery tours/picnics.
Extras Limited wheelchair access. Local airport/station pickup.

QUINAULT

Lake Quinault Lodge 🛏 ✕ ♿
South Shore Road, Box 7, 98575

Tel: 360–288–2571
800–562–6672
Fax: 360–288–2415

Olympic National Park, with an average annual rainfall of almost 150 inches, offers many sights of interest, including the Hoh Rain Forest, filled with massive Douglas firs that are covered with shaggy green moss. The area was set aside as a forest reserve in 1898 by Grover Cleveland and was declared a National Monument by Teddy Roosevelt in 1909. In 1938 it was toured by Franklin Roosevelt (he stayed at the Lake Quinault Lodge), who declared it a national park.

The lodge was built in 1926, in only 10 weeks, at the then-considerable cost of $90,000. All building materials and furnishings had to be hauled over 50 miles of dirt road. Many area artisans were used, and their work can be seen in the stenciled designs on the lobby's beamed ceiling. Much of the wicker lobby furniture is original to the building. ARA Leisure Services of Philadelphia took over the management in 1988, and has substantially improved and upgraded the property since then, including refurbishing of rooms in the main lodge, and the addition of 36 lakeside rooms, decorated with wicker furniture with typical motel layouts.

"Our twin-bedded room in the main lodge was smallish but adequate, with a nice view of the lake. Be sure to reserve ahead for dinner." *(Eileen O'Reilly)* "Lakeside rooms are attractive with good light for reading. Food is a cut above other national park concessions, and service at breakfast, lunch, and dinner was good." *(Tom Wilbanks)* "Wonderful location in the middle of the world's only temperate rain forest." *(Julia & Dennis Mallach)* "Hiking in the area is perfect for beginners." *(Mrs. Arnold Miller)*

"This large cedar-shake building is perched on top of a low hill with grass rolling down to the lake. The lobby is inviting, the staff friendly and eager to please. Nearly all the odd-numbered rooms in the lodge have views of the lake; those that face west offer beautiful sunset views over the mountains and lake. The dining room has large Northwest Coast Indian prints and Navajo rugs on the walls. Breakfast was well done, with lots of choices; excellent homemade strawberry jam. The mist lifted while we were canoeing, revealing the snow-dusted, jagged tops of some of the closer peaks of the Olympic Mountain range. Recommended forays from the lodge include going to the end of the road (the rain forest is overpowering here), driving around to the huge grove of trees on the other side of the lake at July Creek Campground, and taking the rain forest paths that start directly across the street from the Lodge." *(SC)*

Open All year.
Rooms 3 suites, 89 doubles—all with full private bath and/or shower. 16 with gas fireplace; 54 with balcony. Rooms in 3 buildings.
Facilities Dining room, lounge, lobby with fireplace, game room, gift shop. Pianist or singer in lounge summer weekends. 5 acres on lake, with lawns, gazebo, heated indoor swimming pool with hot tub, sauna; interpretive programs in summer. Fishing, canoeing, hunting, hiking nearby.
Location NW WA, Olympic Peninsula. In Olympic National Forest, 40 m N of Aberdeen/Hoquiam, via Hwy. 101N. At Milepost 125, turn right on South Shore Rd. Go 2 m to lodge.
Restrictions Some non-smoking rooms.
Credit cards Amex, MC, Visa.
Rates Room only, $98–220 suite, $49–115 double. Extra person, $10. Children 5 and under, free. Midweek packages. 2-night weekend minimum. Alc breakfast, $5–9; alc lunch, $6–10; alc dinner, $20–30.
Extras Limited wheelchair access. Pets by arrangement in annex, $10. Babysitting by arrangement.

ROCKPORT

Also recommended: Received just as we were going to press was an intriguing report on the **Ross Lake Resort** (Milepost 134, Highway 20, Rockport, 98283; 206–386–4437), accessible only by boat or a two-mile hike. Built in 1950, the resort consists of 13 cabins built on log floats, located on the west side of Ross Lake, just north of Ross Dam. Despite its remote location (no direct road access), it's just a three-hour drive from Seattle to meet the tugboat and truck that delivers you to Ross Lake less than an hour later. The cabins are fully equipped with hot water and electricity, bedding, towels and cookware, but you must bring your own food. Activities include the beautiful hiking trails in the North Cascades National Park, and fishing, canoeing, and boating on the lake (rentals available). Double rates range from $51–77. *(Gene & Roberta Altshuler)*

SAN JUAN ISLANDS

If you can visit only one part of Washington state, choose the San Juans. Depending on the tide, between 175 and 300 rock-cliffed islands dot the area between Puget Sound and Canada. Here you will find secluded bays and densely forested ridges inhabited by eagles. From Anacortes on the mainland, ferries travel to Victoria, Canada, stopping at four of the more populous islands. The largest is Orcas, where you can climb Mt. Constitution for spectacular views of the other islands, Canada, and the Olympic and Cascade mountain ranges. Lopez is perfect for cyclists, and Shaw is known for the nuns who operate its ferry dock. On San Juan Island (namesake for the whole chain) visit the site of the infamous "Pig War" between the U.S. and England; relax in remote Roche Harbor or join the summer crowds in Friday Harbor.

By ferry the islands are three hours north of Seattle and the same distance south of Vancouver and east of Victoria. The ferry from Anacortes takes about an hour. One warning: If you're traveling in the summer, advance reservations for accommodations and ferry passage are *essential.*

Reader tip: "From Memorial Day to Labor Day, don't expect to get the first ferry you try for; they fill up quickly, and you may end up waiting several hours. Don't schedule tight connections." *(Adam Platt)*

SAN JUAN ISLANDS—LOPEZ ISLAND

Just 80 miles north of Seattle, Lopez Island has few places to stay (or even eat), making it a haven for those who want to get away from crowds. Most visitors to this island are fishermen/women and cyclists who peddle the relatively flat back roads.

Information please: We need recent reports on the **Edenwild Inn** (P.O. Box 271, Lopez Island, 98261; 360–468–3238) built in 1990 as an elegant country inn with one room that is "family friendly" and another that is fully equipped for the disabled. The eight guest rooms, all with private bath, overlook Fisherman's Bay, the San Juan Channel, or wooded garden. Breakfast is served family-style in the dining room or delivered to your door; B&B double rates range from $85–140.

Inn at Swifts Bay ¢   *Tel: 360–468–3636*
Port Stanley Road, Route 2, Box 3402, 98261   *Fax: 360–468–3636*

A Tudor-style B&B in a country setting, the Inn at Swifts Bay is owned by Robert Herrmann and Christopher Brandmeir. Both innkeepers left careers in the gourmet food industry to start this B&B. In 1994, they opened the Hunter Bay House, a beautifully decorated private cottage for two at the south end of the island, complete with a hot tub, fireplace, and video library of romantic movies.

"Other innkeepers become jaded after years—Robert and Christopher are as enthusiastic as the day they opened." *(Tony & Val Sharp)* "Robert knows where to find the best food, antiques, and getaways. They are outrageous chefs." *(Evan Teplow)* "Cozy sitting room, filled with books for browsing." *(Dr. Elise Herman)* "Nothing is overlooked: bathrobes and slippers are supplied for trips to the private hot tub, headsets are thoughtfully supplied so guests are not disturbed by the VCR, and the common area has decanters of brandy and a small refrigerator for ice and soda." *(Paul & Pat Stackhouse)* "Though isolated, the location is beautiful with beach access." *(Pam Phillips)* "Robert and Chris met our sea plane, made dinner reservations, loaned backpacks for bike riding, and fed us the most incredible breakfasts each morning—crab cakes with poached eggs, omelets with ham, apples and Brie, hazelnut waffles—plus fresh berries and muffins along with wonderful coffee. Our small room shared a bath and had a comfortable bed. Beautifully landscaped yard with plenty of comfortable lawn chairs for sunning and reading." *(Tanya Bednarski)* "Fully endorse existing entry. Can't find anything that isn't perfect." *(Pat O'Brien)*

Open All year.

Rooms 1 cottage, 3 suites with gas fireplace, 2 doubles—3 with private bath, 2 sharing 1 bath.

Facilities Living room with fireplace, den with piano, TV/VCR, stereo; dining room. 2.6 acres with hot tub. Private beach nearby.

Location NW WA, San Juan Islands. 4 m from village. From ferry landing, heading toward village, take first major left onto Port Stanley Rd, opposite Odlin Park entrance, & go ³⁄₄ m to inn on right.

Restrictions No smoking.

Credit cards Amex, Discover, MC, Visa.

Rates B&B, $195 cottage, $125–155 suite, $85 double. Holiday weekend minimum stay. 2-night minimum in cottage.

Extras Airport/ferry pickup. Portuguese, German spoken. Member, WBBG.

MacKaye Harbor Inn ¢

Alec Bay Road, Route 1,
Box 1940, Lopez Island, 98261

Tel: 360–468–2253
Fax: 360–468–9555

The MacKaye Harbor Inn is a restored 60-year-old, two-story frame Victorian-style home; eagles, deer, seals, and otters are frequently seen on the grounds. Breakfast ranges from cheese blintzes and Dutch baby pancakes, to ranch-style eggs, served with caramel pecan rolls, fruit, and meat dishes. "Delightful little extras—coffee, cookies, and truffles." *(Arlene Kveven-Breed)* "Impeccably clean and charming with antiques to enhance the country look." *(Bill Clemens & Micki Ryan)* "As the storm clouds rolled in, we curled up in front of our fireplace (all we had to do was light a match) to read. The parlor is good place to meet the other guests. Sharon and Brooks are friendly and helpful with information from restaurants to island folklore." *(Marjorie Shoemaker)* "Excellent, well-prepared food. Congenial hosts—including the cat, who is clearly the overall manager." *(John & Anita Lewis)* "I awakened to the smell of cinnamon rolls baking and the sound of tiny waves patty-caking the shore." *(Dan Morris)* "My room faced the inlet bay, with a cool breeze through its windows." *(Michelle McGill)* "Our hosts were around if needed but seemed to disappear when we wanted privacy. The scenery is delightful; the atmosphere inside is equally peaceful. Don't go if you'll miss your TV." *(David Pritchard)* "MacKaye meets all our B&B requirements: no noise, firm beds, and wonderful, varied breakfasts." *(Victoria Symonds)*

Open All year.

Rooms 2 suites, 3 doubles—2 with private shower, 3 share 2½baths. All with desk, fan. 1 with fireplace, 1 with deck.

Facilities Parlor with fireplace, stereo, games; guest refrigerator. 8 acres with lawn, orchard, beach. Rowboat, mountain bike rentals; kayak rentals, instruction, tours. Windsurfing nearby.

Location From ferry, go S at MacKaye Harbor sign & go left onto Center Rd. Go past school & turn left on Mud Bay Rd. Turn right at MacKaye Harbor Rd. to beach & inn.

Restrictions No smoking. "Children over age 9 welcome."

Credit cards MC, Visa.

Rates B&B, $87–115 suite, $69–87 double. Extra person, $18. 2-night minimum June–Sept.

Extras Ferry pickup, $10.

SAN JUAN ISLANDS—ORCAS ISLAND

Orcas Island combines a lively arts community with outdoor recreation opportunities and pampered resort life. It's possible to spend the morning hiking Mt. Constitution, pop into a trendy café for lunch, browse in small galleries and bookstores, then while away the rest of the afternoon beachcombing, fishing, or having a spa treatment.

Also recommended: Received just as we were going to press was an enthusiastic report on **The Old Trout Inn** (Route 1, Box 45A, Eastsound 98245; 360–376–4037), 2½ miles from the ferry landing. This contemporary cedar lodge has five different decks and patios where you can catch island sunsets reflected in the pond. Two doubles and three suites are available at rates of $80–135, including a full breakfast. "Articulate, knowledgeable, pleasant innkeeper; exceptional library; spotless, comfortable accommodations; tasty breakfast, mercifully served at individual tables." *(Gene & Robert Altshuler)*

Spring Bay Inn　　　　　　　　　　　*Tel:* 360–376–5531
Obstruction Pass Trailhead Road　　　　*Fax:* 360–376–2193
P.O. Box 97, Olga 98279

Carl Burger and Sandy Playa share their love of the outdoors (they used to be California State Park rangers) with guests at their cedar-sided home, built in 1993. Over 160 windows take in the natural beauty of the private bay and wooded property, and guest rooms are bright and airy with twelve-foot ceilings. After an eye-opener of hot coffee and muffins, Carl and Sandy lead an early- morning guided kayak trip. Waiting at home is a lovable golden retriever and a 10:30 A.M. vegetarian brunch; a recent meal included carrot juice, a mango smoothie, and huevos rancheros with tortillas.

"The refreshing personalities of Carl and Sandy, the beautiful, tranquil setting, plus the tastefully appointed rooms made for an enjoyable stay. After some basic instruction, off we went for a pleasant two-hour early-morning kayak run on Puget Sound. Upon returning, we freshened up before sitting down to a delightful meal (we'd earned it). A leisurely stroll led us from Spring Bay's park-like trails into the adjoining state park. That evening we relaxed in the great room, with its comfortable couches and two large fireplaces while music played softly in the background. When we retired to our room, the fireplace had been lit." *(Philip Tuson)*

Open All year.
Rooms 4 doubles—all with full private bath, telephone, weather radio, clock, fireplace, refrigerator. 2 with deck.
Facilities Dining/living room with fireplace, books, piano, stereo; guest refrigerator, porch. Campfire sing-alongs. 60 acres on private bay with guided kayaking tours, hiking trails, hot tub, picnic tables, barbecue grills.
Location From ferry follow signs to Obstruction Pass trailhead.
Restrictions No smoking.
Credit cards MC, Visa.

Rates B&B, $165–175 double, $155–165 single. Extra person, $25.
Extras German spoken.

Turtleback Farm Inn &.   *Tel: 360–376–4914*
Crow Valley Road, Route 1, Box 650,
Eastsound, 98245

"The Turtleback Farm Inn is a place to experience the three R's—rest, relaxation, and romance, not necessarily in that order. Peaceful and calm, yet invigorating, the inn is on forest and farmland near Turtleback Mountain. Our favorite room has an expansive view with a private deck, queen-size bed, and antique furnishings. The main living room with its terrific fireplace is a perfect place to relax. During the spring and summer, breakfast is served on the deck overlooking the valley; during the winter and fall, it's presented in the dining room on bone china, with white linen and table flowers. Starting off with fresh fruit, juice and homemade granola, a hearty country breakfast follows; the meals are always fresh, healthful, varied, and quite filling. The long-time owners, Susan and Bill Fletcher, are charming, caring, and informative. They do whatever they can to make your stay more wonderful—from restaurant reservations to sightseeing suggestions." *(Rikki Rothenberg-Klein)*

"Our room overlooked a sheep pasture and was beautifully appointed with a combination of old and new, blending antiques with comfortable furniture." *(Melvyn Greenberg & Carole Malone)* "Beds are wonderfully comfortable. Breakfasts are nourishing and delicious, fueling us for a day's bicycling." *(Elizabeth Shaw)* "Fully confirm existing entry." *(A. Sievers)*

Open All year.
Rooms 7 doubles—all with private bath and/or shower. 6 with radio, 2 with deck.
Facilities Dining room with wet bar, refrigerator. Living room with fireplace, game table. 80 acres with 6 ponds, 1 stocked with trout. Tennis, swimming, hiking nearby.
Location 2.4 m from West Sound Marina, 4 m from Eastsound, 6 m from ferry landing. From ferry, take Horseshoe Hwy.; take first left, then right onto Crow Valley Rd.; inn on right.
Restrictions No smoking. Children 8 and over by arrangement.
Credit cards MC, Visa.
Rates B&B, $70–150 double, $60–140 single. Extra person, $25. Tipping "not expected." 2-night minimum May 1–Oct. 31; also holidays, weekends. Midweek rates, Nov. 1–April 1.
Extras Limited wheelchair access. Airport/ferry pickup.

SAN JUAN ISLANDS—SAN JUAN ISLAND

San Juan Island is the westernmost island in the archipelago. Although its main town, Friday Harbor, is the county seat, it is still a sleepy small town. Among its features are a few shops and galleries, a busy waterfront, the Whale Museum, and a performing arts center. From Friday Harbor, take a drive around the craggy western end of the island for superb views; better yet, follow the popular bike route. Continue on to the site of the "Pig War," which started when an American farmer killed a British pig as part of a general dispute about the western boundary of the U.S. While here, watch out for the hundreds of wild rabbits that live in this area! Be sure to stop at Lime Kiln Park on the west side of the island, the only whale-watching park in the continental U.S.

Also recommended: The *Jacquelyn*, a 60' yacht owned by Bette and Clyde Rice, is home to the **Wharfside B&B** (slip K-13, Port of Friday Harbor, P.O. Box 1212, 98250; 360–378–5661) with two guest rooms. "All the comforts of home, plus a beautiful view of the surrounding islands. Our cabin had a comfortable queen-size bed, complete with a down comforter. The main cabin salon was spacious with a variety of books and games in case the weather didn't cooperate; the deck with ample space for lounging and watching the ferries go in and out. We were entertained by a harbor seal while walking around the marina. Shops, restaurants, and the Whale Museum are all within walking distance. Bette was friendly and gracious, serving breakfast on deck: pineapple filled with fresh fruit, a Mexican-style frittata with fresh salsa, and the best blueberry muffins ever. She let us leave our luggage until it time was time to catch the ferry." *(Chrys Bolk)* "Our 12-year-old found marine plumbing very entertaining. We were cozy and warm under quilts with a mattress warmer and an extra-long bed. Big, friendly dog. Clyde and Bette provide a luggage cart for guest use." *(Mark & Kathy Tyers)*

Information please: The **Mariella Inn & Cottages** (630 Turn Point Road, Friday Harbor 98250; 360–378–6868) has a beautiful location overlooking the sea, just a few blocks from the ferry landing. Rooms, furnished with antiques, have lovely views of the bay or gardens. You can relax on the porch overlooking the water, or curl up with a book before the fireplace in the sitting room. A full breakfast is served in the nicely restored dining room with a sweeping view of the bay. Other amenities include kayaks, badminton, and classic wooden rowboats for the pond. B&B double rates range from $85–150; cottages from $200–275; prix fixe dinners from $25–35, plus service, tax, and wine. Readers have been delighted with the breathtaking setting, and satisfied with the meals, service, and accommodation. One reader loved the water view from her charming room but was less pleased at the rate: $130 for a double-size bed with a light and table on only one side and a minuscule private bath (shower, no tub). Comments welcome.

Moon & Sixpence ¢ 👭 Tel: 360–378–4138
3021 Beaverton Valley Road, Friday Harbor, 98250

Charles and Evelyn Tuller have owned and operated the Moon & Sixpence since 1984. The farmhouse is decorated with American folk art from early settlers, Pennsylvania Dutch country, and from the Navajo and Inuit traditions. Evelyn is an accomplished weaver—guests are welcome to visit her studio, where traditional fabrics are woven from island fleece and locally gathered dyes. A typical breakfast menu might include orange juice, peach parfait, cereal, bread pudding with raspberry sauce or perhaps an egg dish, and Black Forest ham or smoked turkey. Families will be delighted with the Island Suite, with one bedroom for adults, and an adjacent one set up with twin beds and toys for the kids.

"The water tower suite was blissfully quiet with wonderful views from all sides." *(Sarah Morrill)* "Warm hospitality; relaxing atmosphere; exceptionally clean. Charlie gave excellent directions and advice." *(Janet Mecklenberg)* "Breakfasts are delicious; my favorite was a bowl of five varieties of local strawberries." *(Andrew Borges & Sayre Coombs)* "Fresh foods simply served. Extremely comfortable beds, especially the feather pillows. The owners are friendly and open but not intruding." *(Kathleen Heft)*

Open All year.
Rooms 3 doubles—all with private bath, radio, desk.
Facilities Dining room, living room with wood-burning stove, library with piano, game room, porches. Weaving and textile studios. 17 acres with lawns, gardens, croquet.
Location 3 m from town. From ferry dock take Spring Rd to Second St. Turn right. Second St. becomes Guard St. which becomes Beaverton Valley Rd. Go approx. 2½ m. Inn on left, just before Egg Lake Rd.
Restrictions No smoking. Flow restrictors for water conservation.
Credit cards None accepted.
Rates B&B, $90–105 double, $85 single. No tipping. 2-night minimum July, Aug.
Extras Airport/ferry pickup. Member, WBBG.

Olympic Lights ¢
4531A Cattle Point Road, Friday Harbor, 98250

Tel: 360–378–3186

"A carefully restored and sensitively updated 1890s Victorian farmhouse on gently sloping meadowland, open to the southwest with views of the Olympic Mountains and the San Juan Channel, across which the evening lights of Victoria, B.C., twinkle in the clear air. The inn is simply furnished, with a comfy wood-burning stove providing a welcome gathering place in the sitting room. The guest rooms have queen- or king-size beds and down comforters, with light-toned carpets and fresh flowers. Breakfasts are served in the large kitchen/dining room, and include eggs from the family chicken coop, granola, and heart-shaped biscuits." *(Clyde & Lois Coughlin)* "The Ra Room has a glorious bay window facing east; spectacular sunrises." *(Claudia & Gary Weybright)* "The location is perfect, in a meadow near the Sound; nights are star studded and still. Breakfasts include eggs in a variety of herb-laced dishes; scones are light and warm from the oven. Fruit, inventive juice concoctions, and fresh-from-the-garden vegetables are lovingly prepared and served. I have stayed in three of the rooms and all are immaculate, bright, and comfortable. Christian and Lea are personable, interesting and caring hosts. It is evident that they love their life and business." *(Debra Moore)* "Excellent advice about activities; the innkeepers were equally gracious to our two teenagers." *(Robert Boas)* "The walk to the lighthouse shouldn't be missed." *(Caroline & Jim Lloyd)* "Lea's gardens are beautiful, and the inn's cats are unobtrusive. Christian is just about the friendliest innkeeper I've encountered." *(Adam Platt)*

Open All year.
Rooms 5 doubles—1 with full private bath, 4 with maximum of 4 people sharing a bath.
Facilities Dining room/kitchen, living room, parlor, porch. 5 acres with croquet, horseshoes. Scuba diving nearby. Walking distance to American Camp National Park.

Location 5 m S of town. From ferry landing, follow Argyle Rd. S to Cattle Point Rd. to inn.
Restrictions No smoking. Children by prior arrangement. No shoes upstairs.
Credit cards None accepted.
Rates B&B, $70–105 double, $65–100 single. Extra person, $20. No tipping. 2-night holiday/weekend minimum.
Extras Spanish spoken. Member, WBBG.

SEATTLE

Snuggled on six steep hills between Puget Sound and Lake Washington, Seattle is both sophisticated and friendly. It's known as a "city of neighborhoods." Visitors can sample the unusual restaurants and shops in the International District, home to Seattle's Asian population, or stroll through Ballard, the Scandinavian enclave.

On the southern end of downtown Seattle, Pioneer Square Historic District boasts unusual boutiques, the Seattle Children's Museum, and sidewalk cafés. Pike Place Market, in the middle of the business district overlooking Elliot Bay, opened as a farmer's market in 1907. Here you will find fishmongers and fresh produce stands, street musicians and handcrafts, ethnic markets and superb eateries. A few blocks north is Seattle Center, the site of the 1962 World's Fair. Take a ride up the center's 605-foot Space Needle for wonderful views, and take your kids to the excellent exhibits at the Pacific Science Center. Stop by the Center House for a variety of ethnic fast-food choices.

Tour the waterfront by boarding one of the vintage 1927 Australian trolley cars. Be sure to visit the Seattle Aquarium, where an underwater viewing area provides fish-eye views of Puget Sound's sea life. For something really different, take the underground Seattle tour to see 19th-century sidewalks and storefronts left underground when the streets were raised to avoid the spring mud. In the evening visit jazz clubs in the University District or the lively restaurants and nightclubs on Capitol Hill.

Seattle has outstanding public art collections, starting with the 18 works displayed at the airport. Excellent theater can be found at Seattle Repertory Theater, A Contemporary Theater, or The Empty Space. Also worth attending are the Pacific Northwest Ballet and the Seattle Opera's Wagner Festival. The best of Seattle's various festivals include the Seafair Festival in late July, the Bumbershoot street art festival around Labor Day, and the Christmas cruise in December.

Reader tips: "Coffee lovers of the world unite! From the aroma of Starbuck's great coffee greeting you at Sea-Tac airport to shops and vendors around the city, you find wonderful coffee in more great combinations and flavors than Baskin-Robbins has ice cream." *(MW)* And *Joy Suggs* enjoys "the good seafood at Cutters, on the bay, chosen from the smaller bar menu, while watching lovely sunsets. Good seafood can also be found four short blocks from the Market at McCormick & Schmick's."

Also recommended: *Marie Harris* recommends **The Claremont Hotel** (2000/2004 Fourth Avenue at Virginia, 98121; 206–448–8600 or 800–448–8601) as "an ideal compromise between a B&B and an expensive hotel. Located on a quiet street, right on the edge of downtown, an easy walk to shops, museums, galleries, and the Pike Place Market. There's a comfortable lobby and a friendly helpful staff. Many of the reasonably priced suites have kitchens, so you can save by cooking your own breakfast. Extra-long, old-fashioned bath tub, great for soaking." Rates range from $69–129, with the popular kitchen suites at $89; lower rates in February and March, and children under 16 stay free.

A restored Victorian home, the **Bellevue Place B&B** (1111 Bellevue Place East, P.O. Box 12095, 98102; 206–325–9253) has three guest rooms sharing one bath, each with a queen-sized bed and down comforters; the B&B double rate is $85. "Great location for evening walks, water and mountain views. The plentiful, delicious breakfast included egg strata one morning, pancakes the next, plus muffins, fruit, and bacon." *(Cynthia Gibat)*

Restored by the same Kimco Hotel Group that has developed the successful "boutique" hotels of San Francisco and Portland is the 1920s-era **Hotel Vintage Park** (1100 Fifth Avenue, 98101; 206–624–8000 or 800–624–4433). As a salute to the Washington wine industry, each of the 129 suites and doubles (some are small) is named for a winery or vineyard; rich colors predominate in the decor—burgundy (of course), rose, and dark greens. Standard hotel amenities abound, and the restaurant features Italian cuisine.

On the shores of Lake Washington is the **Woodmark Hotel** (1200 Carillon Point, Kirkland, 98033; 206–822–3700 or 800–822–3700) with a marina and public pier. The hotel offers 100 guest rooms complete with an honor bar, refrigerator, TV/VCR with free tapes, coffee maker, and bathrobe, morning paper; most have lake and Olympic Mountain views.

Chambered Nautilus ¢   Tel: 206–522–2536
5005 22nd Avenue Northeast, 98105

Like the seashell it is named for, the Chambered Nautilus offers guests "a home of beauty, warmth, and security." Perched on a hill in the University District, this handsome Georgian Colonial mansion was built in 1915 by one of the early faculty members at the University of Washington; it was bought in 1988 by Connecticut transplants Bunny and Bill Hagemeyer. The Hagemeyers have landscaped the inn's gardens, creating an impressive display of flowers with lovely views of the Cascade Mountains in the distance. A typical breakfast might include cereals, fruits and juices, apple raisin quiche, French toast with homemade syrup, pumpkin-blueberry muffins, and fresh-ground coffee.

"Rooms are decorated with English and American antiques, comforters, and pillows. Each is provided with a Japanese bathrobe, a homemade lollipop, and a guide to 'Seattle's Best.' Hot tea is served in the large living room, where a fire is lit on cold nights." *(Aubrey Wendling)* "Guests are encouraged to feel at home, select a book from the large library, or play the piano. Bunny and Bill's are adept at including all their guests in breakfast conversation." *(Beverly Gordon)* "Breakfast was huge—fresh berry tarts, granola, muffins, French toast and, of course, Starbuck's coffee." *(Lisa Gallagher)* "We missed breakfast our last morning because of an early flight, but coffee, muffins, and fruit had been thoughtfully set out for us. Be prepared to meet their friendly Lab when you arrive." *(Caroline &*

Jim Lloyd) "Softly playing classical music accompanies breakfast." *(Kenneth Poll)*

Open All year.
Rooms 6 doubles—4 with private bath and/or shower, 2 with maximum of 4 people sharing bath. All with radio, desk, fan. 4 with porch.
Facilities Living room with fireplace, piano, books; dining room with fireplace, sun porch, open porches. ½ acre with landscaped gardens, sitting areas. On-street parking. Burke-Gilman Trail, Green Lake, Ravenna Park nearby for jogging, walking. Boating, fishing nearby.
Location University district. 10 min. from downtown Seattle, walking distance to U. of WA. Take exit 169 off I-5 N. Go right (E) on NE 50th St. to stop sign at 20th Ave. NE & turn left. Go 4 blocks to NE 54th St. Turn right, go 2 blocks to 22nd Ave. NE. Turn right to inn at #5005.
Restrictions No smoking. Children under 12 by arrangement. 27 steep steps up to front door. On-street parking.
Credit cards CB, DC, MC, Visa; also AMEX.
Rates B&B, $75–98 double. $68–90 single. Extra person, $15. No tipping. Long-term, winter rates. 2–3-night minimum holiday/weekends.
Extras German spoken. Bus stop nearby.

Gaslight Inn ¢
Tel: 206-325-3654
1727 15th Avenue, 98122

Innkeepers Steve Bennett and Trevor Logan bought and restored the Gaslight in 1981 from the Dwight Christianson family who had built it in 1906. Original oak paneling and bevelled and stained glass are complemented by Arts and Crafts furniture and Northwest Indian artifacts. A continental breakfast is served between 8 and 10:30 A.M.

"Our clean, comfortable room was attractive with turn-of-the-century antiques. Breakfast consisted of scones, croissants, fresh fruit, and good coffee, served in the gorgeous oak dining room. The old brass chandeliers made for both gas and electric light are interesting." *(Emanuel Cassar)* "A large, lovely, old house in the Capitol Hill area. Many stained glass windows—one on the staircase is especially beautiful. Everything gleamed from the highly polished wood floors to the bathroom shower door. Bedrooms are decorated in different styles; ours was Art Deco, while others were Victorian. We shared a bath, but our room had a large mirror and a sink. Robes are provided and the bath towels were huge and fluffy. Steve was helpful with suggestions for dinner—many restaurants and shops are nearby, and it's only 1½ blocks to the bus stop. The parlor, complete with fire going in the fireplace, provided a cozy spot for that first cup of coffee." *(Chrys Bolk)*

Open All year.
Rooms 9 rooms—6 with private bath and/or shower, 3 with maximum of 6 sharing bath. All with radio, clock, TV. 6 with refrigerator, 3 with telephone, fan. 1 with desk, fireplace, or deck.
Facilities Dining room, living rooms, 1 with fireplace; laundry facilities, sun decks. Some off-street parking. Heated swimming pool.
Location In downtown Seattle. On Capitol Hill.
Restrictions No smoking. No children.
Credit cards Amex, MC, Visa.
Rates B&B, $62–98 double. 2-night weekend minimum.

WASHINGTON

Hill House B&B ¢
1113 East John Street, 98102

Tel: 206–720–7161
800–720–7161

From its name, you've probably guessed that this simple Victorian frame home sits on a hill; what might be a surprise is the innovative breakfasts that owners Ken Hayes and Eric Lagasca serve. Salmon quiche and Provençal omelets are two of the entrées that appear on the dining room table. Also pleasing are the queen-size beds with lace cutwork duvets, and the tasteful Victorian decor. Hill House was built in 1903 and was restored as a B&B in 1991. "Beautifully decorated, with antiques, paintings, down comforters, and linen sheets. Breakfast was served on elegant china and crystal, while classical music played, and included a delicious fruit plate, then French toast made with sourdough bread, orange rind and Cointreau, with homemade pecan butter and maple syrup. Ken and Eric were unobtrusive, but extremely helpful when asked for restaurant and sightseeing recommendations." (Cori Dykman)

Open All year.
Rooms 2 suites, 5 doubles—3 with private bath and/or shower, 2 with a maximum of 4 people sharing bath. All with clock. Suites with telephone, radio, TV, desk, fan, private entrance.
Facilities Dining room, living room with CD stereo, books; porch. Off-street parking.
Location Historic Capitol Hill district. Between Broadway & 12th Ave. E.
Restrictions No smoking. Children over 12.
Credit cards Amex, Discover, MC, Visa.
Rates B&B, $95–105 suite, $60–95 double, $60–90 single. 2-night weekend minimum.
Extras Local station pickups. Filipino spoken.

Inn at the Market 🛏 ✕ ♿
86 Pine Street, 98101

Tel: 206–443–3600
800–446–4484
Fax: 206–448–0631

Since its opening in 1985, this small luxury hotel has gained a top reputation. Some have told us once you've stayed here, you won't stay anywhere else in Seattle (if you can afford it), although others prefer a more peaceful atmosphere.

"Extremely accommodating staff. Lovely, big, beautifully decorated rooms with terry robes and lots of big, white fluffy towels." (Joy Sugg) "The restaurant 'Campagne' is fabulous—spectacular food and service. Excellent wine list." (Alice Clarke Roe) "I felt very safe while staying at the hotel, and appreciated the valet parking." (Linda Panveno) "We left feeling that the staff's goal in life was to see that we enjoyed Seattle, and indeed we did." (Ruth Tilsley)

"Great location in the heart of the Pike Place Market area. You can walk out the door for fresh coffee, bakeries, street vendors, and more. Above average housekeeping; rooms are spacious, with ample closet space. The little lobby is inviting, decorated with a country French theme, with two loveseats in front of the big fireplace; coffee and tea are available here each morning." (Pam Phillips) "A place for city-lovers who enjoy the activities of a busy farmers' market and lots of pedestrian traffic." (Donna & David Kmetz)

"From the roof garden we had a great view of the market, the ferries, and the sunset. The market is authentic, not at all posh, with real market nells and wonderful places to buy coffee." *(AF)* "We left the car in the hotel garage and walked, took the trolley, the Metro and boat to wherever we wanted to go." *(Suzanne Chantland)* "Request an upper-floor room with a view." *(Elizabeth Sommer)* "Confirm existing entry. Casually elegant." *(Adam Platt)*

Open All year.

Rooms 9 suites, 56 doubles—all with full private bath, telephone, radio, TV, air-conditioning, refrigerator, coffee maker. Some with microwave.

Facilities Restaurants, lobby, sun deck, inner courtyard. Hair salon, shops. Room service. Valet parking, $12. Health club nearby.

Location Downtown, in Pike Place Market. On 1st Ave. between Pine & Stewart. From I-5 N, take Seneca St. exit on left & continue to 1st Ave. & turn right. Go blocks N to Pine & turn left to inn on right.

Restrictions No smoking in some guest rooms. Street traffic in city-side rooms.

Credit cards Amex, CB, DC, Discover, MC, Visa.

Rates Room only, $200–255 suite, $105–175 double, $95–175 single. Extra person, $15. Children under 16 free in parents' room. Corporate rates. Senior, weekend discounts. Alc breakfast, $5–11.

Extras Wheelchair access; some rooms equipped for disabled. Station pickup; free downtown shuttle service. Small pets by arrangement. Crib, babysitting. French, Spanish, German, Dutch, Chinese, Tagalog spoken.

Prince of Wales B&B ¢ 🏃
133 13th Avenue East, 98102

Tel: 206–325–9692
800–327–9692
Fax: 206–322–6402

A turn-of-the-century Capitol Hill home, the Prince of Wales was bought by Carol Norton in 1903. She has decorated it with a light touch and a sense of humor; the living room has comfortable seating arrangements, lots of green plants, and Gladys—a life-size doll complete with jewelry and high heels.

"The King's Room has a king-size bed with a spectacular view of Space Needle and the Olympic Mountains. The shared bath was immaculate, with extra toiletries, razors, and a hair dryer on a little table. If you peek into the kitchen, you will see Carol's blue glass collection in the window—eye-catching in the sunshine. Breakfast started with a dish of yogurt, granola, bananas, and oranges; a vegetable quiche was accompanied by potatoes with onions, and rolls with jam. The dining room table was beautifully set with cloth napkins and unusual wooden napkin rings." *(Chrys Bolk)* "Close to restaurants, theaters, and shopping. Charming rooms. Friendly, warm atmosphere." *(Davis De Mark)* "My room was clean, nicely furnished and homey. Friendly hostess with terrific touring advice; shared travel stories with other guests at breakfast." *(Pamela South)* "We had to leave at 5 A.M. for the airport but were given a breakfast tray the night before." *(Shelley & Gregg Edelmann)*

Open All year.

Rooms 2 suites, 2 doubles—2 with private bath and/or shower, 2 with maximum of 4 sharing bath. All with radio, clock, fan. 1 with deck.

Facilities Dining room, living room with books, stereo, piano, fireplace; guest refrigerator/microwave/pantry. ¼ acre with garden, parking passes.

Location 1½ m from downtown. In Capitol Hill historic district.

Restrictions Possible traffic noise in front rooms. No smoking. Children over 3.

Credit cards Amex, Discover, MC, Visa.
Rates B&B, $85–100 suite, $75–85 double, $70–80 single. Extra person, $:
2-day minimum, May 1–Nov. 1.
Extras Possible babysitting. Some Italian, Spanish spoken.

Roberta's B&B ¢
1147 16th Avenue East, 98112

Tel: 206–329–33.
Fax: 206–324–21

A classic turn-of-the-century home, Roberta's B&B has been owned I
(surprise) Roberta Barry since 1968; she opened her home to B&B gue
in 1984. She notes that "one of the neatest things about my B&B is th
it's in a nice old neighborhood, convenient to almost everyplace in town
Breakfast starts with a fruit dish, such as peach cobbler or baked appl
next comes juice, freshly baked muffins (maybe apricot walnut or zucchi
walnut) or breads, homemade jam, and a hot entrée that might be
omelet, cheese strata, Dutch babies, French toast, or ginger pancakes wi
lemon sauce.

"Near the Broadway district which is a little like Greenwich Villa
with a wide assortment of people. We felt well taken care of without bei
hovered over, and our teenager enjoyed sleeping in the loft of the Plu
Room. If you're going to explore the area shops and restaurants, go
foot—the parking is terrible." *(SC)* "Although our room was small, it h
ample closet and drawer space, and two good bedside reading lamps. Th
living room was supplied with dozens of up-to-date magazines as well
the Seattle papers and the New York Times." *(Lillian Koltnow)* "Th
resident cat, Wally, is as friendly as his owner and helps make the gues
feel right at home." *(Robert Wolkow)* "Roberta is a wonderful hostes
generous and friendly, and serves a delicious breakfast." *(NL)* "A love
home in a quiet older residential neighborhood. Roberta is warm, brigh
and extremely knowledgeable about Seattle." *(Robert and Julia Youn*
"Roberta's warm, graciously casual inn gets it all right, with very little fu
or pomposity." *(Adam Platt)*

Open All year.
Rooms 1 suite, 4 doubles—4 with private bath and/or shower; 1 with bath in ha
3 with desk; telephone on request.
Facilities Dining room with pot-belly stove, living room with fireplace, pian
books, games. Tennis in Volunteer Park, 1 block away. Golf nearby. 1 1/2 m fro
Lake Washington for swimming and canoeing.
Location Capitol Hill area, 1 block E of Volunteer Park, 1 1/2 m E of downtow
From I-5, take exit 166 to E Olive. Go 3 blocks to E John, turn right. Go 3 bloc
to 15th Ave. E, turn left. Continue on 15th Ave. E to E Prospect and turn righ
Go 1 block to 16th Ave. E, turn left to inn.
Restrictions Smoking on porch only. No children under 12.
Credit cards Amex, DC, MC, Visa.
Rates B&B, $95 suite, $75–90 double, $75–85 single.

The Sorrento Hotel ✕ �👍
900 Madison Street, 98104

Tel: 206–622–640
800–426–126
Fax: 206–343–615

The Sorrento derives its name from its grand façade, designed by Pacif
Northwest architect Harlan Thomas in the tradition of the houses

orrento, Italy, with terra-cotta trim and an Italian fountain. The lobby
rea is paneled in Honduran mahogany, and the fireplace mantel features
a hand-painted tile landscape. Guest rooms have all the luxuries one
xpects in a hotel of this type—antiques, fresh flowers, goose-down
pillows, bathrobes and oversized towels, turndown service, and bedwarm-
ers for chilly nights. The hotel restaurant prepares innovative Pacific
Northwest cuisine as well as traditional American.

"Built in 1909 and still operating with one elevator (a lesson in pa-
ience), the Sorrento is home to the Hunt Club, one of Seattle's finest—
and most expensive—restaurants." *(Laura Scott)* "Afternoon tea is lovely
and can be taken out on the courtyard in summer. Excellent food; the wine
ist has many interesting Washington and Oregon wines. Save room for
dessert." *(Hilary Huebsch Cohen)* "This beautiful red brick building has
finely carved gray stone cornices; rooms above the third floor, on the west
ide, have a fine view of the city and Puget Sound. Service at lunch was
attentive, and my crab meat and salmon sandwich was delicious." *(SHW)*
"Our suite was delightful, perfect for our family. Friendly service." *(M.
Freedman)*

Open All year.

Rooms 42 suites, 34 doubles—all with private bath and/or shower, telephone,
radio, cable TV, desk, air-conditioning, refrigerator, bar. 1 penthouse suite with hot
tub, fireplace, balcony.

Facilities Restaurant, lounge with piano/jazz entertainment, lobby with fireplace.
In-room facsimile machine on request. Valet parking.

Location Downtown; 4 blocks E of downtown business district on First Hill. From
I-5, take exit 165, marked James/Madison St. Continue to Madison, and go right
2 blocks to corner of Madison and Terry.

Restrictions Non-smoking floors available.

Credit cards Amex, DC, Discover, MC, Visa.

Rates Room only, $170–1,000 suite, $130–160 double. Extra person, $15. 10%
AAA discount. Weekend/holiday packages. Alc lunch, $15; alc dinner, $46.

Extras Wheelchair access. Airport/station pickup. Crib, babysitting. Chinese,
French, German, Spanish spoken. Complimentary downtown shuttle service.
Member, Preferred Hotels.

Tugboat Challenger   *Tel: 206–340–1201*
1001 Fairview Avenue North, 98109

The tugboat *Challenger* is a 96-foot-long boat, built in 1944 for the U.S.
Army; until 1983 she plied the waters of Puget Sound doing what all
tugboats do. Then, in 1985, Jerry and Buff Brown bought the rusty vessel
and spent $500,000 rebuilding and remodeling it as a B&B ("bunk &
breakfast"), now permanently moored at Chandler's Cove Marina. There
are single bunk rooms and the more spacious (a relative term) Master's
Cabin on the upper deck, with queen-size bed and private bathtub. Breakfast is served in the main salon (with fireplace and conversation pit), and
might include eggs with crabmeat or pancakes with sausage or bacon, plus
potatoes, pastries, fresh fruit, freshly squeezed orange juice, coffee, tea,
and cocoa. "While tiny, the cabins are charming and well maintained;
mirrors are used to stretch the space. The Brown's have given guests
every view possible using glass and plastic, adjustable for weather condi-

tions, from wide open to snug and tight. Chandler's Cove has nic
restaurants within walking distance. The surrounding boats are spectacu
lar and you can watch the sea planes take off." *(Donna Bocks)*

Open All year.
Rooms 9 doubles—1 with tub only, 5 with shower only, 3 with maximum of
people sharing bath (sinks in all cabins). All with radio-telephone, radio, clock
air-conditioning. 6 with TV/VCR; some with desk, refrigerator. 2 rooms o
separate yacht.
Facilities Main salon with fireplace, books, video library; guest kitchen, laundr
facilities. Free valet parking at head of dock. Boat rentals nearby.
Location 10 blocks from downtown. Take Exit #167 off of I-5. Go right at ligh
onto Fairview. Go 1 block past Chandler's Restaurant & turn left at Yale St
Landing parking lot. Boat at end of dock.
Restrictions No smoking. No shoes inside boat. Children over 8 preferred, b
arrangement.
Credit cards Amex, DC, MC, Visa.
Rates B&B, $75–125 double.

Williams House

1505 Fourth Avenue North, 98109

Tel: 206–285–081(
800–880–081(

"A beautiful turn-of-the-century house, with a magnificent view of th
city lights and the Space Needle. Inside, rich dark wood leads to coz
corners to sit and read or look out onto roses and flowers everywhere
Other little touches include the phone booth on the stairwell landing (n
change needed), the robes and slippers in the bathroom, and, of course
the smell of home-baked muffins wafting its way upstairs each morning.
(Kris Kegg)

"Beds are comfortable, breakfasts are excellent—always lots of fresl
fruit and a great variety of breakfast dishes. Terrific neighborhood fo
walking, safe at night." *(Marilyn Bommer)* "Located in Queen Ann
Hill—a beautiful place; parking was easy. Our light, airy room had a bed
with lace awning, a good mattress and comforter, and a large futon or
which to sit and read." *(Marsi Fein & Todd Miller)* "Sue was accommodat
ing and helpful, the inn well run and spotless." *(VLK)* "The Brass and Satir
Room has a big brass bed and view of the city and Puget Sound. Th
sunrises are worth an early awakening." *(Sarah Ellison)* "The decor is
pleasant mixture of antiques and functional pieces; I thought the Bay
Room was the largest and the prettiest." *(SHW)*

Open All year.
Rooms 5 doubles—2 with private bath, 1 with ½ bath, 3 rooms sharing 2 baths
Facilities Parlor, sun porch, dining room, TV room. Rose garden. Swimming pool
tennis courts nearby.
Location Queen Anne district, 1 m from downtown. From I-5, take Merce
St./Seattle Center exit, follow signs to Seattle Center. Turn right at sign to Oper
House & Space Needle, right onto 5th Ave. Go left on Highland, right on 3rd Ave.
right on Galer St. Inn is at corner of Galer and 4th Ave.
Restrictions Smoking on porch only. Children welcome by prior arrangement
Credit cards Amex, DC, MC, Visa.

Rates B&B, $70–100 double. Extra person, $15. Discount for 5-night stay Oct.–April.
Extras Member, WBBG.

SEAVIEW

Seaview is located on the Long Beach peninsula of southwestern Washington, between the Columbia River and the Pacific Ocean. It's two hours north of Portland, three hours south of Seattle. Endless walks await on 28 miles of beach; the area is also good for sport fishing. For an additional area entry, see **Long Beach.**

Reader tip: "The Longbeach Peninsula is home to a number of small communities which host various festivals and local celebrations, from antique shows to jazz festivals and garlic celebrations. A number of very fine dining spots are at close hand; 'Pastimes' was a good choice." *(DR)*

Gumm's B&B ¢ 👬   *Tel:* 360–642–8887
3310 Highway 101 & 33rd, P.O. Box 447, 98644

"Owned by Mickey Slack, Gumm's is a beautifully restored craftsman-style home with a turn-of-the-century feel. The touches of Stein glass and the walls of wood create a true feel of the Northwest. Our immaculate room had thoughtful touches—fresh flowers, 'Symphony' candy bars, and stamped postcards of the area." *(Betty Norman)* "Handsome folk art, collectibles and antiques. Guest rooms are clean, comfortable and sweet smelling, with down comforters and crisp bed linens. Lights are handy for reading, windows open, doors lock; rooms have individual thermostats, extra blankets and pillows, a basket of soaps and lotions. The carpeting is plush, and I was never disturbed by the sounds of other guests. Mickey's delicious breakfasts (never a repeat) include a hot casserole, waffles or French toast, muffins, fresh fruits, an assortment of juices and hot beverages, as well as sweet rolls. Coffee and munchies are set out in the afternoon. If guests must leave before breakfast, a tasty boxed breakfast awaits in the refrigerator." *(DR)* "The house has some remarkable history behind it, and Mickey pleased to share it. The table settings were beautiful with lace, linen, and china." *(Max Everitt)* "The rooms have brass plates with Mickey's grandchildren's names on them." *(Ruth Reddaway)* "Our four- and six-year-old boys were welcomed, not just tolerated; the bathtubs are supplied with toys! The inviting living room has a wonderful fireplace, built-ins with play dough, puzzles, books, games, and plenty of room to stretch out." *(Karin Roy)*

Area for improvement: "A comfortable reading chair in my room."

Open All year.
Rooms 4 doubles—2 with private bath, 2 sharing 1 bath. All with TV.
Facilities Dining room, living room with fireplace, sun porch, deck, gazebo with hot tub. Garden.
Location Follow Hwy. 101 to town & inn.
Restrictions No smoking. Summer traffic noise in front rooms in early evening.

Credit cards MC, Visa.
Rates B&B, $60–80 double. Extra person, $5. Extended stay discount. Family rate, senior discount.

Shelburne Inn ✕ &.

4415 Pacific Highway, P.O. Box 250, 98644

Tel: 360–642–2442
Fax: 360–642–8904

Built as a hotel in 1896, the Shelburne Inn was purchased in 1977 by Laurie Anderson and David Campiche, who have been fixing it up ever since, adding and refurbishing guest rooms, and enhancing the restaurant and pub with Art Nouveau stained glass windows salvaged from a church in England. The inn is also home to the famous Shoalwater restaurant, specializing in fresh, locally harvested foods and regional wines. Readers are delighted with the inn's breakfasts, served at a large table in the lobby, with such choices as corn, spinach, and bacon frittata, scrambled eggs with salmon, or razor clam fritters, accompanied by fruit, juice, and just-baked pastries.

"Wonderful ambiance and a truly outstanding restaurant. Rooms are in three sections: above the restaurant, above the lobby, and in the new section. The oldest ones have considerable charm, albeit uneven floors. The new section overlooking the herb garden looked appealing, with larger rooms. The pub is lively, but not noisy. The beach is a few blocks to your right going out the front door." *(DCB)*

Areas for improvement: "A living room for guests to gather." And, "Better lights for reading in bed."

Open All year.
Rooms 2 suites, 15 doubles—all with private bath and/or shower.
Facilities Lobby, restaurant, pub. ½ acre with gardens, off-street parking. 3 blocks to beach.
Location Follow Hwy. 101 to Seaview. In Seaview, go N ½ m on Hwy. 103 to inn on left at 45th St.
Restrictions Smoking restricted. "Quiet, well-supervised children welcome." Limited soundproofing in older rooms; summer traffic noise in front rooms in early evening.
Credit cards Amex, MC, Visa.
Rates B&B, $160 suite, $89–130 double, $83–123 single. Extra person, $10. Midweek, off-season packages. Alc dinner, $25–40.
Extras Wheelchair access; 1 room specially equipped. Crib.

SEQUIM

Often overlooked between the well-known towns of Port Townsend and Port Angeles, the sleepy Sequim/Dungeness Valley offers peaceful farmland and lovely water views. Birdwatching is a highlight at the Dungeness National Wildlife refuge, a six-mile sandspit reaching into the Strait of Juan de Fuca; animal lovers will enjoy the Olympic Game Farm, where the buffalo roam (over to your car for a handout). The climate is dry and sunny, with an annual rainfall of only 16 inches (less than half of Seattle's). Sequim (pronounced "Skwim") is located on the Olympic peninsula, 80 miles northwest of Seattle.

SEQUIM

Greywolf Inn
395 Keeler Road, 98382

Tel: 360–683–5889
800–500–5889

Named for the fast-running Greywolf River, the Greywolf was built in 1976, and was renovated as an inn in 1990 by Peggy and Bill Melang, North Carolina retirees. The spacious guest rooms have queen- and king-size four poster, canopy, or king-size sleigh beds, and each has a different decorating theme: Oriental, Bavarian, Southern, and English garden. Breakfast is served from 8–9:30; menus change daily, but include fruit juice, creative fresh fruit plates, hot breads and muffins, and such entrées as eggs scrambled with smoked salmon and chives; wild rice quiche with Parmesan potatoes and stewed apples; or North Carolina country ham with red eye gravy and hot biscuits with scrambled eggs.

"Peggy and Bill are gracious, unassuming, and kind. Their home is charming, clean, and comfortable, set in a pastoral meadow countryside." *(Mark Hale)* "As we soaked in the hot tub one evening, our host brought us a glass of wine." *(Richard Golden)* "Wonderful breakfast of sausage quiche and strawberry sherbert for dessert. Loved the view of their sheep, Hazel, and cows grazing in the meadow. Their two labs made us feel even more welcome." *(Mr. & Mrs. William Cayford)* "Comfortable rooms with firm beds. Easy drive to the National Park, marina, seashore, mountains, animal park, and downtown; owners helpful with area information." *(Joseph Dziados, also Clyde & Wilma Crawford)*

Open All year.
Rooms 1 suite, 4 doubles—all with private bath and/or shower, radio, clock, fan. 4 with desk, 1 with telephone, 1 with TV/VCR, deck.
Facilities Dining room, living room with fireplace, TV/VCR; library with books, games; decks, courtyard. 5 acres with Japanese hut with hot tub, exercise equipment; lawn games, walking trail. Boating, fishing, golf, hiking nearby.
Location 1 m E of town. From Seattle, exit Hwy. 101 at John Wayne Marina (Whitefeather Way). Take next right onto Keeler Road. Go $^4/_{10}$ m to bottom of hill & driveway on left. From west, go through Sequim to Keeler Rd. & turn left.
Restrictions No smoking. Children over 12 preferred.
Credit cards Amex, MC, Visa.
Rates B&B, $135–155 suite, $62–108 double, $52–88 single. Extra person, $20. Senior, AAA discount.
Extras Airport pickup, $25.

Juan de Fuca Cottages ⁑
182 Marine Drive, 98383

Tel: 360–683–4433
800–683–4432

The Juan de Fuca cottages were built in the 1930s, and have been owned by Sheila Ramus since 1983. Most have views of Dungeness Bay, the National Wildlife Refuge, the Dungeness Spit, the Strait of Juan de Fuca, and Victoria, 18 miles across the water, and are equipped with a queen-size and a double bed. Rates include free videotapes and complimentary tea and coffee.

"Cozy, comfortable cottage, with adequate kitchen utensils and such extras such as a pretty tea pot and current magazines." *(Breta Malcorm)* "Spectacular views of the Straits of Juan de Fuca and Canada from the large picture window. Beautiful stone fireplace, skylit Jacuzzi tub, and lovely furniture. Quiet, relaxing, and peaceful." *(Michael & Linda Gooch)* "Outstanding location. Plenty of hiking and beachcombing nearby. Our proprietor was kind and friendly—never intrusive." *(John Marshall)* "Our dog was welcomed as a part of our family." *(Shawna Willan)* "The toaster was gleaming on the shelf like a mirror. Ample closet space." *(Patricia O'Neill)* "Friendly staff and manager. Great book and video library. Plenty of wood for the fireplace." *(Jennifer Hicks & Thomas Johnson)*

Open All year.
Rooms 5 1-2 bedroom cottage, 1 suite—all with private bath (5 with whirlpool tub), radio, clock, TV/VCR, desk, fan, refrigerator, fully equipped kitchen, deck. 1 with fireplace, double Jacuzzi.
Facilities Lobby with video library. 6 acres with off-street parking, swing set, gazebo, lawn games, boat launch, beach.
Location 7 m to Sequim; 7 m N to beach.
Restrictions No smoking.
Credit cards MC, Visa.
Rates Room only, $135–175 2-bedroom cottage, $90–105 1-bedroom cottage. Extra person, $7. 2-night minimum July–Aug. & weekends.
Extras Wheelchair access; 1 step into cottage; bathroom specially equipped. Airport, bus station pickup. Pets by arrangement. Crib.

SNOHOMISH

Eddy's B&B ¢
425 Ninth Street, 98290

Tel: 360–568–7081

With a quiet setting atop a hillside with views of the town, the Cascades, Mt. Rainier, and the Olympics, it's hard to imagine that the "Antiques Capital of the Northwest" (over 400 dealers), is just six blocks away. Eddy's B&B is located in a residential area, surrounded by lovely gardens of lilacs, roses, hydrangeas, and wisteria. Built in 1884, it was renovated in 1989 as a B&B by Ted and Marlene Bosworth. The rooms are furnished with antiques, Grandma's hand-made quilts, and a resident Teddy bear.

"Snohomish is filled with antique shops and antique malls. Eddy's has a peaceful location, away from the intensity of the antique hunt. The lovely common areas have soft rose carpeting, beige wallpaper with tiny blue flowers, and white woodwork with dark blue detailing on it. Clean, airy guest rooms. One has twin beds with a red velvet teddy bear, another has a lace-canopy king-size bed with big lacy pillows, with an enormous teddy bear and a baby. The breakfast of orange juice, melon, blueberry pancakes, blueberry syrup, and ham, was served around an oak dining room table." *(SC)* "Everything is first class—the food, atmosphere, decor, friendly reception, comfort and affordability." *(Caroline Imakire)*

Open All year.
Rooms 1 suite, 2 doubles—all with private bath or shower, radio, clock, desk, fan.
Facilities Dining room, living room, porch. Portable TV available. 1 acre with gardens, orchard, off-street parking, heated swimming pool. Golf, Snohomish River for fishing, boating nearby.
Location 25 m NE of Seattle. From Hwy. 2, turn onto 2nd St. Go right at Ave. A. Go right at 9th St. to Eddy's on right.

Restrictions No smoking. Children over 12.
Credit cards MC, Visa.
Rates B&B, $85–95 suite, $65–85 double, $45–55 single. Senior discount. Jan.–April, 2 nights for 1 midweek. 7th night free.
Extras Airport, station pickup, $25.

SNOQUALMIE

Also recommended: For a place to stay with the family, try the **Summit Inn** (P.O. Box 163, Snoqualmie Pass, 98068; 206–434–6300). "A recently built motor lodge, nicely designed and decorated, with a spacious lobby, plus a hot tub, sauna, outdoor swimming pool, and playground. The front desk staff were friendly and helpful with touring suggestions. The coffee shop next door provided a large and unexpectedly fine breakfast with many choices." *(James Utt)*

Salish Lodge 🛏 ✕ ♿   *Tel:* 206–888–2556
37807 SE Fall City/Snoqualmie Falls Road   800–826–6124
P.O. Box 1109, 98065   *Fax:* 206–888–9634

At the crest of 268-foot Snoqualmie Falls is the Salish Lodge, opened in 1988 under the same ownership and operation as the famous **Salishan Lodge**. The elegant guest rooms are equipped with wood-burning fireplaces and goose-down comforters, while the restaurant claims to offer the finest in game, beef, lamb and seafood, accompanied by an extensive wine list.

"The lodge is tastefully done with lots of windows and wood, and a huge copper chandelier in the lobby. The setting is spectacular, perched on a bluff right at the edge of giant Snoqualmie Falls. Ask for one on the third or fourth floor, with a number in the teens (i.e., #316, 416) if you want more than a glimpse. To see more of the falls, follow the pathway behind the Lodge, along the top pool, or leave from the front door and walk through woods and greenery to the overlooks. Our room was done in Arts & Crafts Movement decor, with subdued wallpaper, fir trim, a king-size bed, an armoire with TV, and ample firewood for the fireplace; turndown service provides cookies, fresh towels, and a little tidying up. We had a table overlooking the falls, and witnessed a spectacular sunset as we ate. Service was prompt, courteous, friendly, and efficient—but never pushy. The food, if possible, was even better." *(SC)*

"Warm country decor, enhanced by a handsome art collection. The library is a jewel—quiet and comfortable, with a glowing fireplace, and shelves filled with old books and interesting magazines and photos. Our room had good bedside reading lights; the large bathroom had a huge Jacuzzi tub, and thick terry robes." *(Mark Mendenhall)* "We could watch the flames in our fireplace while soaking in the Jacuzzi." *(Alice Clarke Roe)* "Exceptionally accommodating staff." *(Mr. & Mrs. E.E. Stewart)*

Minor niggles: "Sometimes boisterous corporate groups and day-trippers clutter the bar and trail." And: "Perhaps we hit an off-night; dinner seemed over-priced and over-rated."

Open All year.
Rooms 4 suites, 87 doubles—all with full private bath, whirlpool tub, telephone, radio, TV, desk, air-conditioning, fan, fireplace, mini-bar. Some with balcony.
Facilities Restaurant, fourth-floor lounge with jazz entertainment Wed. through Sun. Library with fireplace, fitness center, rooftop Jacuzzi. Golf courses, cross country and downhill skiing, hiking, canoeing, fishing, and steam train rides nearby.
Location W WA. 30 min E of Seattle via Rte. 202 E or I-90 W to Rte. 202 W 1 m NW of town.
Credit cards Amex, CB, DC, Discover, JCB, MC, Visa.
Rates Room only, $250–500 suite, $165–225 double. Extra person, $25. Children free in parents' room. 5-course breakfast $17–26; alc lunch $15; alc dinner $50. Ski, winemaking, theme packages.
Extras Wheelchair access. Crib, babysitting. Concierge services.

SOAP LAKE

Notaras Lodge ¢ 🏃 ✕   *Tel: 509–246–046.*
236 East Main Street, Highway 17, P.O. Box 987, 98851

"If you're driving between Seattle and Spokane and want to stop halfway, Soap Lake and Notaras Lodge are perfect jumping-off places to explore the gorgeous Grand Coulee area. The Notaras Lodge was constructed in 1983 (with additions in 1988) of spruce logs from 20 to 65 feet long; the largest are 42 inches in diameter. Even the door handles add to the cattle ranch theme—they're made from yokes used on draft animals or from interlocked horseshoes that form a four-leaf clover shape.

"We were in the Ben Snipes room, named for a prominent local rancher. Our large room had two queen-size beds against a huge wall made of a variety of woods that formed a scene of canyons, hills, and the sun. High up on one side was a cow skull with lighted eye sockets—sort of quietly spooky—and a huge cowhide. Furnishings included a table with a base made from a large knobby tree trunk, and a top made of a slab of wood with a coiled rattlesnake skin, two old spoons, some arrowheads, horseshoes, and an old folding knife buried in epoxy resin. The bathroom was divided into three separate areas. A swinging café door led to the tub/shower with a choice of either Soap Lake mineral water (piped in directly) or regular water. There were lots of towels and a leather-topped half log to sit on. The sink area had pictures of wagons, cattle, and hills burned into the wood walls, with lights hung from an old yoke. One sink counter was embedded with slices of agates and geodes in beautiful colors, with lights underneath to make the agates glow. The Lamplighter Restaurant down the street was a great place for breakfast." *(SC)*

Open All year.
Rooms 8 suites, 8 doubles—all with private bath, telephone, TV, air-condition ing, mini-kitchen with microwave, refrigerator. Suites with whirlpool. 4 rooms in annex.
Facilities Restaurant, bar/lounge with entertainment; bathhouse with sauna, soak ing tubs, massage therapy; playground, horseshoes, basketball, ping pong.
Location Central WA, 6 m N of Ephrata off Rtes. 28 & 17.

strictions Some non-smoking guest rooms.
edit cards MC, Visa.
ates Room only, $90–125 suite, $45 double, $38 single. Extra person, $7.
ildren under 3, free. Commercial rates. 2-3 night weekend/holiday minimum.
tras Crib. Roll away bed.

OUTH CLE ELUM

information please: Built in 1909 to house railroad crews, **The Moore ouse** (P.O. Box 629, 98943; 509–674–5939) offers nine guest rooms d two restored cabooses, decorated to commemorate the inn's railroad-g history. B&B double rates range from $45–105, with a bunk room for ds. "Celebrates America's railroads with wonderful pictures and emorabilia. Welcoming innkeepers; tasty breakfast of fruit, eggs, and uffins." *(Sherrill Brown)*

POKANE

otheringham House ¢   *Tel:* 509–838–1891
128 West Second Avenue, 99204

otheringham House was built in 1891 by Spokane's first mayor; he also uilt the Patsy Clark Mansion across the street. Located in Browne's ddition, a National Historic District, the house is built in an eclectic tick-style." Original to the house are the tin ceilings, most of the glass, e open staircase, and much of the hand-carved woodwork. In 1993, the n was bought by Graham and Jackie Johnson.

"Beautifully redone as a 'painted lady.' Graham and Jackie are wonder-l innkeepers. Graham was born in Spokane and had a long political areer in Olympia, and is a wealth of information. Delicious breakfast of uckleberry pancakes with huckleberry syrup. In the evenings we were elcomed with a pot of Scottish tea and Jackie's homemade truffles." *ennifer Neill)* "Clean, attractive, comfortable, and well furnished. Plentiful reakfast of French toast and broiled grapefruit." *(Allen Hay)* "The inn ces the park, a perfect place to sit, especially in May when the lilacs are bloom. Don't miss having dinner at Patsy Clark's, across the street." *C)* Reports welcome.

pen All year.
ooms 3 doubles—1 with private shower, 2 with maximum of 4 people sharing ath. All with desk, air-conditioning. Additional rooms in Hoover House annex.
acilities 2 living rooms, breakfast rooms, library, porch, veranda. On-street arking. Tennis, jogging across the street. Fishing nearby, skiing 45 min away.
ocation W central WA. Historic District, 1 m from city center. From I-90, take xit 280 & go N to 2nd Ave. Turn left; stay in right lane to inn on right.
estrictions No smoking. Street noise in some rooms. Children over 12 wel-ome; under 12 by arrangement.
redit cards MC, Visa.
ates B&B, $65–70 double, $50–80 single.
xtras Special dietary needs can be met by prior arrangement.

Marianna Stoltz House ¢   *Tel:* 509–483–43
East 427 Indiana Avenue; 99207

A classic American four-square home built in 1908, the Marianna Stol
House has been owned and operated as a B&B by Phyllis and Jim Magui
and Marie McCarter since 1987. The original fir woodwork, high ceilin,
and leaded glass are enhanced by Oriental rugs, period antiques an
reproductions, family quilts made by Phyllis' grandmother, and lace cu
tains. Breakfast favorites include egg and cheese strata and peach mel
parfait, with homemade granola, muffins, juice, coffee, and tea. "Phyl
Maguire grew up in this house and is unpretentious and friendly. Love
the enormous clawfoot tub in the bathroom adjacent to our room, we
supplied with shampoo and huge towels." *(Allen Hay)* "Wonderful brea
fast of Dutch baby pancakes, served with lemon and powdered suga
with homemade apple syrup. After work, I can relax with a cup of hot t
before going out to dinner, and borrow a paperback from Jim for lat
night reading. Clean, neat, and well-maintained." *(Barbara Hargrave)* "Co
fee, tea, chocolate, and cookies are set out in the living room for guest
enjoyment. Phyllis and Jim are friendly and helpful with advice an
information. Convenient to downtown, on a quiet residential street
(Wenche & John Hemphill)

Open All year.
Rooms 1 suite, 3 doubles—2 with private bath, 2 with maximum of 4 peop
sharing bath. All with clock, air-conditioning, TV. 2 with desk, 2 with radio, 1 wi
fan.
Facilities Dining room, living room with books and fireplace, parlor with pian
verandas. Off-street parking.
Location 1½ m from downtown. From I-90, take Trent Hamilton exit & go
on Hamilton. Cross river at Trent, go past Boone Ave. & go left on Indiana to in
on right. 5 blocks from Gonzaga Univ.
Restrictions No smoking. Children over 5.
Credit cards Amex, DC, Discover, MC, Visa.
Rates B&B, $65–70 suite, $60–70 double, $50–60 single. Extra person, $15.
Extras Airport/station pickup. ½ block to bus stop.

Waverly Place ¢   *Tel:* 509–328–185
West 709 Waverly Place, 99205

Facing the greenery of Corbin Park, Waverly Place is a Queen Anr
Victorian house built in 1899. Innkeepers Marge and Tammy Arne
welcome their guests with a hearty breakfast, starting with fresh frui
juice, and coffee, followed by Swedish pancakes with huckleberry sauce o
possibly eggs baked in herbed tomato shells, with sausage and Scandin
vian pastry. Also included in the rates are afternoon tea or lemonade, an
cookies.

"Pretty gray house with green trim and rust accents, surrounded b
gorgeous flowers. The living room has comfortable reading areas and
brick fireplace with interesting ceramic insets and an unusual wood mantl
Anna's Room has a high, four-poster bed covered with pink flowere
sheets and spread. The best part was the turret area with a comfortabl
window seat. The shared bath had a black and white patterned tile floo

342

Jacuzzi tub, and a good shower. Our hosts were pleasant and friendly. Tea and coffee were set out early in a silver service. Breakfast included a fruit compote, followed by a custardy Finnish pancake with berry sauce, served on antique Haviland china." *(Suzanne Carmichael)* "Excellent location—quiet and restful." *(Carol Codd)* "We enjoyed sipping coffee on the front porch while watching the Saturday morning activities in the park." *(Allen Hay)*

Open All year.
Rooms 4 doubles—1 with full private bath, 3 rooms share 2 baths. All with radio, fan.
Facilities Dining room, parlor with fireplace, parlor with library nook, porch. Swimming pool. Park for jogging, tennis.
Location 2 m N of Spokane center. Corbin Park Historic District. From I-90, take Exit 281 & go N on Division St. Go left on Waverly Pl. at Pizza Hut to inn on far left corner of Wall & Waverly. 1 block to bus stop.
Restrictions No smoking in rooms. "Not well designed for children."
Credit cards Amex, Discover, MC, Visa.
Rates B&B, $65–75 double, $60–70 single. Extra person, $10. 2-night minimum, 1st weekend in May.

STEHEKIN

Information please: The **Silver Bay Lodging** (P.O. Box 43, 98852; 509–682–2212, Mon.–Fri.) has "friendly innkeepers who really know the area. They can help with hiking plans, picnics, and more. In the evenings, homemade ice cream was served. One evening, a guitarist played on the deck while we all watched the sunset. Even though the house is contemporary, antiques are mixed in for a pleasant effect." *(Pam Phillips)* Set at the headwaters of Lake Chelan, with spectacular water and mountain views, Randall and Kathy Dinwiddie offer accommodation in a master suite with private bath with soaking tub, sitting room, and decks with lake and river views. Also available are cabins on the lake's edge, furnished with linens, bedding, and utensils; the kitchens have dishwashers and microwaves. Rates range from $75–130, depending on season. Reports appreciated.

STEVENSON

Information please: The **Skamania Lodge** (P.O. Box 189, Stevenson, 98648; 509–427–7700 or 800–221–7117) was constructed in 1992 as a joint project of the U.S. Forest Service, Skamania County, the Columbia River Gorge Commission, and Salishan Lodge (see listing, Gleneden Beach, Oregon). Opened in 1993, Skamania sits on 175 wooded acres, with an 18-hole golf course, horseback riding, tennis, indoor swimming pool, fitness and conference centers, and restaurant. The 195 suites and doubles are housed in the four-story wood lodge designed with heavy timbers, board-and-batten siding, and stone. Double rates range from

$85–155; children under 12 stay free. "Though not little, we thought it was wonderful. Designed to look like a turn-of-the-century rustic lodge, the woodwork, lighting fixtures, and fabrics were all custom designed and handsomely executed. The Pacific Northwest art displayed on the walls is special—everything from paintings to Navajo rugs to fine carvings to rubbings of the petroglyphs found on the walls of the Columbia Gorge. Many rooms offer spectacular views of the Gorge. The dining room is large but attractive and the food was well prepared and presented." *(Lee Todd)* And another opinion: "During our visit, a big convention group dominated the lodge." And "Too many noisy children."

TOKELAND

Tokeland Hotel ¢ 👭 ✖   *Tel: 360–267–7006*
100 Tokeland Road, P.O. Box 223, 98590   *Fax: 360–292–0559*

The development of the Tokeland Hotel parallels the growth of Toke Point; in 1885 it was a simple farmhouse but, by 1889, as the community grew to encompass more beach-oriented visitors, it had become the Kindred Inn. Purchased 100 years later by Scott and Katherine White, and managed by Erin Radke, the hotel has been refurbished with shining wood floors, period furnishings (some original to the inn), and coordinating wallpapers, linens, and towels. Clam-digging and crabbing are popular local activities, and seafood plays a prominent role in the hotel's dining room. Breakfast consists of breakfast meats, eggs cooked to order, French toast, or blueberry pancakes; homemade biscuits are a specialty.

"Rooms are quaint, small, decorated with antiques and period wallpaper. The staff is friendly and courteous. Delicious buttered steamers and clam chowder." *(Barbara & Eric Platz)* "Our room had handmade cross-stitched detailing on the linens, fresh flowers, and a filled pitcher of ice water at night. Coffee in the kitchen for early risers." *(Gloria & Russ Odell)* "Chintz, eyelet lace, and antiques decorated the comfortable rooms." *(Dena Douglas)* "Near the western shoreline of the peninsula, the Tokeland sits facing a good fishing bay." *(JP)* "We felt pampered and comfortable, which made up for the quaint electrical, heating, and plumbing systems. Plenty to do, and the staff had ideas for other area activities." *(Suzanne Helms)* "They welcomed our golden retriever without a thought!" *(Dena Douglas, and others)*

Open All year.
Rooms 2 suites, 16 doubles—1 with full private bath, 17 with a maximum of 8 sharing bath.
Facilities Dining room, grand hall and lobby with organ, living room with fireplace; library with piano, TV/VCR. 3 ½ acres with gazebo, picnic area. Beach, golf, bicycles nearby.
Location S coast. 20 m S of Westport. 20 m W of Raymond. From I-5, take Exit 104 to Hwy. 101 to Aberdeen. Then follow signs to Westport/Hwy. 105 exit. Nearing Westport, follow sign to Tokeland. Travel 15 m S to Tokeland exit. Hotel is 2 m from exit on left.
Restrictions No smoking in guest rooms.
Credit cards Discover, MC, Visa.

Rates B&B, $65–70 suite or double, $60–65 single. Extra person, $10. Off-season, family rates. Alc lunch, $4; alc dinner, $12.
Extras Pets by arrangement. Crib.

WHIDBEY ISLAND

Whidbey Island parallels the upper Puget Sound mainland from Everett north to La Conner. The largest of the many islands that dot the Sound, Whidbey is close enough to Seattle for an easy weekend getaway, yet offers quiet island ambience and small, friendly towns. Scattered between the pleasant hamlets are loganberry farms. The country's main source for this tart-sweet fruit, some of the farms also produce a delightful loganberry liqueur.

Coupeville, just past the center of the island, is one of the state's oldest towns. Nearby is scenic Madrona Drive, which follows the outline of Penn Cove. Langley, on the east side of the southern part of Whidbey island, is a tiny town suspended in the 19th century. It has a charming (and short) main street lined with antique shops and friendly restaurants. From First Street, you can look across Saratoga Passage to the mainland, the Northern Cascade Range, and volcanic Mt. Baker. "Langley is one of those beautiful hamlets on Puget Sound and is a charming place to visit. Lots of great little shops and galleries to knock around in and while away the time." *(Pam Phillips)*

To reach Whidbey Island, take Interstate 5 or 405 north from Seattle approximately 25 miles to the Mukilteo exit 182. Take State Highway 525 west to Mukilteo. Take ferry to Clinton, then follow 525 to the various small towns.

Information please: The well-known **Captain Whidbey Inn** (2072 West Captain Whidbey Inn Road, Coupeville 98239; 360–678–4097 or 800–366–4097), overlooking Penn Cove, offers rooms with antique charm—and shared baths—in the original inn, along with more modern rooms overlooking the lagoon. Although you can no longer arrive directly by steamer from Seattle at the inn's private dock, as did early visitors, the charming, old-fashioned atmosphere here has changed little. The inn's restaurant features such favorites as basil steamed mussels and house-smoked roasted turkey with an apple relish. B&B double rates include a continental breakfast, and range from $85–145 for suites and doubles; and $150–225 for the cabins; a three-course dinner will cost at least $30, plus wine, tip, and taxes. Guests are thrilled with the lovely setting, peaceful atmosphere, warm and friendly service, and delicious food, but several felt that given the rates, more attention to minor areas of maintenance and updating was in order. Some noted that after a wonderful dinner, breakfast was a letdown.

Colonel Crockett Farm ¢   *Tel: 360–678–3711*
1012 South Fort Casey Road, Coupeville, 98239

"Set on a point of land that juts out into a salt marsh, the inn offers wonderful views across Crockett Lake to Puget Sound. Crockett's is a remodeled farmhouse and is one of the oldest houses on the island. It is listed on the National Register of Historic Places, and the land surrounding it is part of Ebey's Landing, a National Historic Reserve. The inn's decor is homey, with Victorian and Edwardian antiques. Breakfasts are served in the dining room, overlooking the garden; guests are seated at separate tables. Owners Bob and Beulah Whitlow, retired academics, are pleasant and friendly. The Crockett Room to the right of the front door and two upstairs rooms are medium in size; two downstairs rooms are very small." *(SHW)*

"Beautiful, immaculate room; quiet, homey atmosphere. Gracious, friendly innkeepers, who went out of their way to make our stay exceptional." *(Lynda & Jim Kuppler)* "We were warmly greeted by the Whitlows (and their two cats), and enjoyed the story of the farm's history and renovation." *(Del & Sylvia Ann Anorbes)* "Extensive library where you can sit and enjoy tea or coffee and meet other guests." *(Harold & Ev Diewert)* "Outstanding breakfast of fresh fruit, poppy seed muffins with homemade jams, an oven omelet, and sausages." *(Linda & Leon Hussey, and others)*

Open All year.
Rooms 5 doubles—all with private bath and/or shower.
Facilities Breakfast room, library with fireplace, solarium. 39 acres with garden, orchard, wishing well. Hiking trails.
Location From ferry at Clinton, go N 22½ m on Hwy. 525, turn left onto Hwy 20 W (sign to Port Townsend Ferry). Go W 1.4 m, turn right onto Wanamaker Rd. Go 1.7 m, turn left onto S. Fort Casey Rd. for 0.2 m, to inn on left.
Restrictions No smoking. No children under 14. Some bathrooms very small.
Credit cards MC, Visa.
Rates B&B, $65–95 double.
Extras Member, WBBG.

Eagle's Nest Inn
3236 E Saratoga Road, Langley, 98260

Tel: 360–221–5331
Fax: 360–221–5331

Although historic inns have a flavor that can't be duplicated, new homes constructed as B&Bs often have a comfort level that's hard to beat. Years of thought and planning went into Eagle's Nest, built by Dale and Nancy Bowman in 1987, and purchased by Joanne and Jerry Lechner in 1994. Breakfasts include kiwi sorbet, pecan praline toast with wild blackberry syrup, and garden scrambled eggs with sausage; or sliced melon, blueberry walnut muffins, and smoked salmon soufflé the next.

"The inn is set high on a hill with spectacular views of the Saratoga Passage; guest rooms are furnished with queen- or king-size beds." *(Caroline & Jim Lloyd)* "The building's octagonal shape was designed with numerous windows to offer mountain and water views from every one." *(Darla Blake-Ilson)* "Our room was the Eagle's Nest, reached by a private stairway, with windows all around." *(SC)* "After a day of seeing the sights we relaxed in the hot tub on the spacious deck." *(Bill & Eileen Youngdahl)* "Our immaculate ground-level room was decorated with a flower theme from the couch pillows to the dried flower arrangement hanging over the bed. Our bathroom was outfitted with shower cap, hairdryer, bathrobes, and lemon-scented shampoo and soap. Breakfast was served at a long table in the kitchen, and talking with the guests from all over the country was a pleasure." *(Sylvia Ann & Del Anorbes)* "After dinner we met friends from Seattle and sat in the living room late into the night by a cozy fire." *(Gerri Yarborough)* Reports appreciated.

Open All year.
Rooms 4 doubles—all with private shower, radio, TV/VCR. 2 with desk, air-conditioning, deck.
Facilities Breakfast room, living room with woodstove, piano; library with games, video library; decks, hot tub. 2½ acres with walking paths, lawn games, canoe. Beach across street. Tennis nearby.
Location Whidbey Is. From ferry at Clinton, go N 2.7 m on Hwy. 525. Turn right on Langley Rd., go 3.7 m to Langley. Turn left on 2nd St. (becomes Saratoga Rd.), go 1.5 m to inn on left.
Restrictions No smoking. No children under 12. No shoes in house.
Credit cards Discover, MC, Visa.
Rates B&B, $95–115 double, $75–95 single. Extra person, $15. No tipping necessary. 2-night holiday/weekend minimum.
Extras Airport/ferry pickup. Member, WBBG.

Guest House Cottages *Tel: 360–678–3115*
3366 South Highway 525, Greenbank, 98253

At this most unusual B&B, which has been awarded a four-diamond rating from AAA for eight years in a row, Don and Mary Jane Creger invite guests to a private getaway. The romantic cottages are built for two or four, scattered about their 25 acres. No one is asked to "rough it" in the woods; each log or frame home is decorated with country antiques and equipped with everything from fireplaces, to featherbeds, to microwave ovens, to "instant hot water" to VCRs.

"Gracious welcome, immaculate cottages. Fresh fruit on the table, candies, sachets, soap in quilted flowery baskets on the bedside table. Terry robes in the ample closets." *(Juanita Dooston)* "Our breakfasts were set up attractively on trays in the refrigerator." *(Mr. & Mrs. C.G. Breeding)* "A fireplace warmed our cozy cabin, and sunlight streamed in through the skylights. Our bed had heaps of fluffy pillows." *(Joy & Sean Hildebrandt)* "A peaceful, quiet, private sanctuary in the woods. We stayed in the Lodge, with a Jacuzzi in the bedroom, set on a platform so you can gaze down at fireplace or out over the pond." *(Gene Baker)* "You can sit on the deck and look out over the lake and watch the ducks and geese." *(Ina Gartenberg)* "Fresh eggs from the resident chickens, and ham and cheese croissants are just a portion of the delicious breakfast." *(Gary Freudenberger)* "No need to lock your doors or even draw your shades." *(Boyce & Tracey Sharf)*

Open All year.
Rooms 7 cottages—all with full private bath, radio, TV/VCR, movie library, kitchen, fireplace, Jacuzzi tub. 3 with desk, 1 with air-conditioning.
Facilities 25 acres with exercise room, heated swimming pool, hot tub, badminton, horseshoes. Ocean, lakes, parks nearby.
Location NW WA. Central Whidbey Island, 10 m S of Coupeville, 1 m S of Greenbank. On the island, follow State Hwy. 525 16 m N of ferry to 3366. Office is at 3366 S. Hwy. 525 in farmhouse, lower level.

Restrictions No smoking. No children.
Credit cards Amex, Discover, MC, Visa.
Rates B&B, $135–265 cottage. 2-night weekend minimum. Midweek winter discount.

Log Castle B&B
Tel: 360–221–5483
3273 East Saratoga Road, Langley, 98260

This is the house that Jack built. No ordinary house, mind you, but a stunning log home designed by Norma Metcalfe and built by her husband, state senator Jack Metcalfe. Highlights include the cathedral-ceilinged common room with fieldstone fireplace, leaded glass windows, a wormwood stairway, and the third-story turret bedroom overlooking the water, beach, mountains, and pasture.

"Ann's Room on the top floor has a private tower magnificently surrounded by log luxury—woodstove, white iron double bed amid the five windows forming the octagon, private balcony with wonderful view of the Cascade Mountains and the water. Lea's Room has a swing on its balcony and excellent views." *(SC)* "The atmosphere in this secluded spot is one of relaxation and quiet, and the Metcalfes are gracious hosts. At 8 A.M. Norma brings coffee, tea, or juice to your room. At 9 A.M., she prepares a fabulous breakfast of homemade cinnamon rolls, eggs, sausage, old-fashioned oatmeal, and hot cottage cheese pancakes. In the evening she serves hot cider and cookies in the living room, with plenty of light and room to read, play cards or do jigsaw puzzles." *(Karen Martin)*

"A comfortable, homey, rustic hunting lodge, right above the water of Saratoga Passage, in splendid isolation. The lodge is built entirely from materials found on the premises. The living room overlooks the water, and there are ample balconies with similar views. The bedrooms are comfortable and attractive, but not posh. The two tower bedrooms have spectacular views; three of the bathrooms are tiny, with custom-made pottery sinks." *(SHW)* "Our room had a basket of fruit and a seashell filled with nuts and chocolates; soft music filled the air, and there was a packet of menus from all the local restaurants. We took a romantic walk on the beach and the trails on their property." *(Susan Springgate)* "Norma and Jack tell wonderful stories about the inn during the fabulous three-course breakfast." *(Alice Clarke Roe)*

Open All year except Christmas.
Rooms 1 suite, 3 doubles—all with private shower and/or bath. 1 with desk, 2 with woodstove, 4 with balcony.
Facilities Common room with fireplace. Balconies with chairs, hammock. 2½ acres with 500 ft. of waterfront on Saratoga Passage. Canoe, rowboat for fishing. Walking trails.
Location 1½ m to village. From Langley, follow Saratoga Rd. to inn on right.
Restrictions No smoking. No alcohol. No children under 10.
Credit cards MC, Visa.
Rates B&B, $85–115 suite, $80–105 double. Extra person, $20. 2-night holiday weekend minimum.
Extras Bus station pickup.

YAKIMA

37 House ¢ ✗

Tel: 509–965–5537

4002 Englewood Avenue, 98908

Built in 1937 for one of the Yakima Valley's first fruit growing families, the 37 House stayed in the family's hands for over 50 years. Restored as an inn by Michael and Rhonda Taylor, it is managed by Chris Chapman. The elegant common areas include a high-ceilinged entry hall with original wallpaper, a sweeping hardwood staircase, and a formal dining room with original cherry wood dining room chairs with hand-woven cushions. The spacious living room is comfortably furnished with traditional decor and an authentic Oriental rug, and the cozy den has knotty pine paneling, a red-tiled floor, and floor-to-ceiling bookcases. The spacious guest rooms are equally inviting, with king-, queen-, and full-size beds, with such custom-made touches as walk-in closets, window seats tucked under sloping eaves, built-in desks with lots of cubby holes, and fully tiled baths. Breakfast is served at guests' convenience between 7:30–10 A.M., and might include eggs Benedict, French toast or waffles.

"This huge stone house is impeccably, luxuriously designed and decorated. The original owner was a creative, innovative woman—she selected a woman architect to design it, the stunning photography in the house is hers, she even wove the fabric for the dining room chairs. Each room is individually and beautifully decorated with antiques. My favorite was the Master Suite with black-tiled bathroom, but all are lovely." *(Suzanne Carmichael)*

Open All year.

Rooms 1 suite, 4 doubles—all with private bath and/or shower, telephone, radio, clock, TV, air-conditioning. Some with desk.

Facilities Dining room, living room, library/den, game room; each with fireplace; balconies. 9 acres with gardens, walks, children's swing, tennis court. Golf nearby.

Location S central WA. Wine country. From I-82, take Hwy 12 W. Exit at 40th Ave. & go S to inn at corner of 40th & Englewood.

Restrictions No smoking.

Credit cards Amex, MC, Visa.

Rates B&B, $120 suite, $65–90 double. Children free in parents' room. Alc lunch $5–7, alc dinner $25–30.

Western Canada

West End Guest House, Vancouver

Canada is a huge and beautiful country, with a number of wonderful places to visit—from the exciting, cosmopolitan cities to the peaceful countryside and rugged interior. Far from being a carbon copy of the United States, western Canada offers visitors subtle "foreign" experiences: the very British city of Victoria, an East Indian enclave in Vancouver, the Indian native peoples along the coast with a sprinkling of German-Russians in Saskatchewan.

Although most of Canada's population is located in metropolitan areas not far from the U.S. border, it's worth wandering farther afield to discover some of the country's most scenic and remote areas. In Western Canada this means going beyond Vancouver and Victoria to sample the Gulf Islands, Vancouver Island, and British Columbia's interior, as well as Alberta's fabled Canadian Rockies.

You have discovered some very wonderful hotels and inns in British Columbia, but we would love to have more suggestions in Alberta as well as Saskatchewan and Manitoba.

A few notes for first-time visitors to Canada: Radar detectors are illegal and seat belts are mandatory. When consulting maps and speed limits, remember that Canada is metric. Also, ask your auto insurance company for a free "Canadian Non-Resident Inter-Provincial Motor Vehicle Liability Insurance Card"—it will speed up immeasurably any procedures if you are involved in an accident. Finally, it is often advantageous to purchase Canadian currency in the U.S.—make some comparison calls first (the rate varies from bank to bank).

Rates quoted in this section are noted in Canadian, not U.S., dollars.

US $1 = Canadian $.76; exchange rates are subject to constant fluctuation.

In 1991, a federal Goods and Services Tax of 7% (GST) went into effect, which also applies to accommodation and restaurant meals, *in addition* to existing sales taxes. Nonresidents are eligible for refunds on most goods and accommodations but not meals, alcohol, or fuel; inquire to obtain appropriate forms or call 800–66VISIT (in Canada) or 613–991–3346. Explanatory GST booklets are available at border crossings, shops, and hotels. Original (not photocopied) bills must accompany your claim for a refund. Refunds can be obtained by mail, or on the spot at Canadian Land Border Duty Free Shops. Charges made on your credit card to a non-Canadian address may circumvent this unpleasantness or facilitate a refund.

Note: The GST and provincial sales taxes do not currently apply to some B&Bs with three guest rooms or less, a significant savings.

Alberta

Alberta is home to the Canadian Rockies; Banff, Jasper, and Lake Louise are the major resorts where most visitors go for hiking and fishing in summer and skiing in winter. Farther south is dramatic Waterton Lakes National Park, which shares its territory with Montana. This province's key cities are Edmonton and Calgary. Though Edmonton is the capital, its major claim to fame seems to be the West Edmonton Mall, a mile-long indoor shopping and recreation complex containing about every imaginable shop and recreation facility, even a 360-room hotel, the Fantasyland, with a selection of theme rooms devoted to different countries and periods (403–444–3000). Calgary is a center for agriculture and oil production. Its most famous event is the annual Stampede, a combination rodeo and state fair; it is also home to a fine collection of museums devoted to telecommunications and energy, along with the more traditional subjects of art and history.

All rates quoted in Canadian dollars, and do not include taxes.

Note: Despite Alberta mailing addresses, entries for **Emerald Lake Lodge** and **Lake O'Hara Lodge**, both located in British Columbia's Yoho National Park, are in fact listed under the town of *Field* in the British Columbia chapter.

BANFF

Also recommended: Although there's nothing little about the **Banff Springs Hotel** (Box 960, Banff T0L 0C0; 403–762–2211 or 800–441–1414), frequent contributor *Marilyn Parker* recommends it as being one of Alberta's best hotels. Built by the Canadian Pacific Railroad, it was modelled after a castle in Scotland. "Huge halls and fireplaces with Elizabethan furniture. Our attractive room faced the river valley. A visit to the Upper Hot Springs pool nearby is very special; go at night when the stars are out, or when it is snowing." Double rates for the 829 rooms (we said it was big) range from $105–337; standard rooms have little or no view. The complex also includes numerous shops, restaurants, and a conference center.

Information please: Under the same management as the Emerald Lake Lodge (see the British Columbia chapter) is the **Buffalo Mountain Lodge** (Tunnel Mountain Road, P.O. Box 1326, Banff T0L 0C0; 403–762–2400 or 800–661–1367). It's within walking distance of The Banff Centre and the Whyte Museum of the Canadian Rockies. The mountain-style main lodge has hand-hewn timbers and a huge fieldstone fireplace; outside is a 14-foot hot tub. With guest rooms in 85 chalets, accommodations range from doubles to two-bedroom suites, most with fireplace and balcony— many have a kitchenette; decor includes custom-made cherry, pine, and bent-willow furniture, and handmade copper and glass light fixtures.

CARDSTON

Badger Valley Ranch ¢ 🏃
P.O. Box 1371, T0K 0K0

Tel: 403–653–2123

"This working cattle and horse ranch is set on rolling green grassland, and is owned by Rod and Joan Shaw. One large duplex cabin allows for two sets of guests. Both sides of the cabin are tastefully furnished in a Western motif; each has a full kitchen and guests are responsible for their own meals. A lush lawn, several ponds, and flower beds surround the cabin. Guests can fish on the stocked ponds, hike up the ridge behind the cabin for a spectacular 50-mile view, relax on the deck, or ride the range on one of the ranch's first-rate horses." *(William Fuerst & Lisa Ottinger)*

Open All year.
Rooms 1 duplex cabin; each side with bedroom, private bath, living room with fireplace, fully equipped kitchen.
Facilities Lodge, barbecue grill, patios. 640 acres with horseback riding, hiking, lawn games, volleyball, playground, children's fishpond. 2–5 day pack trips.
Location S ALB, 45 m E of Waterton Lakes National Park.
Restrictions No smoking. No riding on Sundays.
Credit cards None accepted.
Rates Room only, $65 double. Extra person, $5. Off-season rates.

EDMONTON

Capital of Alberta, Edmonton offers science at the Edmonton Space and Science Centre, history at the Fort Edmonton Park, and shopping (and more) at the West Edmonton Mall, with over 800 shops, an indoor water park, ice skating rink, dolphin show, and deep sea adventure.

Chez Suzanne B&B ¢ 🏃
18603 68 Avenue, T5T 2M8

Tel: 403–487–2071
Tel: 403–483–1845

Suzanne Croteau welcomes guests to the lower level of her home and serves a breakfast of bacon and eggs, homebaked bread, croissants, and pastries, or perhaps yogurt and fruit with crepes and maple syrup.

"Clean, comfortable, homey. Tasty breakfast, with ample choices." *(Mr. & Mrs. Paul Lemire)* "Suzanne loves what she does, and provides bath amenities, fresh flowers, bedtime chocolates, readily available cookies, hot and cold drinks." *(Francine & Berl Biddle)* "Large, airy, well-equipped guest room; comfortable bed. Shared bathroom was very clean, supplied with lots of toiletries and towels. Relaxing guest lounge, perfect after a day on the go. Warm, welcoming hosts are pleased to answer guests' questions fully and pleasantly. Great breakfast—nutritious, filling, varied, served in a lovely dining room—table nicely set, good linens." *(Rollande Smith)* "Quiet residential area. Our rooms were well-lit, with a desk, closet, reading materials and maps of the area." *(Larry & Loreen Scales)*

Open All year.
Rooms 1 suite, 1 double, 1 single—1 with private bath, 2 with shared bath. All with telephone, radio, desk.
Facilities Dining room, sitting room with fireplace, TV/VCR, video library, guest kitchen, games, books; laundry. Deck, lawn games. Off-street parking.
Location W Edmonton. Residential district 5 min. from Edmonton Mall. From Jasper Hwy., go S on 178 St. Turn right onto 69 Ave. Go W to 4-way stop, turn left on 184 St., turn right on 66 Ave., then right on 185 St. to inn midway through large crescent.
Restrictions No smoking.
Credit cards None accepted.
Rates B&B, $75 suite, $50–55 double, $40 single. Extra person, $15. Cot, $15. Family rates. Lunch, $6; dinner, $12.
Extras Airport/station pickup, $5–12. French spoken. Private touring by arrangement.

Hotel Macdonald 🏨 ✕
10065 100th Street, T5J 0N6

Tel: 403–424–5181
Fax: 403–424–8017

A chateau-esque, nine-story grey stone structure built in 1915, the Hotel Macdonald occupies a prime location on a hill overlooking the river valley. Owned by Canadian Pacific Hotels, it was fully restored in 1991. The hotel's lobby and sitting rooms have two-story windows, ornate wrought iron railings, and plenty of seating areas; Oriental rugs, Victorian settees, comfortable wing chairs, and large potted plants highlight the decor. Guest rooms have Queen Anne reproduction furniture, floral-patterned upholstery and quilted bedspreads. The hotel's restaurant, the Harvest Room, has a soaring barrel-vaulted ceiling; a more intimate is the wood-panelled Library Bar.

"Not little, but wonderful. Everything is clean and fresh-looking. Our lovely room looked south across the river. Delicious buffet breakfast in the Harvest Room—juice, granola, yogurt, fruit, muffins, and tea. We enjoyed the swimming pool in the health club." *(Marilyn Parker)*

Open All year.
Rooms 198 suites and doubles—all with private bath, telephone, TV. Some with mini-bar, refrigerator, or whirlpool.
Facilities Restaurant, bar/lounge, lobby, sitting room. Conference rooms, business services. Laundry service, valet parking; garage nearby. Health club with heated indoor swimming pool, wading pool, tennis courts, sun deck, squash courts, whirlpool, sauna, games room, massage therapy.
Location Downtown, directly S of Jasper Ave. 1 block to Convention Centre.
Restrictions Smoking restricted in designated areas.

ALBERTA

Credit cards Amex, CB, DC, Discover, EnRoute, JCB, MC, Visa.
Rates Room only, $119–190 double. Extra adult, $20; children under 18 free in parents' room. Senior, corporate rates.
Extras Small pets by arrangement. Airport pickups; fee charged.

La Boheme B&B ✕   *Tel: 403–474–5693*
6427–112 Avenue   *Fax: 403–479–1871*

"This historic apartment building, constructed in 1912, has an excellent French restaurant with overnight accommodations on the second and third floors. Rooms have antique furniture, canopy beds, and hardwood floors; the bathrooms have old-fashioned tubs. Long-time owners Ernst and Carole Eder have created the charming atmosphere of a Parisian hotel, with Edith Piaf often played over the sound system. Food is carefully prepared, nicely presented and delicious. Service is professional and caring. It's only ten minutes from downtown, and parking is no problem." *(Eileen & Phil Walker)*

Continental breakfast is served beginning at 7 A.M., either in your room or in the restaurant. The dinner menu offers vegetarian and light cuisine in addition to entrées such as rack of lamb with mustard, mint, and balsamic vinegar; pork tenderloin with apple cider cream; and scallops with white wine sauce. The Sunday brunch menu includes eggs Benedict; pan-fried steak marinated with sake; and chicken crepes with curry cream. Reports welcome.

Open All year. Closed Dec. 24, 25.
Rooms 6 suites—all with full private bath, telephone, clock, TV, desk, fan, refrigerator. 3 with deck. 2 with air-conditioning. 1 with radio.
Facilities Restaurant, dining room, bar, porch. 3 on-site parking spaces; off-street parking lot 5 P.M.–9 A.M.
Location Historic district. 5 min to town center. Off Capiland Freeway E at 112 Ave. to 65 St.
Restrictions Street noise in front rooms. No smoking in some dining rooms. No children under 10.
Credit cards Amex, MC, Visa.
Rates MAP, $145 suite. B&B, $95 suite, $75, single. Extra person, $20. Escape packages. Prix fixe dinner, $30. Alc lunch, $10; alc dinner, $30–35. Sunday brunch, $9–12. 15% gratuity suggested for meals.
Extras Limited wheelchair access. French spoken.

HINTON

Black Cat Guest Ranch ¢   *Tel: 403–865–3084*
Box 6267 AW, T7V 1X6   *Fax: 403–865–1924*

Founded over half a century ago, the Black Cat is owned by Jerry and Mary Bond, and managed by their daughter and son-in-law Amber and Perry Hayward. The ranch is set in the forests on the eastern slopes of the Rockies, and guests stay in a modern, natural-wood lodge with balconies overlooking the mountains. Breakfasts consist of eggs or pancakes, bacon or sausage, biscuits or toast, and yogurt, fruits, and juices. A typical lunch includes homemade soup, fresh bread, meats and cheeses, quiche and salads, and homemade cookies. Dinner favorites include roast beef with Yorkshire pudding and creamed onions, or steak barbecue with potato salad and coleslaw with carrot cake for dessert.

"Friendly hosts who are always smiling. Clean, bright, airy rooms. The stables are clean, and wranglers are knowledgeable and sensitive to guests' riding capabilities." *(E. Burns)* "The owners take their meals with guests; the food is plain but tasty, and special diets are accommodated. Coffee, cookies, and fruit are available all day. A large log fire usually burns in the stone fireplace in the living room, with a beautiful view of the Rockies from picture windows facing an open paddock." *(Dennis & Doreen Hillman)*

Open All year.
Rooms 16 doubles—all with private full bath, desk, balcony.
Facilities Dining room, living room with fireplace, piano, books; game room, lounge. Hot tub, lawn games. 480 acres for cross-country skiing, trail rides, hiking, canoeing, lake fishing, bicycling.
Location NW AB. 200 m W of Edmonton; 44 m NE of Jasper. 13 m N of Hwy. 16 (Yellowhead Hwy.). From Hwy. 16, go N on Hwy. 40 toward Grande Cache. Look for green sign for Brule, then brown sign for guest ranch; 200 yards after brown sign, turn left. Go approx. 6.7 m, then turn right at ranch driveway.
Restrictions No smoking in dining room. 6 nonsmoking rooms available. Children over 8 preferred, must be well supervised.
Credit cards MC, Visa.
Rates Full board, $114–150 double, $65–90 single. Extra adult, $50–75. Children, ¾ adult rate. 10% senior discount. Weekend, midweek package rates. Writing, art, photography workshops; mystery weekends; Elderhostel. Prix fixe lunch, $7.50; dinner, $16.50.
Extras Free local station pickup.

JASPER

Also recommended: Too large for a full entry at 450 rooms, is the well-known **Jasper Park Lodge** (Box 40, T0E 1E0; 403–852–3301 or 800–441–1414), set on the shores of Lake Beauvert. Dating back to 1927, it now ranks as a world-class resort, with a full complement of activities, set amid spectacular scenery. Though it caters primarily to tour groups, readers continue to be pleased with the views, cabins, and facilities. Double rates, including breakfast and dinner, range from $181–501.

Another possibility is **Jasper House Bungalows** (Box 817, T0E 1E0; 403–852–4535), overlooking the Athabasca River. Some of the 56 cedar log units have a kitchenette, living room, and Jacuzzi tub. Rates range from $90–$150 (mid-June through mid-September) with discounts off-season. "The restaurant serves delicious area specialties. Cordial staff." *(Nanci & Norm Cairns)* Reports needed.

Pyramid Lake Resort ✕
Box 388, T0E 1E0

Tel: 403–852–4900
Fax: 403–852–7007

The Pyramid Lake Resort, owned by Ernie and Esther Gingera, offers the only accommodations at Pyramid Lake, providing guests with exclusive and unobstructed views. Some units are only 200 feet from the shore, and have large picture windows to provide panoramic vistas. "The lake is relatively small but gorgeous. We heard and saw many loons on the lake and enjoyed the early morning view of Pyramid Mountain just beyond. The accommodations vary in age; the older units are a bit closer to the lake, but are smaller and more Spartan. The newer ones, where we stayed, are attractive and comfortable, though not fancy, with a small kitchenette. Pretty, peaceful birch forests." *(James Utt)*

Open All year. Restaurant open for summer.
Rooms 42 suites and doubles (32 in winter)—all with full private bath, TV, desk. 30 with refrigerator, 16 with fireplace, 10 with whirlpool tub. 10 rooms in motel-style duplex; 32 rooms in 8-plex units with balcony.
Facilities Restaurant, porch, barbecue facility, beach. Boat rentals, fishing equipment and licenses (summer). Hiking, cross-country skiing.
Location 4 m NW of Jasper.
Credit cards MC, Visa; no personal checks.
Rates Room only, $85–172 suite (up to 6 persons), $65–110 double. Extra person, $8. 2-night minimum.
Extras Cribs.

LAKE LOUISE

Also recommended: Although too large for a full entry at 515 rooms, the **Chateau Lake Louise** (403–522–3511 or 800–441–1414) is a must for those who don't mind paying a premium to be right on the lake. "Our small room faced the lake for an incredible mountain view. We enjoyed breakfast in the Poppy room and dinner in the Wine Bar. We were there the week before Christmas; it wasn't crowded and it was great to walk out the door to skate on the lake or cross-country ski along its edge." *(Marilyn Parker)*

The **Deer Lodge** (109 Lake Louise Drive, Box 100, T0L 1E0; 403–522–3747 or 800–661–1595), was built in 1921 as a log and stone teahouse; the first of 73 guest rooms were added in 1925. The handsome, rustic log-beamed restaurant in the original building features hearty soups, homemade breads, and fish, veal and beef entrées. Room rates range in season from $75–$150 for double occupancy; children under 13 stay free. A rooftop hot tub provides a breath-taking spot for viewing Victoria Glacier. One reader noted that the guest rooms in the new addition were "standard HoJo's," but were a good value; the breakfast buffet is recommended.

Baker Creek Chalets 🛬 ✕   *Tel:* 403–522–3761
Highway 1A, Bow Valley Parkway, Box 66, T0L 1E0

Unlike some of the decades-old lodges that dot the area, the Baker Creek Chalets are of recent origin; Mike and Jan Huminuik are the owners. Cedar log cabins dot the grounds beside Baker Creek; a cozy one-room unit has a double bed tucked in an alcove, beams stencilled with flowers, wall-to-wall carpeting, and a combination sink/stove/refrigerator unit in one corner. A one-bedroom chalet has a log ladder leading to a loft with twin beds (the room below has a double bed) plus a more spacious living area. The Baker Creek Bistro dinner menu includes entrées of grilled beef, broiled salmon, roast chicken Florentine, and pasta marinara with shrimp and scallops. During the summer season, breakfast and lunch are also served. "Located off the old highway between Banff and Lake Louise, so there's little traffic, with trees all around. Attractive, spacious cedar log cabins; cozy main lodge with highly regarded restaurant." *(Marilyn Parker)* Reports needed.

Open All year. Restaurant closed Nov., mid April–mid May.
Rooms 25 1–2 bedroom cabins—all with private bath and/or shower, fireplace or woodstove, kitchenette, deck. 7 with loft bedroom.
Facilities Restaurant, library, bar—with fireplace, piano, TV/VCR, stereo. 2.5 acres with cross-country skiing from door. Volleyball. Downhill skiing nearby.
Location 6 m SE of Lake Louise. 25 m W of Banff.
Credit cards MC, Visa.
Rates Room only, $115–145 suite, $100–125 double, $80–100 single. Extra person, $10. Off-season senior discount.
Extras Cribs. Babysitting possible.

Moraine Lake Lodge ✕
Box 70, T0L 1E0

Tel: 403–522–3719
Fax: 604–985–7479

The Moraine Lake Lodge dates back to 1908, when it was built to provide sustenance to tourists on the carriage road between Lake Louise and Moraine Lake. It was expanded over the years to accommodate guests enamored of the azure blue waters and the breathtakingly rugged beauty of the valley. In 1988, under new ownership, the resort was totally redesigned and rebuilt, to blend with the environment and accommodate day visitors while respecting the privacy of overnight guests. It opened in 1991 under the management of David Hutton. Lodge rooms and cabins are decorated with custom-made furniture, and all have magnificent views of the lake, mountains, and glaciers. Most of the staff are university students in hotel/restaurant management programs. Complimentary coffee, tea and homemade cookies are served in the library each afternoon. The glass-walled restaurant has superb views; entrées include veal with Madeira, chicken in green peppercorn sauce, a daily pasta selection, and rainbow trout with almonds. The Café has an informal menu of soups, salads, and sandwiches. "Beautifully designed and appointed rooms, all with views of Moraine Lake. Outstanding cuisine and service." *(Richard Lissner)*

Open June 1–Sept. 30.
Rooms 18 cabins, 14 doubles—all with full private bath, deck. 24 with fireplace. 18 with desk.
Facilities Restaurant with fireplace; coffee shop, lobby with fireplace; library with fireplace. Park naturalist lectures Fri. evening. 5 acres with canoes, fishing, hiking.

Location 8 m S of Lake Louise. Go left off Lake Louise Rd. to inn.
Restrictions Children age 16 and over preferred.
Credit cards Amex, MC, Visa.
Rates Room only, $155–$235 double. Extra person, $25. $2 per day gratuity for housekeeping. Alc lunch, $10–12; alc dinner, $35–45. 15% service suggested on meals.
Extras 1 room wheelchair accessible, equipped for disabled. Station pickups. Cribs. French, German spoken.

Post Hotel 🛏 ✕ ♿

200 Pipestone Road, Box 69, T0L 1E0

Tel: 403–522–3989
800–661–1586
Fax: 403–522–3966

The Post Hotel is comprised of a log building, constructed in 1952, which houses the hotel's restaurant, and a handsomely built yellow cedar and fieldstone addition which houses the luxurious guest rooms. The hotel has been owned and operated since 1978 by the Schwarz family; in 1986 Husky Oil Operations acquired a 50% interest. In 1993 a $3 million renovation added duplex suites in the main lodge, and a separate function facility was constructed on the south end of the lodge.

"Well-planned landscaping and flower beds. The comfortable furnishings and impressive staircase made the lobby feel warm and inviting. The lawn and patio were great places to view the surrounding mountains. Attentive and helpful staff in the restaurant. We had the venison and duck breast terrine, followed by rack of lamb and Atlantic salmon, prepared to perfection. The pool, steam room, and hot tub were welcome after a long day of hiking." *(Ronald & Linda Craddock)* "The chalet-style building is beautifully done—nicely furnished in pine, immaculately clean." *(Marilyn Parker)* "Exceptional service, accommodations, and cuisine. My dinner included lobster bisque, spinach salad with grapefruit vinaigrette, duck with blackberries, and warm apple tart with cinnamon ice cream; even the house wine, a Burgundy, was memorable." *(Mary Beth O'Reilly)*

Open All year. Closed Nov.
Rooms 26 suites, 76 doubles, 2 cabins—all with full private bath, telephone, TV, desk. Some with fireplace, balcony, loft, whirlpool tub, kitchenette. 2 cabins—1 with 4 bedrooms & conference facilities.
Facilities Dining/breakfast rooms, lounge with fireplace, stereo, piano, evening entertainment; bar with TV/VCR, fireplace, stereo; library, conference rooms. 7 acres with Jacuzzi, heated indoor pool, exercise and steam room. Tennis, fishing, trail rides, canoeing, bicycling, downhill, cross-country skiing nearby.
Location SW AB, Banff National Park. 120 m W of Calgary. In Lake Louise village, on Pipestone River.
Restrictions No smoking in some guest rooms. Train noise in some rooms.
Credit cards Amex, MC, Visa.
Rates Room only, $235–360 suite, $100–265 double. No charge for children in parents' room. Ski package rates. 4-night minimum stay Dec. 24–Jan. 2. Prix fixe lunch, $18; prix fixe dinner, $45. Alc breakfast, $13; alc lunch, $13; alc dinner, $40. 15% service.
Extras Wheelchair access. Station pickup. Crib, babysitting. French, Swiss, German, Italian, Spanish spoken. Member, Relais & Châteaux.

WATERTON PARK

Waterton Lake National Park was established on the international boundary between Canada and the United States in 1895; in 1932, in connection with Glacier National Park, it was designated the world's first International Peace Park. Attractions include Upper Waterton Lake, the deepest lake in the Canadian Rockies; high alpine meadows filled with wildflowers during the early summer; a wide variety of fish and wildlife; and such natural attractions as Red Rock Canyon and Cameron Falls.

Also recommended: We've had mixed reports on the **Prince of Wales Hotel** (June–Sept: Waterton Park, T0K 2M0; 406–226–5551 or out-of-season: Glacier Park Inc., Greyhound Tower, Station 5510, Phoenix, AZ, 85077; 602–207–6000), an historic 1920s-era hotel designed in Alpine style, overlooking Waterton Lake. The 82 guest rooms have private baths, and double rates range from $122–156 double. "The most gorgeous setting imaginable, on a high bluff overlooking the lake, mountains, and glaciers. Be sure to ask for a room with a lake view, preferably one with a balcony. Also beautiful views through the floor-to-ceiling windows of the spacious lobby." *(SC)* "Adequately furnished, clean rooms. Enjoyable afternoon tea." *(Nanci & Norm Cairns)* Other readers felt that given the rates, more attention to housekeeping, maintenance, soundproofing and decor would not be amiss.

Kilmorey Lodge 🛉 ✗
117 Evergreen Avenue, Box 100, T0K 2M0

Tel: 403–859–2334
Fax: 403–859–2342

The Kilmorey is a gabled log structure, built in the early 1900s. The interior is paneled in knotty pine and is furnished with antiques and country furniture.

"Friendly, informative staff. Convenient location a ten-minute walk from the boat dock, town, Cameron Falls, and theater. Make dinner reservations; the restaurant is popular. During the summer, drinks and sandwiches are also served in the gazebo. Quiet at night—I was awakened only by the smell of bread baking and coffee brewing." *(Shirley Lieb)* "Our bathroom sparkled, towels were fluffy; a down quilt was on our bed. The owners, Leslie and Gerry Muza, are sincere and hospitable." *(Mavis & Eric Roland)* "Where else can you find mountain sheep lying content at the back door, sheltered from the wind and oblivious to the humans watching them? At breakfast one morning, as we ate our meal, a deer was peering through the window, munching away at his." *(Carol Breakell)* "Our motel-style room on the first floor was clean and comfortable, with a headboard attached to the wall, and a pretty flowered comforter. Service in the restaurant was fine, the food adequate. The town itself is small and manageable, and the area surprisingly untouristy, even in August." *(SC)*

Worth noting: "Accommodations vary in size—our small room was not for the claustrophobic."

Open All year.
Rooms 3 suites, 20 doubles/singles—all with private bath and/or shower, desk, fan.

Facilities Restaurant, bar/lounge with fireplace, TV; library/game room with fireplace; heated gazebo. Picnic tables. Fishing, boating, bicycling, hiking, trail rides, stream fishing, tennis, 18-hole golf course nearby.

Location SE AB, near provincial border with British Columbia and close to US border at Montana. 80 m SW of Lethbridge via Hwy. 5; 145 m S of Calgary via Hwys. 2, 3, & 6. From Glacier National Park, take Hwy. 6N from Chief Mt. Customs; Waterton is 40 m from St. Mary, MT. Lodge faces Emerald Bay on Upper Waterton Lake.

Restrictions No smoking in some guest rooms.

Credit cards Amex, DC, Enroute, MC, Visa; personal checks for advance deposit only.

Rates Room only, $106–129 suite, $72–115 double, single. Extra person, $10. Children under 16 free in parents' room. Cot, $10; playpen, $5. Ski, golf, mystery, romance packages. Alc dinner, $32.

Extras 2 rooms handicap accessible. Airport/station pickup, $30. Crib, babysitting. French, Spanish spoken.

British Columbia

Bordering Washington, Idaho, and part of Montana, British Columbia stretches north to the Yukon and Northwest Territories and west to the Pacific. Although British Columbia is 50 percent larger than Texas, more than 75 percent of its population (of only 2,744,000) lives near the two principal cities, Vancouver and Victoria. Since British Columbia is something of a mouthful to say, just about everyone in Canada and the northwestern U.S. refers to the province as "BC," which is just what we're going to do here.

Summer is very much peak season in BC; we'd strongly recommend making your reservations two to three months ahead.

Vancouver Island is located 40 miles away from the city of Vancouver on the mainland. To get here, take a ferry from Anacortes, Washington, through the beautiful San Juan Islands; from Port Angeles, on Washington's Olympic Peninsula; or from the city of Vancouver. Victoria, the very British capital of BC, sits at the southern tip of Vancouver Island and is the starting point for island explorations. Near Victoria, scattered like jewels off the southeastern coast, are the 100 Gulf Islands, known as bucolic getaways with all the amenities of island life.

Be sure to travel beyond Victoria when visiting Vancouver Island. There are no continuous roads on the west shore of the island, so you must take Route 1 up the east coast. Turn inland near Parksville, then either stop in Port Alberni to board the MV *Lady Rose* for a romantic cruise to Bamfield or visit Pacific Rim National Park, between Tofino and Ucluelet, for beachcombing and scuba diving. For more adventure, take Route 1 to Campbell River, Route 28 to Gold River, and board the MV *Uchuck III*, which sails the remote fjords of the northwest part of the island.

Mainland BC: Plan to spend several days in the city of Vancouver and the surrounding area. For one good side trip, take Route 99 north past a long inlet, then into the Coast Range Mountains, ending at Whistler, an excellent ski area near Garibaldi Provincial Park. For another, follow picturesque Route 101 up the "Sunshine Coast" from Vancouver to Powell River. This route includes crossings on tiny ferries at both Horseshoe Bay and Earls Cove.

Routes 1 and 3, east of Vancouver, lead you to the most interesting interior spots in the province. On Route 7, stop first at historic Harrison Hot Springs (worth a look but not an overnight), then drop south at Agassiz to Route 1 and the multi-layered Bridal Veil Falls. From here you begin seeing the sharply sculptured, snowcapped Cascade Mountains rising directly behind the Fraser River Valley. At Hope you have a choice. Route 3 winds through the mountains and past the apple orchards of the Okanagan Valley to Penticton and Lake Okanagan, a popular but over-crowded resort area. Alternatively, Route 1 follows the Fraser River Canyon past dramatic Hell's Gate (take the tram across the narrow canyon) into the dry, high plains near Kamloops. From there you enter remote forested back country until you reach the spectacular Mt. Revel-stroke and Glacier National Parks; admire their massive sharp peaks, rolling alpine meadows, and hundreds of glaciers. To the north, the remaining two-thirds of interior BC is sparsely populated; with extreme distances between towns and rustic accommodations, it's not high on our must-see list.

Also sparsely populated and relatively unknown, but worth a special trip for the hardy, are the Queen Charlotte Islands, located 75 miles off the coast and 200 miles north of Vancouver Island. These 150 islands (dominated by Graham and Moresby) provide one of the few opportunities to see large Indian totem poles and longhouses *in situ*. Native Haida Indians, following ancestral designs, carve intricate bowls and sculptures out of argillite, a rock found nowhere else. To reach the Queen Charlottes, either fly up from Vancouver or contact BC Ferries at (604) 669–1211 for sailing information.

All rates are quoted in Canadian dollars, and do not include taxes.

ASHCROFT

Sundance Guest Ranch 👤 🏇   *Tel:* 604–453–2422
Box 489, V0K 1A0   604–453–2554
                                  Fax: 604–453–9356

The Rowe family has owned and operated Sundance Ranch since 1978, maintaining a stable of about 100 horses—from gentle to frisky—as well as a herd of American bison. The ranch has a reputation for good food, with lots of cookouts and barbecues; rooms are basic but comfortable.

"From Vancouver you drive east on Route 1 into the beautiful Cascade Mountains; stop to see Bridal Veil Falls. Stay on Route 1 as it turns north through lovely Fraser Canyon, and visit Hell Gate Canyon enroute. At Sundance, the scenery is the major draw, and the ranch buildings blend in perfectly. It can get hot in summer, although evenings cool down nicely." *(MB)* "Clean, comfortable rooms, delicious meals, spirited horses, and pleasant semi-arid climate." *(Glenn Connelly)* "What you find in this climate is sagebrush and evergreens, bears and coyote. An Indian reserve on one side and a cattle ranch on the other make for a quiet and peaceful stay (except for the Saturday night dance). Great kids' lounge, and another one for adults." *(Andrew Molnar)* "Terrific riding, but I have also enjoyed staying behind to read or swim." *(Marcia Knipher)* "Amenities are well-cared for and clean; comfortable without being stuffy; friendly without laying it on too thick." *(Calum Srigley)* "Great riding, great fun; safety conscious—they will not give you more horse than you can handle." *(Maria Schroyens)*

Open All year. Closed 3 days at Christmas.
Rooms 28 doubles—all with private bath and/or shower, air-conditioning. Some with desk, fireplace.
Facilities 2 dining rooms, game room, 2 lounges (1 for adults-byob, 1 for kids) with Sat. night dances. Children's program. Heated swimming pool, tennis court. 1000 + acres for horseback riding, March to Oct. Lakes for fishing.
Location Central BC. Thompson Valley High Country, 220 m NE of Vancouver. Take Hwy. 1 N to Ashcroft Manor, turn right. Go into Ashcroft; after railroad tracks, turn right onto Highland Valley Road. Go 5 min up hill to ranch on right.
Restrictions No smoking in kids' lounge. Weight limitations on riders; cowboy boots required (rentals available).
Credit cards MC, Visa.
Rates Full board, $230–270 double, $130–155 single. Children in parents' room or kids' wing: age 15–18, $100–115; age 8–14, $80–95; under age 8, $10 or less (riding in arena only). 2–3 night weekend, holiday minimum.
Extras Station pickup; fee for Kamloops airport pickup. Crib, babysitting. German, French spoken.

BOSWELL

Destiny Bay Resort ✕ &.
Highway 3A, V0B 1A0

Tel: 604–223–8234

Hanna and Rolf Langerfeld bought this small resort on the shores of Kootenay Lake in 1977 and have been renovating it ever since.

"Hanna's food is extraordinary and Rolf is a master at spending just enough time chatting to make you feel personally welcome and then leaving you to enjoy the peace they have created. The greatest disturbance we encountered was the squabbling among the hummingbirds who dine along with you on the porch of the main lodge." *(Mrs. P. W. Warren)* "We drove a short distance to a beautiful hiking trail up Lockhart Creek, then explored the Kootenay Forge blacksmith and gift shop with hand-crafted native gifts. You can take the free ferry across to Nelson for a day trip." *(Nancy Lindberg, and others)*

"Porches overlook the lake and mountain range behind. Everything is clean and neat, European both in atmosphere and cuisine. It's owned and run by a German couple who retired from Hamburg, then from eastern Canada." *(Penn Fix)* "Bicycling before vistas of snowcapped mountains, beautiful Kootenay Lake, and wildlife at each turn was topped only by the wonderful four-course dinners." *(David & Patricia Smith)* "Great breakfast every morning at 9 A.M., preceded by muffins in a bag delivered at 7 A.M.

to keep body and soul together. Delicious meals—Mediterranean lamb stew was my favorite." *(Bill & Kathy Cole)* "Good, accessible roads. Wildflowers grow on the sod roofs of the cabins." *(Phil & Eileen Walker)* "Our immaculate private cabin had cedar panelling, attractive wallpaper, cathedral ceiling, and a birchwood fire ready to light. Parking in front; flower boxes line the windows." *(Katie Lawler, and others)* "Firm mattresses, adjustable heat, large bath towels, and big bars of soap." *(Rose-Marie & Bob Beasley)* "The decanter of sherry at fireside was doubly warming." *(Maurice Twomey)* "Friendly, helpful, and competent owners and staff." *(Howard & Elinore Schuck)*

Open April–Oct.
Rooms 3 suites, 5 cottages—all with full private bath, desk, porch, refrigerator, patio, coffee maker. 1 suite has fireplace, double whirlpool tub. 3 cottages with fireplace.
Facilities Dining room, sitting room, library. 3 acres with flower gardens, oversized chess game. Private beach with fireplace, sauna, rowboats. Swimming, fishing, hiking. Heli-hiking, golf nearby.
Location SE BC. 30 m N of Creston on Hwy. 3A, 3 hrs. N of Spokane, WA.
Restrictions "We are an adult-oriented resort; children must be properly supervised."
Credit cards MC, Visa.
Rates MAP, $150–190 suite or cottage (double), $110–150 single. Extra person, $40. 2-night minimum. Prix fixe dinner, $24–30.
Extras Wheelchair access. German spoken.

CHEMAINUS

Pacific Shores Inn ¢   Tel: 604–246–4987
9847 Willow Street, Box 958, V0R 1K0   Fax: 604–246–4785

Chemainus has diversified its lumbering and manufacturing-based economy by adding art to its industry. Over 32 larger-than-life murals, emblazoned on the sides of buildings, depict the history of the region. An annual festival, held in July and August, attracts artists and visitors from around the world.

A neo-Victorian home, bearing its own mural (a fishing schooner), Pacific Shores was built in 1990 inn by Dave and Sonia Haberman. "Clean and well-furnished. Close to all points of interest in town." *(Floyd Young)* "The Duchess room is decorated in a French country style accented with several antique pieces." *(Karen Robbins)* "Clean, quiet. Friendly, knowledgeable, and obliging innkeepers; good suggestions for activities and restaurants." *(Wally & Donna Russell)*

Next door is the Haberman's **Little Inn on Willow**, a Victorian cottage straight out of a Beatrix Potter illustration, with stone chimney, conical tower, and luxurious, romantic accommodations. "Small and compact but contains all one could imagine for a romantic stay. The lighting effect the Habermans have achieved makes the room virtually glow at night." *(Mr. & Mrs. Ian Barrigan)* "The chilled champagne upon arrival was the perfect romantic touch." *(Dr. & Mrs. Taggart)* "Great attention to detail in overall decor and furnishings." *(Tim Jacox)*

Open All year.

Rooms Pacific Shores: 3 suites—all with full private bath and/or shower, kitchenette, radio, clock, TV/VCR, desk. 2 with fan, deck. 2 with washer/dryer. Little Inn: 1 cottage with private shower, radio, clock, TV/VCR, double whirlpool tub, air-conditioning, fireplace, refrigerator, patio.

Facilities Video library. Massage therapist. Bicycles. Off-street parking. Golf, beach, playground, lake, Thetis Island ferry nearby.

Location SE Vancouver Is., Inland Passage. 60 m N of Victoria. Town center.

Restrictions No smoking. No children in Little Inn cottage.

Credit cards MC with 4% surcharge.

Rates Room only, Pacific Shores: $75–90 suite; Little Inn: $160 double. Taxes included.

Extras Wheelchair accessible. Station pickup. Babysitting.

CLINTON

Clinton was a lively place to be during the gold rush days; today it serves as a supply center—not for miners panning the Fraser River—but for the surrounding ranches and camps set in the high meadows and pine forests of the region.

Information please: Owners Teresa Hobot and Karl Krammer call **Cariboo Rose Guest Ranch** (P.O. Box 160, Clinton V0K 1K0; 604–459–2255) the smallest guest ranch in BC—with only four guest cabins—but it also has indoor and outdoor riding arenas and 250 miles of riding trails. Rates of $875–980 per person per week (Friday arrival) are all-inclusive, from all-day rides to a relaxing soak in the hot tub. Meals are served family-style, with dinners of roast beef and Yorkshire pudding; baked chicken and fettuccine Alfredo; or steak barbecue with ranch-style potatoes. On a slightly larger scale, is the **Circle H Mountain Lodge** (P.O. Box 7, Clinton V0K 1K0; 604–459–2565 or 604–850–1873), with five rooms in the main lodge and four sleeping cabins. Rates of $590 per person per week include two guided trail rides a day, some all-day trips, all meals, and use of the swimming pool and sauna; children's rates available. Reports?

COURTENAY

Greystone Manor ¢
4014 Haas Road, RR 6, Site 684-C2, V9N 8H9

Tel: 604–338–1422

Mike and Mo Shipton emigrated to Canada from Bath, England, in 1990 and have furnished their 75-year-old home, overlooking Comox Bay, with period decor. The Shiptons are keen gardeners, and the inn's summer floral display grows more beautiful each year. Guests can relax by the living room fireplace, explore the gardens, walk down to the beach to watch harbor seals at play, and possibly spot a bald eagle.

"We awoke to the sound of chirping birds and rustling leaves, took an early morning walk and enjoyed a homemade breakfast of fruit with cream and nuts, fresh muffins and scones, and salmon and broccoli quiche." *(Mrs*

A.J. Wilson) "We received outstanding suggestions and advice regarding the area and the islands. The Shiptons make guests feel at home while respecting their privacy. Comfortable, attractive facilities." *(Liz Diamond & Dennis Brock)* "Excellent breakfast, with great presentation. Superb gardens and grounds." *(D. Fernell)* "Beds are comfortable, and all is spotless." *(Malin & Moira Thompson)*

Open All year.

Rooms 4 doubles share 2 baths.

Facilities Breakfast room, living room with fireplace, books, decks. 1.2 acres with gardens. Fishing, swimming, beach walks, golf nearby. 40 min to downhill, cross-country skiing.

Location E central coast of Vancouver Island. 60 m N of Nanaimo, 150 m N of Victoria. 3 m S of Courtenay. From Island Hwy. N, go ³/₅ m (1 km) past traffic light in Royston, turn right onto Hilton Rd., then left onto Haas Rd.

Restrictions No smoking. No children under 12.

Credit cards MC, Visa.

Rates B&B, $63 double, $49 single, tax included. Extra person, $20.

FIELD

Yoho National Park stretches along the border of Alberta and British Columbia, in the Canadian Rockies just west of the Continental Divide and the resort city of Banff. "Yoho" is the Kootenay Indian exclamation for wonder or astonishment.

Information please: Not far from Emerald Lake lies **Kicking Horse Lodge** (Box 174, V0A 1G0; 604–343–6303), a contemporary two-story ranch-style structure. The fourteen rooms have queen-size beds, TVs, and full private baths; 7 have a porch. A large family unit is available with a kitchenette and whirlpool tub. The restaurant serves three meals daily, from classic burgers and BLTs to chicken crepes at lunch; dinner entrées include Coho salmon with spiced butter and dried fruit; grilled steak with peppercorn sauce; and spinach manicotti. Double rates range from $54–94; no charge for children under 6.

Emerald Lake Lodge 🏃 ✕
P.O. Box 10, Field, BC, V0A 1G0

Tel: 604–343–6321
800–663–6336
Fax: 604–343–6321, ext. 211

Built by the Canadian Pacific Railway in 1902 of hand-hewn logs with massive stone fireplaces, Emerald Lake Lodge was expanded in the 1920s and was totally renovated in 1986. Some original antiques are found in the common areas, while the guest rooms are decorated in pastel colors with natural pine or oak furnishings.

"A secluded slice of heaven in the Canadian Rockies, with a setting that beats that of Chateau Lake Louise in Banff. Above average rooms, with down quilts, fieldstone fireplace, and efficient plumbing. Visit anytime from mid-September to mid-June, except for Christmas week, to avoid peak season rates and large crowds. We preferred the more casual setting of the bar to the restaurant." *(Adam Platt)* "Our comfortably furnished room was one of four in each cabin (two to a floor), with a small bedroom, living room area with fireplace, and a view of the lake." *(Alan & Karen Roseman)*

"The cottages are stocked with logs and kindling, replenished nightly." *(Steve Bond)* "No cars are allowed after dark, so the evenings are wonderfully peaceful." *(William Fuerst & Lisa Ottinger)* "To avoid the peak season crowds that stop to look at the lake but rarely venture far beyond the parking plot, we planned our hiking, rafting, or riding trips for midday. When we returned in the late afternoon, all was peaceful, and we rewarded ourselves with a relaxing soak in the hot tub, surrounded by mountain flowers, with a spectacular view of the lake and surrounding mountains." *(Mary Beth O'Reilly)* "Delicious dinner entrées—Caribou loin steak, Pacific salmon, scallops. We went skating on the lake before breakfast, and in the afternoon skied around it and under the frozen waterfalls." *(Marilyn Parker)*

Areas for improvement: "Better soundproofing; I could hear the neighbors walking around." Also: "During our summer visit, the student staff in the restaurant was not up to par."

Open All year.
Rooms 1 cabin, 6 suites, 78 doubles in 24 cabin-style buildings—all with private bath, fireplace, balcony, coffee maker. Some with mini-bar. Cabin with kitchenette.
Facilities Restaurant, bar/lounge, lobby, game room with billiards, TV/VCR. Clubhouse with exercise room, hot tub, sauna, decks. Conference rooms. Boating, hiking, horseback riding, fishing, whitewater rafting, cross-country skiing, sleigh rides, heli-skiing, dog sledding, snow shoeing, ice skating.
Location SE BC. 125 m W of Calgary, AL; 55 m NW of Banff, 25 m W of Lake Louise. From Field, go W on Trans-Canada Hwy #1 for 1 m to turn-off for Natural Bridge & Emerald Lake. Follow for 5 m to lodge.
Credit cards Amex, Enroute, MC, Visa.
Rates Room only, $210–370 cabin, $150–285 suite, $100–260 double. Extra adult in room, $15. No charge for children under 13 in parents' room.

Lake O'Hara Lodge 🛉

Yoho National Park
Mailing address: P.O. Box 1677, Banff, Alberta T0L 0C0

Tel: 403–762–2118
In summer season: 604–343–6418

On the opposite side of Victoria Glacier from Lake Louise, this two-story wooden lodge was built by the Canadian Pacific Railroad in 1926. At 6,700 feet, it is the highest resort in the Canadian Rockies. It's been owned and managed by Michael and Marsha Laub and Tim and Leslee Wake since 1976. Rooms are furnished simply but comfortably. The food is surprisingly sophisticated: a typical set dinner might consist of a goat cheese tart, tomato salad with basil, prime rib with Yorkshire pudding, and apple tart. Rates also include afternoon tea and cookies or gluhwein. The setting is blissful—the blue waters of Lake O'Hara ringed by dark evergreens and golden larches, with the snowcapped 11,000-foot peaks piercing the bright blue sky. Access is limited, and it's hard to believe that bustling Lake Louise lies just on the other side of the mountains.

"Exceptional food and service." *(Ross & Diane Evans)* "Well-marked and well-kept hiking trails. Limited number of day trippers." *(Maidrid Jonat)* "Lodge rooms have communal bathrooms, one each for men and women.

Plumbing and lighting are surprisingly good considering the remote location. The staff is obviously handpicked and many have been with the lodge for years. Those who are musically or comically gifted put on a Saturday night staff talent show for guests. It's fun to visit around the oversized stone fireplace in the lodge, especially for afternoon tea." *(Patty White)* "Pack lunches consist of sandwiches, fruit, cheese, crackers, carrots and celery, trail mix, a sweet, and lemonade. Our lakeshore cabin was spotless, and the bed luxurious with down pillows and comforters. Towels were thick, and showers hot and strong. The staff is friendly and warm, but professional. The chef's homemade breads, pastries, and muffins are first rate; wine service is excellent, the menu creative and good." *(Cynthia & John O'Hara)*

Open Early June–Oct.1; mid-Jan.–mid-April. Cabins closed in winter.
Rooms 15 1- to 2-room cabins—all with private bath and/or shower. Lodge with 7 doubles, 1 single sharing 2 baths. All with desk.
Facilities Dining room, lounge. Sat. night entertainment in summer. 5 acres. 50 m of hiking trails, fishing, mountain climbing, cross-country skiing.
Location E BC. Yoho National Park, Canadian Rockies. 120 m W of Calgary, 8 m W of Lake Louise. From Lake Louise, take Trans-Canada Hwy. W to Rte. 1A. Turn left and park in O'Hara gate parking lot. In summer, bus makes 3 round-trips to lodge daily; winter access on skis only.
Restrictions No smoking.
Credit cards None accepted.
Rates Full board, $380–425 cabin, $277–310 double, $210–220 single, tax included. Extra adult (over age 15) in cabin, $140. Family rates. No tipping. 2-night minimum. 5% weekly discount.
Extras Station pickup.

FORT STEELE

Wild Horse Farm ¢ 🚶
Highway 93/95, Box 7, V0B 1N0

Tel: 604–426–6000

Wild Horse Farm is an Astor's idea of a log cabin—a spacious, two-story, 12-room country manor with fireplaces in nearly half the rooms and antiques everywhere. It was, in fact, built by a member of the New York Astor family in the early 1900s, and many of the original fixtures are still in use.

"Located in a lush valley, with mountains on all horizons. Somewhat reminiscent of a posh hunting lodge, the huge wood-beamed living room has a large fireplace, leather sofas and chairs, two pianos, and an enormous globe. Our gracious suite had a library with fireplace, a separate bedroom (with a second fireplace), and large bath. Outside, huge pine trees provide a perfect place to sit and read. In the field are horses and shaggy Scottish Highland cows. We awoke to find steaming cups of coffee and tea waiting on a tray. The excellent breakfast included juice, raspberries with whipped cream, eggs and sausage, bacon, an oven-baked pancake with Canadian maple syrup, and homemade rhubarb muffins. Innkeepers Orma and Bob Termuende are gracious, charming, and funny, with great sightseeing suggestions. Without hovering, they make sure guests have everything they need. Although you can't see or hear it from the farm, across the street is the Fort Steele Heritage Town, a pleasant re-creation of a turn-of-the-century village." *(SC)*

"Loved the homemade raspberry juice for an afternoon refreshment. Orma is a warm person with a genius for cooking—breakfasts feature the best from her garden." *(Karen Richardson, also David Tabakman)* "Breakfast was outstanding, with lots of fresh fruit, bacon and ham, and terrific Yorkshire pudding." *(W. Craig Falkenhagen)* "The farm's homey, friendly atmosphere is perfect for kids. Super breakfasts, served when you are ready." *(Vernon Elliott)* "Our children collected eggs from the chicken coop. Our room had plumbing that was circa 1930 but worked fine." *(Peter Laing)* "Bright lights for reading, unusual in a B&B." *(Ned Gilbert)*

Open May 1–Sept. 30.
Rooms 2 suites, 2 doubles—all with private bath and/or shower, radio, desk. TV available. One suite with 2 fireplaces.
Facilities Dining room with fireplace; living room with game table, player piano, TV/VCR, stereo, books; screened veranda. 3 acres with patio, lawns, gardens, volleyball, croquet. Hiking, fishing, boating, golf, tennis nearby.
Location SE BC. 10 m NE of Cranbrook on Rocky Mt. Trench Hwy. 93/95, just across road from Heritage Village of Fort Steele.
Restrictions Smoking restricted to living room.
Credit cards Visa.
Rates B&B, $93 suite, $64–70 double, $48–52 single. Extra adult in suite, $20; child 12 and over, $13; child under 12, $9; tips "not expected." Prix fixe lunch, $7; prix fixe dinner, $20.
Extras Airport/station pickup, $10. Pets by arrangement.

GOLD BRIDGE

TYAX Mountain Lake Resort 🚶 🎿 ♿
Tyaughton Lake Road, V0K 1P0

Tel: 604–238–2221
Fax: 604–238–2528

Located in the southern Chilcotin mountains, TYAX Mountain Lake Resort is the largest modern log-built lodge in western Canada, and was built in 1986. The resort's restaurant boasts a 30-foot-high freestanding stone fireplace, and overlooks the lake and mountains, as do the guest rooms. Each chalet is situated right on the lake, with a section of beach, and is surrounded by two acres of wooded land for privacy. "The lodge sits above manicured lawns that sweep down to a crystal clear, glacier-fed lake. In the background is a circle of tall, craggy mountain peaks dusted with snow even in August. Our spacious room was done in pine, with a large, comfortable sofa, a firm double-sized platform bed with an eider-down quilt and lights on both sides; clean bathroom, and a wonderful porch overlooking the lake. Simple meals are served buffet-style. When we left, we took the 'back route' which came out above Whistler ski area. This was great fun but I'd recommend it only for experienced, hardy drivers." *(SC)*

Open All year.
Rooms 4 3–4 bedroom chalets, 28 doubles—all with private bath and/or shower, desk, balcony. Some with kitchen, TV. 14 rooms in separate buildings.
Facilities Dining room with fireplace, lobby, lounge with occasional weekend

entertainment, TV, fireplace; children's playroom & bicycles; porch. 275 acres; 6000' on lake with beach, fishing, canoes, sailboat, windsurfer, paddle, motor boats. Tennis, hot tub, sauna, fitness center, playground, gazebo, horseshoes, volleyball, hiking, horseback riding, cross-country & heli-skiing, snowmobiling, ice-fishing, sleigh rides. Float-plane trips. White-water rafting nearby.

Location Central BC. 200 m N of Vancouver, 58 m W of Lillooet.

Restrictions No smoking in restaurant, on 3rd floor.

Credit cards Amex, MC, Visa.

Rates Room only, $180–260 chalet, $90–110 double, $80–85 single. Extra person, $20; no charge for children under 12 in parents' room. Crib or cot, $10 per day. Tipping encouraged. Weekly, package rates, also B&B, MAP rates. 2-3 night minimum. Alc lunch, $9; alc dinner, $15–25.

Extras Limited wheelchair access. Pickups: rail, $70 per person.

GOLDEN

Information please: Promising "the ultimate escape from the pressures of the modern, working world," managers Paul Leeson and Russ Younger welcome you to **Purcell Lodge** (P.O. Box 1829, c/o ABC Wilderness Adventures Ltd., V0A 1H0; 604–344–2639). A remote mountain hideaway situated at 7,200 feet on the eastern border of Glacier National Park, the recently constructed lodge occupies an alpine meadow miles from the nearest road. In fact, a 15-minute helicopter flight from Golden is the only access guests have to the resort. Rates for the ten rooms ($280–330 double) include meals, guiding, and instructional services. Meals are hearty; entrées include salmon with almond butter and rice pilaf, pork roast with chili corn, and roast beef with Yorkshire pudding; ricotta cheesecake and apple crisp are dessert favorites. Reports?

GULF ISLANDS

Sitting like giant stepping stones between the mainland and Vancouver Island, the Gulf Islands are wooded hideaways that offer the very best of island life: tiny villages, deserted beaches, sweeping views of the Strait of Georgia and distant snowcapped mountains. Easily accessible by a web of ferry routes, the islands offer a pleasant contrast to the bustling cities of Vancouver and Victoria. Take your choice between northernmost Denman Island and those islands that are only minutes away from Victoria.

Reader tip: "Washington ferries require you to arrive 90 minutes before departure for the trip from Sydney, BC, to Anacortes, Washington. Leaving from Salt Spring Island and going to Tsawwassen via the BC ferry system requires arrival only 30 minutes before departure—and the ferries are cleaner and better appointed."

GULF ISLANDS—GALIANO ISLAND

Galiano Island rests almost in the middle of the Strait of Georgia, between Vancouver Island and the city of Vancouver.

Reader tip: "Galiano Island is shaped like a very long cigar. Although little of the coast is accessible (there's a steep cliff along its western side, almost no public access on the east), there is one superb area at the northern tip called Coon Bay, where sandstone has been carved into areas that look like Swiss cheese and other areas that look like huge gaping lions' mouths."

Woodstone Country Inn ✗ &.   Tel: 604–539–2022
Georgeson Bay Road, R.R. #1, V0N 1P0

The native sandstone formations of Galiano Island and the forest pathways of the surrounding acreage aptly describe this inn's name, Woodstone. Opened in 1989, the Woodstone seeks to offer guests a relaxed atmosphere in which to enjoy the natural beauty of this Gulf island; boots, binoculars, and guidebooks are available so that you can visit the marsh to see what new birds have arrived on their seasonal migrations. Creative, four-course dinners are served; a recent menu included prawns Romesco; tomato and tarragon soup; a choice of lemon-fennel roasted pork or trout with lemon-dill hollandaise; and bread pudding with rum sauce or frozen lemon cream cake with raspberry sauce.

"Peaceful, tranquil setting. Bright, airy common rooms with plenty of windows and skylights. Guest rooms are equally spacious and light with tall windows or French doors, and high ceilings. The spare use of handpainted borders, coupled with antique furniture and floral print duvets creates an elegant ambiance. Food is adventuresome and beautifully done, with a reasonable variety of wine." (DG) "The Woodstone is a new building in a setting which is ideal for quiet, peaceful enjoyment. My room, decorated with country charm, had a very comfortable bed and everything one could want, including a fireplace." (Patrick Walsh)

Open All year. Restaurant closed for dinner Mon., Tues. off-season.
Rooms 12 doubles—all with full private bath. 10 with fireplace, 6 with patio.
Facilities Dining room, living room with fireplace, patio. 9 acres with walking trails. 5 min to beach. Sailing, fishing, kayaking, cycling, horseback riding nearby.
Location S Galiano Is. Take Tsawwassen ferry from mainland or Swartz Bay on Vancver Is. From Sturdies Bay ferry terminal, go NW on Sturdies Bay Rd., turn left on Georgeson Bay Rd. to inn on left.
Restrictions No smoking. "Adults only."
Credit cards Amex, MC, Visa.
Rates B&B, $82–132 double. Extra person, $20. 2-night holiday/weekend minimum. Winter packages. Prix fixe dinner, $26.
Extras Limited wheelchair access. Free ferry pickup.

GULF ISLANDS—MAYNE ISLAND

Mayne Island is in the Gulf Islands of southwestern British Columbia and is approximately 30 miles from both Victoria and Vancouver. It can be reached by ferry from either Tsawwassen (just south of Vancouver) or from Vancouver Island. Heavily wooded, with rolling hills and a tiny village center, Mayne offers a variety of beaches from pebbled ones to small sandy coves surrounded by soft sandstone ledges that jut out into the Strait and have been so scoured by other stones that they resemble lace.

Oceanwood Country Inn ✗

530 Dinner Bay Road, V0N 2J0

Tel: 604–539–5074
Fax: 604–539–3002

Owners Marilyn and Jonathan Chilvers, former residents of Vancouver, summered on Mayne Island for years; in 1990, they began offering their favorite things—good books, good music, good company, and good food and wine—to paying guests. The inn's dining room specializes in North-west food and wine and has received widespread acclaim; the inn's gardens provide many of the vegetables which appear on the menu. Rates include afternoon tea and breakfast with a daily entrée such as poached eggs with salmon and a dilled hollandaise sauce, or blueberry buckwheat pancakes with homemade veal and pork sausage.

"Fresh flowers everywhere. In our bath, the cold water was icy and the hot was truly hot; thick large towels and luxurious terry robes." *(Richard & JoAnn Sheldon)* "Spotlessly clean. Excellent library, good parking facilities." *(Dorothy Westcott)* "Outstanding food, yet accommodating to dietary restrictions." *(Arthur Barran)* "Beautiful location; the island is great for biking—hilly but manageable. Lots of space to sit out on decks and patio." *(Judith Shands)* "Marilyn and Jonathan are pleased to offer advice on day trips, or to chat about gardening, decorating, a favorite opera or whatever. In the afternoon, Jonathan usually plays classical CDs but as night descends, the soft sounds of jazz or swing float through the air." *(George Medovoy)* "From the upper terrace, whales can occasionally be seen spouting and breaching in the waters beyond. The inn is beautifully furnished, with books and binoculars conveniently placed. Each bedroom, furnished with either a queen-size or two twin beds, has a different decor." *(Janice Hughes)*

Open March 1–Dec. 31.
Rooms 8 doubles—all with private bath and/or shower. 4 with whirlpool tub, 3 with fireplace, 5 with balcony or terrace access.
Facilities Living room, dining room, library with fireplaces. Meeting room. 10 acres on ocean with gardens. Swimming, sailing, kayaking, fishing nearby.
Location From ferry, turn right on Dalton Dr. to Dinner Bay Rd.
Restrictions Smoking in library only. No children under 16.
Credit cards MC, Visa.
Rates B&B, $110–200 double, $100–190 single. 2–3 night weekend/holiday minimum. Prix fixe dinner, $32.
Extras Very limited wheelchair access. French spoken.

GULF ISLANDS—SALT SPRING ISLAND

Largest of the Gulf Islands; people come to relax and enjoy the pretty, rustic setting. Activities include all water sports—both ocean and lake—as well as hiking, tennis, horseback riding, and golf.

Salt Spring Island is 20 m north of Victoria and is accessible via ferry from Victoria or Vancouver or float plane from Vancouver or Seattle.

Information please: For a quiet adult retreat four miles from the village of Ganges, **Spindrift** (Welbury Point, R.R. 3, Ganges V0S 1E0; 604–537–5311) offers six oceanfront cottages, set on a six-acre peninsula where paths lead from two white sand beaches to the cottages. Each fully equipped unit has a private bath, kitchen, and fireplace, and rates range from $72–130. "Tranquility, scenic ocean beauty, and an abundance of wildlife, including lots of hummingbirds, tame rabbits, and a herd of small island deer; seals and otters are usually seen in the water." *(Kirstin McDougall)* Reports welcome.

Hastings House ✕ &.

Box 1110, 160 Upper Ganges, V0S 1E0

Tel: 604–537–2362
800–661–9255
Fax: 604–537–5333

Hastings House is an elegant seaside farm estate, composed of five restored buildings—the Manor House, the Farmhouse, Cliffside, the Post, and the Barn. The Tudor-style Manor House contains the inn's dining and common rooms, while the guest rooms and suites are spread out among the inn's buildings. Known for its food, the five-course dinners feature fresh produce and herbs from the inn's gardens, eggs from its hen house, and local lamb and seafood. Possible dinner entrées might be Digby scallops with leeks and mahogany rice; grilled tenderloin with shitake mushrooms; and salmon with tomato risotto and garlic. In 1994, Cate Simpson and Ian Cowley became the innkeepers after long stints at the luxurious Four Seasons hotel group—Cate from a position in marketing at the Vancouver hotel and Ian from a position as chef at the Boston hotel. Both are happy to be back in their native BC.

"Everything is superb, from the personal nameplate on your door, table, and menu to the thermos of coffee and freshly squeezed orange juice that are left outside your door in the early morning, to the fact that when you order cocktails in the beautiful Tudor living room before dinner, the servers will remember and ask you if you want the same the next night." *(Judith Brannen, also Natalie Foster)* Reports needed.

Open March–Nov.
Rooms 8 1- to 2-bedroom suites, 4 doubles—all with private bath, telephone, radio, desk, fireplace, wet bar. TV on request. Guest rooms in several buildings.
Facilities Dining room, library, living room, conference room. 30 acres with lawns, herb and vegetable gardens, croquet, bicycles; 1,000 ft. of waterfront for fishing, boat moorage.
Location SW BC. At N end of Salt Spring Island, at head of Ganges Harbour; 2 m N of town.
Restrictions No smoking in dining room. No children.
Credit cards Amex, MC, Visa.
Rates B&B, $270–420 suite, $220–290 double. Extra person, $65. 2–3-night holiday/weekend minimum. Prix fixe dinner, $55.
Extras Free ferry pickup. Limited wheelchair access. Member, Relais et Châteaux.

Old Farmhouse B&B

RR 4, 1077 North End Road, V0S 1E0

Tel: 604–537–4113
Fax: 604–537–4969

In 1989 Gerti and Karl Fuss bought this renovated 1895 farmhouse and immediately began designing a guest house, a replica of the original farmhouse. Karl built it himself, searching for old doors and windows to

atch those in their home; Gerti sewed the curtains, bedskirts, and pil-
ws. The spacious guest rooms have high dormer windows, down com-
rters, and bright fabrics. Guests dine together at a table set with fine
ina, silver, starched linen, and flowers from the garden. "Quiet and
eaceful with superb, caring owners. Outstanding breakfasts of home-
aked cinnamon buns and croissants, smoked salmon souffle or German
ple pancakes, with apple juice freshly pressed from their own orchard."
DO) Comments appreciated.

pen All year.
ooms 4 doubles—all with full private bath, telephone, desk, deck.
acilities Dining room, living room with fireplace, TV/VCR, stereo, books. 3
res with gazebo, lawn games.
ocation Salt Spring Is. 3 m N of Ganges.
estrictions No smoking. Children over 12 preferred.
redit cards MC, Visa.
ates B&B, $110–135 double. Extra person, $35.
xtras Ferry pickup. German spoken.

ADYSMITH

ellow Point Lodge &
700 Yellow Point Road, RR 3, V0R 2F0

Tel: 604–245–7422

ellow Point Lodge is a country resort that has been owned by the Hill
mily for over 50 years. Rebuilt after a 1985 fire, guests come to the main
dge for meals and to socialize; it's built of massive logs, with natural
ood siding and a large stone fireplace.

"Thoroughly relaxing, with leisurely walks through the woods and
ong the beach. The outdoor hot tub, with its view of the water and
ountains, was spectacular. Driftwood Cabin isn't on the beach, but had
great water view." (Marsi Fein & Todd Miller) "Meals are good and
lentiful, especially the homemade breads and goodies served at tea time
d in the evening. Rooms are clean and comfortable, though not luxuri-
us." (Pamela & C. Adrian Stone) "In the lodge, Room 5 is best (with its
wn balcony), but the cabins are nice and private." (Suzanne Carmichael)
At breakfast, you can order whatever you like, in any combination and
uantity—eggs, bacon, sausages, oatmeal, pancakes, hash browns, and
ore. The seating at tables for 10 allows you to meet new people, yet
ere is ample opportunity for privacy when desired. Although the lounge
rea is huge, with a beautiful view, there are little living room groupings
cattered around. Our White Beach cottage had lovely furniture, including
high bed, from which we could enjoy the view out our window." (PE)

"Fully endorse existing entry in terms of beauty, location, comfort, and
alue. However, the vast majority of guests have been coming for years;
lthough we met others who disagreed, we felt like outsiders and left
arly."

pen All year.
ooms 9 doubles in main lodge, 42 rooms in cabins, cottages. 21 rooms with
rivate bath and/or shower, 7 rooms with a maximum of 6 sharing bath. Also 24
each and field cabins sharing communal-style washrooms.
acilities Living room with dance floor, fireplace; game room; dining room, guest

refrigerator. 180 acres with 1 m waterfront; walking/jogging trails; outdoor saltwater swimming pool, hot tub, sauna, 2 tennis courts, badminton, volleyball, mountain bikes; beach swimming, canoeing, boating, windsurfing. Golf nearby. Midweek cruises.

Location SE BC. SE coast of Vancouver Island, 70 m N of Victoria. 15 m S of Nanaimo. From Nanaimo, take Rte. 1 S 3 m to Cedar Rd. Go left on Cedar 5 m to Yellow Pt. Rd. Turn left & go 7 m to lodge. From Ladysmith, go N 3 m to Cedar Rd. Turn right on Cedar; go 2 m & turn right on Yellow Pt. Rd. 4 m to lodge.

Restrictions Non-smoking areas. No children under 16. Dietary restrictions with 24 hrs. notice.

Credit cards MC, Visa.

Rates Full board, lodge: $153–164 double, $95–105 single. Cabins: $97–164 double, $54–105 single. Extra person in room, $54. 2–3-night holiday/weekend minimum. 20% off-season midweek discount.

Extras Limited wheelchair access. Free ferry, station, airport pickup, by arrangement.

MILL BAY

Information please: An easy 25-mile drive north of Victoria is the **Pine Lodge Farm** (3191 Mutter Road, V0R 2P0; 604–743–4083), overlooking the ocean across acres of farm and woodland. The house, built in 1979 by Cliff and Barbara Clarke of pine logs harvested on the property, was especially designed to show off their collection of antiques. The seven guest rooms have private baths; no smoking is permitted, and $75–85 double rates include a full breakfast. Comments?

POWELL RIVER

Information please: We'd like comments on **Beacon B&B** (3750 Marine Avenue, V8A 2H8; 604–485–5563), owned by Shirley and Roger Randall since 1990, and offering beautiful views of the Straits of Georgia and the mountains of Vancouver Island. The three guest rooms in this contemporary home have full private baths and telephones, and the hot tub is ideal for relaxation. Breakfast possibilities include fruit salad, scones, juice, bacon and eggs, blueberry pancakes, waffles with strawberries and whipped cream, eggs Benedict, omelets, or porridge and muffins. B&B double rates range from $65–$105; massage therapy available.

QUADRA ISLAND

If fishing is your passion, then head for the Inland Passage and Quadra Island where salmon are the game of choice. Quadra is located about 2 miles north of Courtenay, and accessible by ferry from Campbell River.

Information please: You can take a float plane directly to the dock of the **April Point Lodge & Fishing Resort** (P.O. Box 1, Campbell River, V9W 4Z9; 604–285–2222). This 65-room lodge, on 200 acres, offers heli-fishing as well as heli-hiking, native feasts, and barbecue picnics on the beach; guides can take you salmon fishing, and your catch will be prepared for the journey home. Guests choose between cabins or guest rooms, many with fireplace, kitchenettes, or hot tubs. Reports welcome.

Tsa-Kwa-Luten Lodge ✗
P.O. Box 460, Quathiaski Cove, V0P 1N0

Tel: 604–285–2042
Tel: 800–665–7745
Fax: 604–285–2532

Set on Cape Mudge, Tsa-Kwa-Luten Lodge is the only resort in Canada featuring authentic Pacific Coast native food, art and cultural activities. Guests can partake of the area's legendary fishing; they're also invited to take part in ceremonial dances and feasts as a way of learning about the culture of the Kwagiulth People who own and operate the lodge.

"Dramatic lobby with huge timbers and a 45-foot-high ceiling; it's modeled after a traditional native longhouse. Decorations include dramatic carved masks, petroglyph rubbings, a huge carved ceremonial screen, and century-old photos of local villages and ceremonies. Our room, with vaulted ceiling, had tan walls, wine-colored accents, a Northwest Indian artwork, and knotty pine furniture. From our balcony we saw Vancouver Island, fishermen, and cruise ships. The attractive dining room has a superb view; service is pleasant and competent with good food. Unusual breakfast offerings included fiddleheads and mushroom omelets, forest berry crepes, and a hash of seared salmon, peppers, leeks, potatoes, and herbs. A great place for relaxing, walking on the beach, hiking on the island, and visiting the Kwagiulth Museum to learn the history of the native people. The 'ceremonial feast' was served buffet-style with salmon traditionally cooked over a fire, various salads, corn fritters, steamed scallops, and mussels. The ceremonial dancing program included magnificent dancers wearing masks, with explanations of the legends behind each dance." *(SC)* Reports appreciated.

Open All year. Salmon feast, Sat., early July 2–early Sept.
Rooms 1 guest house, 4 2-bedroom cabins, 26 suites—all with full private bath. Cabins with whirlpool bath, fireplace, kitchen.
Facilities Restaurant, lobby, bar/lounge, deck, gift shop. Fitness center with sauna, hot tub. 1,100 acre forest; beach. Bicycles. Kayaking, boat cruises, museum nearby.
Location Quadra Is. Go N from Victoria or Nanaimo on Island Hwy (19) to Campbell River. Take ferry to the island. 5 min. to resort from dock.
Credit cards All major credit cards.
Rates Room only, $450 guest house, $230 cabin, $175–200 suites, $115–150 double. Vacation package, $260 double; includes 2 nights, 2 breakfasts, 1 dinner. Fishing packages.
Extras Pets permitted in cabins only.

QUALICUM BEACH

Blue Willow B&B ¢ 👫
524 Quatna Road, V9K 1B4

Tel: 604–752–9052
Fax: 604–752–9039

The blue and white china, from which the inn gains its name, highlights the decor of this Tudor-style cottage with leaded glass windows and beamed ceilings, owned by John and Arlene England. "Warm ocean currents make the beach a popular location for seaside activities, and the town has a profusion of flowers, small delightful shops, and an excellent art gallery," Arlene reports. Breakfasts, served on the patio amid Arlene's beautiful gardens, include home-baked treats and a choice of a continental or full English breakfast. "Arlene's scrumptious breakfast was carefully prepared with homemade everything; these lovely people never encroached on our privacy." *(Peggy King)* "Serene setting. Ask about the shortcut for a beautiful walk past some gorgeous property on the beach at Judge's Row. Rooms are exceptionally clean and neat; some have a private bath across the hall." *(Owen Halliday)* "Gorgeous, well-kept gardens. But the best feature is the warm, friendly atmosphere provided by Arlene and John." *(Jane McNulty)*

Open All year.
Rooms 1 2-bedroom suite, 3 doubles—all with private bath and/or shower, radio, desk. Suite in separate building.
Facilities Dining/breakfast room, guest lounge with TV/VCR, desk, books. Laundry facility. Off-road parking. Golf, swimming, boat rentals, boat ramps nearby.
Location Vancouver Island. From Victoria or Nanaimo follow Island Hwy. N to Qualicum. Turn left at Qualicum Rd., right on Quatna Rd. to inn.
Restrictions No smoking.
Credit cards MC, Visa.
Rates B&B, $50–70 suite, double. $45–55 single. Extra person, $15. Family rates.
Extras Airport/station pickup. French, German spoken.

REVELSTOKE

Also recommended: *Eileen Walker* reports that the **Three Valley Gap Motor Inn** (Highway 1, Box 860, V0E 2S0; 604–837–2109) is "a popular overnight stop for people coming from Calgary and Edmonton on their way to Vancouver, but it is also a destination in itself. Beautifully located in the Monashee Mountains, 12 miles west of Revelstoke, this resort is built on the shores of the Lake of Three Valleys. There is a ghost town, garden, indoor swimming pool, and hot tub. Comfortable rooms are nicely appointed. Helpful and friendly service. Exploring the property is an adventure." Owned by the Bell family, most of the 117 rooms are in motel-style buildings, all with private bath; the honeymoon suite is built into the rock so the interior is made entirely of stone. The hotel is located on the highway, so light sleepers should ask for a quiet room. Facilities include restaurants, lounges, a theater, gift shop, and guest laundry.

Piano Keep ¢   *Tel:* 604–837–2120
815 Mackenzie Avenue, Box 1893, V0E 2S0   *Fax:* 604–837–2120

The Piano Keep is a 1905 Queen Anne home, owned by Vern and Gwen Enyedy since 1989. Made of Victorian Stone, a manmade block resembling carved stone, the house has an oak entrance door surrounded by stained glass panels; the Eastlake-style cedar central staircase has curved walls, one with curved pocket doors. The B&B takes its name from the Enyedy's collection of antique pianos—squares, uprights, grands. The guest rooms, all on third floor, are decorated with floral wallpapers, antiques, and family pieces.

"Our large, quiet room was spotless, bright and cheery with a skylight and large windows. The bathroom was modern, well lit, with an oversize tub. Our attentive and easygoing hosts spent time getting to know us and making excellent sightseeing suggestions. Breakfast was completely homemade—pancakes made with hand-ground flour, stuffed French toast, fresh fruit, and the most wonderful tea. Vern takes you on a 45-minute tour by actually playing the pianos that he has restored, some 50 in all." *(Kelley & Donald Rowley)* "Heritage home on a quiet street close to town. Our front room was decorated with firm and comfortable beds, plus interesting books and a view of snowcapped mountains. Superb bathroom with luxurious towels, soups, and bubble baths." *(Mary Fox)* "The bed linen had embroidered edging, as did the towels. Breakfast was delicious, served in the second floor breakfast room with our companionable hosts." *(Jean Staniland)*

Open All year.
Rooms 3 doubles—all with full private bath, radio, clock, fan. 2 with desk, air-conditioning.
Facilities Breakfast room with fireplace, library, guest laundry (small fee), porch, piano museum with fireplace. Off-street parking. Golf, tennis, lake, downhill skiing, cross-country skiing, hiking nearby.
Location 325 m W of Calgary, 400 m E of Vancouver. From town center (1st & Mackenzie Ave.), go 7 blocks S to 7th & Mackenzie Ave.
Restrictions No smoking. Children 11 and over.
Credit cards None accepted.
Rates B&B, $65–85 double, $55–65 single. Extra person, $15.
Extras Station/airport pickups.

SMITHERS

Also recommended: Located in northern BC, Smithers sits at the base of Hudson Bay Mountain on the banks of Bulkley River. Set among blue spruce, pine, and tamarack is **The Ptarmigan B&B** (Willow Road at Highway 16 West, V0J 2N0; 604–847–9508). Guests at this alpine-style home can have breakfast in the country kitchen, the dining room, or on the patio. Free ski storage, travel information, and car plug-ins are available. B&B double rates range from $50–$60. "Beautiful house with superb custom woodwork and nice, friendly owners. Our two rooms shared a bath for the price of $75. We were warmly welcomed, even though we arrived late. Breakfast consisted of a fresh fruit plate and French toast made with thick slices of bread." *(Allan Brotherton)*

SOOKE

Sooke sits on a natural harbor formed by the Jordan River; forestry and fishing feature prominently in the economy, and a festival of logging sports is held every July. Located at the southwestern end of Vancouver

Island, an especially scenic portion of Highway 14 runs the 27 miles east from Victoria to Sooke.

Also recommended: With only two rooms, the **Richview House** (7031 Richview Drive, RR #4, V0S 1N0; 604–642–5520) is too small for a full entry, but we've received rave reports about its gracious and informative hosts, Joan and François Gething; the lovely setting overlooking the Strait of Juan de Fuca and the Olympic Mountains; the comfortable, private rooms; and the delicious three-course breakfasts, included in the $175 double rate. "The house is recently built in a timber and stucco style. Each guest room has a queen-sized bed, down comforter, Jacuzzi on a private deck, and a wood-burning fireplace. Just a three-minute walk to the Sooke Harbour House for one of their famous meals." *(Stephanie Pietromonaco).* "Francois' expert carpentry is a work of art, and Joan's decorating and cooking are superb." *(Margaret Sievers, and others)*

Ocean Wilderness Inn
109 West Coast Road, RR #2, V0S 1N0

Tel: 604–646–2116

To commemorate a special occasion, guests at the Ocean Wilderness can plant a tree; owner Marion Rolston will provide the watering can, shovel, and a Douglas fir seedling. Built in 1930, this log home has a wooded oceanfront setting, and was restored as a B&B in 1989; most guest rooms have lovely ocean views from the deck or picture window. Guests can soak in the private hot tub in the Japanese-style gazebo overlooking the ocean and Olympic Mountains. One-half hour before breakfast, a silver service of coffee or tea, is delivered to each guest door. In addition to muffins, juice and fresh fruit, breakfast might include a spinach roulade with grilled tomatoes.

"An old log cabin filled with interesting antiques; guest rooms are new, elegant, and luxurious. My room had a four-poster bed, polished wood floor, beautiful carpets, and a large, spotless bathroom, supplied with fluffy white bathrobes. Marion made us feel right at home. She prepares the food, assisted by her son. On an absolutely beautiful evening, dinner was served on the beach—corn chowder, barbecued salmon, just-caught shrimp and crab; rice pilaf, green salad, fresh fruit, and Marion's wonderful biscuits. The tables were set with white linens, silverware, and fresh flowers. Breakfast was elegantly served in the dining room—endless coffee, fresh fruit, more feather-light biscuits, and individual cheese soufflés." *(Barb Voynovich, and others)*

Open All year.
Rooms 9 doubles—all with full private bath, radio, clock. 8 with refrigerator. 3 with double soaking tub. 2 with deck.
Facilities Dining room, porch, 4 patios. 5 acres with hot tub in gazebo, gardens.
Location 8.5 m from town. From only traffic light in town, go 8.5 m to inn.
Restrictions No smoking.
Credit cards MC, Visa.
Rates B&B, $85–175 double. Extra person, $15–25. Prix fixe dinner by reservation.
Extras One room wheelchair accessible.

Sooke Harbour House ✕ ♿   *Tel:* 604–642–3421
1528 Whiffen Spit Road, RR 4, V0S 1N0   *Fax:* 604–642–6988

Sooke Harbour House, a small white clapboard farmhouse, sits on a bluff overlooking Whiffen Spit. Originally built in the 1930s, the inn was expanded in 1986 to provide additional guest rooms. Rates include breakfast, brought to your room, and lunch (except in August). Frederique and Sinclair Philip, owners of this inn, describe it as being located on the "edge of the wilderness, with whales, otters, seals, bears, cougars, and bald eagles nearby. Honeymooners love the romantic location, while adventurous diners can try the sea urchins, sea cucumber, pickled kelp, lavender ice cream, edible flower salads, and more." Known as one of Canada's best restaurants, menus change daily and feature the freshest possible local organic foods, creatively prepared. The inn's garden is home to hundreds of edible flowers and herbs, along with summer and winter salad greens, vegetables, fresh fruits, and berries. A recent winter dinner included oyster and nasturtium cream soup; veal topped by a pearl onion and honey hyssop glaze, with garlic roasted hubbard squash, or rockfish crusted with crabmeat; and a pear and chocolate pastry with white chocolate cream.

"The 'Edible Blossom' Room has a split-level design, and ceramic tiles to match. Our dinner of fennel soup, oysters, salmon, and braised lamb was marvelous. Hazelnuts featured in our two desserts—cheesecake and chocolate cake." *(Jack & Sue Lane)* "The Beach room is one of the smallest, but was most comfortable, with a decanter of sherry by the bed." *(Lynne Derry)* "Room #1 has a double Jacuzzi, exquisite woodwork, and a balcony overlooking the beautiful water and mountains. The wet bar was complete with canisters of coffee, tea, and fresh cookies." *(Norma & Bob Simon)* "Gracious, helpful staff." *(Jim Trumper)* Comments appreciated.

Open All year.
Rooms 4 suites, 9 doubles—all with private bath, radio, desk, fireplace, balcony, or terrace. Some with Jacuzzi, stocked wet bar, or hot tub.
Facilities Restaurant, dining/breakfast rooms with fireplace, lounge, library, living room. Musical entertainment weekends. 3 acres with herb, flower, vegetable gardens; orchard, beach for water sports. Massage therapists by appointment. Hiking nearby. 2½ hrs. to downhill, cross-country skiing.
Location 1 m from town. Take Hwy. 14 for ³⁄₅ m past Otter Point Rd. (at Gulf station), turn onto Whiffen Spit Rd. to inn.
Restrictions No smoking.
Credit cards Amex, Enroute, MC, Visa.
Rates B&B plus lunch (except Aug.), $195–280 suite, $160–265 double. 15% service. Extra person, $30. Tipping only for meals. Alc dinner, $65.
Extras 1 guest room equipped for disabled. Pets by prior arrangement, $10. Crib by prior arrangement. French, German spoken.

VANCOUVER

Dramatically situated on a peninsula where towering mountains sweep down to the sea, Vancouver is Canada's loveliest city. At once cosmopolitan and amiable, Vancouver offers exciting cultural, shopping, and recreational opportunities. The compact heart of the city is located on a tiny peninsula, one-half of which is Stanley Park, known for its gardens, zoo, golf course, bathing beach, and jogging trails. Downtown Vancouver is a wonderful amalgam of apartment houses, hotels, sidewalk cafés, smart shops, galleries, and office buildings. It is lively, clean, and safe, and bubbles with people late into the night.

Vancouver's rich ethnic mix adds to its charm and makes for diverse shopping and dining adventures. Chinatown and nearby Japantown are a jumble of exotic markets, shops, and restaurants. In south Vancouver (near Main and 49th) is a thriving East Indian community where you can buy beautiful silk saris and outrageously colored sweets. The Greeks and Italians have also left their mark on this wonderful city.

Originally a tidal flat known as Mud Island, Granville Island had developed by 1930 into an industrial park. In the late 1970s the island was the focus of a major waterfront redevelopment project, and it is now home to a variety of commercial and artistic endeavors: a public market, selling everything from mussels to bagels; a kids' market and water-play park; a brewery; two theaters; and a variety of trendy cafés and boutiques, restaurants, and art galleries. Although fun for families and shoppers alike, one reader warned that "parking is impossible, so take the False Creek ferry if you do go." She goes on to note that another restored area is Gastown, "a well-conceived redevelopment area with charming restored buildings and an interesting steam clock."

Do *not* miss a trip to the Museum of Anthropology on the campus of the University of British Columbia. In a dramatic building designed by Arthur Erickson, you will see 40-foot totem poles, ancient canoes, and other items emphasizing the artistic diversity of the Northwest Coast Indians.

For a wonderful view of southeastern British Columbia, go up to the top of 3,900-foot Grouse Mountain where you can see the city of Vancouver, Vancouver Island and the Gulf Islands, the Fraser River, the Strait of Georgia, and, on a clear day, the Olympic Mountains in Washington State. In winter you can ski here in the morning, then lunch in town. Visit Andusen Botanical Gardens for vibrant displays of flowers during the spring and summer.

Vancouver is located in the southwest corner of the mainland of British Columbia.

Information please: The **Lonsdale Quay Hotel** (123 Carrie Cates Court, North Vancouver V7M 3K7; 604–986–6111 or 800–836–6111) is "a modern hotel located on the third floor of the Lonsdale Quay Market, overlooking bustling Burrard Inlet and the skyline of downtown Vancouver. On the first floor of the market complex are rows of food vendors and ethnic takeout food stands. On the second floor are a variety of shops and restaurants. On the third is the hotel. Outside the hotel/market is a huge fountain, with a deck overlooking the harbor. A half-block away is a passenger-only seabus that whizzes you downtown in minutes. Our contemporary-style room was well decorated, with a view of the water and tugboats." *(SC)* Double rates for the 70 rooms range from $130–145; this is a great choice for families; there's even a kids' playroom.

The **Delta Place Hotel** (645 Howe Street, V6C 2Y9; 604–687–1122) has a superb location just a block away from the Vancouver Museum and underground shopping. The 197 suites and doubles have a full complement of amenities, and the restaurants offer a variety of international dining experiences; breakfast entrées include Canadian, Japanese, Chinese, diet, and heart-healthy choices. **O'Doul's Hotel** (1300 Robson Street V6E 1C5; 604–684–8461 or 800–663–5491) is a contemporary West End hotel with 130 guest rooms, a bar and restaurant, an indoor swimming pool, and an excellent location. Double rates range from $140–190, and children under 18 stay free. For a reasonably priced hotel with an excellent West End location consider **The Barclay Hotel** (1348 Robson Street, V6E 1C5; 604–688–8850), built in the 1920s and renovated in 1988. The 85 doubles, singles, and suites have rates of $50–125.

Beautiful B&B ¢
428 West 40 Avenue, V5Y 2R4

Tel: 604–327–1102
Fax: 604–327–1102

A 1984 in Dutch Colonial, the home of Ian and Corinne Sanderson has been a B&B since 1993, and is simply decorated with a comfortable mix of antiques and reproduction furniture. Breakfast is usually served from 7:30–8:30 A.M. and includes eggs to order or perhaps spiced French toast with maple syrup. "Comfortable and warm, spotlessly clean. The lawn was meticulously manicured and an inviting apple tree was loaded with luscious fruit. The aroma of coffee woke us in the morning after a comfortable night's sleep. Breakfast was a feast of bacon, sausage, eggs, toast, scones, biscuits, fruit, and cereal." *(Bob & Gail James)* Comments welcome.

Open All year.
Rooms 1 suite, 2 doubles, 1 single—1 with full private bath, 3 rooms share 1 bath. All with telephone, radio, clock. 3 with desk, deck. 1 with TV, fireplace.
Facilities Dining room, living room with fireplace, piano, TV/VCR, stereo, books; porch. Garden. On-street parking. 3 blocks to park. Swimming pool, tennis, golf hiking nearby.
Location 5 min. to Residential area, 15 min. to downtown. From airport, take Marine Dr. E Exit off bridge into Vancouver. Follow Marine Dr. to Cambie St. & turn left. Go N to W. 40th Ave. & turn right to inn.
Restrictions No smoking. No children under 15. No shoes in house.
Credit cards None accepted.
Rates B&B, $125–150 suite, $60–90 double, $60–75 single. 2-night minimum stay.
Extras French spoken.

Columbia Cottage Guest House
205 West 14th Avenue, V5Y 1X2

Tel: 604–874–5327

"A small neatly-kept Tudor-style cottage devotedly run like a miniature inn. Close to City Hall and a modern shopping complex, it's on a quiet, tree-lined, residential street only blocks from the Cambie Street Bridge. The rooms are well-laid out—ours was a charming upstairs back room, comfortably and tastefully furnished with a king-sized bed, antiques, and well-chosen artwork on the walls. The bath provided a modern shower and an ample supply of luxury towels. A second bedroom was separated from ours by a small, nicely laid-out lounge area and a sink and sideboard for making tea and coffee. Coffee and iced tea are offered during the day as well as sherry and nuts in the early evening in the inviting common room on the main floor. Breakfasts include homemade muffins, omelets, French toast, and fresh fruit. The intimate dining room was set with lace tablecloths, beautiful china, and a pleasant view of the front garden. Classical music quietly plays throughout the day and evening. Special little touches were the homemade cookies at bedside and the robes and slippers for lounging." *(Colin & Kay Bailey)*

Open All year.
Rooms 1 suite, 4 doubles—all with full private bath.
Facilities Dining room, living room, sitting room, guest pantry. Garden with patio, fountain. On-street parking.
Location 7 min. from downtown. At corner of W. 14th Ave. & Columbia St.
Restrictions No smoking.
Credit cards None accepted.
Rates B&B, $110–150 suite, $75–125 double. Extra person, $20.

English Bay Inn
1968 Comox Street, V6G 1R4

Tel: 604–683–8002

"A charming home in Vancouver's residential West End, English Bay Inn is a traditionally and somewhat formally decorated home on a quiet street. Pretty accommodations with Ralph Lauren sheets and good lighting. Owner Bob Chapin serves a delicious, multi-course breakfast in the formal dining room, and his inn is warm and inviting." *(Adam Platt)* "It was readily apparent that Bob had spent considerable time and expense in turning his 1939 Tudor-style house into a comfortable inn. Our immaculate room had an antique mahogany sleigh bed and wardrobe. The living room was furnished with antiques and had a gas fireplace, which was lit every afternoon when we returned from our day's outing. Delectable breakfast served between 7:30 and 9:30 A.M.—quiche, scrambled eggs, and apple cinnamon crepes. Coffee and juice were served liberally throughout." *(Ford & Beth Stephens)* From 4–6 P.M. sherry is served in the living room.

Open All year.
Rooms 1 suite, 4 doubles—all with private bath and/or shower, telephone, radio, clock, balcony. 2 with TV. Suite with whirlpool tub, fireplace.
Facilities Dining room with gas fireplace, TV; living room with gas fireplace. Garden with gazebo. Off-street parking.
Location West End. 20 min. walk to downtown. On corner of Comox & Chilco Sts. 1 block from English Bay & entrance to Stanley Park.
Restrictions No smoking. "Adults only."
Credit cards Amex, Visa.
Rates B&B, $199–210 suite, $125–140 double. 2-night weekend minimum.

Johnson House B&B ¢
2278 West 34th Street, V6M 1G6

Tel: 604–266–4175

Innkeeper Sandy Johnson tells us that "after ten years of renovating we have actually finished restoring our Craftsman-style home and decorating it with an eclectic selection of antiques and collectibles. Our bedrooms have antique king- or queen-size beds with comfortable modern mattresses; the plumbing and wiring are all new, although many old fixtures have been refitted. Breakfast includes good strong coffee, juice, homemade jams, homebaked muffins or scones, bacon or sausage, and whole wheat-oatmeal pancakes, French toast, or eggs. Blueberries, strawberries, raspberries, and grapes grown on the property are served in season. The rock and rhododendron gardens create an incredible spring display with hundreds of flowering bulbs, accented with antique Indonesian sculptures."

"Our bed was comfortable, and the room pleasantly cool for sleeping." *(Claudia Forest)* "Plenty of desk drawer space, lots of hangers, superb homemade cinnamon buns." *(Lorraine Holloway)* "Spacious room; fresh linens daily and the large and airy bathroom was spotlessly clean. The house has plenty of windows, cozy window seats, and interesting antiques—gramophones, carousel horses, brass beds, and antique bureaus. Excellent view of the harbor and mountains; great neighborhood." *(Susan Izumi)* "White wicker furniture, a huge bed with lovely quilt, and big plump pillows." *(Mrs. Dianne Durkin)* "The owners were warm and friendly, giving me advice on what to see in the area; I called them from a number of destinations in Vancouver and they guided me 'home' by local transport." *(Teri Rodabough)*

Minor niggle: "A good reading lamp and bedside table on my side of the bed."

Open All year.
Rooms 1 suite, 3 doubles—2 with full private bath, 2 with maximum of 4 people sharing bath. All with radio, fan; 2 with desk.
Facilities Dining room; living room with fireplace, TV/VCR, stereo, books; porch, deck. Laundry facility. 2 m to ocean, beaches.
Location Kerrisdale district. 10 min. drive from city center. From downtown, go S on Granville, W on 33, S on Vine to inn at corner of 34th & Vine.
Restrictions No smoking. No children under 11.
Credit cards None accepted.
Rates B&B, $75–105 suite, $55–80 double, $45–95 single. Extra person, $20.

Kenya Court Guest House
2230 Cornwall Avenue, V6k 1B5

Tel: 604–738–7085

Overlooking English Bay, with an unobstructed view of Stanley Park, ocean, mountains, and downtown Vancouver, is the Kenya Court Guest House, a three-story heritage building constructed in Art Deco style. Guest rooms have king-, queen- or twin-sized beds, and families will appreciate the separate entrance and spacious two-bedroom suites. The inn is minutes from downtown, and walking distance to the appealing shops of the Granville Market and Fourth Avenue. "Most reasonable rates for a huge two-bedroom apartment complete with kitchen, dining, and living room! The innkeeper, Dorothy McWilliams is a pianist and most elegant hostess. She serves a breakfast of juice, fruit, cereal, fresh breads and croissants, bacon and eggs, in the rooftop solarium with a dazzling view." *(KC)*

Open All year.
Rooms 8 1–2 bedroom suites—all with private bath and/or shower, private entrance. Some with kitchenette.

Facilities Music room with piano, rooftop solarium. Tennis, saltwater swimming pool, jogging trails across the street.
Location On English Bay, across Burrard Bridge. From bridge, take right fork onto Cornwall Ave. to inn.
Restrictions No smoking.
Credit cards None accepted.
Rates B&B, $85–120 double.
Extras Italian, French, German spoken.

Penny Farthing Inn ¢
2855 West 6th Avenue, V6K 1X2

Tel: 604–739–9002
Fax: 604–739–9004

A Craftsman-style house built in 1912, the Penny Farthing has been furnished with English antiques by Lyn Hainstock, who opened this B&B in 1991. Stained glass windows, polished wood floors and woodwork highlight the decor; outside, you might happen upon one of Lyn's cats playing in the garden, overflowing with flowers and herbs. Abigail's Suite is tucked under the eaves, with a skylight and mountain-view sitting room; Sophie's Room has a pine double bed and armoire, forest green walls, and its own porch overlooking the garden. Breakfast, served from 8–9:30 A.M. at the dining room table, includes freshly baked croissants, sourdough bread, and fruit, plus seafood quiche, apple frittata, or perhaps strawberry crepes.

"Varied breakfasts with good conversation and the opportunity to linger. Lyn is warm, open and a helpful guide to restaurants and attractions. This residential neighborhood is good for walking and close to local shopping, restaurants, sightseeing, the bus line and park; the garden area is nicely landscaped and private. Decorating throughout the inn is tastefully done with antiques, books, fresh flowers." *(Dottie Seymour)* "Warm, homey atmosphere. Clean, nicely decorated room with stained glass windows and a pleasing color scheme. Delicious freshly baked croissants; good quality and variety at breakfast. Caring, experienced, helpful owner." *(Stella Lau)*

Area for improvement: "An in-room telephone." And: "A bit more drawer space in my room."

Open All year.
Rooms 2 suites, 2 doubles—2 with private bath and/or shower, 2 with a maximum of 4 people sharing bath. All with clock, fan. Suites with TV. 2 with porch.
Facilities Dining room, living room with stereo, TV/VCR, porches, patio. Garden. Bicycles. On-street parking. 6 blocks from water.
Location 8 min. from downtown. From Hwy. 99 (becomes Oak St.), go to W. 12th Ave. & turn left. Go to MacDonald St. & turn right. Continue to W. 6th Ave. & turn left to inn ½ block on right.
Restrictions No smoking. Children over 12 preferred.
Credit cards None accepted.
Rates B&B, $95–155 suite, $65–75 double, $55–65 single. Extra person, $20; children under 12, $10. 2-night minimum stay.
Extras Airport/station pickups, $20–25. Babysitting by arrangement.

Wedgewood Hotel ✕ 🛏 ♿
845 Hornby Street, V6Z 1V1

Tel: 604–689–7777
800–663–0666
Fax: 604–688–3074

Overlooking charming Robson Square, the Wedgewood Hotel is probably Vancouver's best-known small hotel, and we have received consistently positive reports on the attentive and gracious staff, the attractive rooms, and the excellent location.

"Dinner was superb, from the antipasto with grilled fennel, carpaccio, peppers with lentils, marinated prawns, and goat cheese to the pasta with smoked salmon, asparagus, and green peppercorns. The atmosphere in the dining room is subdued, with light wood chairs, floral cushions, Oriental motif rugs, and nice background music." *(SC)* "Our tenth-floor room was spacious and quiet, with a lovely view looking east over the city; service and amenities are first rate. We had a fully-stocked mini-bar, a patio with deck chairs, and a fresh terry robe every day. Chinatown is only a few minutes drive east and Stanley Park is to the west; the harbor is only a 10-minute walk." *(Joni Hiramoto & Mac Master)* "Guest rooms are available in four price categories; all have luxurious appointments and are decorated with a country French motif with dark red and blue colors. The hotel's prices definitely put it in the splurge category, so be sure to ask if any promotional or off-season rates are in effect when booking." *(SWS)* "In addition to the hotel's fine dining, the helpful concierge recommended an excellent restaurant, Chez Thiery, about a mile away." *(Stephanie Roberts)*

Open All year.
Rooms 34 suites, 60 doubles—all with private bath and/or shower, telephone, radio, TV, air-conditioning, refrigerator, hair dryer. Some with fireplace, balcony.
Facilities Restaurant, lounge with piano bar, coffee shop, meeting rooms. Business, concierge services. 24-hr. room service. Valet parking. Health club. Limousine service.
Location Downtown. On Robson Square, between Smythe & Robson Sts.
Restrictions No smoking in some guest rooms.
Credit cards All major.
Rates Room only, $290–310 suite, $180–240 double, $160–220 single. "Overnighter" rate, $130. Weekend, honeymoon, anniversary packages.
Extras Wheelchair access, one room equipped for disabled. Crib, babysitting. French, Greek spoken.

West End Guest House

1362 Haro Street, V6E 1G2

Tel: 604–681–2889
Fax: 604–688–8812

Built in 1906 for the Edwards family, the West End Guest House is constructed entirely of straight grain cedar (meaning it is without knots). The young Edwards men operated the first photography shop in Vancouver and many of their photographs of interior British Columbia and the Yukon hang in the inn. When the last of the Edwardses died in 1966, the house went into rapid decline as a "hippie" residence. In 1985 it was restored as a B&B, complete with a "Painted Lady" pink and white exterior color scheme. It was purchased in 1991 by Evan Penner, who has furnished the rooms with Victorian antiques and reproductions, keeping the style elegant, light, and uncluttered. Guest rooms are supplied with terry bathrobes and fine linens; the brass beds are fitted with feather mattresses and goose-down comforters. Breakfast is served at the dining room table from 8–9 P.M., and includes fresh fruit, hot and cold cereal, homemade baked goods, coffee and tea, and such entrées as salmon quiche, hazelnut waffles with sausage, or poached eggs on spinach with

385

tarragon hollandaise sauce; in the afternoon tea and cookies are set out, plus sherry in the evening.

"A personal note of welcome and plate of chocolates and fruit awaited in our room. Breakfast was cooked to order and brought guests together to share thoughts about the best of Vancouver. Warm, caring atmosphere." *(Debbie & Michael Swiatek)* "We had the least expensive room, the small-but-cozy Terra Double on the lower level of the house. It was perfect, from the imported linens to the sponge-painted walls to the little armoire. The shared bath was dramatically painted midnight blue with gold accents, and a small table was provided on either side of the sink, holding separate toiletries and towels for each couple. The common rooms are a comfortable mix of traditional and Art Nouveau furniture." *(Anita Epler)* "Fresh cookies on a turned-down bed and sherry in the evening." *(Simon Wonnacott & Jill Hamilton)* "Nice neighborhood for walking, close to the cafes and boutiques of Robson Street, just blocks from Stanley Park." *(Helen Monk)*

Open All year.
Rooms 8 doubles—6 with private bath and/or shower, 2 with maximum of 4 people sharing bath. All with telephone, radio, TV. Some with desk, ceiling fan, sundeck.
Facilities Dining room, living room with books, stereo, games; sun deck, porch. Bicycles. 15 min walk to beach, marina. Off-street parking.
Location 1 block S of Robson & Broughton Sts. 6 blocks W of Robson Sq. Walking distance to Financial District, Stanley Park.
Restrictions No smoking. No children under 13.
Credit cards Amex, Discover, MC, Visa.
Rates B&B, $95–195 double. Extra person, $15. 2-night weekend, holiday minimum.

The Windmill ¢   *Tel: 604–988–0031*
2025 Moody Avenue, North Vancouver V7L 4M6

The Windmill is named not for any resemblance to that towering structure, but to reflect the Dutch origins of owners Mary and John Mulder. John, a building contractor, constructed this contemporary home, with cedar exterior, large windows, and a tile roof. Mary brings a wealth of experience to the business of personal attention, as the mother of five children.

"High on a quiet street overlooking the Burrard Inlet, the Windmill has well-kept gardens front and back. Sheets and towels smell of sunshine, as Mary hangs them outside to dry. Bountiful breakfasts of cereal, bacon and eggs, bran and raisin muffins, jams, and specially blended coffee, served at your convenience." *(Virginia & Henry Hart)* "The Mulders went out of their way to familiarize us with the city and to make suggestions, including tips on getting around and saving money." *(Jordan & Robin Ross)* "Special breakfast needs are not a problem." *(David & Kim Schaeffer)* "Mary obviously enjoys house guests and takes a personal yet unobtrusive interest. The house is within easy reach of the transit system." *(Francis Noronha)* "Extremely clean bathrooms; quiet neighborhood with on-street parking." *(Lynn Pakulak)* "Hospitable, welcoming owners. Although our lower level room was a bit darker than the rest of the house, it was pleasant and private, with our own bath." *(Marsi Fein & Todd Miller)*

Minor niggles: "It took a few tries to get hold of the Mulders, but it was well worth the effort." Also: "The rollaway bed set up in our room was not too comfortable."

Open March 1–Nov.1.
Rooms 3 doubles, 1 single—1 with private shower, 3 with maximum of 5 people sharing bath. All with radio, desk, balcony.
Facilities Family room with TV. On-street parking.
Location N Vancouver. 15 min. to downtown. Bus stop nearby.
Restrictions No smoking. Well-behaved children only.
Credit cards None accepted.
Rates B&B, $40–45 double, $30–35 single. Extra person, $10.
Extras Airport/station pickup. Crib. Dutch spoken.

VICTORIA

Set at the southeastern tip of Vancouver Island, Victoria is known for its British ambience—though with a distinctly un-British mild and sunny climate. Among the city's many beautiful gardens and parks, Butchart Gardens is the most famous of all and is well worth the trip 14 miles north of town. On summer evenings the gardens are illuminated until 11 P.M. Other attractions include the Houses of Parliament, a grand edifice built in 1893; and the Provincial Museum, with an excellent Northwest Coast Indian Collection, along with exhibits on natural history and 19th-century development. The city is small, so be sure to wander through Beacon Hill Park, the Old Town area, the now-compact Chinatown, and explore the shops—those specializing in Indian and Eskimo art and handicrafts as well as those offering the best of British imports. Although there are many excellent restaurants, the Indian and Chinese establishments offer the most interesting dining at the most reasonable prices.

Also recommended: The **Chateau Victoria** (740 Burdett Avenue, V8W 1B2; 604–382–4221 or 800–663–5891) is a luxurious 178-room hotel with an indoor swimming pool and spa, and double rates of $90–190. "We were upgraded to a beautiful, well-equipped suite, immaculately clean and tastefully decorated. Comfortable living room, huge bedroom; matching blue and soft beige decor. Extremely accommodating, friendly staff. We'd recommend the Parrot House Rooftop Restaurant for its gorgeous view, reasonable prices, and good food." *(Maryellen Forde)*

The three guest-room **Dunroamin' B&B** (616 Avalon Road, V8V 1N8; 604–383–4106) is recommended by *Gail Schwartz:* "Lovely, with cute little rooms tucked under the eaves, and an attractive and private flower garden. Nice, friendly owners." Rates of $70–80 double include a breakfast of juice, scones and muffins, fruits, tea and coffee, and an entrée of eggs and bacon or sausage and waffles.

Information please: Long a reader favorite, we need reports on **Abigail's Hotel** (906 McClure Street, V8V 3E7; 604–388–5363) an English Tudor-style building owned by Bill McKechnie, who renovated in 1986. The inn features an elegant country-style look, with lots of soft colors and flowers, and goose-down comforters on the beds. The 16 rooms all with private baths; some have a fireplace and Jacuzzi tub. Guests can enjoy sherry and hors d'oeuvres in the library each evening; in the morning, creative full breakfasts are served family-style in the dining room. A contemporary building in a parklike setting, the 200-room **Laurel Point Inn** (680 Montreal Street, V8V 1Z8; 604–386–8721 or 800–663–7667) offers an unusual combination—a convenient in-town location with resort facilities and atmosphere. You can stroll the flower-lined paths along the harbor, watch the ferries sail by from your bedroom window, or relax in the swimming pool or hot tub. Double rates range from $110–155, and children under 12 stay free.

The **Olde England Inn** (429 Lampson Street, V9A 5Y9; 604–388–4353) offers not only an antique-filled Tudor-style mansion but also an English village containing replicas of Shakespeare's birthplace, Anne Hathaway's cottage, Harvard House, the Garrick Inn, a Tuck (sweet) Shop, and the Olde Curiosity Shoppe—all, of course, set on Chaucer Lane. Staff is dressed in period clothing, most of the 50 guest rooms (all with private bath) have canopy beds; double rates range from $74–145, with suites at $166–190. Breakfast in the restaurant includes scones or crumpets, while dinner features roast beef and Yorkshire pudding, and steak and kidney pie. "The spectacular view of the Strait of Juan de Fuca and the promenade makes **The Sea Rose B&B** (1250 Dallas Road, V8V 1C4; 604–381–7932) ideal for those who long for the sea. This uncluttered home has white walls and modern art accenting the Art Deco-style interior. Our suite had a spacious bedroom, living area, and small kitchen—all squeaky clean. Wonderful breakfasts of juice, muffins or toast, hot or cold cereal, omelets with bacon and hash brown potatoes, tea or coffee." *(Irene Kolbisen)* Owner Karen Young has restored this 1921 Craftsman-style bungalow; she reports that she happily accommodate special diets with advance notice.

The memorably named **Waddling Dog Inn** (2476 Mount Newton Cross Road, Saanichton V0S 1M0; 604–652–1146 or 800–742–9244) is 16 miles north of Victoria, close to Butchart Gardens and the airport. Rates for the 30 rooms range from $70–100. "The half-timbered architecture, furnishings, and lighting had a traditional English flavor, and the bathroom was absolutely spotless. Appealing pub, plus a tasty Sunday brunch. The eponymous canine turned out to be a Bassett hound, sleeping contentedly on the office floor." *(Sylvia Ann Anorbes)* Reports welcome.

The Beaconsfield Inn   Tel: 604–384–4044
998 Humboldt Street, V8V 2Z8   Fax: 604–721–2442

The Beaconsfield is an Edwardian mansion restored as an inn in 1984 and furnished with period antiques in exceptional taste. It was purchased by Con and Judi Sollid in 1993, professionals in the fields of law and dentistry. A recent breakfast, served at individual tables in the dining room, included freshly squeezed orange juice, croissants with raspberry preserves, coffee and tea, baked bananas topped with almond yogurt sauce; and a smoked salmon and Brie strata with dill; cereal, granola and muesli are also available. Tea is served in the inviting Victorian library in the afternoon, with sherry and nibbles offered in the early evening.

"Friendly, welcoming owners and staff. Rooms are clean, bright, and beautifully appointed; excellent lighting and bathroom facilities. Delicious breakfasts; afternoon refreshments provide a wonderful opportunity for guests to chat. Convenient yet fairly quiet location." (J. & E. Gilbert) "The Duchess room has steam-heated towel racks and old-fashioned bathroom fixtures. The Attic Suite takes up the whole top floor and has a double Jacuzzi tub and fireplace—very romantic and private." (MB)

Open All year.
Rooms 1 suite, 10 doubles—all with private bath and/or shower. 6 with desk, 5 with fireplace, 3 with whirlpool tub.
Facilities Dining room with fireplace, library with fireplace, sunroom. $1/2$ acre with off-street parking.
Location Historic district, 4 blocks from center of town. From ferry terminal, go N on Belleville, left on Blanshard, right on Humboldt to inn at corner of Vancouver St.
Restrictions No smoking. "No children please."
Credit cards MC, Visa.
Rates B&B, $200–275 suite, $135–275 double. Extra person, $45. 2-night weekend minimum, April–Oct.

The Bedford ✗ 👭 ♿

1140 Government Street, V8W 1Y2

Tel: 604–384–6835
800–665–6500
Fax: 604–386–8930

Located in the heart of Victoria's Old Town, the Bedford is an elegant small hotel close to Parliament and shopping areas. The hotel restaurant offers continental cuisine with daily pasta and deep-dish quiche specials. A thermos of coffee and the morning paper is delivered to your room by 7 A.M.; breakfast is served from 7–10 A.M.

"An excellent value; European charm. Our courtyard room had a Palladian window filled with a profusion of flowers. Though small, our room didn't feel cramped. It had a small sitting area and a comfortable bed with excellent reading lights. The bathroom was spanking clean. Breakfast offered a choice of cereals, baked goods, juices, and eggs. Excellent location, next to Murchie's, one of BC's oldest coffee and tea merchants, and Munro's, a wonderful bookstore. Adjacent Bastion Square houses several marvelous restaurants; we enjoyed Re-Bar and Camille's." (Carolyn Myles) "A beautiful little hotel in fine condition, with especially pleasant service, handsome rooms, a lovely little dining room where they serve a nice breakfast, and an excellent lunch and dinner. The hotel is so centrally located that we hardly needed the car." (Lee Todd) "Memorable breakfast omelets; light as air and full of ham, cheese, mushrooms, peppers, and green onions. Afternoon tea featured a piping hot scone with a choice of spreads. The lobby had long white columns topped by ram's head cornices to create an elegant atmosphere." (Joni Hiramoto)

Minor niggles: "Our early morning coffee wasn't hot." Also: "The unloading area was congested with delivery vans when we arrived."

Open All year.
Rooms 40 doubles—all with private bath and/or shower, telephone, radio, TV. 12 with Jacuzzi tub, fireplace.
Facilities Dining room with library, bar/lounge with fireplace, TV, stereo, meeting rooms. Valet parking, $5 per day.

Location Central Victoria, near Inner Harbour.
Restrictions Traffic noise in some rooms. No smoking on 2nd & 3rd floors & public areas.
Credit cards Amex, MC, Visa.
Rates B&B, $105–185 double. Extra person, $25. Children under 6 free. Alc lunch, $10; alc dinner, $30.
Extras Limited wheelchair access. Crib, babysitting. French spoken.

Dashwood Seaside Manor ♀♦

1 Cook Street, V8V 3W6

Tel: 604–385–5517
Fax: 604–383–1760

The last ice age some 15,000 years ago made way for the Manor's beautiful bluff-top location. Designed by Samuel Maclure, a renowned architect of the Edwardian era, the inn was completed in 1912. Unfortunately, the good times didn't last, and in 1978, Derek Dashwood rescued this architectural gem from impending demolition. Since then, Derek has spent more than $750,000 on rebuilding and restoration—an ongoing process. Victoria's only seaside inn, it has guest rooms innovatively designed for the building: one suite has a granite fireplace, beamed ceiling, and a chandelier; another has stained glass inserts above each of the large windows; all have antiques and period pieces. Each suite has a kitchen, so guests make their own breakfast from the ingredients provided (juice, hot and cold cereals, fruits, bread, ham, eggs, coffee and tea); also included in the rates is an evening glass of wine or sherry in the library.

"The location, atmosphere, staff, and Derek's accommodating attitude make this place ideal." *(Diane Tyler)* "Beacon Hill Park on one side and the open waterfront on the other provide fantastic vistas. Marvelous walks and close to downtown Victoria." *(D.M. Hughs)* Reports needed.

Open All year.
Rooms 14 suites—all with private bath, radio, TV, kitchenette. Some with desk, fireplace, balcony.
Facilities Library with fireplace. Laundry facility. 2 city lots with off-street parking, croquet. Near public tennis and other recreation.
Location Next to Beacon Hill Park.
Restrictions No smoking.
Credit cards Amex, MC, Visa.
Rates B&B, $75–285 suite. Extra adult, $45; extra child over 12, $25; extra child under 12, $10. 2-night weekend minimum. 10% senior discount.
Extras Crib, babysitting.

Hotel Grand Pacific

450 Quebec Street, V8V 1W5

Tel: 604–386–0450
800–663–7550
Fax: 604–386–8779

"Convenient to the superb Provincial Museum and the Parliament Buildings. There's a pleasant dining room and a bar that serves a light menu, with a great pool table. The hotel, constructed in 1990, seems smaller than the room count indicates, and service is excellent. Be sure to ask for a room facing the Inner Harbor (even-numbered rooms) above the 4th floor so you can see everything. The 7th and 8th floors are non-smoking—so that's the best view—although every room has a small balcony where you can see the Empress Hotel, the Inner Harbor, and the ferry from Port

Angeles. Across the harbor you see the seaplane landing area, and the low mountains up north on Vancouver Island. You can walk off your dinner by strolling around the Inner Harbor listening to all the impromptu street musicians, magicians, fire-eaters and more. Our room was irregularly shaped, with two armchairs, a table, armoire, a king-size bed, TV, desk, and mini-bar, decorated in subdued tones of salmon, beige, and mint green. Good-size bathroom, with a second sink outside the bathroom. The fitness center on the lower level is a great place—no fees except for the two squash courts—and there's a 25-meter lap pool, lots of machines, exercise rooms, plus it's all manned by pleasant staff." *(SC)*

Open All year.
Rooms 19 suites, 130 doubles—all with full private bath, telephone, radio, clock, TV, desk, air-conditioning, mini-bar, balcony. 3 with whirlpool tub, fireplace.
Facilities Restaurant, bar/lounge with TV/VCR, lobby. Meeting rooms. Health club with heated indoor swimming pool, sauna, whirlpool, squash & racquetball courts, exercise classes, massage therapist. Underground parking.
Location Center of town. On Quebec St. between Oswego & Menzies Sts.
Restrictions No smoking in some guest rooms; restricted in restaurant.
Credit cards Amex, DC, MC, Visa.
Rates Room only, $110–260 suite, $169–189 double, $69–89 single. Extra person, $15. Senior discount.
Extras Wheelchair accessible; some rooms equipped for disabled. Airport/station pickups; free to $25. Cribs. Japanese, German spoken.

Prior House B&B
620 St. Charles Street, V8S 3N7

Tel: 604–592–8847
Fax: 604–592–8223

When the King of England's representative to British Columbia needed an appropriately grand home, the Prior House was built in 1910 to meet his specifications: a ballroom and drawing room, stained glass windows, and extensive oak paneling. The inn has period and antique furnishings, accented with crystal chandeliers and sconces. Guest rooms have brass and antique beds, down comforters and pillows, and lavish use of fabrics to create romantic canopies. A full breakfast is served from 8:30–9 A.M., usually in the dining room; tea is served from 4 to 6 P.M.

"Our spacious front bedroom was designer decorated with coordinated draperies and bedding, mirror-backed shutters and sparkling clean windows. The bath was small but adequate. Other rooms are equally gracious, some with ocean views. Tea and sweets are set out in the large living room with port and sherry, too. In the morning, coffee and tea are available before the formal breakfast, which included juice, baked apples, and quiche, served in the bright, large dining room, overlooking the patio and gardens." *(Jean Rees)* "An Edwardian mansion decorated beautifully with antiques; breakfasts are superb." *(Judith Brown)*

Open All year.
Rooms 3 1–2 bedroom suites, 3 doubles—all with private bath and/or shower, radio, clock. Suites with whirlpool tub, fireplace, TV, deck or kitchen. 4 with desk; 2 with deck, 2 with fireplace.
Facilities Dining room, living room, library with piano—all with fireplace; porch, guest refrigerator. 3/4 acre with off-street parking, children's swing set.
Location Center of Victoria, at corner of St. Charles & Rockland.

Restrictions No smoking. Children under 13 in Garden Suite only.
Credit cards MC, Visa.
Rates B&B, $230–250 suite, $135–145 double. Extra person, $25. No charge for children under 6 in Garden Suite. 10% senior, AAA discount.

Sunnymeade House Inn
1002 Fenn Avenue, V8Y 1P3

Tel: 604–658–1414

Nancy Thompson reports that she and her husband Jack "designed and built Sunnymeade House in 1985. We love living on Vancouver Island, being close to such a lovely city and still be able to enjoy the beach—just steps away—country walks, and the local village shops and restaurants. Art galleries, a great bakery, and a world-class golf course are all nearby." The decor features floral draperies and bedspreads (on double, twin, and queen-size beds). Breakfast, which can be enjoyed with other guests or at individual tables, includes homebaked muffins or scones, fresh fruit, home-made jams, and a main dish that varies each day. "Attractive accommodations, pleasant innkeepers." *(Teresa Anderson)* Comments welcome.

Open All year.
Rooms 6 doubles—4 with private shower and/or bath, 2 with sink in room & a maximum of 4 persons sharing bath.
Facilities Breakfast room, living room, lounge, porch. Lawn with gazebo.
Location 10 m from downtown Victoria. From Hwy. 17 turn on Cordova Bay Rd. Follow to Fenn Ave. & turn left to inn.
Restrictions No smoking. "Adult-oriented; children over 10 preferred."
Credit cards None accepted.
Rates B&B, $69–169 double, $59–89 single. Extra person, $35. 2-night minimum stay preferred. Dinners served off-season, by reservation.
Extras Airport/station pickups, $15.

Appendix

STATE AND PROVINCIAL TOURIST OFFICES

Listed here are the addresses and telephone numbers for the tourist offices of the western states and Canadian provinces covered in this book. When you write or call one of these offices, be sure to request a map of the state and a calendar of events. If you will be visiting a particular city or region, or if you have any special interests, be sure to specify this as well.

Alaska Division of Tourism
P.O. Box 110801
Juneau, Alaska 99811–0801
907–465–2010 or 586–2959

California Office of Tourism
801 K Street, suite 1600
Sacramento, California 95814–0189
916–322–1396 or 916–322–2881 or
    800–862–2543

Hawaii Visitors Bureau
2270 Kalakaua Avenue, Suite 801
Honolulu, Hawaii 96815
808–923–1811
New York Office
350 Fifth Avenue, Suite 808
New York, New York 10118
212–947–0717

Oregon Economic Development
    Tourism Division
775 Summer Street, N.E.
Salem, Oregon 97310
503–986–0000 or 800–547–7842 (out

of state) or 800–543–8838 (within
Oregon)

Washington Department of Trade and
    Economic Development
Tourism Division
101 General Administration Building
Olympia, Washington 98504
206–586–2088 or 586–2102 or
    800–562–6138

Travel Alberta
City Centre Building
10155 102 Street
Edmonton, Alberta, Canada T5J 4L6
403–427–4321 or 800–222–6501
    (from Alberta) or 800–661–8888
    (from continental U.S./Canada)

Tourism British Columbia
1117 Wharf Street
Victoria, British Columbia, Canada
    V8V 1X4
604–387–1642 or 800–663–6000
    (from continental U.S./Canada)

_____ Maps

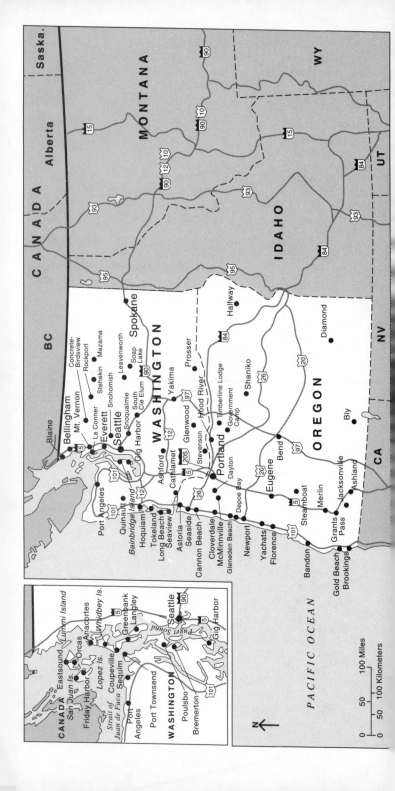

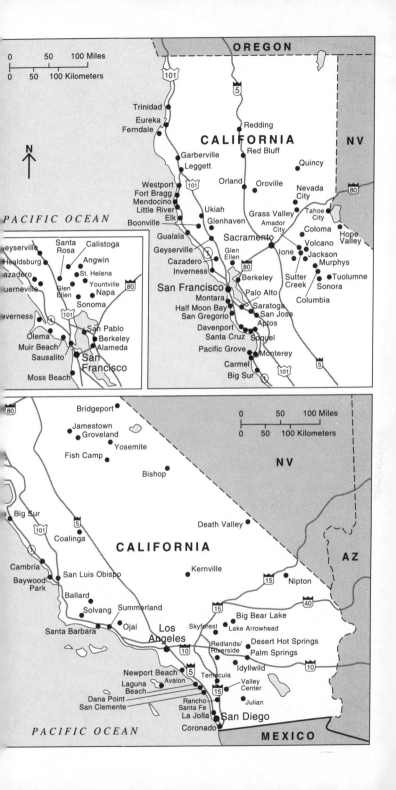

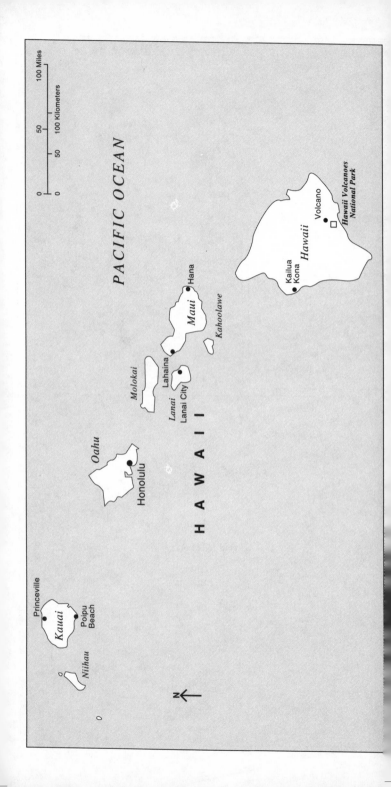

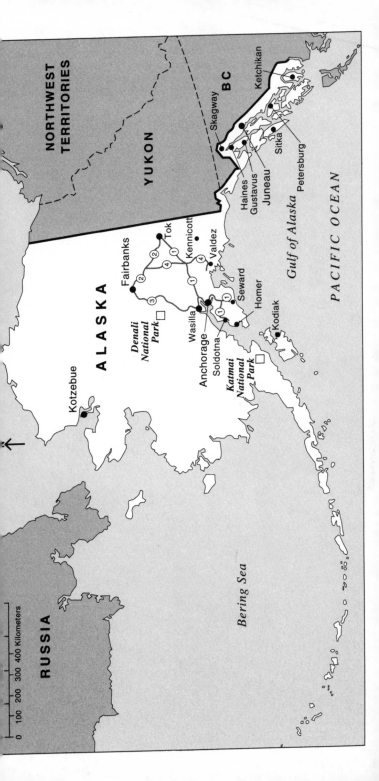

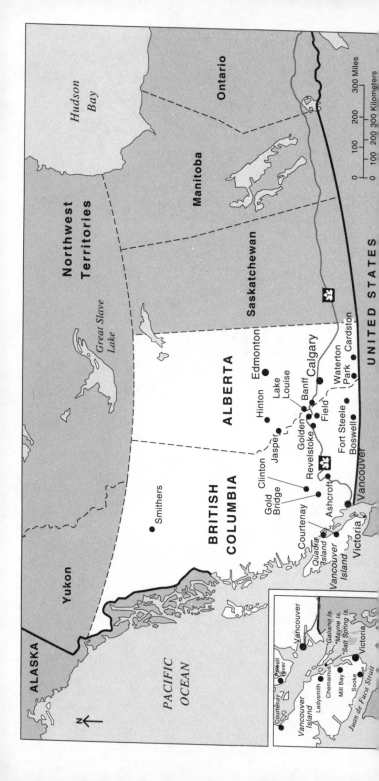

Index of Accommodations

Hotel/Inn Report Forms

The report forms on the following pages may be used to endorse or critique an existing entry or to nominate a hotel or inn that you feel deserves inclusion in the next edition. Don't feel you must restrict yourself to the space available; feel free to use your own stationery. All nominations (each on a separate piece of paper, if possible) should include your name and address, the name and location of the hotel or inn, when you have stayed there, and for how long. Please report only on establishments you have visited in the last eighteen months, unless you are sure that standards have not dropped since your stay. Please be as specific as possible, and critical where appropriate, about the character of the building, the public rooms, the accommodations, the meals, the service, the nightlife, the grounds, and the general atmosphere of the inn and the attitude of its owners. Comments about area restaurants and sights are also appreciated.

Don't feel you need to write at length. A report that merely verifies the accuracy of existing listings is extremely helpful, i.e., "Visited XYZ Inn and found it just as described." There is no need to bother with prices or with routine information about the number of rooms and facilities, although a sample brochure is very helpful for new recommendations.

On the other hand, don't apologize for writing a long report. Although space does not permit us to quote them in toto, the small details provided about furnishings, atmosphere, and cuisine can really make a description come alive, illuminating the special flavor of a particular inn or hotel. Remember that we will again be awarding free copies to our most helpful respondents—last year we mailed over 500 books.

Please note that we print only the names of respondents, never addresses. Those making negative observations are not identified. Although we must always have your full name and address, we will be happy to print your initials, or a pseudonym, if you prefer.

These report forms may also be used, if you wish, to recommend good hotels in Europe to our equivalent publication, *Europe's Wonderful Little Hotels & Inns* (published in Europe as *The Good Hotel Guide*). Reports should be sent to *Europe's Wonderful Little Hotels & Inns*, St. Martin's Press, 175 Fifth Avenue, New York, NY 10010; to P.O. Box 150, Riverside, CT 06878; or directly to *The Good Hotel Guide*, 61 Clarendon Road, London W11 4JE. Readers in the UK can send their letters postage-free to *The Good Hotel Guide*, Freepost, London W11 4 BR.

To: *America's Wonderful Little Hotels & Inns,*
   P.O. Box 150, Riverside, CT 06878.

Name of hotel_____

Address_____

Telephone_____

Date of most recent visit_____ Duration of visit_____

☐ New recommendation   ☐ Comment on existing entry

Please be as specific as possible about furnishings, atmosphere, service, and cuisine. If reporting on an existing entry, please tell us whether you thought it accurate. Unless you tell us not to, we shall assume that we may publish your name in the next edition. Thank you very much for writing; use your own stationery if preferred:

I am not connected with the management/owners.
I would stay here again if returning to the area.

☐ yes   ☐ no
Have you written to us before?

☐ yes   ☐ no

Signed_____

Name_____
                    (Please print)

Address_____
                    (Please print)

WC95